Through the Glass Ceiling

1/29/06

Diana
It was great
serving in the
Senate with you
Enjoy
love
+ Victoria Ford

Sue Wagner

Through the Glass Ceiling

A Life in Nevada Politics

Sue Wagner,
with Victoria Ford

Edited by Richard Hoadley and Kathleen Coles

University of Nevada Oral History Program

Production of *Through the Glass Ceiling* was made possible by an anonymous donor's generous gift through the Nevada Women's History Project. Additional funding was provided by Jim and Loretta McCormick, Maya Miller, and Tom and Joyce King.

All photographs in this volume are courtesy of Sue Wagner.

Publication Staff:
Director: R.T. King
Assistant Director: Mary Larson
Production Manager: Kathleen Coles
Production Assistants: Linda Sommer, Allison Tracy,
and Kathryn Wright-Ross

ISBN: 1-56475-389-1

PREFACE

Founded in 1964, the University of Nevada Oral History Program (UNOHP) records and collects interviews that address significant topics in Nevada's remembered past. The program's chroniclers are primary sources: people who participated in or directly witnessed the events and phenomena that are the subjects of the interviews. Following precedent established by Allan Nevins at Columbia University in 1948, and perpetuated since by academic programs such as ours, these recorded interviews and their transcripts are called oral histories.

Sue Wagner's life and career made her a worthy oral history chronicler, but the UNOHP could not have done the work necessary to produce the book at hand without considerable financial assistance. In 2000, an anonymous donor approached the Nevada Women's History Project (NWHP), offering to fund an oral history with Ms. Wagner. The NWHP contracted with the UNOHP to produce it. Over the next three years, oral historian Victoria Ford conducted a series of interviews with Ms.

Wagner totaling forty-two tape-recorded hours.

This book is crafted from the verbatim transcript of the Ford-Wagner interviews, but it is much easier to read. Remaining faithful to the transcript's content, and adhering as closely as possible to Ms. Wagner's spoken words, Richard Hoadley and Kathleen Coles edited it for clarity. They also gave it chronological and topical organization that are not always found in the raw transcript. Ms. Wagner reviewed their work and affirms that it is an accurate interpretation. Readers who desire access to the unaltered oral history are invited to visit the offices of the UNOHP, where the tapes of the interviews may be heard by appointment.

To add context to written representations of the spoken word, the UNOHP uses certain editorial conventions. Laughter is represented with [laughter] at the end of a sentence in which it occurs; and ellipses are used, not to indicate that material has been deleted, but to indicate that a statement has been interrupted or is incomplete . . . or there is a pause for dramatic effect.

As with all of our oral histories, while
we can vouch for the authenticity of
Through the Glass Ceiling, we advise the
reader to keep in mind that it is a personal
account of a remembered past, and we do
not claim that it is entirely free of error.
Intelligent readers will approach it with the
same anticipation of discovery, tempered
with caution, that they would bring to
government reports, diaries, newspaper
stories, and other interpretations of
historical information.

UNOHP
November 2005

INTRODUCTION

Sue Wagner is a multi-faceted woman, which makes it impossible to write a simple introduction to this oral history of her life as a mother, friend, baseball and sports enthusiast; former Nevada legislator, senator, and lieutenant governor; current gaming commissioner; constant political activist, mentor, teacher, leader . . . and the list goes on. However, through Sue's oral history, what becomes clear is that she has a rare and indomitable spirit.

As a politician, it was impossible to subdue her. She became involved in Nevada's political scene as a young woman— wife of Peter Wagner, a Desert Research Institute (DRI) scientist, and mother of two small children, Kirk and Kristine. Today that description would not raise any eyebrows, but back in the 1970s, when she first ran for public office, there were practically no women in the Nevada legislature, and those who were there did not have small children. Gloria Steinem and the women's movement were still new and definitely considered radical—so new that when Sue heard Betty Friedan (author of *The Feminine Mystique*) speak at her college, she said she could not relate to the idea that women felt prevented from attaining any goal.

When Sue walked door to door in 1974 campaigning to be an assemblywoman— during the same time that the infamous Watergate scandal was unfolding—her goal was to open up government to the people. Her constituents didn't ask about her political views, but instead wanted to know who would care for her children while she worked. When asked about the Equal Rights Amendment (ERA), she joked with voters about baseball's Earned Run Averages. She had yet to fully realize the leading role she would play as a champion of women's rights—especially their right to serve in public office.

She won her first office during an entirely different era. There were no guidebooks or parenting magazines addressing issues facing working mothers, so she did the best she could, just as other working women did. There were no day care facilities, so Peter cared for the children after work, and neighbors filled in during the day.

When she entered the Nevada Assembly chambers as a freshman legislator, she was seated next to the other women, and she thought that many assumed she would be a carbon copy of the two other women there, Jean Ford and Mary Gojack. All were linked with women's issues, whether or not that was their main focus. Little did any of her colleagues know that they were meeting a fighter—a woman with experience, determination, and the ability to cross the gender gap and move through the glass ceiling. She was an able negotiator with both men and women, and over the next twenty-some years, her colleagues came to know and respect her.

In her oral history, Sue shares what her friends already know of the background that shaped her political skills. She was born in Maine, tempered by the cold winters and raised with the sound of foghorns and the smells of a sardine factory. People born in Maine were "very tough, very hardy, very opinionated," she said. Her idol was U.S. Senator Margaret Chase Smith, although she realizes now that she is more like U.S. Senator Olympia Snowe. Snowe also stood up for what she believed and didn't always go along with the Republican leaders, but people knew where she stood on issues at all times.

Sue tells the story of her first door-to-door campaign as a child, selling candy bars for a penny profit each in order to earn the $30 to replace her sister's bike, which Sue borrowed without permission, only to have it run over by a car. That was when she learned how much she likes meeting new people. When her family moved to Arizona for her father's health, she wasted little time being the new kid and instead became a class officer whose favorite subject was government. The only election she ever lost in her life was when she first ran for an office at Girls State, and she lost because she didn't vote for herself. In those same high school

years, one of the experiences that changed her life the most was spending a summer in Germany as a foreign exchange student.

Her father died when Sue was just eighteen, so when she went to college, an uncle offered the financial help she needed to join a sorority. There she acquired more political and people skills, and even then she knew her interest in politics would last a lifetime. How she would accomplish the dream of becoming a politically active adult became a challenge when she found herself, a young wife and new mother, living miles from Reno at Stead, where her husband worked for DRI.

Soon she had two small children and a home. Sue always had unlimited energy and an intelligent mind, so she added to her household duties and began campaigning for Pat Lewis Hardy for Reno City Council. After campaigning for others, she decided to tackle her own run for the Nevada legislature in 1974. From that first win, Sue's oral history covers her Nevada political career in depth, right down to the inner workings of the committees and the powerful people who served with her. Her oral history also recounts the many issues she supported, including safe houses for abused women, prison-system reform, abortion rights, and the fight to ratify the ERA as an amendment to the U.S. Constitution.

But one compelling thread weaves unrelentingly through her life—tragic losses. In 1980, her husband, Peter, was killed in an airplane crash while working for DRI. Sue was entering the Nevada Senate that year, and suddenly, as a single mother of two small children, she needed the job. Amidst her grief and that of her children, she continued working with the aid of neighbors and friends who helped her care for Kirk and Kristine. Her daily reality was a constant pull between the necessity and joy of her career and her feelings of love and responsibility for her children. In spite of the inner conflict, she continued to lay the groundwork for other women to enter political careers.

Then came the second airplane crash in her life. This time, she was a passenger in a small plane returning from the Labor Day Cantaloupe Festival in Fallon, where she was wrapping up a successful campaign to become Nevada's lieutenant governor. For me, the memory of that newscast reporting the plane crash and showing Sue being wheeled into the emergency room is as vivid as my memories of the day when President John F. Kennedy was shot. I remember where I stood in my living room while watching the newscast, and I remember the agony and the sense of loss I felt at a time when I did not know Sue and had never even met her in person. To those of us who were not her friends or family or colleagues, she was still so important. She was our hope. We appreciated the battles she fought for us. We appreciated her honesty and integrity. She had such a bright political career ahead. Seeing her suffer from an airplane crash, one so similar to that which killed her husband just ten years earlier, seemed more than she or any of us could bear. We waited anxiously for news of her recovery.

For Sue, that day was just the beginning of yet another battle, and one she was not willing to lose. Her strong will kept her alive through the painful days ahead and through the even more painful surgery and continued health challenges that resulted from her injuries. She won that campaign and served—against all odds, based on her health—as lieutenant governor.

When Sue announced that she could not seek a second term as lieutenant governor, she did not quit working. Although she no longer runs for Nevada public office or plays baseball, she still serves the state on the Nevada Gaming Commission and through her work with the Washoe Medical Center Advisory Board. When the legislature is in session in alternate years, she places University of Nevada, Reno students as legislative interns and continues to mentor both young men and women as they enter the political arena.

Although she did not get her opportunity to continue running for office—her chance at the Nevada governor's mansion or the U.S. Congress or more—through her continued work for Nevada and through her oral history, she lives her passion every day and continues laying the groundwork for women to join the political process and move through the glass ceiling. She is still making sure that all of our voices are heard in the political arena, and her indomitable spirit won't allow her to quit.

Victoria Ford
November 2005

CONTENTS

1

CHILDHOOD IN MAINE AND ARIZONA

VICTORIA FORD: It is July 3, 2000. I'm here with Sue Wagner in her home in Reno, and we're going to be interviewing Sue about her life. Sue, let's start talking about your childhood. Would you tell me, first of all, when and where you were born?

SUE WAGNER: I was born January 6, 1940 in South Portland, Maine, right near Portland, which is the largest city in the state of Maine.

And is it central, northern coast?

Portland is in the southern part of Maine, about, maybe, an hour's drive from the New Hampshire border. So, it's definitely in the southern part of the state.

And let's talk a little bit about your parents and grandparents. Were your grandparents from Maine?

My entire family, as far back as I have any knowledge of them coming across from England, I guess, were from Maine, lived in Maine. Now, particularly on my mother's side, I know that, because I know where my grandmother and my great grandparents lived in Maine. My mother was born in the premier tourist place in Maine, called Camden, and my sister was born there, as well. My dad was born in a town called Dexter, Maine, where the shoes are made, Dexter shoes, and I'm very loyal to Dexter loafers and Dexter golf shoes. It's a town in the middle of Maine, unlike being on the seacoast, so no one goes there unless they have to.

But my dad is of French Canadian descent, so evidently, some of his relatives came down from Montreal, and in that area a lot of Maine people, particularly in the far northern part of Maine, are very close to French Canadians and come from that background. So a mixture.

Did your grandparents live nearby—of both sides?

I remember meeting my paternal grandmother in Dexter, Maine, several times. Sadie her name was. But my paternal grandfather died before either I was born or I remember, but I have heard that he was a very good tennis player and had his own grass tennis court—just like Wimbledon (that tournament is going on today at the time of this interview) is played on grass—in his backyard and used to play and was evidently quite a player, even in his older age.

My dad had six siblings, all of them but one men, and they all died between the ages of fifty and fifty-seven of heart-related problems, including my grandfather. So, even though he may have taken great care of himself, evidently there was something wrong genetically, I guess. And the grandmother, Sadie, I did meet a couple of times. A very hard worker, I am told.

Now, on the maternal side, I never knew either of my grandfathers. My mother's dad was a doctor in Maine, and I have heard great stories about him being such a wonderful man. He was the mayor of Camden and very involved in politics and, in those days, a doctor who went in his horse and buggy from home to home to home, but I never knew him, and I never knew her stepfather, who obviously was a very nice man, as well. They both died before I was born. My maternal grandmother I knew quite well, the only one I did know. She lived with me for awhile in Tucson, and we'll get to that part, I guess.

What was her name?

Her name was Carrie Newhall at that time. My mother's maiden name was Hooper, but needless to say, my grandmother took her second husband's name.

And she was evidently a very difficult woman. You know, there is a saying about people born in Maine, particularly differentiating them from other people from New England, that they are very tough, very hardy, very opinionated, and she was all of that, but, I guess, a very difficult

woman. I just remember a few things about her, like that she couldn't hear. She lived to be almost a hundred. She was two days shy of a hundred when she died at the nursing home. She had lived with us for awhile until it just became impossible. But they told her she was a hundred. So she just said, "OK. I reached my goal," and just kind of turned off the organs and shut down, because the doctors found no reason for her to die. And of course, my mother is ninety-four, so something is going on there in those women's genes. But I do remember her pretending, and I'll say feigning, the fact that she could not hear. She'd had a hearing aid, but if we'd whisper something like, "We don't care for the dress that Grammy has on."

"*What?*" She could hear that! Absolutely, she could hear that perfectly. [laughter] But if it was something else that she didn't want to hear, wow, she just couldn't turn up that hearing aid high enough. So, I thought she was kind of an interesting person, but someone that I don't really have a lot of memories about, although she lived with us. It was kind of difficult, because I had a brother, myself, and we all lived in a very tiny, little home—on top of a grandmother—so I heard things about her, probably from my mother, which were not always positive.

So, I don't have the same kind of memories that, maybe, my sister does, who's older than I and who knows her in a totally different way.

Have you and your sister talked about it?

Yes, we have.

And how would your view of Grandma differ from your sister's?

Well, I think my sister, first of all, used to go down and stay with her, grew up in Camden, and my grandmother, the woman

I'm speaking of, had an absolutely unbelievable home on Camden Harbor, which, as I say, is this premier place now, and I went by to see the home just last fall when I was back in New England, and it is unbelievable. My sister spent a lot of summers there, and I've also been told that she was my grandmother's favorite, so my sister has pretty good memories and fond memories of her. I don't have memories that are not good. They're just not a lot.

And maybe not quite as close as your sister?

No, not quite as close. And I don't remember my grandmother ever sitting down and talking to me about what her life was like or anything of that sort. So she was just sort of there.

What's the difference in age between you and your sister?

My sister is twelve years older, and I have a brother who's eight years older.

And what are the names?

My sister is Joan Choate. And there's a famous prep school in New England, the Choate School. I think Ted Kennedy, or the Kennedy boys, went there.

And then, you have a brother?

I have a brother, Dick—Richard—who lives in a town called Alamo, near Danville, California. He's retired. He owned some oil companies and has done very well.

Is he also older than you?

He's eight years older.

Eight years older, so you're the baby of the family?

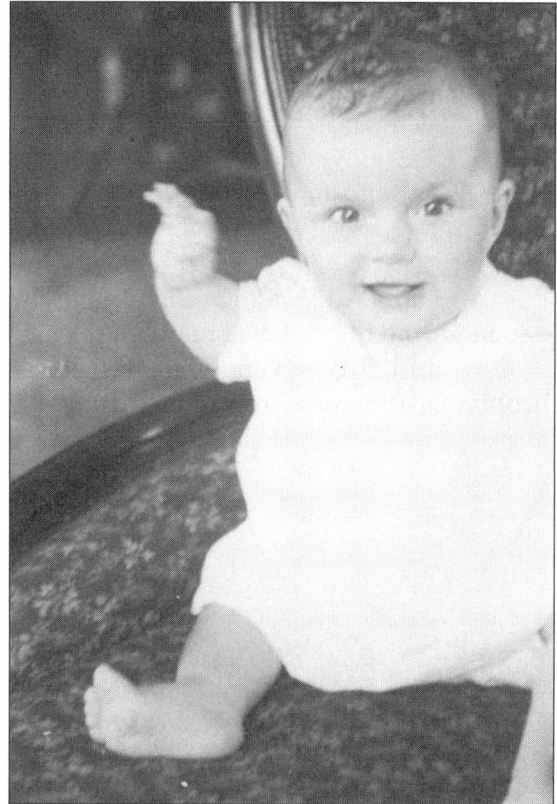

Sue Ellen Pooler. August, 1940.

I am the baby, and very honestly, I've often thought, to be honest with you, that, well, I was born in 1940—times were not good—and I will tell you about what my dad did, but things were rough, and I kept wondering why a family would want another child, when they had a girl and a boy, particularly. Because twelve, eight years, and then all of a sudden this other one. So, I've always kind of felt like I was the runt of the litter, and that may have something to do with what I've accomplished with my life.

And it also sounds like, as you're talking about some of your genetic background with the strong Maine personalities, you may have some of those, too.

Well, I suspect so. [laughter]

We'll get back to that as we go along.

I suspect I do.

And tell me, then, you talked about what your dad did. Did both your mom and your dad work?

Yes. I will tell you a little bit about the education of my parents, because I think that is unusual when you think about their age. My father graduated from college, the Massachusetts College of Pharmacy, which I think is still around, in Brookline, Massachusetts, and he was an athlete. He played baseball and was just very interested in sports, but he was a pharmacist. My mother had an older brother, and she went to college for two years to a music conservatory in Pennsylvania [Engle Music Conservatory, Lebanon Valley College, Annville, Pennsylvania], and when her brother, who was two years younger, got to be college age, she had to quit, because in those days, of course, the boy took precedence over the woman in order to have an advanced degree. He turned out to be a nuclear engineer and was one of the first engineers to work on the first atomic submarine for Westinghouse, and so clearly his education was extremely important to him, and he did something with it, and he was a wonderful, wonderful man. But it did show the difference in the times, yet it also shows that both my mother and father were very interested in education, as, of course, were their parents, and this was in the 1920s when they graduated. So, I think that is somewhat unusual.

More unusual in the 1920s. Not everyone had the opportunity to go to college then.

And particularly, if you remember, my dad had a large family. And all of these guys,

several of them were involved in like . . . editor of a newspaper, attorney—several had professions . . . *professions.*

So, I don't know what it was in that family that was so committed to having these boys and the one girl . . . my Aunt Geneva was the comptroller of the Dexter Shoe Company, which was at that time a pretty decent job. And in fact, when I last saw her, she had just recently retired, so education clearly was important.

It was important on both sides of your family.

On both sides. Yes.

How did you know the story about your mom having to quit when her brother was ready for college?

Because she told me.

Did she tell you how she felt about it?

Yes. I think she felt cheated. Very honestly.

Did she have some dreams that she didn't get to follow then, because of that?

Yes. I think everybody who goes to a music conservatory thinks they're going to be a concert pianist. And of course, what that equated to was becoming a music teacher. When you ask me about them having jobs, yes, they both did. One of the things that my mother did, and I don't remember this as a small child, but, evidently, she was a piano teacher. Certainly, as I got older, after my dad died, that became her source of income. She was able to carry on by doing that in her home. And so, it was extremely important that she had those several years, but I think that her dream was something quite different.

And I think she felt that probably it was unfair, although I did mention that my uncle did, you know, do something extremely important with that degree, and she was very proud of him and loved him very much, but I still think there was definitely that feeling there.

There was an issue for her in that.

Yes, I think so.

Tell me the names of your parents.

My dad was Raymond Augustus Pooler. And that was an Anglicized version. My maiden name is an Anglicized version of the French Canadian name, which was Poulin. And I kept thinking, "Why didn't you pick something better, if you were going to change it, than 'Pooler'?" [laughter] Because I used to get jazzed a lot about that name when I ran for office in high school and college. And my mother's name is Kathryn Hooper Pooler.

Now we kind of have the constellation of your family. Tell me what some of your earliest memories are as a child.

Well, I guess I remember my dad's drugstore, which was in a town called Cape Elizabeth, which was sort of like Incline Village, a resort town south of South Portland. In fact, it's Portland, South Portland, Cape Elizabeth, because I was just there. There's a very famous lighthouse called Cape Elizabeth Lighthouse, which, if you see a picture of one, that's probably it.

So, his drugstore was in a different small town than where you lived?

Yes, but it was like . . . .

Like a suburb?

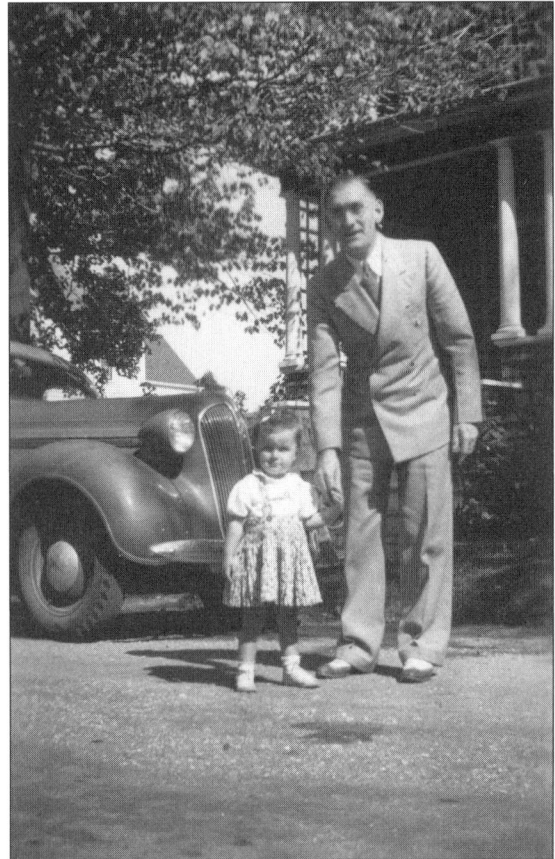

Sue with her father, Raymond Pooler, 1942.

Yes. And in Maine it's just little town after little town. But it was where Bette Davis, the movie actress, was one of his customers, as was her husband Gary Merrill and a lot of these old-time movie stars, and I have no idea if today it is the same. You may have heard of Bar Harbor. Now that's passé, because Camden is the place, but Cape Elizabeth was a place where a lot of people had summer homes or whatever, and it is really beautiful. I lived very close to the Atlantic Ocean.

Anyway, one of the first memories I have is of his drugstore, and I did see it again just recently. Evidently, when I was little, first born, I lived upstairs. My parents lived upstairs of the drugstore, and so, I gather I was left in a little playpen while my mother ran downstairs, and when they were first married, she worked in the drugstore—

versus having the piano lessons; that came a little bit later—helping my dad, because it was tough. I've been told it was very difficult, and a lot of people that were his customers just didn't think you had to pay. My mother just told me this recently, that he just closed on getting this drugstore right after the stock market crashed, so he thought he could get a loan, and all of these financial problems came upon him one after another, which happened to a lot of people at that time, but I guess it was just kind of devastating to their aspirations, and things just didn't work out very well. I do remember her talking about leaving the light bulb on upstairs and leaving me in the playpen and keep running downstairs and coming up and checking on me when I was little.

So, money was a struggle for your parents?

Absolutely. And that has always been.

And were you aware of that as a child? Or is that something that you realized looking back and hearing the stories?

Yes. I think it was something I'd heard about growing up. At a certain time in high school, I definitely got it, that there was a definite demarcation line, but up until that time, it didn't make any difference, and it generally didn't make any difference, even when I recognized it, to me.

What other childhood memories?

Well, I remember growing up in Maine. The snow, the snow, the snow, the snow. It was incredible, and, of course, as a kid it was fabulous, but I guess it wasn't so much for my parents. [laughter] And the other thing, the home that I remember was right across from a cemetery, and that was very

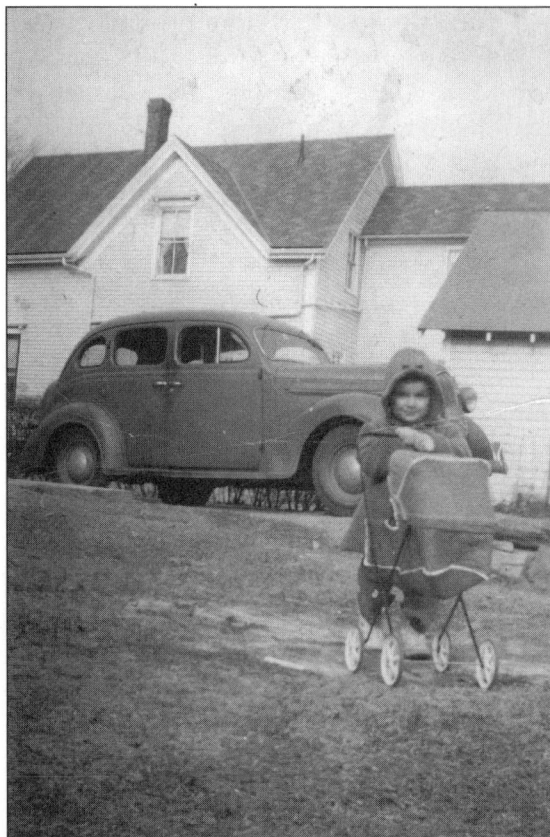

Sue with her doll carriage at home in Maine, 1942.

cool for a kid, [laughter] particularly if you wanted to be near a really scary place, and Halloween was just the best. I'm sorry to say that it's not very nice now, but it was a great place for Halloween. To me it was just that's where I lived. I mean, hey, nobody could build over there. [laughter] That was one way to look at it.

But I do remember snow. I remember that we lived very close to the Atlantic Ocean, and there were sardine factories and foghorns, so you not only heard the foghorn all the time, but after a while it was just like anything that you live close by—you just blotted it out. And of course, the sardine smell—if in the summer the wind happened to blow just right, if you didn't like sardines, it was all over, because the

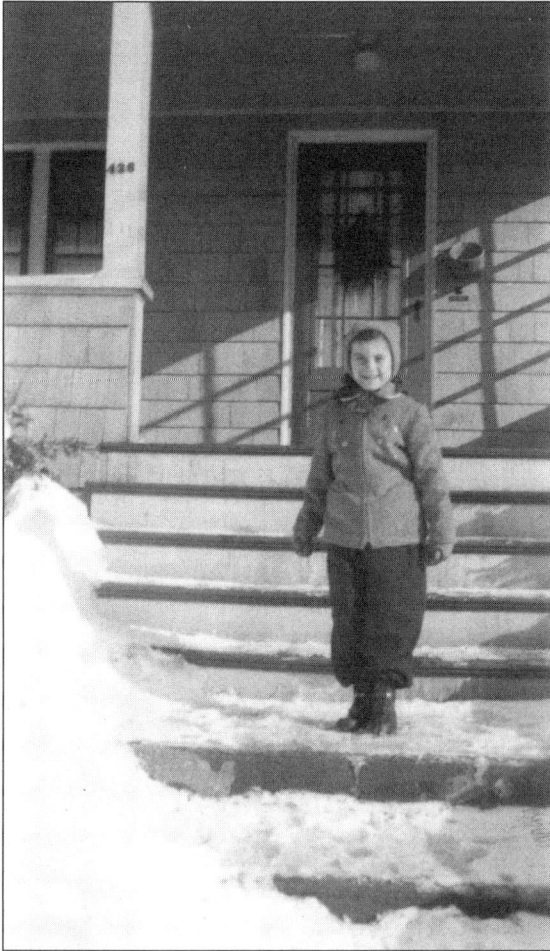

"I remember growing up in Maine. The snow, the snow, the snow . . . ." Sue, age seven.

smell is fairly pungent, one you recognized immediately.

Let me ask you this. When you talked about snow, did you sled? Did you skate? What were some of the things that you did that you liked in the snow?

Yes. My dad, as I mentioned to you, was a good athlete, so he had snowshoes, the old-fashioned kind, that he used to do a lot of trekking around on. Skiing was not a big deal, because Maine, of course, is relatively flat. Now, my sister, being older, she used to go to New Hampshire to ski, but I did a cross-country type, and snowball fights.

Sledding was big. I can remember my sled, and I lived in a neighborhood where there were mainly boys, and so I spent a lot of time playing with guys, playing sports.

I had one girlfriend who was a foster child, Margie Hammond, who lived kitty-corner to me, and she was just my best buddy, and my mother kept saying, "You know, Sue, you better find another friend," because she didn't really, maybe, explain to me what a foster child was, but she told me that she wasn't going to be around for a long time, so I better not just have *one* friend. There were several important messages here. It was don't have just one friend, because that one friend may not be there forever for you, and I remember that, and that's true of my life today.

And secondly, I played a lot with the guys, and there was a place at the end of the street that was next to mine called the Piggery, and I saw it again last fall, fall of 1999, when I went back. The Piggery, of course, was much bigger in one's mind when one was a small child, like everything is—their home, their yard, et cetera.

Like everything, yes.

But the Piggery was still this place in fall of 1999, as it was when I was growing up in the 1940s, that was wild, unkempt. Blueberry bushes grew there, and at one point there were wild pigs that ran around, but it was the most fabulous place for a child, because you would play cowboys—or cowgirls—and Indians or play hide-and-seek, and go hide somewhere. There were little creeks, and there were bushes, and there were trees, and it was like something out of a Disneyland. I mean, it was just for a child the most incredible place to run and play, and I remember the very first time I went back with my husband and my two children. It was in 1972 when we went on a trip to New England, and I told my husband, Peter, "I want you to park at the end of this street, Vincent Street, because I'm going to go run here in the Piggery," because I had told him what it was.

I was gone for like an hour, and everybody was so worried. My husband went out; the kids went out looking for me. And I was just living in the past, hiding behind trees and doing all those things. It was just fabulous.

The one other thing that is a vivid recollection of my childhood, which is *extremely* important to who I am today, was an incident when my sister, twelve years older than I, got a new Schwinn bicycle, which was just something that was revered, wanted, desired by my sister, and expensive for my family. I was told, "Do not touch. Don't go near. Don't breathe on it. Don't even look at it. Don't *think* about it." Needless to say, I took it, and I took it over to the next street, Vincent Street, where the Piggery was, showed it off to all my buddies, and then I got distracted to go play a game, and I put it up on top of a little embankment. I came back, and it wasn't there, but there was a big Buick on the street. Well, unfortunately, the bike was under the Buick, and the bicycle was totally destroyed. The Buick was driven by a very short, little man, who couldn't see over the steering wheel to see a bicycle was there. He smoked a big cigar. He rented a room in this house, and later on I got a clipping from the newspaper that he was an illegal bookmaker. [laughter] Interesting, coming back to my profession today on the Nevada Gaming Commission. [laughter] He was caught by the cops. When this incident occurred I was, of course, hysterical. I knew I was in so much trouble. So we got to talk to the man down at the police station. We explained to him what the situation was. Well, he could have cared less. It wasn't his fault, he said, and it wasn't. He said he couldn't see. He couldn't, and that's all true. However, I wanted him to reach into his wallet and pick out the money and hand it

to me, so I could go buy one, replace it, and no one would ever know that I'd taken it. That didn't happen.

My parents were just very upset. Needless to say, my sister was more angry than ever, and I had to buy her a new one. How did I do that? Well, my dad owned a drugstore. For every candy bar he sold for a nickel—and in those days a Milky Way, whatever, was a nickel—he made a penny. So I had to sell candy door-to-door, and I would make a penny off of every bar I sold. He wouldn't make anything; I'd make the profit, and I had to work to earn whatever a bicycle cost, and I think it was like thirty dollars for the top Schwinn, whatever it was they'd bought her. Well, I had a little basket, and it was all fixed up with a hanky or something in it, a bandana, with an assortment of different kinds of candy bars, and my parents sent me out one day, and I was probably seven or eight years old. They said this is what you have to do, and you must do this.

Well, you can imagine. What little seven or eight-year-old child wants to go knock on total strangers' doors and sell them something that they probably could get at the grocery store or the drugstore. So, I started out, and I told them the story. Obviously, the first door I knocked on, knock, knock, knock, "My name is Sue Pooler. I did this to my sister's bicycle, and my parents are sending me out and making me do this." [laughter] "They're punishing me." I'm sure I embellished on this story. And well, pretty soon, people were waiting for me with this long list of candy bars, because they felt so sorry for me, and if they didn't want them, they bought them anyway. And so, pretty soon, I got so I liked it, and I met a lot of people, and I had little friends along my route, and pretty soon my route got bigger, and finally, I'd gotten to seventeen, eighteen, nineteen dollars, or something, and my parents had ultimately decided somewhere, when I got to a certain point, that was going to be it. I'd learned my lesson, and I think it was half the amount or twenty dollars out of thirty or something. So, one night they just said they needed something in the garage, and so I went out to get it, and there was a *brand new Schwinn bicycle*, just like the one I had ruined. So that was the end of that, but when I think back on it, and I wonder why I like going door to door campaigning, hey, they sent me out on my first door-to-door campaign at seven or eight years old. I told my mother how mean that was of them, and how they didn't seem to think it was that way at all, and she claims that she was very, very upset when she sent me out that first day, but I'm not really sure whether she was or not. [laughter] But it really was a wonderful experience, when one looks back on it, for me.

That's an incredible experience.

But, when you think about parents making a child *do* that. And my dad was a real softy, so I suspect that he would have just been willing to have me do nothing, whereas my mother said, "No. There's a lesson to be learned here." So that was the lesson.

That's a pretty amazing story.

Oh, yes.

It has all sorts of elements of responsibility, and being able to present yourself to strangers, and it's just an incredible experience.

Yes. Going up to a total stranger's home and selling something. First of all, there's a lesson on selling a product. In this case it was a candy bar, purchasing a bicycle. In later life it was selling myself, and the product was better government. You know,

it was not being afraid of strangers, which, unfortunately, so many children are told not to do this very thing, and think of parents today sending out a child going to total strangers' homes. That would probably be unheard of, but fortunately in the 1940s it was not. Although, here we have an illegal bookmaker right next to us, who happened to run over my sister's bicycle. [laughter] We thought we lived in a really nice, little neighborhood. But it did. It taught me responsibility. It taught me when someone says you're not supposed to do something, guess what? You're not supposed to do it, and if you do it, and you break the rules, then you have to pay for that.

So, a real respect for the rules and the laws.

Exactly. A respect for rules, for laws, and even today—my son wanted me to change a law that wouldn't allow him to have a motor bike, I think it was, or a motor scooter or something, until he was a certain age, and he wasn't that age. I said, "Well, Kirk, that's the law."

And he said, "But, Mom, you can change it, because you just put little brackets around it, and you remove that age and put a new age in it." [laughter]

I thought, "Well, he's got that right." But I wasn't going to do it. [laughter] And my point was, "The law is the law, and if you don't like it, change it."

He said, "OK. Change it." [laughter]

But I think, as you say, there are a lot of lessons that I learned in that one experience, although I'm sure I cried and cried and cried when I first went out, and I'm sure it was hard the first week, the second week, the third week, and after awhile it got to be fun. And I do remember exactly. It was like Little Red Riding Hood, going off . . .

With your basket of candy?

. . . with my basket, and then, if I didn't have what they wanted, I'd take orders, for whatever my dad could get. But also, you understand the other part of it, that my dad—and it was to impress me—only made a *penny* out of every candy bar he sold. How much money it took to make some kind of a decent living. Even if you owned your own business, it wasn't all that terrific. Then you had to sell a product in that business, and how little you actually made on whatever it was you sold.

And there was overhead, and what you earned was hard-earned money.

Yes. Right. And I had no overhead. My overhead was a basket, and that was about it, and my dad wasn't making anything off the candy. Of course, as I got near the end, and I got not so mad at my parents, then I would tell them which drugstore my daddy's was, so they might go and continue to buy candy. And then, when I stopped doing it, the people were very upset, because they depended upon me to come around, and some of them were older and didn't like to get out. So then, I think that my dad delivered stuff to them after awhile. But then I decided, "Well, maybe I should promote my dad's drugstore." [laughter]

Keep this all in the family going well.

Yes. Right

Are there any other memories like that from childhood that you'd like to cover? You said your dad was a softy, but your mom was very focused on teaching you things that she thought you would need to know?

Well, in that case.

In that case, only?

But I think that my memories . . . and maybe it's because my dad died young, and I hear a lot from my sister that clearly, for my sister, my father was the one who she very much loved, and that he was nice and kind and easy going. But because my dad died when I was about eighteen, I guess, again, I have great memories of him which I will share as I get on. I was thinking about childhood memories, and I may go back and remember some other things, but I think that my other big memory was when we had to move from Maine to Arizona, the fact that my dad had been told that he was of poor health. He always had been in bad health, evidently, and when he was in college, I guess, he got rheumatic fever, which at that time it was a very bad thing to have and damaged his heart, and he also had a lot of lung problems. Now, I suspect today they'd do a bypass and do other kinds of things with the lungs, and he'd be fine, but in those days they didn't know that sort of thing. So, the doctors told him, because Maine winters were so severe, and the dampness just kind of permeated your body, "You've got to get out of here and go someplace else."

My mother tells me that they looked at Denver and Tucson, [pronounces it "Texan"] better known as Tucson [pronounced "Two-sahn"] to us today, but that's what they called it. There was another place, but they chose Tucson because of the University of Arizona, and my brother was just beginning to go into college back in those days, and I was about in the fifth grade. They felt that it was a public school, and that they would be able to afford to give us college educations.

So, they came out. My mom and dad went out to Tucson for a couple of winters, for a couple of years—at least one year, maybe two—and lived in Tucson, and my dad didn't do anything, except sit in the sun and try to get better, and my mother worked as a sales clerk in a store that would be like

Macy's, called Steinfeld's, in Tucson, which was a family owned, very nice department store, just to be able to live.

My brother and I lived with my sister, who was about nineteen, twenty, who'd just been married and had a baby, and her husband was off in the military—this was during the Korean War. We lived with her, which must have just been awful for her—to have a new baby and a fifth grader and a kid in high school, her brother and sister—but she did it, because it had to be done, and it worked out real well for my mother and father, as far as his health. He got better, so we all moved out to Tucson, and I really was very upset about it, because I had a real network of friends, and I was a very outgoing person even in grammar school and was active in a lot of things. I was very scared because nobody knew what Arizona was. This was in 1950 that we moved. And literally, people thought of Indians and cowboys and snakes and tarantulas, and I used to dream about scorpions and things crawling around, but we had to go.

As I have mentioned to you before, we packed up everything we could, because we always had financial difficulties, and took what we could in the car, in our Pontiac, out to Tucson and bought a home, which my mother still lives in today. My mother tells me it cost $5,000 in 1950, and she's done a lot with it, but it's very small, less than a thousand square feet, and when I told about my grandmother, my brother, and myself, and my mom, and my dad living in there with one, little, tiny bathroom, you can understand, it was a bit crowded.

But anyway, that year with my sister was actually difficult, but also kind of fun, because there was this little baby, my niece, Louise, who's now fifty, who I could feed and kind of take care of when I wanted to, and when I didn't, I could leave and go play or do whatever, because I was just in the fifth grade. That's really the bigger memories I think I have of my time in Maine.

You said that you were very active in grammar school and involved in a lot of things and had a lot of friends. Can you describe that just a little bit?

I can. I can particularly when I get to Tucson in this move that I made.

So, your parents went down, made sure that everything was OK, spent a couple winters there, and then everybody moved—except your sister and your brother?

Yes, my sister and her husband and child stayed in Maine for awhile. My brother had already moved out. They bought this house, I think, or rented it, or whatever, but my brother was out there going to school. He started at the University of Arizona when we got there, and I would have been in the fifth grade, and there was an elementary school as close as the one I live near now, Jessie Beck, called Cragin Elementary School.

When I first went there, of course, I'm sure I was very nervous, but I've never been that kind of person who's been incredibly . . . maybe it goes back to selling the candy door to door, I don't know, but new things have never really bothered me that much. Right away I got elected to do all these things that this teacher (Mr. Palmer was one of my favorite teachers, fifth grade teacher) had somebody do—the weather, somebody do the news, somebody do everything to begin the day. Right away I got selected to do all this, and I thought, "Phew, everybody really likes me." Well, I later learned that it had something to do with my funny accent, and that they all liked hearing me and laughing at me. [laughter] Not *with* me, but *at* me, because I had a very definite Maine accent, and if you've ever heard one, which I don't now have, it is *very* different, and particularly for kids in Arizona who had nothing, no accent. I mean, people had come from some place, or even at that point in 1950, most of the kids were born there, so they just had a kind of bland accent. So I sounded really strange, and that was the reason that I had been elected or selected to do all these things.

But then we get back to the sports thing and my playing and being a tomboy, I guess, with all these kids in Maine. Mr. Palmer, our teacher, was very big on this, and we played softball every recess, before school, after school. I lived so close to my school, and the first person to tag up in the morning got to say what they wanted to do, what position they wanted to play. Of course, being a girl, nobody wanted to pick me, but pretty soon they realized I was pretty good, and I always wanted to be the pitcher, which, of course, was the star of the team. [laughter] So I'd be the first one to tag up in the morning, and I was always the pitcher. And we will later find out, as we move along through my story, that I was the pitcher for the powder puff team of Theta Pi Phi, for the assembly softball team, the senate softball team in Nevada. So all these things, I guess, in one's life, come back to play a part in their later years.

Those are not the kinds of things that you normally think are going to be important in a political career, are they?

[laughter] No, that's, hey, the big stuff. I think so, because then that also got me in with the kids: "Oh, that new person," blah-blah, "with the funny voice. She did the pitching," and so on. So by the time I went to middle school they made this major change—which they also did here in Reno at the time my kids were moving on from elementary school to junior high—of moving sixth grade into middle school. And

so then, by being in a new school and then having to go to another new school, which a lot of elementary schools fed into, of course, this was a whole new arena of kids.

You weren't the only new kid, then, because this was a new constellation of kids?

That's true, but you had your little Gertrude Cragin group, which moved on, but for some reason, there were other junior high schools where the kids tended to be different. They tended to be, I think, maybe more affluent, dressed nicer, just a different economic level, and there, then, you saw this distinction between who were popular, who were the class leaders, and I evidently noted that, and I know I did, because I remember telling my mother that I didn't have, at that time, the popular clothes. I remember one of the styles was called Lanz dresses, I think, from like the Swiss. It was like a little Swiss type of a deal with rickrack and things on it, and that was very in, and one of the gals who went to our school—her parents owned this department store called Levy's, which was, again, one of the premier family-owned businesses in Tucson at the time. So she and her friends, obviously, had all the matching cashmere outfits and things. There were also some shoes, Capezio shoes, I think, was the brand. If you didn't have Capezios . . . . Of course, I had none of those things. So my mother, I do remember, sewed, and so she did try to make me things that looked like these Lanz dresses, but I'm sure you could tell. But, hey, for me, that was close enough. And so, at some level, I think I noted those things, but they weren't an overriding thing to me.

As time went on in this middle school, I became a class officer, and I was a very good student, and I mean very, very good grades, top five or whatever in the class, and a leader. But I was also somewhat of a

Sue pitching for the Nevada state senate softball team. *"I was always the pitcher."*

troublemaker, and my parents never knew this, because everything looked good coming home, until, I remember, my mother went to parents' night, and one of the teachers said something. I had been punished one year, having to make an entire tennis court by hand by myself, and of course it wasn't cement. It was ground, but I had to go out and measure it, level it, put lime all around, and do all of this. And I don't remember what it was I did. It wasn't anything *really* bad, but it was a prank, which everybody thought was very funny. See, I thought I was very funny, and everybody thought I was very funny, which obviously made me more popular and a comedian type, and the teachers just didn't think it was as funny as the kids did. [laughter] My mother didn't think it was funny, at all. And that's the last time she

ever went to a parents' night. As punishment, I had to make a tennis court at the junior high school. It was all dirt, and I poured lime for the outlines. I had to level it, and I remember working with the level.

Oh, really?

She said, "That's it. I will never go again." She may not remember it quite that same way now, but that is true.

Because that's when she learned about what you were doing?

That's when she learned that I was there doing this tennis court thing, not because I was a good kid, but because I had to. I had to do it to clear my record of some such.

This is an interesting story, a sideline. When I graduated from the University of Arizona, I won this award as being the outstanding student, woman student, and the principal of the junior high wrote me a letter saying, "We knew you had it in you." [laughter] It was harking back to those days.

Never thought you would do that.

That I would actually . . . yes. I mean, I was in the student government and good grades, but there was this little rebellious thing going on. Clearly, by the time I'd graduated from college, either I'd covered it up, or I'd outgrown it.

Found more acceptable pranks, maybe?

Right. Right.

What were some of the pranks? Do you remember any of them?

I don't. I remember something in high school, because I continued to do these things in high school, same pattern.

So building a tennis court didn't slow you down any?

No. But I would do things like, if we had chicken for lunch, then I would take the chicken bones and stick them inside the grading book of the teacher, and she would open it up, and, of course, everything was greased, so she couldn't see anybody's grades or attendance marks, anything like that. Then, she would ask who'd done it, and, of course, no one would ever guess me, because I was a very good student and behaved myself in class. It was just that I would do these things, and then I'd get egged on, and then I'd do it even more.
I know in one case I fessed up, and the teacher absolutely didn't believe me,

thought I was just saying it, because I was covering up.

To save somebody else, maybe?

Yes. I said, "No. I really did it." ·
"No, no, no, no."
It would be dumb stuff like that. But the kids thought it wasn't dumb.

Thought it was great.

We thought it was *fabulous.* Particularly, the kids who didn't have good grades. [laughter]

What classes were most interesting to you? Do you recall?

Yes. In middle school . . . wait a minute. Maybe that was in high school. Foreign languages and government, anything dealing with government. Oh, and I have to go back to my childhood again. My interests for government—not just going door to door, but my real interests—my father was very involved in Republican politics in Maine as I was growing up, and he was like our county chairman, our state chairman. Our U.S. senator, when I was a little girl, was Margaret Chase Smith, the only woman senator, and I got to meet her, and even at that time I knew *that's* what I wanted to be. She was my idol. I just visited her library again on this last trip in the fall of 1999. Margaret Chase Smith represented everything that even women today . . . we have two women senators from Maine today, Olympia Snow and Susan Collins. The only other state besides California whose two U.S. senators are both women. And those women, both Republicans, are exactly, I would think, like Margaret Chase Smith, like myself, who are a different kind of Republicans than we normally think of, more definitely moderately social and fiscally conservative. They could do things and vote differently, or feel that way and maybe lead their people, whichever way you want to look at it, that they were more interested in the individual, and government out of our lives, et cetera, those kinds of things. And so, to me, Margaret Chase Smith was my role model. Today Olympia Snow is the one that I would pick out. A lot of people had not heard of her, but she is just a class act. Anyone in the Senate will tell you that, *and* they will say, "She stands up for what she believes is right. She may be a maverick, may not go along with all the Republican leadership, but we know where she is all the time." That's what's been said about me, and I believe that comes from my upbringing in Maine and understanding that that's an acceptable thing to do, and probably, in my mind, a good thing to do.

But my dad was very involved. Our dinner conversations at our table were often about government and politics and what was going on in our community. Not very long ago, when I was visiting my mom, she had an envelope full of things of my dad, which I read—newspaper clippings and things—and it was amazing some of the things that he had done and been involved in. I remember at that time political conventions used to hang on to the last moment, because they used to count up the votes. None of these presidential primaries where you know a year in advance who your candidate is going to be, and it was all done on the radio, and I remember us really, literally gathering around the radio with little tabulation, vote tallies, as they were saying, "And I'm from the State of Puerto Rico, and we cast . . . ." We'd write it down and add it up and, of course, by hand, because there were no such things as calculators or anything, and that was a big deal, and I *loved* it, and even as a kid, I would watch *Meet the Press* and

those kinds of things more than anything. Well, my friends would think I was a bit odd. Even in college, when I was so involved in, not just campus politics, which I was, but big picture politics, they just thought, "Oh," and they're not surprised what I've done with my life. Let me put it that way.

But those were the classes I was interested in: government, languages and sports and gym.

Not English, not math?

Yes, English.

English was good?

Oh, yes. English, reading, yes. Books, all that.

OK. You liked math?

No, not math. Not math, not science. Hated them. Hated them. Algebra, trigonometry, had to get through. Didn't like them. Liked science a little bit better, because it was a little more interesting—chemistry and stuff—but not a lot. No.

That's interesting that you knew at such a young age, because you probably met Margaret Chase Smith, when you were about how old?

Yes, I did. Oh, well, I had to be less than ten.

It would have been less than ten. And you knew then that you just had a passion for this?

I just thought *that's* what I want to be, a U.S. senator. I had no idea she was the only woman. I didn't get that until quite a bit later, that she was *one* out of a *hundred*. That was startling to me, and clearly, that made a difference in my understanding of women and their role and how far they had to go.

Do you recall when you started to understand that?

No. I don't.

Somewhere later, though, definitely.

Yes. Certainly, it was later.

But to you as a child that looked possible, because she had done it.

Absolutely. And besides that, I didn't realize she was the only one. So I thought, "Well, that's something." Besides, I was *so* interested in politics. My family was; my mother was, and my brother—very. It wasn't just my dad. It was just this whole thing. My sister has been involved, like being precinct captain and that sort of thing, when that was a big deal, but not to the point of actually running for office. Both of them probably could have and would have done a good job, but it's a lot to give up. Anyway, that was something very important that I thought about, as far as my childhood memories.

And it's very much a part of your family, then, if your dad was involved in politics.

Yes. And if you remember, my grandfather was as well, and I don't know about my paternal grandfather, because, as I say, I just remember his tennis prowess, and the fact that my dad was a good athlete. My dad was very small. I think he was a shortstop on the baseball team, but he was very short. I can't remember how tall he was. My brother is six foot, but my mother is tiny, and my dad, I would say, isn't more than five' seven", five' eight", a really small guy. And it's interesting, because I married

such a tall guy, and so did my sister. But anyway, that was a very important aspect of my childhood, the political.

The other thing does tie in to the radio, but I do remember as a child, which is nothing unusual, probably, for any child at that age, was all of the radio shows—*The Shadow, Sky King*—where you would get box tops and send things in, get the secret decoder. Oh, man, and the Hardy Boys and the Nancy Drew novels—I could hardly wait to read every Nancy Drew, and when I got all through those, I read all my brother's Hardy Boys books. They were just the same, except they had two guys rather than a girl. [laughter]

Different gender. Yes.

Or a girl and a guy, or whatever. I just think back. I thought I had a pretty good childhood. There wasn't anything atypical about it. We didn't have a lot, but I didn't know that at the time. It didn't seem to matter. As I said, as I got a little older, I saw more of a class distinction in junior high and high school, but it's interesting. I don't know which letters that you're reading, because probably not a lot of them are from people that I went to high school or college with.

Yes, only two from college—of the letters when you retired.

OK. Because I suspect that the person who organized this . . . I don't know who it was. I could guess, maybe, that the governor got it going, so maybe it was on our advertising. Normally, sometimes they will do that. Then they'll ask people, and they'll get a list, not from me, because I didn't know anything about it. So they'll be people they know here in Nevada.

But I think the one thing that people would say—and I will give you some examples—is that I seem to be able to make friends or have friends across the board, whether they were Greasers in those days, guys who worked on their cars, like in the movie *Grease* . . . . That was of my era, the 1950s, when I went to high school. And with the DA's haircuts, and I had a lot of buddies in that group. I was a class officer every year. I've got yearbooks—I looked pretty awful, but I was still elected, and yet I was very involved in sports, but not as much, I don't think, in high school.

That was earlier—sports?

Yes. I don't seem to remember. I was always on the tennis team. I was on the Catalina High School tennis team.

It seems to me as if my actual personal involvement in athletics, which I was very involved in earlier, tended to be put in the background there in high school, because I think I was just *so* involved in government—student government. I really have to say that when I went to high school we all went to Tucson High School as freshman, which was at that time the largest high school in the United States, because Tucson had gone through this incredible growth. And this, again, would have been in the late 1950s.

When you say the largest, about how many students?

The high school had 1,000 graduating seniors. And seniors is the smallest class. So at that time there were three high schools being built in different parts of the town. So my sophomore year, everybody in my area went to Catalina High School, and that was considered "the best," because it was in the more affluent part of town, and I guess they thought that was the best, I don't know. The sophomore year we had an opportunity to be involved in a big way in student government, because then you had diluted the size of the pool, but when I

went to Tucson High School, I went on a bus, and I have to tell you, I was a geek, a female geek. I had big, thick glasses—well, I actually have big, thick glasses on right now as we're talking, but these were worse. [laughter] There were no contact lenses. I had flat feet, so I had to have orthopedic shoes, and they only had one shoe—like this big, ugly, saddle shoe—and I had to wear that saddle shoe. [laughter] And we were talking about the Capezio shoes—forget that. Even if I could afford them.

You couldn't walk in them.

I couldn't, no, because I would get leg aches from having these flat feet, so I either put up with the pain, or I had to do something about it. So I had these little things put in and so on.

Then I had to have braces, because I had a jaw that came with my family, an under bite, so they had to shove my whole jaw back. Now, there was only one orthodontist in Tucson at the time, Dr. Tweed, and I went to school with his daughter, Perry Tweed, and he was just, of course, making money hand over fist, because at that time people were starting to think about things like braces, and so he had this young man with him. I got him, and, in fact, later on he got a Fulbright based upon the work in my mouth—of how it was before and after, that it hadn't gone back, that what he did kept itself in position my entire life.

So here you have this person that was just unbelievable: orthopedic shoes, thick glasses, braces, not clothes that anybody else wore, going on a school bus. [laughter] And you know what? I went down to that high school, and I ran for vice president of the freshman class in this huge high school, and I didn't even think about what I looked like. I mean, I only know what I looked like now by looking at pictures. I guess I must have recognized it, but it just didn't . . . why would I have run for vice president of the class and then made the finals, had to get up there in this auditorium in front of everybody, and give a talk? The girl I ran against, Lynn . . . I can't remember her last name, but she was the epitome: short, cute, little, blonde hair, cheerleader, freshman cheerleader, darling . . . da dat di dat. I beat her, and I was the vice president of the freshman class. I just don't know if everybody voted for me because they felt sorry for me, or why, or what kind of speech I gave. Have no idea, but I won, and that was the beginning, I guess, even though I'd done this in middle school, this was now a different arena, and where looks and appearance and all that were becoming more important. I understood that.

Yes. The high school cliques were very in with . . . .

Yes. But you know what? It didn't seem to matter to me. I guess not. Because then, all of a sudden, once I did that, then I started becoming friends with all these people who were "like this girl," but I also had all these other friends, too. Then we go off to this new high school where, clearly, if you'd been able to do this thing at Tucson High School, you were immediately chosen to be on the first student council, to set up the government, et cetera, and that led to other things. Because I've always liked people, regardless of who they were, I'm sure that's why I had these friends in different groups, never looked down on anybody. I thought everybody had something interesting. I just was that way.

So I obviously got elected to stuff in high school, and high school was just an unbelievable time for me, because everything seemed to go right. I won everything. The American Field Service Exchange Student Program was very, very big in Tucson, and from Tucson High School,

wow, the most outstanding person got to go. [stated with humor] We had the first year at Catalina. All the outstanding kids applied. I got to go. I was the only one chosen to go. I could remember, every time, particularly my senior year, someone would come from the principal's office with a note for me, it was almost always something good. It was never being called in to do something because I was bad.

Because you were in trouble?

No. It was always, "You've won this award. You've done this. You've gotten . . . . " It was just like I was so lucky. It was just good. It was just kind of about the best thing.

Let me ask about the American Field Service exchange student experience. Where did you go and for how long?

I went to Germany for the summer. They only had a summer program at that time. I lived with a German family in Heilbronn on Neckar.

Between which years? Sophomore to junior?

It's your junior summer year. My daughter did it, too, from Reno High School, as a matter of fact. She did exactly the same things I did. I went in 1957, I believe, the summer of 1957.

Tell me about that experience before we go on. There're a lot of good things happening here.

Too many things going on in high school.

Yes. Let's stop and talk about some of them. Tell me first about the summer in Germany.

When you asked me back awhile ago what classes I liked the best, I had a French teacher in high school, and first I thought she was middle school, but she wasn't, and I corresponded with her until she just died recently, and she taught French, so she was the one that encouraged me to apply for this. She was on the selection committee, and I'm sure that she was very helpful in picking me out of a lot of very outstanding kids. Any one of them could have been chosen and done a good job. She also was very influential in having me apply to Mount Holyoke, which was her alma mater. Her father was the world's authority on Balzac, a French author, and very academic—you would expect to see her as a professor on a college campus. She obviously didn't have a Ph.D., but she encouraged my interest in foreign languages and a variety of other kinds of more academic intellectual pursuits, and I got chosen for this.

Of course, I wanted to go to France, because I was taking French, and that didn't work out. It hardly ever does. So, anyway, I got to go to Germany.

I had discussed this with my parents before I'd ever applied, that if I won, would we be able to come up with some of the money? There was a chapter that raised money, as well, an AFS chapter, but because this was a new school, the chapter wasn't as large or as into money raising as the one at Tucson High School had been. But my dad talked to me and told me, of course, they were so proud of me, and that it would work out, and it did.

When I left to go on this big excursion, it was the first time I'd ever been on a plane—a lot of firsts. They put me on a plane, and I flew to Detroit, and in Detroit I met thousands of other AFS kids, and we then, I think, got on to the Saint Lawrence River. I guess you can do that in Detroit by going over to Windsor or Toronto. So we got on a boat, the *Arosa Kulm*, and that was an American Field Service, AFS, boat. The

AFS at that time was the premier foreign exchange program. It may have been the only one. It grew out of an ambulance service in World War I in France, but it was a very, very reputable, very well-known exchange program. So there were hundreds of great kids who went on this—thousands, probably—throughout the world, but at that time it was pretty much focused on Europe. So we met all these kids in Detroit, got on this boat, went up the Saint Lawrence River, which was in itself a fabulous experience, and then ultimately crossed the Atlantic.

So, you went by boat all of the way, rather than flying?

Yes. In those days they had their own boat. Now, I'm sure that . . . . The boat sank. [laughter] It sank, in fact, later on. There were pictures of the *Arosa Kulm* going [smack] like that direction into the ocean. The North Sea was the one experience you remember, because it was so unbelievably bad. [laughter] And talk about upchuck—all the time. The food, I gather, was pretty darn good even for a kid boat, but it was just thousands of kids and a few counselors to try to keep track of these kids running around. [laughter] I mean, how much better to put us on a plane. But I don't think intercontinental . . . this was in 1957. I don't think there was a lot of that. It probably was unbelievably expensive. And the boat, they could just pack us in like sardines and send us on our way.

So, once you got through the North Sea, where most of us spent the time at the rail, because it was a really bad storm we ran into, as well, we landed in Bremerhaven or Düsseldorf. I don't remember now—I'd have to look on my map of Germany. Anyway, it was way, of course, on the North Sea or the channel that comes in there. Then you disperse. I was going down to southern Germany, right near Heidelberg, where the university is. It's called Heilbronn on Neckar, on the Neckar River, which Heidelberg is also on the Neckar River. We didn't know anybody. I didn't speak the language. And all of a sudden I was then sent with a few other kids, and that first night we actually had dinner on a floating restaurant on the Rhine River. Whew! This was just unbelievable. And the people were wonderful. I didn't want to leave. I wanted to stay with them. Then we got on a train and went down along the Rhine until I got down to my home in Heilbronn, and there were a number of other kids there. I have pictures of some of my buddies who lived in the city, not many, but maybe five or six. There had been an army base right close by, a U.S. Army base. Remember, this is 1957, not long after the end of World War II.

Right. Ten years, twelve years.

Yes. That's not long after something like this. Some of the city was still bombed out, although Germany was incredible in terms of reconstructing themselves versus France, which, like many places, looked like World War II, still. They just hadn't gotten around to it. At that point it really clicked in my brain what a difference between the German people and the French people in terms of their industriousness or their commitment to cleaning up or taking orders, or whatever.

The family I lived with . . . I found that most families take you for a reason, normally very personalized. They wanted their daughter to learn how to speak English well enough to get to go back on the AFS program to America, which was fine, and the gal was just great, Ulrika Gast, Uli. And *Mudi* was Mom and *Fadi* was Dad, although I never saw Dad the entire summer until the last weekend, and I kept wondering why, and I was told that he was a traveling salesman. The family was very middle class,

no refrigerator. Every day we went to market and got what we needed for that day, and the one thing that the AFS people rammed into your head was, "Don't cause any problems. Go along." And they had people you could contact if things didn't work out, if you had to change families. My family was not perfect, but I was very homesick, as everybody was. You're sixteen years old; you're sent over there; you don't know a *person.* I bet I wrote a letter home every day, saying, "I want to come home. I want to come home. I want to come home." I know all this because of my daughter going through the same thing thirty years later.

But I didn't come home. You did what your family did. Well, because they didn't have a lot of money, we didn't do much, except the gal was really cool. She had a neat boyfriend, Peter, who was really hoping to be some kind of an Olympic track star or something. A handsome, young boy, looked like your typical Aryan type of a kid—blonde and good looking. We did a lot of things. Like we'd sneak out at night, Uli and I, and go off. She'd take me to a *Biergarten,* which, of course, we weren't supposed to do. I collected all these little *Bierdeckels,* coasters that you put your beer mug on. There were all these old guys in these *Biergartens,* except the two of us. [laughter] She was the same age as I was. Then we'd smoke cigarettes. We'd go to vending machines, and I'd buy cigarettes, like I was not supposed to do. [laughter] Drink and smoke. I got that out of my system, because you could do that over there. Of course, at meals they would drink wine or beer, and I gained *thirty pounds* in one summer, because I kept saying, "Well, they told me to do it." [laughter] So, it was eat, and Germans aren't known for delicate meals. [laughter] Heavy stuff. And just dah, dah, dah, just piled it in, and loved every single thing. *Wiener Schnitzel,* oh man. Just thought that was the best. And for breakfast you'd have rolls and meat, like blood sausage and ugly stuff that I probably would hate today, but thought it was fabulous then. Jams and stuff.

You were there during the summer, so they were out of school, like they were in America?

No, to some extent. She was in school quite a bit.

And did you go to school?

Yes. I did. Yes. But I went to school only as sort of a novelty, because everything was in German, and I didn't know any German, so I went just to see how the school was run and so on.

You didn't have homework or grading or any of that?

No. No. That was not part of the assignment.

Could you tell that the schools were different from American schools?

Yes. I did feel the same way that most people thought, that they were further ahead than we were in English. She had a very good command of the English language, was taking French, of course, understood German, her own language—languages by far. I thought she had a pretty good understanding of American government, where I had hardly any about Germany until I got ready to go there and did some reading. But, yes, I'd say I was pretty impressed, and yes, the school system was not exactly on the same shift, so she was gone a lot, and I was alone a lot. And Mudi—she didn't speak any English, so we just kind of like . . . that's why I ate a lot, I think, because it was something else to do.

And then, the organizer in Heilbronn, the town, wasn't, I think, as good as it could have been for AFS students. I think that the number of us should have gotten together more often than we did, because we all felt exactly the same way. When we got together we'd talk about things, and we had the same problems, the same difficulties, and we wanted to share more, but we weren't able to do that very often.

We did go on a huge bike trip down to the Boden Sea, which is called Lake Constance, which divides Switzerland, Austria, and Germany. It's a huge resort area, and we biked down there, all of us, which was fabulous fun. I felt that it was the most maturing experience anybody could ever have, because I grew up so much in terms of understanding, and again, how to get along in difficult situations and how to tough it out. I really felt that for the Germans there was really a lot of negative feelings toward Americans. Actually—one horrifying experience—I was in a department store with my mother and my sister, and a woman knew that someone had pointed me out as an American, and had a dog and let it loose on me, and said, "Sic, sic, sic. Sic her." They had to haul the dog off. When I would go into people's homes, occasionally, not all homes, but I'd see a picture of Hitler in their room, still. It was just kind of eye opening to me.

I remember one particular instance with my German sister. We were standing at a train station for some reason, and a man got off, and she said, "Oh, that guy is an American."

I said, "How do you know that?"

She said, "Look at his suit. It's all wrinkled."

I said, "Well, how would you know?"

She said, "Well, your material is so inferior to ours."

I just remembered that comment, and there were many, many things like that, but I still felt close to her and really loved her. I did finally meet the father, as I said, on my last weekend, and when he walked in I thought he was Hitler. He looked *exactly* like him, and I thought, *"That's* the reason he's been gone all summer!" [laughter]

It's really Hitler.

My imagination just went crazy. He'd been hiding away! He had the little mustache; he had the hair. He was exactly . . . . And then, I noticed—and this was an interesting observation—how Mudi waited on him, and I didn't like that. There was something about that that didn't set right with me, even when I was in high school, that a woman should not run around and put the slippers on, have them there. I don't know, probably there isn't anything wrong with that, but to me, it wasn't right.

You'd never seen that in your own home?

No. No. I thought it was too subservient. I just chalked it off to being a different culture, but it stuck in my mind as being something, and I hadn't seen that, of course, because he hadn't been there until he came home, and maybe it just happened because I was there, or because he had just come home. I don't know, but anyway, to me it was probably the most *defining* time of my life in terms of maturing, because when I came back, all the kids, all my friends, were at the airport to meet me. Hardly any of them recognized me, because I'd gained so much weight. [laughter]

"Where's Sue? Where's Sue? Oh, my God, look at her. She rolled off the plane." [laughter]

Worse than that first year at college?

Yes.

They always talk about the dorm food in college.

No, I had that experience at the camp in Wisconsin. That was my other fattening experience. But I realized when I got back to my senior year, I was interested in totally different things, and they were still in cheerleading, and I thought, "I'm way beyond that." I had to really kind of rein myself in, because I didn't want to sound like I was a snob, or I was more educated than they.

Or worldly?

Or more worldly, more sophisticated. When kids asked me, "How was it?"

I'd just say, "Great!" And that's all they needed to hear.

But I did work on the newspaper, so I got a chance to write stories about it and so on, which was good, because that way I could get it out. If they wanted to read it, they could. If they didn't, they didn't have to. But it was an incredible experience in terms of, in my own mind, thinking what's really important and what isn't.

And what kinds of things did you decide, when you were defining what's important, what isn't?

I guess I'd say one of the things I didn't find important was who was going to make the cheerleading squad, or who Dick Bowser had invited to the prom, or who Jim Seal was dating. I kept thinking, "Why don't they care about what's going on in our country? Do they understand that these people over there, some of them still revere Hitler?" And bigger things, I thought. And why should they? How could they? I kept saying that to myself, "It's not that big a deal. You've had an experience they haven't." It just made me see, in my mind, the bigger picture.

But even though that was all going on, my senior year was just great, and at the time, junior year, also, you are elected to go to Girls State. I did mention that. And I went to Girls State, and I was elected mayor. And you move up. You start at the local level of government, and you learn about city government, county government. Then you choose whatever you want to run for, and you don't have to run for anything, I guess, but I wound up running for governor. I was the gubernatorial candidate of my party, and, boy, another big learning experience, which paid off later on in life.

What things?

Well, I had to give a speech to the assembled crowd, and I was very nervous, because this was a big deal, the governor of Girls State. I had a friend whom I met there, who had gone to Girls Nation. They select two girls to be the U.S. senators to go on to Washington. So they come back. They're a year ahead. They come back and kind of are the big mentors, counselors. So she helped me with my speech, and she decided that I should get beyond this traditional stuff and do something big. I did. It didn't work.

Besides that I was scared to death. My knees knocked together so much, they were black and blue by the time I was done. The little, old ladies at the American Legion, who sponsored this, were sitting back there, I'm sure, just looking at those knees. [laughter] I lost by one vote. I didn't vote for myself; that was the one vote that would have caused a tie. I later on thought, "Well, if you thought you were good enough to be governor, why wouldn't you vote for yourself?" I never voted for myself in high school, because I thought it was arrogant, although it was a secret ballot. What the

heck? Who knew? "And besides that, you're running. Why don't you vote for yourself?"

So, two things I learned here. One was that you should vote for yourself, and the other was that I needed some help in public speaking. Although it never seemed to bother me before, clearly, it did. So, my senior year I took public speaking, hated every minute of it, *but* learned a whole lot. Secondly, of course, I always voted for myself thereafter. In fact, I know Bill Raggio already knows this, but when I first ran for the senate, we both ran at large, so people could vote for two, and it had always been Bill Raggio and Cliff Young who ran as a team. When Cliff decided not to run, he endorsed me, so it was Bill and I and some other people. So not only did I vote for myself, but the campaign staff decided on women to single shot me—meaning, even though these women could vote for two, they'd only vote for one—which meant Sue would get twice as many votes in the end. So I beat Bill Raggio in total number of votes, after all these many years of his running, and my being a first-time senate candidate.

So you take one experience, and you turn it around, and even turn it around to be more than just voting for yourself. [laughter] My senior year, when I did take the public-speaking class, ultimately, I spoke at graduation, and my sister said to me, just several weeks ago when she was up here, she still remembers what an incredible speech I gave and how nothing seemed to bother me, and that I hadn't even started writing it until a couple of days before, which is very unlike me. Even now I do prepare quite extensively, and practice and everything, but then, I guess, I didn't. But, clearly, the class made a huge difference, because I do enjoy it. It's one of the things I really like to do is speak publicly. I feel it's extremely important in order to get a message over, and I think if you can speak in front of two, two hundred, two thousand, twenty thousand, it doesn't make any difference: it's really the same thing. But I learned that was true by not doing a good job and losing the only race I've ever lost.

I tell the story when I go to Girls State. I was asked to go this year, because somebody dropped out, and they know they can call on me. They have a city at Girls State, named the Sue Wagner City.

Did you take other public speaking after high school?

No. That was it.

That did it? That was what you needed?

Yes. It was the ability to get up. Paul McCready, the teacher, would make us get up, and he'd point a finger—no eye contact—and you would sink down in your desk, hoping nobody would see you. Of course, that's what you were there for. [laughter] And he'd say, "OK. Talk about . . . " just some absurd thing like a leaf, like a caterpillar becoming a butterfly. You'd just have to think about something very off the subject and then get up and talk about it, and then, of course, all your friends were in the class. They'd go, "nyah, nyah."

Making faces and giving you a hard time?

Making funny faces. Yes.

Making it as hard as possible?

And doing all those kinds of . . . . [laughter] So if you could get through that, then you could get through anything. Clearly, obviously, he must have told us how to prepare, how to put your thoughts together, and that kind of thing, because that's the only experience I've ever had, and personally, I just think it takes something like that and practice, practice,

Sue's high-school portrait.

practice. And you get the practice by doing it, by having the opportunities to do it. So, I had a lot of opportunities, not only in high school, but then on into college, and we haven't even gotten to college yet. [laughter]

Now, I want to make sure we cover everything in high school. You also mentioned being on a tennis team?

Yes, I was on the Catalina High School tennis team. They'd have a ladder. You could challenge somebody above you, and if you knocked him or her off, you'd move up. I think I was probably fourth or fifth. I was not the best, but I was on the team, won my letter, but I don't remember a lot

Sue at Girls State, which she attended twenty-three years in a row. *"They have a city at Girls State, named Sue Wagner City."*

of other organized activities that I was in—athletic activities, that is.

I don't remember a lot of team sports for girls in high school, although there's a GAA, the Girls Athletic Association, so there must have been, but it's certainly *nothing* like today, where it's absolutely wonderful for girls. Tonight is the soccer, USA versus Brazil—not the World Cup, but getting ready for the Olympics.

It was a different time, then. That was what I was wondering.

It *was* a totally different time.

You graduated in 1958, so in the 1950s and early 1960s, even still, that was a time when girls' sports had not developed.

Not until the 1970s. I'm going to say 1973, but that was *Roe v. Wade*. I don't know when Title IX came into play, but it was in the 1970s, because it was under Richard Nixon, and Caspar Weinberger actually was the Secretary of Health, Education and Welfare, and he's the one who really recommended this change—equity for women, for gender equity in athletics, which is the single most important thing that's happened for young women, in terms of learning all about team sports and participating in everything.

Say a little bit more about that, the single most important thing for girls.

Well, I think there are many important things that have happened to women in my time. I was thinking about what we called the women's movement the other day. I personally think Gloria Steinem and Betty Friedan were revolutionaries. They made this movement, they started it, and then it was taken over by AAUW, American Association of University Women, and BPW, Business and Professional Women—groups that were definitely mainstream. Once that was accepted, it became like any other revolution after years, a part of our consciousness and mainstream. But if it wasn't "radicals" like those women, nothing happens. There aren't those, then, groups.

You would take it all the way to the extreme, so that you could get the real work.

You got to have them be out there. Somebody, whoever it may be, whether it's Thomas Paine, Thomas Jefferson, or whoever starts something, that is, in my mind, a revolution. But I think it's mainly seen in two areas: politics, where I think you can make the most difference for women, and because it's so visible, more than in business, actually; and in athletics. I think that that has just become an incredible change. We now see men who have daughters who totally thought things were different when they were in college, and now it's their daughters who have taken precedence in their lives. She deserves a scholarship, and they want to go to her games, and that's transformed a very important part of our lives, and, of course, as you know, I'm so interested in athletics and politics, government, so to me they're two doubly important things that have happened.

But I think with women's sports, you have individual sports, and you have team sports. Now, my daughter, Kristi, for example, was a fabulous golfer, an individual sport, and she also played basketball, but I'd say golf

was by far the more important thing. My son Kirk, the same thing, golf and basketball. But I think we all hear about the team concept, that girls never had that opportunity to learn how to share and work things out, win, lose, and that that's what's given men the edge in many ways over women, that we never had that opportunity. That may be true. I suspect there is a lot of truth to that, but we clearly have become a world of thinking that women's sports are just OK, and the fact that women have muscles and have defined bodies, is not weird and obnoxious. We see Brandy Chastain, the soccer player, who ripped off her T-shirt and showed her sports bra to the world and her fabulous abs. If only we could have abs that looked like that. [laughter] But then, I don't want to work out like that, or I can't work out like that. That was just unbelievable. And nothing was wrong with that, except was she doing it for Nike? Or what were her real motives? But that had nothing to do with her body and looking like she did.

And none of that would have happened in the 1950s or the 1960s.

None of that happened before the advent of Title IX. The fact that these girls got scholarships, and it was acceptable, and it was great, and you had an entire stadium of 100,000 people watching this game, and millions of people watching it on television in the World Cup, and the fact that it was great, and that WNBA, Women's National Basketball Association—people are watching that in droves. In fact, our former UNR basketball coach, Sonny Allen, now is the coach of the Sacramento women's team, and every time they're on TV I watch them, because I see Sonny, and I wish him well, and here's a *guy* guy, who'd only done men's coaching, now coaching a professional women's team, and doing the same things, having great success. You don't see a lot of women dunking, but you see just about everything else.

Now, my mother has a difficult time with seeing women basketball players, although, she's just a *big* Arizona basketball guys' fan, and now sends me clippings on the women's golf and softball and other things I've gotten her into. But the basketball—they're a little too muscular for her, I think. Maybe she wonders about crossing the gender line there, but I don't think that's much of an issue these days, and it was, if you were just like some big hunk, I suspect, if you looked like Babe Zaharias. I think she was just selected as the century's outstanding woman athlete, when they just did all those things a while ago. She was a fabulous golfer, javelin thrower—all of these different things. She was married, but there were all these questions about her and her sexuality. Even to this day, there are some about the German swimmers, and particularly when we had the wall between East and West Germany and so on. There were always questions about what kind of drugs they were getting over there, and we now learn that some of them *were* getting steroids, male hormones, and things that they shouldn't have. They didn't know about it in some instances, and it was a terrible shame to do that to their bodies, but I don't think that's so much an issue anymore, which is good.

So, it's just interesting, too, that you liked sports all the way through, but high school was sort of the time when you did about the least, maybe, in sports.

Yes. Tennis.

And that was about it?

Yes. Same in college. I know the only sport I was involved in was tennis in college.

Except for when I became the pitcher for my sorority team, and then the Thetas took on the Pi Phi's, and the Thetas always won, because I was the pitcher, [laughter] but that was the only time that I did anything like that, and I guess it was because it just wasn't . . . I don't know. In my sorority there were many girls who were . . . interestingly enough, the Thetas had kind of an interesting grouping of people. There were the beauty queens, and there were the athletes, and there were the campus leaders, and there were just a variety of different girls who did different things. Each of them excelled in their own areas, the academics, and that's what I liked about that particular sorority, but I think sports, to me, became more of a passive thing than an active thing.

I will say this, when I was younger, middle school, particularly, the Cleveland Indians did spring training in Tucson, and my dad, if you remember, played baseball in college, and he was a great sports fan. We only had a little black-and-white TV in the 1950s, and the only thing that was on was boxing. I remember my dad sitting in the chair and moving around, ducking with every body movement. My mom says to this day that if Daddy were alive, and you had all this morning-to-night sports, he would just be in fat city. But he and I used to go to the Cleveland Indians spring-training games, which were free—beautiful weather, sit out in the sun—knew all the players, and they were famous. They'd just won the World Series in the late 1950s, when we went. He'd pick me up after school, and I'd go with him, and so that was a real bond I had with my dad, and also encouraged my interest in sports. That was a big connection. The politics and the sports, I guess, I could really relate back to my father, and doing things with him with those two interests of mine. But I never had an interest in becoming a softball player, for example, except in these charity type or fun type of things, but I am a *great* sports fan watching it, and watching my team, and so on, and I've mentioned my Cleveland Indian connection with my friend, Assemblywoman Jan Evans—we're Cleveland Indian fans—and how we used to kind of broadcast the games to each other on the phone and so on, but that interest came from my dad taking me and getting to know all of that, and him explaining everything to me, how the game was played and all that. So it was important, but as far as my participating in it, it kind of dwindled at that point.

Let's talk a little bit more about high school. You went to Girls State, came back as a senior. Was there anything else from your earlier years that really struck a chord, or shall we talk about graduation and when you get ready for college?

Well, I think the thing was my moving into high school freshman year at this huge high school, then kind of organizing my sophomore, junior years, getting very involved in just about everything. I was never president of the class. I was always vice president of the class. Never ran for president, because it was always a boy thing.

Did you think of running for president of the class?

Yes, but I figured I wouldn't win.

Because you could clearly see it was a guy who got that.

Yes. And I didn't want to be secretary, because that was too much of a woman thing, but I wanted to be, interestingly enough, lieutenant governor! [laughter] I wanted to be as close as I could to the thing that maybe I couldn't be. I don't know, but

I would *never* have run for secretary. I think I was vice president of my class every year. I definitely was the freshman year. My senior year I was president of what was called Girls League, which was like the girls student body, and then I was also vice president of the senior class, and I think I was vice president of the junior class, I'm pretty sure. But I was very involved in the student newspaper. I was involved in a lot of things.

And you said that you gave the commencement address when you graduated?

Yes. I had two cousins who are my exact age, and we all were graduation speakers—all in different parts of the country—and my mother used to tell me, "The two of them were valedictorians, and you were elected." [laughter] Which is true. In my school they elected their speakers, and you had to be in the top five to ten percent or something like that. I probably was twentieth out of my class of four hundred or something, but not number one. But then, they elected you to give the speech, and there were four of us, I think.

Four students who gave talks?

Yes. I think so. Two or four. I think there were four.

Do you remember that address?

No.

You don't? Your sister does, though.

I don't think she remembers what it was, but she remembers how well I gave it, in her mind, and she's always been very proud of me and very supportive of everything I've done. She was just amazed at my calmness about it, and this would be very difficult for her. She's just not the same kind of person at all.

You'd developed some poise by this time?

Yes. Evidently.

The knees weren't knocking anymore?

No. No more knee knocking. But see, I took that experience and then did something about it. I think that I did that in a lot of cases throughout my life. I don't know what made me do that, but if I saw some kind of deficiency . . . in my mind it was a deficiency. Now, a lot of people wouldn't have cared, because they figured, "Hey, I don't care. I'm not going to do this again." But for some reason I thought I would.

You overcame it.

I thought I would need this skill, and I thought it was an important skill. I thought there were two really important skills. One was to learn how to write well and the other to speak well, and I suspect that was my traditional liberal arts upbringing, that those were real keys to doing well in the liberal arts course, I guess.

I want to ask you a couple of more things about your family during these years up to your graduation, things we haven't covered. One is religion, and the other is work. Let's start with work. Did you work at all during high school after the candy-selling job?

Well, that was, of course, way back in elementary school. I'm trying to think of the different jobs I had. One job that was pretty important to me was working at Burns' Floral Shop, which is still a pretty nice florist place there in Tucson. I worked there every holiday. I know I had some

other jobs, but this is one that stands out in my mind. Anyway, I worked on holidays, and then I worked in the summers at this floral shop, and basically, it wasn't making things—it was selling. It was really great, and I did this through college, as well, because guys would come in and get corsages for dates and so on, so I knew who everybody was taking. [laughter]

You knew what everybody was doing?

Yes, and I knew who was taking who, because I'd made the corsage, and they had to be delivered and all that sort of thing. So that was kind of fun. I liked it a lot. But what I think I liked about it was the people. And I remember I did not like . . . and I always say this to people, even to this day, when I go somewhere. I was at the Name Droppers just the other day, over here in Arlington Gardens, and somebody was just hanging around, and she said, "Oh, I'm just bored."
I said, "Are you clock watching?"
And she said, "Yes."
I said, "Well, when it's slow, and you're not busy, it seems like it drags on forever, but I remember when I worked," and I was thinking of my floral days, "that when you were busy, whew! Time just flew. But when you were just standing around, standing around, standing around, and there wasn't anybody there, it seemed to drag on."
But I think it was also the connection with people. I do remember one thing my mother had said about me, and probably if you called her today, she'd say the same thing, "My daughter, Sue, could speak to a cotton picker, turn around, and speak to the president of the United States, within the same five-minute period of time, and each would be involved in a conversation that was totally relevant." To the Maricopa County cotton picker, because that's where the best cotton came from, Pima County cotton, Pima cotton, and the president of the United States. That's exactly how I

perceive myself, and I was perceived in high school, as I say, and in college of having all these different friends from different groups and so on. My daughter feels very strongly that she's the same way. She will say to me that to this day, when she was in high school, she had the same kind of career I did, same thing at the university, that she sees herself as being well liked across the board.

But as far as jobs, it's the one that stands out in my mind. I must have had others. I will say that one of the reasons I did get scholarships to Mount Holyoke—I had mentioned my French teacher. I also got a scholarship to Pomona, but they weren't enough. They weren't a full ride, so I couldn't take them, and besides, Mount Holyoke was so far away. So I went to the University of Arizona. It was very close, and I think one of the reasons I didn't have to work full time was because I got all these scholarships and full-ride tuition. We didn't have enough money. I did join a sorority, but I couldn't live in the sorority house, because it was too expensive, and my house was very close. So that's the only one that really stands out right now in my mind.

The other question I had was about religion, and maybe touch also on any family traditions, holidays. Somehow that all connects in my mind. It may or may not when you think about it.

Well, my father was Catholic, and my mother was like Congregationalist or something that was very New England, but we all became Episcopalians, which, I guess, was the thing that seemed to satisfy everybody as a moderate choice, but I grew up being an Episcopalian. Now, my dad's drugstore in Maine, going back as a little child, is right across the street from St. Alban's Episcopal Church, so my dad was very active in the church, and my mother

was, probably, too. I just remember my dad being on the vestry, and that was kind of like the council that made the decisions. Even if he couldn't go to church with me, then he would drop me off when he went to open up the drugstore, so I had perfect attendance all through elementary school. We were all pretty involved in the Episcopal Church.

Then, when we moved to Tucson we became members of a beautiful Episcopal Church called St. Philip's in the Hills, which my mother is still very active in, and my daughter goes now, takes my mother. I don't remember being as involved, although we went to church, but in the fifth grade I don't remember being as involved in Sunday school and things like that, but we've always been very active. The Episcopal Church, though, is not one that you become fervent about, I don't believe. George Bush is an Episcopalian, for example, and it's very New England. The perfect description, I said, a New England, Republican Episcopalian. That's pretty standard. The Episcopal Church is very open. It's very close to the Catholic Church, in terms of their ritual, which I like, but it also isn't something that you get all exercised about like Catholics. Look at Mexico. They just had the Mexican election, and I believe they upset the PRI party [Institutional Revolutionary Party] yesterday. I went to Mexico. I was down there as a guest of the PRI party in 1975, so I have a great interest in Mexico and their elections, but for the very first time, I believe in, I don't know, centuries, have they lost, because they had the first open election and had people there making sure everybody got a chance to vote.

So the church was there, but it wasn't . . . .

Right.

You were more passionate, it sounds like, about your student government and that type of thing.

Yes, yes.

The church was there, though, for your family.

I think that's a fair assessment to make, that church was something we did. In fact, at this church in Tucson, St. Philip's, you had to get like a ticket to go to Christmas Eve service, because it was such an unbelievable church, and particularly on those big holidays, everybody wanted to go, and getting a ticket to go to your own church kind of . . . I don't know. But it was a church where the rector didn't reach out to kids. It just wasn't . . . I don't want to say a senior citizen church, because I don't mean that at all. The rector was more theatrical and dramatic, and you never thought about going to him if you had a problem. Now the church is totally different. It has got a rector for every possible thing going on down there. It sounds wonderful. I was married in that church. My husband was Episcopalian as well. His father happened to be Catholic and changed, because neither one of our dads believed in certain things and couldn't buy into certain practices. So it was perfect. But even though my kids have been baptized and confirmed, and I feel very strongly about that, none of my granddaughters have, and I keep mentioning that to my son, without being pushy, and nothing's happened. So religion, even though I'm a lay reader . . . . I will say this, in my church here, Trinity Parish, I was the first woman lay reader in the 1970s, and then I became the first woman to pass a chalice, and that was a big deal, and I think I was hand selected, personally, because I was an elected official, and somehow it would go down better if I broke the barrier, and it

did. Even though I do that, I have to admit I have really reached for a spirituality that I haven't found. And I try. I really do, but I think part of it is my church. We had a woman rector there, but she got squeezed out, and that doesn't really make me feel good either, even though, you read in the paper, we're one of the mainstream churches that will accept gays, lesbians— we don't ostracize them. So in many ways, they're very open, but they've got a way to go, but that's not the reason. It's just me. When I went through so much difficulty in my own life after a plane crash and being paralyzed, I realized that a lot of people turn to God when they have these traumatic things happen to them, and they can't . . . they make promises.

I do believe that that is true. I've seen this with many of my friends who have had problems, that they've tried everything, and it doesn't work, and so they finally turn to God or to Jesus, and it works for them. For me, I really did not realize in my plane crash what it would be like at the end. I thought I'd be just like I was before, so needless to say, this thought didn't occur, but when I had Guillain-Barré, that was real scary, and I was totally awake and realized that I was becoming paralyzed. I thought to myself, staring up at the ceiling, "This is the time for me to make a commitment to God, that if I become not paralyzed and can walk and do everything again, I will dedicate my life to him or whatever." I couldn't do that. Actually, I just had this conversation with my neighbor today.

She said, "Oh, I couldn't do that, either." She's Methodist or Presbyterian or something like that, but, I don't know. My sister is *very* . . . she's a "born again," I would say. In fact, she went off from the Episcopal Church and did some missionary work and so on, but she and I don't talk about this much, because we realize we have a totally different view on spirituality and religion.

I've talked to my mother about this, because she goes to church every Sunday. She feels the same way I do, and she's talked to her Episcopal priest. There's a little poem she gave to me which I have in my room. I can read it to you. If it's important, I will get it and do it, but it's very short. Basically, it just says, "Please forgive my unbelieving." And that's pretty much where I am, and that's pretty much where I think a lot of Episcopalians are, to be honest with you. I certainly don't want to go off and become a member of another church. Never would do that, but it's not something I have not thought about. I've given it a lot of thought. I've talked to a lot of people. I've talked to my friend, Jean Ford, about how she felt about it, particularly near the end of her life, but at the church that she belonged to—talk about being free and not having any structure.

She was with the Unitarian Church.

Yes. Yes, she was with the Unitarian Church, so they didn't even have a pastor or rector or priest or anybody, so there's no structure, and so, she pretty much just kind of believed what she wanted.

Since I am in more of an organized, structured church, I pretty much do the same thing, but on the surface it is a part of my life. Internally, it's not an important part of my life. I wish it were. I think it would be easier to deal with getting old, to deal with pain.

All kinds of limitations, all kinds of things.

Yes. But I just can't get there, yet.

What about family traditions, holidays? Were there some things like that that were important in your family?

Now, are you speaking of my immediate family, or my mother-father-type family?

Let's talk about your mother and father's family, the family you grew up in, at this point, because we'll come back to this question when we talk about your children. Any things that, during the time you were growing up, where Christmas is special?

Christmas was big, big, big.

Birthdays, Easter?

Yes. I'd say those three. I think Christmas was huge, and particularly because it was in Maine: snow and trees, and even today I notice every single card I select looks like a house, a scene, or something in New England. Absolutely, I know it to this day, I go and look directly at that, because it's memory of my childhood. To me that was perfect. I think Maine is just perfect, except the weather. I mean that it's perfect on the Christmas card.

It's very cold?

But even the summers, if you get a few nice days . . . When I was there we ran into Hurricane Floyd, the last terrible hurricane we had. It was right behind our shoulders all the way we went, so it kind of ruined the trip, and that was just last year, the fall of 1999. So, you do take your chances, but I guess for every kid your childhood memories, if you had a fairly decent childhood, they become bigger than life. My husband grew up in Alaska—the same kind of thing.

I think Christmas was just marvelous, and we did decorate. We also had a basement in the house that I lived in. I just took a picture of my old house, and it's been kept up really well, the one across from the cemetery, and the basement my mother used to decorate up for parties and things, and I can remember having Halloween parties down there, and it would be like a haunted house, and there would be black things hanging down. It was like spiders or things. And then, we had a lot of wonderful things taken from a boat that had sunk in Camden Harbor, like an anchor and a bell, and they were in our basement. So our basement was all decorated in a maritime kind of scene, even though it was hand painted by all of us and so on. It looked like waves on the wall and things, but she'd do a really good job, I think, of decorating. The basement, even though it had a big furnace that you shoveled coal into, was used for parties and things.

Birthday parties—my mother made a big effort in celebrating our birthdays, and of course, I only remember mine, and a little bit of my brother's, because my sister was married when I was seven, so she was gone, and I was happy, because I got the bedroom to myself.

You didn't have to share.

Right, because she was married when she was nineteen. Easter, because we were very involved in the church, again, we had Easter baskets. Now, a big day when I was little was May Day. May first is May Day, and that was a huge thing, and you would make little May baskets and go leave them on people's doorsteps or on their doorknobs. I don't know if you're familiar with this.

I am. We had the same where I was growing up in Iowa. It was a big thing for the kids. We loved it.

Yes. Right. Right. Me, too, but that is not even a thing, and no one even heard of May Day, except in the Soviet Union, where they have the big parade honoring the Kremlin, Stalin and everybody. But that was big, and we used to make all these cute, little baskets, I remember. And Easter, with all the little heart candies and things, and Halloween—very big. I used to have

homemade costumes. One time, I was at a Halloween with my sister. I have a picture. In fact, I'll show it to you. It's on my wall. She decorated me as a pirate. My sister went to an interior design school, after she graduated from high school, in Boston to become a, I don't know, either a clothes designer or maybe a designer of displays in stores, but she's got a real artistic talent, and, boy, you should have seen this pirate thing I had. Whew! Silk bandanas and big eye patch and the sword. Really looked great, but nothing you buy in a store. So, Halloween was big, too, and, of course, I carried that on in my own family, but I think May Day, Easter, Halloween . . .

Real celebration times?

Yes.

And were they a special time for your family or a time for family with friends? Sort of sounds like family with friends, maybe.

No, I don't remember myself my parents having a lot of other friends, couple friends. I don't remember that at all. And I don't know if it's because all they did was work, either at the drugstore or piano teaching or what. I just don't remember that. Maybe my sister would, but I don't. I do remember I had a wonderful godmother, and she was a close friend of my mother's. Ruth Barstow her name was, a lovely woman, lived in a great house in the woods, birch trees. I can see it in Maine, Cape Elizabeth. My mother did a lot of "home" things, like she knitted. She was a beautiful knitter. Made us lots of sweaters and things, and my sister carried on that tradition, still does a very nice job, and my mother and sister are both great seamstresses. I'm none of those things. That's pretty much, I think, all that I can remember right now.

And then also, I think it sounds like a family tradition that your evening meals were spent talking politics and world events, community events and so on.

Yes. Yes.

So it sounds like you had special times with your family.

Yes. I think so. And of course, it was different, because I was pretty much an only child at that time. I remember my brother was in high school, gone, working, other friends. I was just a pest.

The younger kid sister.

Sometimes they, yes, had to baby-sit or something like that. And my sister was pretty good. My brother—I was telling somebody about this the other day. When my brother would baby-sit, he would get a cigarette, tie me to a chair and see how close he could get to burning my flesh. He was just *mean*. And then, he would scare me to death after I'd gone to bed, come in dressed up like some monster. I'd tell my parents about this. "Oh, he wouldn't do that." Sort of like what *I* used to do in school. [laughter] But nobody would believe it.

My brother and I are really pretty good friends now, but he was just a . . . I was sure I was just a pain in the butt. I was for my sister, too, because I remember she had a lot of hot dates in high school. My sister was quite the hottie, I guess, and she used to have to drive me around. I remember going to the beach and stuff with them, and I'd catch them doing stuff. [laughter] Oh, she would just cut off my tongue if I ever said anything to my mother. My sister and I, as I have told you, and we will probably talk about later . . . my sister has been very important to my life in times when I have needed somebody. But at that time I didn't

know her. I really didn't know her until I got married and had more in common with her, and I think that's probably pretty typical.

Yes. With such an age difference.

Yes. It was just pretty big.

It was almost like an aunt or uncle or something.

Yes. Twelve years old. She just loved having this little baby. I see pictures of my being in the basket on the bicycle and she riding me around, and it was great fun for her to have a baby to play with, because twelve—that's a great age. My brother I don't remember.

2

COLLEGE YEARS

If you feel like we're finished with high school and early years, we'll start with the college years.

College was pretty big, too.

So, you were going to your hometown university because of your scholarship situation?

Right. I had said, I believe, that I had a couple of opportunities: one to New England to Mount Holyoke, and one to Pomona, but neither one of the scholarships were full rides, and that's what they had to be in order for me to go away. So I went to my home school, which was just really, literally, a mile away from where I lived, and I was somewhat disappointed by that, because it was, again, another public school, and I kind of had dreams of going to one of the Seven Sisters, as they were called, the women's universities in New England: Barnard, Wellesley, Bryn Mawr, Mount Holyoke, Vassar, Radcliffe, and Smith. I don't know if I've got them all, but those are the schools.

And you were especially interested in a couple of those, you said?

Yes, I was particularly interested in Wellesley or Smith, and I don't really know why. Maybe, I'd read about somebody who had been there, although, I did have that partial scholarship to Mount Holyoke.

But it wasn't enough to make it possible for you to go?

No. It wasn't, so I didn't go there. Anyway, the University of Arizona . . . . Of course, I was lucky to have a school in my town, but that really is the reason my mother and father moved in 1950 from Maine to Tucson, because my brother would be able to continue his college education, and so, clearly, they were thinking of me, as well. And that was great, because there was a school there. It was much smaller than it is now, but still a pretty good size university.

Now, was your brother finished with his college by the time you went?

Yes. My brother is eight years older than I am.

That's what I thought. So he would have been out by then.

He was gone. Actually, he got an M.B.A. and worked for an oil company. In fact, he went to the same school my daughter went to, to get her M.B.A., as it turns out, called the Thunderbird School. He was interested in foreign trade and foreign corporations and things such as that, as was my daughter. Anyway, he was long gone, and I really didn't pay much attention to what he did in college, because I was mucking around in middle school and high school and things like that.

But anyway, the big things for me at the university at that time were either, probably, to continue my political career on campus . . . or the big deal was the Greek system, and that was a thing for me, because I felt I needed a place on campus. I just wouldn't go to class, and take notes, go home, study, go to another class, and have no connection with anybody, because that really was very important to me, to always have connections with people. And it just wasn't available.

And you mentioned what students were called if they stayed at home.

Yes. If you lived in Tucson and did what I just described, you were called a "Townie," which I'm sure is the case in a lot of university communities, where, if you don't live in a dorm or a sorority house, you are considered that. As it turns out, I really did live at home three years, all except for my last year—and I'll talk about that when we get to that point, what happened and what allowed me to live on campus in the sorority house, because that was not the plan to begin with. It was enough for my parents just to pay the fees to belong to a

sorority, much less stay there, but something happened that allowed me to do that.

OK. So, the big thing was, then, rush?

Oh, I have to talk about that. Rush was pretty exciting. It was always done before school started, so it wouldn't interfere with classes or orientation or any of those kinds of things, but lots of kids from my high school went through rush. So most of my friends did, with the exception of, maybe, one who was a good friend of mine, just because she didn't like that whole idea. But it was pretty exciting, and of course, the big deal was you knew what the sororities were that you wanted to be in, practically before you even set foot on the campus, because somebody's sister was in one, or because we lived in Tucson we knew . . . I didn't, because I was never attuned to that whole life, but my friends had sisters, or they were much more sophisticated than I, and maybe had already gone to things on campus or something. But it was clear right from the get-go what the buzz was, as you would expect. There were a lot of houses on the University of Arizona campus, even in those days, maybe fifteen plus.

Oh, really? That many?

Yes. It was very big. The Greek system was very, very big at Arizona, still is, and it was big in the 1950s everywhere; and it's had its ups and downs, but Arizona has been pretty much a Greek place. So anyway, it was pretty exciting to go through rush.

Do you remember what kinds of activities happened during rush?

Yes, I do, vividly. I was just speaking with a friend of mine who is a housemother for the Thetas at Berkeley, just a couple of weeks ago. She came back to Reno, and I had lunch with her, comparing how things are today and then, and they have changed considerably, particularly at Berkeley, which is not a big, big sorority campus, as you might imagine, but that was the house that I happened to be a sorority member of, Kappa Alpha Theta.

But anyway, you got organized, and you were put in a group, I think, by virtue of maybe your last name or a number or something of that sort, but I might have been in a group with none of my friends. You first go to every single sorority, and then you had this system, which now, of course, is all computerized, but in those days it was done by hand, I'm sure. You would put down whom you wanted to go back to, and they would do the same thing, and then they would match up, and you hoped that it would match. In some cases it didn't, and there have been horror stories about young women, and even men, who didn't get in fraternities or sororities that they wanted to be in. Tragic things happened, because it was too important to them, I suspect.

Anyway, for me, particularly because I came from Tucson, and because there were a lot of alums who lived in Tucson of different sororities who would tell their sororities, "You must look at Sue Wagner, Mary Lou Doolen, Mary Helen Richardson," or whoever the girls were, that they were people who the alums in that community wanted. So I had, if you will, a head's up on, maybe, other people, because I did come from Tucson. Although, if you were well known in Boulder, Colorado, or somewhere else, there clearly was going to be a conduit into a sorority or fraternity, but it was easier, I think, for somebody from Tucson. But anyway, to me it was very exciting, and I was very fortunate, because I didn't get cut by any sororities, so I ultimately got down to deciding the two that I really wanted the most, and that was Kappa Alpha Theta and Kappa Kappa Gamma, better known as Theta and Kappa.

What they do is, you go through these different parties, and there would be theme parties, and each sorority would try to outdo the other in terms of having girls come away and say, "Wow! Was the Theta party the best?" Or because they'd all talk, and most of them lived in dorms, they'd all go back to the dorm, and even though they wanted to be in a sorority, you still got to live on campus when you're a freshman. And so, they would all buzz, buzz. I didn't, of course, because I was at home. But you still shared some of those experiences and what was going on. I can remember even some of the parties and some of the people, and now I understand how it all worked, because I've been involved on the other side—how you were able to meet so many girls, and different girls, within a very short period of time. It's all worked out into a system, and some did it much better than others.

In fact, there was in one instance an electrical storm, because this was the time of year when you got a lot of those in Tucson, in late August, when all the power went out, and I was stuck in a house, one I would not have preferred to be a member of. I wound up over there for hours, literally, and I was rushing them almost, going around and talking to all the girls in the sorority house, because they didn't have anything else to talk about, and so I kind of took over. I was telling my daughter that, and she was horrified [laughter] that I had done anything like that. She said, "Mom, you really didn't!" And then she thought about it. She said, "Yes, yes. You probably did!" [laughter]

As though you represented the house?

Yes, exactly. [laughter] I was asking *them* the questions [laughter] whether we really want *you* or not, because it dragged on interminably long, because they wouldn't let us leave while the power was out. I wasn't rude, but I could have been a little quieter, I guess, about it. But anyway, when it gets down to the last number of choices, it becomes more difficult, because there are people you know in all of these places, or sisters of somebody, or you meet somebody who's a real hotshot on campus, and particularly if they know that's what you're interested in, they'll make sure that you meet that person. For example, in the Theta house, the person who was assigned to me the very last evening, which was the most important one, when you get down to a choice of two, was the president of Mortar Board. Now, Mortar Board at that time was an all-girls' senior women's honorary, where maybe the top ten senior girls were selected to become members of, and to be president of Mortar Board was like the pinnacle for a woman.

She was assigned to me, and we are still friends to this day, and in the Kappa house it was another friend of mine still to this day, who is my son's godmother, as a matter of fact, and she was the first Hispanic woman taken, I believe, by any college sorority. [Edith Sayre Auslander] But anyway, so those were the two choices, and it is all a very exciting time, because everything is focused on *you*, particularly if you are wanted. Then you feel, wow! Can this be any better? [laughter] And then if you think maybe they don't want you as much, then you worry about that, particularly. It's just this time for all kinds of emotions and things that go on.

Of course, my parents didn't really know anything at all about it, and they were sort of interested, but not really. They were interested to the effect that they hoped I would get what I wanted. Clearly, they would be that interested.

But they didn't have any experience with it.

None at all. No. But there was a friend who used to do business at my dad's drugstore in Tucson where he worked. When we moved from Maine to Tucson he didn't own a drugstore any longer, of course, because he was out here several years recuperating. So he just worked somewhere. But there was a woman who was very well known in Tucson who used to get her prescriptions there and used to talk about me and ask how it was going, and did I like the Thetas, et cetera, et cetera, and my dad didn't know, and I told my dad, "Don't tell anybody," anyway. [laughter] And people like that or maybe someone at church would ask, but other than that . . . and it went on for quite a long time, a couple of weeks.

So this was a rather long period of time, and you got very tired, but the girls in the house got more tired, now that I realize how it works on the other end, because after all, the girls they want to have join go home. Then the girls in the house sit down and go over each and every one of them, and the ones who met them will give input, and, of course, they have written information on them and so on—grade point average, what activities they were involved in, in high school, and that kind of thing. So, ultimately, the final decisions are made, and you go back and look inside an envelope and find out who you get, and you know yourself whether you got your first choice or not.

And were the Thetas your first choice?

Yes, they were.

So, you were pleased with that?

Oh, thrilled. Yes. And I would have been happy with the other house, but to me there was a clear difference. The thing I liked about the Thetas—and I still do, even though I think they have a reputation nationally of being rather snobby, or they did at that time, although, on almost every campus they're good—the one thing I liked about them at Arizona is that they seemed to have . . . and I now know they made a concerted effort to get a part of their house of girls that would run for office, girls who would be involved in sports, girls who would be probably valedictorians or in the top ten academically (girls who might make Phi Beta Kappa, that same group), girls who would go out for cheerleading, girls who would be homecoming queen potential candidates. So, there was this huge conglomeration of just about everybody, every kind of different girl. So you'd always find somebody you could be a friend with.

They were trying to be represented in every part of campus life?

Yes, exactly. And you could tell that as you went through, because I met this girl— she was not going to be a beauty queen. She wasn't interested in running for office, but her dad was a doctor. She wanted to be a doctor. And I found out, because she was in the little group that I met, that she was a Phi Beta Kappa, so that impressed me. So you get the sense of even going through there . . . not to say that some of the others weren't similar to that, but I didn't get that same sense. But the Kappas were the ones who were the most similar, I thought, at that time, and probably still do. But anyway, it was real exciting, and that was very important to me. I know a lot of people pooh-pooh the Greek system and fraternity life. To me it was very important, and I would never disavow that I was ever a member or say, "Oh, golly, that was just something I did when I was young." I think it was very important to me, because, again, it gave me a group of girls—of women, who many had the same interests I did. Many didn't, clearly.

Didn't have much in common at all, but that was OK, and that was a place where you could come home. Even though I lived at home, I could have lunch there. It was a place to go between classes, study. They had study tables, and I had to become part of that, even though I lived at home, to make sure everybody did well grade-wise, because the Thetas also had the best grades on campus. That was something else that impressed me a lot, and I believe that the Kappas were number two. And that's been pretty much consistent for twenty, thirty years, as a matter of fact.

So I can understand—the study tables were where you had study partners? Or was it just a matter of you could join any group, as long as you came and studied?

No. It was a very certain time at night or something of that sort. You had to be there, and at that time it was only for the freshman, to make sure they made their grades. Then, if you did poorly as an older sorority member, then you had to participate in them, too, and that was something you didn't want to do, because you were with all the freshman.

And besides, you stuck out like a sore thumb. If you had to go Monday night, and you had to go somewhere else besides— out some place—if you lied about it and said, "Oh, I got to go," you wound up at the study table, and everybody would know. [laughter]

But one did it in order to make grades, because if you don't make your grades you can't become a member of the sorority. And also they were very interested in winning the scholarship trophy. So, there was this real drive. As I said, they always had won it. The four years I was there, they won it every year. So, there was not only a drive for the young girls to make their grades to become full-fledged members, but it also was to win the scholarship trophy. So there were proctors, if you will, older sorority girls who were there to oversee the scholarship, and it might have been the vice president of scholarship, for example, who might have been in charge of that.

And when you say you weren't ashamed or embarrassed to have been a Theta . . . you started college what year?

Let's see, I graduated in 1962, so it would have been 1958, I think. The early 1960s I would have been in college.

And that was still a time before flower children and lots of social movements that kind of changed some of the thinking.

Yes. Yes, I think so, because I remember in the middle of my college years, one of the big races was Nixon versus Kennedy. I remember watching those debates on the TV at the sorority house, and I was one of four or five who were sitting down there watching them.

Really? That's how many were interested in it?

Yes. Many weren't too interested. And of course, I remember when L.B.J. [Lyndon Baines Johnson] came to our campus. I guess it was when he was campaigning as a vice presidential candidate, and he had the Speaker of the House of Representatives in Congress, nationally. Carl Hayden, his name was, and Carl Hayden from Arizona was the oldest living member, and is even older than Strom Thurmond, I believe, or whoever is older. I guess Strom Thurmond is the oldest person now, in his nineties. He was like ninety-six, Carl Hayden was, and he was a Democrat, and he was with L.B.J. and Mo Udall, our Congressman from Pima City. They were down at the gate of the university campus, and, of course, I went

down to see them, and I'd gotten there early, so I was right up next to their convertible, and when Carl Hayden was introduced [laughter] he turned to me and said, "Young lady, would you help me up?"

I was so *appalled* that I had to *help up* this *old* guy, who was *third* in line to be president of our country, that I ran back to the sorority house and told everybody, and everybody went, "So?" [laughter] "Big deal." [laughter]

Just weren't concerned.

No. I just described the house as being this composite of everybody. But there were not that many people as interested in politics as I was. And that's for sure. You know, on *that* level. They might have been interested in getting *me* elected to an office on campus, but that was pretty different.

They weren't tuned in to the national . . . .

No.

I'm curious to know, when you were watching the debates with Nixon and Kennedy, what were your thoughts?

Oh, I supported Nixon. Absolutely, because my father had been chairman of the Republican Party in Maine, and it never occurred to me that I would be anything but a Republican, and you had to be twenty-one, of course, at that time, to be eligible to vote.

This would have been before you were twenty-one?

That was my first election, and I did vote for Nixon. It never occurred to me . . . and I do remember all the other girls who watched it. There were more, because it was J.F.K., I do remember. It was the incident with Carl Hayden that I got a terrible response on. Nobody knew who he was.

Or how important his position could become.

No. No. No. And it was unlikely that he would ever be president, just like Denny Hastert [current Speaker of the House] today. Do we really think he'll ever be president? I don't think so.

So anyway, I'm getting back to the sorority business. I will say that that was a very, very important part of my life, because I was able to have a base there on campus rather than, as I described, just going in and out. I think you do lose a tremendous amount of your college life, if you don't have that opportunity to somehow be connected. And since I didn't live on campus, this allowed me at least an opportunity, although not to know the girls as well as if you lived there all the time, at least a better opportunity. And of course, starting right in, I was president of the pledge class. Then that started the whole deal with running for freshman class office, and I did that, and I was freshman class vice president, and that started that whole role.

Now, at that point you have maybe a Theta running against a Pi Phi or a Kappa, another sorority house, or another guy, but it would be difficult in those days to win, if you did not belong to a fraternity or a sorority. Even if you belonged in a dorm, it was very hard for them to be organized enough to make posters, to do all these things. And then, you could go from sorority to sorority to fraternity to fraternity during Monday nights' meals and go in and make a short speech, for example, and interrupt their Monday night meals.

I remember, from the money I paid, you got lunches and also your Monday night meal, because Monday night was the night that you had your study tables, and all the activities that took place at the sorority. So

that was important to me, as well. You had to make your grades to become a member of the sorority. I mentioned that, and you also had to go through . . . not rush. I can't remember what it's called now, but people think of it as hazing, and I cannot grab the word right now.

It will probably come to us, but there's some sort of initiation period. Is that right?

Yes. After you make your grades, then you're still not a legitimate member of the sorority or fraternity. And this has changed considerably, of course, through the years, because of things that have happened in hazing, but it wasn't all that bad. The biggest problem was that you didn't know whether it was morning or night, because you didn't know what time it was. You had to remove your watches, and all the clocks were covered, and things like that. They made you do dumb things, but there wasn't anything that was life threatening or anything of that sort.

Or dangerous.

Some of it was sort of humiliating, because they thought that was cool. The older girls lived for the time that they could humiliate, particularly, some of the freshman who were kind of wise-asses, wiseacres who, maybe, thought they were too beautiful or too this or too that. They really waited for this time. [laughter] This was their chance to get back. But anyway, it was a fun thing when it was all over, because the Theta pin is in the shape of a kite, and everything around is a kite shape, so we had to make kites and then leave them there, but we didn't know what for, but at the end, we went out and flew kites.

I'm jumping around here, because it just is that kind of a thought process here during college and sorority life, that after you're

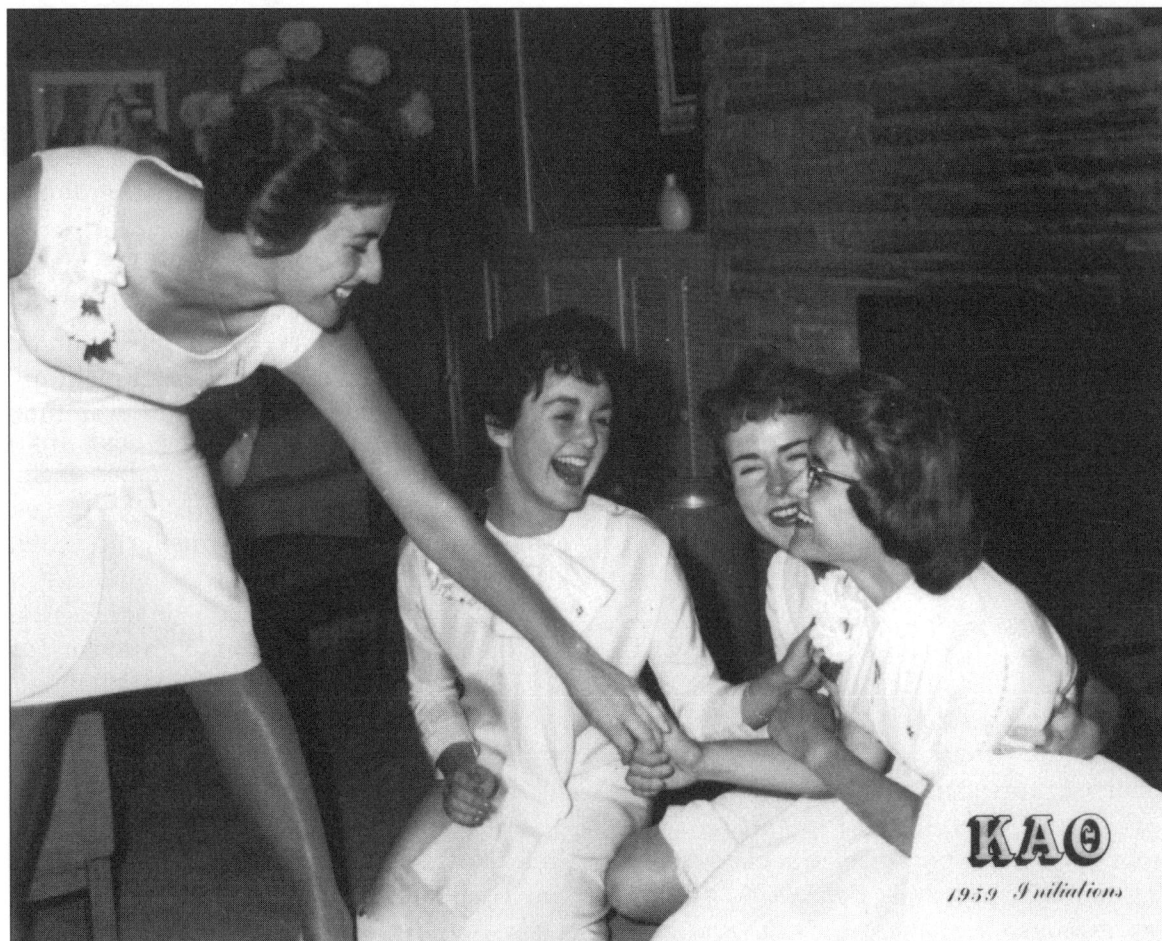

Sue (far right) with sorority sisters at Kappa Alpha Theta initiation, 1959. Sue was chosen outstanding pledge.

selected, you're assigned a pledge mother, somebody who is responsible to make sure you get your grades, that if you are interested in running for office, that people know about it, that you're taking the right classes, et cetera. That person for me was the president of Mortar Board. She was assigned to be my pledge mother. And then you would do some things at the end of this period of time with your pledge mother, and that was important, and I've had some wonderful girls and women who are my pledge daughters, who I still keep in touch with to this day.

I will mention this now, although it's not in chronological order, because my parents,

basically, all they could afford was the dues, but my uncle, my mother's brother, Charles Hooper, who I've referred to before, the electrical engineer with Westinghouse, had made a commitment to my mother that when I became a senior, he wanted to pay for me to stay in the sorority house. He had a daughter my exact age. In fact, I think I had mentioned to you I had two cousins the same age, and we all were graduation speakers, but the two of them were valedictorians, and I was elected.

Well, this was the dad of one of those cousins. But she was very different than I am, although I keep in touch with her still to this day. We're the same age, of course, or close to it. She and her husband used to both teach at the University of Maryland in math. But because she was not someone who would run for office or was more of an introspective person, a quiet person, I guess my uncle thought that I deserved this opportunity to live on campus, since by the time I was a senior, he could see that I was doing the same things, running for office and being very involved, that it would be nice to do this, and he could afford to do this. Since his daughter wasn't doing this sort of thing, he would like to do it for his sister's daughter, so it was very, very nice.

I'm not sure when I actually knew about that. As a matter of fact, I know why it happened, because my dad died. My parents had decided they were going to do this for me when I got to be a senior, and then my dad died when I was about a sophomore in college, and so that changed everything. That's when my uncle entered the picture and said that he would do it, because that was something my mother and dad had wanted to do for me, and she was not able to do that, even that one year, so he decided to pick it up.

I was wondering what was happening with your family. Was your father getting more ill as time went on?

During this period, I would see them all the time, because I was living at home, of course. My dad had some very good years, and I think I have explained on a previous tape how my dad and I used to go to baseball games together, and we did a lot of those kinds of things, but still, he had been through some very tough physical problems. He wasn't able to go out and play baseball or anything of that sort, but then he was getting older, but he would always catch for me when I was preparing for the Theta Pi Phi game or something like that. I think he got to go to one of those to see me,

and he did enjoy going. But he did OK, and of course, the climate was so much better for him. Remember, we moved there in 1950, so we're now talking about ten years later, and at that point they had said he would not make it through another year. So, we're talking about him having another decade or ten to twelve years of life left by moving to Tucson and being in a totally different climate—dry, warm, nice winters.

And so, I remember the exact night my dad died. [crying] He and I were watching a boxing match, and I mentioned to you about watching TV, how he'd kind of move around and duck when somebody on the tube was hitting somebody else. Anyway, my mom didn't, of course, like that, and I would sit up and watch this with my dad, and besides, television was rather new in the 1950s. We hadn't gotten one until later on, anyway, so it was interesting to watch anything, usually. [laughter]

Although I hated boxing, I'd stay up with my dad, and my dad had had a heart attack prior to this and had been at a hospital and had been discharged and sent home as being all well, so he was pretty much taking it easy, but we were watching one of these boxing matches one night, and I went to bed. He went out and sat in the living room. Now, my dad continued to smoke cigars, and he was not supposed to do that; my brother and sister and my mother would urge my dad to give up cigars. He never did. And we'd try to get him to at least give them up for Lent, and he would give up things like cotton candy, which, of course, he never ate, [laughter] ridiculous things that he never, never, never . . . would be no big deal to give them up. He wouldn't do anything with the cigars, and the smell was just awful. When my parents would take me on a big trip—our big trips were once a year to Boston, maybe to see the Red Sox or the Ringling Brothers Barnum and Bailey Circus, because those big things didn't come to Portland, but they'd go to Boston— we'd have to sit in the car with the windows rolled up, because it was normally cold, and my mother would always wonder why I would get sick. Well, it was because of the awful cigar smell. But that night I do remember my dad going out into the living room and having a cigar and smoking it, and I went to bed, and something *made* me get up.

In fact, I was just looking on the back of a picture. I think I was nineteen or twenty. Something made me get up and go out and tell my dad how much I loved him. That night he died. [crying] And sometimes when you're that age, you don't do that, although my daughter tells me all the time, but I guess *I* didn't. But I did that night.

Anyway, my dad died, and that changed a lot of things, because we had, of course, no savings. I don't think anything had been put in my mother's name. I don't think people thought about doing those things in those days. My dad was relatively young— he was fifty-five, fifty-six—although he was not well. He had just had a heart attack, but that had only been two weeks before. So, they should never have discharged him from the hospital, I'm sure, but in those days, clearly, science and medical technology was not what it is today.

Anyway, my sister, who was twelve years older than I (and since I was nineteen, twenty, she would have been in her early thirties) pretty much took charge of things, and although I do vaguely remember things that happened during that period of time. My brother at that point, [sighs] probably was in New York. I can't remember at what age my brother was married, but my brother went to New York to work for Texaco Oil after his experience with this school, Thunderbird School. So we had to even tighten the belt more, financially speaking, because the only income mom had was based upon her piano teaching,

because, of course, my dad didn't even have health insurance. There wasn't anything like that, because he was pretty ill all the time. I didn't drop out of school or anything like that, because, clearly, I was right there. I didn't have to come home or anything of that sort.

It was a big financial pressure for your family.

Yes. Yes, it was, but as I had mentioned before, I was fortunate and received enough scholarship money and everything that that pretty much took care of all of the expenses, including, I think, the sorority house, because I had a number of different scholarships. But, clearly, living in the sorority house was not part of it. You had asked me about working, and of course, this all went on during this period of time, too, working at the florist shop, Burns Flower Shop and so on. In fact, it was even more important at this point. But the same thing—the big dances and all those things were still applicable; I'd know who was going with whom.

But while I was going to the University of Arizona, it was really important for me, as it always was, and as it must have been for my family, to get good grades, to do well in school. Now, at this point, a major thing occurred, because I really wanted to go into the Foreign Service. That's where I was headed. My mother told me that it was now time to get serious and to become a teacher, because of what happened to her, that something could happen to me, and I might need to . . . . And I really didn't want to become a teacher, to be honest with you, because that was about one of the only options open for girls at that time, still. That's what you were kind of pushed into.

Nurses, teachers, secretaries.

Yes, and I didn't want to do that, and if I'd *really* had my druthers, I would have gone to law school, but that seemed to be *way* out there. I didn't even attempt to do something like that, but I was interested in the Foreign Service and in taking the Foreign Service exam. I was prepared, and I was taking courses that would lead to doing well, I thought, in that, but my mother had said, "This is it," and I didn't argue. I did what she wanted me to do.

So, you switched then and got your teaching . . . ?

Yes. I went into education. It was hard for me to tell her no right after this happened. Needless to say, little did I believe that it would happen to me, that something like this [having a husband die at a young age] would *happen*. But you're not going to argue. So anyway, I did that, and I really didn't like it. Very honestly (although I just got some honor from the education school at the university), it wasn't very tough, really was not that difficult. But I was able to go on to graduate school, which we will get to at a later time, I guess.

So that was a big change in your sophomore year.

That was a *big* change.

That was a huge change.

Yes, it was a big change, but that was the biggest change that occurred, I think, in terms of what was going on during those college years.

My life on campus was the thing that really kept things happy, pleasant, fun, because now my mother lived by herself, and of course, I still lived with her, still took my laundry home and things like that and would see her, but that was a big change for her, too, of course. My sister and her

family and children lived there at this point in time. They had moved to Tucson, because they heard so much about Tucson and how wonderful the weather was, and by then, my brother-in-law—the Korean war was over—and he was home, and it seemed like, "Why not?" There wasn't anything in Maine holding them there. So they all moved out. That was good to have our whole family there, except for my brother who was off making his life.

Do you remember your father's funeral or any of the details of that time?

No.

Kind of a blur?

I don't remember. No. I just don't remember a thing about it. I think my sister pretty much took care of most all of those things with my mother. I don't know why. I just don't. I think it's become mixed up with my husband's. I don't remember anything at all about it.

Could very well be. You just know changes at home, but school kept you going?

Yes. Yes.

That was the main thing, but you had to change into this education focus.

Yes. I changed what I wanted to do, which, to this day I regret, and in a way, resent it, to be honest with you, because it's not what I wanted to do with my life. I have been very good about my kids. My daughter has changed several times, and I have supported her every single time, because I think it's *her* life. It's not mine. And even though she realizes that this could happen, that could happen, this could happen, that could happen. As it turns out, when my own husband died, I did not go back to teach. That isn't what I opted to do to support myself.

A law degree would have been a good thing.

It would have been a great thing. Because I already would have been into that area [when I had to go to work]. But anyway, in thinking back, my collegiate life was pretty much a replica of what life was in high school; it was everything good. Everything good happened. I never lost an election, which was important. Obviously, that was what was the deal to me.

As I was explaining, one of the ways you got to meet even more people was going around to all of these different living places, whether it was fraternities, sororities, dorms, or whatever, and talk about yourself and why they should elect you. You got to meet a lot of new people that way, too. Then the sorority would, of course, do all of the work. They would do the signs and put the signs up, just like we have today in Reno, where the signs are on people's corner lots or whatever. If there was not a member of a different sorority running against you, then you'd try to get signs up in their windows or in their yard or cars, and I can't remember all the things that were done, but there were certain things that could be done and other things that were off limits.

I do remember one. My junior year I was running for a student-body office, and it was an office designed for a junior. You had to be a sophomore to run for it, because it was a junior position, and they expected that person then probably to be a student-body officer the next year. It was called junior councilwoman. A good friend of mine, who was in the sorority across the street—she and I were the two finalists. The Theta house had a dinner that evening. They planned it—spareribs. My name was Pooler, and you couldn't get away with this today, but they blackened their faces up

and put the sparerib bones in their hair and had flaming torches, and it was late at night, and they went around in this like conga line—and there were like a hundred and plus girls in the house—many saying, "Boola, boola. Vote for Pooler. Boola, boola . . . ." [laughter] It was just this big deal, and everybody the next day was repeating it [the slogan], and it was a close race between this friend of mine—Susie Palmer her name was—and myself, and that probably was what got me over the top. [laughter] But it was pretty funny.

Talk about having a campaign committee ready made?

Oh, absolutely incredible, incredible, and they really pitched in, too. That was part of the obligation when you became a member of that sorority. I'm sure others would be the same. You're expected to do this, and then at homecoming—huge floats, and maybe I'll see if I can find a picture of one of them. Sharon Disney, Walt Disney's daughter, was a member of the sorority I was in, on my campus, many years before, but I don't know how many: eight, six. But anyway, everybody used to say that Walt Disney used to design our floats, because we always used to win, because they were *incredible*. Of course, they were all made out of paper flowers, but you couldn't believe these things. I look at what the University of Reno has, and you cannot believe what the University of Arizona had in those days. Even when I go down now—and I've been there at homecoming—the floats are *nothing* like what we had. They were incredible spectacles, really—the themes, the colors. We would have to work days and weeks, and then somebody would design them. Then you'd have somebody do the chicken wire all over the float, and the trucks, and the cars. Some of them would be humongous, like an eighteen-wheeler long. The girls would be sitting on different levels depending upon the theme and the colors, and we'd all have to make the flowers and stick them in night after night.

Everybody was assigned certain obligations, whether it was working on a campaign, or you just did these things, and that was expected as a member of the sorority, and that was good. I will talk about my academic life, as well, but my senior year I lived in the house, which was just great fun, and it was a huge difference. I really did notice the change from living at home. Even though, being as involved as I was, it was still fun. The president [I was vice president] got a room of her own for one semester, and then the other half of the year, she and I lived together, and then some other friends and I stayed together. And as you got older, you got to choose which room you wanted. You could put dibs on it. Or if you were an officer or something—I don't remember all the protocol—but whatever, you got to choose.

You had your eye on certain things, and I knew about the rooms just by being there, but then, a lot of people slept on the sleeping porch, which in itself was fun. You really got to know people really well that way [laughter] by laying there and listening to what they'd be talking about, when they'd come in.

What was the sleeping porch?

Well, there were very few rooms that were big enough to have the bunks and things in the room, so you could put more girls in a room, and because there were so many and the houses were so large, a hundred plus members, and maybe only thirty or forty, roughly those numbers, could actually live in the house. So, if you had a big porch where you had bunk beds and just jammed them all in, then you had a lot more people that could sleep in the house. In Tucson it was just screened in,

because, of course, it was so warm. They would have a room, but the room would not have a place to sleep. You'd have your bookcases and your desks and things in there. Maybe we'd get four girls, versus two, into a room that way, if you didn't have the beds in there, for example.

In addition to that, it meant more money coming into the house. These places were big, big homes and you had to keep repairing, painting.

But the sleeping porch was also fun, just for listening to other various conversations?

Oh, yes. Oh, yes. If somebody got drunk, and you found somebody on the sleeping porch at nine a.m. [laughter] or at one p.m., when you happened to go out to the porch and pick something up, and a couple of gals were zeeing out, and you thought, "Mm. They had a hard night," or whatever. It was just fun.

You were probably very ready to be living at the sorority house by your senior year.

Oh, very much so, *having* to live at home, and then having to live with my mother during a difficult time. I realize that I was a help to my mother in many ways, and I was glad to do that, but it also my only time in college. So it was good that I had that balance.

I was a good student. I was a political science major, and I think the difference between the University of Arizona and Northwestern, where I went to graduate school, was that the U of A, even though it was a huge school compared to Northwestern, which still is very small, is that you got known. You were known by running for office, or you were known by virtue of maybe being selected as outstanding freshman, sophomore, whatever, and even the professors knew that. If you did well in your department they knew that, too. To be honest I believe I probably got better grades than I probably deserved, because of that, because, well, "You're going to have Sue Pooler in your class, and she's one of my better students, blah, blah." So maybe that mind-set is already there, or maybe if they'd looked at it critically, maybe I shouldn't have gotten an A without a little more analysis, I guess, because I realize when I went to Northwestern, it was a totally different world. That's why I say that. If I'd never had a chance to go to a topnotch graduate school, I probably wouldn't have ever known the difference.

Well, you were very busy, if you were working, doing sorority and attending classes.

And involved in all these outside extracurricular activities, and there were lots of those.

Serving on the government.

I was on the tennis team, and there were a lot of things going on, all the proms and the social environment, and, again, I have to say, that by being a member of a sorority, you had a much more active social life than if you hadn't been, on that campus, because if a fraternity, the Sigma Chi, had a pirate party or whatever, the dates are going to come from within the sorority system. I don't remember too many independents. I think it was pretty rare, because the normal thing was to ask, "What fraternity is he in? What house is he?" Not even fraternity. So it really was dominated by that, and it was probably not fair. It gave me a base, and I enjoyed it, and I think it was a natural thing for me to do. Although, I would have been fine being an independent. I could have made it, I'm sure.

What do you think were some of the most important things you learned from being in the sorority in college?

Oh, the big thing, because I came from a rather small family—I was like an only child being young—was the cooperation, learning to live together, learning to give, take. There were rules; you had to abide by them whether you liked them or not. It might have been that maybe someone else was chosen to do something, and you thought it should have been you—too bad. That other person got to do it, and you'd better cooperate, participate, do the best you can for that individual, whatever it may be. Also the stress on academics—although, I think, a lot of these things would have happened to me, anyway—*that* would have, certainly.

The learning to get along with a whole variety of people in a living situation?

Yes. That was big. And the learning about the different kinds of people, that was important to me, the jocks and the queens and the leaders and the mixture. And the feeling of, I guess, comfort, security, safety, companionship, if you will, by a very large campus, on having a place to identify with. I think that's really important. I think it would be very difficult to be on a very, very large campus of forty, fifty thousand people, and not have that. And of course, everybody finds a place. We hope they do, whether it's the Newman Center, whether it's a religious organization, whether it's a dorm, whatever it may be, but sometimes they don't, and sometimes people go through a collegiate life feeling really rather lonely. I think that's a real shame.

I wanted to ask you a little bit more about your academics—two specific questions.

One is about how heavy a load you took through college, and then, also, any mentors?

Well, I took fifteen or eighteen credits every semester. As I mentioned, I think, I majored in political science and minored in French, because my goal, of course, was to go into the Foreign Service. When I switched to education, it was then my objective to teach government or something of that sort, because I clearly knew I would be teaching upper grades. I had no interest in teaching elementary school, because my whole academic life was geared to those kinds of classes that would fit into a high school or junior high classroom curriculum.

I'm curious about the Foreign Service, although you didn't go that direction. Was it difficult to get in at that time?

Yes.

So, there were some things that you knew you had to accomplish, if you were going to do it?

Oh, yes. It wasn't a slam-dunk that I would get accepted or make it, because the Foreign Service exam was considered to be very difficult to pass. Of course, you now hear people say that that life is not really as exciting as one might think, and I have no idea what it might have been like in the 1960s, probably pretty exciting, depending upon where you were sent.

But in terms of the Cold War and other things going on internationally, war and that sort of thing, where today we're a little more concerned with terrorism, I guess, but there was nothing that guaranteed my getting in. But I felt comfortable that I would have been able to achieve that goal.

The other thing I was interested in, I did mention, was law, but one of the things that was missing, although I did have a mentor that was very important to me, was any kind of guidance and true counseling for women at that time. I will particularly address this when I mention that I won this one fellowship to go anywhere I wanted, to do anything I wanted to do, as long as I got admitted. There was *no* counseling, even at that level for, "This is what's available to you, Sue. You could go to law school, if you can get in, and here are the schools that might be good." Nothing of that sort, and I'm not too sure it was available for guys, either. I'm not saying that it was something that was gender related. I just don't think that it was available. Parents were supposed to do it, or somebody else was supposed to do it. I don't know. But I did have several very important influences. Of course, girls who were older than I were always influences, and when I was a freshman, my pledge mother who, as I mentioned, was the president of Mortar Board, was only there that one year. She was a senior.

And what was her name?

Her name was Shelby Porter. She lives in San Diego now and has a son who is about thirty or a little older. Shelby and I correspond, and I've seen Shelby a couple times when I've been to San Diego. Anyway, Shelby was just a real straight arrow. She wouldn't have even thought of doing anything wrong—*thought* of it, much less do it—and a very good influence and just a really nice person and very active, obviously, because she was president of Mortar Board, which is a national senior honorary.

Now they have men in it, which, even to me, is a surprise, because at the

University of Arizona they have a day in May, or maybe April, called Women's Day. They used to. And on the University of Arizona campus, as most campuses have one building that sort of personifies this college, it's called Old Main, and there is a big grassy area—huge—out in front of it. Before the sun came up on a day assigned as Women's Day, women would go out and stand in a huge circle, and that was the time for just the Mortar Board to be selected. There was an honorary for each year. Spurs was for sophomores. Chimes was for juniors—and these are national. They're not just at Arizona. They're at other colleges, as well. Spurs, Chimes, and Mortar Board are the national honoraries for each class, but Mortar Boards, of course, is the smallest and for seniors, so it's more difficult. But women were dressed in white, and usually sororities or groups would come over together and stand in a group. The outgoing Mortar Board members would walk around in a circle, and then each one would go off and look for someone in the crowd and tap someone. We'd get tapped to be a member of Mortar Board, and it was a pretty big deal.

The president of Mortar Board, as I said, was my pledge mother, but the woman who tapped *me* to be Mortar Board president—and you did get tapped to even be the officer—was the girl who'd taken me through the Kappa house, who I had told you was one of my good friends now today, who's my son's godmother. Her name was Edith Sayre, and her name now is Sayre Auslander. Edith, I might add, was president of the board of regents in Arizona, and her husband was, up until just a month or so ago, editor of the *Arizona Daily Star*, which is the largest newspaper in Tucson. It's the morning newspaper. She was vice president of Tucson Newspapers, Incorporated, which is the Gannett paper in the evening, and he's the editor of the morning paper (and I think it's a Pulitzer paper).

Pulitzer prize winner?

No, it's a Pulitzer family paper, I think. But anyway, this couple, they're the power couple in Tucson.

Edith tapped me, and I became Mortar Board president, but that was a big tradition that they had, which was a very, very important one, and a very lovely one. Now, I don't know if that [continues]. I've gone back to a couple of Mortar Board breakfasts when I've been there at homecoming, and as I said, there are guys in it now, so I suspect they don't do this Women's Day thing, and they don't, probably, select them in the same way. I'm sure the guys wouldn't stand out there in white. [laughter] The Sigma Chi's wouldn't all get out there early in the morning and stand around in white shorts and T-shirts. So I suspect it's somewhat different, but I guess you do lose some of those things, when things become coed.

I would say, Shelby and some of the older girls in the sorority were mentors, but the other mentor was the assistant dean of women, and the dean of women, and again, at that time they had a dean of men, dean of women. Now, it's just dean of students.

But the dean of women was like the adviser to Mortar Board and did a lot of other advising of other activities, and because of that I got to know her. Now, she had an assistant who became much closer to me, because she was much younger, and she went with Edith and I off to a Mortar Board convention in Oklahoma, and it was Edith's first trip on an airplane, and we took all of our Mortar Board stuff to be put into awards and scrapbooks and things.

Unfortunately, Edith vomited on the plane, and it went all over the stuff, because we had stashed it under our seats. [laughter] This guy flying our plane—now, remember, this was in the 1960s—decided that we should all see Tombstone, which was nice, but from 20,000 feet down to about a hundred, wasn't a real good idea. [laughter] Because it appears to me like we could actually read the Tombstones. [laughter] What it said on them. It was just like . . . [makes sound like "waaaang" with gesture for airplane diving] Edith just couldn't quite make it at that dip, so when we got home and we got off the plane, we had to kind of stuff . . . . [laughter] I don't even want to get into it. It got kind of gross.

Anyway, it kind of went downward that way when we were landing, so we got rid of some of the vomit, but everything had to be cleaned, and I'm sure some of that was not salvaged, but because of those kinds of experiences, then, you got to know somebody better, and because she was older, and in fact, she became very important in my life, because she called the dean of women at Northwestern and got me a job, when I went there, as a resident assistant in a dormitory, so I got my board paid for, for example. And then, from there, when I went to Ohio State [University], I became an assistant dean of women and ran a whole dormitory, so it started way back at the University of Arizona with this help in moving me on throughout my academic life.

And the dean?

Her name was Jean Wilson. This is the assistant dean, the one I was the closest to who did these things for me. Jean Wilson Smith, because she got married at some point in there. I actually thought at one time of maybe getting my degree in personnel and guidance and doing this very thing. Because I thought that it would be just really fun, and I think that it would be something I could relate to and do well, but I didn't. I stuck with political science.

So, Jean was an important mentor?

Yes, and I do still keep in touch with her. She lives south of Tucson.

Any professors stand out in your mind, or mentors, or classes you particularly enjoyed?

Oh, yes. There were professors, but I wouldn't put them in the mentor category.

Not the same as the mentors?

Yes. There was one I was talking to my mother about yesterday, as a matter of fact, when we were talking about Catholicism. I'm sorry, I don't remember his name. He taught Western Civilization, which we all had to take as freshmen, a huge lecture course, but for some reason, I got to know him better, from the big lecture hall to a small group, I don't know how I got there. But anyway, he'd have maybe two, three, or four kids over to his apartment, wherever he lived. I remember he went to Harvard. He was a Harvard graduate, young man, and of course, I was a freshman, and I was very interested in the subject, anyway.

When I went to Northwestern, if I'd had a choice, I would have gotten my degree in European intellectual history, because that's what my interest really was, in that area, and that's kind of like the Western Civ[ilization] type of approach, anyway. But he was really important to me just by virtue of the fact that he would take it upon himself to have these small groups of students come over, which you don't find on a large campus like that very often, particularly when he taught such a huge class. And then all the small sections were taught by graduate assistants, as they are now, but I'm sure there were other teachers. I remember the instructors I had at Northwestern far better than I did at Arizona.

Graduation, University of Arizona, Tucson, May 1962.

Did you go straight from your bachelor's degree on to grad school?

Yes. I did. I went one year right after the next.

To Northwestern, and Northwestern is located . . . ?

In Evanston, Illinois.

You had a fellowship, and this is where you went with that fellowship?

Well, the fellowship was given by Phelps Dodge, a large copper-mining corporation, and, of course, Arizona was the largest copper-producing state in the nation at that time, so they did a lot of things like this. This was the one fellowship everybody

applied for that allowed you to go anywhere that you could get in, and it didn't matter what subject, as long as you did well, and they paid it. They didn't pay everything. I think I already alluded to how I got the rest paid for. But I applied, and I got admitted to Stanford, Berkeley, Duke, Northwestern, and there might have been one other, but I only chose Duke because it had a great history department, and I had originally planned to get my master's in political science, and I only knew about that because somebody mentioned it to me. As I say, I had *no* help. I could have taken the scholarship and gone to law school. I got admitted to all these schools, and so, I don't know, maybe it would have been harder to get admitted to law school, but I suspect, for a woman at that time, not, because I was like twenty-fifth in my class out of thousands of kids, and, again, that's somewhere in my records, in that scrapbook that I will try to find.

But there was just no help, and I ask myself, "Why did I go to Northwestern?" I have to tell you, for the worst reason. Why didn't I go to Stanford? Why didn't I go to Berkeley? Here they were on the West Coast. It never occurred to me. No one ever said to me that it would make more sense, if you're thinking of coming back to live in the West—and of course, I figured I'd come back to Tucson, which I did—why wouldn't I go to one of those schools? Duke was way out of it, because that was so far away. I picked Northwestern because I'd never been to Chicago. Now tell me, is that good? No. It's a terrible reason, and that shows that there was *no* help. And my mother didn't know. It wasn't her fault, she just didn't have any background in terms of helping me make this decision. There wasn't anybody there, and clearly, Jean . . . evidently, I don't know what happened there, why that didn't connect. She was helpful, I think, and because all the outstanding seniors applied for this fellowship, and I was selected. I was also selected as the Merrill P. Freeman Medal winner, and I did win that. There was a young man, Matt Hanala, who I remember to this day, who won the men's outstanding senior award. He's a well-known dentist in Phoenix today, maybe retired by now, but just a great guy, well known in Arizona. And there were a lot of people like that, and they *all* would have been equally qualified for this. I think that Jean, again, had something to do with, maybe, maneuvering me, I don't know, because he clearly was, as a guy, as qualified as I was, and there were other girls and other guys who would have been right up there, as well.

Would you have been able to go on to graduate school without it?

No. No. Now, Matt probably would have, because I think he came from . . . but there were several others who I knew didn't go on to graduate school because of that. I don't know if need was a big part of it. I can't remember.

So much as academic.

But I do know it was based on what you'd done on campus. It was your activities, all the kinds of things that I was involved in.

The whole thing, not just academics.

Right. But of all these people, there were four or five who would have been easily qualified.

I can't say I picked the wrong school, because Northwestern is in the top ten in every single category you look at, whether it is in liberal arts, medicine, business, law. You know of Northwestern, I'm sure. It's like the Stanford of the Midwest. Anybody in the Midwest, that's where they would want to go.

Now, why I chose it, I told you, it's a very poor reason. And if I did it all over again, I would not do the same thing. I would, first of all, look at and have a clear idea of what it was that I was getting my master's in, because I went there, and realized their political science department was not anything like what I was interested in. So, I moved from political science into history.

I'm sorry. I had it reversed the other way around when I say I went there for history first. That's not true.

You were hoping for political science?

Yes, because that's what I'd gotten my undergraduate degree in, but I got it in history, because political science was called behavioral political science, and at that time it was the very beginning—and I didn't understand this at the time—it was brand new, really, of poll-taking. It was going door-to-door and figuring out the behavior of people. Now, of course, I clearly understand what it was all about, but then, it sounded like the most boring thing, and that's not what I went there for. I was very much more interested in political theory and things like that, and that was not their strength, but I didn't know that. So I switched, and I had enough credits to get into the history department, and again, in the history department they didn't have anything really like what I wanted. They had this intellectual European history, but you had to do it all in a foreign language. So I would have had to have done everything in French, every bit of reading, every bit of it. I'd still be there! [laughter] Working on my master's degree! So, I got my degree in Civil War military history, which has done me a heck of a lot of good. [laughter] And the reason I chose that is because there were four other people in the department, so I figured I'd get a lot of attention. You'd *really* get to know the professors well.

In downtown Chicago was the Newberry Library, and you had to do everything in primary sources, of course, at this level, particularly at a school like Northwestern. Maybe at Arizona, you wouldn't have had to, but the Newberry Library had the papers of George McClellan, the Civil War military general. I was excited about that. I thought that was hot stuff. I was really interested in history and doing primary sources, but when I went to look at his papers, very honestly, it looked like a chicken had gotten into ink and run across a piece of paper. It was the *worst mess* I'd ever seen, and I had to read it and then, of course, make something out of it.

It was, again, a very interesting experience. It didn't equate to my undergraduate days in terms of good memories. But you can go back and say if,

if, if. But if I had been channeled even into knowing that if I went to Stanford political science or Berkeley or even another school that I hadn't applied to, that I could have applied to, that this is what you're interested in, this is where you should go. And maybe, partly, it was my fault. I maybe should have gone back to the political science department, but it was a big deal that I'd won this award on campus, and what was I going to do?

I would have thought maybe someone might have called me, but nobody did, so maybe that was for me to have gone and found the right people. Maybe I should have gone to each of the departments and asked them, but I didn't do that.

When you look back, it's easy to see why there might be regrets, when you think about what was happening in the political area. For example, on the Berkeley campus about that time, it would have been just your cup of tea.

Absolutely.

Because there was some very innovative thinking going on.

Right, but I didn't understand that at all. I just don't remember any input. But really, my choice would have been to go to law school. Think of, even on the West Coast, the opportunities of law schools—just great. Any of the schools I just mentioned to you, if I could have gotten into any of their law schools, it would have been great. Because today they're still in the top ten, every one of them, except maybe Duke.

And as you say, it's partly a comment on the time period, where the guidance was not a strong thing for college students. You were kind of supposed to know what you were doing when you got there or something.

I guess. I guess. Yes.

That's a much more developed part of college systems today.

Oh, much more so. But, as I said, even though I had one of the people in that area, who I would consider my top mentor, somehow that didn't click, or maybe her advice was . . . maybe that's when she was getting married. I can't remember. But certainly, she plugged me in to where I was going, and maybe she encouraged me to go to Northwestern because she was real good friends with the dean of women there and would be able to get me the room and board. I don't know. I don't remember. But for whatever reason, I did not feel that I talked to anybody who suggested anything, except exactly what I had decided myself— which was not a poor choice. It's not like I went to a terrible school. You mention Northwestern—almost everybody really thinks of it as a very top academic school, but it was not the kind of education that I really went there to get, although it was a real shock to the system—the demands on you and the expectations on you. Wow!

Quite a contrast?

Even harder than going from high school to college. Way more. In going from Arizona to Northwestern.

Did you struggle that first year with the academics?

Absolutely. I was only there a year.

Oh, you got your master's in a year?

Yes.

Wow! Now, did you say you'd gotten through college in three years or four years?

Four years. I graduated in 1962, and actually my master's was awarded in 1964, but I had finished my work in 1963 and moved on to Ohio State in 1964. I'll talk a little bit more about Northwestern, but getting back, I'm trying to think if there are any other things. I'm sure there are just a jillion funny, funny things at college, but in your mind we've pretty much covered it, I suspect.

I think so. We talked about what was the most important thing about the sorority. Was there anything else important about college that you feel, even though the academics didn't exactly fit with what you later did with your life? Were there other important lessons you think you learned during those college years that did benefit you as you went on? You talked about in the sorority, getting along with such a variety of people.

Well, I would say that, generally, I could make that whole argument for the entire campus, because it was such a diverse campus, because it was a public institution, and that was the good part of that, is the fact that you had just about a little bit of everybody there, and I have to say, at that time . . . Arizona probably is perceived to be a better academic institution now, because it does rate a lot more highly in a variety of areas than probably it did then. They didn't have *U.S. News & World Report* doing their thing then.

A lot of people came from very wealthy families, who wanted to be in the sun and probably play a little bit, and there were other schools that had bigger reputations for play schools, but this certainly ranked up there, I suspect. But I was happy and even then I realized that I was lucky that I was able to go to college, and that my college was so close to me, because, if I hadn't, it would have changed my life. Just think about the differences that would have made, and I am such a loyal Wildcat supporter, much more so than Northwestern. The fact that I don't think that it was a top ten school when I went there doesn't matter to me at all. Because I think you can get out of college what you need to at that time. Although, as I say, I did notice a big jump in expectations. Part of that, I think, was because I'd built up this reputation and kind of maybe slid along on that. I recognize things that happened to me that made life easier, and I'm willing to acknowledge those things.

We've gone through how you chose Northwestern, but tell me a little bit more about your time there and what you gained at Northwestern for your master's degree.

First of all, I did get this fellowship, the Phelps-Dodge fellowship, which provided tuition, books, and fees, but didn't provide for room and board, so the assistant dean called ahead and talked to the dean of women at Northwestern, and I was in charge of a floor in a brand new freshman dormitory there at Northwestern, and also was in charge of certain nights at the switchboard. That provided me the room and the board, because I had a room on the floor that I was in charge of. It was interesting, because at Northwestern, the first thing I confronted was sorority rush. So, by my having been part of that, I was able to help some of the girls, and I could not believe it. It was a *huge* deal at Northwestern—big, big, big, big, big. Northwestern is a small college—it still is today—probably a total of eight to nine thousand student body, divided pretty much in half, undergraduates and graduates, maybe more on the graduate side than the undergraduate side. It's very comparable to Stanford in size and academics and liberal arts.

It's the only private school in the Big Ten, and that's why they always come in last in every single athletic endeavor. They have always come in last in basketball. Their football team wins like 0-10—maybe one win a year, nine losses, or something, because they don't care, really. It's not a big deal, although a couple years ago they went to the Rose Bowl, and everybody sent me . . . I have lots of T-shirts and sweatshirts and things like that, because it probably would be the only year that they'll do that, because they're very academically oriented.

I'd never been to Chicago, as I mentioned, and the Evanston campus is unbelievably gorgeous. It's right on Lake Michigan, and it's beautiful. It looks like an Ivy League—old rock, stone, and of course, being in Chicago it has an unbelievable endowment. I think it's third in the nation in terms of endowments, and that's a lot, because it's smaller, really, than Harvard and Yale, but I think it's third after them. You've got the Chicago base and many of the movers and shakers in Chicago past, present, and probably future, are Northwestern graduates. That's the school to go to if you're in that area. University of Chicago is just a fine academic institution, but it's a totally different kind of college. In fact, I'd thought about applying there and was talked out of it, because it was in south Chicago, and I was a single woman, and Evanston was in the North Shore, where all the ritzy suburbs are, including Evanston. The campus is beautiful. It's small. I did have another connection in this dormitory, so I immediately had people I knew, although in graduate school, it's not necessarily that important, because in my mind you're there to get your degree, and that's about it. You're not participating in government and things like that.

Not like the social whirl of the undergraduate in the politics.

Sue in graduate school at Northwestern Univesrity, 1963.

No. No. None of that. It was to do it, and to do it as soon as you could. But I did then get into the history, into Civil War military history, and I did do my thesis on George McClellan, comparing him to other Civil War military generals, and I really did find it rather interesting. My adviser was a very good guy and had written a number of books on Civil War military history that we used.

There were two professors. The first was Richard Leopold, who is just very famous. There were very many, very famous history people, much more so than the political science department. Richard Leopold was still in American diplomatic history, probably one of the two or three best-known historians in that era. He's now died, but even to this day he's still one of the top two or three. And the professor I had for French history, Richard Brace, was just a wonderful guy, and I liked him very much. He served

on my oral history exams, and fortunately, I did not have Dr. Leopold. [laughter] Everybody would have felt that way. He was very, very tough, and very scary, but everybody who had him really remembered him, because he was just topnotch.

I was wondering if some of these things like comparing military careers or the American diplomatic history, if those had some interest for you, even though they weren't the political science that you loved.

Oh, they did!

This was more your type of thing.

Oh, yes. As I said, I really loved it. It was just *very* difficult, and I started dating a young man who had gone to

Northwestern as an undergraduate and was getting his master's, and he told me that it was just like at Arizona. I go back to thinking about maybe Arizona professors who got to know me—same thing at Northwestern. Can't say it's any different, because when he explained to me how . . . let's take a certain professor and how he liked to have his book reports done, because we might have had three book reports a week. There was like a little form, and he got it figured out as an undergraduate, that Dr. So-and-So liked to open with a beginning paragraph, a quote from the first part of the book, and then you develop that, and somebody else wanted it done this way. Once I got that, then I was like getting C's on everything, and C's in graduate school was not good.

I was really upset, and I didn't understand it, because I would have gotten A's as an undergraduate. Once he explained to me how this worked—well, I went right from C's to B or some A's. It was just, again, a matter of figuring out that individual professor.

One of the things that was interesting at Northwestern, and I don't know if this is true of other schools, but you never called anybody "doctor." Everybody was Mr. Leopold, Mr. Brace, because everybody was a doctor. No one was hired there that did not have a Ph.D. So, they never went by anything. There was no pretense or pretension about anybody.

Once I got that figured out, things went a lot better, but I was really rather lonely, I think, because I just didn't have this group of friends. The girls, the young girls, were the closest thing I had to that. Their mothers, when they'd find out pecan pie was my favorite, when they went home for the weekend or for spring, they'd come back, and I'd find a pecan pie by my door or whatever. I really loved the girls. They were fun. As you might imagine, I did enjoy that, but being so far away from all my friends I'd had my whole life was a bit of an adjustment, and the climate in Chicago was just awful. No matter what time of year it was, it was awful. [laughter]

It's the extremes, isn't it, compared to Tucson, Arizona?

Well, it was. Living right on Lake Michigan, and the dorm I was in was practically *on* the Lake, and in the winter the wind would come off Lake Michigan, and you talk about the "windy city" in Chicago, it's because it's on the lake, but having the campus on the lake, it was unreal, and the waves would lash up, and it was cold, cold, cold and windy. Then, in the summer when I was there doing my paper, it was *so humid*. It was incredible. I'd forgotten, growing up in Maine, but I didn't care for the climate, and the one thing about living near Chicago and taking advantage of all the opportunities, I never had time. I worked all the time, either with the girls, going to class, or as I mentioned, I had to work at the switchboard, and we didn't get done until two a.m. by the time we'd closed up everything.

Then, I'd go out with my guy I was going with, and Evanston is a dry town. That's where the Women's Christian Temperance Union had their headquarters, which was a horrible thought, coming from Arizona, so we'd have to go down to a place called Howard Street, which divided Evanston from Chicago, and it was a lineup of bars, up and down the street, and there was one place that we used to go to, because he was in charge of what's called Stadium Dorm, where all the jocks lived.

So, we pretty much had a comparable environment, and not only in terms of our parents and everything, but what we were doing on campus. We'd go out after two a.m. to go down and have a drink and talk and see one another, so it was just that kind of a life.

I remember going home at Christmas, because I wanted to go home and see my mom and my sister and my family, and I could not afford to go, but I had enough money saved from the scholarship to do two extra things. One was to get contact lenses, and this was when they first were out, and all the girls had them. To go to Northwestern is expensive to begin with, because it's a private school, and the tuition is rather high, so most of the girls there came from affluent families. They all had contact lenses, and they encouraged me to go get them, and there was a place there that was run by some guy from like China or Taiwan or something. At that time, they were the people who were putting in contact lenses, not ophthalmologists, just contact lens guys who tended to be from Southeast Asia, for some reason.

I was a little concerned about it, but I did it, and that's how I spent some of my fellowship money, and the other was getting a Greyhound bus ticket home to Tucson. And I'd never do that again, either. [laughter] There were a lot of things I learned about this experience that are "never doers"—that aren't keepers, as they say.

Why no more Greyhound bus tickets?

Oh, God, it was just the worst. It was about a five-day trip: four or five-nights, six-days or whatever.

Stopping everywhere?

Everywhere. And then, the thought was when I got home, I had to go *back again* on it. That was the worst part. [laughter]

Once you knew what it was?

There was some excitement of getting home for Christmas and surprising my mother. She didn't know I was coming. But

I couldn't afford the plane. And then, to think about going back. I remember spending New Year's Eve in the bus depot in El Paso, Texas, and when you get on the Greyhound bus that long, and you don't shower, you can't change your clothes. I guess people do go into restrooms and do that, but I was not an experienced bus traveler. [laughter] So I didn't know about those things.

So, it was something that I would not do again. But anyway, I did get through the program. I did very much like working with the girls, and at that time, really thought about maybe getting an advanced degree in personnel and guidance and going into that field. The dean of women at Northwestern was just a lovely gal. Then I decided to go on to Ohio State to work on my Ph.D.

Now, in the middle of this, let me see if there was anything else that I should talk about Northwestern. Well, of course the el is very famous in the Chicago area. That's how you get from Evanston and the suburbs to downtown Chicago. As I said, I didn't go very often. [laughter] I did go to see Joan Baez. My ticket, I remember, wherever it was, was up so high that I looked down, and all I could see was the part in her hair. [laughter] She had the straight, long hair that hung down. It was just parted in the middle, and I looked right down on top of the part, so I was up quite a ways.

That was just really the only kind of social activity. Oh, I did go to a bunch of the football games because of my boyfriend, because he had the Stadium Dorm, so I used to go over early, and one time I ate lunch with the guys. [laughter] Oh, that was the most incredible experience. Excuse me, I'm ahead of myself. That's at Ohio State. When my boyfriend, who I met at Northwestern—he and I both went to Ohio State together. The one that I have just described that was in charge of the Stadium Dorm, that was not at Northwestern. He was in charge of, like I was, a floor or something of that sort.

A floor. Yes. What was this boyfriend's name?

Well, I knew you were going to ask me that question: Bruce Larson, from Kansas. I want to remember the name of the town, because I went there, stayed with his family during spring vacation, and they were just fabulous people. His dad was the superintendent of schools, and I know the name as well as anything, and if I looked on a map I could find it. It's outside of Kansas City. I have a picture of him in that album

Yes. There's a lot of towns around there. Now did you finish your master's degree in just one year? And was that usual to finish in just a year?

I don't know if it was usual, but what happened was that I finished all the course work and wrote my paper, but then I had to come back for an oral exam, which was very difficult, and I went home between the summer of going from Northwestern to Ohio State and spent the entire summer doing practically nothing but studying for this oral exam, because you did not know who was going to be on your committee, and depending upon, if you walked into the room and saw the French guy, it's going to be French history, but if you found a guy on, I don't know, European intellectual history, then, guess what? That's what it was going to be. There would be three people, but you did not know the area of history.

You didn't choose him. You didn't get to choose your committee?

No. My daughter has been able to do that, but I was not.

Had to be ready for anything.

I know I was told that I had to be ready for American history from the War of 1812 on. Well, that's quite a bit. And Europe from the French Revolution on—1789 on. One of the questions I did not get was some question dealing with a French country and their colony in Africa, so it really was African history, but I didn't pay any attention to that when they said European History from 1789. You tended to focus on Europe, and of course, America, because I had that from 1812, but I didn't think about . . . .

Colonies?

France had control over this African colony, which has totally changed names by now, and what relationship that had. And when that question was asked, I had no clue, couldn't even guess.

You got through it? You passed the orals anyway?

Got through it. Yes. And that was done when I was at Ohio State. I came back to do that. They did tell me, when I got done, that I passed, and I remember, there was a gal at Ohio State, whose name I don't remember, who had a comparable job to mine, who loaned me her convertible to drive back from Columbus to Chicago to take the exam, and I did go back and stayed overnight with a friend of mine who was in charge of a dorm—it was in some dorm someplace—and the next morning went and took the exam, got done, went down to Howard Street, and only could have one drink, because then I was going to drive back in the convertible—and boy was I excited! Oh, man!

Because you knew you'd passed.

Was I excited! Because that was huge, to walk in and see who was in the room was like [catches breath] and then your mind started thinking, "OK. French. Ta dat ta dat ta dat."

But anyway, I did go to Ohio State, mainly because I was going with this guy, and I really didn't have any other aspirations at that time. I hadn't decided . . . see, I now have a master's degree in history, but I really wasn't interested in teaching, because I really didn't want to do that. So, I decided, well, might as well get a Ph.D., so Bruce and I went off to Ohio State, and I got a job running a whole dormitory there, and he was in charge of the Stadium Dorm. Mine was called Oxley Hall. It was the oldest living residence on the campus and had been closed for a number of years to bring it up to fire code and things like that. That was an interesting experience at Ohio State—in many ways more interesting actually than at Northwestern.

So maybe you can give a little background on your going to Ohio State University and tell us about that experience.

It was interesting, I guess, the beginning of what we would call today a women's network. I was in charge of a floor in one of the dormitories there at Northwestern, and then when I made plans to go on to Ohio State to continue my work on a Ph.D. the dean of women at Northwestern contacted her friend who was the dean of women at Ohio State and said, "I've got a student coming down, and she needs to have some financial support, and could you find her a place there?" At that point she thought that I could move up in the ranks, so to speak, and run an entire residence hall, which would mean a lot more to me in terms of finances, because it would mean room and board, plus I would get my own apartment, which is quite different than just another dormitory room. So that was done, and that did happen.

That was interesting to me, now, looking back on it, that that was really a women's network, because almost the entire field of personnel and guidance was dominated by women. I didn't know that, and it didn't mean anything to me, even if I did know it, but clearly that was an area that was open to women, and when I got to Ohio State, I had thought about going in that direction, rather than continuing in either history or political science, because I did like it. I enjoyed working with students, kids, and, obviously, it must have registered somewhere in my mind that this would be something that was possible for me, doable. Probably, very honestly, it wouldn't be as challenging academically as political science or history would have been to get a Ph.D., but I chose not to do that, and I don't remember why, exactly. I think it's because I probably felt that I wanted the extra challenge, because there wasn't any reason for me not to go into that. But I went off to Ohio State, and as I said, the guy I was dating at that time, Bruce, also went to Ohio State, and that clearly was the reason. It wasn't one of them; it was *the* reason.

The reason.

The reason, because Ohio State was not noted for some great department in political science that I had to go there. It just wasn't. It was a great place, particularly because Bruce was in charge of Stadium Dormitory, and at Ohio State, football was king, queen, court, everything. [laughter] It was pretty incredible. The coach was named Woody Hayes, and he is one of the most famous football coaches ever. Even today, people know who Woody is. Woody would get behind one touchdown—maybe at halftime he was down 14 to 7—and the blimp would go over, and it would say, "Goodbye, Woody." They were serious. [laughter] I couldn't even believe this, but my dormitory, Oxley Hall, was on Neil Road, and there was such a difference between living out here or in Arizona compared to the Midwest, where on a Saturday afternoon, when you live in a college town, it is football, football, football, and people started going by my dormitory early in the morning with their blankets and, I suspect, their flasks underneath the blankets, and with the leaves falling down. I can even hear the crunch of the leaves as they're shuffling on their way to the stadium. It was just big, and the stadium held almost a hundred thousand people.

Columbus, Ohio, probably didn't have more than a hundred thousand people in the town, but, if you had season tickets to Ohio State, you were lucky, and it was big. So, because Bruce ran Stadium Dorm, which was underneath the stadium—inside the bowels of the stadium somewhere, where all the jocks lived—I got to go to lunch occasionally *with the guys*, [laughter] which was just an incredible experience. Did I talk about this—how they ate and what they ate?

I don't think you went into any details.

OK. We think of a nice little steak. Literally, this would cover the plate, and just tons and tons of food.

Huge portions?

Yes. Big, like a Basque dinner, you'd think of, but it would be like one Basque dinner for one guy—what we would think of for a whole table. [laughter]

I'm sure there were certain things that they were supposed to eat prior to a football game, just metabolically speaking, and I'm not sure if they were into all that in the mid-1960s. They didn't seem to be that concerned about quantity, anyway, I have to say. [laughter]

They loaded up.

But it was kind of fun, and we obviously had really good seats, better than the average student. I had a separate apartment, and that was one of the luxuries of being in charge of a residence hall. Mine was the oldest one on campus and had actually been closed down for a number of years, in order to have all kinds of improvements done to it, because it was so old, but they didn't want to demolish it and build a brand new, squarish box-type thing. This looked more like a home, so it was more old-fashioned looking and different looking, but inside the apartment I had, it was very nice, and because they had just done some work on it, everything was pretty modern for those days. It was a really interesting experience for me to run a dormitory, because I was in charge of everything—the food, the academics—and there was pressure to make sure girls stayed in school. If there was a problem, you took care of it immediately. If a youngster was in distress, you tried to find out what the problem was.

It was interesting, because it was, I'm sure, mentioned to us, but it became very clear that, because Columbus, Ohio, is not noted for it's climate . . . and I was not made aware of this, I have to say, at Northwestern, but at Ohio State they made it clear to us that when winter came, and when it became gray and overcast, that there were going to be more and more problems, and stealing would occur. All these other kinds of things would happen, and that was extremely true. You never saw the sun, and no blue skies like we're used to. That was after the nice, crisp falls that I've already described. When winter settled in, and it was raining or snowing and gray and overcast—which it certainly was in Chicago, too, but I don't remember that being noted to us, nor did it register that if I had problems with the girls, that might have been one of the reasons—we were directed at Ohio State to watch out for that sort of thing. It's something that stayed with me all this time, that there were incredible problems that arose by having that many girls live together who couldn't go out—not that there were people into jogging all that much at that time, but just to get out and take a walk or go outside and do something. They were always enclosed, or they'd run off in sleet and crummy weather and go off to their class and come back, but it did fester and foster problems that we were responsible for, and there was an occasional serious problem—someone attempting to take their life or something like that. So there was a lot of, I felt, responsibility on us, because we were the adults, supposedly, the adults in charge, and in many cases I was not much older than some of the students, because I was a student myself.

Did you have those kinds of situations?

Yes, I did.

Like stealing and suicide?

Yes. All of those things. Absolutely. That's why I'm saying this, because I did have them in my dorm. And that's what was so surprising to me, that if I did have them in Chicago, I don't remember them.

But you really remember Ohio.

I remember them, and I think it's because *I* was the one totally responsible, so everything funneled to me, whereas, maybe because I only had a floor at Northwestern, and I maybe didn't have those big of problems on my floor, or maybe I did, and I didn't know about them, and they got directed to the head person, I don't know, but I think I would have known about it.

Were you still interested in the idea of guidance after seeing those kinds of problems? Did that change your opinion of that at all?

You know, I'm not sure. No, I think it must have been before that, Vikki, because I obviously had to register for classes, which I was taking. Not a lot, because this job was really full time. But I did take a couple of classes, and I had to sign up for those, and there was nothing in the personnel and guidance field, so I must have made that decision between those two campuses.

I think, even before I got to Ohio State, my relationship with Bruce had kind of fallen apart, because I know when I got there, well, I had met Peter, my [future] husband, that summer, between Northwestern and Ohio State, because, if you remember, I had said I had to go home and study. I studied the whole summer to get ready for the oral exams. And at that time I met Peter.

So, you met him in Tucson, then? You were back in Tucson.

Yes. Well, I went home and stayed where I grew up in Tucson to study.

Do you want to stop and tell about meeting Peter that summer?

Yes. Yes. I had met Peter. Actually, my sister, Joan, had talked to me about Peter when I was at the University of Arizona as a senior. She had met him. He had graduated from Stanford and had come to Arizona to work on his Ph.D., because they had a department in atmospheric physics, which very few colleges had at that time. He was getting a Ph.D. in electrical engineering, but he wanted to get one in atmospheric physics, as well, or a combination, and that was one of the few places he could do that.

He was a big skier, and my sister lived on the top of a mountain in Tucson, called Mount Lemmon, and taught skiing up there. The season was rather short, [laughter] but they advertise that you can golf in the morning and go up and ski in the afternoon, which is true in Tucson. It was a nice, little ski area, but kind of homey and for families and that kind of thing. Anyway, Peter used to go, occasionally, to Bishop, because that's where he went while at Stanford. In fact, my sister went with him one time there, met him up there, and talked to me about him when I was a senior. But when I was a senior, you have to remember, I was a big hot dog, and there was no way I was going to date somebody who was a double E major, because in those days they had slide rules that attached to their belts, [laughter] and that would have just been too much.

They were more the nerds at that time, were they?

Absolutely. Absolutely. The Bill Gateses of today, the Bill Gateses of his time.

Although my husband would be today about sixty-two or three. Oh, yes. Absolutely. No way. [laughter] In fact, when we'd go by the double E building, walking from the Theta house to campus, I would just *pray* that somehow this guy would not come out. I had not met him, but I would hope that he wouldn't come out—because he knew who I was—and say, "Oh, hi, Sue," because I would just be *humiliated*. [laughter] I knew I'd just die.

So I told my sister, "Out of here. No way! Bye. Good. See you around." And, of course, I went off to Northwestern. Then I came home. And my sister kept, oh, promoting it, promoting it, promoting it. She just thought he was just the greatest guy—smart—and I think at one time I had this idea that it would be really neat to marry a

college professor and live in a college town, but Reno was not what I had in mind. I mean, like Hanover, New Hampshire, where Dartmouth is, which is just the idyllic place, isolated and just a campus town. So maybe I said something like that to her, and here he was, getting his Ph.D. I don't know, but she thought he was just the nicest guy, and obviously he was smart, and she knew that I would want someone smarter than I, or at least as smart, and he was an athlete and da da da.

When I came home she continued to persist, and since I was just there for the summer without anything to do, really, except study for the exams, I kind of relented, and then my *mother* thought he was wonderful. [laughter] I'm sure my mother was getting a little nervous that I hadn't been married by then, because at that time, you have to remember, *all* my friends were married, and I was in everybody's wedding when I graduated from college. I don't know how many bridesmaid's outfits I had, but having been in the sorority house and all of that, you can guess that I'd have a lot of friends that I would be part of their wedding parties, and I do remember that most everybody did not go to graduate school. Hardly anybody did in that day—a woman. Hardly any men did. And so, maybe my mother was saying, "This guy looks good." [laughter] I don't know.

But anyway, I went out with Peter that summer, and then I thought he was very nice, and I was interested, but nothing like, "Oh, wow! This is it." Slam, bang! No, it was not that kind of thing. I think I was very concerned about passing the exams, and that was really my goal and my objective, and it would not have been *me* to have just flitted away the summer, forget about this and think, "I'll deal with this later on. I'll just have a good time this summer." I'm just not that kind of person. I would never have done that.

So your focus was on the exams, and there wasn't much else that was going to deter your attention?

Absolutely. No. And too much had been invested in terms of my time, money, all of these kinds of things, that nothing was going to deter me, but anyway, I did realize that I thought Peter was pretty special, too. So, by the time I got back to Ohio State, at least I realized that I was not going to be committed only to Bruce, and I did take the exam, as we've talked about, passed it, and it's terrible to say, but I do not remember exactly when I was engaged. [laughter] I can't remember, but I do know, anyway, that this relationship . . . and then I thought, "My gosh, here I am at Ohio State, and I really came for a different reason. I didn't come here, necessarily, to pursue an academic life." And since I was interested in Peter—he was getting his Ph.D.—I figured, "Wow!" To have two people in a family work on their Ph.D.'s at that time, I thought, was pretty unusual and would be pretty tough to do. So I don't think that I overloaded—and I didn't, I know—in terms of academic classes. I can't remember exactly what I did take, but a couple of classes, as I say. So my focus at Ohio State was more on the work than the academics.

I do remember that this was the year that John Kennedy was shot in Dallas, and I remember, because I had my own little apartment with a TV and everything in there. There were two things that occurred that affected Peter and I. One was the assassination, and you really wanted to talk to somebody about that. You didn't want to just be in a place all by yourself to sort of internalize it.

And the girls, oh, they were very upset, but I didn't feel it was my role to kind of talk to them about very personal feelings. I guess I felt that there had to be some difference . . . although I was always very

Sue Wagner, engagement portrait.

friendly to them, but there had to be a relationship that I was the boss so to speak, and the buck stopped there.

So that was difficult, I remember, and Peter and I talked a lot on the phone during that period of time. The other thing that occurred, there was a huge earthquake in Alaska in 1964, and it was in Anchorage, but it was just the worst one this continent has had in the last, probably, fifty years, at least. And it devastated the town where Peter's parents lived, Seward. I was in constant touch with him, and I called the Red Cross and tried to find out what I could about his parents, although I hadn't met them or anything, but I thought it was just so incredible. It was a big one—6.5 or 6.6 or something like that on the Richter Scale. Anyway, those were two things that I remember specifically that we spent a great deal of time talking about on the phone. Also during that period of time, obviously, our relationship developed, and we found out what things were important and not important to each of us, and as I told you, in looking for this scrapbook, which I haven't looked for this week, I found all these letters Peter had sent me that I've saved through all these years. So someday when I have some time I will find them. Many of them were sent there, to Ohio State, because, see, I was gone then, and after Ohio State I went back to Tucson and got married, and there were no other letters until he went off to get his Ph.D. in Boulder, but that probably would tell me even more than I remember now.

That's great that you have them. So, were you there for one full year or longer? One full school year?

Yes.

And that was during the time when the earthquake occurred, and Kennedy was shot in the fall?

That's when these things happened, 1964. Wait a minute. No, it would have been 1963-64, because John Kennedy was shot in November of 1963, I believe.

That's right.

I remember I actually got my master's in 1964, and that would have been in May of 1964, but I'd done the exam and everything in the fall of 1963, so that would have been 1963-64.

The other big thing, I guess, that happened to me on that campus was, the dean of students, Ruth Weimer, had a friend who had just written a book, and her name was Betty Friedan. The name of the book was *The Feminine Mystique*. So she invited

all her assistants to come to lunch and meet this woman and hear about this book, and we all *had* to go. I remember I didn't want to go. I had something else I wanted to do— maybe a football game, I don't know—but anyway, I went, and I thought, "What is she talking about?" I had *no clue*. She was talking about a life that I had no connection with. She was talking about women who were married, basically, and were at home and needed to feel . . . needed something else in their life. I wasn't there yet. I had a life. I was doing things. I was going to class. I was in charge of a dorm. I had more things to do. I was falling in love with a guy. All these things were going on, and what she talked to us about . . . I just went out of the room saying, "Huh?" basically.

Just couldn't connect to it at all, relate to it?

Could not connect. Nope. Couldn't relate, couldn't connect. And I really don't know how some of the other assistants felt. We were able to ask questions. I do remember that, but it would have been nice to have small groups or have us all sit around and talk about it, and then I would have known if anybody felt the same way I did. I'm sure they did, because there wasn't anybody there who was married and had a family.

It was the wrong audience for the kind of things she wrote about.

Well, to me, I think it was. I think it was. But it had just been published, and it was her friend, so I think that she wanted to expose us to that. And clearly, several years later on, [laughter] it just really clicked in. I thought, "Now I know what she was talking about."

At that time, I didn't, but that was another big thing in terms of that time that happened to me, because there aren't that many people who heard Betty Friedan right out of the chute.

To hear her speak.

Later on, yes. Because I've met her a number of times in other venues later in my life, but not when she was unknown. Her book, it hadn't even been discussed or anything of that sort. So, that became very important to me later, but I found it interesting that it had no connection with me *at all* when I heard her speak and talk about it. The life she had described in that book just wasn't my life. And I suspect it wasn't any of the other lives, either, if we'd sat around and talked about it.

It's interesting to hear you assess how that affected you at that time and then later affected you. What about President Kennedy's death? You said you talked to Peter about it a lot. How did that affect you at that time?

I think that was just devastating to me. Well, being a political science *major*, and somebody who was interested in that, it was devastating, although, I didn't vote for him, as I told you. It was devastating to me that he was the president of our country, and someone had slain him, and then there were all those things that happened afterwards—Jack Ruby and Oswald and all of these things that just sounded so bizarre, that you knew there was something else up. It just seemed like this really was contrived, to say the least, but I think the thing that struck me in thinking about it was that this system of government, our country, could go on, and Lyndon Johnson, who we all knew they didn't like—either Jackie or Jack—was sworn in as the next president on a plane flying back to D.C., and that he took over, and there was maybe

a few blips on the radar screen, and that was it. It's pretty incredible. That really stuck with me, that, those framers of the Constitution were pretty smart guys.

Because in any other country, the death of a president is a revolutionary type of act.

Oh, it would have been, particularly one who was just a hundred days in, and everybody—most political pundits, anyway, except for maybe diehard Republicans— expected great things from him, and felt he was . . . who knows? I suspect now that revisionist historians look at some of his presidency and feel that he had made some mistakes already—the Bay of Pigs and a number of other kinds of things that are questionable in terms of who he relied upon and the advice he chose and even Vietnam. But at that time, that was a different feeling, and regardless of whom it had been, except maybe Richard Nixon, because I think there was just so much animosity to him at that time. Well, no. I would say Richard Nixon, not at that time, but later on. Because that was in the 1970s.

But if Richard Nixon had been the person . . . regardless of the president, whether you voted for him or not, Democrat or Republican, it was a devastating thing to happen, because none of us in our lifetimes had experienced an assassination, although there had been some, but we weren't really around for them. Probably the other one was Abraham Lincoln. That was just so incredible, but one only reads about it or might go to the theater and look and see where John Wilkes Booth jumped down and that sort of thing, but this we all lived, and particularly, because everyone had television, and we watched it, just as I said. I was totally occupied by this. I, in my living room area, just watching all the time what was going on, and that was a first, as well.

Those were pretty amazing times, and you've just named two really important things: the Betty Friedan book, The Feminine Mystique, *and the assassination of John F. Kennedy. Those were life-changing events at that point.*

That's true, although one did not understand that Betty Friedan's book was going to be life-changing, not only for me, but for women, and everything that's happened in our country since then, whether it was Gloria Steinem, if one wants to point to her, or Betty Friedan or both of them together.

I think the one thing that did not occur to me, when this happened to John Kennedy, nothing happened to me in terms of, I made a decision about running for office, or I wouldn't want to run for office, because this might happen to you. None of that. That was not part of my thought process at that time. I thought maybe you might ask me that question. Personally, it didn't affect me. Clearly it did, as I've described, but not in terms of what I chose to do later in life.

Your future career, because you hadn't made a decision to do anything politically at that point.

No, but I think that I'm about ready to get married here soon. But when I did get married, I think my husband realized that some time I would be running for office. So, I think that was not something that . . . .

Wasn't a big surprise?

No, no, no. Not at all.

3

MARRIAGE

I went back to Tucson after that year was up, and my husband and I, we were married in August of 1964, so at some point earlier than that we were engaged—I think it might have been at Christmas time when I came home. So that summer there were wedding plans, and, of course, my mother, being the mother of the bride, had most of the responsibility, so I helped her with that. Of course, my sister had been married when she was nineteen, many, many, many years ago, and I was then twenty-four, so my mother getting involved in this had had a long period of time in between. So I really don't know how she felt about that, but I think I was there to help her do many of these things. Many of the gals, who I had been in their weddings, were then in mine—many of my college friends.

Did you have a large, traditional wedding?

Yes, and it was in the Episcopal Church that I had gone to. I have an album around here. I just cannot find all that, must have put them in a box, because I have a lot of boxes in my crawl space downstairs, and they must be there because I showed it to my daughter a couple of years ago.

I do remember that the wedding dress I wore was worn by one of my good friends, whose wedding I was in, and her husband was not part of the wedding party, but she was, and she was president of the Theta house, and she was just a sweetheart. She was, I don't know, homecoming queen or something like that. But anyway, I'd lost a lot of weight. I was much thinner than I am now, so I was able to get into her wedding dress. [laughter] She was kind of light. Her husband, I remember, said, "Where have those love handles gone?" I can remember him saying that, and I'd never heard that term before, and he was so surprised, I guess, that I could wear it. Her name was Joanie Johnson Hill, and it was just awfully nice of her to offer, because this was an expense for my mother to have a big wedding, and this was one thing she didn't have to buy. It had only been worn once, and it seemed like a good idea to me. It was silly. To me, that was no big deal, to wear someone else's wedding dress. Now, some people might just be so appalled by the thought of doing that, but to me it was just great. I loved her. She was in my wedding. She was my friend, and the wedding dress was beautiful.

My sister was my matron of honor, and I'm trying to remember. Let me see, I had Ellen. I had Mary Helen. I had Gwynne. I had Joanie. So that's four bridesmaids, and then my sister made five. And there might have been more. My friend, Edith, who I think I mentioned to you before, was the board of regents president in Arizona, she, I think, was in charge of my book, the registration book.

Then my husband's best man was an attorney in town, Wes Carlson. My wedding party, even when I was forty or forty-two, almost half of them were dead. And that is a pretty incredible thing to say when you're that young. All of them were my age or a few years older.

My husband's best man, as I said, was an attorney, [and although] his father was a doctor, he evidently went around to different doctors. He wasn't feeling well, and he had just married a woman who was in my wedding party. They'd met as a result of our wedding. In fact, they married a couple of weeks before we did. He ultimately died of cancer when he was about, maybe, thirty-five or something like that, but I won't get into it. I'll just say that. And then, one of the other guys in our wedding party, ultimately, turned out later on to be the mayor of Tucson. Then, I think maybe there was a guy or two that had been in his fraternity at Stanford. When I see the pictures, I'll be able to remember better.

I remember exactly who mine were. But I do remember it was a very traditional wedding. It was in the evening, because Tucson is so hot, and it was in August. I remember the bridesmaids' dresses were, like, aquamarine. I remember the color, and I remember where the reception was and where the wedding was, and I remember my brother gave me away,

because my father was dead, and I think I did mention, maybe, that he brought down two of his children. He has six children now, and they are all grown and married, but at that time they were just a couple of little squirts, and they came down and were the ring bearer and the flower girl. But they had never seen lightning before, and they were scared to death the whole time they were there. So that was the one thing that disrupted the wedding, [laughter] was this crackling of lightning and their fear of it, because they came from the Bay area, and they just hadn't ever heard anything like that.

So you were married in a storm?

Well, there are always storms at that time of year in Tucson, but they're usually over by that time, and the reception was sort of indoor-outdoor, knowing that does happen at that time of year.

Did you have a honeymoon at that time?

Peter and I, oh, we went on a pretty incredible honeymoon. We went to Alaska. His parents drove down, and this was the first time I had met them. They actually bought a brand new car, coming down from Alaska. They usually come down to Seattle or Portland to buy a car, and he was a dentist—his dad—on the Kenai Peninsula, the only dentist on the Kenai Peninsula at that time. They drove down and bought a new Chrysler station wagon, because they had bought an Airstream trailer, and he was going to retire. They had come to Tucson and thought, "Wow!" Man, they couldn't believe the climate, compared to Alaska, where they had lived since 1929, so they decided it was time to retire and go travel. He had to fly back after the wedding, because he was president of the Alaskan Dental Association, and he was in charge of the convention. They had to get right back, so they had this car there, and that's what we used on our honeymoon. Oh, it was just really nice: leather seats and everything. Anyway, what we did was, we camped from Tucson to the Kenai Peninsula through national parks. That was our honeymoon.

Had you ever camped before?

No. I had never camped before, but I thought it sounded like a great idea, until about the second camping night out. [laughter] Geez! I remember people had given some funny wedding shower presents, like flannel underwear with trapdoors in all different kinds of places. [laughter] And they just had a lot of fun with the whole idea. And I thought it sounded more fun than it was. [laughter]

It took us thirteen days. It was a long trip. You're talking from southern Arizona. And then we had to go over what is called the Alcan Highway, and today that's pretty nice, but in 1964 it was *incredible*. It was pothole after pothole after pothole, and it was several thousand miles long. It took us forever to get over that, and in those days—and probably today, although I've not been on it for many years—you had a book, the milepost book, and you have to plan ahead, and there was nothing in 1964 on the Alcan Highway, even to camp, even if you wanted to have sort of a campground. We might have wanted to have stopped in a little cabin or something, and there just wasn't much. But remember, we were traveling in a brand new, beautiful car. When you hit those potholes, it was as nice as it could be.

After the national parks, we went to the town of Prince Rupert and caught the State of Alaska ferry. We slept in the car two nights (the ferry only had a few rooms) and then were dropped off onto the Alcan

Highway to Anchorage. That shortened the trip on the way there.

We got to Anchorage. We stopped at his parents' best friends' home—their age—and it was in the evening, and they had been waiting and waiting and waiting for us, I think, expecting us to be there at dinnertime, and it was much later than that. They had this *unbelievable* table prepared of, oh my, king Alaska crab and all these wonderful delicacies, particularly seafood, and it was just wonderful, but it was like ten or eleven o'clock at night, I think, when we got to Peter's home. Now, this was right after the earthquake. Seward used to be a place where big ships came in and unloaded canned goods and, I don't know, not cars maybe, but big stuff.

Big shipping center?

Big shipping center. The earthquake totally destroyed what they called their big harbor. The typhoons, or the big waves—I guess that's what they call them, typhoons—that's usually what comes in after an earthquake. Then all these tidal waves came in and devastated the big harbor. I guess they had a big harbor and a small harbor. And it wasn't there! It was totally destroyed, and it was never rebuilt. So they lost, in that evening or several days, their entire source of economic being.

So, the little harbor was still there, the small-boat harbor where people had their own private boats or small fishing boats. I did get the chance to see that, and we stayed there, I can't remember how long, but I'd say at least a week, maybe, with his parents. They had saved up for us moose meat, caribou. Of course, Peter grew up on this, and besides that, they didn't eat all that stuff all the time, but they had saved it up for me, and, of course, I had to like everything.

Then we went to meet all his parents' friends, and I remember, somehow they *all* made something called dandelion wine, which was just the world's worst. It was so awful. [laughter] Well, you can imagine—dandelions? It was so bitter. Oh, they just could hardly wait to open that bottle. It was an excuse for them, I'm sure, because, hey, look, in Alaska the winters are pretty long. [laughter] And Seward was very isolated. There was no really good road from it almost to Anchorage. When Peter was small, they used to fly in and fly out, because that was really, at one point, the only way you could. Then a lot of the road was washed out because of the earthquake and the tidal waves. So we had a difficult time even getting in, but we were able to. But that was just really a time to get to know his parents better and to see where he had been raised, and it was a very small, little town. I graduated from this huge high school, which I've described, the size of Tucson High School's graduating class, and Catalina High School I don't remember now, but a thousand. Big like the schools are here today, I'm sure. This was quite a long time ago. But his high school was twenty or thirty.

He knew all of his class really well.

Oh, twenty or thirty, period! That's it. His mother was president of the school board, and there was another boy right before him that got to go to Stanford, too. So, from this tiny, little high school, to have two boys—and the other boy was a good friend of his—who had gone off to Stanford. And Peter's dad was a real outdoorsman, loved to hunt and fish, and Peter did, as well. That's what they did, growing up there. Peter, when he went to Stanford, came home in the summers and worked for the National Forest Service and helped to make roads and paths and that sort of thing on the land.

So, this camping trip all the way from Tucson to Alaska was just more natural to him, because he was an outdoorsman?

Oh, yes. Oh, absolutely.

This was a big, new adventure for you?

Exactly. And it continues after we get there. [laughter] But when we're all done with this trip, all of a sudden—how are we getting home? [laughter]

You didn't have a plan for that?

Well, I hadn't thought about it, but he had. [laughter] And guess what? Dad had a 1959 GMC truck, and Peter was going to get the truck. That was part of the wedding present that I was unaware of. Now, I'd never been in a truck. It's not the way I normally travel, and to go on the Alcan Highway that I just described. Also, that whole distance from Alaska to Tucson that we had come up in the best of cars, the Chrysler, and then to go back in this truck and bom bomp—oh, it was terrible. It really was.

Very bumpy?

It was not an experience I'd wish on anybody. There were times in our marriage that if you got through those periods—and there were others that were worse that come up—then you figured you were going to make it. This was one, right in the first month! [laughter]

You were introduced early.

Yes.

So this was quite an introduction—the 1959 GMC truck all the way back? Another thirteen days back, was it?

No, we made it faster, because . . . . [laughter]

You didn't stop as often?

We had to get home, because it was just awful. I remember, though, when we hit pavement . . . see, the Alcan Highway was not paved at that time, either. It was dirt. And I'm telling you, it's like twenty-five hundred miles long. I got out in the middle of the road and broke open a bottle of wine that we had, a champagne or something, and just sat right flat in the middle of the road and went, "Yes!" [laughter] And finally made it.

Glad to meet pavement!

Oh, man! And going home, we didn't camp out as much. I do remember that we threw the sleeping bags and stuff in the back of the truck, of course, but I think we stopped in motels along the way, because we were in more of a hurry, because we stayed there longer. Peter had to get back to work, get back to school, and during that time, I also was seeking a job, because Peter had a graduate assistantship, but that was hardly enough to keep two people alive on. I had my teaching certificate. If you remember, that was one of the things that my mother had wanted me to do.

Things were getting late, of course, you see. And I didn't start when I got back. I started before the wedding, I'm sure, to try to get a job, but it still is late to get a teaching job.

In August?

I called my friend. She was the assistant dean of women at the University of Arizona, because I'd had this experience, and I thought, "Ah, well, maybe I don't have a degree, but maybe they would hire me if there was a job."

"Absolutely, no question," she said. "Oh, my gosh, we would hire you in a minute, because you have enough to justify us hiring you," but there was no job.

So, OK. Didn't have a job. So, in Tucson—and I have to remember how this worked—say I wanted a job at a certain high school. If they called in to the school board or the school district or whatever, and said, "We would like Sue Wagner to teach. We've got an opening at this high school, and we would like to have her," I think that's pretty much how it worked. So I called the high school where I had gone, and the dean of girls there was a good friend of mine, and, of course, I'd gone there, and it had only been, what, four or five years later? So, they were very happy to try to get me a job, and they did. The next day I got a call from the assistant dean of women saying there was an opening, and I wanted to do that in the worst way, but I could *not* . . . and only she knew that, and my husband. I was devastated, because I really thought that that could have been a career for me, because we were always going to be on college campuses, because of my husband's work, and that could have been a career for me, and really, as I've told you, I was *not* that excited about teaching. I wasn't from the get-go. I did it because my mother wanted me to do it.

So, I just thought it would be very unfair, though, to the high school dean of girls, who had gone to some lengths, I think, to get me this job. At least, I felt that way, and I thought maybe if I'd called her and said, "Hey, this is what happened," she would have said, "Oh, fine." But I guess at that time I didn't think it was the right thing to do. I know I anguished over it, because I really wanted the other job. I wanted to be on the college campus. I wanted to do whatever this job description was, but anyway, I didn't, and that opportunity came and went, so I did teach, and actually, I did enjoy it. I taught American government, American history, and world history. That was the biggest challenge, to have *three* totally different subjects, and you had to be prepared. It takes a lot of work, particularly when you're brand new, to have lesson plans and do all of the things that one does in high school, versus college, where you don't have to turn in lesson plans and that kind of thing, although you have to have them, or you should have them in college.

Did you have all the high school grades then? And was that sophomore through senior, or was that freshman?

Well, seniors was American government only. Everything I taught, they had to take in order to graduate, so that was another thing that people didn't like.

So, you had freshman all the way through senior?

I'm trying to think. Yes. American government was seniors only. They had to take it in order to graduate. And world history, I think, might have been freshman and sophomore. Maybe you could take world geography instead. I really don't remember. American history was mandated, and I think that was juniors. They had to take that in their junior year. But anyway, the point is, yes, I had all ages, but the biggest problem was that I had three totally different subjects, books, everything, and that's why, I think, I got the job, probably, and that there was a variety of openings, and they figured they could plug one person in, because it was really hard to get a job teaching school.

I was very lucky to get one, because most people didn't, who applied, but it was

just a tremendous amount of work, and even if you loved teaching, and it's everything you wanted to do, that does tend to make it somewhat discouraging, because that's *all* I did. I was totally dedicated to work again, even though I was just married, because it just took all the time I had after classes, in the evenings, weekends, whatever, to read the books, to get everything ready, to think of things that were different. Remember, I'm teaching at the same school that I went to a number of years before. I didn't think some of the teachers I had were very exciting or made me very interested in the subject. It's just that I liked the subject matter so much that I overcame their . . . .

Lack of style?

Yes. I didn't want to repeat that. It would have been nice if you'd had a teacher that said, "Wow! Mr. or Mrs. So-and-So was fabulous. I will go . . . ." And I did. I went. The head of the department was a good friend of mine who I'd had as a teacher, Miss Korfhage, her name was. The dean of girls who I mentioned before was Myrtle Brown, and she was called Brownie, when you knew her well enough. I didn't. I called her Mrs. Brown or Dean Brown, but later on I called her Brownie. Nona Korfhage was the chairman of our department, and she was helpful, but she had her own classes to teach.

I have to say, one of the memories I had during that time, was I was extremely disillusioned with many of the teachers that I had had or knew. There was a teachers' lounge, and you'd go down there and have lunch or sit around and talk or, in those days, smoke, and a couple of things I remember distinctly was the fact that having these three courses and getting around to grading finals, for example, it was incredible. I had teachers tell me, "You grade them?" They said, "We just have them do them, but then we throw them away." They already had the grades all made out.

I was shocked! I said, "That is so *unfair!*" I said, "Those kids could be studying for a *real* test that *really* counts, rather than waste time on studying for yours, when you don't even count it." I said, "If you don't count it, fine. That's a decision you make, but I think they should be aware of that, rather than *trick* them," in my mind. It really left me with a very negative feeling towards, not only individual teachers, but in certain cases, I think, probably many teachers. We hear about many teachers—coaches—getting jobs, and coaching being the most important thing, particularly in the social studies department, and that was very, very clear to me in those days, that there were many guys that—as I said, by sitting in those lounges and listening to what was going on and picking up on stuff—that was very, very important to them.

Because I taught seniors in the American government class, every Friday I had to approve who was going to play in the football game that night, and you talk about pressure—it was incredible. I not only got it from the kids, their parents, but other teachers, who might have been a coach or an assistant coach. If they were some big linebacker—I've already talked to you about how much I enjoy sports—and if they didn't pass the test, or if they didn't get the right grade, they didn't play.

That's big. That's a lot of pressure, especially for a brand new teacher.

I guess when you think about sports and politics, they all seem to always be intertwined in my life, one way or the other, whether I'm participating in them, or they affect me in some way.

And in this case it was both, right?

When I think about it, it was both, exactly. As far as the positive things, I don't want to leave the impression I did teaching as something that I just had to do. The kids were great. I loved the students, and again, that's what attracted me to the personnel and guidance, were the kids. I'm sure, if I learned more about that field, in terms of the bureaucracy, there'd be things that I didn't like about that, as well. It's just that I didn't as much, or the memories weren't as vivid, but I think that I had some amazing students, because I did teach in a high school that at that time was zoned where you got the best and the brightest, and most of their parents, maybe, taught at the university, so I was blessed in that way.

Let me think if there's anything about the teaching experience that I would want to remember . . . but I believe I skipped an entire year, because I worked at the newspaper, and that was prior to my teaching. There were some other interesting things that occurred because of that reason, and I guess, while they're on my mind, I'll talk about it.

I did have a lot of drug problems, and this high school was written up in *Good Housekeeping* magazine. This was now maybe 1965, 1966, something like that, where drugs were *just* starting to creep into our high school, into our school system, and this was the first time any national article had ever been written about a high school and drugs—or school and drugs, I guess I should say. They chose this one, and we were all horrified and disappointed and shocked, et cetera, but the reason being is that Tucson is so close to Mexico, and clearly, drugs, just as they are today, that's where they came from, and that's where they were cheap—cheapest, I guess. I'd heard about this, and we all discussed this, of course, the teachers, this horrifying thing that was national news now. I decided that in my class it would be pertinent to have a discussion on some of these subjects.

I tell you, I was so unsophisticated and so out of this mainstream, I guess, of the 1960s, that I didn't even know what a "narc" meant, but I did get a narcotics agent to come to my class. I'd had him recommended to me by somebody else as being somebody who was *really* a spellbinder and someone that kids would get excited about. Before this guy came I'd asked the kids how many of them were interested in taking drugs—not how many *did*, because there was no laws even, I don't think, at that time, I suspect. Maybe so. I don't know, but anyway, almost all the hands went up, so I decided this was right to have a "narc" come, and he did, and, oh my God, scared the heck out of me! Stories of incredible, personal . . . maybe even personal to him. And he might have worked for that DEA [Drug Enforcement Administration] or whatever the federal thing is drugs and whatever. I don't remember, but anyway, after he had come and gone, and we discussed it and everything, then I asked how many were interested in taking drugs—same number. Practically the same number!

Still?

I couldn't believe it. It impacted practically nobody but *me*. [laughter] I was just blown away. And there were some of my really square kids, just like I was and who wanted to do everything right, who didn't raise their hands, but for the most part, it was not a lot of effect. That was, of course, my desire, to scare them or do whatever to make them really think that this was not the way they wanted to go.

I had a student whose father did teach at the University of Arizona, and he was one of my brightest, and he was so demanding of attention that he would come to school with silly little things like just a T-shirt on, and there were dress codes in those days, like our principal made all the boys wear belts, because everybody wore Levis, Levi Strauss, and you had to wear belts, because I gather that the Levis would kind of ride too low on the hips or something like that. [laughter] Look at today!

Nothing compared to today, by any means.

No, and there were all these, what we would think of even then as being kind of silly, but this guy came with just a T-shirt, and you could not wear an undershirt without a shirt on top with a tie. He was a tall, thin boy, I remember, but *really* smart as heck, and was planning to go to Princeton, had been admitted to Princeton. Living in Tucson, a lot of the kids did not apply to schools that far away. They would look for something, maybe, on the West Coast, if they were a very good student, possibly. He was not a popular boy, but a big kid. People would not intimidate him by size, but then he did other kinds of things. I do remember that. I think one time he came to school without any shirt on, so you'd have to keep sending him down to the office. Ultimately, one day he came with a slip for me to sign for him to leave school, and I said, "You mean, you are quitting?" It was like *two months* before graduation.
"Yes."
I said, "You're on your way to Princeton," all of these things.
He was going to go down to the Yucatan Peninsula to grow his *own* drugs. I will never forget that day, signing that, thinking, "What a waste. What a waste of a human being." But then, that was just the beginning. I saw it in my school at the very first, and just now, that that refrain has been repeated so many times over and over again, but to me, that was my first experience with it, and it was the first one

in our school. It was a big, big discussion among the teachers about this particular boy, and I know he had an older brother who was a star, and in his mind, I believe it was just the old refrain—he didn't get enough attention, even though his father . . . I can't remember what field, but he was a well-respected and renowned guy, and it was a liberal arts type of a discipline. He had been brought from some other school to the University of Arizona. And he was gone. Never saw him again, never heard about him again, and I did ask, and nobody had heard from him, and I never did meet his parents. They never came to school to find out what was going on.

And 1965 was before some people even realized there was a drug problem, at least in other parts of the country. Probably, as you say, close to Mexico, that was a little different. You were seeing the beginning wave of it.

Oh, yes. Yes. As I said, in the first national publication we were the first school. It mainly said about this school, more than most in Tucson, that the kids used drugs more, because they could afford it. They could go to Mexico. They had extra money, because they were more affluent than some of the other high schools in town. That was all true, and it was just a real shock, particularly because there were so many good kids, and he was a good kid. He kind of wanted attention and kind of got it.

Did things to attract attention?

They weren't any big deal. It wasn't anything to get upset about, and also, he was not *in*, just like we hear about, in any particular group, and I'm sure he felt left out, ostracized, and all the kind of things that we hear about today lead to worse

things than that, affecting other people's lives.

I taught for about three or four years, I think, and during that time, Peter was working on his Ph.D., and, as I said, he had this graduate assistantship. Somehow, in one of my classes, someone had been late for class or something, or didn't start until later, because some of the seniors didn't have early classes, but, as I said, they had to take mine, so they had seen my husband somewhere. I can't remember exactly the sequence of events, but I think that's what it was, and they were talking to him, and he had said he just got up or something, and they were *so upset* that I was out teaching, like at seven a.m. through three or four, and he was still in bed. So they, unbeknownst to me, started calling my home early in the morning, after I was at school, and letting the phone ring and waking my husband up and hanging up. [laughter]

And these were the kids, your students?

These were the kids, yes, because they thought it was so *unfair* that my husband got to sleep in while I was out working. They didn't think it was fair. So I guess that was the beginning of equality or something. [laughter]

Equal rights?

I know. But I found out. I'd come home, and he'd say something, and I'd say, "Well, I don't know what that was all about." Never, never, never did we put this together, until one of the kids said something. That was kind of funny. It came and went.

The other unfortunate thing that happened was that I got pregnant, and of course, in those days, you could not be pregnant and teach—you had to quit, resign. It seems like not that long ago, in terms of how far we've come and things like that. I never did understand what the reason was. I kept asking them why that was, when I turned in my resignation. It was like, did they think that woman went home and did something with her husband that we're not supposed to know goes on? What is it about this deal that you don't want them knowing that I'm carrying a baby? There was no rational explanation ever given to me.

Well, I did turn in my resignation, and unfortunately, right after that my senior kids—American government—came in, and they were hee-hawing about somebody who got the measles. Needless to say, I was very concerned, and of course, the kids didn't know at that time, because I'd just turned in my resignation to the administration. I was going to wait to tell them. I told my doctor, and at that time, there wasn't anything they could do. I'd suspect there is not anything they could do now, I don't know, except give you gamma globulin, and they did do that. But I'd already resigned, and then I did lose the baby and had to have a D and C. The doctor told me that it was a good thing I'd lost the baby, that it was nature's way, evidently, but I must have probably picked up something from the kids. I don't know.

Of course, when that happened, I immediately tried to get my job back, because we needed it, but it was too late. It was just at this strange time, like a few weeks or maybe a month at the most. They'd already hired somebody else, so I was out of a job, and I had to substitute teach that next year. And talk about bad—that is the worst. [laughter] Besides, in Tucson they were on double shifts, again, because schools had gotten overcrowded one more time, so the early classes, you got called like at four, four-thirty in the morning to go for the early shift at seven, and you had no life. And then you would not know whether you were going to get called or not.

Then you would know whether to go to bed early.

Yes, and there was just no life, and besides, kids always give substitutes a hard time, particularly a little woman, somebody who's not a big guy. And then it all depended upon where you went, which part of town, very honestly, and what kinds of classes they were. We needed everything we could get, but after awhile, my husband said, "You got to limit this to certain places," because it was getting rough. It was, and people will tell you that today—nobody enjoys substitute teaching.

It's interesting when you look at women's history that there was a period of time in the 1800s and early 1900s where women couldn't teach if they were married.

Well, that was my mother-in-law in 1929 in Alaska. She couldn't smoke, and she could not date. She had to date my father-in-law on the q.t., and then when she got married, they must have been mad about that.

That was it. You couldn't teach. And then, here it was in the 1960s, where you think we've evolved some, and you couldn't be pregnant and teach at the same time. You said being in the teachers' lounge and so on left you kind of a bad taste about teachers in general.

Some of them.

Would you say that that's still true today, or was that just for that time? Do you still have concerns about the quality of teachers?

Oh, absolutely. Sure. I can't imagine that wasn't anything that was time-driven. The specific example I gave you was about grading of final exams. There would be some people who would feel the same way. They may do something, shortchange the kids in some other way. I also sincerely believe that teachers are *so* poorly paid, that if we think kids are this important, and we listen to every politician talk about education, children, and yet, they're not willing to pay someone who's guiding kids from five to eighteen years of age and spending more time with them than their parents.

The most formative years.

That they don't want to acknowledge that in a way that other professions are acknowledged. If you understand a computer or something, you can write your ticket, and I don't have a problem with that, but I think it's appalling that we do not appreciate teachers, and part of it, I think, is because of the very thing that I described to you. I think that's unfortunate, because I have to believe that's just a few rotten apples in a very large barrel of people who really care.

In fact, I just went in to some teachers recently, who are almost near retirement. One just retired. I saw her down at the gym the other day, and she was telling me what she was doing in the summer. She just retired in May. She was teaching—and she's been teaching since the 1950s—and her eyes lit up, because she said, this summer she was teaching *little* kids. Like she normally taught fifth graders, and they were like second graders. I went away thinking, isn't that fabulous? She lives in my neighborhood. I saw that real joy and excitement on her face, describing the fact. She'd just retired and was very happy that she'd retired, but would have this other opportunity. There are, hopefully, many, many more of them, and I have to believe there are more of them, who really care about teaching.

But I think that there was a feeling, and then I think that was partly my kind of

hang-up with having an education degree, was that if you can't do anything else, you can get to be a teacher. That *was* thought of. I know that from my sorority house living that girls would talk about it.

That was an attitude of that time, and it's maybe not so much now?

I hope not.

You still hear it occasionally.

Oh, I'm sure. There was this old adage on whether you should know your subject matter, like how much do you know about political science and about government and about history and the kinds of things that you're teaching, particularly when you get into middle school and high school years, versus teaching methods, the methods classes and so on. I think they're both equally important. Because, as I said, I had teachers in high school who were teaching the same classes I did, who knew the stuff cold, but just didn't know how to get it across to the students.

Yes, did not excite them.

In fact, one of my high-school teachers, who I later taught with—I would read ahead in the chapters, just a couple ahead, and then I'd ask questions in the class, and he wouldn't know the answers. That was another prank I would play even when I was older. I mean, that wasn't anything bad, but in a way it was, because the teacher knew exactly what I was doing, and it made him look like you know what, and it also made him look like that in front of the whole class. I didn't do it quietly off to the side. I did it on purpose, and I know that. Then, of course, I wound up teaching with him. [laughter] That I did *not* know was going to happen at the time, but it was *appalling*. He hadn't read chapter six, and we're on chapter four. And he'd been teaching the class—it wasn't his first year.

I definitely do not want to leave the impression that I did not enjoy it. I enjoyed high school. If I had been around longer, if we had not moved, and I hadn't had to resign I would have gotten very involved in being an adviser to different groups and that kind of thing, but I was only there for a short period of time. I think you had to teach three years before you were kind of approved, not like tenure, but something of that sort.

Sort of like off probation or something, yes.

Yes, something like that.

You'd been objecting to being a teacher all the way through college after you'd made the change, but you actually found a lot that you liked about it when you got out and did it?

Oh, yes. The kids were the biggest thing. There were several things, and one of them was that anybody can do it type of thing, and I certainly did not want to feel like that's what I went to college to have that said about me.

I think that was more elementary school, because you'd see the girls in the house cutting out different color Kleenexes and doing designs for their bulletin boards and things. [laughter] And I think, "Oh, my gosh." But I suspect in whatever grades in elementary school, that's important, to have attractive bulletin boards and things, with what's on there, so the kids will read them. It just wasn't my thing, particularly elementary school. I very honestly could not teach elementary school.

You like the older students?

Yes. Yes.

Tell me about the newspaper job you had prior to teaching.

Well, that was my first job, and the description I gave you between the dean of women and that occurred a year later, because when I first got married, when I came back, I could not get a job. I was thinking to myself while I was talking, "How was I able to get that job so late, teaching?" Well, I wasn't, but that's why I was able to get it the next year, because they knew that I was on the look. And that's why I was able to get in at the high school that I taught in, because I didn't have anything. I had a couple of friends who worked on what was known as the women's page. In those days, they had a special page for women, and it was mainly a society type of page: who was going to what parties and that sort of thing, and cooking and things that appealed to women at that time, because most women didn't work in the 1960s.

A couple of my friends from the high school that I went to, or from college and the sorority or whatever, worked on this page, and they said, "Oh, we work for the editor," blah, blah, "and she'll hire you." The pay wasn't very good, but it was a job, and it sounded fun. The first thing I had to do was to type a wedding, and they thought that would be cute, since I'd just been married, you see. So I had been told, probably, that that would be what they'd ask me. Betty Milburn was the name of the woman who was the women's editor, and I don't know if she's still alive or not. Her husband was the publisher of the newspaper, Bill Milburn, but they said it would probably be most likely that's what she would ask me to do. It would be a test. If you couldn't do that, you probably wouldn't get the job. So I read. I cut out all the weddings, and the first paragraph said that and this, and then the gown was trailing, and then the altar was covered in gladiolus or a wreath, so I kind of had this in mind. So when I got there, that's exactly what she asked me to do, and she gave me a scenario. These are the circumstances. This is when the wedding occurred; this was the time, and describe it. And, whew, I did pretty well, so I got the job, and it was just so much fun.

First of all, I knew all the other people, practically, and if I didn't, we all were like in one room with desks. Since I was the new person and had never done this before, I got all the worst things, what no one else wanted, like editing the *Heloise* columns, and the stuff we did not use—you would not believe what people sent in—or what the *Heloise* people from wherever would send out to newspapers, that you could not use. They were just garbage, so you had to toss those out.

There was another column—oh, I know, *Dear Abby*, yes, which we still have. We still have *Heloise* and *Dear Abby*. They are still around. Well, those were the worst, in terms of what people would write in and *share*—their problems—with some strange person that they've never known, that might get published in newspapers all across the country. But anyway, what they did was, they would send you lots of different options, and then you could choose what to use for your own paper. Some may be totally appropriate for one part of the country, not another, or whatever. So anyway, I did that and had to edit them, and really mind-boggling things, and then I did the recipes. See, these are things that were just a joke for me, and everybody would laugh, because I was much more interested in more worldly things, but it was fun, and the people I worked with were fun, and that was part of what made the job one you enjoyed going to every day.

You probably would have liked to have covered city hall as a reporter?

Oh, yes. Well, I'll tell you later on.

Oh, OK. You got a chance to?

Yes. Not exactly, but something. You would get an opportunity, if you came up with a great idea to do a feature, and I had some, like April Fool's I had all these recipes on what to do with your leftover buffalo meat and venison and things, because I had gotten these recipe books in Alaska when I was there.

Then I did a thing on what kids wrote to each other in high school yearbooks. I remember that was a *really* popular one, in terms of what people wrote in, and because I had connections, still, in high school and was going to be a teacher pretty soon, I was able to get some real popular kids' yearbooks, and I promised them, though, that I would not put in print something I read that would be very inappropriate, that would *shock* their parents or anything like that, because they made me *swear*. [laughter]

Remember the time when . . . ?

Yes. [laughter] They made me promise. I could do funny stuff, but they did not have the right to edit it or anything of that sort. I said, "You're just going to have to trust me."

And then, of course, everybody else in the room wanted to read them, and they'd say, "Oh, listen to this one!" [laughter]

"Can't use it. Can't use it."

And, oh, I don't know. I can't remember any of the other things, but it was a fun job, and it was a job where the editor went to all the social events, and she had her little column, "In and About Tucson," or whatever.

Tucson was a very social place at that time, because it was growing. I don't want to say it was like Las Vegas, because nothing's like Las Vegas, but it was a growth thing, and people were very social, and things were going on all the time, so it was interesting. I did not go to any of those, and Peter would not have wanted to, and of course, she got to go to them. Sometimes we'd have to, if she couldn't, or if there were two or three things going on at once, then the rest of us would have to take over. One of the women who I worked with now is the editor and has been for many years. I see her, very often, when I go back to Tucson, and we have lunches with people. She edits a magazine called the *Tucsonian* or something like that, which is a big deal. She obviously took her journalistic experience and turned it into something. Her husband is an attorney in town, so I think they do many of the same things that Betty did, in a way. There was a little party/social part of it, and then she is also a very good writer and very smart. A lot of stories. But the other people, I'm not sure where all of them are. I think some of them don't live in Tucson any longer, those I worked with.

The one other big thing that happened there was the passage the Civil Rights Act of 1964, I believe. And the expectation of that—because I remember that very day—was that women went cheering through the newspaper, thinking they will now be paid the same as men, and one of the things that I knew—and I was one of those people running through the newspaper cheering—was the fact that there was a young man in the sports department who got twice as much a week as I did. I had a master's degree, and he hadn't even finished his B.A., and we recognized right away, even without all the women's movement—because this was, again, 1964, 1963—that that was absolutely wrong. There was something *wrong* in American society if that could happen. That probably was the first light bulb that went on in my mind—not the Betty Friedan book, but that, that happened to me personally—that didn't

seem right and didn't seem fair. I think it was the Civil Rights Act of 1964. It was under Lyndon Johnson, so it does all fit together.

That would take care of that problem, and many of the women talked about that exact case of mine being so unfair. Neither one of the jobs were that big a deal. I got seventy-five dollars a week, and I think he got a hundred and fifty, or close to it, but it was just not fair. He didn't even have the amount of education that I did. Mine was not a master's degree in journalism, and his may have been a degree that he was working on in journalism, but after awhile, what you're doing there is a matter of form, and you learn that right away.

And you were both probably in the position also of being the main breadwinner for your family, if your husband was on a fellowship.

I was. I don't know about the young man. He might have been just a single guy, working his way through college. I have no idea, don't remember much about him, except for the fact that I remember the amount of money he made, versus the amount that I made.

Twice as much?

Exactly. This was a big deal, and that was supposedly going to change everything, and we now know today, as we speak in the year 2000, that that has not yet been accomplished.

So, whatever the intentions of the act in 1964 were, they have not yet been seen. Maybe the expectations were too high. Maybe it was misread as to what the intentions were, I don't know, but that was what came down, and here I worked for a newspaper. So, clearly, this was the buzz and the message coming down through the newspaper that this is what was going to happen. So I have to believe this was a *real* expectation.

And it gives a sense, too, of the kind of expectation that was going on at that time in terms of expectations of President Kennedy changing things, expectations the Civil Rights Act would change things.

And I have to say, that really was Lyndon, LBJ.

Yes. This was under . . . . I was just kind of saying, that's kind of the attitude at that time, the sense of hope for change.

Yes, there was change going on. Now, it wasn't really change for women. It was change, and it was basically based upon race, much more than gender. And that was yet to come, but clearly, as you say, there was a movement on for change, reform, in a variety of different segments of our society. But that was a big deal. I remember that specifically.

I do not believe—not just because we were a small women's department where only women worked—that we had imagined this or blew it out of proportion. I don't believe that for a moment, because the city editor and the editor were right around the corner, and clearly we got our information on things like that from them, from the newspaper. The women who worked there, who were all bright, capable—I would say none of them were really what you would call today a feminist, because people weren't that tuned in to inequity, but that was just beginning, because clearly we recognize that as being an inequity.

I guess, maybe it hit me that it was gender based, or at least that I believed that, because I believe that I was better educated than he, and yet I was getting less, so what was the difference here? Sex. So, that had to be it. But it wasn't like I ran

right out and created a chapter of something or other. [laughter] I just thought it had been taken care of. When LBJ signs that, it's going to make everything better.

So, from the newspaper job, then you went and taught, and then, had to quit, and then substitute teaching, and about how long were you substitute teaching, then?

Well, we moved here in 1969. I would say, probably, a year. And my husband, when he got near the time when he had to do some heavy research with computer work to finalize what he was doing, he had to go to Boulder, the National Center for Atmospheric Research. It's called NCAR. The computer filled an entire basement of this building. It was huge. Now, we have them sitting on our desks, and he never lived to see that, which was one of my big regrets, that just as this entire revolution occurred, that he just wasn't here at that point. Because of his background it would have been something he would have just eaten up.

He was gone for long periods of time, like an entire summer working on this, and I finally decided that this was not good for our marriage. At that time, I then became pregnant again, and I got approval to go to Boulder from my doctor, even though I'd lost the other baby. He felt it was because of the measles business. So, I flew to Boulder, and he had a little apartment there, and his parents were there, as well. His mother and father had come up to visit him, and you have to keep in perspective here— this is something that was real important throughout our life—that he was an only child.

Whatever happened to him, whether it was his marriage, who he married, what he did with his life, his death, and everything, were unbelievably important, because that's all they had. I never thought that I was the person that they really wanted him to marry. I was just too much, too aggressive. The fact that I didn't stay home and went out and ran for office and those kinds of things. But they were there, I do remember, and we had a little tiny apartment at this point upstairs in some place, and it was hot, hot, hot, I remember. I started to have . . . I started to bleed, and I was about three months pregnant, so I called my doctor, and he said, "You got to get home immediately." He thought maybe it was the altitude change. Of course, there wasn't a lot that they knew about things like that at that time.

Anyway, I did come home. And of course, his parents stayed there for weeks or whatever, because they were retired. They didn't have any commitments or places they had to be. Things got pretty tough at home. I used to take care of everything. I'd do the yard work, but I couldn't at that point. The doctor did not want me mowing the lawn—it's one of those pull things.

Pull things to start?

Yes. So, the yard got to be so *bad* that I finally had some guy come and knock on the door and say, "We didn't know there was anybody living here. We thought maybe it had been vacated." [laughter] That was so embarrassing to me, because I used to trim mine and get it, as you can imagine, perfect. I was just humiliated, so I told Peter that we had to hire somebody to do this. We didn't have money for that sort of thing, but at least they had to do it once in awhile, because he was gone for, I would have to say, a month or two. It was a long period of time, and it was not good, because he had a tendency to get very preoccupied with what he was doing and wouldn't call and do those things, and I was just there. I couldn't *do* anything. I couldn't work. I wasn't working. It was in the summer, I do remember that. I could hardly do anything,

because the doctor had been very concerned about me.

Since we'd lost the other baby, we really did not know what was going on here. I think that it got to be around the Fourth of July, because I remember that. It must have been the end of June in some year. Let's see, it might have been in the year of 1968. He was pretty much winding up with what he was doing in Boulder, and his parents wanted to take him on a tour, a trip of the Western United States, for doing all this work. That didn't set too well with me, to be honest with you.

No. You were already struggling.

You can imagine what hit the fan. I was really upset, and I told him that if he did that, that might be it. He seemed to have no understanding of what it was like for a mother-to-be to lose one baby and then be called home for this one. So, he made the right decision and came home, I think it was July third, July second, and the day after, one of those people in my wedding party was killed in a car crash on July 4, 1968.

Her husband was the D.A. of Pima County, where Tucson was, and they were coming back from Fort Huachuca, I think it was, which is an army base down in the southern part of Arizona, to go to a big fireworks display at the Tucson Country Club. In Tucson there are little dips in the road, where, when the flash floods come, the water can rush through. I guess they were late. She had one little baby, a little girl, and she had just had another baby. Her husband was driving, and he pulled out to pass somebody, and there was a car in the ditch—hit them head on. She was killed. The baby was killed. The little girl in the back seat lived. After he had plastic surgery done, it looked like a television show of a man who had gone in and had a total makeover done to disguise himself.

I was not really totally in the loop, because I had all this stuff going on in my own life, but her friends could not forgive him, because anybody who lives in Tucson knows signs, "Dip Ahead." I mean, why he would ever have done that, and they blamed him for taking her life. Her name was Gwynne. Her maiden name was Barthels, and her married name was Pedersen. And Lars was her husband. He had been through a tremendous . . . he was barely alive, I guess, and had to have all this plastic surgery, and he had lost his wife and a baby. And the little girl, her name was Ann Eve. She was, like, three.

Then, this is a little hazy with me, but I believe she was kind of raised off and on by different parents in that group, because he had a lot of problems, and not only physical, but also mental, to deal with all of this. I wouldn't say every one of her friends kind of held him responsible, but there were some. Later on, I think they understood that that was not a fair thing to do and kind of rallied round. But the point of all this with me was, if that had happened when Peter was out on a trip, and I didn't have anybody there . . . . [long pause] [crying]

Anyway, that brings us back to him finishing up his work. Of course in those days you had to type a dissertation exactly. Everything had to be perfect. We had a hundred dollars, I remember, and we could either buy a new Royal electric typewriter, which was about a hundred dollars, or pay somebody to do the dissertation. Well, of course, Peter thought we should buy the typewriter, and I could type it, and then we would have the typewriter when we were done. So we did that. That was another one of those experiences. [laughter] By the time I'm typing this dissertation it's fall, and I can hardly reach the typewriter, because, as it turns out, the pregnancy went OK after that first problem, and the doctor just assumed it was because of the altitude or some change or something.

Anyway, I typed it, and you have to understand . . . I'll show, maybe, at some point when we wind up, Peter's papers, because we have all this. There's hardly a word you understand in this; there were all these signs that have to be drawn in by hand, mathematical signs and so on. I didn't understand what I was typing, in addition to the fact that I'd done about four or five chapters—a lot. It was in the days where you just couldn't go back and get rid of something. You had to do the whiteout, and then, you couldn't do that, not on the original. You had to be perfect. He came home one day, and he did not know how he was going to tell me that he had made a mistake, and the indentations were supposed to be nine spaces, and he had told me eight—or vice versa. That meant that I had to throw those all out and start all over again. [laughter]

Definitely the days before computers, too, when footnotes were very hard to estimate.

Oh, oh, footnotes. Absolutely. That's a very good point. Because you didn't put those at the back. They had to be at the bottom of that page. You had to guess. You had to figure up all that spacing before. It was just hell. There was no other way I can describe it. The only good thing about bad experiences in your life—and this was hardly the worst one I've ever had—you forget about them. They become hazy, or they become, hopefully, humorous, if that.

Anyway, it did get done on time, and then Peter graduated. Now, this is a time when there was not any demand for people in electrical engineering. It's hard to believe. Today, with his education, he would have just been, wow, snapped up by everybody and everywhere, but that was not the case. In fact, there is that old line about somebody getting a Ph.D. and having to drive a cab. That did happen to some people in his class, but because he had this atmospheric physics part of it, at least he had a couple of job offers. Otherwise, he wouldn't. One was here at the Desert Research Institute. One was in Rapid City, South Dakota, and it was a school of science and technology. I don't remember the name. They were very nice. They flew us both there, and they really wanted Peter to come, and they took me around and showed me homes and, my gosh, we'd never looked for jobs before, but I thought this was pretty nice, and the people were delightful, very friendly and nice, but it was just like in the middle of nowhere, because we'd been in Tucson, and that was a fairly good-size city. Peter's first choice would have been to go back to the University of Alaska in Anchorage, but that was sort of ruled out after the honeymoon. [laughter]

After the honeymoon, you didn't think you wanted to live in Alaska.

No. And so I did . . . I was very open-minded. I sent for the Chamber of Commerce literature and looked at all their materials, and I told Peter, "I can't believe the chamber is sending out this stuff. It says the average daytime temperature in the winter was like minus eighty-five." [laughter] I said, "This is the Chamber of Commerce sending this out." [laughter] "They've got to put their best foot forward and think about what it's really like." And there were stories, and this was true, that you had to wear ski parkas, which came from that whole idea of what you wear in that kind of a climate, but you have to have a certain material, because it catches all the ice crystals, so you don't breathe them in, because then you'd never go outside at certain times, certain low temperatures, because of that. It would freeze your lungs.

It just did not sound like a place that you'd want to live and raise your kids, and he realized that that was a long shot. Rapid City, even he was not, I don't think, as interested, but when you think back on it, it probably was much more like, oh, the memories of the days you had of growing up in the 1950s, a small town, people knowing one another. As I said, people were very nice, and it seemed to me as if whatever they were offering him as a salary that you could get a nice house, because they were showing things that were reasonable, that we could get. Of course, it was near Mount Rushmore, so it was that kind of terrain. It was pretty, to my memory.

There were some trees and . . . ?

Yes. And I think there was a river that went through there, too. Anyway, then I didn't come to Reno, and the other place was Boulder, but that job was with General Electric. It was not with the university, and there was something about that that he was not as interested in, although we both would have picked Boulder as the place we would have gone, because we both liked to ski; we liked to do all the outside things and felt that would be a really nice place to live. He had been there, and I had been there to see him, if ever so briefly, but at least, I got a chance to see what Boulder was like, and they were very much into, at that time, green open space. That started in the early 1960s. They had elected a city council of students from the University of Boulder, so they kind of took over the town, because it's a small town, and you could actually do that. The population base of the university could dictate the politics, so they had all this open space and everything, and it was really nice, but the job was not to his liking.

4

SETTLING IN RENO

That left Reno and DRI, so he accepted the job, and I had to stay in Tucson. I could not travel, because at this time, it was getting close to the time that I would deliver, and they didn't want you traveling at that time, in your eight or ninth month. He moved up here, moved to Stead, because he worked out at the Atmospheric Sciences Center, which was at Stead. There was a big gray building out there, which was used by the air force as a bomb shelter, and there's one window in the entire building. It's a concrete slab, with walls I don't know how many feet thick. There was some place where they would store secret papers, if something happened or whatever.

He rented officer housing at Stead. Of course, I did not know where any of this was. You remember, I'd lived in Tucson now, since 1950, for eighteen years, all my growing up years, high school and college, and my friends, they were just, "Reno?" I mean, hardly a place to live, to go from Tucson, at least in their mind.

This year, in 1968, there was a terrible Asian flu that was killing many people in our country, much worse than anything we've seen since then. There were nurses in the hospital, in the nursery, who had caught it and died and had given it to some of the babies, and fortunately, that did not happen with mine.

I don't know how specific you want to get. I'll tell you, and you know, obviously, but I had started dilating way too soon, and that was another reason I didn't come. That was the big reason. I had to lie flat, and I couldn't even go to the bathroom or anything, so I had to stay with my mom, and of course, she was teaching her piano students. She had taken over my brother's bedroom and made it into a little studio. I had a little bell that I had to ring, if I needed anything, and I tried not to bother her when she was teaching, but there just wasn't much you could do, just laying flat on your back in bed.

Anyway, so Peter moved up here, and I was there, and as it happens, as it gets closer to Christmas, my doctor, a very popular gynecologist, had a lot of people due around the holidays, and evidently he was going on a vacation, so he decided that everybody was going to be induced, so he

Peter Wagner at the Desert Research Institute.

could get out of town. I was one of those people, and here I am, restricted to bed, because the baby might come too soon, and now he's bringing the baby sooner, because he wants to go on a vacation. [laughter] But certainly he wouldn't have done it, if it hadn't been healthy enough, or the right weight and all that.

I remember calling Peter one morning and telling him, "I'm going in today to have our baby." We didn't know, of course, what sex it was. "You can get a plane and get down here as soon as you can." It was kind of strange that I knew that day—didn't know the day before, though, so I could have given him a little advanced notice. I know he bought this little dog—which Kirk

has, which he's, I'm sure, given to one of his daughters—bought it at JCPenney here in town on his way down to Tucson.

Little stuffed animal?

Little stuffed animal. Yes. A little reddish, cute little dog that's sitting, and he got there after the baby had already been born—Kirk—and my mother was with me, and Peter could not . . . no one could come in, because of this Asian flu.

We got him out of the hospital and got him home to my mother's house. My sister was allowed in and Peter, but even Peter's parents . . . we had to move the bassinet up next to the window. We arranged my mother's house. She had a big picture window in her living room and we moved the baby up there, so people could come in and look. It was a big disappointment for me, because I was going to move as soon as I could leave, and I was leaving all my friends, my life, everything behind, and they couldn't even come in and see the baby. I couldn't really get out to talk to them either, because if I went out and picked it up and came back . . . .

The day Nixon was sworn in was the day I left to fly to Reno, because as I left, I remember he was taking his oath of office, so that would be January 20, 1969, I believe. I think Kirk was one month old to the day. Now, the trip here was another adventure. I'd only been on a plane once, and that was to go on my AFS experience I had talked about, to Detroit. So, now I have this little, tiny baby.

This was your second airplane ride, is that right?

Yes.

And with the baby?

Yes. Now, this was in 1969, as I said, and it was not that common to take children on planes and so on, particularly just a month-old baby, so we got a lot of attention from people, "How sweet," and I got involved in a lot of conversations. The plane left from Tucson to Vegas, and then I made a plane change there to Reno, and unfortunately, that did not occur. The plane did not arrive in time to make the connection. It was Hughes Air West Airline, and they said, "Oh, not to worry. Not to worry. We're going to put everybody up overnight, and we'll get you on a plane in the morning." Well, I was not prepared with diapers, with formula, with anything. I never traveled. I never knew this kind of thing happened. My parents didn't. I know

Sue and Kirk, January 24, 1969.

nothing about babies. [laughter] I read Dr. Spock. That's about everything we knew. So, we get to Vegas, and they're acting like it's no big deal. Of course, they have to act that way, but most people were pretty upset, because I don't think this happened a lot, I don't know, but it was late at night, and I remember I got into one of the Hughes properties called the Castaways. When I think about it now, I am regulating the gaming industry. [laughter]

And the Castaways probably felt just about appropriate for how you were with a baby and no supplies, too.

Well, I didn't know what to do, so I put the baby . . . . [laughter] This is just so funny, now, when I think back on it. I put the baby in the middle of the bed, and I didn't sleep all night. I sat up and watched him, because I was afraid it would roll off. [laughter] Well, one-month-old babies don't roll, but I didn't know that. I could have gotten in there and slept with the baby all night long and been very comfortable. But I was so afraid I was going to do something wrong. Oh! My life would be devastated.

I don't know about diapers. I know they did not have disposable diapers. I do remember that. I remember the first month when I was there, someone had given me a month of the diaper service, so we didn't have to mess around with it. They were expensive, those disposable diapers in those days, so we did buy some for the trip. I'm guessing, maybe, I had enough to get by, I don't know, but anyway, I got by, somehow, and the next morning I arrived in Reno.

Of course, it was January 21, and it had been snowing or something, but Peter picked me up and drove me right downtown on Virginia Street out to Stead, and I'd never seen a place that was more *ugly* in my whole life. [laughter] Every neon sign on at ten in the morning, or whatever it was, and slush and dirty snow, even more so than you would normally find here in the winter. Then, we got to Stead. [laughter] It was so far out, without anything in between at that time. You know, Gray Reid's . . . and I don't know how long you've lived here.

The department store, Gray Reid's? Yes.

Yes. Gray Reid's department store. It was downtown. And that was pretty much the end. You had the university there, and then that was it. Then, it was just nothing from there to Stead, pretty much, and Stead itself was a place that would not be my choice of where to live.

What was it like then in 1969? Was it similar to today?

No. There were no buildings, nothing else out there, except the air force housing, pretty much. No warehouses, no school, nothing, nothing, nothing. It was just barren. You're driving along, and it wasn't a big freeway. All of a sudden there's this, as I said, miles of nothingness, and then there's this place, and you can't really see the

housing from the road. So, you didn't see anything until you got off and went up, and then the first part, lower Stead, they were really into signs of success. [laughter]

Lower and upper Stead?

Right. Lower and upper Stead. Yes. Upper Stead, of course, was, quote, "air force housing." We made the best of it, and Peter could walk home for lunch, and that's what he liked, but the winter was a very bad winter, and the housing was very poorly built, and the wind would whip through there, and there was no way you could heat it to keep it warm. We had no furniture. Well, we had nothing. We had no money, so it was just pretty depressing, and nobody, none of the neighbors, had any similar interest that I had.

I decided that I had to make some friends, so I decided I was going to join all of these alumni groups that I belong to, because, clearly, I'm somebody driven by having friends and being involved, and I wasn't just going to sit out there and feel sorry for myself. I'd done that, and I just remember I *loved* having a little baby. I have always loved having little babies. I could have been a baby factory. I could have produced a lot of babies, but then, I wouldn't have wanted them for their entire lives. Someone else would have had to have taken them.

But you liked that—tiny babies?

They just felt incredibly cute, and I remember Kirk and looking at every little hair on his head and just thinking how marvelous it was, the little fingernails, and everything was just so perfect. So that was just an awesome experience in that way. Because I was there all alone, pretty much by myself, I had a lot of time to think about that, what an awesome, incredible deal this was.

Kirk Wagner

Then, as I said, I decided I needed to do something besides. We didn't get lots of magazines, and then, because I'd come from Tucson, I was very unfamiliar with driving in snow, and I have to tell you, there was something about that winter, because there was a lot of ice on the road. So we both didn't think it was a good idea for me to go back and forth into town, because it was a trek. I'm not saying it was like wilderness, but there weren't the freeways. They didn't clear the roads and all that sort of stuff. And there was nothing else out there, except this building where Peter worked, and the houses. That was it. No grocery store, nothing. To get groceries, we had to drive all the way into town, so we'd do that together and make a big deal out of it.

At some point, a little later on—I was still at Stead, I know—I joined the Theta,

the sorority, because, see, that was on campus, and that was fairly close, the alumni group.

I didn't mention in Tucson I was a member of the Junior League, that I was the first working woman that the Tucson Junior League had chosen. I was a teacher at that time, and I think it was because I was pretty well known. I've got to toot my horn, but I had grown up there. I was involved in campus politics, and then I worked for the newspaper, and I was teaching at that time, I remember. The society—most of the women were wives, spouses of well-known men in town who were affluent. So that was a pretty big step for them, I think, to select somebody who didn't fit that description, so to speak.

So, when I got here, I knew I wasn't going to be there long, because I'd told somebody that would be the case. I would not be a long-time member, and that was too bad, because they only took so many.

So, Junior League—you did that?

Yes. When I got here, I decided to see if there was a Junior League, and there was not. There was another group that was hoping to become a Junior League, but I didn't get involved in that until I moved into this house. We stayed at Stead for about a year. Let's see.

You got there in January?

I think we bought this house in May of 1969.

Just a few months in Stead?

Yes. So, we started looking around for a house. See, I got off track there, but I was talking about joining organizations. I attempted to do that in order to make new friends.

And I will say this, the people were not warm to someone who had come to this town from outside, and it is not that way today, because so many people have moved here, but in the late 1960s, and I'm sure, early 1970s—I've heard people say this, who moved here at the same time, that unless you'd gone to UNR, gone to Reno High, da dat da dat da dah—that was it. I found that to be the case, and I don't want to point fingers specifically at the Theta alumni group, but that was very apparent.

Real distinction between locals and outsiders?

Absolutely. And there were very few outsiders. I was one of the few who had rung the doorbell and offered to help. So I did, and they assigned me, of course, the worst job, which is being the rush adviser, which I've described, and I don't know if you have been in a sorority or not.

No, I haven't, but you described how hectic it is.

When I was talking about that, I should have asked you if you were familiar with everything I was talking about, because I went into it in a lot of detail, and maybe I didn't need to.

No, that's what is usual in a life history, is to go into some detail. Because we have to assume there will be people studying this, who haven't been in one, so it's important to describe it. Yes.

That's right. Besides that, my experience is going to be totally different from your experience, of course. Anyway, so I did become the rush adviser, which meant late nights and so on, and I was pretty impressed with the young ladies here, that they were very sensible, and, I thought, were looking for the right kind of girls and

considered the kind of qualities that I thought they should look at. I was pretty impressed. I did that for a couple of years, but then you get really tired of doing that

At that point, we were moving, and Peter knew a lot about building and knew a lot about a lot of things, but particularly about just how to build a house. We looked at a certain price range that we were familiar with in Tucson, where you could get a really nice place. We were just amazed. We would rather not buy something than get what we would get for that. And he knew what he was looking for. Two by fours. When he walked across the floor and found out that he heard everything, then it was structurally questionable, so we had to go up in our price range in order to find anything that *he* thought was good enough for us to buy, and he wanted certain things. He wanted a basement. He wanted a place for the trailer. I wanted a dining room, and you'll notice what we have now, and what we don't have. [laughter]

There's your basement.

I have a basement. I also have a cement pad over here for the trailer.

Let's see . . . I can't remember. He even wanted the garage to not face the street, because he had all his tools, woodworking tools, in there, and he was afraid that somebody might see them and rip them off. I remember that was a concern. So, we found this house, and we found one that Tom Jensen, who built it, is still living in it, a couple of blocks over, and they just kept it up so nicely, too. I don't remember exactly what happened. I guess this was a bit bigger or something, but this house, this was all added on.

This section we're sitting in now, a large family room and an office, was added on?

Yes. Yes. It stopped at where the sink was. I'd say it was about sixteen hundred square feet, maybe, I guess. But anyway, the house cost, I think, $31,000, and what we had originally looked for was about $25,000. So, we moved into this house. It was fairly new, only one home owner. It was built in 1965, and this was 1969, and the homeowner was the daughter of the Scott Motor Cadillac dealer. They had bought this house for her and her husband for a wedding present. I guess maybe they were buying them another house in South Hills, which at that time was way out—South Hills. Because this was really the end of a lot of the development in the late 1960s.

And we're just off of Plumb Lane.

So, everything out there has been added, pretty much, since then.

Since you moved in here?

Yes. But South Hills, that was something that somebody must have had a dream, to place something way out there. But anyway, that's where they lived.

The Realtor, I remember, had told Peggy Brown, that she *had* to get this house in better shape. The yard was *unbelievable.* It was like they were raising hollyhocks to sell or something. It was just awful, and the house was a mess, and he said, "If you would fix it up, you could get more money for it." But the house had been given to them, so what the heck.

So, they didn't do that. And we thought we were spending a fortune for the house. My husband's parents bought the house, basically, and we then paid them our monthly mortgage payment. When I said how close he was to his parents, that was another . . . that was the only real problem that we had in our marriage, because, basically, we didn't have much. Neither one

of us cared about having a lot. So it wasn't like one of us wanted things and the other couldn't provide it, and that became a bone of contention or anything of that sort. It's just that we paid his parents twice as much mortgage payment as anybody else in the neighborhood was paying, and he believed that he wanted them to have that money while they were alive so they could spend it, but the irony is, they didn't need it. They were pretty wealthy. And secondly, we didn't have anything and never went anywhere, because we didn't have anything, and he died, and they were both alive. So, we didn't need to pay them that much.

Yes, but he felt . . . .

He insisted on it. And that was it. After awhile I didn't discuss it, because I realized that's just what it was going to be.

But because Peter could do so many things, we got in here and just tore the place apart, basically. We did the entire back yard over ourselves, brought a Caterpillar in here and just dug everything up, because, of course, he used to drive those things when he worked for the Forest Service in Alaska. I think our lot is about a third of an acre, but the backyard is pretty good size. We dug up the whole backyard, and we measured it to such a degree that we took a string, he and I, and moved it along to make sure it was absolutely level, to make sure there wasn't a rise there or a bump there, before we seeded it. I cannot believe the stuff we did.

Then, while all these projects are going on, I have another baby, Kristina. She was born in 1970, August 1—she'll be thirty in a couple of weeks—thirty years ago. And the same thing happened in that pregnancy. I had to go to bed the last month or so, so I think my mother came up for awhile. I remember, of course, this cement pad. This

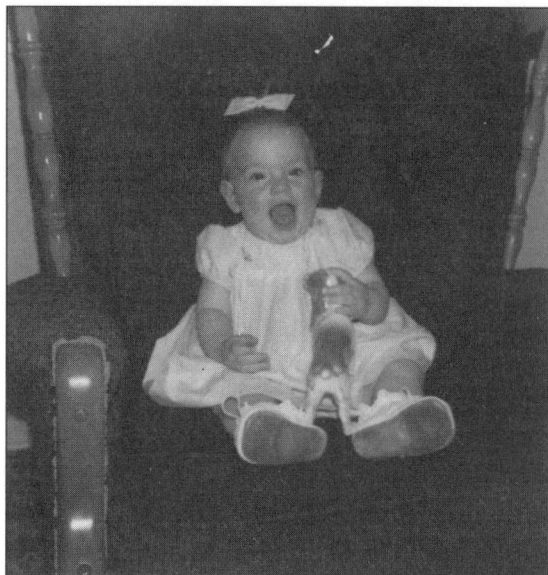

Kristina Wagner, 1971, age eight months.

was not part of the house, so Peter would take me out in the morning, lift me up and put me on, like, a chaise lounge, so I could be outside. I'd bring books and things, and Kirk was eighteen months old, running around all over the place. It was just tough, being in bed and not having any help or anything, but anyway, you make it.

Since that was going to be our last child, and he had missed the first one, and he was ready to go on a big scientific experiment, which he did—he was gone a lot in our marriage—I can't remember if it was Germany or where, but someplace, I said, "You know, this is it. Don't you want to be there for the birth of one of your children?" So, Dr. Stapleton in town decided that he would induce me, so Peter would be there for the birth. So both babies, I never went through these waking-up-in-the-middle-of-the-night deals. It was just a certain day, went into Saint Mary's. So, Peter watched this birth with great interest and charted all the contractions I had, as only a mathematician would. Finally, he went down to grab a hamburger in the cafeteria, and, of course, that's when the baby was born, so he missed that, too.

I remember the day I brought Kristina home. My neighbor next door, who is still my neighbor, had Kirk. Peter had come to pick me up, and Kirk was so cute. Oh, we had the cutest kids! Just jumping up and down, so excited, as little kids are, and they don't realize that that's not going away. Now, that's going to stay there forever.

It's going to stay there, and we have to divide the attention.

Right, right. But I guess the early part of our marriage, really, was devoted to working on the house, plans for the home. Of course, a lot of this was done about nine to ten years later, the big massive improvements, because we realized, as the kids were getting bigger, there wasn't going to be enough room, and by then, I was in the legislature, and we couldn't really move. I had a district I had to live in, and most all the rest of the neighborhoods were too expensive. We couldn't afford them. So we decided to add on here. But it seems to me as if, particularly in the early years, Peter was gone a lot, as I said, on experiments.

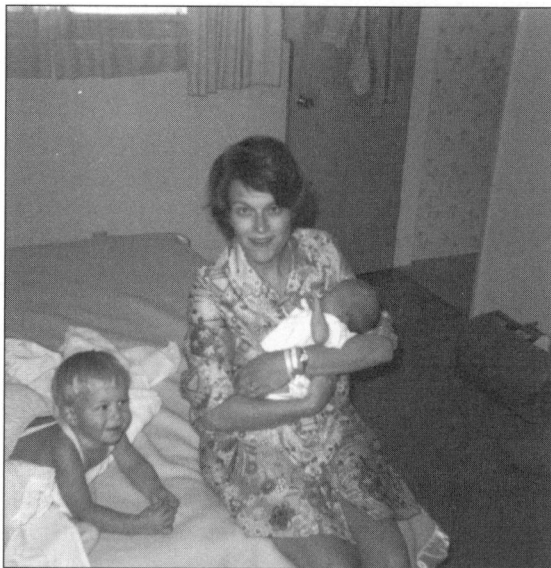

"I remember the day we brought Kristina home." Kirk (left), Sue holding Kristina, who is three days old, August 4, 1970.

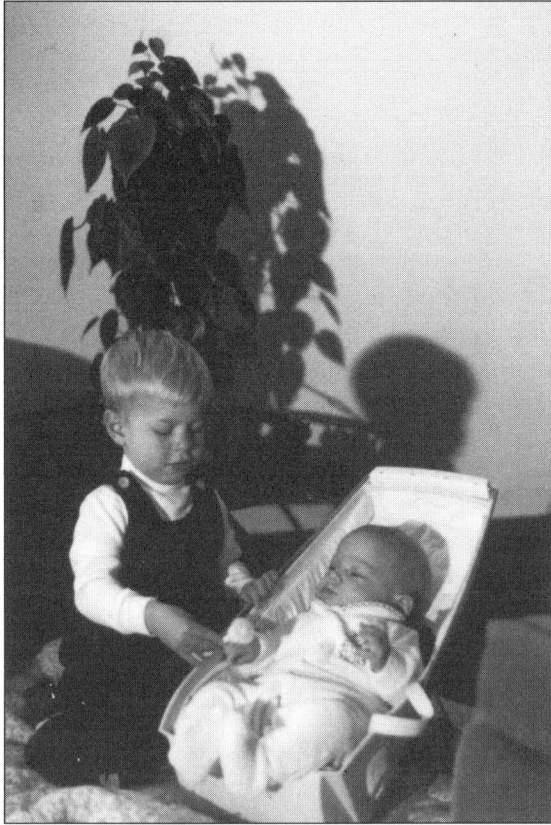

Kirk and Kristina, 1970.

I had a number of good friends, and we all decided that we were going to have our husbands join the Elks Club, and we didn't care if they ever went. We knew they'd never go to a meeting, but they had a great swimming pool over there. We'd all take our little kids. We all had children about the same age, and we would talk, and we would play bridge, and we would do whatever, and they could swim and have fun together, and that would be how we'd while away our summer days.

So I remember—he's now a president of a bank—Wayne Condon, and Peter, and I think that Mike Blakely was already a member. There was another man; his name was Harbison. He was with IBM here, and they moved around a lot—Ann and Bobby Harbison. We got our three husbands to join, and I have to say, we were rather cynical about the whole thing, and they were rather cynical about it, too, but the wives had to go to the initiation, only part of it, because, of course, it was an all-male organization. We had to go too, and it was all we could do not to laugh. We couldn't look at each other, or we'd start laughing. And all we knew—it would get us into the pool.

Were there other pools available at that time?

No. No.

There were no pools in Reno?

Nothing like that. No. I don't even think that . . . well, Hidden Valley Country Club wasn't built, but you had to then become a member. It was a private club. There was nothing else like this. You could get lunch there. You could bring your own food. And it was *very* inexpensive. It was a fabulous place, and *everybody*-well, not everybody went there. Everybody at that time, it seemed, belonged to the Elks Club. It was a big deal. If you had a separation between those who could join a private club and those who couldn't, this is where those who couldn't went, but a lot of those who could went there, too, because there wasn't anything else. There was no private place in town, I don't believe. I can't think of any. So, they never, ever went to a meeting, except for the initiation meeting, and that was the understanding, that if they did this, they would never have to do anything.

Do anything more. That was it.

My neighbor across the street, who was one of my dearest friends before he died—his son-in-law now lives around the corner—became the Grand Exalted Pooh-Bah. I called him the Great Exalted Ruler. I would never tell this. If my neighbor across the street ever reads this, she's going to be so shocked, [laughter] because all she knows is, I've told her one story that was not good, that I did tell her. The minute Peter died, I mean, literally, within the next month I got a letter saying, "You are now not a member of the Elks Club." And I found that to be so cruel. I realize that it was an all-male club, but I thought they could have done it differently. The letter itself is just this form thing.

And the timing was awful, as well.

Oh, it was horrible. I have fond memories of the times I had with my friends and their kids, but not of the organization, to be honest with you. I have no idea what the Elks Club is like anymore. I used to go there all the time to give speeches, because there were a lot of rooms they rented out to groups during the years. I don't know if that's the case anymore. I don't think so.

I think they do still rent some spaces.

Do they still?

I've been there within the last year.

Because when you see meeting announcements, I don't often see, "at the Elks Club." And it used to be *all* the time. They were very, very busy.

So, I would go out there, then, but other than that, after I got that letter, obviously, I couldn't go. I wasn't wanted. At that time the kids were nine and ten, I guess, and probably that wasn't a big thing in their life, anyway.

Yes. But when they were little—preschool—that was a fun thing to do for little kids.

Yes. Yes. It was great. And even when they got a little bit older, I can't remember to what extent, how old they were, but in

thinking about this period of time, I guess, that's where we are.

So the early years of your marriage here in Reno, were really working on the house, raising the children.

Yes, just what everybody does. I had a lot of friends in the neighborhood, and one of my best friends, still, who came down to look at the skunks the other night, Martha Romero, she is a graduate of Stanford and went to Stanford with Peter, although, I don't believe they knew each other at that time. Peter knew Spike Wilson and a number of other people who went to Stanford when he did, and there was a very active Stanford alumni club in town that he belonged to.

Peter was really focused on his work and building things. That was more than a hobby. The television is sitting on a coffee table, but he built that.

Oh, my, it's beautiful.

This lamp over here, he built the whole thing, the electrical part, everything. That is some kind of a wood that came from Bolivia, but it was just this big, old stump. It's all distressed. And you can see it; it's just absolutely beautiful. And then he built the bureau that we had put that thing on top of, and all the cabinets in here.

It's very fine cabinetry and very skilled carpentry work.

Oh, he could do . . . oh, you should take a look at that before you go, with the routing and everything that was done.

Oh, yes. Very beautiful work.

But anyway, that's what he liked to do, and I'm sure, for him, that was a release from work. That's why the basement was so nice, much better than the garage, actually, because we had a truck, the 1959 GMC.

The 1959 GMC was still with you?

Yes, and Peter's parents decided that they didn't like the Airstream trailer. It was brand new, and they went on one trip, or two, and Russell, my father-in-law, whom I love dearly, didn't like hauling it and didn't like getting out and hooking it all up. And the Airstream was the Cadillac of trailers. It probably still is.

They gave it to us. The unfortunate thing is, we only used it once, but it was a great trip, which I will talk about, so don't let me forget to do that—when Kristi was two.

We moved into this house in, I think it was, May of 1969. We'd only lived in Stead, actually, for a very short period of time, because I remember telling you that I had come to Reno in January of 1969, leaving the day that Nixon was inaugurated. And only I would relate to things about a political event, right? Particularly, that one. So that was, maybe, what—four or five months, I guess?

Living in Stead was just too isolated for me, and I just didn't connect. So anyway, we started looking around at homes. We found this home. We moved in, and as I think I mentioned to you, there was a lot of work that needed to be done in this house, but one of the things we liked particularly, was there seemed to be a neighborhood feeling.

I remember the very first day I moved into this house. I had Kirk, my son, who was only six months old at the time, in a little infant seat. I don't even know if they have those anymore. In fact, I haven't seen my granddaughters in anything similar, so they must not. I had him on, like a bar, that

we don't now have in my house, but my neighbor up the street, who is still one of my very good friends, who, in fact, is going off with me for a day trip in a week or so—Martha Romero, whom I think I mentioned before—came into my house the very first day I was here. She said, "Hi, I'm Martha. Don't you know any better—that you're not supposed to keep your child up in an infant seat on this bar?" She said, "You should put him on the floor." [laughter]

I just thought, "*Wow*! What a nice neighbor." [laughter] The first thing she says is a criticism. And here it is, thirty-some years later, and we're still good friends. So I think that that is what is unique about the area I live in, not only Martha, but, with the exception of *one* person, everyone is the same individuals living beside me as did thirty-some years ago, when we bought this house. They have decided, for the same reason I have, that they like the area, the location, the neighbors, the landscaping, the size of the lot, whatever, the way the houses are built better in those days than now, and they've decided to stay here. So it's made it very much a neighborhood in the old Mayberry, RFD kind of mode. There are two times each year—and I'm slipping, because I haven't done it this summer, yet—where I have all the women who are widows—and that's almost everybody, and there are several that I invite who are not—to get together, and that's because one of my buddies died around Christmas time, so I didn't want his wife . . . I wanted to have something going on. So the next year I had her and some other women over, and I do that once in the summer and once around the holiday season. I've had other parties in my backyard, and everybody is invited.

I just learned last night, as a matter of fact—and this is around the first of September here in 2000—in stopping to visit with one of my neighbors about some issue dealing with recycling, that there were six young people, well, moderately young, who have bought their parents' homes in my neighborhood, where they grew up. I was just amazed to learn that. They are all professional people, and they've all come back, really, it appears, for the same sense that they grew up here, that the same schools are still rated as high as they were when they were young people, and they want their kids to grow up here. It was just a real interesting sense. I don't think you find that in many other places in Reno. I really don't.

In this day and age, I wonder how often that ever happens.

Oh, it probably doesn't happen very often anywhere.

Anywhere, yes, but here in Reno.

But I suspect it might happen in like a Midwest . . . I get the feeling, you keep thinking of the Midwest and a little town in Iowa or something like a farming community, but then, those people tend to take off and go see the big city. So, I don't know.

But Reno, especially, with its image as a transient town—people coming and going all the time.

Yes. It was interesting to me, because the husband and wife with whom I was speaking were saying, "Oh, I went to school . . . ." I said, something about somebody down the street, and they said, "Oh, well, I know who you're talking about, because I went to grammar school with that person," or " Yes, I was in high school with the person who was on the plane when you were involved in a plane crash," and da dat da dat. So clearly, all of these people were born here and are native Nevadans

and have lived here their whole life, because they are all connected in one way or the other, and all the guys—there were four or five—who seemed to play in the city basketball team together, and I don't know if it's they knew each other before, or if they got the team together because they all lived on the same street or what. But it was kind of really eye-opening to me and does speak to the same thing that I'm talking about that's just around the corner from where I live. And it's kind of a nice feeling, I think.

That same feeling that you had early on, that certainly panned out the way you thought it would—the feeling of neighborhood here.

Oh, yes. Exactly. And I think that's one of the big reasons I have no interest in moving. There is one overwhelming reason I would move, and I don't think I'll get into that here, or if I do, I think it might need to be edited out. I don't know. One of the neighbors has a foster child who, after my husband died, my kids and I and one of their friends, caught him in my house stealing things. I had noted things being lost for a long period of time before that—a calculator here and a watch there and whatever kind of games kids had at that time—because kids were in and out all the time, and I never even thought that somebody would take things. I just thought we had misplaced them, but when we caught him in our house, then that precipitated quite a to-do between the neighbors and myself, and I did have a man, a bank president friend of mine, come to my home and sit with me while I visited with the father of this boy, or the stepfather or the adoptive father, because I wanted someone else to be there. He apologized profusely and said they would take care of it and send him away, and about two weeks later he came over and told me that I had made it all up, and it was a big lie, and that the son hadn't, of course, done anything at all, and that I had somehow concocted this story. [laughter] I was just amazed that somebody would think I had the time to do that sort of thing, or the inclination, or to even think of something that terrible. Later on, I went off to the legislature, and it was right before a session, I think, came back, and found out he was in prison, or in jail, maybe, at that time, for going up Skyline Boulevard and ripping off house after house, so evidently, his parents understood that I had told the truth in the beginning. Unfortunately, in their mind, everybody else is to blame—school districts or the judges or the prison system or whatever. And that's, in my mind, part of the problem. But anyway, that's another issue. That would be the only reason I'd probably move from here, unless the house did not meet in some needs that I had to have, health-wise or something like that. That would be the only reason.

If he would return to this neighborhood?

If he would return here. Now, it's clear when I came here my husband and I were the youngest people to move in, with a little baby, and another one on the way. So, they're all older than I. As time moves on, clearly the houses may change hands, although none of them really have the inclination or the desire to do that at this time. We've all pretty much settled in here for the duration. So that's nice. That's a good feeling of stability to me.

So, you moved in here, and Kirk was how old?

Kirk was six months old.

And another baby on the way?

Yes, just about.

Was Kristina on the way at that point?

Well, Kristina is eighteen months younger, so just pretty much, just about.

Real close, yes.

She was born in August of 1970.

OK. So, you'd been here a year and a few months.

Yes. When we moved in here, Peter was very busy at DRI, but we did get started on doing a lot of things, particularly the yard during that summer. When he actually rented a tractor and drove it in our backyard and ripped up the whole thing and literally started all over again, I think the neighbors either thought we were insane or, "Wow! Are they an industrious couple." Probably a little bit of both. [laughter] I guess we were probably a little bit of both. Of course, the joke was when we got married that the only things that he had when we married were a king-size bed and a drill press. Well, and any little bit of money we had extra, which was not much, he bought another tool, and with those tools he made more things for our house or fixed things or did whatever, because he could really pretty much do everything. So that pretty much occupied our lives during those early years, was all work, really, either work for him at home, work for me as a young housewife and mother, or work on the home.

Did you work on the home together, or was it pretty much his part?

Well, I have to say, most of it was him, but including the yard, it was both of us, because I remember that he was such a

Sue and Peter.

perfectionist that we took that string from one end to the other, and our yard is pretty big. There were these small, little things that were done that no one would ever appreciate, except myself now, looking out in my backyard, and knowing all of the work that went into it.

I would have to say that pretty much most of the work he did, even a little later on, after we had Kristina, when we were thinking that we might need a bigger house, we did look in the district. And I say the district, because at that time I was in the legislature—getting ahead of myself here—and so I had to stay in Assembly District 25, and most everything was too expensive. So he really designed this room that we added on to our house and did a lot of the work himself, but, of course, had to hire a contractor to do a lot of the outside work. It wasn't quite finished when he died, but his dad came up and finished off some of the things. Some of it still isn't finished yet.

So, a lot of work as a young couple?

Yes. That's pretty much what our life was. We didn't have any vacations, I don't remember, with the exception of going down to visit my mother and his parents, who live fairly close to each other in Tucson and Green Valley, Arizona. I believe I mentioned his parents moved out of Alaska after the wedding.

When his parents came down for our wedding they couldn't believe Tucson— what kind of a climate it was, and how beautiful it was, in a very different way from Alaska, where they'd lived since 1929. But they decided that he would sell his dental practice and move.

So, when you traveled to visit parents, they were both in one location, then.

They were. They were very close, because they had moved to a new retirement area called Green Valley, south of Tucson, maybe forty miles, and it was one of the first retirement places in Arizona, where you could buy these free-standing, single-family homes—three bedrooms—but you did have to be a certain age and that sort of thing. They were building golf courses, just starting, and that would have been in the mid-1960s.

So, that's basically the only vacations we had, and that was a drive. You know how far it is from here to Vegas, plus further on down to Tucson, with the kids and Christmas presents, and that was about it.

And then Kristina was born in August of 1970. Now, with both my children, I had to go to bed the last six weeks of my pregnancy, because I started dilating too soon, according to the doctors. So, in Kristina's case it was more difficult, because I had a little tot around, Kirk, and plus, Peter was gone to work every day, so he would kind of set me up with everything in bed, and just that's the way I'd be until he

Kirk and Kristina with the grandparents, Russell and Beryl Wagner, May, 1971.

got home, because I wasn't supposed to put any weight on myself or anything.

How did you manage Kirk from bed?

It was pretty tough. It was very tough. He just kind of had to stay in the yard, stay around the house, but near the end, I know my mother came up, because I remember my husband would take me outdoors, would lift me up and take me outdoors and put me in the chaise lounge, because it was very hot that summer, and I look at all the temperatures, when they say the "highest temperature," and I keep thinking it must have been 1970, because it was like 103 and 104, and, of course, she was born in the first part of August. So it was just incredibly warm. But anyway, he was not around when Kirk was born.

He was going on another experiment. Germany, I think it was. Some really far place. I talked to my OB-GYN at the time and told him we were only going to have two children, and I really wanted him to be there for one of them. So, I'm sure I mentioned in the first one that I was induced? Well, the same thing happened here; he missed that too, because he was down getting lunch. But he actually was around, far more than he was for Kirk.

I remember when I brought Kristina home from the hospital. My neighbor was seated out on my steps, on my porch, and Kirk was real excited, again, like any little child, as we know. But all little children lose interest immediately thereafter, when they realize that Mom's time is basically spent with this new person. Because he was only eighteen months old at the time. And Peter

Beryl and Russell Wagner at their fiftieth wedding anniversary party, given by Sue (right). January 25, 1985.

and I thought at that time, that things were pretty darn good. It appeared we had a great life in front of us. We had two beautiful kids, both a boy and a girl, which weren't overriding concerns to either one of us, that we had one of each gender, but as it turns out, we did, and I'm so happy that that's the way it worked out, because they were so different.

At that time—and it may be true today—the health departments in our state send out to families of any newborn, pieces of paper that you would put in the diaper, and they would run a urine test, and hardly anybody knew what it was for. I later learned it was to test for what was called PKU, which is a fairly well-known metabolic genetic disorder. And the unique thing about a metabolic genetic disorder is, because it's metabolic, that if you find it, you can change a diet. It has something to do with what's going into your body and what isn't going into your body, and how much or how little, and you can regulate it, if you understand it well enough. With

PKU they did, and so that's why every state in the union mandated that this be tested, because if you didn't catch it, then the baby would grow up to be severely mentally retarded.

So, I got the pieces of paper. I'm sure I did with Kirk, as well, except he was born in Tucson, so maybe it was done in a different way. I don't remember it exactly. But with Kristina the health department sent back a letter saying that it came out with an odd pattern, so we had to do it again. Well, I got to thinking about it, and oh, my gosh, it must have fallen on the floor; Kirk must have touched it; or something must have happened. We did it again, and again it came back in an inappropriate way, so they called my pediatrician, and in those days there were very few pediatricians or doctors in the town. This was in 1970. There was like a pediatric clinic, and there were three doctors, and that was about it.

The doctor's name was Emanuel Berger, and Dr. Berger was noted for being very disagreeable, and not being nice at all to mothers, didn't like mothers, just thought they were in the way, but loved kids, and he did a great job and enjoyed children.

I had chosen him out of the three, because his name was given to me by a doctor in Tucson. So I had Dr. Berger for Kirk, as a pediatrician. Anyway, the health department contacted him and told my husband and I that our daughter had PKU, and that we had to go over there immediately, which we did, and so Dr. Berger gave her a blood test and sent us home and said we'd find out in a couple of days or so. He wanted to do this blood test, because that was conclusive. He believed that the urine samples were an indicator, but not conclusive. The blood test came back negative. It was not PKU, so if we had put her on the diet, it would have been a terrible thing to do, because it's just as bad to do something wrong, because it's a formula that you have instead of milk, and she needed milk at that time, not this formula. So, fortunately, he was a little more careful than some might have been, but then he realized there was something wrong. What was it? It wasn't this, so it had to be something else. So he really went overboard in terms of trying to find out what was wrong. He contacted the man, Dr. Guthrie his name was, in New York State, who discovered PKU and created the test, and sent him Kristina's results, and he didn't know what to make of it, either. And there was a period of time there when there were a lot of doctors around the country doing a lot of calling and talking about the results of my daughter.

Finally, Dr. Berger remembered he had heard someone in a seminar here that came to Reno from Children's Hospital in L.A., so he called him, and he was quite interested and asked us to come down to see them, and that they had a grant to look at certain metabolic genetic disorders, and this might be one. So my husband and I took Kristina down to L.A., and we had to leave Kirk with . . . no, I think we took Kirk with us that first time. Anyway, Children's Hospital in L.A. is located in Burbank, and it's in a very rough area, and there was like one motel there. In fact, it's still there. It's the only one today, because my daughter just went down there a couple of months ago. It was all barred over the windows with padlocks on it, and we weren't used to anything like that, but we just stayed overnight there, and we went in the next day and went to these grueling interviews on pregnancy and any kind of things in our family history and all of these kinds of questions that researchers would be interested in. I'm sure they did at that time some tests on Kristina, and the reason I don't remember is because I then went back many, many times thereafter. So I can't remember exactly what happened on one trip versus another.

Kristina was about six weeks old at this time. And the bottom line was that we all came home, and then I went back many times after. Peter didn't, but I took Kristina back to be tested, and it was just [long pause] [crying] really tough. Because she was such a cute little baby, and they'd have to tie her down in a crib and put a catheter in her and give her certain foods and then see what came out in the urine, and they would test it that way. Anyway, I had to leave her there for a couple of weeks at one time, and I stayed with the gal who was in my wedding. I mentioned her name—Joanie Johnson Hill. She and her husband were living in Tustin, I think it was called. It was in Orange County, and it was quite a drive, even then, but I stayed with them at night and then drove in to the hospital in the day, because I certainly didn't want to stay in that motel for several weeks.

They decided that she had something called Hartnips, and she was the first person in this country to be diagnosed with this. The name was taken from a family in England, where all of these kids seemed to have it, and it was a metabolic genetic disorder where certain amino acids are not assimilated in the body, and, of course, if you don't have those building blocks as a young baby, then you're not going to grow up to be right. So because she was the first, they really didn't know what to tell me what to do, or what might happen. It was just all guess work.

She was so tiny when all these tests were being done—only six weeks old?

Yes. But this went on for some time.

Over how long, a couple of months?

Well, oh, yes, and years. And she just went back at the age of thirty, but that had been like a long, long time since she'd been back. Even as she got older, in high school, she went back every year or so to be tested.

But the early years, of course, are the most critical, and they told me the only thing they knew to do was to give her an excess amount of protein. In those days, you just had the Gerber jars of baby food of like meat or liver. They were horrible. I got this giant tube, like a hypodermic needle, but a giant one, where I'd put this stuff in and then just shoot it into her, and, fortunately, she was a pretty good eater, because if she hadn't been, it might have been a big, big problem, but all they knew to do was to do that, because she wasn't assimilating certain amino acids in protein. She needed to get more, and that's the only way they knew. They did not know whether she would sit up, whether she would walk, whether she would talk, because if this worked, then she probably would; if this didn't work, she probably wouldn't.

We were looking at photos, and I'm just amazed—she was such a tiny child—but this was the first time ever in the United States, so there must have been a lot of testing and studying of her.

There was. As I said, I went back many times. I don't remember how often. When she was small, a lot, because that was important, and they would measure her each time she was there, and I'd have to take fasting samples here, and then feed her certain things, and keep a record of all of that: how many ounces of this, and weigh everything. And then, when we were down there, they would do the same thing. They would have her get up and come over and do testing, and then after lunch, and so on. As she grew, clearly they were very happy, and you can imagine how Peter and I felt, but we didn't realize the—I guess the word would be significance—it had to Kristi, negatively. [crying]

To be so observed and tested.

And to be thought of as odd and the only one in the United States. It really affected her a lot, unbeknownst to us, psychologically. But physically and mentally, it was just incredible, because she was a star in every way as she grew up. As it happened, there was another family here in town, a well-known family, who had a child that had been sent down there and had been diagnosed with Hartnips Disorder. So I had arranged for the mother of the child to come over and have coffee with me and just kind of be here, and she could observe Kristina, unbeknownst to Kristina why she was here, so she could see what somebody could turn out like if she gave her a lot of protein.

I'm told by the doctors at Children's Hospital that they didn't do that, and it was amazing, because the grandfather of this child was a doctor, and the child, evidently, was a fussy eater, and I'm sure it was much more difficult. They just didn't do it, and the child did not develop the way that you would hope. So there was some connection between protein and development.

As you get to certain ages, you are less willing to eat what you're supposed to, and they told Kristina she should have so many grams of protein all the time. Well, at certain times, that's just not that important. And that did happen, and I really don't know if it made any difference to her or not. I believe it did. I made her go down, when she was in high school one time, because I have a letter to that effect, and they were not happy at all, and she'd not been back since, until just recently—just the day before her thirtieth birthday. They did a work-up on her, and she's now very diligently eating protein and is concerned because she's put on weight, of course, more weight than she would normally have, because I think, she was pretty much a vegetarian before, which, at one time in your life, if you're thinking about maybe getting married and having children, that that's very important to start thinking about other things.

I guess that's where she is sort of now, so that's good, I think. But when my son got married, we went through this, and I told him that he probably should have some genetic counseling and talk about this, and he thought that was a good idea. I don't know if he did or not, and I didn't ask. I figured it was not my business after that, but I explained that to him. Of course, my daughter will, because she understands that she had it. And the odds are it's one in four. It was a recessive gene. We know that. This is caused by two recessive genes, so I had to have one, and my husband had to have one. So the chances of them marrying anyone with it are rare.

But we did ask all our family members to send in urine samples to Children's Hospital, because obviously, they were interested in tracing it back, and many of them refused to do it, because they just did not believe that there could have been any problem on their side of the family, so to speak. So I don't know if they got the information—I think they did not—that they wanted.

To trace it down and actually see. So, from what you're saying, she went through it as a child, and you could get high protein into her, and then teenage years, when you're trying to be like everyone else, that wasn't so important?

Yes. That's correct.

But now, as she's getting older, she's returning to it, and it's more acceptable?

Yes. Yes. Understanding that this is very important, particularly, if she wants to have a child, if ever, that that's who she has to think of first. But in the midst of all this is how, today I think, if I were having children,

I would certainly be a lot more attuned and have a lot more tools at my disposal, in learning how to deal with crisis, and I've had a lot in my life, and I probably didn't deal with any of them very well.

[Long pause] [Crying] This has been very difficult, and one doesn't always realize those things, even as a mother, about the fact that in those days it was true, that normally the assumption was made that if things happened to you at an early age, they were things you just forgot about and didn't have to worry, that they would not be a recurring thing in one's life, and their affecting them in any way, mentally or physically.

Well, physically, in this case, possibly. And today, we now know that's not at all true. It's just the opposite. And there are so many more tools available to mother's today, to parents today, in terms of how to deal with things. If we'd all known those things then, we might have done a better job, but I do know that Kristina was very distraught at trying to explain why she was gone, when she had to take a couple of weeks off to go down to Children's Hospital. Who wants to tell their little friends in the third grade that they're flying off to L.A. to go to a hospital?

"What's wrong with you?"

Well, you couldn't point to anything and say, "I have a broken arm," or something. And it wasn't *her* fault. Of course, Mom and Dad felt extremely guilty, because we're the ones who gave it to her. So it does affect people in different ways. That was really the first crisis the Wagner family had, and it was one that is still ongoing to this day. However, the positive side—and there always is; you have to look at that—is that she did grow up to be an absolutely beautiful, bright, talented girl, and that's what I always tell her. That's what she should remember out of all this, is the positives.

This, again, was going on at the same time that Peter and I were just getting going here as a young couple.

And working so hard on the house and the whole thing.

Yes, and I remember the reason we had our children so close together was, we had these great plans of living here. We had chosen this place, because we liked the outdoor things, and we had thought, by having them so close together—Peter was a fabulous skier—that he could teach them how to ski, and they would be about the same level at the same time, and they could go do all of these things together, and we could go backpacking, and we wouldn't have to wait four years, while the other one caught up to the older one. And all these great things that just never did happen, but it was a good idea. During this time then, not only did we try to have some kind of a normal life as a couple, but these kinds of things . . . . I'm trying to think what it was that we did to have a normal life. [laughter]

Did you get to have outings as a family? You said no vacations that you could remember?

No. When Kristina turned two, I think it was on that day, prior to that we took off on a six-week trailer trip across the country. At that point, we had not gone anywhere. I don't think, at that point, we had even gone to Tucson for Christmas. We just had not done anything. Peter had gone off to a lot of places, exotic places, to do experiments, but I finally said, "You know, we've got to have a vacation." So, we built the vacation around some of his experiments, which were on Lake Ontario.

His parents had bought a travel trailer when they retired and moved to Tucson, thinking they would travel, and it was the

early part of this whole RV world in the 1960s. They bought the Airstream, and they went on one trip. [laughter] His dad, Russell, who I just adored, just thought it was the *worst* experience. He didn't want to have to mess around with hooking the thing up and doing all the things that one had to do, and have a special vehicle to haul it, although they had bought a new car. So he gave it to us. And we got an International Harvester, and it was like the first of the big . . . what you'd call a Suburban, today, squarish, and it was made by International Harvester, which made combines, or those kinds of things.

Yes, combines, and tractors.

Yes. But it was like a big Scout, like a giant Scout. And the reason I know it was about her birthday, August 1, was because I knew we were going to be gone for a very long time, six weeks, and I wanted her potty trained, and of course, at that time, you tried to get them potty trained around two years of age. Well, we almost made it, but we did have to take some disposable diapers. You could see, on a trip like that, you really didn't want to have to mess around with that, if you didn't have to.

I remember leaving, driving out of the driveway, my neighbors—who, again, are still my neighbors—thought, "Poor Sue! She thinks this is going to be a vacation. Six weeks in a trailer with the *two kids*, two and three and a half!" [laughter]

We drove across the state the first day, and it was just awful, because all they did was fight, and in their seat belts, and this and that, and we realized we had no sense of six weeks. What's that mean? But after they got the drift, that this was going to be the way it was going to be every day, it got much better. The unfortunate thing was, neither one of them remember *a thing* about the trip. In one way, you say they'd

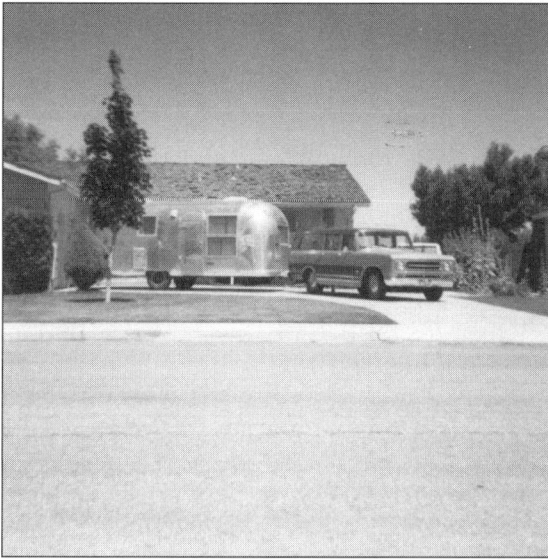

"I remember leaving, driving out of the driveway, my neighbors... thought, 'Poor Sue! Six weeks in a trailer with the two kids, two and three and a half!'"

forget everything. Unfortunately, they forget the good things.

The good things that you were trying to do to show them the world.

Right. And I guess we didn't quite have an understanding of how really young they were, and what they would not remember, but it was a fabulous experience, really, to go across the country, and I won't go through the whole thing, of course, but we did go up into Minnesota, because Peter had an aunt and an uncle, who had a beautiful farm, and what I would think of as Minnesota, these beautiful rolling hills in upstate. His parents were there and surprised us; they had driven up. It's RR-1, Rural Route One, and she has her own lane that's called Clear Acre Lane in Underwood, Minnesota. So, as we went into this little, tiny town in this big pre-Suburban, with this thirty-two-foot-long Airstream trailer rolling into town, everybody knew, "Whoa! What is that?" [laughter] And his parents surprised us, so that was a nice experience.

That, of course, was my mother-in-law's sister, who we were visiting, In fact, I still correspond with his aunt.

We stayed with them a while, and then trekked off, and ultimately went up to Lake Ontario, where we stopped in a camping ground. This was at a time when gas was sixteen and seventeen cents a gallon, so we could afford to do it, because we didn't have much money, and this was the only way we could travel. Most of the campgrounds, even if they were parks, were very cheap. It was fun, because wherever you stayed, there were other campers and other kids. Of course, they were a brother and a sister, and that was better, because they had themselves, even if there wasn't anybody else, or they'd get out, and there would be other kids, and a ball game would start, or something would happen. So, if they did have memories of it, they would be good ones. Unfortunately, they don't seem to.

But we did stay at this campground for several weeks up on Lake Ontario, which was near Niagara Falls and Fort Niagara. Peter flew out of the Buffalo airport, I think, doing his experiments, and so we were sort of left there, because we didn't have a car or anything, so we had to just make do with what we could during that two-week period. After that, we went up into Montreal, and then, of course, came down through Maine, where I was born, and then spent time in New England, and headed on back. I think we went, maybe, thirteen thousand miles. Thirteen. Yes. We put in a lot of miles, and I do remember one other significant thing—well, I remember many—but I cooked every meal *in the trailer*, with the exception of one in Maine, and I said, "Now, I'm tired of this." When my neighbors said this wasn't a vacation, were they right! [laughter] I said, "In Maine, I'm getting a lobster dinner, at a minimum," and that did occur. I remember Hamburger Helper and

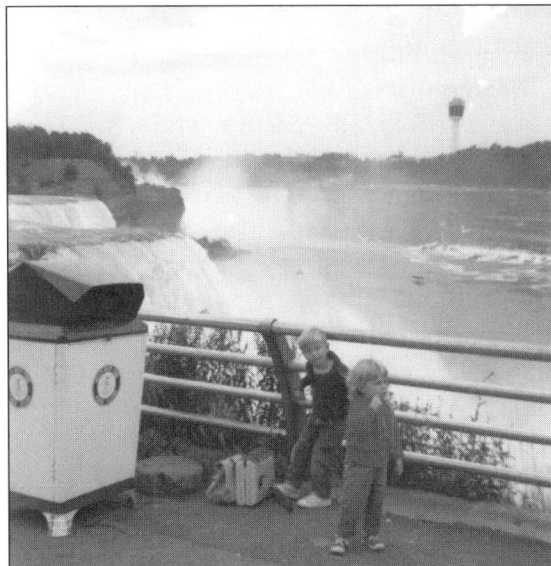

Kirk and Kristina at Niagara Falls, 1972.

those kinds of things were used a lot on that trip.

Did you have relatives, still, in Maine, who you visited while you were there?

Yes. I did have an aunt, who lived in Dexter, Maine, where they made shoes called Dexter—golf shoes and sporting shoes.

Walking shoes. Yes.

Yes. Loafers and things. And she was a comptroller for the company. So I did not have her address, but when we got there, we asked, and, of course, it was a little, tiny town in Maine, so everybody pointed us in the right direction, and she was so excited to see us. Other than that, my family has either moved out of Maine, or has died.

We did visit other relatives of, maybe, Peter's, or other folks along the way. I do remember in Cincinnati we stayed with some, and we stayed with some of my sorority sisters, or visited them. But that was the only vacation we, actually, ever did

have, and that was the only time the trailer was ever used, because that was in 1972.

Now, you mentioned to me, Desolation Valley. Was that any part of that trip?

Oh, no. But you're right. That occurred before that time. That was a vacation—of sorts. And I take that back. This camping trip came after Peter had some experiments in Barbados, and that would have been in 1969. Yes, it was July, and we decided that that would be a time for me to go with him. So we planned it, saved the money, in fact, even bought a ticket for my sister to come out, because Kirk would have been an infant—we'd just moved into the house. We moved here in May, and we asked my sister to come up. In fact, she wanted to bring her son, so we had him come as well, to babysit while we were gone.

Well, Peter was in Miami, and he called me—I was really, literally, on my way to pick up my sister at the airport—telling me that . . . and I should know this, because the big, huge computer or whatever. . . . Remember, this was way pre-computer times, that we know. It was made by Litton Company in L.A., and they used to make, I believe, ovens and things like that. But they made this huge mainframe computer that he did a lot of his work on. Well, there were always problems, *always*, and I don't know why I would have thought this would have been any different. It wasn't, because he called from Miami saying something was wrong with the computer, and the trip was off. Well, my sister was already on her way here, so she arrived, and we changed plans, and he decided that it would be nice to go backpacking. Since I'd never been on a hike, I had no idea what was in store for me, but we took the money that we saved and bought, at that time, the lightest weight tent and backpacks and the kind of things that you could buy.

We left the day after Neil Armstrong landed on the moon, because we were gathered around the television in my living room, and Kirk in his infant seat—same infant seat that I mentioned before—in front of the TV, thinking maybe he'd absorb some of this, you see, at six months, that this man landed on the moon. And the next day we took off for this trip.

Now, I got out all these shorts and T-shirts, and Peter had told me we've got to carry everything, and, of course, he'd done all this stuff in Alaska, and I never had. So I had this and this and this and this, and put it all together, and I could hardly move. So out went all of the stuff. We had to wear the same thing every day. We were gone for ten days, and Desolation Valley, you go up and off of Fallen Leaf Lake, and then you go up into the John Muir Trail, and it's absolutely incredible. But for me, the first day was incredible, too, because I had never done anything like this, and when we went to park our truck and just left, and Peter had all these maps from the Forest Service and so on, and we never saw a human being in ten days, not another human being. Saw a lot of animals, and even in July it was freezing up at some of the higher levels, snow on the ground.

The first night, I couldn't move. I was so exhausted, and I just laid down, flat on the ground. It started raining, and Peter said, "Hurry, and get up, and put up the tent!" What, a tent? I don't care about a tent. [laughter] I just let the rain fall down, but anyway, then after the second and the third day, I got the gist of it, and it got to be more interesting, and a lot more fun. I remember we went to all these places. When I see names or things, I think about this trip. But we got back to South Lake Tahoe, or wherever it was, because we were up at Fallen Leaf where we started, [laughter] and we went in to get pizza, because we hadn't had anything to eat except dried stuff for so long, or whatever

he cooked on this little campfire. He had gone in, and he had toilet paper hanging out of the back of his shorts, because we'd just gone outside all this time, and stuffed stuff in the back of our pockets. And there he was at whatever it was—the pizza place, I can't remember—with toilet paper hanging out.

That was not exactly what I had in mind for the vacation, in lieu of Barbados, but that's what we did, and, in fact, I still have one of the backpacks we had bought, and I'm sure now, it would be like very heavy compared to what you would get, because I just bought a new golf cart, and I had one, probably, fifteen years old, and I couldn't even believe the difference. You just touch it, and it practically goes by itself. It's so lightweight, but at that time, we did have the lightest, because we were carrying it all, and so that did precede the trailer trip. So they both were sort of outdoorsy trips.

You had a whole string of experiences with your husband, starting with your honeymoon up to Alaska, and then, your Desolation Valley backpacking, and then your six weeks in an Airstream trailer.

I don't know why I should have expected anything different. [laughter] And actually, it wasn't as if I didn't like it, because I was an outdoorsy person myself. It's just that most of the things I hadn't had any experience with, because my parents weren't . . . .

And backpacking is quite a bit harder than you first imagined, to haul all that stuff for a whole day?

Oh, wow! Yes. Even if you think you get it all situated, and it's all on your hips right and all that, then you lug it day after day, for two or three miles every day, or whatever it was.

Yes. Over rough country. I imagine Desolation was really rough.

Oh, it was. Oh, it was very, very rugged. And now, I understand there's so many people, as you would expect, that you've got to go through Ticketron.

Right, to get a chance to go.

They only allow so many people in. And then, we just drove up and got in and went.

And no one else was there.

Not a soul, not another human being in ten days. That's the one thing I remember about it. It was just incredible. It was so still. You could hear for a hundred miles, it seems. Every little pebble dropping, or whatever.

When you think of that, in comparison to how you have to get a ticket to go do it today, with hundreds of others.

I don't think I could bear to do it, even if I physically could do it. I just couldn't.

What a precious trip that was, when you look back at it now.

Oh, it was. Just to think about how times have changed. When I first heard about that, that people had to sign up, I thought, you've got to be kidding. Who would want to do that? But again, it's all relative. That is an experience for people today, that probably is meaningful to them, based upon the compactness of our lives, as it would be for ourselves at that time.

It's also a real measure of the difference in the times. In 1970, when you were first here, Reno was also very small. Going to Desolation Wilderness, you were on your own. All of that gives quite a picture of the

space and the lack of congestion in this whole area, compared to now.

Yes, it does. Do you know where Fallen Leaf Lake is?

Yes, on the southwest end of Lake Tahoe. It's a beautiful area where you take off.

Right there is the Stanford Camp, and Peter had graduated from Stanford. So, we walked back in and looked around, thinking when we got older we would take the kids back there at some time, because they have great experiences in the summertime, where you have visiting professors and everybody come.

One of the other things that you mentioned is how much you enjoyed your children when they were youngsters, that you really liked children as babies. Did you stay at home with the children all the time, until they went to grade school?

I stayed home with the kids all the time until I ran for office, and I really enjoyed it, but times were changing. I sewed; I made all the kid's clothes, and Kristina, particularly, jokes about the fact that they all had the same thing in different patterns, but it was one thing that I could make, a bubble suit, which was absolutely the truth. But I really didn't like it. It wasn't something I enjoyed doing. I canned and made applesauce, apple butter, cherry jam, because I had all these trees in my back yard, and I did all that. I made home-made bread. I did all these things that people wouldn't believe I did. To some extent, I enjoyed it. To some extent, I didn't. To some extent I did it because it was something to do, because I found that my days were not quite as intellectually challenging as I would liked for them to have been. I did love the kids. We did everything people do with little kids.

I've told you about the Elks Club, but I had a birthday party for Kirk, because his birthday was at Christmas. I started when he was very young, to make a big deal about it, to separate his birthday from Christmas.

So, you're saying that you did the kinds of things that women did who stayed home in those days?

Well, I think I even did more. I don't remember all my friends canning and making all their kids' clothes. But I think maybe I did that for two reasons: one, I guess, to prove that I could do it, because I hadn't done anything like those kinds of things before, although my mother and sister are very handy. They knit, and my sister is a very talented seamstress, and I'd say the most so, in my family. My mother painted and did crewel, needlepoint, those kinds of things. I didn't do any of those things, although my sister did teach me how to knit, and maybe someday I'll get back to doing that again. That would be something good to do, I think, now. But I did do all those things, as I say: one, I guess, to show that I could do it, and secondly, because it did occupy myself, and it was something a little bit challenging. I liked to cook a lot in those days, because that, to me, was the most creative thing you could do around the house. And the kids and I, we'd go down to the park. There were not that many kids in the neighborhood: the one next door, the foster boy, who was fine until he grew up, and there were a couple of little guys up the street who the kids were very friendly with, and there were always some kids around, and then I mentioned the friends and their children.

But I'm just trying to think. The kids were in Little League and basketball and Indian Guides and I think they had a pretty typical life. Both kids were active. They could walk to their particular school, Jessie

Beck, and it had a ski program in elementary school, where they learned how to ski. They got off on Thursdays, because one mother was always willing to drive, and so they got to start earlier than the Reno Ski Program. All of the kinds of things that kids do. Today I look at my grandchildren and see that they've had this lesson and that lesson and this and that, and it boggles your mind. I don't think in those days it was quite that pressure to learn how to do something. Through the Reno Rec, as the kids got older, there were opportunities to learn how to play tennis in the summer, if they wanted to, and they were very good golfers, as I mentioned, but that came a little bit later. I don't know if you want me to talk about my kids now, or just up until that period of life, until I decided to run for office.

I think we'll just come back from time to time and kind of get up to date with where the kids are.

5

RUNNING FOR PUBLIC OFFICE

Was this about the time that you began to think about running for office?

Yes, because, see, we're talking about this trip being in 1972. Well, in 1973 Pat Hardy Lewis ran for the Reno City Council, the next year. So I was invited to a coffee by, I believe, Pat. Her name was Pat Gothberg, at the time. No, that's not correct. That wasn't her last name, but she just recently retired from being head of the Sierra Arts Foundation.

Oh, Smith. She's Pat Smith now.

Pat Smith. That's right. And her husband is Ron, with Channel Five. But at that time, when I first met Pat, she was married to Roy . . . his name escapes me. Somehow I met her, and she invited me to a coffee, and she got me involved with Mary Gojack, too, because she was Mary Gojack's friend. I went to this coffee, and it was over where Pat lived. I don't know who the hostess was, but anyway, Pat Hardy Lewis was the person for whom it was given.

So I was just taken, the minute I walked into that room. It was like the light bulb

went off in my head. I realized that this is what I was interested in. I liked the candidate. That was good, even though there wasn't this big thing about it, at that point. None of the issues related to women. It was a city council seat. But clearly, I got involved in the campaign. I don't remember exactly what I started out doing, but that's what I did in my spare time. Then, it became so that I pretty much was literally in charge of running all of the precinct, walking for her campaign. I became *very* involved.

So you organized all of that, organized the volunteers to go out and walk the precinct?

It seemed like I was, yes. See, this was the first time. This was like an explosion, in terms of politics. No one had done this before. Nobody had gone door to door. It was just incredible, the number of volunteers she had, and that they were everywhere. Her opponent just was crazy, because they were there; they were here this day, that day, that evening, everybody handing out things for this woman.

Who was the opponent?

I know his name well, because he ran against me the following year, Alex Kanwetz. He was an insurance agent, a nice guy, very good friend of Frank Fahrenkopf. Does that name ring a bell?

Yes, it does.

Frank was active in Republican politics and became state chairman here in Nevada and then went off to Washington and became national chairman of the Republican National Committee in D.C., when Laxalt was in the Senate, and when Reagan was president, and now is president of the American Gaming Association, which really is the lobbying arm of Nevada's gaming interests, but also represents other gaming interests throughout the country, and has been very successful. Frank is just a good guy in my mind and never forgets his Nevada friends.

Anyway, he had this buddy. They were young, early thirties, and they were going to be very involved in politics, and I didn't know Alex Kanwetz, but I did like this woman and got involved, as I said. So anyway, she won, and she did the thing that we all, as women, should do, and I have always done since, or tried to, and that is that she was on a number of committees and positions, and had kind of got herself, before she ran for the city council, in a position to run, and so she, in turn, appointed me to many of the positions that she left. By virtue of her being now on the city council, she had certain positions, and they weren't huge, but I turned them into something. She appointed me to what was called the Mayor's Advisory Committee. What it became was a city charter review, and then I took some of that information and turned it into legislation when I was in the assembly, but she also appointed me to a Blue Ribbon Task Force, and those were

very big. Bob Rusk was very involved, he of the recent pony tail. And that's where I first met Bob.

We're referring, just for background, to the pony tail: he had sworn he wouldn't cut off his hair until there was some resolution.

The city council had done something with the homeless concerns, because Bob Rusk owns a . . . well, it's not a motel, exactly. It's right on the river, but it's more of a week-to-week rental type of place, I'd say. I've been in it before, because there was a physical trainer, who came from San Diego, who I used to meet there, because there's sort of a semi-gym in the building.

Anyway, this was called the Blue Ribbon Task Force that the city set up to project what the city was going to look like ten, fifteen years down the line, and what it should look like. I was appointed to the one on housing. I went to this meeting, and almost everybody had an interest in housing—builders, developers. And I'm just this person. I don't know one, single person there, literally. All men. I'm sitting next to a guy named Harold Bigler. He and his wife, Dorothy, were Realtors, and there were a lot of Realtors, of course, involved. I got talking to Harold, and, by gosh, he nominates me to chair this panel. I don't remember the other sequence of events, but I wound up being chair of this committee, which was the *best* thing possible for someone interested in going on, because when the reports were all done, then you had television time, and the chair, of course, came and represented the committee and the results of their particular committee. And we did a lot. I flew . . . [quick exhale] thinking about it . . . on a small, little plane over to Woodland, California, and saw how a mobile home was made, and the whole issue of stick-built homes versus mobile homes. These are all issues I dealt with at the legislature later on in my life.

So it was good background.

Oh, absolutely. Everything that I had an opportunity to do was educational for me. But these were opportunities that Pat really gave to me, and as happenstance, she didn't get me to be chair, as just . . . that was the best, single, most important thing.

I just remember Harold and Dorothy—Harold, particularly. I always used to tell Harold that he started my political career. He just loves to hear that, thinks that's just the best. In fact, I saw Dorothy the other day—she's getting, oh, of course, quite a bit older—in the grocery store.

Anyway, so those two things I remember specifically as happening in this time period. Now, I'm going to talk about politics, what was going on in my life that way. I do remember one very disconcerting thing, and it does concern Pat Hardy Lewis. She came by my house one night, and I remember I had in my living room set up my card table where I had my sewing machine, and I was making another one of those bubble suits, I'm sure. I was telling her I was seriously thinking about running for the assembly. She was just shocked. She just couldn't believe that I thought that I was qualified to run. I was shocked that she felt that way. She says, "Well, what do you know about issues at the state legislature?"

I said, "Well, what did *you* know about issues at the city council level?" I said, "I have a degree in political science. I certainly learned so much from your own campaign, how to campaign." I said, "Firstly, I think that I intend to do research. I intend to find out what the issues are, important to my district. What else does anybody do? There are people, probably, who run, that never even think about, are they qualified." And it struck me. "Why are we, as women, sitting here, and you asking

me this question? Do you think two guys are sitting somewhere else, in some bar downtown, with the cigars, asking themselves, 'Do you think you're qualified?' Of course not!"

I don't know why I had that thought at that day, because nothing I'd ever read had suggested to me that women would look at things in a different way, but it just was such a shock to me.

I expected her to say, "I think that's fabulous! Whatever I can do to help you." It just wasn't that way. However, I have to say that since that time, I don't think she has any idea, really, how it affected me negatively, but whenever she's in an audience, and I've given a speech, I always introduce her and tell everybody how important she was, and that is true. Even though I probably haven't seen her for five, six years, whenever I would see her, I'd know that she feels very strongly that I did a good job. I don't think she even thought about that evening, since then.

Do you think it had something more to do with just the overall political climate for women at that time, in general?

I don't know. I don't know.

Was it still unusual for women to run for state legislature?

Yes. But I think, if that had been the case, I would have thought she would have said that, or she would have said, "My God, your kids are so little!" But I didn't get that feeling. I got the sense that she didn't think that I was qualified, and that hurt. That was very personal.

So the question didn't come out. Yes. That came out personal.

Yes. But anyway, clearly, when I got that thought, that became just an incredible thing that went on in our household, with my husband and me. My husband never once discouraged me, never once. I think he believed that when he married me, because of my already history of running for office and things, and being involved in politics, that this would happen. I think he felt that it probably wouldn't happen quite that soon. And the kids in 1973, 1974, they would have been four and five. So this was a pretty huge decision, because there was not a woman in the state who had run for office with children of that age. They were both preschoolers. And what would it mean to our family? Just our family structure? The relationships? All those questions were very important. I had far more doubts about it than my husband did. It was the worst. I agonized over this so much. One day I would feel absolutely sure it was the right thing to do. The next day, totally different view. Back and forth, back and forth, without any input, without saying anything to anybody, except to Peter, just in my own mind.

Some of the things that I thought about were really silly: like I could just see my son going off to school with his hair all stuck straight out, because my husband hadn't combed it, [laughter] or hadn't wet it down, or he hadn't had a shower, or whatever. So what? But that was important to me, to make sure my kids had clean clothes, etc. and had their little lunches packed. And, oh, I worried about all that. [Gasps] What was he going to put in their lunch bag?

Because he would have to take over some of the responsibility for the children?

Oh, *huge* responsibilities he would have to take over, particularly at the end of the session. The only reason I even thought about this particular office, was that it was every other year. I felt very strongly that the state legislature was a place for women who were mothers, because they could

have that time off. As it turns out, I did really do it full time, but not in the sense of going down there and going from morning to night, morning to night.

Like when the legislature is in session. Yes.

Yes. Oh, yes. That's just so consuming. And you can do what you want in the off time. But that to me was the appropriate place.

Even the city council that Pat was on, it was really an ongoing thing, and you had all these other committees, in addition.

Week after week.

You had to be on the parks board or this or that. And she was older. Her children were grown when she ran. I think she might have been still married. I can't remember. I think she got a divorce somewhere in between that, which again, was, of course, something that was always raised, that your marriage would not be able to survive this.

And there's no question. If I had been married to anybody other than Peter, probably, it wouldn't have. Because it is such a tug on your self-esteem, because, clearly, someone else is now the person that people know, not the traditional husband, and it's Mrs. So-and-So. It's no Mrs. anymore; it's Sue, not Mrs. Peter. So you've got to have the right person, who feels pretty good about themselves and isn't in competition with you in any way. And I think that's what gets some of the other relationships. I had often wondered without thinking through this that if I'd been married to, say, an attorney, how much more we would have had in common. And on second thought, how much worse that would have been.

Yes. Because in a way, you're in the same field competing with each other.

Absolutely. Yes. And Peter had a real interest in a lot of issues and gave me a lot of good advice, but it wasn't like he wanted to be down there and do this.

Anyway, I will get back here to the whole decision-making process, which was very, very difficult. I have to say, almost no one supported my attempt to do this. None of my friends.

Outside of Peter?

Yes. I remember my mother wrote me a long letter when I was in the deciding point, and went through the 150 reasons why I shouldn't run, and then wound up saying, "But I know you're going to, and here's your first campaign contribution." [laughter]

And my mother-in-law was not real happy about it, although, to her credit, she never really said anything or would interfere. But they were traditional mothers, and I think that they found it was a very untraditional thing to do. My friends, I asked a few, of course, my few close friends. They all said, "It isn't the right time." And the biggest thing was the age of my children. It was not the right time. "Why don't you wait until . . . ?" The most liberal said, "Until they're in school." Then it got, "Until they're out of high school, or until they're out of *college*, or until they're *married*, or until you're a *grandmother*." [laughter] As it kept going up.

Kept pushing it back?

Yes. And when you look back at those times, it's just on the cusp of changing, because almost every woman who wanted a political career, wound up on the school board. That's where it was, and most of them, because it was involved in mother things, children things, and it was part time. It usually was for no pay, which was another

thing that women always seem to gravitate to, a little step up from volunteerism.

One step above PTA.

Yes. You had a little policy-making position, and also, you normally did this after your kids were out of school. The traditional was high school. That was pretty much the bell-weather time.

Even Nancy Gomes—and I'm sure you've heard of Nancy Gomes—who was probably one of the more liberal people I ever knew, didn't run until she was older, and she started out at the school-board level. So that's pretty much what my friends were concerned about, the same thing. But they were *really* concerned. I mean, they had our interests at heart.

Now, I think that Lynn Atcheson . . . I had just met Lynn, and she was very interested in politics, I could tell. So when I had made up my mind to run, I asked her if she would be involved in my campaign, and she said no, she couldn't be, because she had just signed on board to be very involved in her college buddy, Jim Santini's, campaign. Of course, Jim was running for Congress, and that was a much bigger office, and if he won, it would mean something pretty significant for her, i.e. a job. So here was someone else, whose kids were about my age: Nicki, her daughter, is Kristina's age. I'm the godmother, I think I mentioned to you, of all her kids. So clearly, here's someone else who is not necessarily putting herself out there on the line, but has some of the similar interests. And of course, there were women like that who supported me, once I made this decision. But my close friends, in asking their advice, "Should I run?" I don't remember anybody saying yes.

I don't want to say unequivocally, because someone may read this and say, "Don't you remember?"

Sue (right) with friend, Lynn Atcheson.

Then they'll say, "She doesn't remember me."

"I was there, the first person." [laughter] But it wasn't resounding.

So what you feel was a sense of going out on your own, really, without that support?

Well, I think people now know me well enough to know that I went into this for the right reasons. I didn't go into it to make money, to get a bigger job, to build up my business, none of those things. I went into it for issues. What really pushed me over was not only what I've already described as something missing here at home, and I just mean intellectually—it was Watergate.

It was the fact that government . . . as I've already told you, I have been interested in politics and government from a tiny child, and particularly, as a Republican, when I saw what was going on, and no one had any respect. Now, of course, hardly anybody does, but in those days, that was not the case.

We'd had John F. Kennedy just prior to this. Now you have Richard Nixon, who's lied, lied, lied. And all these things are going on. The Watergate hearings were going on as I was going door to door, knocking on doors, asking people to vote for me. I was so appalled at that. That's the reason. I had all of these ideas that I wanted to open up government.

In fact, I got this Common Cause book called *Secrecy No More*. I think that was the name of it. Just say a Common Cause book, I guess. *Money and Power*. There were a lot of those I read. But basically, it pointed to the fact that they believed—and Common Cause was a major supporter of these concepts—that if you let people know where you're getting your money, and how much you're spending, and who you're spending it on, how you're spending it, and you have open meetings, and all of this openness in government, and campaign reform, then things would be better. And boy, that just struck me, and that's what I ran on. Those were my issues in this district, which were very unpopular in this district, as it turns out, but anyway, they were important to me. That is really one of the major reasons I did it at that time. I just felt like I knew myself. I knew I wanted to do the right thing. I knew I would do the right thing, and I felt that I was one of those people who, in a little, bitty, tiny way could make a difference, and have people at least respect somebody, even if it was just their local legislator. I know that sounds so idealistic, but that is exactly who I was, and who I was even in the legislature. I really irritated a lot of people, because I was so idealistic and really believed how these things could happen for a long time.

I'd like to go into your campaign in a little more detail. You mentioned you were going door to door in your campaigning. Would you tell me a little bit about the kinds of questions you were greeted with from the voters, as you knocked on doors?

Well, I guess the general impression that I have of that first campaign following on the heels of another woman having done that same thing—Pat Hardy Lewis, who we have already discussed—clearly it was easier, I suspect, for me to do this kind of campaign, because she had done it. Indeed,

I felt I had a sense of how to do it, from my experience with her. I don't know if I've talked about how I even made the decision to get involved, how I went to Dr. Broadbent, who was the incumbent?

No. I don't believe you did.

Well, I think we'd better talk about that, because we're getting to the point where I'm going door to door, and yet, we haven't even come to the part where I've decided to run.

Right, because the things we did talk about running, were more about the family issues, that your husband was always supportive of you, that you had some friends who were, and some who weren't.

Right. But the political decision of whether I should even get involved—because that was clearly as important, if not more important, in my making a decision, because if I felt I could not ever win, I probably wouldn't have gotten involved, but I might have.

The incumbent in this district, Assembly District 25, southwest Reno, was Dr. Bob Broadbent. Now, that was a very well-known name in the entire community at that time, Dr. Broadbent. In fact, it's a very well-known statewide name, because there's another Bob Broadbent who was chairman of the county commission in Clark County and was head of the airport authority. He now is head of the group—as we speak, on the day Vikki just tagged in here—that was just able to get the largest bond revenue issue through the board of finance, I guess you call it, where the governor sits, and the treasurer of the state, and some other people, for a monorail that's going down the Strip in Las Vegas. So, that Bob Broadbent was a power in the Republican Party, and everybody expected him to ultimately run for governor. This Bob

Broadbent, who was the incumbent in my district, is a different one with the same name, and he was equally as important and as politically popular in Reno as the other Bob Broadbent in Las Vegas. I know that's an aside, but it seemed to be interesting, because they are totally different guys with the same name.

Not related.

It's not a common name. In fact, the sister of Bob Broadbent in Clark County lived around the corner from me, and she was married to a man named George Siri, who owned part of the Eldorado Hotel downtown, because they're related to the Caranos. It's a small state—and a small community.

Anyway, Dr. Broadbent was the incumbent in this district, and we had just gone from running from a slate at large in this community—and probably communities throughout the country—until the Supreme Court decision of "one man, one vote," when they had to break up running at large, where you had a list of Republicans and Democrats, and the highest number of Republicans and/or Democrats came out, and then you voted on a ticket. They ran it as a sort of a team. But Dr. Broadbent was, I believe, the first assemblyperson—man—from Assembly District 25, once the district had been broken up. I think so, but I'm not sure about that.

Anyway, he was the incumbent and very popular. The assumption was he would run again, but there was this undercurrent that he was a doctor, and he was just appalled by what he saw at the legislature, that his profession was such that he said something, and people did it. If you have a patient, you say, "Listen, this is what's wrong with you. Here's a prescription. You go get it filled, and you'll feel better." And when you get to the legislature, you can't

get out on the floor of the assembly and say, "Listen, this is a bill that I think is important, and we all should pass it. And you listen to me, because I'm the doctor, and you're the patients—all the rest of you out here. You get it? You go do what I say." [laughter] It didn't work like that, and he realized that he was one of—at that point, I guess it would have been—forty. Now there are forty-two.

So the other thirty-nine said, "Huh? If we don't like it, we're just not going to do it, doctor." [laughter] And there were some medical issues. I think it was acupuncture, because I think I did not deal with that. No, I didn't deal with acupuncture. I dealt with laetrile and Gerovital—mark that down, because that is an important one I want to talk about.

I'm going to talk about this, because it leads up to why I was able to run, or how, in fact, I was able to win, basically, because he didn't like the attitude of the other legislators, that they didn't listen to him as the authority. This acupuncture bill came through during his time, and, of course, he was very opposed to it, as you would suspect a traditional doctor would be, even more so in the 1970s than today, and they still are, but not quite as much. So Dr. Broadbent was very opposed to acupuncture.

Well, the acupuncture lobbyist was Jim Joyce, who unfortunately has passed away, but an incredible guy in terms of my relationship with him, and how it started out, and how it ended up, but the premier lobbyist of all time, most people say, in the legislature. Anyway, if Jim Joyce had something, you could almost bet it was going to pass, or if he was opposed to it, it wasn't going to pass. He got somebody to sponsor the acupuncture bill.

Dr. Broadbent, of course, thought this was appalling and tried to get it killed, and everybody looked at him as I've described, and it passed. So acupuncture became legal in our state—first state in the nation, only state in the nation, which was in my mind, of course, par for the course, because we always did things like that. I got very much on my high horse about stuff like this, when I first got into the legislature, as did Dr. Broadbent, because in a way, I guess, we came from this district, and we were representing, in a sense, not only ourselves, but also the district. Many doctors, many lawyers, and many more affluent people lived in Assembly District 25, more established, traditional people, that may not have liked that sort of thing, but Dr. Broadbent was clearly representing his own traditional medical views.

So when he got done with that session, there were rumblings, and I was hardly in the mainstream of politics. I didn't know anybody. I didn't go to Republican events. I didn't even know where they were, but somebody had told me he might not run, because he disliked it so much. It just wasn't what he had thought it would be. He couldn't make the kind of impact that he thought he would like to make.

So, when I got to thinking about running, and I guess I've talked a little bit about that, that I thought about this on my own, without anybody . . . because I had no advisers. I didn't know anything, and none of my friends did, either, so I thought that I should probably go and visit with Dr. Broadbent and tell him I was interested in running, and get a sense of whether he might run. I wanted to tell him who I was, because he clearly would have no idea. I remember walking right outside of where we are right now, kind of rehearsing what I was going to say to Dr. Broadbent when I went to his office, which was located very close to my home, because I remember just going down here on Plumb Lane somewhere, and he lived right over across Plumb Lane on Dartmouth Drive, which is over here by a little pond.

I went to visit him, and he just was as nice as could be, but I was just petrified,

because I realized that this was very important to me—what I said, how I acted, how he interpreted me to be. So I didn't want to come across as being too aggressive, but tough enough that he wouldn't think, "Oh, if I'm not going to run, I'm going to turn it over to this little, wussy woman?" [laughter]

So it was kind of this balancing act, and it was the best thing I did. It was absolutely the most important thing, probably, in terms of that election, in terms of my winning, in addition to going door to door and those other things. But I did go to visit him, and he asked me some questions, and I had done some research on things he had introduced, things he had voted for and against, and so on. You don't have research like this [rustles papers] at that time. Besides, I was a nobody, so I couldn't get this kind of thing done—and I'm pointing to all the lists of bills that I have introduced during my time in the legislature, while I'm talking at this moment to Vikki.

Yes, because you've gotten those out of the Legislative Counsel Bureau.

Yes. I got this from LCB, and, of course, at that time I wasn't a part of the legislature, and they didn't have the sophisticated system of retrieval, or any of those kinds of things.

I was able to find out a little bit about the doctor, and so I could talk about a few things that he was interested in, and one was how mobile homes were taxed, because this district did not have one mobile home. It was *all* single-family residences, not one apartment, not one condo. I don't even think there were things called "condos" in the early 1970s. There was not anything in Assembly District 25 but single-family homes. Now, that is incredible. There was no other district in the state of Nevada that was so homogeneous.

Think about it—not even an apartment building!

No rentals at all?

Now that's not true today.

Well, a single-family home might have been a rental, but that's different from apartments or mobile home parks and so on.

Yes. Well, I don't know if they were rented or bought, but you couldn't tell that by knocking on somebody's door. Structurally, it was a single-family home on a lot. There wasn't anything that was more than one floor. [laughter] There were no two floors of apartments, nothing. So anyway, he was very interested in mobile home property tax, so that was on a list of things I was going to talk to him about. He asked me some questions about me, personally, and I told him why I would run, and I told him that I might run, even if he did, that there were a number of women who were very supportive of getting a woman elected. It was time, and we had so few women in the legislature, which he certainly was aware of, that I wanted to come and meet him, but I hadn't made up my mind about that, but if he did not run, then I certainly would run, but I might run, even if he did. I was pretty up-front about that, and that was taking somewhat of a risk, because I did not know this man, at all. Anyway, we talked about issues, and I came away feeling like I really liked him, and I felt that, because of that, he probably liked me. I felt pretty good about the interview, if you will, and it was an interview. He told me that he was going to make up his mind like within the next week or so, and that he would get back to me. Indeed, he did, and he told me he was not going to run, so I immediately asked him if he would endorse me, and he said no, he would not, that he

felt that he probably would stay out of the race, totally, which was the best thing. I mean, if he couldn't endorse me, the best thing was, he was going to stay out of it.

He did make that commitment to me, because, I think I've already said, that Frank Fahrenkopf's best friend, Alex Kanwetz, was one of the people who ran against me. Frank Fahrenkopf at that time was a major player in the Republican Party, a young man, but somebody who was definitely going to be a major player. We did not realize what a major player he was, but he turned out to be head of the Republican Party in the state of Nevada, and then, when Paul Laxalt got elected to the U.S. Senate, and Ronald Reagan got elected President, he then became Chairman of the Republican National Committee, and still is in Washington. He is now head of the American Gaming Association, AGA, but has been a major player in politics all his life.

Probably his best friend from middle school, Alex Kanwetz, had been defeated by Pat Hardy Lewis in the race for city council, so he turned right around—and of course, that's a good thing to do sometimes, to run again when your name identification is somewhat higher than maybe normal—to run for the legislature, which he intended to do. So Frank went to Dr. Broadbent right after I had visited him—and he had made this announcement he wasn't going to run—to really pressure him into supporting Alex, and he said no, because he had met this young woman, whom he didn't know very well, but was pretty impressed with her, and had committed to her that he wasn't going to support anybody. So in that way, that was incredibly important to me, that I had taken it upon myself to go and do this, because, clearly, he would have probably endorsed him, otherwise. There's no reason for me not to think he wouldn't have, if I hadn't gone, because why wouldn't he? He would have. I believe he told me that—or Frank did. Somebody told me that he would have endorsed Alex, but he met another candidate, and so that was an important thing I did.

Anyway, after that, I hit the road, so to speak, but I did it in a methodical way, and probably that was because of Pat Hardy Lewis's experience. I realized there were thirty-one precincts in my district at that time, and I figured I could probably do a precinct a day. I wasn't sure about that, but that was my plan, so I moved out thirty-one days, plus a few, back from election day, to make sure I hit every single precinct.

Now, AAUW, the American Association of University Women, was the most instrumental organization in my district and race, bar none. Hands down, they helped me win this election, because there was someone that met me here at my home, or in the district somewhere—thirty-one women, at least—who committed that they would meet me on a day and help me walk that precinct. I did not want to go by myself, because you did not know who you were going to meet, and it was possible a number of things could happen to you if you were alone, not only bad things, but you would get hung up too much in one house, and you would never get out, and you'd only do two houses in the allotted time you wanted to do a precinct. You had to move along, because, if you started too soon, then other people would come after you, because now, after the 1973 election, people decided when Pat Hardy Lewis won this election going door to door, that that's what you had to do. So starting that election in 1974 everybody was going to do it, because they figured, if they did it, they'd win. If they didn't do anything else, they would win. So if you started too soon, someone would come after you, and they would forget you if you just came in three months before. So you had to time this within a reasonable period of time. I felt so, anyway. So I had AAUW women meeting me and had a schedule and had all of that, and to a person, there was only one instance when someone did not meet me, during the entire primary.

Then I did this all over again in the general, so I walked my district twice, even though I probably didn't need to. I didn't know that at the time. I didn't believe what people told me at the time, and I wanted to make absolutely sure that I was going to win this, and not listen to what other people said. So the person and I—and I can remember many of them to this day—went walking, and for example, we had certain things that we left at each home in the district.

I remember the very first precinct I walked with Judy Dankel. This is an aside, but as a matter of fact, I just read in the paper, her husband died a week or so ago, and I've cut it out, and I've got to write her a note, but I haven't seen her for years and years. She and I went walking up near Court Street in my first precinct ever. People said that what I should do is get a list from the registrar of voters, and it would have the name of the person who lived in that house. You'd go up and say, "Hi, Mrs. Ford. How are you today?" or "Hi, Mrs. Wagner. I know you're a registered voter, and you're a Republican, and I'm running." Blah blah blah.

Well, the first four houses I hit, "Mrs. Wagner" didn't live there any longer, or she just died the week before, or she was a Democrat, not a Republican, and so I said, "Phooey with this," because it messed everything up, and they thought we didn't know what we were doing, and so we just didn't use names, so all of the lists I had purchased were of no value, and maybe it was just in that particular precinct, but I told everybody else we were just going to knock on the door and introduce ourselves and hand out and move on.

They obviously weren't up to date.

They had not been purged. They weren't correct. They weren't accurate. And it may have been that particular precinct, and I might not have found that to be the case in others, but we spent a lot of time finding out where we were on the list, and it wasn't as well organized for the use of a walker. Later on they had walking lists that were better, but this wasn't quite as efficient a use of our time. Time was wasted finding names, so it was better to move along.

As far as what I ran into going door to door, it was really a mix, I suspect, of what a young woman would find at that time anywhere. You have to understand, there were no other women running for office in this state, or I would wager to say probably—I don't know if I could make this statement, but pretty darn close to it—any in the country who were in the same situation I was, that had two preschoolers. This was unheard of anywhere, politically. I know that, because there were many stories written about this campaign and our kids and the ages of my children, because of what I've said before, that women waited until kids were grown. That was the acceptable thing. So, to leave your family behind, in the minds of many people, was just unheard of, and not well taken by many women, and particularly women who were mothers and felt that that was just not the thing to do. We're talking about the early 1970s. Now we're doing this in the year 2000. An incredible attitudinal change has occurred during that period of time.

Can you describe what the attitude was like in the early 1970s when you were doing that, because it is very different?

Yes. The attitude was basically that there were very few women who worked, period, outside the home. Women were homemakers. That's what they did. And there was just this beginning of movement outside of the home—maybe real estate, which you could do on a part-time basis. There were some little inklings, but to go out and be an attorney was just difficult. I think I know one woman who's a friend of mine today, Margo Piscevich, who was the first . . . no, I think Nada Novacovich was the first woman attorney in town, but Margo was the second, I believe. And that would have been, probably, 1975. I could have told you there were two women attorneys in town. There were probably no women doctors.

The way I reached people campaigning, you couldn't do today, and that was, women had coffees in their home at about ten o'clock in the morning, and so I would go, and I would speak to all these women. This was the other main campaign vehicle that men and women had. Everybody had. In the evening you might have a wine and cheese tasting party, where you would have husbands and wives, but if you wanted to get to the women, you went to a coffee. I used to jokingly say to the LDS members, because I live in an LDS district here, "orange juicers," because, of course, they didn't drink coffee. And I did have one Mormon orange juicer, which wasn't too successful, in my neighborhood, but because women were at home. Women didn't work, and that's how you visited with them. You couldn't possibly do anything like that today.

You could, I suppose, among certain groups of women, and they would be probably religiously oriented, but I don't even think that would be the case, because many women . . . I'm just thinking of women who home school their kids, for example. They would have to be at home in order to do that. And they, at least from my understanding, tend to maybe be of more of a religious orientation, but that's not necessarily true. I was just reading some articles about home schooling, that a lot of times it has to do with just their attitudes about public schools, that they're so in an upheaval, but when it first started out, it was more of a religious movement for home schooling. Now I don't think it is quite, but you just can't find many women at home today during the day.

It was just a totally different world. And I'm not that old. I don't think of myself as being that old—sixty. But I was thirty-four at the time. I was very young. There were two things I had against me. One, I was very young. I was the youngest woman elected in Nevada when I got elected, and I was the only woman in the country, I believe, who had preschool children, who was successful in an election.

So, when you went and met with people, say, at a coffee, was that issue always brought up?

Well, yes. I was going to get to what I found out door to door, and then I'll get to the coffee thing. The door-to-door experience—some people would be pleasant and just accept whatever you were handing out, but that would be it. Then, there would be a group of people who would want you to come in and visit for a long time. I would say they tended to be older people, who probably were a bit lonely, and wanted to visit with somebody. Also, it was very interesting—this district was the most politically smart and astute district, I would suspect, of all of them. The other district might have been one that included Lake Tahoe. My senate district did include Incline Village.

But people sometimes wanted to visit with you all evening, if they could, and then that's when you had your other person come by in the number of minutes that had been agreed on, and knock and say we had to move on. If somebody wasn't home, I hand-wrote a note on each of the little, inexpensive brochures that I had, that were

only one color, because I couldn't afford anything more than one color.

A friend of mine, Renate Neumann, who is now a well-known artist in town has started a non-profit called Angel Kiss—somebody just gave me a brochure on it the other day, but it's a foundation for young children who have cancer, and to help their parents do some of the testing and some of the medical things that are necessary. Renate—I went to school with her husband at the University of Arizona, Pete Neumann, who is a well-known attorney in town. My husband knew Pete pretty well, because they skied together and knew each other in Arizona, as well. Renate offered to do some graphic work for me, and that was one of the things that women did in my campaign. I'm going to digress here a moment, because the whole campaign was based upon volunteer work.

Jean Stoess, who's still involved in editing books and magazines and things like that, offered to do any kind of press releases for me, because she had a lot of contacts with the press. She had a journalism background. So I had Jean Stoess and Lynn Atcheson, and, I believe, Barbara Weinberg—I can't remember everyone—Renate, who did certain things; that's where their expertise rested. Also, there were many women who would do things, who would offer to make like a casserole for dinner as their contribution, because I'd be out walking, so Peter and the kids would have something to eat. Or someone would offer to give me a massage, because they might have been a masseuse, and they figured after I'd done a lot of walking . . . . Whenever I gave a speech during that campaign where there was an audience, there would be some woman who would rise up and say, "I could offer to do this. I can't walk a district, but I could cook meals for you," or "I could give you a massage," or "I could do this." And that was the way that they contributed to the campaign. That was the beginning of that sort of networking that began in those days, which I don't think you see today; maybe you do, but I think not. I think money is the exchange rate today, rather than someone's expertise and background and services in a volunteer way.

Getting back to the door-to-door business, the people I met who I found to be the least interested, I guess—but I didn't know this at the time—were women my own age. They were not the most supportive, but they didn't say so, necessarily, at the door. Some did. Some just outright said, "You should be at home with your kids."

There were many men who were the Archie Bunker types, and Archie Bunker was very big at that time on television. He was rather bigoted about just everything, and they would just slam the door and tell me I should get home, and what business did I have with running around doing this sort of thing? They were pretty outspoken about it. Older people—if I could put a general turn on it—I think older men and women, generally speaking, were the nicest and seemed to be the most supportive. I thought a lot about that, and I'm guessing that older women thought that time had passed them by, and that there was something going on in this country, that people couldn't quite put their finger on yet, but it was opening up, or people were trying—or I was trying. In my case, it was somebody out there running for office, but things were changing, and the opposite was true, evidently, I later learned, of women my own age. So I met all kinds, and I really do enjoy so much meeting people and going door to door, that it was a pleasure for me, even if I had a slammed door in my face. It didn't really affect me all that much—I'd just go to the next door. But I thoroughly enjoyed that experience.

When I wasn't able to run for lieutenant governor again, I was told by at least one major player, Billy Vassiliadis, who owns R&R Advertising, that he could get me reelected by video, by my not having to go to all these places that I had gone to, because of my neck and back—because Governor Miller wanted me to run again for lieutenant governor. I told him that he missed the point, that that is what I enjoyed about politics, was meeting people, and I would not enjoy sitting at home, even if you could do it by video, paid advertisements.

Even if you could do it, which I didn't think you were yet able to do that in Nevada, the people in Winnemucca and Fallon and Ely expected you to be there, and I still think they do expect that, even today. Even if you could, I wouldn't have wanted it that way, because I do get an adrenaline rush, if you will, from meeting people. I enjoy people—whether it's good, bad, or indifferent—hearing what they have to say, and talking about what my issues were, what was most important to me, about opening up the process. It wasn't much to do with women and women's issues, because that really hadn't registered

Sue with Billy Vassiliadis, President, R&R Partners.

with me. I was the personification of that, but I didn't realize that at the time. I just realized that I felt women had something to bring to the process, and there weren't very many there, and, as I mentioned, I felt that this was one job that you could do on a part-time basis, which I later did not do. But it was an unbelievable experience, because I got a sense of the district, and I got a sense of wonderful people, generally speaking, who lived in the district.

Now, the other way I reached people was, as I mentioned, at these coffees. Now, that was a real mixed bag, because all of those people were women, who were at home during the day, and here I was saying I was not going to be at home all the time. So I tried to talk about issues, and I had a file cabinet in my basement full of every issue, and I had done a lot of research and felt that I was really on top of the major issues.

The big gripes about me were that I hadn't lived here long enough, that you had to be a native Nevadan in order to understand Nevada. That, of course, has also changed, because we have so many people moving to our state, but at that time you really had to have been here, in order to understand what the issues were that affected Northern Nevada and/or the state. Having just come here in 1969 and running for office in 1974, which would have been five years, was not good enough. So that was one of the big things against me.

The other was my sex. The other big one was my kids' age, and fourth, believe it or not, would be the fact that my husband was probably some liberal professor at the university, because that was the image of people at the university, that they were all liberal, and there were issues going on at that time at the university that fed into that. You would have to go back, I can't remember. I sort of remember one where students ran out in the street and laid down in front of the car of the president of the university, because he had canned a professor, and so on. So there were issues that fed into that image of professors. My husband had a beard, and that immediately was identified as being, at that time, a leftover from the 1960s, I guess you know, and even a more liberal image. Of course, they didn't understand an engineer. By training, he would be pretty conservative. So you can't go around telling people that, and I certainly wasn't going to ask Peter to shave off his beard, if he didn't want to. [laughter]

Anyway, those were a lot of obstacles that I had to overcome. I realized all of them, at one point before I started, to be things I'd have to deal with. As you notice, the first picture that I have, we put the kids up in a tree, because my husband was so tall—six foot, seven inches—and they were so tiny that we didn't want to make them look that small, so we put them up in the tree, so we couldn't tell the difference between their height and my husband's, and point out even more the fact that they were tiny. So we recognized that that was an issue.

We also put on that brochure, I believe, that he was a graduate of Stanford, because there were a lot of Stanford alums in this district, and we felt that anything we could identify with people, I needed to do. The fact that I had gone to Arizona and Northwestern were not that much of a tie-in, because not that many people lived here from Northwestern, certainly. I think we put on there—and I'd have to look; I've got a copy of it—is the fact that I had a master's degree. Whatever we felt we could click in, because we realized we had these other handicaps.

Peter, ultimately, walked with me whenever he could, and that was very important. Of course, I always mentioned that when he didn't. If somebody would ask how did my husband feel about this, "Well, of course, he supports me, or else I wouldn't

Family photo taken for Sue's first assembly campaign. (left to right) Kristina, Sue, Kirk, Peter. "...we put the kids up in a tree because my husband was so tall ... and they were so tiny...." 1974.

be running, and he walks with me on the weekends or at night or whenever." Of course, he was gone almost the entire summer, back to Cape Cod doing experiments. He was gone this entire period when I was out walking, so my sister Joan came up and stayed with the kids, and she would feed them, and then when we came back, when we were done, normally it was kind of too late, and we weren't very hungry, but she would have something for myself and the precinct walker, if they wanted it.

I have to say, I have never been in such good condition, walking every single day, mile after mile after mile, and then it wasn't as good, because by then it was so late, I didn't have as much to eat. I lost some weight, and not only was I thin, but I was also strong, because of all the walking.

The coffees—I distinctly remember two of them that were negative, and it's interesting to remember the negativity and not the positives, because there were many that were positive. There was one that I thought went very well, but, evidently— and I cannot believe I would say this— someone claimed that I had commented on a woman, saying she was *just* a housewife. Now, I would never have used that term, and I know myself. First of all, I'm politically smart enough to know not to use that term, because I wouldn't want to hurt anybody's feelings. And it was somebody, I guess I knew. I even remember the person to this day, after all these many years. So I recognized that, whether that was true or not, I called her, apologized, but it was done in a coffee, evidently. I don't

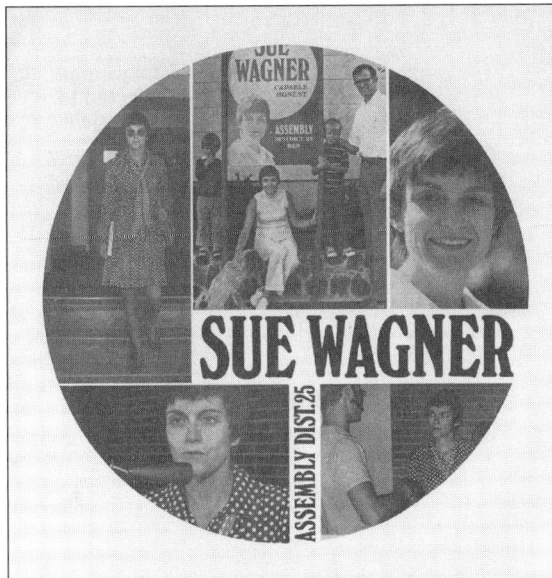

Campaign flyer, 1974.

remember that, and I'm sure I didn't do it, but I didn't think the woman liked me personally and didn't want me to win, probably didn't vote for me, anyway, but she started this little rumble. So it was really hard to put those kinds of things out.

The other terrible experience that happened to me . . . and I don't believe I'm going to name the people, because they are very well known in town—their daughter babysat for Peter and I. We had gone out one night and come back early, decided not to go to the movie, and we found the babysitter and her boyfriend, who was not supposed to be here, in bed. We were *shocked*, absolutely shocked. I mean, we were pretty square people. I talked to her and said, "Look, I'm not going to go to your parents, but if you do this again, if we *ever* . . . then the ax is going to fall." I think we used her once more, and then Peter said he didn't . . . I can't remember all of the happenstances, but *she* decided to take the offensive and went to her parents and said we abused our children, because she realized that if I ever came back to her parents, who, as I said, are well known in

our community today, that they wouldn't believe me, because I did this terrible thing.

So, from her mother's mouth, this went throughout the entire community, and I didn't know it. So I go to this coffee, and someone raises the question, and . . . I know what it was. I did know it, and, I remember, I was sleeping in the basement, because I gave my sister my bedroom, and I got up that morning, and I said I just couldn't go to this coffee, because I knew what was going to happen. My sister said, "You just got to go. You've got to confront it and deal with it."

So I walked into the room, and it was just like, if venom could have come out of these people's mouths and teeth, it would, and I just knew that. So I just brought it up, and it was hard, because what are you going to say? I couldn't go to the place. I was not going to put this girl in jeopardy, so I just said that what they had heard was not true, and I didn't get into any of the specifics that we caught this girl in bed with somebody. I just didn't think that was appropriate. She was a young girl, and I didn't want to ruin her life. I realized she was a brat. I just brought up the issue of child abuse, and then you wonder whether you should do that, because a lot of people might not have heard it.

My sister and I talked about that a long time. We decided that I would have to feel it out when I went to this first coffee, so I did, but after that I never raised it again.

My husband was back in Massachusetts, and then the rumor was that he had left me, and that was the other rumor that went around, that we were getting a divorce, and that's what happens to women who try to break out of the normal confines of being a homemaker and a housewife. When you do that, it upsets everything in the traditional home. So that's what's happened—Pete's gone off, and he hasn't been out. No one's seen him. That's why, when he came back from doing these experiments, he had to go out with me. I remember walking Juniper Hills and all of these districts that were big and spread out, that we hadn't done. They were left at the end, because they were harder to do, and they took more time. We had to drive a car, rather than walk. I think about it, that these are two ways that people who don't want you to get elected can get to a woman.

Through smear tactics.

Yes. The way they can get to somebody, a woman, not a man, is, "She's a bad mother. She's a bad wife." And that's what they did. [Crying] Even now it bothers me, needless to say, but you can imagine how it affected me then. I was just absolutely crushed. It was so untrue, and it was so hard to deal with that sort of thing, which is rumor, and it's just word of mouth, and if anybody was against you for any reason, or had a question—[smacks hands together] that's it, boy! That seals the lid.

Then I had Mary Gojack's husband, at that time, John T. Gojack, who was a story in himself. [laughter] But John T. was involved in a group at that time called Citizens for Private Enterprise, CPE. Now, CPE was huge at this time. It had hundreds and hundreds and hundreds of members, and it was the major business group. There isn't anything comparable today that I can think of, although there may be a CPE. CPE endorsed candidates, was very influential, as I say, and most everybody that was in CPE lived in my district, because of the makeup of my district. So, John T. called me one day and told me—when all this other stuff was going on—that someone at CPE got up and said something like, the one thing we have to do is defeat this pinko, commie, leftist woman in southwest Reno district. And the reason was because I was going after them, many of them, who were

lobbyists, on how much did you give, or to whom did you give it. You got to fill out a form. I think lobbyists should register—all of this stuff.

I was told this by—I want to get back to the tenor of the times—Lucy and Marvin Humphrey; they were really big in the Republican Party. Lucy was the National Republican Committeewoman and had been forever, and was forever after. Everything kind of went through her, and she lived in my district, of course. So I took it upon myself to get to know Lucy, and Lucy was very nice. She wasn't a hundred percent for me, but she certainly wasn't throwing things in my way, either. She did invite me over. I remember she invited Kristina and me over to swim. She had a pool. She lived out on West Plumb. She also introduced me to some big guys who ran Republican campaigns, which, of course, now that's nothing to me, but in those days I didn't know there were people that did those kinds of things for pay—political consultants and so on.

They told me that the issues I was running on were the worst, that I had to get rid of these issues (Watergate, Nixon, the GOP), because they did affect so many people in my district, just as the CPE deal came home to me, that they affected lobbyists, and that's who was in District 25. I told them that was the reason I was running. I wasn't going to suddenly ditch these things, and that I felt really strongly about them, and I was going to continue with them. So they just kind of felt that I was not at all someone who would listen and do what they said, which was good and bad, but they just felt that I didn't have a chance. They told Lucy, "She's not going to win, because she's too dug in, and these are the wrong issues for the district," et cetera, et cetera.

So there was all this stuff going on. My neighbor, Patsy Redmond, who lives on the next street from me, is very, very involved in the Republican Party—young, about my age. I happened to sit next to her at a precinct meeting. I decided I had to go to the Republican convention and some of these things at the time I was running, so I could get to know people. It was pretty scary, because I didn't know anybody. I just went from this precinct, and Patsy, living on the next street from me, was in my precinct. So I met her, I believe, at our precinct meeting, and then went to the state convention, which was in Carson City, and I sat next to her, because they had little signs for the precincts, and Patsy couldn't have been nicer. She took me around and introduced me to absolutely everybody, and Patsy knew *everybody*. She was friends with Frank Fahrenkopf, with Lucy Humphrey, with all these people, and that's how I actually met them. Patsy was just a godsend and such a good support system. As it turns out, she ran my campaign for the senate in 1984. But Patsy was probably the most supportive of all the Republicans I met at that time, because, I think, what I've just described to you, that the political consultants told me, was pretty much the view.

So you have this campaign made up of myself going door to door, now, with other women, and so there are no men, except for my husband. No, I take that back. Paul Page, who's now vice president of the university, and his wife Jeanne walked for me as a couple out in Juniper Hills where they lived, and so did Don and Martha Jessup, and they're both active. I notice Don is now on the board of that theater coalition, the Lear Theater. So Martha and Don walked as a couple, and there were maybe a few others, but basically, it was women, women, women. It was something new, something different, and AAUW was just committed, and all those women came from AAUW, as I said.

So, what you're describing is that you ran into, not only the issue of gender, but also the issue of the political system that was in place, that you were supporting unpopular issues for the people in your district.

Yes.

And you were getting some pressure from all different directions to start changing your mind about these issues, if you wanted to win.

Yes. And part of it was because I was new to the community. As I've already mentioned, that was a downer for a lot of people, but that was for different reasons, but because I was new to the community, I didn't know all these people. So I was a stranger to them, and that was scary. I can understand that. If the Republican Party, the movers and shakers, didn't know who this Republican was, running, it concerned them. It bothered them. They didn't know exactly what she was going to do, who she was, where she came from. They could read what my background was, but that didn't tell them a whole lot, and so, for somebody like Patsy, who was one of those players, to be so supportive of me, was very important, and there were not too many people like that.

Did you start to feel a change, then, in this pressure, once some of the people in the Republican committee got to know you a little bit, and Patsy introduced you around? Did you notice?

No.

No change, immediately?

I don't think so.

You were still the untried newcomer?

Yes. I didn't get any help from the Republican Party. There wasn't any of that, because, as I said, you had Alex Kanwetz, who was a friend of Frank Fahrenkopf's. Well, he was the inside candidate. He was the person that everybody knew. He had just run against Pat Hardy Lewis and lost. Frank was the most insider of insiders, even at that time. So who were you going to support? The only reason some of them even included me in anything was probably to find out more from me, because I was never going to be their candidate.

Besides that, on the very last day, another man files in the Republican primary—Ted Moore, who's a stockbroker in town, who again fits that image of being established. His father had served in the legislature from Ely. He was a native Nevadan, although he was not as inside as Alex, because of Frank Fahrenkopf's friendship with Alex. Ted wasn't that established, in that sense, but he was certainly . . . . We were all about the same age, thirty-four, thirty-five. He was a young man on his way up the business ladder, as was Alex. So, I was the different one, and that's what won me the election. I really have to give Ted Moore a lot of the credit for my winning, because if he hadn't gotten in at the last moment, it might have been a different race, because if you didn't want a woman, you had two men to choose from, and they both were pretty much alike. One's a stockbroker; one's an insurance agent; they're both the same age. Both had young children. We all had young children, but it was different if you were a man with young children than a woman with young children, because you weren't a mother, and you weren't expected to stay at home. I really dealt with that at these coffees by being very up-front about it and saying, "Did you ever ask yourself when Bill Raggio," or I'd use some name in town, "got elected, oh, what's Dottie going to do, now that Bill's not home with these small children?"

Of course, "No," they never thought of it, because it was different, because the husband *was* supposed to go out and do these things, and the wife *was* supposed to stay home and take care of the kids. But I kept saying if you said it enough, maybe you'd have somebody start thinking about it, that maybe, hmm, that wasn't quite fair.

The issues really boiled down to less about policy—hardly anybody asked about issues, about what my position was on education or the growth of the state or whatever was going on at the time—but it was about, "What are you going to do with your children? How does your husband feel about this? I heard your husband had left you this summer." Da, da, da, da, da, da, da. It just was incredible.

I had one man, and I remember exactly where he lived. He opened the door, and he said, "Ah, look at you!" He said, "You're so *little*!" He said, "How do you expect to go down there and take on those big guys?"

I said, "Give me one chance, and I'll show you that I can do it, and then I'll come back, and you'll tell me if I did an OK job."

So he said, "Well, that's fair." I mean, I remember this conversation.

Then I met people who didn't have any clothes on, and I said, "Well, that was when you had good eye-to-eye contact," when you met a guy who was nude. [laughter] And boy, you met all kinds. I thought about it, as the election got closer. Well, the election was the primary, because this was a Republican district. The old saying had been—although it was not old, because Bob Broadbent, I think, was the first elected person from an established district, rather than running at large—that if you won the Republican primary, you were going to win, because the registration was so lopsided, 75 percent to 25, or something incredible. It is still the same today.

So that was the race. I remember the teacher's association guy at the time, Ed Morgan, and Kim, his daughter—she's now head of the legal division at LCB, but he was the head of the Washoe County Teachers Association, WCTA. He told me one time, "What you need is another opponent in the primary." He said, "Can you think of somebody?"

I was just horrified that anyone would think of that. Then this guy announces on the very last day, and I think, "I wonder if the teachers got this guy to run?" I always have wondered that, and I don't remember whether I asked or not, but there didn't seem to be any connection to them.

So that kind of helped split up that vote?

Oh, absolutely. If you looked at the results on primary night, you saw that, maybe, I had two hundred, and each of them had a hundred, let's say, as an example. So clearly, the election could have been totally different, and subsequent to that, I see Ted a lot, because he and I go to the same church, and Ted has told me time and time again—we're good friends—that he never would have worked as hard as I did. I have seen Alex Kanwetz once or twice, and he has told me the same thing. And it's nice, because there wasn't all this bitterness. At the time, I'm sure that they were bitter, particularly Alex, because now he'd lost twice to women—once to Pat and once to myself. He was done. He never ran again. I really never saw them much, except, as I said, I do see Ted and his wife Carol, who, I would say, have become good friends since then. I do believe that is the reason I won.

After that race, then, things were totally different. Those issues never became issues again, because my husband didn't leave me. The kids, as they grew older, both were excellent students and active in sports and extra curricular activities. My daughter was everything at Reno High School: student body this and top golfer and the song leader. All those things they said—they were going

to become juvenile delinquents because mother wasn't there—didn't happen.

Actually, in the next election I had a Democrat no one had ever heard of. [laughter] I remember that Bob Barengo—who at that time was speaker, or maybe majority leader, because he was a Democrat in the assembly—called me right near the end of the election. My opponent—I can't remember his name, but he hadn't done anything at all. So Bob calls me, and I just was so compulsive that I went out and walked my district all over. Even though this guy had no name—no one knew who he was—I still did the same thing again. Besides that, when you run every two years it's good to have people know you didn't do it just once, that you're going to go back, even though you didn't have major opposition, and hear what they have to say, see if they thought you did a good job or not, or whatever. So that would just be my MO ever after.

I remember Bob called me right near the end and said, "Oh, Sue, I just need to tell you that the Democratic Central Committee just voted to give your opponent twenty thousand dollars," or some huge amount of money. "And he's going to . . .

Wagner family with campaign poster, 1974.

everything is prepared. I'm just letting you know this," because he and I were friends, "But there's going to be television going on," and no one ever did that, "and radio, and the signs are already going up. I saw one over by blah blah in such and such GOP district."

I was just horrified. It was just a big joke. He was just putting me on. [laughter] Because he knew I'd just have a fit. [laughter] I said, "Bob, you're *kidding* me! How could the Democrats *do* this!" And da da da da da da.

He said, "Nyah, nyah, nyah, nyah!" [laughter] It was so stupid. Like, "Get real. Do you think the Democrats would do anything for this unknown?"

It wasn't even a race. By the end of my running for the assembly—I ran three times, 1974, 1976, 1978—the last time I didn't have any opponent, but I still walked my district, and some use that as the example.

That was a part of something I felt very strongly about, because I really believe that, as a woman, particularly, coming with the baggage that was hanging around my neck, which was unfair, that I wanted to do the very best job in *every* way, not only by working very hard at the legislature. I got all kinds of awards after the first session. In fact, I remember Dennis Myers, who's still on Channel 8, had done a story about me in the paper, that I had introduced thirteen bills, and twelve became law—or some incredible thing like that—my first session. I also wanted to show other women that, "You can do this and make things work." That was really important to me. So the fact that these personal issues went away and were not as important, that was an important statement for other women and attitudinal changes.

Now, about getting back to women my age, who didn't support me, Ella Grasso, which is a name you probably are not familiar with, at that time was governor of

Connecticut. She only ran one time, I believe. I think maybe her husband died, and he was the governor, and she assumed . . . I don't know. She ran in her own right at one time, and she wrote a book later on, and she was appalled by the fact that she learned that women her own age, and Italian women, didn't support her. I thought it was the same thing happened to me. It was right about the same time, and of course, "Italian women, even more than women in my district," she said, "thought I should be home making pasta." I think I remember her, "Making spaghetti," she said, "and having kids," and doing all the things that her culture said were the kinds of things that women should do.

So that was not an anomaly. It was the time, I think, the fact it was the early 1970s. Things were going on, but they weren't quite sure what they were, and they weren't sure whether they liked them or not. It was unsettling to many women, because things were changing, and they didn't know if they wanted to be part of it, or if they would be part of it, what it might mean to their relationships with men, their husbands. What would happen when women were out there in the work force with their husbands? They were at home, and their husbands weren't working with just guys, anymore, and saying they had to work late at night, and it was with a bunch of guys. They might be there working late at night with men and women, or with just women. All these things were going on, and women just didn't quite know how they felt about it. I personally have always felt, when I've listened to women come before me in testimony at the legislature, that it was a sense of insecurity, that if they did not feel confident about their own relationship, it was sad. I mean, I felt that way.

When I heard women, regardless of where they were from, like the Eagle Forum—we never agreed on anything—if they would come and say these things like on the Equal Rights Amendment that, oh, women were going to be firefighters who'd be living in the firehouse together, and what would they be doing together at night? Or they would be in a foxhole. I kept thinking, "Why do you think that way?" Well, they think that way, because evidently . . . I mean, no one's ever written a book about it. This is just my own supposition, that for someone to think like that, there's got to be some lack of confidence in their relationship with their husband, or a lack of self-confidence about themselves, to feel the *worst* might happen. I felt it was too bad they felt this way.

And the part that you described about not knowing, the women's movement was there, but many women didn't know what was going to be expected of them, either. Would they have to go out and work, if they'd rather stay home?

Yes. There was.

So uncertain.

Definitely, at that time, there was this huge uncertainty, but I would suspect that most felt, later on in the 1970s, as the movement became stronger, there was clearly a feeling that homemaking was just pffft. If you stayed home, you were lower on the ladder of self-respect. And that was not true. You've seen this whole swing come around now, and I think it's now in the right balance.

My daughter-in-law has stayed home, had three children, and now is starting to think about a job, but I think that when people now can make their own decision, it's fine, whatever it is. You have flex-time people now who can divide their jobs in half and work half time, and then split it off with another woman, and they both have families. So they can stay home. You have maternity leave. All of these things just were

not available, but there was this period of time, when the women's movement was *it*. And I'm sure it made a lot of women feel insecure and uncertain. But that was not the way it was in 1974, when I'm talking about my first race. Those issues had not risen to that level, yet. I would say that happened, maybe, two or three or four years later.

It was still so new.

But clearly, that's true, and Jean Ford and I had talked about this with our own children, and the fact that we felt this sense of almost obligation to go out and *do* this thing, *make* this work in the political arena, because politics was our love. But it was something new for women. We felt it was where *huge* change could occur. Clearly, we were right, because you could, by the stroke of a pen, by the change of a piece of legislation, and the governor's signature, affect change that could be applicable to *every mother*—from testing newborn infants, which I did—or for every attorney or for every woman who wanted to own her own business.

At one time in the 1970s, you could not become the sole owner of a business, as a single woman. You had to get your father's signature or your husband's signature. Well, we immediately scrapped that. Mary Gojack was the main sponsor, and Jean Ford and I helped her get rid of that. These things were happening not that long ago—not allowing a woman to have credit in her name.

We felt that this is where you could make the most change, and so just something like that, get a change for every woman who wanted to own her own business. We weren't scary. We weren't there to do damage. We were there to try to do positive things for women. Now, some women might think those things were scary, but if you didn't want to own a business, or whatever, then it doesn't apply to you. If you wanted to own a business, it did apply to you, if you weren't married, for heaven's sakes, or if you didn't want to have your husband sign with you. You wanted to do it on your own. Maybe you had twenty million dollars, and he had a dollar fifty.

So I think that many people misread, potentially, what women wanted to do, but clearly, as a woman, you immediately were identified with women's issues, either for or agin. At that time there is no way to describe how *unbelievably* important the Equal Rights Amendment was. Then, subsequent to that was the abortion issue. But the Equal Rights Amendment issue was the most important. To me, it was more traumatic than the choice issue ever has been.

Mary Gojack (left) with Sue and Florence Lehners (right), celebrating the Nineteenth Amendment which gave women the right to vote.

So, let me understand, because those were not issues that you went into with this campaign. You were going in with open government as your main issue, but you're saying that the ERA and the abortion issue soon became the most important issue?

Well, what I'm saying is that, first of all, ERA became an issue immediately in the legislature, but it wasn't an issue I dealt with in the campaign. Hardly anybody asked me about it. It was an issue I really didn't know enough about. It was just being formed as an issue in my mind, I guess. The World Series was on while I campaigned and I used to joke about ERA standing for earned run average, a baseball term. I sometimes joked about it to disarm people, because I knew about baseball.

If somebody had said, "Do you think women should have equal rights with men?" of course I would have said yes. But if they asked what the amendment itself said, I probably wouldn't have known. By the time I got to the legislature in 1975, 1977—and I don't remember when it stopped—it was *the* issue, the most contentious issue, particularly for women, because it was perceived as a women's issue. It didn't matter if you were the speaker of the house, and you were a guy— of course, you would be, because there's been no woman speaker—you hardly ever got asked how you felt about the Equal Rights Amendment, but as a woman you were front page on all those issues, because people identified that as a women's issue. That's part of the women's movement. They want this. They want to be paid the same. They want to have equal rights here. They want this constitutional amendment. Blah, blah, blah, blah. And so you became the face of it, for it or agin it.

That's interesting, because Jean Ford described a similar kind of thing as what you said. She had very little awareness of it, before she got into the legislature, and when presented, "Do you believe women ought to be paid the same?" it made sense to her, and then everything just kind of exploded, because you were so attached to the ERA, just simply because you were a woman legislator.

Yes. That's exactly right. That is very true. And it was very, very emotional. I was interviewed. *Ms. Magazine*, which was a big magazine at the time started by Gloria Steinem, sent out a reporter who stayed with me, and oh, man, I was quoted big time in that article, which, obviously, other guys got a hold of it when it was published in Nevada, and they weren't happy with some of the things that were said, but they were true. It was, in my mind, a trade-off, that it got traded off for other issues, and that many of the leaders and the men didn't care that much one way or the other, and just could use it.

There were buttons, and probably Jean has said something more about this. I can't remember how many there were who lied, and they had buttons, because, evidently, there were certain members of the assembly who had promised that they would vote for it, and they didn't. I didn't get into that stuff much, because they were people I worked with, and I was very, very, *very* angry, and very upset with people. They hadn't lied to me, but the whole issue was so incredibly traumatic to me. I didn't set these guys aside separately and be mad at them, because I wasn't involved in that particular piece of business, and they're people that I liked, maybe, in a different way on another issue. One of the things you have to learn—and it's very hard when you become *very* emotional and involved with something that means so much to you and to women in America—is to be able to say, "OK. Tomorrow, now, we're going to have postcard voter registration," or something like that, "and then I'm going to have to

work with Assemblyman So-and-So or Senator So-and-So," who totally disagreed with me on the Equal Rights Amendment the day before, because life goes on, even though, particularly with the Equal Rights Amendment, you are building to try to get three-quarters of the states to ratify this amendment, and you're very close. Everybody is looking at Nevada as a potential vote to put in the column and get over the top, and so much happened in the senate with Bob Rose as president of the senate. The powers that be really didn't allow him to break a tie. All of this went on, and so there was just so much politics.

Down in my basement, hanging on my wall, because I have pictures and plaques and things down there, is a telegram from Betty Ford, who was First Lady. It was pertaining to my vote in the judiciary committee, complimenting me on being a Republican and being in favor of the Equal Rights Amendment and voting for it to get out of the judiciary committee.

I remember that Virgil Getto from Fallon was our minority leader, and he got called off the floor in the middle of the Equal Rights Amendment debate. Now, usually, if you left the floor, too bad. You missed the votes. You missed whatever happened. No one stopped for you. But in this case, I guess, someone let him know it was the First Lady of the United States. So maybe we didn't. Maybe we kept right on going. As a matter of fact, I think we did, because he didn't know who it was. He went out to a pay phone, because we didn't have offices in those days. So he went out and trotted back in, and he could hardly wait to get to his microphone to tell us who it was, Betty Ford, who had called him, urging him to change his mind and support the Equal Rights Amendment. He was very proud to say that no set of circumstances, not even the First Lady, could change his mind, and he intended to vote no, regardless of who was on the other end of the phone. "I just want you all to know, I don't care what she said. I'm voting no." And it was a big deal, like he'd turned down the First Lady.

Virgil and I are dear friends. He took my kids out to Fallon after Peter died and took each of them out there for a week, or they could have gone out all summer and lived on the farm and milked cows and had a wonderfully different kind of experience. [laughter] I just can't even believe him saying something like that.

But I guess that's the thing that you learn in politics. I, today, cannot look back and think of someone that I dislike, because there are people I respect, and there are people I don't respect too much, but because we've all been through a lot of different situations . . . and I know that I was far more naive politically than a lot of other players, because I just didn't do all of this stuff and trade off things. I just didn't do that through my entire political career. I have to say, because of that, I do like everybody, because I do think we went through all of these difficult times together. They all affected us in one way or the other, but once you've been through a legislative session or sessions, as I have, and you go through this time, and that's all you work with are the same people day in and day out, and you're up all night at the end of the session, you've got to have this feeling that we have shared an experience that very few people have ever shared. And that's how I look back on my whole political career. I don't think, really, honestly, there are too many people who would not have good things to say. They may not have liked some of the issues I supported, but I really don't think anyone said I ever did anything underhanded. I became a part of the leadership by ultimately being in the majority party and chairing the senate judiciary committee, which was the first time for a woman, and it's one of the major committees, I suspect, second only to finance. So, when I look back, I think I had,

despite these traumatic experiences that happened, a really pretty good experience in the legislative process.

Yes. The question I'm curious about, since we got into the whole ERA, even though you were in the forefront, being interviewed on it and so on, were you also able to keep your reputation as an assemblyperson separate from the Equal Rights Amendment vote, and how that went?

I think that probably to some extent. You mean, in terms of my image?

Yes.

I think that because the Equal Rights Amendment has kind of gone in the background now . . . . I mean, you say ERA. [laughter] I was telling somebody the other day that some of the students in my class weren't even *born* when I was involved in some of these issues, and they probably think it's a real estate agency. I think that after a while that was not part of my image or makeup. There are so many things I could say that I spent *much* more time on than this, like prison reform, campaign reform. But I would have to say that probably, if people were asked, "What do you remember about Sue Wagner?" I suspect they would have said, "She supported women's issues," because they were so magnified; they were so controversial. Then, immediately following that, was the abortion issue, the choice issue.

That was another issue that was just as contentious, just as hard fought, just as visible, and there I was. I had friends who were not in favor of my position on the choice issue, some of them good friends to this day, tell me, "Please, please, please, we know how you're going to vote, but please don't say anything, or don't be on the front page."

I said, "I can't make that promise, but we'll see what happens." Well, it was clear that I felt I had to, because at one point, I was the only woman in the assembly who was pro-choice, and I was always the only Republican woman, if I remember correctly, when I served. I mean, Joanie Lambert was a Republican pro-choice, but that was when I was in the senate. I'm thinking back in these days, and you couldn't let every woman in the assembly get up and speak against it, and not have another woman's perspective from the other side.

So what did wind up in the paper? It was Senator Jim Gibson—who was the majority leader and who was not on the Apostles of Thirteen, but on the next level down, twenty-four, very high up in the Mormon Church—and me. Those were the two people picked out as the antagonists, and we always were, whether it was sex education in the schools or other issues, it was he and I. Needless to say, being majority leader and chairman of senate finance, he had far more . . . . [laughter] I was not in the same league in terms of being able to do much, in terms of getting votes and things, but in some cases, I do believe there were votes, in particular with the Equal Rights Amendment, that if you want such and such passed, I want you to vote no.

Senator Gibson ran again in order to kill the Equal Rights Amendment, on orders from the Mormon Church. I'm going to say that, because it's true. When he died I went to his funeral in Henderson, and I was sitting in a row with Spike Wilson on one side and Nick Horn on the other. Nick was his protégé, a Mormon senator, but we were all friends. Somebody from the Mormon Church came and spoke and said to this *huge* assembly of people who came to his funeral, that they had told him that he must run again for the last time, when he wasn't

feeling very well, on orders from the church in Salt Lake to get this thing killed. And all these elbows went into my side. [laughter] One from Spike, and one from Nick Horn, who said, "You knew it all the time." [laughter] One from a Mormon and one from a non. I always felt that it was *so* important to the church, and the church was *so* heavily involved in politics, particularly in my day. I think that, because the state has gotten so large, that their base of political support, particularly statewide, is not as large.

Now, I suspect it still is, in certain districts, and I get the *Ralston Report*, which is a private newsletter thing, and very rarely will it say that the church has gotten all their support behind Mr. X or Miss X or Ms. X, or whatever, but in my day they were incredibly important. I had been told I could never, never, *never* run for a statewide office and win, because they would mount such an offense against me, because of all of my visibility on these issues that they were very, very opposed to. But at the end of the day, when I was in the senate, one of their lobbyists came up and said, "I really admire you and really like you far more than some of the people who are on our side, because I really can't ever depend on them, and I can always depend on you. You're always going to be wrong!" [laughter]

I'd like to get just some details about the ending of the campaign, the first campaign. Obviously, you won the primary, and then won the general election.

The general election, though, we did go out and do the thirty-one precincts all over again with AAUW, even though I had been told, as I mentioned, that a Republican who won the primary always won the general— because I was such a different Republican, we weren't quite sure about that. The

Democrat was not that well known, but did campaign.

The one thing I will mention here is that the guys who ran against me in the primary really believed that they were going to win, particularly Alex Kanwetz. Well, I don't know. Lynn Atcheson told me that Ted Moore, whom she knew from high school on, told her that he was going to win, because everybody said positive things to him at the door. I just laughed, because I never took . . . if somebody said, "I wish you well," that doesn't mean they're going to vote for me.

I'm curious about the celebration, once you knew you had won your first election at the primary. Tell me what you remember of that.

Well, I remember very vividly that it was practically nothing. Lynn Atcheson, who I had told you, I think, before, I'd asked her to be involved in my campaign, but she was very involved in Jim Santini's first run for Congress. I was invited over to a celebration, a party for Santini, at Lynn's house, but it was very clear the party was for Santini. So I was really very disappointed, to be honest with you, that all these people who worked on my campaign weren't doing anything, and they were a lot of the same people, even though he was a Democrat, and I was a Republican. So anyway, my sister and I went over, and we got to the door, and I opened it, and there was this big, "Surprise!" [laughter]

Oh! It was for you and Santini?

Yes. And so it was just to make me really, I guess, appreciate the fact. It was just a surprise. It was great. And, of course, we had no idea, really, what was going to happen. There were a lot of the same mix of people, but I think Santini's election was pretty much of a sure thing, because mine

was not. But as these numbers came in, as I said, they split, and I was about twice as much. We could see this pattern develop, and so that was the primary. The TV anchors analyzed the elections a lot more, although I have been on television analyzing elections in past years.

So these numbers were coming to the party by television?

Yes, by TV, and it seemed to me they spent more time on that than they do now, I think, and, particularly, because this was a primary, but we could see this pattern develop. So anyway, it was a party with a lot of the people.

And this was at the primary then, that you had the surprise party?

This was the primary. Yes, and that was the big election. The general election, all I remember is at that point what we used to do is go around from one television station to another and be interviewed. My husband was with me, and it was really interesting, because at that time when you walked in, they were just all over you and very, very nice, but if you weren't the candidate or the person who had won, you could just disappear. Of course, my husband could not just disappear, being so big, but it was very interesting, because I realized at that very moment that there would never be a problem with Peter because all the attention was on his wife. It didn't matter to him.

It was OK? No jealousy or needing someone?

No. No. Absolutely not. I didn't think there ever would be. But that struck me at that moment, that it wasn't going to make a bit of difference to Peter.

That's pretty special. Not every partner, male or female, can offer that.

Dennis Myers is somebody you should talk to, because he has the most incredible history of the legislative process and my involvement in it, because he's always been supportive of women, particularly, a woman such as myself. You know him? You know who he is?

I do know him, yes. I know him, especially from working on the history of the YWCA—his mother was involved there—and also with Jean Ford. So I know he's very well informed.

Yes, he is, and he and I go back a long way. We still send things back and forth through the mail, and if I have something, anything that deals with issues, he always calls me to this day. But anyway, Dennis has always said this publicly, that my husband was the absolute ideal for any woman legislator to have, that if he were still alive, he'd be president of the spouse club, or he would know how to deal and talk to men whose wives had just been elected to office, to understand how to deal with it, because he just *did*. I remember Dennis being just so impressed by this, that there was never a problem. Most every other woman, from Vivian Freeman to Nancy Gomes to Mary Gojack to almost everybody, Diana Glomb, oh, my God . . . I've even spoken to Richard Freeman and Diana's former spouse, who was county manager at one time here. But anyway, my point is that almost every other woman I have known has had some difficulty. Their husbands have not been able to adjust to the fact that the wife was the visible spouse. In Diana's case, it was more of a problem, because her husband was the county manager, or assistant county manager. He was in the paper all the time, and he had a

real problem with it, and they ultimately divorced. But at that moment in time, after that first race, I realized, I knew it all in my heart of hearts.

You saw it in action?

Yes. It was a very telling moment, and as I said, other people recognized it and understood it, as well.

Sue, why don't you go back and tell us a few of the highlights that you think of now at this point where you've won the election.

Vikki, what I think I might do is even go back further and make sure that I have covered major events from a historical perspective, as far as myself as a new legislator, as a woman legislator, as a young woman, as a mother, and how those events affected me. Certainly, this would be the case, I believe, of any other woman running for office and being in a similar situation in the country at that time.

So when I go back to the time when I even thought about running in the early 1970s, one of the interesting things was the fact that I was a very young woman, thirty-four. However, I was the oldest person in our delegation from Washoe County, out of eight or ten people. All the rest were men, of course. Excuse me. I was the oldest with the exception of Don Mello at that time, which was very interesting. We had little puppies running—little guy puppies—like Patrick Murphy, et al, who were in their twenties. So even at thirty-four, I was not the youngest, but as a woman I was the youngest, and I believe the youngest in the state, and certainly the youngest with pre-school children. That's an important point, and I believe we've covered that fairly well.

The other interesting thing we have covered, I believe, is the role of a woman,

Sue (center) with Assemblywoman Nancy Gomes (left) and Senator Mary Gojack, January 1978.

such as I've described, which is myself, and how she was treated in the campaign, how people viewed her, how they viewed this woman with these pre-school children, going out and doing something that had not been done in Washoe County, for sure, if not for the rest of the state.

Because you were met with questions about being a wife and a mother.

Oh, very much so.

And that would not happen today.

No. And very few people talked about substantive issues, because *these* issues were, in their minds, the substantive issues. It wasn't education policy or campaign reform or legislative reform. It was the age of my kids, my husband, our relationship, our marriage, et cetera, which were very personal and private things, but then, I guess, if you look at today's political campaigns, people still want to muck around in personal lives. So maybe not a lot has changed. I don't know. [laughter]

But I also would point out here something which I don't think we've talked about. I *have* talked about the fact that I was amazed that women my own age— same gender, same age, or similar—were not in support of me. I did talk about that, but I did not, I believe, talk about the fact that interest groups who interviewed candidates, who endorsed candidates, if they did not want me to get elected, it seemed to be that the way you attacked someone such as myself, was to demean them in their role as a mother and as a wife. There wasn't anything else. I had no record. There was nothing. I had lived here a relatively short period of time, so they *could* make it an issue that I hadn't been a real Nevadan, that I didn't understand the issues. That was used, but the way that people who did not want to see someone such as myself elected, was to attack me that I was a bad mother, and that I was a terrible wife, and our divorce was imminent. Our children would grow up to be juvenile delinquents. I think that is an extremely important point to make, because men did not have to deal with this issue.

As I mentioned, many of the Washoe legislators who were elected that year in 1975 were younger than I, but they didn't get asked these kinds of questions, because a woman is perceived differently, particularly if she is a mother. Then, if she's not a mother and not married, oh, my! Heavens to Betsy! A single woman who was thirty-four probably would have *never* been elected, because there would have been suspicions about why she wasn't married and why she didn't have kids. That would have been an issue in itself. I do not believe a single woman who was thirty-four could have been elected. I think the reason I was elected, because at least I had the semblance of normality about me, that I was married, and I did have two children, even though that was in itself unique, but at least it seemed "normal."

Today the other issue would not be an issue. I know women who have been elected in this state who fit that category. There are questions raised—sexual preference is what I'm talking about. But it has not lost an election for anybody that I know of.

There's been major progress in that twenty-five years, from the time you first ran, to today, in terms of young women with children no longer being greeted with

that as the main question, "What are you doing as a wife and a mom?"

That's correct.

They might still be asked it, though?

They still may be asked, and I know there are young women who have contacted me, who have run. I don't think I should mention their names here. Some of them were Democrats, and I think, probably, in the perspective of this book it doesn't make much difference who they were, but they have called and asked my advice, not only about the issues and how to handle themselves in a campaign, in a debate, for example—maybe they were running for a statewide office—but they had young children, and how that all fell out. Did I feel good about that, looking back on it? Now, as my children are entering their thirties, did I have regrets, and so on? Actually, they didn't ask me that. I might have brought it up to them. They felt there would be no problem, because they've seen other women do this with young children and move along in political careers, if you will.

I have mentioned before that anyone has to start out at a relatively young age—except for our present governor, as we're speaking in the year 2000. Governor Kenny Guinn—this is the first office he ever ran for, and he was elected to the top spot. I do not believe in this year that a woman could do that, that a woman could run for governor right out of the chute, never having held public office before, and get elected governor. Wouldn't happen. We haven't even seen a woman governor, period, in the year 2000, even if that woman has gone up the ladder of a political career. It hasn't worked out that way.

So, today the inequity isn't about personal life as much as it is about having paid your dues, for a man doesn't necessarily have to pay his dues, but a woman still has to pay her dues.

But a woman can pay her dues and still not get there. That's my point. Even despite that, that a woman has paid her dues. But that probably may not be fair to say. I'm thinking about the governor's race, that there have been extraneous circumstances, such as Jan Jones having served as Mayor of Las Vegas, the largest city in the state, running for governor twice in successive elections. However, coming in late, running in a Democratic Primary against the incumbent—those are hard, hard obstacles to overcome for anybody.

Frankie Sue Del Papa certainly has paid her way up the political ladder, dropped out, because in her mind, she wasn't going to get financial support. She did this twice, once in a U.S. Senate race, and then just the next year for the governor's race, same thing. But she did climb up the political ladder. I cannot address the issue of money, because it boggles my mind, and I have said this to her personally, because her polling data looked very, very good, and I have to believe that at the end of the day, when it got down to the end, that people who she didn't think she'd get money from would contribute to her, because she might win! [laughter] And my gosh, you want to be on the side of the winner.

However, obviously, she made a decision that she didn't want to take that chance. So there are those inequities that still exist today, whether one works their way up or not, but there certainly are great inequities in terms of what you have said, that a woman could not just jump into and run for the U.S. Senate or the governorship as their first office. Even lieutenant governor, going down the ladder. I certainly had a lot of experience before.

Lorraine Hunt, who currently is lieutenant-governor, was on the Clark County Commission, a big job, much more important in my mind than being lieutenant-governor of the state, basically, running Clark County, the largest county. And the county commissioners, they are everything. They're the airport authority. They're the water authority. They're every other bullet—unlike our county commissioners here. So she had experience. Rose McKinney James, who ran against her, had never served in public office before, but had been head of one of the largest state agencies in government.

However, I think part of the reason that she didn't win—I think Lorraine Hunt was an excellent candidate—here were two women running against each other, which was terrific. We knew a woman was going to get elected. Either it was a "D" or an "R." They both were, in my mind, very qualified. Even though most of my friends supported Rose McKinney James, I knew Lorraine Hunt, and I felt, considering what her job responsibilities were—economic development and tourism—she would do a crack-up job, and I believe she has. But Rose, I believe, partly because she had not run for office before, and she was running for a statewide office, didn't understand some of the skills one has to have, in terms of debating on television, in terms of making a decision on who to run the campaign. What issues should I focus on? What's this job really all about? Some of those questions, that when one has run before, by the time they get to that top job, they know.

Another distinction, however, and this has just come about in the last week or two, is that there's a new book out called *The Anointed One*, which is written by Jon Ralston who is a political columnist, and he's carried both in the Las Vegas newspapers and in the *Reno Gazette-Journal*. He just published a book by that title, and I've called the publisher to get a copy of it. It's about how our current governor was elected, and it really focuses on behind-the-scenes people and how they were able to get Kenny Guinn elected. I haven't read it, so I can't speak to it, but I have read a few clippings. I've talked to Jon about it myself, and I don't think any woman in this state could get that same set of people behind her for governorship at this time.

I must say, though, that some of those people were behind me for the lieutenant-governor's race and urged me to run again when I was thinking about not running—or after I decided not to. Because I worked well with Bob Miller, they wanted me to serve again as lieutenant governor. Now, if I'd done that, and if I had felt miraculously well four years later, which would have been, I guess, in the year 2000, would I have run for governor? If I felt well, I probably would have. Yes. But would those people who supported Kenny Guinn have said, "Well, we're going to support Sue Wagner, because she's been an excellent lieutenant-governor, worked well with the governor, despite party differences?"

"No, we're not going to. We're going to support this guy over here."

Don't know that. I do know that Governor Kenny Guinn called me early on and asked me if I was running for governor and cleared the boards of any other Republican that he felt might possibly run and that he might have a primary race against. If I'd said yes, I don't know what the answer would have been. Don't know that. But to his credit, he did call, and I'm sure he did that with any other potential opponent, as well.

It leaves a big question mark, doesn't it? Because I think there were a lot of people saying Sue would be the first woman governor.

Well, I think they thought either Frankie Sue or Sue. I think that they felt it possibly could be the two of us against each other—just as Lorraine Hunt and Rose McKinney James. People would have said, "Well, at least we would have a woman governor," in that case.

That could have been very possible, but I'm really trying now to get back to my main theme, which I have a tendency to digress from, for the mileposts along the way in my life, trying to put a handle on some of the main things women confronted that men didn't have to, or men had to and women didn't have to, but I couldn't think of any of those. Maybe you can get the important people behind the scenes to help you in a campaign, but women can't. [laughter] Maybe that's one. Maybe there are some if I switched it around.

So there's this progress, but there's not an end to the fact that women still can't do what men can do in this state.

Well, they still have not. When you look at it today, there are only two women governors, one in New Hampshire, who's a Democrat, and one in New Jersey, who's a Republican. Christina Todd Whitman is not running again. She chose not to run for the U.S. Senate, about the same time Frankie Sue didn't, and I do not know why. I get clippings from the New Jersey newspapers, gaming clippings, of course, because I asked the New Jersey regulators if we could exchange clippings, so we'd be able to keep up on each other's business. That's really the only connection we have with New Jersey in that light. But Christina Todd Whitman chose not to run. She was hands-down the front runner, and it just really concerns me.

So, I'm thinking, trying to go through what we've already discussed, in some ways, of some of the obstacles that women had to deal with that men didn't have to, during this period of time. One of the things I'd like to comment on at this moment is that, as you've pointed out, there are some significant improvements that have occurred, but in my mind, we're *not yet there*.

I think we will even see more headway made this coming session, the year 2001 of the legislature. We have a minority leader woman in the senate, Dina Titus. She has been in that position for a number of sessions. This session we will have the first woman majority leader in the assembly, which is *very* significant. There's a big difference between being a minority leader and being a majority leader, and it will be Barbara Buckley—she's been waiting for a couple of sessions here. Richard Perkins will become speaker. Joe Dini will bow out of that position, and Clark County will take over, but that will be, again, a movement up the ladder of our power, and there's nothing wrong with women having power, but that's another whole subject I would like to talk about at some time. But now we're talking about women and what offices they can actually seek and how they're treated, how they're able to raise money or not raise money, or have the credentials, or not, to achieve whatever they have staked out. And I still think there are differences.

Another thing I'd like to bring out, is that women are identified with issues that are perceived to be women's issues, whether they want to be or not, whether they have any interest in them or not, whether they really have a position on them or not—they are *hung* with them. I say it in that way, because sometimes it's like a moving train coming at you, and there's no way to avoid the train, because you're going to get hit. [laughter] And that is a fact.

It's something you don't think about, "Oh, this is a man's issue. Oh, I wonder who's going to lead the fight on this *male* issue."

Every issue is a human issue, but there are certain issues—clearly, when you talk about abortion, you could say, "Well, *that* really is a woman's issue, because we're talking about a woman's *body*."

"Yes, but it's a family issue."

And if you look at the number of organizations that fight abortion, they're mainly led by men, not by women.

Based on the family issue?

No, they're not. In many ways, they're not. They're based upon life—when life begins.

What women should do? OK.

The fact that the fetus is a human being. That's what you really hear. I don't find that to be a family issue, in a way. I find that to be an issue of life or death, an issue that would make the same argument of, not euthanasia, but at the other end of the spectrum, does a person have any right to make a decision on when they should take their own life? The answer for them would be no.

So I respect people who have the same philosophy and are consistent, but it is very clear that Operation Rescue, and many of the same groups that do not want women going into Planned Parenthood or abortion clinics, are led by men. Women are behind the ropes, carrying the signs, but they're mainly men. So I can't really say it's a totally woman issue, because it is a woman's body and her health and her life, but it also is, if she's married—or, obviously, there was a male involved here. Hopefully, it was a significant other, to say the least, that they had some conversation about it, or she and her doctor did, or whatever, but there are very few issues that I really believe are women's issues.

I'm going to say that the two biggest in my lifetime as a legislator were the Equal Rights Amendment and all the choice issues, because they were *so* confrontational, *so* volatile, that I've never seen anything like them. They really marked you as a liberal or a conservative, even though they had *nothing* to do with finances, and that's how I define whether you're a liberal or a conservative, whether you watch out for the money, and you don't spend things that you don't have. Are you a conservative fiscally, or not? And personally, I'm a conservative in my mind by supporting issues such as pro-choice, because I don't think government should be involved in our lives, and that is a very conservative approach, but because I took those positions—I was for the Equal Rights Amendment, and I was for the choice issue—I was perceived as a liberal, even when I served on the money committees, and I was much more conservative than some of the men, who are perceived to be the most conservative in the Nevada senate. That was not ever registered. It was these two issues that defined me forever as a *way* liberal Republican, and I don't see it that way at all. But anyway, those are very important, and they defined not just me, but other women, as well, whether they were for or agin the issue, but more so if you were for it, and if you were outspoken on it, of course, then you were clearly identified, as you would suspect you would be.

As you're talking about this, and how this defined you, and the fact that there were "women's issues", did that come as a surprise to you as you went into the legislature at that time? Do you recall?

Oh, when I first entered the legislature, absolutely, yes, because, of course, they weren't even issues then to me, because the Equal Rights Amendment—I didn't even really address it very much in my first campaign, because it hadn't registered with me on the radar screen, yet. So when I got into it, and it was not just one session; it was a number of sessions. Then my position was rather firm, and I realized, because of all the press attention given to it, that it was

a big issue and certainly confrontational, because of all of the letters and phone calls and things I received, and the people who came to testify; but in terms of how it branded me, no, I had no clue.

You didn't expect that?

No. Never. And it didn't really occur to me until later on.

You realized how it had happened?

Yes. And why. Why it happened, what caused it, what caused this liberal tag wrapped around my neck. But in terms of getting back to the issue of when I ran with small children and then being successful, I did talk about the fact that if groups didn't want you elected, they went after you as a woman and as a mother, because that's where they felt you were the most vulnerable. That is really a sad comment to make in my mind, that that's all you can do, and then to make things up is even worse.

One of the problems that a mother has, having been successful, is then what child care is available? This is a problem today, even, for women to go into the work force—what do you do about child care? But in early 1970s, there was hardly *any* child care, and my husband and I couldn't afford it, anyway, but it was something clearly I had thought about before I ran, because I didn't run to lose; I ran to win.

In fact, I thought about this the other day, and I was commenting on it to somebody, that the reason I felt comfortable in running for the legislature when I was so young with small children, is that it was a part-time job. This was something that was a selling point in my own mind, my own head, and with my husband. It was every other year. It was biennial sessions. If it had been annual sessions, I would never have thought about it. I'll be honest with you.

That's why I chose to run for the state legislature, and not the city council or the county commission.

Even today, I was just asked a couple months ago to run for the county commission, and in speaking with a friend of mine who is on the county commission, she was telling me how busy she is. Why, she's got to go here and there; she's on so many different other committees, besides just going to the county commission meetings. I really didn't think about it seriously, anyway, but the point is that they are much more time consuming, in terms of the spin offs—on city council, as well—than the legislature. You go, you do your thing, then you can pretty much choose whether you want to be on interim committees—and they were in vogue at the time in the 1970s—or if you want to go out and do speaking engagements and that kind

Family photo for Sue's campaign.

of thing. That's your choice. If you want to win again, then probably you'd have to do some of those things, just like happens in any other position, but to me, I really didn't understand the implications of running again. I had not ever thought of re-election. I ran to get elected, and that was about it, at that time. Never even talked about it. I was so apolitical, that I didn't think about that.

But anyway, that was a big selling point for a woman, for a mother, because it was part time. Now it's more time constrained, because it's 120 days, as of a recent constitutional amendment, but in the 1970s it could go on and on and on. Whenever it got done, it got done. And as the years went on, it did go on and on and on. Way past the Fourth of July. But it was a positive, or at least a subjective, reason for deciding upon that race, rather than others.

It's an interesting point that child care in general was not readily available in those days, in the 1970s.

Well, I think not, Vikki. I can't really speak definitively to that, because we really didn't look, my husband and I, because it was just too expensive. So we had worked out an arrangement with my next-door neighbor, who took in foster children when we first moved into this house. She had foster children, and certainly she did before we moved in here and a few years after. So I asked her if she could take the children during the day until my husband came home, or I got back from Carson City, and I had no idea what time involvement there would be in this job, at first.

I talked to Jean Ford, for example, to Mary Gojack, to get some feel for it, but they were in a different capacity. Mary didn't have children. I mean, they were much, much older. I even think they might not have both been living with her at that time, I can't remember, but Jean was even away from her domicile. She lived in Vegas, and she had a room at the Ormsby House. So that wasn't even a concern to her, how much time she spent. She spent whatever it took and then walked across the street.

So it wasn't an issue. There weren't really any other women I thought I could talk with. There weren't any others who were in the same situation. So I didn't know that. But anyway, that's what my husband and I did. Now, it worked out pretty well, but my daughter, particularly, addresses a lot of issues today. I've really not talked to my son about it much, and he, maybe being a boy, just has never offered anything about how he felt about his mother being in the legislature, whether he wished she wouldn't have, whether he wished she would have stayed home, particularly, after their Dad died. Of course, they were so young when I ran that they really didn't understand the implications of what I was doing, whether I told people that we had a family meeting, and they all supported my running, which was true, they really didn't understand what that meant. They didn't understand it until they saw a campaign sign up, and they realized it when they saw my picture on a sign. I think I mentioned this, I don't know, that my husband built all the signs himself in the garage?

Oh, did he? No, I don't think you mentioned that.

We made them. We bought a piece of plywood, and he was a cabinet maker—this was his hobby—so he felt he could make the signs, even put a picture on them, silk-screening them to some extent. We bought pieces of plywood. He cut them; he sprayed them. Well, we did have some work done by a silk-screener place. I take that back. But there's still some yellow paint stains on my garage floor that are remnants from my first couple of campaigns. But I'm digressing here. I'm talking about child care. And I do

want to get back to the involvement of our family in the campaign.

Yes, because they wouldn't have understood at those ages. And you didn't know exactly how much time it was going to take?

No. But when they saw the sign, and they saw Mommy's picture on the sign, that was my point. They didn't see any other mommy's pictures on signs—little Jerry across the street, or Jimmy who they went to school with, or Catherine, or whomever. They started asking me questions like, "Where is their mommy's sign?"

I told them that their mommy wasn't going to have a sign, because she wasn't doing what I'm doing. Then maybe they thought this wasn't as great an idea as they initially thought, because then they realized not only wasn't it Jerry's mom or Catherine's mom, it wasn't *anybody's* mom. There wasn't another mom doing this.

So then, this meant they were going to be different.

Yes, exactly. Then they realized that *they* were going to be different. Anyway, I think that even though the children were very young, they did get the fact that there were not that many mommies doing this. I'm not sure if I told them I was the only mom, but I made it clear to them that they probably wouldn't see any other mommies' pictures on signs. Well, first of all, a lot of people didn't have their pictures on signs. But even if there were other mommies . . . there weren't any others, let me put it that way. So they weren't going to see that. And that was probably in their mind, five minutes of concern, and then they went on to something else. Went out and played or something.

But when the campaign was over—and I did address this before, I'm sure—the angst

I went through, and the real anguish I went through in making a decision whether to run or not, because of the kids—my husband was very, very instrumental in encouraging me to do this and in convincing me that he could take care of the household, his job, and the kids. I really can't stress this too much, because every time I wavered, he was there to say, "What are you worried about? We can do all this."

The things I worried about were just so miniscule. They weren't the big things. They were small, little, silly things. Like, would this affect their lives? [laughter] We didn't talk about that, because people didn't discuss things like that. No one thought about big issues like that. There weren't books and things written by doctors and psychologists saying, "If you do this, it might affect your child negatively. If you do this, it might affect your child positively." There just weren't those things available, so we didn't even think about that.

But anyway, in terms of the child care, that was important, and I thought it went as well as could be expected. There were always kids to play with, having other children around, and that was a positive. Sometimes they weren't always the kids you would choose for your children, maybe, to play with, because they were foster kids, and they'd come from a variety of different places. Some were older, had already developed, I don't know, behavioral problems. But that's what you dealt with, because that's the only option you had, or you didn't do it. Clearly, those things maybe didn't show up ever, but they were things my husband and I talked about as time went on.

My daughter, today—and I might as well bring this up now—tells me, not to a great extent, that that wasn't the best deal in terms of her growing up, and she didn't like it. She wished I hadn't done it. We'll get into that probably at some other point, as well,

but I'm just talking about the child care arrangement.

Yes. But at the time it seemed to be going OK?

I guess. I'm sure there must have been times when she told me how much she didn't like it, and the food wasn't any good, and all that sort of stuff that you hear.

I also may have said this, but I did recognize that when I stayed in Carson City, when it got towards the end of the session or whenever, my daughter would scream and cry and really throw a temper tantrum if I went back on a Sunday night, say. My husband would always tell me, "She stops crying the minute you get in the car and go around the corner. Don't worry about it." And I did, and I could hardly wait to get to Carson City to call and talk to her and find out how everything was. He'd say, "She stopped crying, just as I told you." Whether that was true or not . . . . And it was, I know, because now my daughter tells me it was, but it made me feel so guilty. I cannot tell you the guilt I felt. I have talked about this before.

You had this struggle, or at least I did, and I know Jean Ford felt the same way, to some extent, that we really felt at that time that women needed to be in these positions. Women needed to be there, or these issues that we cared about would never be dealt with by men, because they would not be on their radar screens. Yes, the Equal Rights Amendment would have come up, because it was a Constitutional Amendment. They had to deal with it. But would they have heard another side? Would they have dealt with domestic violence? Would they have dealt with the Sole Trader Act that only allowed men to own businesses? Would they have dealt with all the sex discrimination that was pervasive throughout our Nevada Revised Statutes?

Probably not—because they were all led by women.

So, I think, because of the women's movement, it was a real tug for me to not run again, let's say, once I got in office and saw what could be done, versus, if my child said, "I don't want you to ever, ever run." And I really didn't get that sense, when I think back on it, that there was this big lobbying effort at home not to do this again. I think my kids really did pretty well. They should be complimented highly on being able to survive in probably not the best of circumstances, in terms of the ideal, where you could have a nanny come into your own home and do all those things. That just wasn't the set of circumstances.

Clearly, I was told by some of my neighbors that Peter sometimes didn't get home until nine or ten at night, and the kids might not have gotten fed until nine-thirty or ten at night. But they should have been in bed hours before that, so maybe he was more of a concern than the kids. [laughter] But that happened when I was home, too, so it wasn't anything out of the ordinary, but I do know the kids would talk about, "Oh, Daddy just went into the refrigerator and took all these leftovers and put them together in a pan and cooked them up, and that's what we ate." [laughter] That did sound pretty yucky, even to me. One of my neighbors did confide later that Peter did sometimes come home rather late, and that's how I knew. He didn't tell me. And I don't even think the kids did, really.

I have to say, there was a positive to all of this, and I really believe this, particularly in light of what happened. [long pause . . . crying] Peter had a chance of being a father, of having to deal with his kids, seeing what it was like raising them, being around them, participating in their activities, because very honestly, I really don't think he would have done that to any extent, if he hadn't had to. He became a Little

League coach, was Indian Guides medicine man, was the WJBA coach, which was Washoe Junior Basketball Association. Of course, he was an all-state basketball player when he was in high school—all-territory because Alaska was a territory at that time—[laughter] and hoped to play basketball at Stanford, actually, when he went there, but he was too small at six foot seven. And also, he just couldn't keep up with it, with an electrical engineering program. But he did do those things, and I think that knowing the commitment he had to his job at DRI and the hours he spent and what our life was like before this occurred, and even when I wasn't in the legislature, that his work came first, I really felt. I told him several times that if he didn't wake up, that the kids were going to grow up, and he's going to turn around like we hear so often, "Oh, what happened to them? What happened to their life?" [long pause . . . crying] So he was forced to play a part in their lives, and I say that not in a negative way, because he was a . . . . [crying]

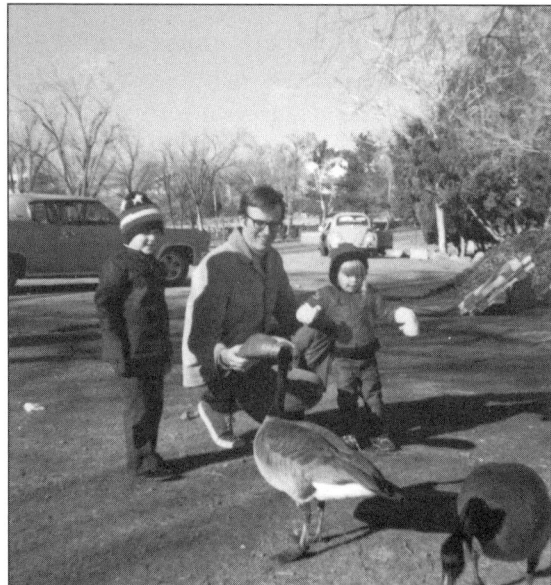

Kirk, Peter, and Kristina feed geese at Virginia Lake, Reno.

Peter coaching youth basketball. *"He became a Little League coach, was Indian Guides medicine man, was the WJBA coach . . . ."*

Well, because he died so young, he wouldn't have had that chance any other way, to have that really close time with them.

Wouldn't have had it. And I do think, even if he would have had it later on . . . and this happens to so many men, that all of a sudden, when they get more manageable, or they're doing things that *they* like to do, like, "Oh, well, now we can go skiing together, or we can go hunting." And Kirk was just getting to that age, which is, again, very sad that they did not have that opportunity to do that more together, but that happens with so many dads, I think, today. It happened then, probably will happen in the future. Hopefully, things have changed to some extent, but until it comes to a time when they, either in their own

careers they feel secure or . . . and I understand all this. I'm not making judgments about it.

Right, because there's pressure for them to make their next mark.

Right. Even with Peter, he had to publish, he had to do certain things, had to get patents, so there was all that pressure. I understand that, but you've only got one family, and you're only going to have these two children, and all of a sudden . . . and I can say this for myself, too, that I missed a lot by being in the legislature, and giving up time that I could have spent with my kids.

But in this case it was good for Peter to have that experience and opportunity, and for even my kids, who to this day do not remember their dad very well, and they wouldn't have remembered him at all, if they hadn't done these things. [crying]

The other thing that you mentioned was that it was almost equal pulls, in that you felt concerned about your children and leaving them, but you also could see the things that needed to be done for women, and there was no other way but for some women to get out there and do it, to make some changes in how women's issues were being dealt with.

I did feel that way.

Jean Ford talked about that same sense of responsibility.

Yes, I know, because Jean and I talked about that when she was going through the oral history process with you, as well, because we got to thinking about things, experiences we had had together, and I did feel that way. There was this kind of dichotomy and this chasm that existed between those women who did something different and those who didn't, at that time.

Now, I think we've come to a point where women don't have to feel that they have to carry the gauntlet for women to make inroads in the legislative process, in the political process. That is not to say, as I've already addressed, that women don't still have a way to go, because they have not reached that top spot in very many cases. How few women there are in the U.S. Senate. How few women there are as governors. I've already addressed that. How few women there are in Congress. Yes, the numbers creakily go up, maybe, slightly, but I don't believe there have ever been more than three women governors at one time. As I think back, I think that was the case when Ann Richards and Christina Todd Whitman were governors, and I think there

was Joan Finney of Kansas, who was not a strong woman leader and was not supportive of women's issues, at all. There were three of that gender, I believe, at the same time, but that's it! Now, there are two. We've slipped back one, and it's out of fifty. That's not what you call high numbers.

It's not fifty-fifty, like the population is, pretty close to fifty-fifty.

No. And nothing is close. Actually, Nevada has a pretty good percentage of women in the legislature among most states in this nation, proportionately speaking. Actually, it's one of the top five, or was in the last couple of sessions. So that's good, considering we are what you call a conservative Western state.

Whereas, of course, California has two women senators, and Maine has two women senators—U.S. senators, that is. Both their entire delegations are women, but that's pretty unheard of, and they're both ends of the country, one a New England, Republican-oriented state, but liberal; and California—hey, that's all over the map in terms of political philosophy—but they're both Democrats, so they kind of balance each other out.

But I think that in getting back to the pressure on someone such as myself, or someone in that same position—and of course, Jean's kids were older, too. Mine were at a very formative age, and to be honest with you, I didn't understand that at the time. There were not, as I said, books on parenting. The only book out was Dr. Spock's book. That was the *only* book on the market that dealt with children, and that was babies.

And how to raise them.

How to raise them. There were not books about, "Well, if you play music to them, and Beethoven, particularly, da da da da." Or the fact that, if you don't hold them and nurture them by the time they're three, then their entire life is—forget it. [laughter] Then there are some things that are ridiculous, but there are a lot of things that are very good, that any mother, if you don't read them today, you should be spanked. You really should. Because you should assimilate all this and then see what you think is important in your own judgment. But there's a lot of stuff out there that I think is really very informative for mothers.

It wasn't available to you.

There wasn't anything available. I think every mother does the best they can. I think to most extents you'd want to believe that mothers do the best they can. We all hear the old adage that there are no courses on how to be a parent. There are no classes on how to become a good mother. Absolutely true. Parents do the very best they can, but there are certain things you know you shouldn't be doing. In this case, this wasn't one of them, but I did feel, when my daughter would throw herself in front of the door and cry and carry on and wished I wasn't gone, that clearly, wow, talk about killing you inside, that was it. But then I had, on the other hand, my husband, who was telling me, "She's just trying to pull your strings, which she obviously is doing very, very well. Forget about it. We're getting along fine. Everything is going great." I don't believe he *ever* had a complaint, during that entire time. So whatever was happening, I think, in retrospect, was good, that he did have a role. He did play that role that I think was needed, because I don't think it would have happened. I can't say that he wouldn't have been maybe a Little League coach along the way, but it was very. . . .

But to be responsible for the kids every day after school, that type of thing would not have happened.

Well, at least when he came home from work. But he was there, and they realize that he was the main man. He was the main person in this family. It wasn't Mom always all the time, anymore. But child care was important, and we did the best we could. Now, getting back, I guess we can move on to the first session.

I'm interested in, yes, the first days of the first session, what it was like for you.

Well, I think, even before then, getting to put how you're even perceived before you even step inside the legislative building as a newly-elected woman even puts you in a different class. I was labeled—and I didn't know this at the time—as, "Here comes another Mary Gojack. Here comes another Jean Ford." So, they already knew who I was going to be, even though that was not at all true. But again, getting back to the issue, we ultimately supported the Equal Rights Amendment, and we're all three pro-choice. So again, to a large extent, those were defining issues, and issues similar to that, but those were the two big ones that put you in boxes.

So even before you started, you were not seen as Sue Wagner.

Absolutely not.

You had to somehow separate yourself.

I was going to be another Jean Ford in the assembly. Then Mary Gojack got elected to go down to the senate, and to top it all off, I was assigned to Mary Gojack's seat in the assembly, which was seated next to Jean Ford. So that just coupled the feeling that

Jean was going to tell me everything to do, that she was going to clue me in on everything.

Actually, Jean did hardly any of that, because she was such a serious person, that when she sat down at her desk, she totally was consumed with what was going on on her desk or getting prepared to vote or reading bills or whatever, because in 1975 there were no offices, very few offices for anyone. The desk on the floor was our office. So everything happened down there. There were no phones for us. We had to go use phone booths, just like everybody else.

You look at the legislative building today, and it is absolutely palatial—it really is—because I've gone through many other capitols, and most of them, the legislative chambers are in capitol buildings in most places in the country. There are very few states that have separate legislative buildings, period, but certainly ones, after we just had a remodel, that are as elegant as ours is. Everybody has staff. Most states don't. Well, I can't say that.

Now, they have separate offices?

Everybody has an office.

Offices, staff, phones?

Oh, yes. Plus, they all have their own secretaries. I never got a secretary, or anybody to help me, until 1987, when I became chair of senate judiciary committee. That was what—twelve years after I had been in the legislature?

Yes.

Never had anyone who worked for me, except an intern from the university. Never had any space of my own. You were a sitting target down there on the floor. By having no place to go and just shut your door, you couldn't even leave anything on your desk, because everybody would rifle through it and read it. It could be a fellow colleague. It could be a lobbyist. It could be anybody. But the point is that Jean sitting next to me, because everything did happen down there, really spent very little time with me. I could have used, probably, more from her as a mentor, than she offered me, to be honest with you. I had to ask her if I really wanted something.

I remember one very good piece of advice that she did give me, but, as I say, this is one of few that I can remember. It wasn't like there was this conduit of information coming over to me, at all. There was a very controversial issue dealing with collective bargaining of teachers. I'd been endorsed by the teachers' association, because I really pushed them to do it, to be honest with you, in my first campaign. I assumed, because I was a former teacher, that I would get their endorsement, and I had a great interview, but for some reason, they were going to endorse Alex Kanwetz, who I've mentioned before in a previous session. This was in the primary, and as I have commented, I believe, the primary was my race, because it was a Republican district, and we had these three guys running. So I kind of pushed the teachers, when I found out I might not get their endorsement to do that, and so there was this big bill, and this was *their* big bill. Collective bargaining always is a big issue for them, what issues they can go to on their contract, but I represented this very conservative district, and didn't like unions, didn't like collective bargaining.

So Jean, representing a university neighborhood, a UNLV neighborhood, immediately knew. Besides, she'd been there one previous session, and she was much more liberal than I.

And this was one point that she made for me. The fact is she had made up her mind on this bill right off the bat, for the reasons that I've already told you. So she didn't have any mail on this subject, or hardly any. My desk was so full of mail, pro and con, that it was incredible. Of course, I had this policy that I would respond to every single letter I received, which today is no big deal, but in those days it was, because we didn't have the staff. Maybe if you came up with a form letter, you'd sign them and send them out, particularly if you had hundreds and hundreds. You couldn't write all those people personally, but you tried. In those days you had to try. But anyway, I kept saying, "Look at all this mail I have!"

Jean said, "That's because you have not made up your mind. You're going to be one of the last people to decide how you're going to vote. So people are going to pummel you with pros and cons, because they think you're still moveable, one way or the other. So, if you can make up your mind early on, particularly when it's an issue as important as this, do so. But if you can't, then obviously. . . ."

I said, "Well, in this case, I haven't even heard the discussion on the floor of the assembly." But clearly, I understood the issues, because you listened to the lobbyists

Sue with Senator Jean Ford (left).

on this side and the other, and that's pretty much what you were going to hear on the floor, I thought, and that was true. That's generally what happened. So that was one good piece of advice she gave me, but to say that because we sat next to each other, and because we were women, and because we were members of AAUW, or that we were interested in campaign reform, that we were then going to be exactly alike . . . or because Mary Gojack had urged me to run for the assembly, which indeed she did, and I think I spoke to that, and that she was a Democrat, and here she was encouraging a Republican to run. Clearly, that must have meant she had quizzed me pretty carefully and felt that we were very similar, or she wouldn't have gone out and gotten any Republican to run. I can't tell you whether that was true or not, but, clearly, as I told you, my mind on the Equal Rights Amendment wasn't even established at that point. Although I did hear about it, I'm sure, from both Mary and Jean at that time. I can't pinpoint that I did for sure, but I suspect I did, but pretty much everybody knew they had different districts, and the districts were quite different, in terms of the composition of the constituency, and that's who you represented. So I don't think there was any particular push to support one thing or another.

Now, you just mentioned the ERA, and originally we were talking about the teachers' collective bargaining, so was it the same for both of those issues, this philosophy that if you haven't made up your mind, then you're going to get tons of mail? Did you experience the same for both of those issues?

Oh, well, there would be no comparison in terms of the kind of input you got on Equal Rights Amendment, versus collective bargaining. It would be national in nature, on the Equal Rights Amendment, because it was an amendment to the national Constitution.

You had even more.

You have to get thirty-eight states, and we would be thirty-six or thirty-seven. So the entire nation was focused on Nevada, but I cannot remember at that time, because I was on the committee that always heard the Equal Rights Amendment, the judiciary committee, and it seems to me, by the time the hearing came about, I had made up my mind that I would be pro-ERA. So, at that point, the answer would be yes. I wouldn't have received hardly any mail on it, because I was *very* identified, right from the beginning, of being pro-ERA, and, in fact, was always asked to defend it or speak on its behalf.

And to go back, I want to just touch on this comment about this bit of advice that Jean gave you, before we get back into how things turned out for the teachers.

Well, that's irrelevant, how it came out.

OK. The important thing was this tip. And it almost sounds like a way to control the amount of input that you're going to have to deal with, to make up your mind early. Was that what she was intending?

No.

Because, what I'm thinking is that somebody might read this and say, "Well, it doesn't make any difference if we write or try to give information to our legislators, because they're simply going to make up their mind early, and then they won't have all that mail."

No. But that's a good point. I think I would never have read it that same way,

but, of course, you're hearing this for the first time. No. As I mentioned, Jean had represented a district that had a lot of teachers in it, and you support your constituents.

She'd also voted on a collective bargaining bill in the session before. She'd been there before me. She had established a record of sorts. The Equal Rights Amendment doesn't change. It's the same language. You either support the Constitutional Amendment, or you don't. So once you decide, if you change, then you don't have much of a philosophy of equality—if you can become pro-ERA, and then the next session not, and that did happen to quite a few people. Well, to me, that says something quite different than, "Hey, I want some more input on this." And as far as another issue, you really didn't receive a tremendous amount of mail, unless it was a big issue like those that I've identified, and at some point, you've made up your mind, so you don't get that kind of input. You might get people who berate you for never listening to them, or they think you never have heard their side of the story, and they say, "Won't you please change your mind, even though you voted that way three times before?" Maybe the fourth time they'll get lucky.

But, in terms of most issues, you do listen, and as your constituency grows . . . when I became a senator, then my district was quite different than this very, I'd say, conservative Republican Assembly District 25. Then I represented from the Oregon border, Lemon Valley, Sun Valley, all the way to Incline Village. Well, you had all political spectrums, and all economic bases, and so then, your view can become more broad.

Then, when I represented the state of Nevada as lieutenant-governor, I didn't vote in that same way, but if I had to vote in the case of a tie, or what I might have taken on as causes, or if I'd been governor, for example, then you represent the whole state. So it becomes different.

So her comment wasn't a matter of how to control things, but just simply that if you're at this stage of the process, where you've already made up your mind, you won't have all that mail to deal with.

Right. And clearly, she herself had already done this before, been there, done that, so to speak. Maybe it was another issue for the teachers to put on the collective bargaining list, but she was very supportive of collective bargaining, and was very supportive of union issues, as a philosophy, versus management. So this would be a normal thing for her to come down on.

Now, I was not. I was more management oriented, and even probably am today. And that's a marked difference between myself and Mary Gojack and Jean Ford. So, you see, people labeled me, and they were wrong. But they didn't know that, and they probably really didn't care, because they just assumed that this was going to be another one of "those women."

A carbon copy, and that you would always vote the same, and you would be identical to Jean, even though you were quite different on other issues.

I think at one time, Jean and I, or somebody, had analyzed our voting records to see, and there were very few differences, but there were very few differences on most everybody, because most every bill passes, by the time it gets amended and gets out of committee. You read in the newspaper today there are very few bills that pass eleven to ten, or nine to three, whatever it adds up to. That just doesn't happen very often. And the issues that we did disagree on were pretty big ones. They were like collective bargaining, or they might have

been some other issue that was very appropriate for my district and very appropriate for her district, but our districts were very different. So, what she was saying was that as you develop a pattern and a history and a record, then this will not happen to you.

It becomes more manageable then?

But while you're debating this and deciding and being torn between, very honestly, being endorsed by the teachers, and really kind of asking for their endorsement, but yet representing a management more oriented district, then that was a struggle for me.

That's a political lesson. That's a political dilemma that people face. After a number of sessions, when you're in the legislature, pretty much people have an idea of probably where you're going to come down on major issues, because it may be labor-management. I can't think, right now, of any other major kind of classes. Well, I can't think of any other large groups of people that would be diametrically opposed to each other all the time. Maybe the governor's budget, versus state employee pay raises or something of that sort. But that, again, is a union-management issue, in the same sense. I can't really think of another class, but generally speaking, as time goes on, although each issue is different, and in some cases—and we'll use labor-management— even representing a district that had a lot of labor representation in it, I might have voted with management on one bill, and in another totally different bill, on the other side.

On the merits of the bill itself?

Based upon what the policy was of that particular issue. Anyway, that's a good point.

Wrapping up, the perception was that you were going to be exactly like Mary Gojack and Jean Ford, because of a number of different things, and you were going to start to tell me about that.

Well, one of them was because I did sit in Mary Gojack's old seat, as I mentioned, and she moved on to the senate, and the seat did happen to be next to Jean Ford. I have discussed one of the pearls of wisdom that I can remember Jean ever shared with me. I'm sure there were more than that, but that's really the only thing that stands out. And because I think we very honestly were not members of a conservative religious organization or group, I was not probably going to be perceived as a major conservative Republican, because I ran on campaign reform. That was in itself not a conservative Republican issue. I was told not to do that, if you remember.

I talked about consultants telling me that I wouldn't win in my district. I didn't pay attention to them, which said I must be headstrong, or not controllable. The other thing was I went right ahead and campaigned on those issues, which obviously did resonate to some extent with this constituency, and those other things— that I was running while raising small children, et cetera, et cetera—all set me out and apart from other women. Other women, as I've explained, did not run. Even Mary and Jean were in an older age bracket than me, and they didn't run until other things had been done that were expected of them in their lives. So there was something about me that was going to be different, and if I was going to be different, I must be like them, because they were different, too.

So, less probably to do with issues at that time, but suspecting, probably, the issues would be similar. Sometimes they were; sometimes they weren't. But it was this,

probably, I'd say, control issue. I wasn't going to be as controllable—more of a maverick. Let me use the term maverick.

6

FIRST LEGISLATIVE SESSION—1975

Tell me how long it was before you sort of felt like you knew your way around the assembly that first year, a completely different experience for you.

What was the first day like? That was a big, big deal—to be elected to the legislature, first time out, under what I'd call obstacles that I had to overcome, and I think they were obstacles. There weren't a lot of positives, when we think back on it, except that I think that people, when they met me, believed me and knew that I was being sincere, and they believed I'd probably be very honest. Those are big positives, but that's because I did hard work in order to meet them face to face, so they could have that impression about me.

The first day was a big deal. My children all got dressed up. My husband was with me. I had some friends, and we had lunch, and we took pictures, and it was *very* long, and the poor kids—it was just awful for them, because I had no idea what it was going to be like, but it dragged on and on and on and on. Still this day, it takes really all day. If I'd known that, I probably would

have taken them down for a short time, and then taken them home.

It's a lot of ceremony, is that correct?

Very, very ceremonial, and a lot of waiting around for committees to go out and report, and a committee must be sent to the governor's office and tell him that we're ready to do business, and then that committee and other committees have to go to the senate and say we're organized and ready to do business, and vice versa, and all of this sort of thing. It doesn't move at a rapid pace without breaks. There are a lot of breaks that go on, and that's what drags it out. It takes pretty much a day. They begin at noon. So pretty much it extends to the end of the afternoon. For little preschoolers, that was just awful, and it could well be that Peter finally took them home, I don't remember, but it was very exciting to me.

The fact that I really didn't know my way around, even in the building—I remember the first time I ever went down to the legislature, I had to ask somebody,

"Which side? Where was the assembly chambers?" [laughter] I had no idea. So, needless to say, I was not like Jean Ford, who probably had the whole thing scoped out before. [laughter] Probably had her seat picked out and everything.

Now, I was just sort of new to the whole thing, and I think I would have felt rather presumptuous, to be honest with you, to have gone down before I'd been elected, for sure, to even see what the legislature was like. This does go back in time, but I did have an opportunity to go down and testify, because AAUW—if you remember I told you how much they were involved in my campaign—decided that since I was the legislative chair for AAUW, I would go down and testify on legislative reform, which was a committee Joe Dini chaired on how do we make the legislature more efficient. Jean Ford was on that committee. I went down, and this was right before I decided to run. They thought this would be really good. Maybe I'd already decided to run, I don't remember, but it was early on, anyway, that AAUW thought it would be good for me to go down and testify, so that some of these legislators could see me, and then I could maybe meet some of them, or whatever. So, I did do that, and, of course, Jean Ford did see who I was, and I had been told to look for her, because she was instrumental in this issue, and this was one of AAUW's key issues. It was on campaign reform, but also legislative reform.

That was the first time I'd been in the building, but that was like on the second floor, where the hearing was held, and I know I didn't go down and look at the chambers, because I didn't know where it was until I'd come back. As I said, I think I would have thought it was presumptuous to assume that I might be there, and clearly, after I'd been elected, it wouldn't have been, between November and January, but I didn't do it then, either.

So, this was all pretty exciting stuff, and in those days, even to go down to the senate—I just didn't go down to the senate side—I mean, they were, like, whew! That was the upper house. The senators didn't have any problem coming down to the assembly, but anyway, I felt that way. In fact, there was one woman who served in the senate, and I would have to look her name up right now, but I saw her one day, and I didn't even know who she was, because I'd never been down to the senate, and she had on this long skirt. I remember she wore that all the time—long dresses or long skirts, very formal. Clearly, I knew Cliff Young and some of the people like that from Washoe County, but many of them I would not have recognized, except from pictures hanging on the wall. Maybe that was just me, that I thought it was too presumptuous to go down and say, "Hi. Guess what? Here I am! The answer to all your prayers!" [laughter] So the whole first session was a huge learning curve, a huge learning experience.

Oh, I have to say, Jean did help me in terms of giving me some advice on what committees to serve on, what committees did, and even though you might have read the general purpose, what bills really got sent there. Would that committee be of interest to my district, for example, or not? What were my particular interests or my background, and that kind of thing? But once you got a schedule down and so on, pretty much, it became like anything else. The more you do, the more familiar you become with the procedures and the rules and things, and the process is pretty much the same, over and over.

My routine is also varied, because each issue is different. That's what I think is so exciting about it, is that each bill has a different perspective and affects different groups of people or individuals, some positively, some negatively, and you have to look at it from many different angles. The first session, everything was exciting and new, and many times I got snookered by very good friends of mine, including my friend Joe Dini, who I just reminisced with this about him on the phone not long ago, that he had sent me down to the senate on a campaign bill that he had.

I don't think I've mentioned this, that I was known as a little, old campaign reformer, and see, the press loved that. I have to say, those were issues that were just geared to the press, because those were issues that appeared, and they certainly were opening up the process, so the public—the people who elected you—could find out what was going on, learn more about who was funding your campaigns.

Lobbyist registration—lobbyists were taking you to lunch, dinner—how often? How much would they spend? What did they buy for you? All those kinds of things. Clearly I had no understanding of that, and also I'd been a reporter at an earlier age, so I had a real appreciation for their role, as well, so that was another positive for me, in terms of my relations with the press. I always returned every call, was always available, regardless of whether I wanted to talk to them, or not. Maybe I didn't want to revisit the Equal Rights Amendment, or something, again one more time, but I did. All those things, I think, were building up a relationship that was beneficial to, hopefully, my constituents, the public—by reading the newspaper—and myself personally.

And so Joe Dini sent you on this?

Joe Dini sent me, because I was noted as this campaign reformer, so he had this bill in that dealt with an ethics commission, which he wouldn't pass. Ultimately, my bill from the senate side became the ethics

commission, which we now know, but he wanted part of it. It passed the assembly, because . . . . No, this wasn't in 1975. Maybe it was 1977. I could be wrong. Doesn't matter.

The point was that you got snookered.

The fact was that I got snookered, and sometimes that happens to you when you're not keenly aware of everything that's going on, and he sent me down to testify on it in the senate. Well, I found out why. Because they hated it. It was never going to go anywhere in the senate, and he just didn't want to go down and listen to them all beat up on him, but thought that probably it would be good experience for me, to put it nicely. [laughter]

One of the things that it would make you do, if you were an attorney, was to disclose who your clients were. To this day that is not our law. And everybody on this committee was an attorney: Thomas R.C. "Spike" Wilson, Norman "Ty" Hilbrecht, Melvin D. "Mel" Close Jr. These are names that some people will be familiar with. Lots of attorneys. And of course, they zeroed right in on that. I said whatever it was that I said, but, clearly, Joe knew full well this never had a prayer's chance.

So I was very pleased, however, you see, that he had handpicked me to go down and do this, because he was the speaker, or whatever position he was in at that time, maybe majority leader of the Democratic Party, see? I should not have been surprised that he would pick a Republican to go down? [laughter] Oh, no. No, no, no. I was young and naive. [laughter] But I learned a lesson. So you chalk up those experiences.

When I talked about the press, that was a positive and a negative, because I had so *much* press, literally speaking, in my freshman term. I'm not kidding you.

Probably, if everybody didn't dislike me, I'm surprised why not, because I'd have full-page stories of me and the kids, me and Peter— full color—or that I was selected as outstanding freshman, or something, but on and on and on, where I would think that if I were my age, or I came in at the same time, I would really resent it. And they would say, "Well, she just is a woman. She's getting all this attention because she's a woman." That probably was true to some extent, because this was an unusual thing, not that it was unusual for, necessarily, a woman, because you had Mary Gojack, you had Mary Frazzini, but nobody with little kids. And I did have all of this legislation that was very attuned to the public. I didn't think about it at the time, that I could understand in retrospect, but I'm sure there were some people who felt that way, but that did not play out to a very great extent in my life. Certainly, as time went on, it didn't, because I'd built up real friendships, I believe, in the legislature.

One of the things you said is that you ran on campaign reform. How successful were you in getting bills introduced and passed that first session, or within the first few sessions?

Well, I can't exactly remember, but I think I introduced fifteen, and thirteen passed. I do know that O'Callaghan took one of the bills I had introduced, where I had a disclosure of campaign contributions of fifty dollars and above, and he added another zero onto it and made it five hundred dollars or above.

Made it five hundred and above?

Right. Rather than fifty. I believe that passed. That was in the state of the state message, I think. And that wasn't quite what I had in mind, but I'm going to say that's still the law today, but I'm not sure about

that, because, since I haven't been in the legislature, I'm not too sure. A lot of things have changed, in terms of disclosure.

There were various things on legislative reform, and lobbyist registration is one that did pass. You didn't introduce that, but you had a comment about lobbying in general.

Well, I guess the only bills I actually attempted to get drafted and introduced my first session were things that I had had some experience with, because I'd already been through a campaign cycle. And since I really hadn't any experience with issues related to lobbyists yet, in terms of whether they should register, and what that was all about, that wouldn't have been something I would have tackled.

Because why? Because you didn't have experience?

Because I hadn't had the experience, so it would have been presumptuous of me. In fact, some people thought it was pretty presumptuous for me to come down and try to suggest that even in campaigns you should file more times than you did already, or that you should even have a figure, a number, that you should disclose. But at least I'd been through a campaign before and had run on those issues and felt that those were very legitimate. Because I hadn't had any experience on how lobbyists operated and such, I didn't think that would be appropriate, although I did sign on, because it fit right in with exactly what I was talking about. I would have never been the prime sponsor and had it drafted, and there's a distinction there, because clearly, if you're asking for a drafting to take place, that's going to be something that you feel very important, not that you wouldn't other things, but that somebody's contacted you about, or you've experienced yourself. In this case, since we're talking about campaign reform, clearly, I had that experience and felt that those things needed to be changed, and that's what I ran on. I told my constituents that's what I was going down there to do, so, needless to say, I did have those introduced.

Some of them didn't do very well, but that's not that surprising, because the legislature really didn't want to do anything more than they absolutely had to. But because it was after or during Watergate, then, clearly, there was *much* more focus on it than there ever would have been, and none of these things would have ever seen the light of day, if not for Watergate. One of the main reasons I ran was because of Watergate. So it all goes together, that it made very good sense for me to introduce these things, because that's why I got involved in the first place. That's what I said I'd do, so I did it.

Whether it passed or not—many times you have to keep on trying, and later on we'll see that some of these things ultimately did pass. It might have taken me a session or two. Sometimes, even when I got to the senate, I think I was still fighting some of these battles. In fact, in one case, I believe that after I left the senate and became lieutenant-governor, another senator took it on, and he got it passed, because he was a Democrat, and the Democrats had more votes, and they were more supportive of it, I guess. I don't remember why. But anyway, all the work had been done. The point is, if you feel strongly enough, you keep on trying, and you try to get it done.

In that case, I do remember that at one time, there was no way to tell, really, if you did not have a series of disclosure statements. Somebody could give you all this money after a primary, or after the general election, when the election cycle was all over, and you'd be able to pay off your debts. If you were able to pay for radio

spots—I never had any of that stuff—but if you used those, then they could contribute to you after the fact, and there was no form for you to fill out then, so no one would ever know that special group x, whether it was the teachers or the chamber of commerce or whoever, had given you a lot of money. Well, the chamber doesn't usually give money, but somebody, you know.

Or an individual business.

Yes, businesses that gave you money, say, the Associated General Contractors (AGC) or the labor union. We'll take those two, because they're usually the opposite on issues. Either one could give you money at the end of a campaign, and the way the law was written then, there were no disclosure statements. So what I attempted to do through my years in the legislature, was to have you file one before the primary, and this is the way it is now, and that's why you see these articles in the paper as it gets closer to election, how much money has been contributed to the mayor or to Senator Blank, or whoever it may be. In fact, they just had them in the paper not very long ago, and they showed the difference between Senator Raggio and his opponent, for example. But his opponent is really unknown, and Raggio is the majority leader. Besides that, when you're in that position, you tend to give some of that money to other candidates that you want to win, so you will be still the majority leader.

But anyway, the point is that now you have to fill out these forms before the primary, after the primary, before the general, and after the general. So there is no way, hopefully, that there isn't at least a reporting period before and after every election cycle. People, if they're interested, can read the reports in their newspapers— and very often they don't print them all— or they can contact the secretary of state's office or whomever and get these reports sent to them. If they're interested they can find out. And that was one thing that I thought was very important.

The attempt at lobbyist registration was the same kind of thing, to have them register, and then, I think, at some point, to have them say how much money they spent and upon whom it was spent. Believe me, they fought that very hard, particularly, some of the older, more established lobbyists, because they came from a time when none of that was expected. This was all new to everybody, new to the legislative process, new to lobbyists, to have to disclose anything at all.

Really, I have to say, it was not only because of groups like Common Cause that had public scrutiny at its heart, or the reason for being, I guess, but because of Watergate. That sort of opened the floodgates of, "We better take a closer look at what's going on here." It wasn't that Richard Nixon didn't fail to file a disclosure statement. It didn't have anything to do with the specific points. It was that it shed more light on what was going on in government. "My goodness sakes, look what's going on!"

And the need for more knowledge about what was going on in government.

Yes. Yes.

Because when I looked at that list, and it said the lobbyist registration bill had passed, and some of these other things did not pass, I was interested in why that was possible in 1975. It was just interesting to me.

Well, I think one of the reasons was because, first of all, legislators are voting on things that affect them. They're not lobbyists. I mean, they are lobbyists. They're the ultimate lobbyists—we lobby our own bills among ourselves—but we're

not lobbyists from some group x, and that's the person who comes to mind. This didn't come to be the definitive answer now on the reason one did or one didn't, but . . . .

But it was the beginning of the change.

Yes.

Common Cause, Watergate. It was the beginning of changes.

Oh, yes. Probably, if you looked in the 1993 session, there wasn't a bill introduced on any of these subjects, I suspect. I don't know, but I would suspect that's true, because Watergate happened in 1974, if I remember correctly.

Yes, while you were campaigning.

Yes.

Some of the other topics I jotted down: some health issues, some equity issues, mobile home property tax, children and licensing preschools, and so on. Were there other things about that first year that you'd like to go into?

I can definitely tell you about the preschool licensing. I think this is what happens when you go back too far, but it seems to me as if in 1975, then, my kids would have been in preschool, and we talked about my next-door neighbor. Obviously, preschool for little kids isn't all day, so that's where they went after, but they went to Trinity Montessori Preschool, which was in the basement of Trinity Episcopal Church. It was the only Montessori preschool here, which is a different philosophy of teaching. There were several bigger names preschools here in town. One was Merry Berry, I remember. Almost all my friends had their kids there. It was like, "This is where your child must go." The other was Child Garden, and they're both still around, and I think they're both still run by the same people, actually. Then there was Trinity Montessori, and I went to Trinity Church, and I heard very good things about it, and I liked the whole concept of Montessori. I went down and talked to the head of it, who was Barbara Krueger. She ran Trinity Montessori School for a very, very long time, and it got an excellent reputation as the years went on. I don't know how long it had been set up when I took my kids there. It wasn't nearly as established as the other two I mentioned. There were other preschools around, certainly. I know there was Noah's Ark, which had a good reputation, which was up in the northwest part of town, but anyway, I chose Trinity Montessori.

Now, Barbara Krueger, the head of Trinity Montessori School, came to me and talked to me about the fact that there was no licensing that went on with preschools, that some schools could call themselves a "preschool" and use the word "school" in their name, when all they were were babysitting agencies. Drop your child off. They would be given an apple. Bring their lunch. And they might have coloring books and things, but there was no school going on. She felt that was misinformation, that the public wasn't getting the correct information. This all sounded reasonable to me, so I talked to the two that I mentioned, maybe the three, and they all said, "Absolutely. Totally, absolutely right."

"And would you support it?"

"Yes."

So that's about what I did. [laughter] Oh, my! Talk about a buzz saw. Every other "preschool" that used the word school in their name, was adamantly opposed to it and flooded the hearing room. When I walked in I could not believe the room, the education committee room—I couldn't even hardly get into it. It was packed, and there was hardly anybody in favor of it. I

cannot remember the Department of Education, who, of course, had no jurisdiction, at all, over this, because there was no jurisdiction. They didn't have anything. I'm not sure if they supported it, or not. See, these are other lessons I learned, that when you introduce a bill that affects an agency, you better make sure you talk to them first and get them to buy off on it, or you're going to have opposition on your hands, because they're going to say, "Well, it's going to cost us so much money. We're going to have to add two staff people," and on and on and on and on, whatever they want to say. That may be true. I'm not saying it isn't, but these are lessons that one learns, and I did learn from this.

The hard way?

See, these come out as we talk about other issues, and there may be a million things that I'm forgetting here. Anyway, I remember a friend of mine, Jean Stoess, who was a Washoe County commissioner during this period of time, appointed by Governor Mike O'Callaghan, and then ran for that office later on. Jean, for some reason, was down there with me on this day of the hearing, and she'd bought some Tootsie-Pop lollipops to suck on, I guess, while I was listening to all the people against it. She thought that very clever, since we were discussing this, and she thought it was so funny that I dealt with preschools, or something. She had been a journalism major and did press releases for me. She edits books now, actually.

One thing I did learn, another step, that if you're going to send it to the education committee, you should try to get them to be your co-sponsors, because they're the ones who are going to vote on it. I think all of them had. And when they heard the testimony, boy, did they take notice! [snaps fingers] I mean, I wanted to jump right out of the window. I had to explain, well, I didn't know, because it was like, clearly, a hundred to one. What it told me was that the ones who legitimately could say they were teaching the kids something weren't afraid of having to go through a process, because there was a process involved, and I can't remember exactly what it was. I'd have to take a look at the bill, but there was some process that the Department of Education would come in and determine whether you actually were teaching the kids anything, or not, and whether you should be called a school. Then there was another term—I don't remember what. There were three different terms, I think.

Three levels, so to speak?

Yes. One was a school.

Day care?

Day care, probably. And maybe there were just two. I don't remember. I thought, hey, if day care was what you wanted, what you needed, fine. There was no kind of elitism, "But one is better than another." It's just that one is doing different things than another, or, financially, you could afford one or the other. I suspect Merry Berry was more expensive, but sometimes this was not the case, as Humpty Dumpty. I remember that was one of the names— Jack and Jill, Humpty Dumpty. [laughter] We had a great discussion of this on the floor. I remember talking about all the names, because everybody kept getting in and saying, "I've got a bunch of telegrams on Humpty Dumpty, Jack and Jill, Little Brown Bear, Red Riding Hood, Snow White. [laughter] Who *are* all these people, Assemblywoman Wagner?! They were all saying to vote no on your bill." [laughter]

Anyway, there's another lesson learned, that a) you better get the agency, and b) you better not talk to . . . but I had no idea. I just talked to the ones I had called and

contacted, because those are what I was interested in, but I didn't know that ones that had school in their name, there wasn't anything really going on there, until wow! You could tell. And I was, maybe, cynical enough at that point to realize, if you had such a problem with this, there was a reason why this group over here didn't have a problem, but all these people over here did?

Of course, when questioned, they said, "Oh, of course, we do this and this." Well, when the heads of these three or four got up and talked, it was clear to the people on the panel that there was a huge distinction, but they didn't want to go vote. It was such a buzz saw, and the numbers were so against it that it died. I believe that must have died in committee. [laughter] I'm sure, it must have died in committee. [laughter]

Yes, it did. It died in committee. So, yes, amazing.

It was always learning experiences. I felt that if I introduced the bill, I was going to do every single thing I could to get it passed, because I never introduced a bill, if I myself could not vote for it. If one of my constituents called me and asked me to introduce something dealing with motorcycle helmets or let's say, kids, instead of at sixteen being allowed to ride a moped or a motor scooter, having it reduced to fourteen—if I don't want my son or daughter doing that, then I would say, "No, I can't introduce that, but I'll give you the name of somebody else who might be more interested." But I explained to them, "Yes, I am your legislator, but I can't vote for that. I'll be voting no, if it should get to the floor. So I'm not going to do that, so here's somebody who I think will help you." So I felt very committed, and I certainly didn't sit around and laugh about it that day. [laughter]

Probably not.

I was probably pretty devastated, [laughter] to tell you the truth, because I took this stuff pretty seriously, particularly my first session.

At some point did a similar type of legislation go through, or not?

I don't think so.

It never has?

I don't think so.

They can use "school" if they want to?

I really cannot answer that question affirmatively, but I don't think I reintroduced it, because I think I went back and talked to the schools I named, and we decided that it was not going to happen, at least not the next session. I think after that I didn't do it. It didn't pass, to my knowledge, while I was in the legislature, because I would have gone and testified on it. If it had been someone else's, I would have testified for it. So, I really don't know if that is the case today.

One of the others that seemed interesting was the gender equity type of thing, that wages, hours, working conditions be uniform among employers, without regard to sex. And that would have come in the same year that the Equal Rights Amendment was there in front of you, too, AB219 in 1975.

And who was the main sponsor of that? Basically, what you're reading from here, I might say, is coming from the Legislative Counsel Bureau. They were able to provide us with a copy of every piece of legislation that I sponsored, either as the main sponsor or as a co-sponsor. Being a main sponsor

means you are the first person on the bill. That meant you most likely got the bill drafted. It is in your package of bills that you're introducing that particular session. Although, sometimes that is not the case, and we read about that in Jean Ford's own life story, that she sometimes had to get other people to introduce bills, although she might have gotten them drafted. But normally that is the process, that you are the main sponsor. That's what that term means. You could be a co-sponsor, because you support the idea or the concept of the bill. So all of the things that we're referring to now have come from the Legislative Counsel Bureau, Research Division. I want to give them credit for this, in that they have sent to us a list of every bill that I've either been a main sponsor or co-sponsor of, from every legislative session from 1975 through 1989. We're looking at 1975 session right now. [pages turning]

I'm picking out some that were significant.

We're just talking about some that either give a general tone of the session or ones that were of particular importance to me, or that I introduced as the main sponsor, or some that I was just a co-sponsor of.

This one, that I was a co-sponsor of, did become law. And what it says in the title is that it makes certain provisions on wages, hours, and working conditions apply uniformly to employees without regard to sex. And your question to me was do I remember much about it, because it did pass, and my answer was no. When I read it, I find that I don't remember anything about it, and if you look at the title that we're reading here, it doesn't even add up, because, clearly, there's nowhere in this country where wages, hours, and working conditions are comparable. Just take the word "wages." We know for a fact that wages are not comparable anywhere in this country. We keep hearing in this presidential campaign, whether it's seventy-three cents on the dollar, seventy-five cents on the dollar, but when these bills were introduced, it wasn't even anywhere close to that. It was less than fifty cents on the dollar, and so that is not a true statement, so somehow this bill means something other than what it's saying here in its title. And that in itself is a lesson, because sometimes the bill gets amended significantly. I'm not saying this one is, but the title doesn't change, so it may not identify exactly what's happening in the text of the bill itself.

OK. And then we did spot several that you wanted to talk a little bit about, and maybe we'll just take them in order. AB54, which was regarding the issuance of degrees or diplomas.

Yes. That was, again, introduced in my first session, and this was called the "Mail-Order Degree Bill" for a short term description of the bill, because there were people putting Ph.D.'s and law degrees and other degrees on their walls, when they just paid a certain amount of money and wrote off and got the degree back in the mail, and this fell under the jurisdiction, again, of the Department of Education, I'm sure. Nobody really could not support this bill, although there were groups that came down and testified against it, basically saying that we were mislabeling them, and so on, that they required certain things of people in order to get these degrees, and I suppose there may be still some of that that people might say goes on today, that it's less challenging to get a degree under some set of circumstances than under others. I don't know whether that's true or not, but in this case there really was a diploma mill, that you could send away and get some kind of a degree. So that was clamped down upon as being not in the best interests of the consumer, because, of course, they

believed, if someone called themselves a doctor, whether they were a real doctor of philosophy or a doctor of medicine, hey, they could have just paid for that.

Just ordered it. Another one that was significant was AB85, about advance notice.

Yes, this was a bill that just was the precursor of things to come, dealing with the open-meeting law, basically. This bill did not pass, and I was not the main sponsor, but I was a co-sponsor. It did pass, however, in the assembly. Let me also add this caveat, that sometimes bills pass one house and not the other, knowing full well they're not going to pass the other house. The house that introduces them, or the person that introduces them, if they can get one more than half to pass it, people will say, "Well, I'm going to vote for this, because it looks good, and I won't be against this idea, but I know it's not going to go anywhere down the other end of the hall." And that does happen. That's the political process. It goes on today, goes on in Washington, goes on everywhere, I'm sure.

This bill did die in the senate, but this was a forerunner, as I said, of the open-meeting law, which we hear a lot about all the time, and also provides for public access to meetings and records thereof, basically meaning that minutes should be available to people, and minutes should be taken. Minutes weren't even taken in some instances. I have to say that Nevada really did a pretty good job in this area, however, in terms of record keeping. Not all of us have secretaries, but all the committees did, and, depending upon the expertise of the secretary, of course, depended upon the validity and the value of the minutes. Some were very brief; some were very good. Some were used for Supreme Court decisions, to base cases upon, in terms of what was the record, public record. Some couldn't be used, but some states didn't do that. And we certainly have seen progress in this state, in terms of the Internet and having access to public meetings.

And then you wanted to talk about AB106.

AB106 was a bill that came to me from some constituents, and, basically, it requires the confidentiality of customer records and information obtained by banks and savings and loan associations. In other words, the people could not go in—including district attorneys—and look at somebody's financial records; and this was part of the problem, I think. The bill did die in the senate. It did pass the assembly, that without just cause, to go in and look through somebody's financial records tells a lot about a person.

No. I remember why I did this bill. I received in the mail a bank statement with canceled checks belonging to somebody else, and without knowing, I opened it up, started going through it, and realized this wasn't mine, but, to be honest with you, I went through the whole thing, and I got a *very* clear picture of this individual. I got a picture of magazines they subscribed to, because in this bank statement came their checks for, obviously, subscriptions to magazines. Their renewal was obviously up. A lot of things that weren't as important, where they ate, where they may have stayed, where they traveled, how much they spent, how much they had in the bank at that time. There were a lot of religious affiliations.

I remember, I made a list of everything from this one bank statement that I learned about this individual. Needless to say, I called the bank and told them mine went someplace else, and I'd like mine back, and I think that this should go to this individual. It wasn't even like my next-door neighbor. Needless to say, the minute I saw that, I wouldn't have gone through it, but I did, and it doesn't matter why I did. I don't know

if it was because I thought this might make an interesting bill—probably not, at the time. But anyway, it *did* turn out to make an interesting bill, because that's the reason I introduced it, because I realized how much somebody, anybody, could learn about another individual from looking at bank records.

Then I was approached by the district attorney saying, "Well, we have to do this," and I realized that in many cases—and I don't want to really pinpoint in on the D.A.'s here—but people had access to bank records without a whole lot of documentation to show why they needed it, what the purpose was, and just to get it, because there might have been a trial going on, or something else. Somebody might have broken the law, for whatever reason, I don't know. That was not sufficient grounds. You had to have a pretty good reason. But you didn't want somebody going on a fishing expedition, just going through somebody's records for no reason, at all.

It appeared to me that the banks didn't like it, but I'm not sure. I can't remember exactly who was opposed to it at this time, to be honest with you, but that was the purpose. Again, to me, this was a consumer protection bill. Clearly, I was taking on the banks and their right to give these records out to whoever *they* felt, but I didn't think that that was responsible. I wound up, later on, being on a bank board of directors.

Which bank?

First Interstate Bank (FIB). But that was many years later. But I was just amazed. I never thought about it, when you're balancing your own checkbook, you just check it off and make sure it's been returned and that you can balance your checkbook and move on. But my goodness, it was really eye-opening to me and produced this bill. Ultimately, something did pass later on, I believe, in another session, which we may wind up seeing later on.

The last one dealt with the date of the statewide primary election. It has gone back and forth through the years, and right now it's back *exactly* where it was before this bill was even introduced. The reason I felt that that was important, the reason I changed it from the date, was because the primary was held, and currently is held, on the Tuesday right after Labor Day. Very often, people go on a three-day or longer weekend, and they may not get back in time, and school sometimes didn't then begin until after Labor Day, and very often, depending upon how important the class was, if you had a second or third grader, maybe you didn't bother to get right back on the first day of school. And so you might miss the election all together. The primary to me is very important and can make or break a race.

In fact, we look at my own assembly district today, where the current assemblywoman, Dawn Gibbons, won in the primary, based upon a new law, which says if there are only people running in your own party, and there's no general election, because there's only people in your own party, and you win, then you've won the election in the primary. She won by six or nine votes over Patty Cafferata, and I don't remember if it was six or nine, but that's a pretty important primary.

The point is that the reason I changed the date is because it comes too close after Labor Day weekend, and some people don't bother to come back in time to even vote, or they come back in time to get their kids in school, but forget about voting, because they've been gone that weekend, or they don't know the issues, or they figure the primary is not that important. So I got it changed on consulting with the Education Association, everybody involved in the school district. I did go out and get some input from people, particularly teachers,

because they were the ones who gave me the information on how many were in the class at that time. This was really what was driving me—the time and schools. They all agreed to it, so we postponed it a week, which meant that by moving it even further into September one week, then you scrunch up the time between the primary and the general, even more. You'd only have six weeks or something. That was the big argument against it.

It was on the books for a couple of years, a couple of campaign cycles, elections, and then has gone back to the way it was before. The reason is the lack of time for the primary winner to run against the other primary winner of the parties, to mount a campaign before the general, because we don't have that much time. A lot of states have their primaries in June, as California does, I believe, and other dates.

Ours is only two months apart.

Right. And that is the least amount of time anywhere in the nation. I thought we'd get a better turnout, and numbers did show the turnout was better by moving the date, but the candidates didn't like it.

We talked about 1975, your first time in the legislature, and the measures you introduced, and also, other bills that were important in that session. We also wanted to talk about the Equal Rights Amendment, which was one of the things you dealt with right away, as you went into the legislature. So, Sue, maybe you could start and talk a little bit about how you became aware of it, and what involvement you had.

Well, it's hard for me to remember exactly when I first learned about ERA, because I do remember going door to door, and it was about this time of year, in October, when the World Series was going on, or when the playoffs were going on, and ERA in baseball terminology means "earned run average." My being such a big sports fan, I do remember at one time kidding somebody at the door about that. When they asked me about the ERA, I said, "Oh, you mean," whatever pitcher's it was at that time, "earned run average?" And they just thought that was very funny. That totally distracted this person to what the Equal Rights Amendment was all about. I don't remember if that was in my first campaign. I don't think so, because I really don't think I was very aware of it, or at least not to the point of having a position on it. After I had already taken a position on it, which would have been in my first session and was fairly well known, then it wouldn't have mattered to me whether someone asked me a question. So maybe I had heard about it in 1975, through other candidates, but not to the extent where I knew enough—strange as that may seem, for a woman running for office for the first time.

So, you had heard of it, but had limited awareness of it? Is that what you're saying?

Well, I guess so.

That's sort of the way everybody's awareness begins.

Well, we're talking at this time about when I was campaigning, not when I got to the legislative session.

Not about once you got to the session?

No. Because by that time I was on the assembly judiciary committee, through which constitutional amendments went. I think that probably was the *only* constitutional amendment then, because we don't have very many to the United States Constitution. Oh, there was one

dealing with a balanced budget. That was the only other one in that twenty years, I think, of my life. Anyway, so I'm only talking about the campaign period, when I was not at that point of taking a position on it.

Maybe that I had some familiarity with the subject. I'm sure I must have, but by the time the session came around, it became clear that I was in favor of the Equal Rights Amendment for a variety of reasons. The main argument, basically, was that it treated individuals in this country, regardless of sex, equally. Basically, that's the bottom line of the amendment. It was like twenty-three words long. I don't remember exactly how many, but it was very succinct and to the point. The opposition to the amendment discussed the fact that if you pass something like this, it then leads to bureaucracy. It then leads to the interpretation of each and every word. What does that mean? And who's to know? Because it has not passed. And none of these things have come to pass, historically. In fact, yesterday there was a march in Washington, D.C., that took sort of second place to the Million Man March, I guess, because I saw it on the national news last night. In fact, one of the women who was seated by my desk in either 1975 or 1977 was Eleanor Smeal, who at that time was president of NOW, which I had never been a member of, interestingly enough, but I guess I was the only person whose desk she could sit by. [laughter] That's how slim the supporters were for women in the assembly, anyway, because in addition to that, I was a Republican, and she's pretty well known as being a pretty liberal Democrat. Anyway, I saw Eleanor Smeal yesterday leading this parade with other women. I saw signs that said, "We need the ERA now." So it's still an issue. I know that it is still an issue with business and professional women nationally.

I think that's true of every congressional session, though, that there are certain congressmen—congresspersons—who start the process. To get an amendment out of Congress into the states is really very difficult, and then you have to get it ratified by thirty-eight states, I think it is. So it's very tough. And by now people have dug in their heels, in terms of whether they're for it or against it. Or you may have a whole new generation starting all over again, who would have a fresh mind and a fresh attitude toward it. Who's to say?

Anyway, in some of the memories I have, I cannot determine whether they were in 1975, 1977, or even maybe in 1979, but they all occurred when I was in the assembly. That's where most of the action occurred in my life. Clearly, for Mary Gojack and other people, because she was in the senate, it occurred there, but for Jean Ford and I, it pretty much was happening down in the assembly.

Going back to that comment I made about people sitting at my desk, it was interesting. I think maybe they were seated between Jean and me, because Jean sat next to me. As I mentioned, they would have been seated with her, because she was a Democrat and also as committed to the passage of the Equal Rights Amendment as I was.

What do you remember of Eleanor Smeal, when she was there?

Yes, I'll get to that part. And maybe it would be an appropriate thing to get, to see if we can get the remarks that were entered into the journals on those days in 1975 and 1977 to see what it was that was said. But different things happened in different sessions, and one of them, I think, in 1975, was a clear vote on the ERA, and I wished I had the information with me now, because I don't know how many votes there were for and agin it.

We'll add some exact information about the vote and some of the remarks that were made, since that's available. You remembered in 1975, your first session, that there was a vote, that you did vote on it?

Yes. I'm pretty sure Bob Barengo, who was chairman of the assembly judiciary committee—I was a member of that committee—was the main sponsor of the assembly resolution, which would have ratified the national amendment to the Constitution. It seems to me that it did pass the assembly and went over to the senate, and I really don't remember what happened there. It obviously didn't pass, because, if it had, then we would have been the thirty-sixth or thirty-seventh state to have ratified it, because there were just two or three left to make this an amendment to the United States Constitution. We were so incredibly close.

It's my understanding, if my memory serves me, that this did pass the assembly, did not pass the senate. It couldn't have, because if it passed both houses in the same language . . . and you can't change the language of a national amendment to a constitution. So it didn't pass the senate. When the first states right out of the chute sent out the Equal Rights Amendment to states to ratify—who'd be opposed to something that's twenty-three or twenty-eight words long, however many it might have been, that says, "Equality shall not be denied based upon sex or gender"? No one is going to be opposed to that. So, many, many states ratified it right off the bat.

Then, as time went on and opposition grew, there were some, in my mind, not really reasonable arguments. You could make an argument that we don't know what this exactly means, so there probably will be an agency set up that will have to regulate this, et cetera. Now that I'm a regulator, I can maybe understand that a little bit more. But some of the arguments were, "Everybody is going to be forced to go to war and be in a foxhole together." I think I mentioned this before, dealing with state equal pay for equal work, or something, that other women were very upset that possibly they would be forced to go out to work.

Right, when they didn't want to.

And that they didn't want to. Well, no way is that going to happen. Even if this was passed, it didn't say every single woman would have to go out into the work force and make exactly the same amount of money as a man. It says that if you *are* doing the same job, then you should be paid the same wage. I just don't see an argument against that, but my point is that when this started out, there were a lot of states that rapidly ratified it. So you got up to twenties and thirties rather quickly, in terms of numbers of states. Then the opposition started settling in, and using some arguments such as I've just mentioned, and some that were more reasonable arguments. So there was a very large, rather well-organized opposition to the Equal Rights Amendment, and as the states became closer to the thirty-eight, the magic number, the opposition was bigger and more. Even if you were Nevada—the amount of attention given to our state from national organizations was incredible—those that wanted it ratified, those that didn't want it ratified—because we were getting very close to the thirty-eighth state, and by that time there had been a legitimate opposition organized. So they would move from state to state as it got closer to the thirty-eight. It seems to me like there was maybe one other state at that time debating this, but there weren't that many at that very

moment that we were, so a lot of attention could be brought to bear on Nevada.

It was pretty much organized by the Eagle Forum. The opposition was led by the Eagle Forum and Phyllis Schlafly, a national conservative leader in our country, who is connected with the Eagle Forum, and, actually got her start in the Federation of Republican Women. She was moving up the ladder, if you will, to become the national president or chair, and she didn't get it. They chose somebody else at a convention, so she walked out, and she's still a Republican, but she formed this new organization called the Eagle Forum, which was more conservative than the Republican women's group, and much of it was done because she was angry, and it was in protest, but they were very well organized.

I do know that there were groups that organized in our state in favor of the Equal Rights Amendment, because many people I still know today got their start in politics by being involved in that organization, but they weren't as well organized, I don't believe, and also you had organized religion involved in this. In my mind, mainly the LDS Church seemed to be very involved.

There was an overlap, to some extent, between the Eagle Forum and the LDS Church, but not totally. They were very much opposed, because, clearly, if you look at their religious dogma, or doctrine—I don't know exactly what the correct term is—you will note that they do not really perceive women to be equal. Women cannot become priests. Women cannot play an active role in their church. They have their Relief Societies, and they have other groups for women in the LDS Church, but they cannot become a religious leader. Even to this day, they can't, this many years later. They did not allow blacks, African-Americans, either, but they've changed that, and there will be some people who will argue the reason they did that is because they needed to go out and proselytize in Africa. Clearly, it would not have worked, if they wouldn't have allowed Africans, whichever country they lived in, to be able to participate in the church. I don't know whether that's true or not, but that is something that has been said. I don't believe, however, that this was the year—I may be wrong—that all the national leaders came to Nevada.

Nineteen seventy-five, your first year?

I don't think so, but I don't remember, and I have to go and find some records that would tell me that. Because I believe that I have voted on it twice, and the second time it failed. It did pass the assembly, I believe, in 1975, and failed in the senate.

So the first time did not have all the attention of the national leaders, but by 1977 . . . .

Well, I think not. I'm not really sure. Now, in one of these sessions, and it must have been in 1977, there was a huge debate on the senate floor, and it was at night. One of the things that I have not addressed, and I'm going to go back, is that I was on the committee that processed this, so in many cases I heard far more than what other people did, because we had all the hearings. So the hearings might have been days of allowing everybody who wanted to testify do so, for and against.

We did have one time in the assembly— and I think it was 1977—when we finally had to have the hearing held in the assembly chambers, because there were so many people, and we had them lined up in rows, where the proponents would be in one line at one mike, and the opponents at the other. They decided who they wanted to go first and who second and so on, to make the most valid points, and then after they felt they had made the points they

wanted to, after the first three or four speakers, let's say—and they all had a certain amount of time to testify—then it would just be whoever wanted to testify, even if they repeated what someone else had said. Many people felt rather strongly about this and had come, maybe, from other communities, and if they had made that trek to Carson City, they certainly had a right to speak, even if we'd heard it two or three or four or ten or twenty times.

I do remember in one session, Phyllis Schlafly was the leadoff speaker for the opponents, and that's what I meant by having a lot of national attention. Now, I'm trying to remember who the leadoff speaker that particular session was for the proponents. I don't think we had any person who was well known, who would be able to have a press conference on their own, as Phyllis Schlafly always had a tendency to do, and did that very well for her side.

I do remember a friend of mine, Margo Piscevich, who is an attorney in town, was one of the leadoff speakers in favor of it. She was raised in a Mormon family, and her mother happened to see me in the hall that day and came up to me and took her handbag and hit me, and I didn't know who she was. I had no idea who this woman was, what her name was, why she was hitting me, and later on I found out it was Margo Piscevich's mother, and I couldn't understand why she was beating up on me like that. Well, it appears that Margo was one of the lead-off speakers in *favor* of it, and her mother was adamantly opposed, and she felt that I had had something to do with convincing her daughter that she should be pro ERA, which I had had nothing to do with. If anyone knows Margo Piscevich, they pretty much know she has a mind of her own, and she came to this conclusion on her own. In fact, I was very surprised to see her testify there, because many people might have supported it, but were somewhat reluctant to come out in a public arena like that, if for a religious reason or something of that sort.

There was a neighbor here, who lived on the next street from me, who was very active in the LDS Church. I do have a stake very close to my home, on the next block, so I have a lot of neighbors who are members of the church. They do like to live close, because there's a basketball gym and a variety of activities that they participate in. In fact, my husband played on their basketball team, since he was 6' 7" they went out and recruited him. [laughter] Actually, he did bring a lot to their team, I might add. But this neighbor of mine decided she would have a function for me so I could explain this in a reasonable, rational way, which she did, and it went pretty well as far as I was concerned, but not for her. She was called on the carpet after that by leaders in the church. In addition to doing that for me, she also came down and testified, pregnant. Now, I'm not sure if she was pregnant when she testified on behalf of the Equal Rights Amendment, and holding another baby in her arms, or if that was on the choice issue. I believe she did it on both issues and got into a great deal of difficulty and basically was told she really had to stop doing this—she was bringing embarrassment to the church— or she'd have to leave the church. So she made a choice, and I haven't seen her for, probably, fifteen years or more and never heard from her, didn't even know she'd moved, actually. Yes, I did know she'd moved.

So, she's now moved out of this neighborhood, even?

She doesn't live that far away, but, no, she does not live on the street next to mine. So she has never appeared. Never seen her at the legislature. Never had any conversation with her, letter from her,

anything of that sort. But this is basically what happened, which is a real shame. I felt that one could not have their own opinion, even though it might have been in opposition to church, and there are many people today, Catholics, who do not support the Roman Catholic position on abortion, and yet they're, at this time in America, anyway, not driven out of the church.

But it does illustrate how strongly feelings were running on this issue at that time, in terms of the pros and cons. You probably saw that in these committee hearings?

Yes. I did, but I have to say, I don't think the feelings were that much different than on the choice issue, maybe. Maybe a bit more so, I don't know, because it was pretty new. This was a new idea, to make people equal. Funny that we'd call it a new idea in America, but, clearly, the Supreme Court had not ever viewed any previous amendment to include women, and so that is the reason for the effort made. But I think it was because the issues were a little less clear-cut, in terms of knowing what the results might be, or the fact that things could be said, and no one could really refute it, except, "Well, how silly that is. Of course, that's not going to happen," or, "That's not true."

But there weren't any concrete reasons that you could give, or examples that you could say, "Well, it didn't happen in x state or y state, and they've had an amendment like this on their books for years."

I think, with the issue of choice, which we'll get to later, that people understand the issue better. There may be no way of ever agreeing, but I think they understand what a trimester is and what can happen in the first trimester versus the second.

This was different. This was new, and so there was a lot of misinformation, I guess, and some of it, I'm sure that they wouldn't believe was misinformation. Many of these people that I heard in the hearings, I felt very sorry for, very honestly, because I felt that they were very insecure, because they seemed to feel that if they let their husbands out of their sight, something *awful* could happen. If their husband was a fireman, and you were going to have a woman fireperson, which did happen and is the case without the Equal Rights Amendment . . . . They'll make the argument that you don't need it, because these things have happened. Well, that is true to some extent, but certainly, we don't have the same wages, and there are a variety of things that we don't have. I don't know of too many CEO's in Forbes 500 who are women, but that really is a social attitude, an attitudinal change, and I think that is happening. I don't think it would have happened, if we hadn't had all this discussion about the Equal Rights Amendment, very honestly. I think that did cause much of the change in our country. But many of these women I heard during the hearings, I felt really sorry for. Some people might have thought they were laughable. I did not, because I felt that they very honestly came believing what they said—many of them. Some of them, I don't think, did. I think some of them knew that they were probably stretching it quite a bit, but I think those who were sent in by organized groups, really felt they were told by their leaders of whatever organization, whether it be religious or political, that they believed that, and they were very, very scared. But it did suggest to me an insecurity in their relationships with their spouses, and in this case it would be husbands, which I found to be rather sad, to say the least.

So a lot of fear in the comments that were made in the committee hearing, by those opposed to the Equal Rights Amendment?

Yes, there was a lot of fear. Whether it was justified or not is very questionable, but there was a lot of fear, and that I found to be unfortunate.

Were these some of your first committee hearings, also, on the Equal Rights Amendment? Or had you gone through enough to have a sense of the assembly judiciary committee hearings before that? I'm just trying to get a sense of you as a new legislator.

I don't remember, chronologically, where the Equal Rights Amendment came in 1975. Whether it was the second week or the second month, I have no idea. I could look at the date when it was introduced and when the hearing was held, when I get the record and know exactly. But it wouldn't have mattered really, because I remember one of the very first bills, AB67, something like that, AB6 or AB7, that dealt with silicone being injected into breasts, and I couldn't believe I was the only woman on the committee. This was the first week or two, when I was a brand new legislator. That I do remember, and all of the national television networks, ABC, NBC, CBS, were there from New York, with cameras set up in our room, because no one had ever dealt with this issue. It was an emergency measure, and it was introduced by a Las Vegas assemblyman, because a supply of silicone was coming across from Mexico, and in those days they just injected it into your body. They weren't placed in a packet. They were very concerned that this would be very dangerous. They had gotten word that this was impure silicone coming up from Mexico, and, of course, it would be utilized by a lot of showgirls in the clubs in Las Vegas. So that was the nature of doing this in a real hurry.

Now, I do remember during the hearing that the plastic surgeons, who also were testifying, were showing us—the members of the committee—these implants, saying we need to have these placed in these implants, so that they would not be injected right into the body, that they would be contained, and it would be safer. They passed these around, and I remember I was the least senior person, because I'd just been elected, so I was at the very end. Of course, all these guys are handling this, and all the national TV cameras are focused on them, thinking this was just absolutely the funniest thing—made great television—to see all these guys handling some breast that hadn't yet got into a woman. I'm the last one, and I took it and threw it out into the audience at one of the TV cameramen. [laughter] So all the other cameras got me throwing it out to this other guy! I didn't know what to do with it, actually, since I was the only woman on there. I didn't want to touch it, to be honest with you.

In answer to your question, that was one of the first issues I dealt with in the first week. After that, everything else seemed to pale in comparison. So I got toughened up right away. That was another issue, and if you hadn't asked that question, though, I probably would not have thought about that particular bill. That's what I'm talking about, when I'm saying to you, that if something triggers my memory, it brings back another whole thing, which might be interesting, historically. Clearly, now, we think about breast implants as being saline.

Right. Rather than silicone.

So you've gone from direct injections—and they showed pictures of women who had this injected, and there's growth all over their body in places that weren't even close to the breast. It was just horrifying, but they did it in order to look better, and it's a shame that we still deal with the issues of women trying to look better and doing things that are probably not very good for their bodies,

either eating not enough, or eating the wrong things. It doesn't seem to change much. We have at least changed that, but I'm not too sure. I've never been a believer, even if it's saline solution in an implant, that it's all that safe. After I saw those slides and went through that hearing, I will never, ever believe that.

Anyway, that was one of the first issues I dealt with, and it was totally different from the Equal Rights Amendment, because there was no one *opposed* to this issue. It was just could we immediately make it illegal so it would not come across the border, and we could look at the better way of doing things. But we found out that wasn't all that perfect either, and that's why we've gone to a different solution.

It wasn't the first thing, then, that you'd heard the pros and cons of?

It wasn't. Oh, no, because any bill that you had in, you would have heard the pros and cons. I do know that we did have some well-known people who came in, either to testify, or to be there when the vote on the Equal Rights Amendment was held. When it appeared in the senate, which, I guess, would have been 1977, Bob Rose was the lieutenant governor. Of course, I was then lieutenant governor later on, so this is an issue that procedurally was very important to me, because he broke the tie.

Now, it was not, theoretically, a tie. Several people abstained. They knew the opponents to the Equal Rights Amendment. I remember one of them was Rick Blakemore [Richard E. Blakemore] from Tonopah. He abstained, and there were two or three that did that so it wouldn't be a tie vote. If they had voted no, it would have been an outright tie, I believe, and if they abstained, then you are counted—it's basically a no vote—because you're not on record as voting yes. In that case there were twenty senators, so in order to pass something you had to get eleven. It allowed them not to have it be an equal number of ten yes's and ten no's. It was, I think, ten yeses, very close to having the majority, and that's why we need to look at the record, but I do remember that two or three senators abstained from voting, pushing their yellow buttons, rather than their red or green, in order to take away the right of the lieutenant-governor to break a tie. They were concerned he probably would vote that way, because he was known as a proponent of the Equal Rights Amendment. The two people who abstained were known opponents of the Equal Rights Amendment, and, thus, they felt by voting that way it would take the lieutenant governor out of the process.

It did not. He did it, anyway. He made a decision that an abstention is a no vote. I'm pretty sure this is the way it went, that he made this decision. There was a great deal of discussion about what was constitutionally correct, what did the rules of the senate say, and the bottom line was that the lieutenant governor did believe and felt very strongly that by not voting, you were really casting a "no" vote, and thus created the tie where he could break the tie vote with his vote being cast in the affirmative. The senators were very, very angry at the lieutenant governor for ruling that way. I think he ruled that way, but I know that he voted in favor of it to break the tie and send it down to the assembly.

Now, after that, the majority leader, Jim Gibson, [James I. Gibson] had our legal counsel of the Legislative Counsel Bureau, Frank Daykin, write an opinion that the lieutenant-governor could not vote in case of a tie, and it was a result of that vote. So, even though people said, when I was lieutenant-governor, if I ever had an opportunity, I was going to vote to break a tie, to take it to the supreme court, but pretty much people knew I'd do that, so they would make sure that I didn't preside on

the day when it might be a tie-breaking vote. I did break the tie once on an amendment, but that was not found to be the same as voting to break a tie on a bill. So that wasn't good enough to take it to the supreme court. I always used to kid around with Bob Rose that I would hope that he would definitely support my position, when it got there, since he was chief justice of the supreme court, last session. He said he certainly would, since he got into all that trouble because of it, and he not only got into trouble in the senate, but it was a big issue in his political campaign when he ran for governor the next session, and he lost that election. It was an issue—I don't know if it was the issue that defeated him, but it was an important issue in his campaign.

I believe that we voted again in the assembly, because there were a number of assemblymen, mainly from Clark County, who evidently had promised both sides, or something of that sort, perhaps not expecting that they would have to vote on it again. I'm really not sure about that now, but it would have been in 1977, I guess. I remember one of them was Jack Jeffrey, [John E. Jeffrey] whom I always liked. He was from Henderson and was big in the labor union movement and is very involved in the labor union now that he's not in the legislature. He and I got along real well, but he was one of those guys, along with some others from Clark County. There were little buttons that went around, saying something about the seven or the nine or however many it was who lied.

I believe it was that session, rather than 1975, when there were national leaders out there, because I think they had come out there for the senate, as well as the assembly. One of them was Eleanor Smeal, because I do have pictures somewhere. At that time she was president of NOW, National Organization for Women. She's still involved in another group, but I don't know the name of it. I think I didn't get a chance to know her well. She was just there, and she sat at my desk during the debate on the assembly floor, and I don't remember who else was there, but I do know I became really, really upset about it. There were pictures. One newspaper—I think it was the *Nevada Appeal*—did a whole page of photos of just me at different times during that debate, for example, looking at the board when it showed that it hadn't passed. That's why I know Eleanor Smeal was there, because, I think, her picture was in the paper, and maybe Mary Gojack brought her down, because Mary sat at my seat, and she, of course, had come down from the senate.

When I was in the senate, the assembly chambers were much bigger, because there were more assembly people, twice as many as senators. Then, you get invited down, and you go down and sit with an assemblyperson, when you have a joint hearing, or if you have, maybe, a United States senator come and address the legislature. That's how it works. So, in this case, then, probably Mary sat with me and then brought these people with her. I remember Mary giving me some kind of nerve pill, and I'm going to say it was Valium, but it was something like that, which I'd never taken before, have never taken since, but I took it on that day. Don't ask me why. I became more emotional than normal, and I thought it was supposed to make you not so emotional. [laughter] To kind of level you out.

Calm you down?

Yes. But it didn't do that for me. Medicines don't work the way they're supposed to on me, anyway, so I've later learned. We were discussing here, equality of rights for me, for every other woman in the state, in this country. It's a pretty overwhelming and empowering kind of an issue, far more than a silicone implant, to be honest with you. I mean, that was an important health issue, but hardly on the scale of being treated equally under the law in the United States Constitution. The thing that made me the most angry was that other people didn't see it the same way I did—not that they had to see it as passionately, affirmatively, as I did, but they didn't even feel passionate about it, period. They were willing to trade it off, or promise both sides that they would vote for it, and we're talking about equality of rights guaranteed by the United States Constitution for every woman, every young girl, every granddaughter. It just seems to me to be something that I could not quite understand how people—men—didn't think of their own wives or their daughters or their mothers in this way, that it would be guaranteeing them something very, very important that *they* had. I guess it's just they took it all for granted, because, hey, everything worked out OK for them. Not everything always worked out OK for everybody, but they never had any obstacles legally, hurdles in their way. So maybe they didn't quite see it the same way, but I really did and really, really became very passionate about this issue, and felt very, very strongly about it and was always labeled, along with the choice issue, as being pro ERA.

Now, it's not even mentioned by my name, because that constitutional amendment has come and gone. As I say, there are people even talking about resurrecting it again. Of course, it would have to start all over. It has to get out of the committee in Congress and then start out through the states. You can imagine it would probably have a more difficult time now, because there would already be all this organized opposition, right out of the chute, because nothing's changed. The language should be the same. I would guess that's why it was so important to pick up those two or three remaining states at that time.

Because it was so close?

Because it was so very, very close. But as I explained to you why—it went pretty rapidly through some of the states.

Right. The early states.

I think now that would not be the case, because you'd have this organized opposition right from the get-go, right the minute it had its first hearing in the U.S. House of Representatives. That's where you'd have the first opposition, and I have no idea what it was like back when it first came out of a committee in Congress.

Several other things happened that stick out in my mind, dealing with the Equal Rights Amendment. I was asked to go to the airport to pick up Maureen Reagan, Ronald Reagan's daughter, and this was, I believe, when he was President of the United States. We'd have to figure out what year that was, versus Gerald Ford, because Gerald Ford was president for a very short period of time. When he ran, he lost, and then Reagan became the standard-bearer and won. But anyway, I got a call one weekend that Maureen Reagan was coming to town—she and Judy Carter, Jimmy Carter's daughter. They both were pro ERA, and they thought this would be a dynamic duo. They were both young women at the time, and they did a routine together. They got together, and I don't know if we are the first state they did this in or not, but later on, I know they went to many other states as a duo, because one was a Democrat, and one was a Republican. Both dads were presidents at one time or running for president. As I say, I don't remember the timetable here, but anyway, I was asked to go pick up Maureen at the airport, who I, of course, did not know, but the reason I was asked was because I was the only Republican woman who was in favor of the Equal Rights Amendment.

So she came into Reno, and she had sort of a little entourage with her, even at that time, although not huge, but a few folks. [laughter] I hardly recognized her, because I guess I had gotten an idea of what she looked like, but she had an incredible personality, just a dynamite person, in terms of being outgoing, and just like she'd known you your whole life. I could see how she would just go into a state and just bowl everybody over and go to another one and do the same thing all over again. But I do remember, she had no makeup on, and that was one of the reasons I didn't recognize her, because I don't wear much, anyway, so it doesn't matter. She had a driver. I do remember that, and I don't remember who the driver was, if I got somebody, or what. I was not the driver. I was in the back seat of the car, and she was in the passenger seat, and somebody was driving the car, and I think there was somebody else in the back seat.

Anyway, on the way to Carson City, Maureen took out this big case of makeup as she was talking and carrying on and figuring out who was who and what she should do, and she was coming to, basically, speak at a luncheon that all the legislators had been invited to. I do remember that, and that she was going to be my guest on the floor of the assembly. Judy Carter was going to meet her there. I don't remember Judy Carter, just meeting her somewhere along the line that day. Maureen Reagan and Judy Carter were going to speak at a luncheon at the Ormsby House, promoting, of course, the Equal Rights Amendment. I do remember Maureen on the way to Carson City getting out this big makeup bag, which looked like a suitcase to me. She put on all this stuff, and she looked like a million bucks by the time she got there, like a totally different person. I kept thinking to myself, "Maybe I could change my look that much, if I did that, too." But this has been thirty years later, and I haven't done much about it.

I had her as my guest on the floor of the assembly, and I think that probably was at eleven o'clock, because that's usually the time we go in on the floor, prior to the lunch. I had introduced her, and this is the only reason I think it might have been in the afternoon, but it really doesn't matter. Governor O'Callaghan was having a dinner that evening for these two women, but particularly Judy Carter, because she was Jimmy Carter's daughter, and they were both Democrats, but clearly he was going to invite Maureen Reagan, as well, to dinner. Well, I wasn't invited to the dinner, although I'd been asked to pick up Maureen Reagan and all of this. As it turns out, on the floor of the assembly we decided we were going to horse around a little bit, and we were going to pretend like we were very, very long, lost friends. How lost? She had told me a little bit about her family and that one of her brothers—I think she had two— had gone to school in Arizona at a private school outside of Phoenix. So we got to talking about that, and the fact that I'd grown up in Tucson. So we just thought we would poke some fun. Who's ever going to know, right? So when I introduced her, I went on about this and embellished it quite a bit. Needless to say, I'd just met her a few hours before, but, of course, no one was going to know that. So then, I heard about this dinner, and someone obviously contacted the governor's office and said, "You better invite Sue, because she and Maureen are really close." So I was invited. [laughter]

One of those times you got to snooker somebody else?

Exactly. Actually, Maureen came back and did a fund-raiser for me, when I ran for the senate, I believe, the first time, or maybe it was for the assembly, over at JoAnne Bond's home. JoAnne is on the county commission right now, and was last year chair of Washoe County Commission, and her husband, Lee Bond—she's now a widow—was the chairman of the Republican Party. They had a beautiful home, and they were very nice to offer their home. Since I'd met Maureen in this way, through this ERA experience, I was able to contact her, and she came and did a fund-raiser for my campaign. I used to keep in touch with her on a more regular basis, because there's someone here in town who worked for Congressman Gibbons's campaign, who is very close to Maureen. They used to both live in Sacramento, and Maureen used to do some lobbying and things in the California legislature. But anyway, they did a great job at this luncheon—the two of them. Judy Carter was a very lovely gal, but it was very clear that I would not want to be on the same podium with Maureen, because she just can absolutely dominate everything. Her mother was an actress, and you could definitely see she had all of the dramatic tendencies. She just was an actress and an excellent speaker.

Then, that night we had the dinner. It didn't change anybody's vote, I'm sorry to say, but it did bring some attention to the issue, as far as the press was concerned, and the public.

Another incident occurred, related to the Equal Rights Amendment, although it didn't happen exactly in this time period. It would have happened, however, when I was in the assembly. I was interviewed by *Ms. Magazine*, which was at that time a pretty hot publication. The publisher and founder was Gloria Steinem. They sent out some reporter to do a story on the Equal Rights Amendment and why it failed in Nevada. This reporter stayed in the same motel where I was staying, and it was at the end of the session. I don't remember who it was. I probably have a copy of the article some place. She was in my room interviewing me. The governor calls me in my motel room while she's interviewing me, and I pick up the phone and say, "Hi, Governor."

He said, "I'm having this meeting tomorrow at 5:00 a.m." I know Governor O'Callaghan was noted for doing things like that, getting up very early and getting a lot of work done before anybody else had even thought about getting out of bed.

O'Callaghan was planning a 5:00 a.m. meeting?

Yes. It was a real early morning meeting about the water-meter legislation, which had nothing to do with the Equal Rights Amendment. It's only that this woman happened to be there from *Ms. Magazine* at the time that I got the phone call about the meeting. I didn't want to get up at 5:00 a.m. Besides that, I was the one who had a bill in my drawer on mandating water meters. I really didn't want to have anything to do with the issue, because prior to that I had gotten it drafted, because there was a neighbor of mine, who still is a neighbor of mine, who left her water on all one day— this was in the 1970s, when I was in the assembly—and it was running down the backyard. I'm pointing at it right now. Our backyards are slightly sloped, and right behind her is a woman who has a swimming

Sue with Governor Mike O'Callaghan

pool, so all of the dirt was going under the fence into her pool. The woman who lives on the street with the pool caught my attention, asking me to help, since she couldn't get my neighbor's attention. I went over, and there wasn't anybody home, so I said, "I'll try to find where the key is and turn it off." I couldn't find where the gizmo was to turn it off, I waited until they came home, and I went over right away and told them. Their response was, "Well, I really don't care much, because I'm really not paying any more for it."

That's what triggered all this in my mind, that it was so unfair to waste water, and it wasn't equitable. You should pay for what you use. My husband told me, "Bad, bad, bad idea," although he agreed with me, but he just knew, politically, it was *not* going to be a good thing for me. But I'm just headstrong, and I decided it was the right thing to do, so I was going to do it anyway, until all the talk radio guys found out about it, and they had people call in to the legislature and to my home, asking only for me—hundreds of phone calls a day telling me that I would never see Carson City again, because it was the dumbest idea I'd ever had. [laughter] I had others before, but this was the worst. [laughter] So, I realized my husband was right, and I put it in my drawer.

Then the governor calls while I'm being interviewed for the ERA, wanting me to come over. I didn't want to have anything to do with this. So he said, "Do you have this bill in your desk drawer?"

I said, "Yes, I do."

He said, "Well, I'll find somebody else to introduce it." Because I told him I wasn't going to, and he said, "OK. I'll get somebody else to do it."

So I said, "Fine." And that was that, and I will get back and finish that story.

The point was that the woman could not *believe* that I was having this conversation with the governor, that the governor would actually call, himself, to a motel room and try to get me over there at five o'clock in the morning. I mean, she couldn't even believe it. The governor had stated his support of the Equal Rights Amendment, because, of course, he'd had Judy Carter and Maureen Reagan as his guests. I don't know to what extent Governor O'Callaghan twisted people's arms—Democrat arms—to get people to change their minds. It might have been an issue that he couldn't get anybody to change their minds on. That's possible. I don't know. But I do know that he was on the record as being in favor of it, so she was even more impressed by that, too. But I told him that there was this reporter here, and I just could not make this morning meeting for the reasons that I've already described.

So they did do a story in *Ms. Magazine* on what happened to the Equal Rights Amendment in Nevada, and they talked about these people who had changed their minds—the seven who lied, or the nine, or whatever the number was. They talked, also, about the LDS church and its involvement in this issue. That was a fairly prominent piece. Of course, when it hit the newsstands here in Nevada it was debatable as to which side . . . of course, they took the wrong side, according to the church, and that sort of thing, so it started that debate all over again.

But those were some of the more memorable instances at this time that I can think of, dealing with the Equal Rights Amendment. Although, I have to say that I was very impressed with Lieutenant-Governor Bob Rose for having the courage to do what he did in the senate to break the tie in the way he did. I don't think he had a clue as to the extent of the anger that some people would hold for him, but he did show a great deal of courage in my mind in breaking the tie and allowing it to go down to the assembly again.

Senator and Mrs. Paul Laxalt; President Ronald Reagan and First Lady Nancy Reagan; Sue and Peter Wagner; Senator and Mrs. Jake Garn of Utah.

We discussed Maureen Reagan and how we cooked up this little story, if you will, in my introducing her, that we were long-time, personal friends. When that word got out, of course, the governor felt obligated to include me, because he was really hosting a dinner for Judy Carter who was, of course, the daughter of then president, Jimmy Carter, and Maureen went with him, and it was kind of a dog-and-pony show representing both political parties and daughters of two presidents, although Ronald Reagan—wait a minute—had not been president yet at that time.

Right, but he would have been governor of California already, wouldn't he?

Well, I don't really know. I don't think so. This would have been in the 1970's, and I believe he was elected president in 1980. He came after Jimmy Carter. Because Gerald Ford and Jimmy Carter ran against each other, and Gerald Ford lost, basically, they believe, because of his pardoning of Richard Nixon.

Reagan was elected in 1980, so Maureen Reagan was just the daughter of two movie stars: Ronald Reagan and Jane Wyman. In fact, this is not really relevant, but I have a picture up there, that I found in the garage when I was cleaning yesterday, of my daughter—who will die if anybody sees the picture—when she was a little kid hugging Maureen Reagan, because she had come for this fund-raiser for me.

OK, so you'd cooked up this ploy that you were going to introduce her as your long-time, personal friend.

Yes, I did, and that's when the governor got wind of that. Of course, he included me in this party, a dinner he was having for the two women at the governor's mansion at that time.

In looking back on this, you can just look at the voting record and see how, if it passed in one house, oh, something happened to it in the other. If it passed in the assembly, oh, it didn't pass in the senate. So, it was like this ping-pong ball back and forth, and, clearly, those of us who were very committed to the issue of equality felt that that was not an appropriate way to deal with the proposed constitutional amendment. Of course, you need thirty-eight states to ratify a resolution for a constitutional amendment, and I think thirty-four states, at that time, had ratified it.

In one of the sessions—I think it may have been in 1977—one of the senators had made reference to South Carolina having just ratified it that day or the day before, very close to the time that Nevada was voting. The reason this took on national attention was twofold. First of all, it was an amendment to the national constitution and not the state constitution, and, secondly, we were very close to the thirty-eight. Time was running out. You only have a certain number of years, and I think it's seven, but very honestly I did not read that last night, and so I'm not sure.

Many states had amended it to their state constitutions—and many of these fears expressed by the opponents had never happened in any of those states. To me, honestly, some of the senior senators who

said the most *outrageous* things are men who I thought knew better. The fact that there was no guarantee in the language of this amendment for homemakers, somehow, to separate them out from women who were in the workforce—the concept had nothing to do with those who worked and those who didn't. You would not have equality of rights for everybody who went into the workforce, except homemakers, and then some other, different kind of rights for them. The real fear that the opponents had was that men and women would be fighting in foxholes together, and maybe they would actually be fire-persons, and they'd have to sleep in the fire station together. These things had not happened in the states where this very similar language had been passed—in a myriad of states, some in the West, some maybe as conservative, politically, as Nevada.

In addition to that, my thought was, as I was listening to these many women, "Oh, give me a break! That's not going to happen." But to be more fair about it, I really felt sorry for women who did not trust their husbands any more than that; that they would somehow live in fear that if they ran into a woman in the workplace, whether it be in a law firm, which now in today's age is *very* common, or male and female going to medical school together, or firefighters, that somehow bad things were going to happen because of the proximity of two genders. So, in a way, I really had a feeling of empathy for many of the people who felt diametrically opposed to my own position, because I thought, "This is where this fear must come from."

There were some legislators who were Jewish and talked about the armed forces in Israel, that men and women were expected to serve in the military when they reached a certain age, and things seemed to move along rather normally there. It worked out fairly well. Needless to say, most women probably are not going to select the military, and those who do should have every right to move on and advance as men do. Until very recently, because there was not a national amendment, women could not ever reach a certain rank, because they did not serve in combat. That's the big distinction made in the military. The more years you serve in wartime, whether in Korea, Vietnam, the Gulf Storm, or World War II, the more quickly you move up the military ladder. In this case, because these restrictions were placed on women—they could not be in combat, they could not fly a fighter plane, et cetera—it precluded them.

That is now changing, I think, because of some progressive people who served in the Pentagon. I did serve on a committee that was selected by Caspar Weinberger, then Secretary of Defense, and it was called Defense Advisory Committee on Women in the Armed Services, DACOWITS. That was the big stumbling block that I saw. We traveled around the country visiting at different military bases, and I always had meetings with enlisted women and commissioned officer women. There were big distinctions as to what they thought the major issues were for them. The enlisted women were more concerned about pregnancy coverage, childcare, housing, and that's not to say the female officers were not, but they were more interested in their careers, and that there were opportunities. It was clear to me that that was very significant. And there was this— not a glass ceiling—a *wall* that was put there until just recently, and some services were a little more open than others.

So that would have been one of the direct results of the ERA not passing?

I think so.

Yes, because they could have those rules that separated who got promoted and who didn't.

The Equal Rights Amendment states in Section One that, "Equality of rights under the law shall not be denied or abridged by the United States or by any state on account of sex."

Section Two is very important, "That Congress shall have the power to enforce by appropriate legislation the provisions of this article." Now, that is what the opponents focused on, that this gargantuan bureaucracy would be set up, and we would never know what was going on. It is interesting to point out that Senator Spike Wilson, on the floor of the senate, I believe in 1977, spoke to that issue and went through all of the different amendments in the Constitution that had *exactly* the same language. Indeed, a few did take some kind of direction, but nothing to the extent that the opponents were suggesting.

Thirdly, Section Three says, "The amendment shall take effect two years after the date of ratification," the purpose being then you could go back to state legislatures and make equality changes. It was *not* going to be immediately taken over by the federal government in Washington D.C. The opportunity would occur at the state level, because it was closer to the people. So it was difficult for me to really understand the *incredible* opposition to this.

At some point we're going to discuss a bill I introduced dealing with high-school students' freedom of press—the First Amendment issues—because that was the only time really that the Mormon Church, the LDS church, issued a public letter saying this was a very bad idea, and they were adamantly opposed to it.

Next to the ERA, correct?

But even in the ERA days, there was nothing you could put your hands on. There was no press release or publicly noted letter. Clearly, we understood where the opposition rested. It was with many conservative organizations and the Church of Latter-day Saints.

And they were not only opposed, they were pretty organized by the time this came to Nevada, correct?

Very. In the case of the other bill, which we'll get to at some other time, it did say they represented 65,000 members of the church at that time. I was always told I could never win a statewide race, because every social issue they cared about, I was on the wrong side of, and so they would support anybody but myself. That did not turn out to be the case, but that was the claim made at that time.

Yes, kind of more like a threat.

It was. I did think about it, to tell you the truth, because particularly in the southern part of our state, which has been the residential area for many members of the Mormon Church, they came early to Las Vegas.

Right. And then we had talked a little bit about the final vote on this, but was it the final vote? You pointed out that there was a point where it seemed to switch completely.

Well, it certainly appeared that way to me, because my first session in 1975, there were twenty-seven "yes" votes in the assembly, the body I was in at that time, and thirteen "no" votes. In the senate, there were eight "yes" votes and twelve "no" votes. In 1977, SJR-5 was originated in the senate, and that was the year when

the president of the senate, the lieutenant governor, broke the tie. That's where the eleven votes came from, because he cast his vote, and it did pass the senate, by virtue of the president of the senate, Bob Rose, who now, of course, is a justice on the supreme court.

Also, after this vote of his, he did run for governor, and he lost. I suspect this vote may have put him at somewhat of a disadvantage in certain political areas that would have made the same impact on my own political career. At least, it was suggested it would. At that time in the assembly, then, there were fifteen "yes" votes, whereas two years before, there were twenty-seven; there were twenty-four "no" votes, whereas in the previous session there were only thirteen.

So, well, what occurred? There may have been different people, and I'd have to go back and analyze that, but there were a lot of people who supported it at one time and then didn't, and it seemed to be this yes, no, yes, no. If it passed in one, then the other side somehow was able to kill it, and I think I've discussed that to some extent.

Just could not get to the point of getting it passed then?

No, and, of course, time was running out nationally.

Yes. One of the things I'm interested in—and you mentioned it with Bob Rose—is the impact that the votes on the ERA had on careers. You were new in the assembly in 1975. Maybe, you'd like to talk a little bit about just your own career, and what impact you saw, and then if you saw some others, too, you might mention those.

Well, the longer I stayed in the legislature, particularly on this issue and several others, it was clear I was not gaining a lot of friends, but I certainly did from people who supported this. Sometimes the proponents kind of take you somewhat for granted at some point in your career, although at the polling booths, of course, they'd be voting for you. But I was told often through the years, beginning with the Equal Rights Amendment, that I would never be able to win statewide office, because, well, religious groups, particularly, members of the Roman Catholic Church and the Church of Latter-day Saints, would not support me because they were *very much* in opposition to this. Of course, later on, we get to other issues, which compounded my problem, but, needless to say, that did not hold true for my getting elected to the lieutenant governorship. Now, that may be because it got me out of the senate, where I couldn't vote anymore, [laughter] possibly, or the fact that they would be waiting if I went to anything else and really nail me. I don't know, because I didn't do that.

In addition to that, we may go back and talk a little bit about the tie-breaking vote, but to get this off the legislators' backs— Senator Neal, I believe, said that he had received twenty to thirty *thousand* pieces of mail on this issue, during that particular session.

But all of you were getting inundated with mail.

Yes, right, but he happened to mention it in a debate. Now, in 1978, because of this, the assumption was, "Well, let's let the people decide." So there was a ballot advisory question, Question 5, where, clearly, my position was *way* outnumbered by the opposition. The "yes" votes in that election were, say, 62,000, and the "no" votes were 124,000. So, it was almost double. That would have been in the

assembly. My own assembly district, I believe, had mostly "no" votes, as well, so I was not representing my constituency, if you took that to mean that's the way you're supposed to vote, and a lot of people do.

But in looking ahead, when I ran for the senate, there were only a couple of precincts in my new senate district, at Incline Village, where they voted for it or came very, very close. A lot of people suggest that support of the Equal Rights Amendment may be relevant to one's education, and I don't know if that's true or not, but that suggestion has been made, particularly, because if you look at the people who live at Incline Village, I think there probably is a correlation between their residency and their education level.

I don't remember if I talked to you about Senator Gibson and I having lunch together, dealing with this advisory question?

No, I don't believe you did.

Well, Senator Jim Gibson at this time in my life was the senate majority leader, a Democrat from Henderson, and also chairman of the Senate Finance Committee, exactly the same two positions that are currently held by Senator Bill Raggio, a Republican from Washoe County. Senator Gibson was a member of the LDS church, and, in fact, I learned this in a very public way. After he died I did fly down with many of my colleagues from northern Nevada to attend his funeral, because I really did feel he was a very astute political figure and had made a major difference, despite the fact that we didn't agree on *a lot* of questions.

But during that service, there was a high-ranking person in the LDS church who had flown in from Salt Lake, and he said, to my utter amazement, that Senator Gibson had been urged to run again and again in order to defeat this amendment. I sat in an LDS church, temple, I don't remember, stake, that was packed full, and I had two men on each side of me who gave me the elbow when that was said—one who had the same position I did, and one who was a member of that church, the Mormon Church. "Wow, listen to what this man is saying." Well, needless to say, I heard it loudly and clearly. In terms of the fact that they hadn't published a letter, that was pretty public, I would say.

It was clearly not only the people at that service who heard it. It was not, of course, a news item, but Senator Gibson and I had had lunch at one time prior to this vote in 1978, and he said to me, "You know, I believe we'll probably be the only two people who will vote our conscience regardless of the advisory vote." He said, "I'm going to vote no, even if it passes." And he said, "I'm sure you're going to vote yes, even if it's defeated."

I said, "Exactly."

The underlying premise of that comment to me was that we philosophically feel so strongly in our position, *unlike* a lot of other people in the legislature who would say, "Oh, well I would have voted for it, but 125,000 people said no," or, "I wasn't going to vote for it at all, but, hey, my constituency proved I was right."

There are two political thoughts of how people should represent their constituents. The one I have always adhered to, having a degree in political science, was the one that people elected you to do a job for them, but they know that you are going to have more information on any one topic—or they hope you do—and they hope you read a lot and assimilate and understand the issues and will vote how you feel it's important to vote. Whether they agree with you, every two or four years, they'll tell you about that at the ballot box. The other

school of thought is, that, somehow, and maybe now with the Internet, you wouldn't even really *need* elected representatives. Everybody would just go in and push a button on any issue, and that's what you're supposed to do. Maybe in today's telecommunication world that may be more possible than it ever was when I served, although, I guess you get down to the bottom line: what's the purpose of having a representative form of government?

At that time, there were a lot of polls taken, and then people used to stack up all their mail on their desks, and one pile might be three feet high, and one might be two feet high and ten inches, and they would go with the three-foot-high pile. So that told me that this really was not an important issue to them. It was a political issue, not a philosophical issue.

Were there other ways this had an impact on your career? Was the Equal Rights Amendment a priority to you in your first session? You must have gone in as a representative of your district with some ideas of things that were of importance to you—was this one of them? Or did that change during all of this process?

It was not one of the issues that I ran on, because the very first time it was introduced was the previous session, in 1973, and in the senate it only received four "yes" votes and sixteen "no." That same year it was introduced in the assembly and died in the judiciary committee. So it did not have a long life. To be honest with you, my focus that first session and what I campaigned on in my district, was opening up the government so more people would have a better understanding of who had supported the individual, how much they'd spent. Should lobbyists, should everybody, know whom they represent? This was all new, and it really was a result of Watergate, but I wasn't really identified with this issue. I was more identified as a mother with small children. Biggest issue in my campaign.

After I got to the legislature, it became so clear to me that this was something that I would definitely support. The more I read, and the more I listened, it became very clear that I felt really strongly about it. It's probably one of the ways that I'm identified. Probably less so today than maybe another major women's issue, because the students I have in my classes now weren't *born* when I was voting on these things. [laughter] I used to laugh, because ERA to most them, probably, is the name of a realty firm. In fact, when my daughter was, say, nine or ten, there was an ERA Realtor up the street, and they had the big signs on the side of their car, because they could use it as a business deduction, if they identified their car in such a way. Kristina came *running* home to tell me that Mrs. So-and-so up the street supported the ERA too! [laughter] Unfortunately, she was having a visit by a Realtor. But Kristina was very close.

Yes, and I think it probably did change people's view of you, and you became very connected to the Equal Rights Amendment. Do you think also to women's and children's issues, in general, or do you think that happened early on from the standpoint of you being a mother and so on?

I think it had more to do with just who I was. There is that well-known school of thought that says if you do involve women in any process, whether it be political or in a business, that they do come with different ways of looking at things and their own wealth of experiences, whether they're a mother, whether they're a wife. Those kinds of things do make a difference, and, clearly, I believe that, because it did for me. I did not go to the legislature as well defined as I

came out. That process and my view of the role of women significantly evolved.

Was it the first session that this started to happen, and you knew already that you felt strongly, or do you think it went on over a longer period of time as you dealt with the testimony and the information that you were reading and so on?

Well, I guess I could generally say that the longer I served, the more sessions I was a member of—it was a continuum—that, yes, I began to feel more and more strongly by virtue of experiences I had, maybe conferences I attended, seminars, my own colleagues' reading material. I would have to believe that it did start in that first session. As sessions went on, it became clear, if I just look at the bills I introduced, what I became interested in, that I had probably become identified with women's issues. We were talking about this feeling of representation of women's and children's issues. When did it start? I'm looking here at the bills I introduced in 1975, and it's clear that if I use this as a gauge, I think there were thirteen bills that I introduced that session. There's one that deals with children's issues, I would say, and that did not pass.

AB424 was a bill I introduced in 1975, and in flipping through the bills that I sponsored, I see this one as standing out, dealing with children. It would require preschools to be licensed and regulated by the state Board of Education. You can tell the success, or lack thereof, or the contentiousness of an issue, by just looking at their history. In this case, I remember this quite well, and the co-sponsors I had were all members of the assembly education committee, because that's where this bill was going to be heard. Of course, these are the things you learn when you get in the legislature—I had people who clued me into these things—that you want to get the committee members who are going to vote on it first to be co-sponsors. Well, I think they regretted it without question once the bill had a hearing. [laughter]

This fits right into the fact of talking about what the women bring to the process. Well, here's a perfect example. I'm looking at preschools for my own children. Clearly, that's of interest to me. If I was a man, I probably would have left this for my wife to do and might not know anything about them. It became clear to me that there were, maybe, a handful of preschools that I would want to send my child to, but if you looked in the Yellow Pages, they all had school in their name. Some might have only been a drop-in, or childcare. My point was that I wanted to make a distinction that, if it said "school," then there should be something going on there, some kind of education, depending upon their age and what was age appropriate.

As opposed to just a straight child-care facility.

Well, they might have coloring books and crayons and just kept busy, but at that time, you remember, there were not all that many women in the workforce, and so the women who would send their kids to this kind of experience, were hoping, I would suspect, that they might have a head start—and I use that term advisedly—before they got to kindergarten.

I discussed this with the director of the Montessori school. In fact, I believe it was she, Barbara Krueger, who brought this to my attention. I then discussed it with the directors of the other preschools that I had been looking at for my own children, and they all thought this was a terrific idea, and they were going to support it. Well, how about all the rest? [laughter] All the rest did *not* think it was a very good idea.

These kinds of experiences taught me that if you're going to introduce something like this, you'd better think about where the opposition is going to come from and, maybe, how you could dilute that opposition to some extent by visiting with people, explaining what you have in mind, rather than waiting to the day of the hearing. I honestly don't remember if I'd gone to the state Board of Education, because they were named in the bill. Of course, they knew to be there, because they were going to have another added responsibility. But the real concern was all the rest who thought this was an elitist kind of legislation. Who was going to make the decision as to what was a school and what was not? I don't remember all the specifics of the bill, but wow! That was a baptism by fire, because it got killed immediately, and maybe they just left it in somebody's desk and didn't have me go through the agony of defeat. It just went to the committee, and that's where it ended.

It died in committee?

It died in committee. It was introduced, and then it was read the first time, which it has to be in order to refer it, and then, I don't know what happened to it after that.

To this day, I still don't think it's a bad idea that there be *some* way for the mother, or the person who's responsible for preschoolers, to get a sense of what's going on in these different places. That's not to say that one is not good, but it serves a different purpose.

It was just a consumer kind of bill, in my mind, to let people know. And it maybe costs more. There may be a financial difference between a preschool and a drop-in center. I certainly would think so. Probably there should be, because you've got to have different training.

To actually teach.

I would hope. I do know that many of the national chains—and I don't want to use any particular name—will hire high-school girls more as babysitters, and that's fine, if the parents know, "Hey, this is what I need. The girl gets paid minimum wage, but I just want to make sure they're in a place and safe while I'm out doing whatever."

As I said, from each of these things, you do learn something. I don't believe that anything ever happened with this idea. I didn't introduce it again because the problems raised were ones that I, evidently, was not able to address in a way that would make the opponents feel comfortable, even though I had very good intentions.

Getting back to the basic question—I'm looking in 1975—it appears that that may be one of many bills that I was the main sponsor of, and I may have co-sponsored a number of other bills.

You mentioned various bills relating to women and children, and I can remember in talking to Jean Ford about it that she basically said, "Well, after the ERA did not pass, we went on to try to work on other kinds of legislation that would address the inequalities for women and for women's issues." Do you feel like there were other pieces of legislation you can point to that you got involved in because of that? Since there was not going to be an ERA, were there other kinds of things that could be brought into force that you were involved in?

Yes. One of the arguments given early on was, "Well, why don't we just have the bill drafters go through and take out everything that seems to be an inequality in our law, and then we will introduce separate bills to correct that?" That was introduced by a woman, a Mormon woman, a Democrat from Clark County, and it did pass. Of course, I supported it, and it did

come out at the end of the session or before the next session with the suggested changes.

We started kind of talking a little bit about other laws. There were just things that bill-drafters had to go through.

Yes, and getting back to that, yes, they did do that, and I don't know if they got everything. Ultimately, we think they did, and I'll bring you right up to date as to last session. There was something still remaining, but the bill drafters had to find this, and, clearly, none of us are going to go through them all and make sure they caught everything. Some of them were not terribly important, and it cut both ways. If a woman got a special something-or-other, then it should be given to the other gender. I mean, the whole idea of this is gender equality. It doesn't mean it's *always* women that need to be elevated. In some cases, it needs to be more equal for the male, as well.

I remember Mary Gojack had a very important part of this, and I don't believe it came from this study—it may have. It dealt with credit, the whole experience of a woman maintaining a credit card or establishing credit *in her own right*, without her husband or her father or an uncle or someone else, if she was not married. That was rampant in those days. It was almost impossible for women to establish their own credit. Today we find that probably a bit ludicrous, but I guess that's what's happened in this period of time. I suspect people would today say, "Well, you didn't need the Equal Rights Amendment, because look at all these changes that have been made." There have been a lot of changes, and I'm sure part of it *was* due to, quote, "the Women's Movement."

The other important thing that Mary was very involved with was called the Sole Trader Act. I believe that's the correct term. Basically, the bottom line was that a woman could not own a business in her own right without the signature—I don't know if it was a signature, or if it was more substantial than that—of a male, i.e. father, husband. She could not do that, and it ties in with the whole credit thing, to some extent. You tell people today that, and they cannot believe it.

They can't believe it was so recent.

That only happened twenty, twenty-five years ago. Really, that's not a long period of time in our nation's history. But those were substantial things that I would suspect came as a result of this. There were things, for example, that a woman could not serve on a posse. Well, we didn't have a lot of posses then, and we have less today, so we made that equal. However, just last session, when I was down at the legislature, I got a call from KOLO Channel 8 reporter Dennis Myers asking me about a bill that was introduced that made it equal for widowers to be treated the same way as widows in terms of a property tax exemption of a thousand dollars. That number has not changed in the past thirty years, but it was granted to women and was until last session, and I'm assuming it passed, to make that equal for men. And it should have been.

There are still those things that are popping up.

Well, he thought that that was the last time on this issue, and Dennis has had a real interest in this kind of legislation, so I suspect if he thought it, it probably was.

He'd done his homework.

But he did mention that, and, of course, I was not on camera or anything, but he did say he'd talked to me over the phone. People kept calling me about this, and I thought, "I just told Dennis that on the phone."

It surprised me that that had not been taken care of, and maybe it didn't come out in this report, because I suspect if it had, we would have done it. That has more merit than the posse bill, I think.

Did that happen right during that session?

No.

That happened later.

In most cases, resolutions are introduced to create a committee during the interim. For example, in 1975, I had one that sort of applies a little bit here to women, I suppose, that was calling for a study of skilled nursing facilities, ACR-33. That did pass, and that study was established. A committee was set up, and I believe I may have chaired that. I'm pretty sure I did. Many, many supporters, co-sponsors, and it did pass.

Of course, in general terms, women tend to outlive men, so you see more women in skilled nursing facilities. I cannot tell what precipitated my introducing the bill, but something occurred, I think, when I was going door to door. There was a nursing a facility in my district, on Idlewild Drive, down near the river, I remember, at that time. One of the things that I was very interested in doing was to have surprise visits, unannounced, so we could see what the place was really like. They did not have advanced notice that a committee from the legislature was coming. Unfortunately, there was one person on my committee who seemed to feel it incumbent upon himself to let the nursing facilities know before we came—even though it was very clear I did not want that to be done—in case they wanted to put up some more paintings on the wall, clean it up, whatever. It certainly focused on that issue, and I really cannot remember exactly the number of bills.

To answer your question, under normal circumstances very few of these resolutions pass, because it takes staff time, it takes legislators' time. To just get on the committee—even if you introduced the resolution that created it, that doesn't mean you necessarily will get on it or even chair it. Again, it depends on the politics and the legislative commission, and I would assume we've talked about interim finance and legislative commission, the two bodies that maintain the legislature during the interim. One is a money committee of course, IFC, and they're supposed to act only in emergency situations, "It needs to be done now. We can't wait for the next session."

Same thing with the legislative commission. It deals with more policy issues, but, clearly, twelve people should not be representing the entire will of a body. The legislative commission is the group that decides who's going to serve on which committee, who's going to chair it, et cetera.

The policy committee in the legislature has changed its name. In those days it was called Legislative Affairs, which is a good name for it, I suppose. [laughter] Legislative Functions, basically, is concerned with issues that deal with the legislature as an institution.

But, most of those, that's how it occurs. In this case, the one dealing with cleaning up any inequalities would be done by staff time. There's no point in having a hearing on that, because what could we add? However they did it in those days, now would be pretty easy, huh?

Yes. Just flip through the computer. It would be great.

Right, but that was not possible.

It was probably all by hand.

I suspect it was.

And so that was one of the things that happened. I don't know if we're entirely done with 1975, but can you point to maybe one or two really big lessons that you feel like you learned during that first session as a brand new legislator?

Well, I think I've already talked about one, figuring out who your opposition might be and trying to work that out beforehand with those people.

And that's not to say that somehow violates the open-meeting law. We didn't have an open-meeting law in those days, but even if we did, that doesn't suggest there's anything wrong with doing that. In fact, I suppose a legislator could go to a school on a certain time of day and say, "Everybody interested in this bill . . . . " Put out press releases, have them come over. You'd put a tape recorder on and get some kind of view or take notes or whatever. I suppose you probably would not be able to take a secretary from the legislature, just you, yourself. But I think that's one lesson is to try to figure out what the opposition is and make sure of the people involved, for instance, State Board of Education in that last bill, and talking with them. The other lesson might be, well, to be sure you don't make enemies right off the bat! [laughter]

Try really hard not to do that!

Try really hard. But you know that's going to happen. I think the more passionately you feel about something, probably, the more it's going to happen.

Well, I've always said in my own mind, I believe that you have two constituencies: one that sent you to the legislature, and then the constituency within the legislature. Even if you totally disagree with somebody, and this is really hard to be able to get yourself programmed to do this, to not hold grudges against the person voting against something you cared very much about, because you've got to work with them. The old saying is, "You're going to probably meet them the next day," and that is absolutely true. Let's say one of these Equal Rights Amendment hearings was late at night. You probably had a long day, the place was packed, and the fireworks were going off. The rules were being quoted, and people thought they were the wrong rules, and all of these kinds of things, but when it's over, it's over, and you go on to another day. I think it's important for you to get to stake out how you want to be perceived by the press, the people you represent, and your fellow colleagues.

I think you don't want to appear too smart, either. You *don't* want to be *condescending* to any of your colleagues, because they all perceive themselves as being equal to you, and they are. They represent the same number of constituents, or as close as you can get during redistricting and reapportionment. But nobody wants to think, "I'm getting lectured by somebody," whether they've been there for two years or twenty years. As I say, you could have the greatest ideas and be elected by 80 percent of your district and not get a bill through. And that was something I learned.

Another thing I learned was that, if it is a bill that certain groups want, and there's a lot of interest in the bill, then the longer you wait, the *more mail* you're going to get, and you're going to receive a swarm of phone calls. Now, you may wait because you legitimately need more information. I'll give an example. On the two last things, this one, I remember, was a bill that dealt with collective bargaining items of the Nevada State Education Association. Now, Jean Ford, who sat next to me in those days, knew immediately how she was going to vote, so she had hardly anything on her desk. I didn't. I was endorsed by them, but I represented a district that was not what you call "labor oriented," and collective

bargaining is basically a labor-management kind of bill, even though it's teachers versus an AFL-CIO worker. That was something I learned. However, if you don't know, then you don't want to jump to a conclusion, just so you won't receive a lot of phone calls and mail.

I think the specific problem that I had, the lesson I learned was that because there were not that many women in the legislature and not that many women who were pro-ERA, pro-choice, that kind of philosophy, then you tended to become friends with those who were, and I joined two others, both Democrats. No, at that time, I believe Jean Ford was a Republican, and she switched later on, yes, during her first defeat for the senate. But Mary Gojack, who had been very instrumental in getting me to run, was in the senate. I'd say that Jean, because she sat next to me and was also the same party, was perceived as being a rather liberal Republican, just like I was stamped right before I got there. I was another Jean Ford, another Mary Gojack. I didn't realize that, of course, but I learned rather quickly, so I needed to establish who I was, that I was not the same. I represented a different district.

Jean, as a matter of fact, represented the University of Nevada, Las Vegas area, which tended to be more liberal and more Democratic. I didn't. I represented southwest Reno, and at that time, of course, it didn't go from here to the Mount Rose highway, but it was a more business oriented, more professional kind of district and more conservative. That was important to me, because at some point you don't go down there and just do whatever you want and say "Oh, well, I can take care of it in November, two years from now." You want to represent your district as how you perceive it, and there was not one mobile home in my district, and not one apartment in that district at that time. That is really incredible. I think that was the only district in the state that had only single-family residences. It was incredible.

I introduced a bill dealing with mobile-home law, that is, depreciation of taxes. That was directly geared to my constituency of single-family homes and really came from a discussion I had had with a former assemblyman from this district, Robert Broadbent, who was a physician. He also understood the district in terms of the single-family residence, getting a handle on mobile-home taxation, because it was perceived to be personal property rather than real property. So, he and I had had a discussion about that when I went to introduce myself to him. We did talk about that. He kind of liked that idea, and I'm not suggesting that he didn't contribute to the process, because I'm sure he did at that time.

So, I think that those kinds of things, then, will set me apart from the two people, Jean and Mary in my case, who I tended to be grouped with or coupled with. There are other things, I'm sure, that I could point out, as well.

For example, the bill I just talked about on collective bargaining, to be honest with you, I don't remember how I voted. The group had endorsed me, and they weren't going to. I had raised a stink with them, because the Teacher's Association was going to support somebody, a male Republican, and when I found that out I called them and said I was a former schoolteacher, for goodness sakes. So I'd have to go back and look at the record.

See how that all went.

Yes, and I know later on, when I represented the senate, because it was a bigger district and more diverse representation, that I felt a little more comfortable maybe supporting a bill on mobile-home depreciation taxes. But I'm guessing that probably I didn't, which would

have very much set me apart from Jean. In fact, I always made the point that Jean and I agreed on probably 95 percent of the things, as I did with most everybody in the assembly. But it's the 5 percent that sets people apart from each other, and that's just a ballpark percentage.

Sounds like it was a really intense learning time for you that first session.

It was. I learned another thing this session. I had also been endorsed by the State of Nevada Employees Association, the state workers. When you go for interviews, you're asked, how do you feel about this, about that? This was all *new* to me. Half this stuff I didn't even know. They were quoting NRS233.102. I didn't know what that was. I had no NRS here at home. So all I could do was give them general kinds of answers. In the one case, I had said that I would support something of the state employees. It was a very close vote, and I did not vote the way I said I was going to, because it had been amended in committee and did something quite different. However, guess what? I did not go to Bob Gagnier, who was then head of the State of Nevada Employees Association, and tell him.

Tell him why.

Yes. All of a sudden, it was there, and they were very, very upset. To me, it was clear as anything. The bill wasn't the same as I said I was going to support, but, again, it's that learning to go out and explain things. Be honest, but explain, "Hey, are you counting me for this? But this isn't the same thing."

So you kind of grew in awareness of all the people you needed to communicate with if you changed your vote, and the reasoning that you did it, and so on, as you went along.

Or you went to do something, and it affected different groups. There are a lot of things, I think, that dealt with better accessibility—that's not quite the word— better communication.

Another thing I learned, which is kind of in the inverse, is that when you're first elected, and, I'm sure, every session, you're sent the annual report of every state agency, and I thought I had to read them all and understand them all. I took all this stuff with me to Tucson, because we went down to spend Christmas with my in-laws and my mother, and that's all I did. Well, I couldn't even remember half of it. Besides I wasn't even on half of the committees that the Department of Transportation bi-annual report had anything to do with. I wasn't on the transportation committee. Big learning experience. Needless to say, not a veteran person had told me that. Or did I ask. Both ways.

You just made an assumption that you should know as much as you could about everything, rather than focusing.

Right, but I could have focused only on the things on which committee I was on, because by then I would have known.

7

1977 SESSION

Now, did you have to do another campaign between the 1975 session and the 1977, or were you there for the two sessions based on that one campaign?

Oh, no. After the 1975 session, then I had to go out and do that all over again. That's the advantage, or disadvantage, of being in the assembly. They are two-year terms, where the senate is a four-year term. I say "advantage" because the advantage is that you're out there exposing yourself, visiting with your constituents pretty much all the time. I spent a lot of time giving speeches, going to every place I was invited, not because I was thinking about running for anything else, but because I thought that's what you're supposed to do.

Very honestly, when I think back, one of the reasons I did run for the state legislature was because it was biennial, and I figured it would only be a hundred plus days every other year, and I felt that a mother of small children could do that. But, as it turns out, I made it full-time, and it was much more full-time than I had thought it would be. So both those things probably came into play.

Another thing I learned, but there wasn't much I could do about it, was the fact that because I was the first mother to be elected at such a young age with small children, and because I'd been a former reporter, I got a lot of press. A lot, a lot of press. I knew that would offend and tick off a lot of other people, but I didn't understand that, or I was certainly not going to say to somebody, "I'm sorry, I can't do this feature with you because I might offend somebody in my party."

That is very clear, and I look today, as an analogy, at John McCain, the Senate Republican from Arizona. The press *loves* John McCain, because he is accessible to them, because he knows how to deal with the press, and because he has issues that the press likes. Since I had been a reporter, I was going to be sympathetic to their issues, like the shield law that had to do with not telling who your sources were.

Protecting your sources?

Yes, I'll probably find it somewhere in this mess. Steve Coulter introduced the bill, and I think I was the only other co-sponsor.

It's right on the tip of my tongue. But those things presented themselves to me. Or they would do a feature on my family—I can think of pictures right now—with all of us getting on our bicycles in the driveway, or the kids out lifting a bottle of milk and bringing it in the house, because I was a different kind of legislator. That was good and bad. It got me the press, but it also . . . .

Raised some jealousies?

Yes, or issues with other people. So there's a lot of learning that went on in that first session.

By the time you had finished the session, did you know you wanted to run again, or did you know that way back when you ran the first time, that if you won, and you could, you'd like to keep going?

No. I had no idea. The first time, no, never thought of it, because, see, this was all kind of a learning experience, and I really, honestly felt that if I should lose, then it was one heck of a great experience, because I'd only lived here for four or five years, and I knocked on every single door twice in my district. I met *so* many nice people, some people who weren't so nice, but really, generally, way more nice people than not. It was just a terrific experience. Now, I probably wouldn't have said with as much surety after I'd been in there four or five terms, "Well, if I lose, what the heck?"

Then you had more invested.

Exactly. And maybe more lofty goals in a sense of running for something that would get you maybe into a different position. Between each legislative session, it was a help to me to be in so many stories in the newspaper, because people learned, even outside of my own district, who I was. I did

get out. I didn't always look at something and say, "Oh, this doesn't have anything to do with District 25. I'm not going to go do it." If it was a meeting at the airport, for example, I would have gone even though the airport was not in my district.

When it came time, after the first session, to make a decision about running again, was your family involved in that decision? Can you tell me a little bit about how you came to that decision and then started through the process for the second round?

I'll, first of all, say that probably the stiffest opposition I had was the first time I ran, because as sessions went on the opposition was minimal, or sometimes I didn't have anybody. I know I felt at the end of each session that I cannot possibly run again. It just is too demanding. I'm too tired. I am being pulled in too many different directions. But I think that that is a fairly normal feeling to have at the end of an absolutely incredible pressure-cooker period of time. Particularly, I have to say, I put a lot of pressure on myself, and I worked way harder than probably 98 percent of the legislators, and I probably didn't need to. But, even if I understood that, I wouldn't have done it any differently.

I really don't know, except for that initial feeling, how long it took for me not to feel that way. But the next race in 1977, I think I remember the man's name, and I do remember I had some of my Democratic friends who lived here in Washoe County who would tease me about how they'd seen at the Democratic Central Committee that everybody had decided to support my opponent, about 80 percent. He was really sharp, et cetera, et cetera, and they're just letting me know that he's planning to do this wide-spread television campaign, and signs are going to go up on such and such a day. Of course, I just bought it, big time. [laughter] And the guy didn't even get out of his house! Nobody knew him. He had two dollars to spend. [laughter]

That could get a rise out of you?

Oh, yes. And they knew that, of course, and so it was done. I remember Bob Barengo used to do that to me all the time. He was chairman of the judiciary committee in the assembly, which I was a member of.

This is just some other little side note, but, thinking about Bob, I did ask a *tremendous* number of questions. I was known for that, and at the end of my first session, all the chairmen got little gag gifts for members. A party is given at the end of the session for each committee, and I was given a T-shirt that said, "Just Two Questions Sue," because I'd always say, "I have a couple of questions!" [laughter] Always! And there were way more than two!

Assemblyman Bob Weise was elected at the same time I was from the district that was contiguous to mine from, say, Moana Lane down to Carson City. He and I, on the floor, would ask an unbelievable number of questions if we hadn't been on the committee that had heard that bill. I remember the speaker at that time said, "We've gone now ten extra days this session because of Wagner and Weise." [laughter]

Asking all their questions.

Yes. Yes. But, getting back to the campaign, I think it was in 1977 that Bob Barengo described to me the non-existent Democrat as a fabulous opponent. In the next campaign in 1979, I don't think I had anybody. Then we get into the senate after that.

How did your family feel about you running again?

Well, I think, probably, my kids would not have liked it. To be fair, I don't remember anything specific, but I was gone a lot. I'd been home all the time up until that point, and I think my husband was so agreeable, that I think he realized this was something I really enjoyed, and he thought I really had done a good job, and he was willing to do the extra—and it was a big extra with two small kids. I think he felt that when there was a new Congressional seat, that I should run for that, because he could get a job in Washington, so he was very, very supportive.

In fact, getting back to reporter Dennis Myers, he always used to say at meetings, "Pete Wagner was the model husband for a woman legislator to have." Not in competition with me, supportive, but gave me a lot of advice about issues—advice that I sometimes took and sometimes didn't. Having a full time job and also, in many cases, being responsible for the kids, he was the role model.

Let me make sure that we've touched on all the 1975 issues.

You've spotted one bill that says, "By Request," that you sponsored?

Yes, and that probably should be explained. It has only my name on it. I didn't get any co-sponsors, and it does say "By Request." It's a bill that changes the reference date used for determining representation in county political conventions. This was a bill I was asked to introduce by the Republican Party, which describes the way one was chosen to go to the county convention. The "By Request" basically sends out a message, if you will, to your fellow colleagues that you are doing this as a courtesy to a group of people. I guess you could go through every single bill and say, "Well, somebody got me interested in this, so I introduced it." But this is done only if you think probably nobody else would be particularly interested in being a sponsor with you, and that it's just different—I don't know how to explain it—being requested, say, by the Republican Party versus being requested by the Motorcycle Dealers Association. There is a difference.

A difference in terms of communicating some priority and importance?

Yes. You could say that.

So "By Request" would mean it was more important than just something that had very limited interest?

No, I'd say this had very limited interest.

This had very limited interest. OK. That's what I was trying to figure out.

Yes. Yes. Limited interests and, also, if you killed it, it's not the end of the world.

One of the things you've mentioned is that you ran your campaign and went into the 1975 session based on the idea of more openness in government, and I think we're looking at the list of bills you introduced, and maybe you can comment overall on some of the things you were trying to accomplish that first session in that direction.

Yes, that's true. I'm sure we've discussed my great interest in opening up the process, and really this is the reason I ran—because of Watergate—as a Republican. I was just so totally appalled with Richard Nixon and the cover-up. "Cover-up" to me suggested, "Let's not allow a cover-up to occur." So how do you do that? Well, it seemed to me you should let people know how you spent your money, your campaign expenses, and who contributed, who gave you money in order to spend it, if you will.

My success rate wasn't very good, because I looked at those two bills, and they have a very short history, meaning they didn't go very far. I do believe at that point Governor O'Callaghan had some of these concepts in his "State of the State" message, and so, clearly, they would be parceled out to Democratic members of the assembly and the senate, because that's how that works. If the governor has a package of bills, he will give it to people in his own party—or *her* own party. Maybe, someday there'll be woman governor. So mine weren't going to be the vehicle to get this kind of a change, because I was a Republican freshman.

You were new and of the opposite party.

Yes. However, on a bill titled, or numerically numbered, AB84, which sets a limit on legislative campaign expenses for primary and general election periods combined, this has a whole page of dates, which means it went over and up and down and around and under and every which way. This is one of the longer histories I've seen. However, on May 20, it went to enrollment, although, it doesn't say "signed by the governor." That may have been because it went to enrollment. In fact, there's an issue going on right now in the supreme court on whether a bill passed between twelve midnight and one a.m. is enrolled. When it's enrolled, that is a procedure that occurs first. Then it goes to the governor for a signature. I'm sure the governor signed this, but it had a very long history.

Now, this would have set a limit on how much one could spend in either the primary or the general, and that is an issue that is even current today. Can you legally put a cap on how much any person can spend? As we all know, there are people who are very wealthy in their own right. The Supreme Court has decided through the years, including one major case called *Buckley v. Vallejo*, that there's a way of getting around putting caps on the amount of money you spend in a campaign. I don't remember the date, but, obviously, it was no later than the early 1970s that the Supreme Court decided you cannot put a cap on what an individual can spend on himself or herself, and that's why you see very wealthy people, in many cases, bankrolling their own campaigns. That is allowable based upon the Supreme Court decisions.

There was a United States senator just elected from New Jersey. I don't remember his name, but he was an investment banker at Goldman Sachs, and he spent like twenty-four million dollars of his own money to get elected, and that is OK, based upon Supreme Court decisions.

But there was a way of dealing with this issue, and I know I'm getting a little vague here, but it may have been that this was passed, and then we found out it wasn't constitutional, after the fact, I really don't know. I guess the basic underlying premise, and maybe you could look that up, is that a large number of my bills dealt with exactly what I campaigned on.

Sue, you wanted to specifically go into a summary of some of the things that happened about the vote and Lieutenant Governor Bob Rose's role in that.

I did. In 1977, SJR5 was the vehicle to hopefully wind its way through the legislature in order to ratify the Equal Rights Amendment. Now, interestingly, as it turns out, I was there that evening in the senate watching, and it was quite emotional. It was late at night. I read this just recently, but I think they recessed until, maybe, seven o'clock at night, and I don't think it got done until about ten. There is a different feel in a body, whether or not the sun is shining, although, there are not a lot of windows in the legislative building, but you do get a different sense, I think, at night. People have gone out. Some of them may have had a couple of drinks, to be honest with you, and come back, and they may not speak quite as well as they might have in the afternoon. [laughter] Or maybe they don't speak at all. Thank goodness, if they don't! But it was an emotional and interesting time for the lieutenant governor to cast the vote and then ship it down to the assembly.

It's interesting that I then became the lieutenant governor, the president of the senate in the 1990s. I waited for an opportunity to cast a tie-breaking vote, and I was hoping then that they would appeal it to the supreme court, because at that time, Bob Rose was chief justice of the supreme court. [laughter] Myron Leavitt, another former lieutenant governor, was on the supreme court, as well. Even though he was not in favor of the Equal Rights Amendment, he had told me when I asked that he would vote in favor of the lieutenant governor casting a tie-breaking vote. So, I guess, what comes around goes around, what goes around comes around, or whatever. But anyway, it was an interesting procedure.

Did you get the opportunity to cast a tie-breaking vote?

I was able to cast a tie-breaking vote on an amendment, and that was somewhat different in importance. I thought it was close. The amendment was not substantive enough to make much of a difference.

There was one bill that came out of the senate judiciary committee—I don't remember if it was 1991 or 1993, or who introduced it—but it would make a lawsuit settlement public, so everyone would know what the jury had done. I, of course, had just gone through a trial. The settlement was not public, although, I think there was a headline, but I felt that that would be a conflict of interest for me, and I would not be voting on that. It was very close, but it did not become a tie.

Now, let me just finish up with the SJR5 of the 1977 session to ratify ERA. It then went down to the assembly where there were fifteen "yes" votes cast and twenty-four "no" votes. I think we talked about how those numbers had totally switched from 1975. I believe that's the time when the seven or nine who'd lied changed their vote. That's why those buttons showed up during that session. It just demonstrated that people were not very committed to a principle of equality, if you could change your mind two years later.

The people who did not want to have to deal with this very emotional and contentious issue one more time, decided to leave it up to the people of Nevada, with a ballot advisory question. In fact, several of us, I believe, voted against that, because amending the national Constitution should not be done that way. It had never been done before, and clearly it was just a political move. It was soundly defeated, 124,000 "no" to about 62,000 "yes." In the district which became my senate district when I was elected to the senate in 1980, only a couple of precincts up at Incline Village, around the lake, supported the Equal Rights Amendment.

We've talked about education level and the connection with the ERA vote.

Right, and we talked about Senator Gibson and me having lunch.

Yes, he said that only the two of you would be voting your true feelings on that.

Right. Interestingly enough, another tactic occurred in the previous sessions, in 1979 and in 1981. A resolution was introduced in both sessions. In fact, in 1979

it was SJR1, and I'm sure people would understand that the numbers are in chronological order, so that would be the first senate joint resolution introduced that session. Interestingly enough, it was introduced, and then the prime sponsor moved for no further consideration. That basically meant that this bill was dead. This resolution, this opportunity to amend the national Constitution, was dead for that session.

Is that usual, to have a sponsor move against his or her own bill?

No, no it wasn't. It was done as a tactical move by an opponent of the Equal Rights Amendment. I think it was Senator Floyd Lamb who introduced it, and immediately after the reading of the resolution he moved for no further consideration. That was done as a tactic to take it out of the legislators' hands, so they wouldn't have to deal with that anymore.

However, it then appears in the assembly, that same session, only two days later. Again, the same motion is made. I remember, I spoke to this, asking why they would bother to go through it. It could never pass because the senate had already taken it out of the political jurisdiction for that entire session. Well, no one answered my question. The senate resolution passed. The one that I mentioned was introduced by Floyd Lamb, I think. Fourteen "yes" votes, three "no" votes, and three absent. In the assembly, it does not show any record of voting, and I'd have to go back and reread it again, to see why the senate actually took a vote on "no further consideration," whereas the assembly did not.

Getting back to the point, however, it was really redundant and not necessary. However, in discussing this on the assembly floor, I do remember that one legislator from Clark County was very happy that this was done, so he could make his speech about opposing it for the record. He could use that, probably, to send back to his constituents and members of his church, showing where he stood on this particular issue.

In 1981, the same thing occurred. Introduced in the senate, SJR7, and a motion for no further consideration, and there was no vote taken on that, either. That meant it was dead, and by that time the period of time had expired for a resolution to be viable. A certain number of years for ratification—I think it was seven, but I really don't remember. Then I think they were given an extension, but it would mean that you'd have to start all over again. At that point there had been thirty-four states, and now the opposition was so much better organized. The Eagle Forum was out in all the states, particularly, in the southeastern part of our country, and so, probably, you're not going to get thirty-four states, to be honest with you, because by now, in my mind, the arguments that didn't have very much merit had kind of warped people's images of what this was going to do. It was going to "ruin the lives of homemakers," when in reality it would have no bearing on them at all. We weren't going to rip them out of their homes and send them into the workplace. If they wanted to go, hopefully, they'd be treated in an equal fashion. But, I really think we might have exhausted this topic.

I think we've covered that one.

Although, in my mind, it's never exhausted.

It is never exhausted. [laughter] Do you ever see that Equal Rights Amendment being revived in any way?

It is often talked about in Congress to this day. As a matter of fact, BPW, Business and Professional Women, a large, national organization—it's still one of their top priorities, and they call for it being introduced each time Congress goes into session. I think it may have actually started, but not with any real fervor or commitment, because, probably, it would be difficult to get a sufficient number of votes, honestly, having Republicans in control almost in the Senate at this moment.

Probably, when we started taping this, maybe, they were. [laughter] We should make a note about why I made that silly comment—because it was a tie between Democrats and Republicans, and this is in the congressional session of the year 2001. Fifty of each, and the president of the Senate, of course, is the vice president— just as lieutenant governor in our state presides over the senate—and he then could become a tie-casting vote in favor of the Republicans. However, a Republican senator from the state of Vermont, Jim Jeffords, did not really believe very much in the Republican platform and principles anymore, and so he left the Republican Party to become an Independent. However, he voted with the Democrats in terms of organizing the United States Senate, and that meant that all the people, all the Republicans, their staffs, who were on a Tuesday in charge, on a Wednesday were not. The Democrats took over, brought all their staff people in and will dictate the agenda for the Senate. Even though it seems, "Well, who cares," it is a huge, huge advantage to be in power in the majority party, not only because you chair all the major committees, but also because, in the Congress, unlike in our state senate, they can actually dictate what goes to the floor.

So, for Nevada, it's terrific, because our United States Senator, Harry Reid, is second in command in the Senate. So, many of the things we want, hopefully, will be done, and things we don't want—and the agenda of Nevada is a defensive one in terms of the nuclear waste dump and sports betting— they are not going to happen this time.

This has been such a tremendous thing. Has it ever happened before?

It has never, ever happened in our nation's history. There *have* been people who have switched parties. In fact, one we might mention here is United States Senator Phil Gramm from Texas. He was a Democrat, but rather a conservative Democrat, and switched his party affiliation to the Republican party. However, he didn't *run* as a Republican immediately thereafter, so that people in Texas could have a chance to either affirm that decision of switching parties or say, "You did the wrong thing," and vote against him.

But to actually change the entire majority to minority political leadership in the Senate—that has never happened. However, having come from a New England state, I felt very comfortable, and I'm sure Senator Jeffords did too, that for the people of Vermont, that was not a problem to most of them. In fact, I believe that from the state of Vermont, currently there is a congressman who is a socialist party member in our United States Congress. So that shows you, or shows the readers possibly, that they are really moderate to liberal in their views.

OK, so it does not look like the ERA is going to be back, even though the topic has never entirely gone away.

That's true. I think another thing people might say, "Well, look at all the improvements for women." 50 percent of law school enrollees are women, or close to it. That's definitely true. I think it would not have occurred without certain women who led the movement, and the fact that this almost became an amendment to our Constitution. So there was a really serious look at why was this necessary, and what can we do about it, even though we didn't get it placed in the Constitution.

We also talked about follow-up legislation in Nevada, different things that came forward, and I'm sure we'll come back to that as we go along. I did want to talk a little bit more about other issues that came up in the 1977 legislature, and there are several to choose from. One of them you wanted to discuss was the cancer treatment, laetrile. We are now in the 1977 legislative session on a bill that you did not introduce, but had a lot of controversy about it at the time. Is that correct?

It is. The bill was introduced initially legalizing laetrile, which is an extract from apricot pits.

And it was used for cancer treatment.

It was an idea that, I believe, came from Mexico and some of the places down close to the border that people went to who just felt that there was no hope left for them. And remember, this is in 1977. I think it still goes on, but you don't hear much about it, anymore. I can understand the position that people would be in who felt like they'd done everything there was, and there just was no hope. People wore copper bracelets; people did a lot of things. This was the first bill introduced in any state legislature to legalize this product. I think it came in liquid form, and the man who had the sole distributorship rights in this country, had moved from California to Nevada. He couldn't get it on in California, so he thought it would probably be easier to get it passed in Nevada, which in my mind doesn't say a lot for the image of the Nevada legislature around the country, or maybe it was because it has fewer members. So, this was something that the proponents would argue would give people hope. However, during the procedure, quite late at night—and it was in the assembly committee first, commerce and labor—suddenly there was an amendment. It was placed on this bill, and it was another product called Gerovital.

This sounded to me like snake oil in the old days where people in the back of a covered wagon would open up the flaps and shout, "Hey, come right up, step right up! I got something here that's going to grow hair on your head, and if you don't want hair, it'll take it off. It'll close valves after open-heart surgery! And it will do just about anything." [laughter] Well, the way it was placed on this bill raised some suspicions, and I believe that it really was Gerovital, and not laetrile, that was the main issue here. They wanted to get that through, and they felt that they had a better chance amending it on to a bill that had sympathy attached to it.

I had been apprized by, at that time, United States Congressman Jim Santini's office to keep an eye on this bill. So, I had my little antenna up to begin with. Then when I was hearing what was happening, I really had my antenna up. It came to the assembly floor, and I was adamantly opposed to it, because I had serious concerns about Gerovital in relationship to the consumer. Now, I suppose you could say, "Well, buyer beware," but I was looking at the process and what we were responsible for at the Nevada legislature, and this was not what I thought we should be doing. We really didn't know much about "medicines," and there was certainly very little testimony for that on that subject.

The man who owned the dealership—not the dealership—the distributorship . . . . [laughter] Dealership might be better description. It was a lemon! [laughter] His name is Marvin Kratter. It turns out that at one time he had owned the Boston Celtics, and there were some slight positives to his resume, such as that, but then there were some other things in that vita that didn't look so good.

Everybody supported this. I think there were two "no" votes—there might have

been three—against this bill, mine being one, and I think that Assemblyman Jim Kosinski voted against it. He represented like Sun Valley, Lemon Valley, Golden Valley area, the north valleys here in Reno. Kosinski had been a former bill drafter, by the way. He was very good. He was a very good legislator. I think there might have been one other.

I was really exercised about this bill. As a matter of fact, it reminds me of a recent applicant for a gaming license; that's why we were talking about his resume. Marvin Kratter owned the Boston Celtics from 1965-1968. Their home was Boston Garden.

Anyway, most everybody thought this was a wonderful bill, and Jim Joyce was the lobbyist for it. I always had a record with Jim—never supporting much of his legislation until near the end of my career, because it was things like this. I felt he kind of marginalized things in the legislature. I really didn't think it was appropriate, and I didn't like what we were doing, because I didn't think we were the right people to do this kind of thing. Maybe a pharmacist would've been a more knowledgeable person.

But anyway, the bill did pass, and I remember making my comments. I think that I said something about, "This bill is the best that money can buy," and that it was brought to our state because, of course, it was much easier to get through the Nevada legislature. I got ruled out of order by the speaker because I shouldn't be saying things like that about our body, the body of which I was a member. But I kept right on going, and, of course, it passed thirty-seven to three, or something like that. The one thing that Marvin Kratter said was that this could only be done by prescription, so that gave it a sense of the "Good Housekeeping Seal of Approval."

Interestingly enough, it ran into a lot more trouble in the senate and still passed, but there were *way* more "no" votes. I believe that Nevada Supreme Court Justice Cliff Young, who was in the senate at that time, was very much opposed to this, for many of the same reasons I was.

The next session, ah, here comes Mr. Kratter back. Now he doesn't want a prescription. He thinks that it should be just sold over the counter, and who is going to benefit from this? Well, of course, he will, and there's nothing *wrong* with that. I mean, we introduce bills for bankers and gamers, but this was an individual. He had said just two years before that this wasn't going to be easily obtainable, that there would some legitimate medical professional writing that prescription.

Well, now, we see that there's no prescription necessary. That would be 1979. I served on ways and means committee under Chairman Don Mello, and it was a very large committee, like thirteen people on it, in order to give everybody their first choice of committees and that kind of thing—some of them became very large, too large. But, in comes this bill. Now, why was it going to ways and means? Well, gosh darn, that's kind of weird, because they only deal with bills that take money away and distribute money.

We have to surmise that probably it was there because they had a lot of votes to get it out of committee. The night before the bill was to be heard in ways and means in the assembly, there were FBI agents out videotaping and audio taping—such as we're doing here today—comments made by certain legislators. I happened to be up at Lake Tahoe that night having dinner with two assemblymen, and I don't remember who else was there. Well, I didn't know anything about this until the following morning when all these cameras started to come into the room, and Marvin Kratter is sitting right there in the front row. One of the assemblymen started talking about this entrapment that had occurred with the FBI

agents. I looked around. I sat *way* at the end, because I didn't have a lot of seniority, of course, and I saw all these people's faces turn like green and want to slide under the seat. Marvin Kratter got up and tried to get out of the room. Skullduggery going on with this bill, and all I could think of was, "I was right from the very get-go." [laughter]

After that, I really cannot tell you what happened. I know this is a teaser to not complete the entire story, but no one was arrested. There were a lot of rumors floating around, and, in fact, there is a book—and I've got to get a copy of that, because I just ran into a woman who had read it—called *Power and Money*. She said that any suspicions I had, "Read the book, and you'll find out that they are true." [laughter] I'm not too sure if this was part of it, but it's written by Sara Denton, and I know it's out right now. [*The Money and the Power: The Making of Las Vegas and Its Hold on America, 1947-2000,* by Sally Denton and Roger Morris.] Unfortunately, it's hardback, and I have a little problem with that.

So, I'm not sure I understand about the entrapment. Sometimes you have to draw me a picture on these kinds of things.

No, that's OK, it's a little confusing.

The FBI agents were interviewing people who were supporting the bill?

That had to do with this bill, yes, exactly. It had something to do with a violation of interstate commerce, I believe. It was a national issue, because the FBI was there, but I am slightly fuzzy, because I wasn't a participant in any of this, so all I could do was observe what was happening.

Later on that session, when the Department of Health's budget came to us—this was where the agency responsible for distribution of laetrile and Gerovital was housed—I was looking through the budget, and I noticed there was only one individual dealing with this. I asked how many people were producing this product, and there was only one. To my understanding it has never made money. I've never heard anything more about it. I do know that it was in the newspaper. There was a man named Foster Church, who wrote for the *Reno Gazette-Journal*, and at that time I think it was the *Nevada State Journal*. It was two newspapers, I believe.

Anyway, Foster Church had a column, and in that column he wrote my opposition to this, and I had a lot of phone calls from people who had cancer who were very, very mad at me. In fact, I have now a friend on the United Way Board, and I saw her yesterday, and I was thinking about that. She was really upset with me, and I tried to explain to her that laetrile was just an excuse to get this other medicinal something-or-other through, and that probably laetrile would never be produced in this state, because that really wasn't the objective, at all. People, I'm sure, remembered that, and I'm so thankful that whatever cancer she had, of course, she doesn't have it. So, she survived, because that was in 1979.

It's that kind of issue that's very emotional that can really color people's opinions of you as their legislator.

You're right.

Did you have concerns about that then when you were getting this attention?

No. No, I didn't, because I really believed I *was* doing the right thing, that the people who sponsored the legislation, didn't have their feelings in mind, at all. My view of it was that they were interested only in a financial windfall, and that it really was

Gerovital that was the issue and not laetrile. I tried to explain to those people who called me, and whether they accepted it or not, I really don't know. In a way, I was sorry he put it in the paper, because I received all those calls, but on the other hand, that was how I was going to vote.

It gave you a chance to explain what was going on.

Yes, it did. I hope people at least understood there was a different view of this, although, when you're only one of three, it doesn't look like that had much impact on the body as a whole. I do know, after the vote in 1979, that a *lot* of guys were all excited because they were going to the NCAA March Madness—and I don't know if it was the finals or a regional—on Mr. Kratter's airplane. I wasn't invited, and I'm a big basketball fan! [laughter]

There must have been some connection.

Must have been. I don't know, but it seems to me like you could draw a conclusion, anyway!

Let me ask you, this is one of those times when you were going against the majority, and it sounded like you were going on what you've studied and also some intuition that this was not on the up and up. It wasn't what it appeared to be?

I really believe that. I believe the real issue was not laetrile. It was done for marketing purposes, if you will. And many people will say, "Well, if you're only going to be one or two votes out of a large group, why do you do it?"

Well, I suppose, you don't want to do it a lot, and I guess you want to do it because you feel strongly about it. You believe you're right, and, particularly, you want your remarks entered into the journal so you can go back, if you need to, to show people what your reasons were. "Go along to get along" is a slogan often used, that you don't raise people's disgust or feelings—ill feelings—towards you, both out in the public who vote for you, but also the people you work with.

Clearly, when I said some of those things about the legislature, it was not what people wanted to hear. And following that vote I did have many of the leaders—at that time it was the Democratic Party—accuse me of voting that way because I had a lot of doctors who I represented. I did have a lot of doctors in my district, but I never was contacted by them. Because my dad was a pharmacist, I think it had much more bearing in importance to me than who I represented at that time. I don't really remember getting a lot of phone calls or mail about this. I did get the phone calls that I've already referred to, of people I knew personally, but that was about it, and I don't really remember how much press attention was given to this. I would have guessed quite a bit.

Yes, it would be interesting to know, because I think a lot of people remember the term "laetrile" and the connection as an alternative cancer treatment that hasn't been available in the states.

That was very big at that time—the Mexican cancer clinics. In fact, in the legislature as a whole, there has been a lot of interest and support for alternative medicine. I think of homeopathic. I think of naturopathy. And we want to mention those two at some time, as well. That comes more with the senate.

There are different levels of medical treatment, if you will, by those two, but there were many senators, particularly, and

probably assemblymen—but at that time I was in the senate—who actually used some of these doctors, rather than a medical doctor, an M.D. Some homeopathic doctors are M.D.'s, I think, but certainly not naturopathy.

Anyway, getting back to your question of being a minority, it does have repercussions for you after the fact, but then I've been there for a session at least, maybe two. I think it was in 1979, and I don't think it was unusual for me to be in a very small minority, but there is some decision making as to how often you do that and on what you do it. Is it really going to make an impact? You're certainly not going to change the outcome of the vote. Why is it that you want to do that? I think you have to think about that internally as to how externally it's going to be perceived. I've learned a lot of lessons, there's no question about it. I've not been a person who went in there knowing *exactly* what to do, and I certainly don't think I would ever go back, if I relived it, and vote differently on many of these things, but I might not have said some of the things I did that were like red flags. Like really incite the bull, and you're the matador. [laughter] I'm sure in my mind that that is exactly the perception in what happened.

It's the old cliché about choosing your battles, then, really, is what you're talking about.

Exactly. I am. That's very good. Yes, if one week, or one session, you had eighty-five votes where it was thirty-nine to one, I think you would really question that. I think, probably, we see this even today, there are legislators who vote "no" all the time, and people say, "What are they there for? They just always vote 'no.'"

That is totally different than what I'm talking about. Those are people who voted against a bill, for example, to fund domestic violence shelters, because they really believed it was an abortion clinic behind closed doors. Now, that is a bit farfetched, to say the least, but there have been many legislators I've known who just vote no, no, no, no. Let's say, anything having the state governments involved in things—they really think it should be locally controlled or no taxes or no fees. Even those are more understandable, I think, if you have a basic philosophy that everything should go to the vote of the people if you're going to raise taxes. I personally don't support that, but I can understand someone who does and does it consistently. But that's not the category I put myself in. Very often, I voted "no" on something like this.

Now, maybe the previous session before I got there, in 1973, this same lobbyist introduced a bill to legalize acupuncture. We were the first state in the nation to do that, and you have to remember almost thirty years ago that this was *way* outside the envelope, way out there. It went through just like the laetrile and Gerovital did. At that time, Assembly District 25 was represented by a medical doctor, Dr. Bob Broadbent, and he was totally, absolutely, unequivocally, opposed to this bill because he was a traditional medical doctor.

He was opposed to the acupuncture bill?

Yes, he was. The next session I had taken his place, so he was not there for laetrile or Gerovital, but I wouldn't have any doubt that he would have voted against that, as well. To be honest with you, I never thought about medical doctors. I was really thinking about the pharmacy angle and my own dad, who probably would have rolled over a couple of times, wherever he is, in thinking that I would have voted for something like that.

Because it wasn't valid medically?

Yes, I'm sure. My dad went to a college of pharmacy. He was traditionally trained in Massachusetts, and I can't believe he would think that this was an appropriate thing to do. We knew nothing about it. There were no medical tests. The FDA didn't know anything about it. I know people don't care for the FDA, but it gives you some sense of authority, some sense of safety. They've tested it; they have some expectation of what it can do and what the results might be. There was none of that, and it was just something that sounded good, that was going to make money for somebody.

And so the laetrile did actually pass both houses?

Oh, yes. I explained that at the next session, they came back and wanted it over the counter. Then I explained that when I was on the money committee I asked the Department of Health how many people were involved in it. There was one, but the answer was, it was not doing very much. They'd never heard about it.

So it's still on the books, as far as you know?

I'm sure it probably still is. There was never a repeal, unless it came in from a Department of Health agency bill that got rid of a bunch of stuff that was outdated in one fell swoop.

But it didn't come back as the big issue that it was back then?

I don't remember. No. After all of that stuff, you never heard much about it.

I know another topic that was a hot one for you in that year, and that was the water-meter topic.

I have it here: "Prohibits local government approval of subdivision map without plan for installing water meters." That passed. I guess I should start with the basic water-meter problem. This is something that did pass. So this was important, but it was after the fact. I had a bill drafted to mandate water meters in Washoe County. It's interesting, there was some legislation passed a long time ago, and I'm not sure of the years, in the 1930s, maybe, that just carved out Reno and one other community, that prohibited them from having water meters. Prohibited them! For every place else the law was silent, so the result was that water meters would be appropriate for those communities. I think we need to check on this, honestly, but I believe it did not talk about Sparks. I don't think it talked about Washoe County. It only talked about Reno, the City of Reno, I believe. So, in order to have water meters installed you had to remove this prohibition.

I had a bill drafted, and the reason I did that is because, clearly, this is an arid community that we live in. I used water rather liberally, because I paid one fee based upon the size of my pipe, but what really got me thinking about this as a major issue and a basic policy question was my next door neighbors who had left the water on all day long. They let all the water run down hour after hour after hour and right next to the fence. Between my neighbor's yard and the individual with a swimming pool was a garden. All that dirt finally worked its way under the fence and went into the people's pool or into their yard. They came over to find out what was going on. My neighbors were gone, but I did know where the sprinkler valve was, so I got a

key and turned it off. Now, that was it, but it wasn't it, because I wanted to talk to my neighbors, in a nice way, and tell them what had happened, and that maybe they should put in a timer.

They didn't care, because they just paid one fee for the water, so what the heck? That attitude just hit me in the head, hit me in the heart, hit me in the wallet. It just was not a good explanation, and I thought how many more people there are in this community who feel that way. So, that's the reason, really, that I got the bill drafted. I started doing a lot of research on it, or had research done for me, and decided what needed to be done. I believe we've touched on this slightly, by the *Ms. Magazine* business.

And just briefly you mentioned that your husband cautioned you about water meters being a hot topic.

Right. My husband, as a research scientist at DRI, really gave me a lot of good input on many bills, and this was one of them. He said, "You are right Sue, but politically it is a horrible, horrible thing." He said, "You know, almost everybody you talk to doesn't want water meters. But you're right. It is an equitable thing to do."

So I did it. I had a bill drafted. Now, the governor at the time was Mike O'Callaghan, and for whatever reason—and I'm not going to get into this—he supported this. He knew I had a bill in my drawer that was all done, ready to go. Right about that time, I had the person coming to visit me from *Ms. Magazine*, which was a fairly big magazine at that time. So during that time, the governor called a meeting for all the Washoe County legislators. The purpose was to get them all on board with the water-meter legislation of Sue's.

I didn't go to the meeting. It was like at 5:45 a.m. The governor, Mike, got up very early, got a lot of work done early in the morning, and if he called a meeting, you were expected to be there. Well, I knew what it was about, and I had this person interviewing me, and the woman—and I don't remember her name—thought it was amazing that the governor himself called at the motel room, and I told the governor "no". [laughter] She thought this was very interesting. She put it in her article. But the point of the meeting was the water-meter legislation, and people were really scared of it, because of the political ramifications.

The chairman of government affairs in the assembly at that time was another Irishman who was a real favorite of Governor Mike O'Callaghan's. His name was Patrick Murphy, and this is where that bill would go, to government affairs. So, the governor thought it would be a good thing for Patrick to introduce this bill, and Patrick, I'm sure, wanted to do what the governor wanted him to do. Same party, Irishman, and chairman of the right committee, so he came over and asked me for the bill. Well, Patrick was a nice young man. He was young, much younger than I, and I was hardly old at the time, but I told him, I said, "Pat, you're in the Democratic Party. Da dat da da. We're friends. We're from Washoe County." I said, "I wouldn't put your name on this bill." I said, "You're going to get more heartache and headache than you've ever imagined, and you don't want that." So I was giving him a clue to re-introduce it as a committee bill, which is what I suggested he do. Committee on government affairs, so no one's name is on there. You could criticize the committee members, and he, of course, was the chairman of the committee. Well, the hearing on the bill, as you can imagine, was a real circus, and I wasn't there, because I didn't have anything to do with the bill anymore. He's got my bill.

I wasn't mean about it. I told him exactly what to expect. The bill didn't pass. During all this involvement with this bill—and I still believed it was the right thing—I learned that the least we could do, is when a new subdivision is built, then the water-meter boxes should be put in for a later date—whenever this community decided that water meters were necessary.

That was introduced in 1977, and Patrick Murphy is the second name on the bill of which I'm the prime sponsor. It did pass, effective May 15, 1977. It actually doesn't have a long history. Registered here, meaning it had a fairly good, smooth ride through the legislative process, but it prohibits local governments' approval of subdivision maps without a plan for installing water meters. That was, I believe, a very good thing, because we're going to be on water meters, and they won't have to tear up someone's yard or sidewalk or whatever to put them in. In fact, a couple years ago, when they did over my street totally, not just resurfaced it, they put in water meter boxes while they were repairing sidewalks.

So back to that, it did pass at that point, and that was when subdivisions had to start making provisions for water meters.

It was effective May of 1977. Right. And that was the reason for it, which I thought was reasonable, and obviously the legislature did, because it passed.

Right, so that one went through. You said it was not a popular position, but when it went through in 1977, it was acceptable then, or was it still a hot topic?

Well, it was different. It was just for the new subdivisions. The other was water meters to be installed, period.

New subdivisions. It wasn't for everyone.

I remember that on the bill, the total bill, the water meters. See, this occurred right about the time that, I believe, that all these casinos went up. We better check the date on that. Somehow, I remember 1979 when the Hilton and all those casinos opened. Well, I got to thinking about it, that if we saved a lot of water by using water meters, who is it going to be saved for? And I thought, "It's going to be saved for this giant MGM and these others tourists who keep taxes low." That was not a good thing. It should be saved for the people who live here.

So, the bill drafter gave me some amendments to that bill. I think it was called "Prior Water Rights," where that would exactly happen, that those people who lived here on a certain date would get first rights to the water. Now, I wasn't sure if that was constitutional or not, but he was a bill drafter for the legislature, and he said it was, so I wasn't going to ask questions. I assumed it was legal. I don't know how it would really work, but it didn't pass. The amendment did, but the bill itself didn't. I'm pretty sure the amendment did. That's when my friend, Nancy Gomes, was in the legislature, and she thought that was really a good thing, because she was kind of no-growther. So that directly fits into how they would feel. They'd say, "Water for who?"

Anyway, sometimes you do things because you think it's right, and you take the guff. To me, that's what people should be doing. I guess people elect you because they think you will be a leader, and if you don't take advantage of that, at least have discussions about these issues. If it doesn't pass, it doesn't pass, but the press would be involved. You would get different opinions from people in the community. I think that's a good thing. Whether it ever becomes a reality, the discussion would probably direct individuals to either acceptance or not. I've always kind of objected to people jumping all over somebody when maybe they had a

good intention in mind. Maybe that's all they wanted. Maybe you should ask them.

The art of discussion—that's a whole different topic. We probably don't need to get into that, but it seems that our Democratic form of government is based on discussion and freedom of information and so on, and sometimes it seems the art of discussion has gotten lost by people trying to get somebody who doesn't have the same opinion to stop saying their opinion.

It's true. It's true. That's exactly what I'm saying. I think that's unfortunate. I don't think people should be necessarily ridiculed. First of all, you should find out what the purpose is, and maybe it's a fairly decent idea that needs to be changed a little bit. Maybe you don't think it's a good idea, but I think I have always had the problem with people getting ridiculed about something without knowing more about it. In this case, I wasn't ridiculed. I was just chastised for a long time.

You know all the call-in radio talk shows? Wow. The message center lights were blinking all over the place, particularly, for me. [laughter] But, hey, it raised the level again to discuss this issue.

And something got passed.

Yes. A good first step.

How long do you think you heard about the water-meter issue?

Even when it was introduced through the government affairs, I think I still was getting phone calls, because unless people kept up with every little nuance to the progress of this bill, they would miss it. Because the radio people said "Assemblywoman Sue Wagner," or probably "Assemblyman," and the phone number,

which was exactly what my husband told
me was going to happen. [laughter]

And it did! OK.

But he still thought I'd done the right
thing. I did, too.

8

1979 SESSION

We're now going to talk about the 1979 legislative session. You were saying the Duck Stamp was a very big deal, so would you tell me that story?

Yes, it was, and as I'm looking at this list of sponsors, besides myself, I notice that they're all men. I guess I must have made a conscious effort to do that, thinking that maybe they'd know what the Duck Stamp was about. Actually, Cliff Young, who's now on the supreme court, had introduced this bill several times when he was in the senate, because Cliff had been president of the National Wildlife Federation. He was noted as a real conservation person and somebody very interested in hunting and all those good things. Well, he couldn't get this bill through, so some of the groups that were involved in wildlife activities in our state came and asked me. They figured as a joke, "Who would be the most unlikely person to introduce something dealing with the state Duck Stamp?" And they picked me out. So, they explained to me what it was, and I thought it was a terrific idea.

If you impose a state Duck Stamp program in your state, two things happen.

One, it creates a stamp—a state Duck Stamp that you must affix to your hunting license in order to go hunting for ducks. For every certain amount of money that's raised—and I don't remember now what the proportion is—that money is utilized for maintaining migratory waterfowl. So, it's a big conservation item. The other thing that happens, which I didn't know anything about until after the bill had passed, was that an artist is selected to create the Duck Stamp in a painting, and some kind of a panel selects the artist who will do it and what the theme will be.

Well, our first state Duck Stamp was the "tule decoy" which was found in a cave, and it was totally preserved. It had been made by a Native American tribe thousands of years ago. That was the design that each artist that wanted to get involved in our program did. Well, after that is selected, then prints are made of that, and then they are sold, and they become a very heavy-duty item to purchase, to have a copy of, particularly, if it's the first year, because those are worth quite a bit.

I had the opportunity to get several of these, because I ultimately became the person who did get it through the legislature, and I'll explain what happened after I finish what I'm talking about now. I had several given to me, one from a conservation group, and then one—I had a fund-raiser done by the Stremmels, Turkey and Peter Stremmel, who have an art gallery in town. I'm not sure if they did know the artist or not, but they tracked the artist down, because they had a fund-raiser for me at their gallery, and they decided to have it during the opening that they were having on Western art. The artist of that particular stamp—I think his name was Larry Hayden—was not able to come to the opening, but right in the front when you came into the fund-raiser, they had this particular print on an easel, and he had done a re-mark of it for me, which means that he did in a pencil or pen, the head. In this case, he did the head of the duck as something special, so that would be worth even more. I also got another one that I think was number two, because I think they gave the first one to the governor, and that I gave to my son when he turned twenty-one, because I thought it would be nice for each of my kids to have something very special when they were twenty-one. My son is a big hunter and still comes up here with a bunch of his buddies. They were up here just several years ago, to go to Fallon on opening duck season day. I've bought other ones for him, but every year there's another duck stamp, and after awhile I could have my whole house, the ceiling, covered with them, and I could have linoleum made out of them so I could walk on them and look at them. [laughter]But I didn't do that; I just had the first one. That's probably worth quite a bit now. Ten thousand dollars. They really get to be quite valuable, particularly, as I said, the first edition.

The reason Cliff Young had so much trouble getting it through the legislature—and certainly I was not as consummate a politician as Cliff—but Floyd Lamb, who also served in the senate with Cliff, would always get it into his committee, the senate finance committee, claiming it had a fiscal impact. Well, it did, but it was a positive one. It was actually giving money to the state, not taking it away. So there should have been no reason that it needed to go there. But, for some reason, he always got it in senate finance, and it never got out. So, knowing that, I believe we talked to everybody on the senate finance committee, explaining that this was just an attempt by Floyd to kill it, for whatever reason. We never really did understand what his objections were, but anyway, he didn't get it; he did try, but we had enough votes on the senate, and the guys who helped me were just great. They were the "guys" type who could talk to other guys and get them to go along because they were well-liked guys, and they were hunter guys.

Kind of spoke the same language?

Yes. It actually gave me a whole group of new friends who, when I ran again, of course, were very, very supportive and supported anything I ever did after that.

That's key. I think people think of me as only being involved in women's issues, and that's one reason among many I'm glad I'm doing this oral history.

That was one of my questions, too. Where along the way did you begin to distinguish your own individual self and style? Because we talked about how, when you first came in, you were kind of lumped with "those women legislators," kind of considered a carbon copy of Jean Ford and so on.

Yes. And Mary.

And Mary Gojack. So maybe this was one of those things where you started to distinguish, at least with your colleagues, that there was more to Sue Wagner.

Well, actually, that's a good question, but I don't think so. When I think back on it, it was the decision of mine to run for the Legislative Commission, and Jean wanted to be on the Legislative Commission. Bob Weise, who was the minority leader in the assembly at that time, came to me and said Jean and I were the only women in the Republican caucus. There are two interim groups that meet when the legislature is not in session to make policy for the legislature. It's supposed to be only in emergency situations. One is the Interim Finance Committee, IFC. You may go to them and ask for money that when it is an emergency and cannot wait until the next legislative session. That's the reason why we have these interim bodies. The other one is the Legislative Commission which works on semi-policy questions, but, clearly, not to abrogate the responsibility of the whole legislature, because it wouldn't be fair for twelve people to be making policy for everybody else.

They fill those spaces between.

Yes, that's why we don't have special sessions a lot. The assembly minority leader at that time, Bob Weise, really felt that both of these bodies were probably unconstitutional, and I think he had a good point, because it could be considered to be unconstitutional, unless every time they made it clear that it was an emergency. Otherwise, they would be really acting as a legislature for the whole. He was not real keen on them, and he certainly didn't want to serve on them. Jean Ford wanted very much to be on the Legislative Commission, the group that made the policy decisions in emergency situations. Bob Weise came and told me she wasn't going to get it, because the other legislators didn't like her,

and that I could have it, and he would make sure that I got it, and I said, "Well, I know Jean wants it."

And he said, "Well, look, if you don't take it, she's not going to get it. One of the other guys will, so you have to decide."

So, I did. I said, "Yes. I will accept it."

I did talk to Jean about that, obviously, to tell her. I do believe I've touched on the fact that she did have a problem with some of the legislators, and that she had to bury her name on certain bills and so on. Well, I think this is probably among the Republicans, and I imagine that those guys talked to others, to Democratic ones, as well. I think I would have to go back to that decision that would suggest to them that, yes, she would do things on her own. When it was clear to me that there was no way she was going to get it, I did accept Bob Weise's description of that, because he was a pretty competent assembly minority leader and was very young. I always expected him to keep on going, but he really didn't like politics all that well. He developed Lakeview Estates, out here by the golf course.

Oh, that's right. He's the developer.

Yes, and his dad owned all that property at one time. But anyway, I would have to say that probably was the thing more than the fact that I introduced different kinds of bills.

Anyway, I think I probably finished what I was going to say about the Duck Stamp. Now, the next thing down here, I do remember this, too. This was to make certain minors eligible for I.D. cards without driver's licenses. There was a young man in my district who I'd never heard of before or since, who told me that he didn't drive. He never wanted to drive. He didn't care to drive. I cannot remember at this time why not. It wasn't a disability, or it wasn't religious. I do know those two things. So, I don't know what the reason was, but he would go in to cash a check or do a lot of things, and he had no I.D. with his picture on it, so people gave him a hard time. I thought, "Hey, I'm sure there are people who don't have driver's licenses that would like to have check cashing privileges, and that was the one that he had mentioned. So, we introduced a bill, and it did pass, and it was utilized by not a lot of people, but some people. It was kind of promoted at that time.

Did it go through the DMV or some other state agency?

It went through the DMV. Yes, it did.

All right. We're looking at our list, and AB151 is services for displaced homemakers, and you said there was some interesting information on that.

Yes, that was a major thing. I believe that Truckee Meadows Community College still does this.

Yes, it does re-entry programs.

Well, that's what it is. This is what created them. On the front of *Time* magazine, about the same time that a hearing was held in the assembly, there was a picture of a woman who had opened the first displaced homemakers center in the country in Oakland, California. I had called her, and she came over to testify on this bill I had drafted to set up centers on the two community college campuses at that time. Well, I believe that maybe it only went into Clark County, which was some other name of a community college at that time.

Clark County was the Community College of Southern Nevada. Oh, it was something else to begin with?

Yes, I think so. And it might have gone into Truckee Meadows, too, at the time. I just don't remember.

This was a big focus of women in 1979. A woman lost her husband by any of these ways: by death, by disability, or by divorce. The women could have been married for fifteen years, twenty years, might have had a profession before. There weren't that many women involved at that time, but let's assume she was a school teacher. She got married and left the teaching profession, had been married for eighteen years. Her husband died, or she and her husband got a divorce, and she then had to go into the workforce again, and she didn't have the correct skills for that particular time, eighteen years later. This would get her back into that stream and get her skills up to par for whatever was necessary. Of course, at that time, we had never even heard of the Internet, so computer skills were not appropriate at that time, but something else would have been. The whole idea was to not only teach her new skills, but to show her how to write a résumé and all kinds of skills, so she would not be just out of the workplace forever. Somebody would offer a helping hand to her and get her back into the workforce again. So, the places I thought were the most appropriate for this, where maybe a lot of women would try to get more education, if that was necessary, would be on the community college campuses.

Was there any opposition to it?

Yes, there was, but I wanted to talk about somebody who supported it. The one thing I feel comfortable in saying was, actually, that this did come back to the assembly, and you could see it started out in January, and it didn't go over to the assembly until May 14. So that was practically at the end of the session. I remember that this very obnoxious assemblyman came up to me and said, "You know, if you want that bill, then you've got to do such-and-such."

I said, "Well, I guess I don't want it that much." And I guess he gave up, so it passed even though I didn't go along with whatever he wanted.

But it was very disappointing to me that there was a woman in this state who was very politically active who would not come over and testify on this. She was so interested in this, sat across the street in the Ormsby Hotel, and had somebody come back and tell her what was going on. But because I was a Republican, she wasn't going to have anything to do with it—even though I was the one who got the bill drafted, did all the work, got it passed. Sometimes partisan politics—I don't understand it.

I'm curious, too, because we don't hear as much about that term, "displaced homemakers," now as we did then. It was sort of a movement at that time that there were a lot of women that this was happening to, and there were no accommodations for them.

Of course, now it's probably called "re-entry." This is the same time as the women's movement was just beginning. Some were saying, "Well, look at all these women. They have their whole lives ahead of them and need help, but because of this or this or that, they can't get a decent job." So, probably, there were women who maybe fell into the same brackets ten years before, but nothing was done about it, because not much focus was given to women—period—particularly women in the workplace, or getting back to the workplace. So I'm sure it was focused on the women's movement.

It was sort of a beginning of accommodating that situation for women at that point.

Oh, it was. It was the first time. That's why this woman, whose name I don't remember now, who was on the front of *Time* magazine, came over to testify and explain, because this was the first one. That's where I read about it. Anyway, it was really a good thing, and still is around.

Yes, it's interesting because I'm working at TMCC now, and just a couple of weeks ago we had one of the women who was in the re-entry program, and she's gone through the dental assisting program. TV cameras came and talked to them about this re-entry program and the services they have, such as babysitting, help with transportation—everything they need in order to get the training. It really made it possible for her life to be quite different.

The last time I was over in the shopping center, Old Town Mall—it's up on the second floor there—I was going to the library, maybe, so I dropped in and introduced myself. They showed me around, showed me what they were doing. This was, oh, last year, maybe. I hadn't really thought about it too much, but when I saw their little sign, "Women's Re-entry," I thought, "Oh."

Still going.

Yes, still going on. Now, the money in that bill was very small, but we figured, "Well, it's a start." Women had to scramble around, and in some cases they probably thought they had sell their souls to get something on. I was on the Ways and Means Committee this particular session, and so almost everybody on the Ways and Means Committee got to pick a bill for whatever they wanted, and it was almost guaranteed to pass. I probably should have gone for something a lot more lucrative than this. The fiscal amount on this was rather small, if I remember correctly, but this was the thing that I wanted the most.

I'll bet there are a lot of women who are really glad that you did.

Who knows how many women have gone through a program like this since 1979? It's almost twenty-five years. Well, it's nice that people are still utilizing the services.

Let's see, the next bills are regarding domestic violence, three of them.

Yes, I had read a book called *The Battered Wife*. Somebody had mailed it to me or something. This is just the third session I'd been in the legislature, 1979. I read this, and I just couldn't *believe* that this actually happened, and hardly anybody did. This was like the first book that had ever been written about this horrifying social problem that we still have today, even in this country. So, I looked in the phone book, and, for some reason, I came across the Committee to Aid Abused Women. So, I called, and they had *just* started. One person—Joni Kaiser—had started this with the help of her mother, Phyllis Kaiser, who was very active in American Friends, the Quaker group. In fact, if I remember correctly, Joni had gone to a college in Ohio that I think was a Quaker school. I can't remember the name of it right now. I told her that I had read this book, and I was in the legislature, and I'd like to do something, but I didn't know what it was that needed to be done. Well, clearly she was excited.

We probably needed to deal with looking at the criminal laws, to begin with, because it was much further down the road until

we got around to funding for shelters. So, there were three bills introduced, and some of them were fairly clear, what they do. One is to actually have a new penalty, or a penalty, period, for battery against an adult member of a defendant's household. The other one I will talk a little bit about, which didn't pass, was reporting of apparent incidences. There was an attempt to set up a registry of the number of incidences and where they occurred. That just actually passed a little while ago, first introduced in 1979, and I think it took at least twenty years to get that particular proposal through.

This was such an eye-opening, incredible experience for me, not only to have read this book, but to understand what this was all about. You have to imagine the hostility that these bills met along the way by mainly a male-dominated legislature. Even people I thought were somewhat open-minded were just appalled at this stuff—could not imagine—and kept asking me over and over, "Well, why don't they just get out? If they get beaten, why do they stay around?"

Needless to say, this was something new. We were one of the first states to even introduce anything, at all. I at one time thought it would be a very good idea if we could actually have some victims come and testify. Well, the problem was, getting any victim to *come* out and have the courage to actually come over to the legislature and let everybody know she was a victim. It was a *very* difficult road to travel because, as I say, no one had ever heard of this before. To find people—women—who at all were interested in testifying was pretty tough, because this was not something you wanted to advertise. This was not something people knew anything about. So, to get victims to actually come over to the legislature and testify, certain guarantees had to be made to them, and they were. Once I had that set up, they felt a little more comfortable. One was that there was to be no names in the newspaper print stories, and there was to be no televising of these women, except from the back, so they would not be identified that way, either, to not only the person who had battered them, but also to their neighbors and their employers and friends, family. It was up to the victim to let them know if they wanted them to know, but not by being a testifier in the legislature.

So the main thing was to try to get someone who would be willing to come and testify, because it was so new and so dangerous for them, is that correct, to come and testify?

Yes. We did guarantee these safeguards for the victims if they were willing to come forward.

The other thing is that when this hit the newspapers, my phone absolutely rang off the hook—from women all over the state, people I knew who swore me to secrecy, people in the most upscale neighborhoods in the state who, they told me, had been beaten all their lives. [long pause] It amazed me that this was all coming out at this time. It *just unbelievably* boggled my mind. In fact, when I think back on some of the people I know quite well, I could not imagine. I have seen the guys along the way in this town, and it's all I could do to say hello to them, because they don't know I know. [sighs]

But, anyway, we finally did get some victims to testify. Some of the horror stories, as I've said, were just unbelievable. All this was new to me. The biggest problem I had was with my fellow colleagues, with legislators themselves, particularly male legislators, and particularly in the senate. At this time I was in the assembly. It appeared that certain male legislators had a real problem with this. I would hope that

it was because they didn't quite understand it, but there are certain legislators who have *continued* to have a problem with this for the last many, many years. Because of the Criminal Code being changed, the bills all had to go through certain committees, one of which was the judiciary committee, where most everybody was an attorney, and most everybody was male. So that was another obstacle.

I have to say that if the victims had not come over to testify, I don't think the bills ever would have passed. I think it would have been very easy to have said, "We don't get this. We don't think it's necessary, so let's kill it." *But* we put a personal face on each one of these bills and explained the trauma of being beaten by your husband— and mostly at that time it was husbands rather than people living together, because I don't think that was as commonly done in those days as it may be today. It was a real eye-opening experience for *me*, even, to meet these victims. One of them happened to be a woman who had a very high position in the supreme court, and so many of the people had heard of her or knew her, and she knew she'd probably run into some people she might know, and this totally put a different complexion on their relationship with this person.

Another person was from Carson City. Her husband worked for the Carson City Police Department, and this was the first time we had *understood* what a police department can *do* to *bury* certain forms, reports, information. This woman had persisted on calling the Carson City P.D. to report on her husband, and they gave her no credibility. She called in twice to report it, and what they would do, she said, "They'd just say, 'uh-huh,'" and would throw the reports in the wastebasket, because they were protecting one of their own, one of their buddies, one of the guys they worked with.

She finally decided to come forward, because she finally was in a truck with this guy, and I remember she was drinking a Coca-Cola or something. He took the bottle and broke it and then slashed her with the cut of the empty bottle of Coke and carved her up and dumped her out in the desert to die. But she didn't die. Fortunately, she did not. She crawled back and showed up, and she was one who was able to show her scars and talk about this terrible thing that had happened to her. After that, clearly, when it was told that this woman had been hurt this badly, people were going to figure out who it was, because she hadn't had plastic surgery yet, and she had big scars. She'd done everything that was right, which was to report it to authorities, even though it wasn't a crime at that time. I think that that was so *awesome*, the story she had to tell, that nobody could ever justify not supporting one of these two bills at that point. I mean, they would have looked like they were *totally* inhumane and non-compassionate at the best. So that's when I say that these women who testified were *really* instrumental. They were instrumental; they were what demanded the legislature to respond to this new kind of crime.

Incredible, the different layers that that particular victim crossed with, the local city police department and then all the way up, in bringing this information forward. Pretty difficult to ignore a witness like that.

Yes. It was very difficult. They couldn't ignore her. And it appeared from the witness that she was a very credible witness, was articulate, explained what she had done to try to report this, so this would not happen, but got nowhere. And it also shone some light on police departments, if you will, law enforcement, that there might

be something going on there that wasn't a very good thing, at all. So I think that was a benefit, as well.

It was really the victims who carried the day, because when people heard their stories there wasn't much that they could say. They didn't have the guts to ask them a question that would somehow suggest they weren't believing them. They may have felt, maybe after they'd gone away, they'd start chipping away at the bill, and some of them did do that, but there were several women who came and testified again on the condition of being totally anonymous.

There is one story I'm going to tell here, and that's the one I remember clearly because it was so horrific. She was an absolutely incredible person, and she had a very important job with the supreme court. Many people did recognize her, but she realized that that was OK. I told them we would *never* have gotten these things through if I'd gone in there and talked about it from a good public policy point of view. I had a hard enough time even with these women. The only reason they passed it is because these women had had the courage to come out and say these things.

When I started dealing with some of the guys, particularly in the senate even, interestingly enough, who I knew pretty well, oh, they just hated this stuff. I've always asked in the back of my mind, "I wonder why they get so upset about these issues?" There's always that big question mark, that maybe I'm just hitting a little too close to home. I don't know. One particular person I'm thinking of right now, he just couldn't support this. I always wondered why somebody like that individual, who's well educated and good every other way, had such a difficult time with this.

Did he believe it didn't happen? Or did he believe that it was the right of the man to do that?

Yes, I think that may be what I thought, and I thought that maybe it was happening in his home.

Thinking possibly some of the legislators themselves?

Oh, yes, that's very possible. To be a legislator doesn't mean you have to be better than the average person. And when I found out how *many* people this touched, I just *couldn't believe* it. My God, I thought I was lucky in finding these women to come and testify. Of course, none of these people who called would have come and testified. When I asked them, they said, "Oh I can't. I wouldn't dare."

They'd be terrified.

Oh, they'd be terrified. And even if I told them, "No one will reveal your identity." No, that wasn't good enough. They just wanted me to know that they really supported these bills. It's never happened with any other bills I've introduced. Displaced homemakers? Yes, but it's not too terrifying. I don't think somebody's going to feel embarrassed or feel like they don't want to tell anybody that they're getting a divorce or their husband has a disability. I mean, we want to help them, but this is an entirely different thing.

I did read something, and I remember this. I've got so many books. I was just reading today some clippings of some things that were in that book of letters. I've never read them, and I opened it up for some reason, and I saw some of the letters. I didn't know that person had even written me one. So when my daughter came home, I said, "Say, I looked through some scrapbooks, and I think some of these things stuck in my mind."

This was something that was just hitting Nevada for the first time. In fact, when I

went to conferences—like the National Conference of State Legislators, NCSL—we were way at the top. We were considered to be further ahead, the most speedy state in the nation dealing with this issue. It really started from reading a book and then calling the Committee to Aid Abused Women, and then getting legislators to understand that we were talking about changing the criminal code here. That was nowhere near as important as finding a funding mechanism for them. But, it was on the path to bringing it out of the closet. As I said, when I started off, I read this poem that was found on the doors in a motel chain. It was some cute little thing. Basically, it says, "You know, you just treat your wife like a piece of property."

I read that, and I said, "This is hanging in a motel chain across our country?"

The guys were like, "So, what's she talking about?" They didn't get it.

Yes. Seemed normal to them.

Yes.

It's amazing, because I think younger people today would not realize that that was the first time, as you said, that people were becoming aware of it.

There had never been a bill introduced—*ever.*

Nobody talked about it.

This was the first time. The book, I'm pretty sure, had been written in 1975, *The Battered Wife.* When I read in the papers now, see something about somebody doing this for domestic violence, I say, "So?" I mean now, it's a totally acceptable thing.

The number of bills that were introduced last session dealing with this, Joni told me, half of them they didn't even want. They were bad. Everybody wants to do something, but that's not the way it was in the beginning. It was like being in support of the "choice" issue. It was not something that people said, "Oh, good we need to introduce something about that." No way. It was not as widely received as the state duck stamp bill, for example.

[laughter] It's amazing how you had to fight that battle, and now it's commonplace, it's accepted, and there's no quarrel with the issue involved.

It is. Yes. Well, in fact, October is Domestic Violence Month. The governor and the attorney-general just yesterday—there's an article in the paper about it today—had a press conference talking about all the things they were doing in this area. I'm certainly glad he's continuing, but it's certainly quite a different issue than it was twenty-five years ago.

Not the hot topic that it was then.

No. No, and that's probably a good thing. It's a bad thing that we still have to deal with it. The number of cases that were reported in this state was just *incredible*.

Even recently?

Yes, it was in the article in today's paper—just appalling. As domestic violence bills have wound their way through the legislative process, the police have *often* been an obstacle. Sometimes it was for no fault of their own, but in some cases it was. There's a lot of training that now goes on, and people, including peace officers, are very attuned to this particular crime. Until other bills were passed later on, when they had to make an arrest, sometimes they'd just walk away, and the easy thing to say was, "This is a family matter. You don't want to get involved." That was the basic description given to these kinds of crimes

then, "We don't want to get involved. We don't *need* to make this a crime, because it just should be handled within the confines of their home." Well, we could see what happens when that kind of attitude prevails. Needless to say, you don't want a police force barging down the front doors of people, invading their privacy; but on the other hand, you have to have some kind of balance between really helping somebody . . . and they normally are the first caller for something like that.

Actually today, being on the Gaming Commission, I see *so* many of these kinds of cases in people's backgrounds, and I have to really think about whether it is serious enough for me *not* to give them a gaming license, because somebody would say, "Well, what has that got to do with a gaming license?" Well, it would have something to do with it in my mind if the person clearly did not uphold a law, did not listen to somebody in authority, because clearly, if they don't do that, then they're not going to be listening to people in authority, i.e. gaming regulators, or paying their fees, their taxes, and that kind of thing. If they had that kind of a track record, then I think that I would not vote for them to have a gaming license. Other people might think it has no relevancy at all and support them. But we have had some cases that, because of my own experience with this, we have been able to deny somebody—a couple of people—on this *alone*, and I think it was absolutely justified at that time. There may be some other comments I want to make on this whole issue when we get to the senate, when I introduced the bill that set up the funding mechanism for domestic violence shelters.

We can come back to that. It's interesting, though, that so much has changed in the twenty-some years since this bill was introduced, in that no one really disputes that there is domestic violence anymore, and that it crosses all social levels, and yet there's still some hesitancy to consider it as that big a deal, if it comes to someone applying for a gaming license. It could be easily passed over—without an advocate on the board bringing that to their attention.

Yes, that's true. When I think about this, to comprehend where we've come in that period of time, from 1979 being the first time people have even heard this *term* used, until today when people are just introducing bills all over the place in order to correct some wrong. In fact, when I was at the legislature last session—this would be the 2001 session—Joni Kaiser told me some of the bills that they really had to come down and *oppose* because they were *not* helpful at all, but somebody wanted to *appear* good and probably felt that they were doing something positive. At least I did the right thing by contacting an abuse shelter to find out what it was that they needed, rather than for me to imagine what they needed, because I wouldn't know. Most of these legislators don't really know and in some cases, probably, would be better off not introducing some things, at all, but for whatever reason, feel that it's an important thing to do.

The next one we want to talk about is overcrowding in prisons.

Yes, it's one of the things, probably, I'm noted for. If somebody was asked, "What do you remember about Sue?" they'd probably say women's issues and prisons.

I talked briefly about getting on the Legislative Commission. One of the things that the Legislative Commission did was to choose all the interim studies that were done between sessions and make appointments to those committees and choose the chairs of those committees. From my being in the minority party for

such a long time, from 1975 to 1987, the only experience I had—and it was very valuable experience—was to chair interim committees. You normally had a better chance of it if you were on the commission, because you could go around and lobby everybody, or you could find out what somebody else wanted to chair, and kind of do that, or you at least were able to get on a committee.

Sometimes it was rather hard because that came out of a budget, and you had so many people who had to get paid to fly here and there and go back and forth, because there was no teleconferencing in those days. So this was one of the opportunities I had to learn some leadership skills in how to run meetings, and it also directed my interest in the prison system and incarceration. I can generally say at this point that I introduced legislation that set up halfway houses, restitution centers, house arrest, and I think there's one other alternative, but maybe I'll remember that at some other point.

Now, again, these were brand new things that we hadn't done in our state. I'm going to mention these all at the same time I'm thinking about it—that made people put a fiscal note on bills that created a new crime or enhanced a penalty, so we could have some idea of how many more prisoners that would mean in our very overcrowded prison system at that time. In the 1970s we ranked as first in the nation, so it was something that, in my mind, ate up a lot of money that could be spent better on education or a variety of other things.

People warned me that if I got too aligned with this issue, I'd always be perceived to be soft on crime. Well, I'll talk about something I voted against at some other point, which didn't make any difference at all. I was really noted for this sort of stuff—and still am today. Dennis Myers, who's a reporter on Channel 8,

KOLO, just last week sent me a clipping about prison overcrowding.

I will say that the two staff people I had from the very beginning of this were very important to me and, interestingly enough, to where I've gone in politics. One was Bill Bible, who at that time worked for the legislature in the fiscal division of the Legislative Counsel Bureau. He then became the budget director for the governor, and he then became the chairman of the Gaming Control Board, when I became a member of the Gaming Commission.

The other staff person I had—her name was Judy Mateucci at that time. Now her name is Judy Sheldrew. She took almost the same path that Bible had. She became budget director and also chair of the Public Utilities Commission. They were two very smart people, who I worked together with very closely, and as it turns out, I was in that sense, both Bill's and Judy's boss, because they did work for LCB, Legislative Council Bureau in the fiscal division. They were very interested, as I was, in trying to do something about sending everybody to jail and eating away at the budgets of both the executive branch and what the legislature wanted to do. So they went away from being just staff persons for legislative committees. This was something that they *also* were very interested in, and that's why they were assigned to that committee, because that's what they wanted to do; they had the same philosophy that I did. So we worked well together.

I remember there was a particular warden, named Chuck Wolff. Don Mello was on my committee at that time; he then was the chairman of the ways and means committee. Mr. Wolff had done something really stupid, and somebody got this memo to me from out of his file cabinet calling some of his employees crybabies. So it got the media's attention, and Mr. Wolff had to resign his job. I didn't feel too badly about

that because he was really not, in my mind, a very progressive warden.

He ultimately did come back after he lost his job and ran the maximum security facility in Ely. I think he may still be there, as a matter of fact. He wasn't hired, and I found out that once a warden, you're always a warden, because you go to the North American Association of Wardens and Superintendents, which is their kind of professional group, and just get yourself hired by some other state that has just dumped their warden. They just get recycled.

There were some things that I was able to do. The fiscal note was kind of interesting, because when I wound up chairing the judiciary committee, where all these bills went in the senate, then I was able to start hiring these people from San Francisco to come over and speak to the committees. In fact, when Bob Sader chaired the judiciary committee in the assembly, and I did in the senate, I told him I was going to pull out all the bills that had any impact on the prison system, save them until the very end of the session, and then have these guys come and tell us in their best estimate, and also our own prison people, how many new inmates this would mean. Clearly, they didn't know, because they were going to be new things, but they would have a pretty good idea, because other states had implemented them in terms of what kind of a rate it would make.

It was the first time anybody had ever really done anything to try to systematically figure out what impact this was going to have. Before then, everybody said, "Oh, good, it's going to go from a misdemeanor to a felony." Well, that's like going from a county jail to the state prison system. In addition to that, if you go from a misdemeanor to a gross misdemeanor to a felony, there are all these other implications, and people don't think about that. They just think that they want to be tougher than the next person.

So, I guess what I'm hearing is that being tough on crime—people didn't necessarily then equate that with needing larger or more space?

Oh, no, no.

So when you were trying to say to them, "We need to find alternatives, or else we need to give money, and we need to think of this with every new criminal law," people weren't wanting to hear that financial part.

No, that's right. They didn't, because if something happened in their district, for example, and they said, "If you elect me, I'll go down and do that," well, they're going to go do that. They probably feel a responsibility to do that. Sometimes they may just want to do it for no reason. They just think it would be a good thing for their constituents to know about—that they did this.

And "tough on crime" is always popular.

It has always been. Interestingly enough, though, I never had anybody run against me on that basis. I've said this over and over again, that I believe—and we should begin this oral history and probably end with this—that if somebody has a specific philosophy and stands up for what they believe, they're almost always going to get elected and reelected. People get so nervous about supporting things, and I think the constituents only care that you *do* support things, whether they're pro-life, and you're pro-choice, at least you're consistent, and they know where you come from, and they're not surprised. I really do believe that.

Needless to say, you've got to work hard, and somebody was talking about me at a dinner last night and said, "She's the only person I ever knew who would walk her district when she didn't have anybody running against her." I suppose that probably had something to do with it, too, but I do think it had something to do with people knowing who you are and what you believe in, whether they always agree with you or not.

And that really came true, at least in this issue where you were told you would be seen as soft on crime. Your constituents saw that you were taking action, and you were taking it with some reason and working hard on the issues.

Yes, and maybe they didn't read the article in the paper or something, I don't know. There just wasn't any opinion. It never came back to affect me.

That reputation?

No, it didn't.

And that's something that you worked on off and on all through the years, the prison system?

Oh, yes, probably three or four different sessions, because all these things didn't happen in one session. I just lumped them together. The fiscal note thing sounded good, but then, after it got on, because I had to pass that as a bill to include a fiscal note, they realized, "Oh, my gosh, that's that thing she was talking about last session. I don't want them to put a hundred and fifty people that it's going to impact, so I don't want to see that." Then there was a lot of pressure for the prison, our own prison guys, not to know. That's why I had some other people come from outside the state.

Yes, to be able to give you the support.

Yes. Actually, the best time was when Bob Sader and I met together jointly. We went over to see the governor—or maybe Bob did—because it was Dick Bryan at the time. I remember that he basically said what he could live with, and that's what we passed out of the joint committees. They all passed and got signed, so that was a most progressive time in terms of actually getting changes made.

After that, in my mind, it's gotten worse. In fact, I was just talking to somebody about maybe running for attorney-general here last evening, and I asked him what was his view on the prison system in terms of overcrowding and so on. I realize that that's a very difficult question to ask somebody running for AG, just a general statement like that.

A certain senator introduced a bill, something I didn't really support, but it did pass, and it was after my day when I had the chance to vote on it anyway. It was called "determinate sentencing," where you would take away a lot of the judicial discretion, and you would say, "Mr. Judge, if you find that this is the crime, then you must find between three and, let's say, seven." You must have a minimum of three years; you cannot give him any less, and he will get a maximum of seven years. You will have some discretion between any of those two dates, but you can't go below, and you won't go above. I don't know if I would have supported that or not, but my feeling was that they get a report from probation in terms of what they think is a reasonable penalty, and it seems to me like that's what we elect judges to do, to hear cases and to make decisions. As I said, I don't know if I would have supported that or not.

This last thing that's listed in here in 1979 is a resolution, but I'm going to talk a little bit about it. It commends the University of Nevada, Reno swimming and diving team on victory in the national championships. There's an interesting story behind this, too. This seems like a very innocuous little thing. In fact, several years ago, I had this particular resolution enameled on a piece of parchment, or board, and given to a woman who was being inducted into the UNR Athletic Hall of Fame at a Pack PAWS dinner, which is an organization for women in sports at UNR. I told this group of hundreds of people there about the gal who was getting into the Hall of Fame. Her name was Karen Petersen, and she was a photographer here in town who did a lot of well-known people on their CD covers or album covers and met a lot of people. She had a studio in the MGM, and so she met a lot of entertainers over there. She's a really good photographer. I'd met her because she did a picture for my lieutenant governor's campaign that I used on the billboards and other things. Anyway, she was a member of this first national championship that UNR ever had as a diver.

The interesting thing was that I had requested this, and I was told by the chief of the legal division at LCB that we didn't do things like this. This was not important enough. Well, it happens that just the week before, they'd done something for Bishop Gorman High School in Las Vegas for a football team. I said, "What is this? This is a university team, and this is the first time UNR's *ever* won a national championship in *anything*. This was just a high school football season?" Well, it was that this was a *women's* team.

I could not believe that he would have . . . I don't know what to say. That he would have the guts—I don't know, there's another word I want to use—to tell me that? So, anyway, I was telling this story at this large gathering, and the woman, Karen, knew that I had gotten up and left. She'd seen me—I was sitting at a table next to hers. So, she gets up to accept her deal, and she says, "Thank you," to all the people who had something to do with this. She was going to thank me, and when she looked down, I wasn't there. Well, that's because I was standing behind her. She was too shocked.

So, I told a story, and it happens that the guy who I'd called at research in LCB lived down the street from where Karen grew up in Carson City. They went through all these inordinate procedures to get this thing all done in a proper form for me to have that evening, because I hadn't thought about it until, maybe, a few days before. Of course, all these women—I mean there were men in there—but the women just *loved* the story. The fact that I could do that—they couldn't believe that!

I said, "Hey, it wasn't that long ago when . . . . You have to always be vigilant."

It really has not been that long ago, has it?

No, it hasn't. But anyway, I thought that was a little interesting story.

That's a very interesting story. We're going to continue talking about the 1979 legislative year.

The first bill I see here in 1979 that I introduced, that I thought wanted some attention, was AB110, which provides a penalty for the failure of a parent or the guardian of a child to show to the school district that a child had the required immunizations. I think it is apparent even in today's time that some parents *don't* want their children to get the normal vaccinations, because they think that there may be some tie-in with autism. So there is a segment of parental groups that don't want to do that.

However, it clearly puts the student in a different class in terms of if they come to

school, and they *don't* have their immunizations, then they obviously can expose themselves and other people at that public school, or private school, for that matter, to disease. But in this case, it would only be applicable to public schools. That was in 1979, and there still are echoes of that same philosophy in today's world.

And really an issue of public health, then.

Yes, it really is, I think.

The next one is AB117.

Yes, that makes certain minors eligible for I.D. cards without a driver's license. This was brought to my attention by a young man who lived in my district, who did not drive a car, did not *want* to drive a car, probably would *never* drive a car or own one, *but* very often you're asked for some kind of identification.

It's even more apparent today, I guess, than in 1979, that the kind of universal identification card became a driver's license, and if people did *not* drive, and did not intend to drive, they had no way to verify who they were. So this was an attempt, which did pass and become law, that would allow somebody who was either under age, or someone who was older and chose not to drive, to have that identification.

There was some attempt made to have the identification cards for drivers to be faced forward and these people to be faced in a profile, if I remember correctly, to show that there was a distinction involved in that. But probably a lot of people haven't taken advantage of it, because they don't fall into that class of persons, but for those who did, it would be important for them, particularly today, in light of the tragedies that occurred in our country on September 11. There's now a discussion about having a *federal* identification card based upon something through each state DMV, which is exactly what we were talking about. When it comes to identification cards, though, I am concerned about privacy issues.

Some of the bills that I introduced in 1979, I think, do not warrant any specific attention, so I'm going to skip over those. There is one bill here that was a good idea, whose time, I guess, has never come, even from 1979 until 2001, and that's a bill that required a biennial report from the governor to the legislature on the management of executive departments. You could see the names of people that co-sponsored this. You'll see it was about everybody in the assembly. However, this was probably an intrusion into another branch of government. As you can see, it didn't pass, and thus, even some of the legislators didn't think it was appropriate.

It seemed as if this was a session where I did a number of bills having to do with the executive grant. When I come to AB190, again, this was co-sponsored by almost everybody in the assembly. It requires the governor to do something *else*, and that's to publish notice of vacancies before appointing persons to fill them. I thought this was a very good idea then. I think it's a very good idea *today*, because there are many people who would like to participate in government, but who never know that there's been an opening on a professional board, for example, that might oversee architects or structural engineers or dentists or something of that sort.

In addition to that, there are a lot of commissions that you *don't* have to have any specific professional background to become a member of, such as the Gaming Commission on which I currently serve, or the Public Utilities Commission, although it's positive if appointees do have some background. But people are not aware that there are openings. They don't even know, probably, that a vacancy has occurred. So the whole idea was to have the public realize that there were these vacancies, and that they could apply for them.

Was that part of your focus on more openness in government?

Oh, yes, absolutely. It's a shame that it didn't pass. I guess the people in the executive branch did not think that the legislature should, again, be telling them what they should or should not do when they have the authority to appoint people. So that didn't go very far, either. I still think it would be a good thing to do.

Moving along, I note that I also introduced AB273, which revises the law in compensation to victims of crime. There is a fund in our state, a certain amount of money in a pot to give out to victims of crime, which they can apply for. Again, I don't know how many people even know about *that*. But this was tweaking the amount of money that could be given to each or any applicant. There is a cap on that, and I have no idea what it is today, but the attempt that I made in 1979 was to increase the amount that each person could *request* from this group that decided whether a victim should be compensated at all and how much they should receive. And that, again, did not pass.

This was the session that I had introduced a number of bills— the first time any bills had been introduced in our state— dealing with domestic violence. I have to look at the people that co-sponsored those bills with me and say, "Good for you." We really did feel that this was an important area. Now it's become so assimilated into mainstream America that no one thinks of it as being something on the cutting edge, but in 1979 it certainly was perceived that way.

I note that two out of the three bills that I introduced that session did pass. I'll spend a little bit of time talking about this because the whole area is very important. These two bills, AB79 and AB80, actually changed the criminal code to even have a crime be involved with domestic violence; for example, providing a penalty for battery against an adult member of a defendant's household. There was no such thing at that time where someone who was in a relationship, i.e. marriage, could ever be found guilty of a crime against another person in that marriage. As I say, this was a first in our state. Actually, we were one of the states in the forefront of this in the nation.

I found this to be a very, very important area for me to be involved in, and I knew nothing about it until I read a book. I can't remember how I'd got the book, but I read it, and I believe it was called *The Battered Wife*, and I *just* couldn't believe what I read in there.

I heard about CAAW, Committee to Aid Abused Women, in our community, and it was just beginning. There were maybe two or three people who even knew about it. For some reason I heard how Joni Kaiser and her mother, Phyllis Kaiser, had helped establish this committee, because they saw this as a real social problem, and, indeed, it was. Having read the book, I called Joni, who still *is* the head of Committee to Aid Abused Women, and told her I would be very interested in doing something for them. I really didn't know what they needed to have done, and I didn't want to go ahead and come up with some idea of mine when it may not have been *beneficial* to their needs, at all.

So we came across these three areas, and I'm going to just mention that two had changed the Criminal Code. The third that did not pass, I believe, finally passed last session at the legislature, and that was a database, if you will, of reporting incidences of domestic violence, so there could be some kind of a central registry. That was

not perceived to be necessary in 1979, but the other two bills were.

Another bill that I thought was kind of interesting in the 1979 session was AB523, which provides for termination of certain boards, commissions, and the like, in the executive branch of government. This actually did pass on another attempt at the legislative branch intruding into the second branch of government, I guess. This was an attempt, I *believe*, that was twofold, and I think this bill might have done both of these things. One was to sunset certain boards and commissions, unless they could justify their existence before the legislative branch of government. In other words, they would be sunsetted maybe five years out or seven years out.

The other was an attempt at consolidating similar boards and commissions together, so they would have one administrative assistant, who would sort of be the staff person for two or three professional boards, for example, dentists, doctors, nurses—something of that sort— so each one didn't have a little area of territory that they were protecting. It would save on a variety of administrative costs. This was a GOP idea.

Would that be something that affected, for example, the Commission on Economic Development and Tourism? Wasn't there a joint board on that?

Well that was created under Bob Cashell's governorship. That would not have happened until the 1980s.

So it's a little ways down the road.

Yes, it is.

This would have paved the way.

No, not exactly.

No? That's something different?

Maybe you remembered that from talking with Jean Ford about the Commission on Tourism and Economic Development?

Right, and I worked for Broedeur-Martin public relations firm, and they had the account at one point for the Commission on Tourism, and so I was familiar with the fact that the two were linked together often.

Yes, they were. In fact, I tried to get them linked together my last session when I chaired both of those, and it wouldn't go through.

So they still have their own separate boards, do they?

Yes, they do. Anyway, what I just described did become law, and hopefully, it's making some difference at some point, *somewhere*. The next bill that has some passing reference had just passed, as well, and that was to provide free hunting and fishing licenses for senior citizens in our state, and that seemed to be something that people thought was a good thing.

In 1979 I had introduced a resolution, which is not a bill, but it suggests certain things, and it urges people to do certain things. In this case, I wanted to establish a system of time when bills had to be out of certain committees, had to be voted upon by the floor of the house of origin, and a certain date that they would have to have accomplished that and move over to the second house. The whole idea was to have a flow of bills, so the chairman of the committee couldn't hold all these things to chip away and bargain at the end of the session.

Well, needless to say, that was not perceived very well by my colleagues,

because I was taking power away from people—but this is *exactly* what we do today. Of course, this died a very quick death in the assembly that year. But it's interesting that this was something that the people have actually voted upon by saying, "We only want the legislature to meet for 120 days." Because of that they had to devise this flow chart, which seemed to have its time in the year 1999 and 2000, I guess, the 2001 session, but not back in 1979. It suggests that sometimes an idea might have some merit, but it takes awhile to get a consensus that it is something that needs to be done.

I've talked about prison overcrowding and my involvement with prisons.

You did. I was going to ask you, it was an interim study committee, is that correct?

That's correct. ACR41 did create a study on the Nevada prison system and alternatives to incarceration, and that did become one of the study committees, and I did chair that. That was, I guess, the beginning of my interest in prisons, which I really had throughout my entire legislative career.

It began a personal interest for you? Had you known much about prisons before that?

Not at all, but I was on the judiciary committee, so all prison policy came through that committee, and I had decided that we spent way, way too much money on building prisons. If you build one, it'll be filled. Judges will find reasons to fill them. And out of a pie chart the public safety budget kept growing and growing and growing. When that happens, it takes away money from education or from a variety of other things that I thought were more important, and there needed to be some real evaluation on who deserved to be a felon, because felons go to the state prison system, and misdemeanants go to the county jail. That was the first real inquiry made of that issue.

Many of these bills that were agreed to by members of that particular interim committee had their day in court, so to speak, at the next legislative session. Halfway houses, house arrest—where an ankle bracelet is put on somebody—all of these things had their genesis in that interim committee. Restitution Center is another example of a halfway house.

In fact, even today you occasionally see people coming before the Gaming Commission. It was somebody just two or three months ago who was able to get the day *off* from his halfway house to come down to testify that he wanted a restricted license once he was allowed to be paroled from the halfway house. Anyway, it was nice to see that they're still serving a real purpose. Needless to say, hardcore criminals don't go to those places, but people who serve lighter sentences wind up there.

I just remembered something I would like to add to my story here. After my friend Pat Hardy Lewis got elected to the city council—I think it was in 1973—she then opened the door for me to get appointed to a number of committees that gave me the opportunity to meet a number of people who were interested in policy issues and get my name better known on the outside chance I might be interested in running for some office in the future, which, indeed, I did.

One of those was to chair the City of Reno Charter Commission, and the charter is like a state constitution for the city. One of the things that we debated—and all these things had to be acknowledged by the city council before they went to the state legislature—was electing the mayor at large. Up until that time, it was done by the people elected to the city council. If there were five people or seven people, then *those* people selected the mayor from among themselves. Well, it occurred to me that that potentially could be a problem, because we voted for people from each ward, but we had no input to who that top person was going to be. So somebody could promise certain things to only four people, for example, get four votes, and they would be the mayor. It seemed to me a better idea that the mayor be elected at large. I guess the arguments were good, because the city council approved it, and it went on to the state legislature. So I introduced some other charter changes, but that was probably the major one— that the City of Reno, from that point on, elected our mayor.

The first mayor to be elected at large was Barbara Bennett. It was a very close race, and of course, it was business interests versus non-business interests, if you will. That was the first time someone like a Barbara Bennett could be elected in the City of Reno, and it was followed by *other* people who might not have won and might not have been mayor under any other format.

When you say business versus non-business, was it also growth versus non-growth at that time, or was it just really limited to pro-business?

Well, the business interests *would* want to grow, so they were similar. It would be hard to make a distinction between those groups. Clearly, Barbara Bennett is known for being slow growth. That would be, in my mind, other interests, because driving the business community would be the interest of more people, more buildings, more apartments, more shopping malls, more casinos, for that matter.

Yes. More tax money.

Yes. So I think that that's a good point. I think they both go hand in hand. As it turns out, it was pretty clear-cut as to who supported what issues as a result of that election.

Were there other things from the City of Reno Charter Commission that you took on?

The other things were probably very small, because this was the big issue.

A big change for Reno.

Right. And it still has been the big change. There's nothing else that has ever risen to a level of people being interested in any charter changes. They tend to bring forward anything that they think needs to be changed at each legislative session, and since we haven't heard about any yet, I guess there's not.

Just happy with the way they are.

There were some changes made last session to the representation on the airport authority, for example, and that's because the two cities—Sparks and Reno—and the county appoint certain people to that airport authority. Some people didn't like the way it was working, so they added some other folks to it.

We have one more piece from the 1979 legislative year. You want to fill me in?

Yes, I do, Vikki. I happened to notice an editorial or a story about cancer registries in our state and the fact that people in Fallon, of course, were quite upset with the fact there hadn't been certain data collected by the cancer registry. I do remember the 1979 session was the one session when I was on the money committee, ways and means, in the

assembly. I remember that some people came before a subcommittee I was on, dealing with this new idea they had about a cancer registry. I thought it sounded like an important idea, and, evidently, it had a rough row to hoe, because I remember, as a first-time member on the money committee, I was the one who kind of carried it and explained it to other members of the money committees. I felt this would be a good thing to have to compare different kinds of cancer, in different areas of the state, whatever kinds of things that they would find important to keep. Needless to say, it just rang my bell the other day when I was reading this article about the Fallon cancer cluster, and I did want to just mention that. This is what happens when you're involved over a long period of time, you do forget, unless you can see something in print that reminds you of a bill or something that you were involved in.

Well, it's one that is very current because of the leukemia cluster in Fallon, and so you're also having an opportunity to see an end result of something that you worked on?

Yes, that's true, and that's what reminded me of it, when I read these stories about Fallon. But I believe the articles were pointing out that there wasn't the appropriate information kept. They were very disappointed that more money was being spent in the budget each year, yet, the statistics did not prove to be of much use for the purposes that would be of importance to Fallon and the cancer cluster in that community. I think that's what was just in the newspaper the other day.

That sometimes it doesn't work?

Yes. Well, it would have worked, and other states are doing what should have

been done. People always had a reason—
not enough staff, et cetera, et cetera. I
certainly don't know what the appropriate
reason is, why certain information was not
being kept. But I do know that the state
epidemiologist, Dr. Randall Todd, was being
interviewed about this. Maybe I saw it on
television, I don't remember. I do remember
seeing Dr. Todd on, not only for the anthrax
scare, but also for this reason, and the fact
that he felt that they were doing a good job.
Clearly, whoever was looking at the data
did not feel that way. So, hopefully this will
be a jump-start to, again, take a look at that
and make sure that it is dealing with
information that will be useful in purposes
that it was designed for.

*Right, because this would be exactly the
kind of thing it was meant to catch.*

I would think so, hopefully. Clearly,
they're having to go out of state now in
order to have people come in here to do
some testing and that kind of thing. So, I
guess that ends 1979.

9

Run for the Senate

We're now, I guess, up to the 1981 session. I ran for the senate in 1980. But before that happened, I had served three terms in the assembly and I had, with my husband's encouragement, decided I would be running for the senate for very easy reasons to understand. One, you have a four-year term, and your district is larger; you do have to get out in a much wider area. Two, you're in a smaller body. At that time there were twenty people, and that was half the size of the assembly. So that meant your vote was really twice as important, in a sense—that eleven votes tended to rule.

However, during that period of time, before I had made up my mind to publicly announce my run for the senate, my husband was killed in a plane crash in a DRI weather-modification plane, on March 2, 1980, and that changed my life totally. My children at that time were only nine and ten—or eight and nine—depending upon what date I would use to record their age at that particular moment. Because of that, I needed to get a job, which I had not had before. Even though my husband didn't make a lot, we were able to exist on it, and

I was staying home most of the time with my kids. But this changed things.

So I had a number of job offers, one from the then governor Bob List, who offered to put me in charge of an agency or something in state government. I really didn't want to do that because that's a full-time job being in state government. Other people thought I should go back to teaching school, which would have necessitated my taking some other classes, because I had not taught since I had moved from Arizona to Reno.

At some point, the Desert Research Institute offered me a job to be assistant to the president, a position which was soon to be open because of soon-to-be chancellor of the university, Mark Dawson, and other people. Alessandro Dandini was another assistant to the president of DRI. I did take that job, although I had really mixed feelings about it, because in some ways I felt them responsible for my husband's death. But it did allow me the opportunity to work three-quarter time, so I had time to be involved with my legislative work and family, and it worked out pretty well for about ten years.

Sue with Governor Bob List.

At that time I hadn't decided whether I really thought it was possible to run again or not. In fact, I was talking to my sister just last night, and this is November 4, I guess. My sister was here after my husband died taking care of everything and making sure I was back ready to be involved in life again, I guess. After my husband's funeral at Trinity Episcopal Church, my neighbors had—I don't know what you call it—a wake. You go after the funeral to somebody's home, and it was mine. They had laid out *huge* tables of food and everything in my kitchen, which is still pretty large, and there were several hundred people in my house.

My sister overheard a couple of guys, at my own husband's funeral, talking about the fact that now I wouldn't be able to run for the senate, and that they probably would. It made my sister angry. I'm certainly not placing the blame on my sister, because clearly I have a mind of my own, but she really did make me, almost for spite, want to run and *not* let those guys get involved. Again, I say—and underline it for about the third time—that that was not a very good reason, but it was something that did enter my mind at the time in deciding to run.

Needless to say, there were other, better reasons, and I have mentioned some of those. I don't want to say that it would make for better government. Well, you can't make better government in the senate than you can in the assembly. I was very honest in the fact that it was a four-year term, that you had more power in the senate than you do in the assembly, and I *did* announce I was going to run for the senate.

We ran at large, which meant that it was all of Washoe County, except for a small part of Sparks, unlike today where it is not as large. Up until that time, Bill Raggio and Cliff Young had been the two state senators from Washoe County. Cliff Young had told me at least a year before that he was not going to run again in 1980, and that he wanted me to have his seat, because he felt that I was the most close to his own ideology. He was a Republican; both he and Bill were. Cliff was very popular and went to the state Republican convention and announced that he was not running anymore, but he was going to support me, which was a *huge* plus at a statewide convention, or at the county convention, to say that. And to anoint someone to take their place never had been done before. Clearly, the people who supported me and wanted him to do that suggested it to him, and he accepted. He didn't have any problem with doing that, at all. So that was very helpful.

You could vote for two at that time, as it turns out, and Bill and Cliff had always run together as a team and had put out in a newspaper two pages where people could fill in what they thought were the big issues of the legislature and mail them back to the two of them. I assume they had somebody compile them and announce the results of their polling. Because Cliff was not now going to run, I don't think Bill knew exactly *what* to do. I'm pretty sure he did ask me to participate in this, but I chose not to do that, and I can't really remember now why. I think it was because I really wanted to kind of run on my own. As I said, we elected two, so a lot of people in my campaign thought people should single shot. That means that even though you can vote for two, you only vote for one, so that makes that vote have almost twice the significance that it would if you divided it up. As a result of the election, I beat Bill, and that was not probably quite the way a lot of people thought the vote should have come out. I think part of that was because of the single

shot that a lot of women did in that election.

So, a lot of the women only voted for you, and not for two?

That's right. Yes. I suspect that may have had some aftermath that I was not really aware of.

So I think it might have created some hard feelings.

I suppose it did, although it was not ever . . . .

Not openly, right?

Yes, not openly. But I think it did. Surely, the people who thought this was a good idea didn't ever realize that that might happen.

They probably thought they were helping you, and instead, created a little tension, at the very least.

Yes. I think that's probably fair to say. I did want to make those comments about why I ran and the fact that I did pursue it. I guess you could always say that my husband would have wanted me to have done that. I think that is absolutely true, because my husband had made a commitment to me that if a new congressional seat opened up, that he would want me to run for that, because he felt he could get a job in Washington with his background. He and I had already talked about running for the senate before his death. So that wasn't anything that I thought would not be a good thing. I'm not so sure it was a really great thing for my family, though, because to have lost their dad, and then to have their mother be elected to *another* office and be campaigning during that period of time, was probably difficult for them. It was difficult for all of us, but it's hard to understand what's going on in someone's head, and certainly in children's. They may not be as open as you'd like them to be, and they may not voice their concerns, as maybe would have been a good thing.

Very honestly, I had spoken to a psychologist I happened to see at the gym not very long ago about a mutual friend of ours who had just lost a family member. I was talking about it, and she said, "Well, they had had some grief counseling."

I thought, "Wow, that would have been something that would have been very good for our family." She wanted me to recognize the fact that in 1980 there was no such school of thought that you would even go, that there would be any help needed to get through a grieving period. So that wasn't anything that I shirked responsibility of; it just wasn't there. Nobody would have suggested it, because it wasn't done. She did mention that the kind of textbooks on this didn't even get published until the late 1980s, at the earliest.

Anyway, I did run, and as I've already alluded to, I did win, and I have to say that Bill and I had only opposition that was *minimal*. One was a Libertarian, and the other person was a perennial candidate, and no one really expected either one of them to win.

So then, I guess, began my time in the senate. People had told me it would be very different. In fact, people in the assembly kept saying, "Why do you want to go down to the senate?" There was a big difference between the tone and the way business was handled between the two houses, and the assembly has a much more laid-back, I guess, fun type of attitude, and a lot of jokes occur, and that really is *not* the way the senate is run. That's not to say there's not some levity and some joking around, but, *clearly*, not in the same way as occurs in the assembly.

More formal, was it?

The senate is much more formal, much more businesslike, and much more committee oriented. When things come out of committee, it's pretty much that it's going to pass the senate, because it's gone through this committee structure. Well, that's the same way the assembly is run, too, but it's not quite the same feeling that just because it got out of the committee, that it's not necessarily been anointed, so to speak. But the committee system was very, very omnipotent in the senate. I was placed on, and did want to be part of, the judiciary committee again. Government affairs and legislative functions, I believe it was called at that time, which really is a committee that almost all the quote, "leadership," serves on. I certainly was not in any way part of the leadership, because I was a freshman senator in the minority party, but I did get appointed to that committee. It was an interesting one, because it does oversee the legislature as a branch of government.

It was interesting to me that Jean Ford and I were both in the senate together, and we both wound up on the same three committees. Jean had been led to believe that the other members of the committees, who were, of course, all male, were *really* concerned about the *two* of us being on the same committees together. Like we had any power or anything—we didn't—but they just were concerned that there might be something afoot with the women getting together, like both of us. [laughter] It wasn't anything to be really concerned about, and, needless to say, we didn't think of it that way, at all.

Obviously, you wouldn't have had 50 percent of the vote on a committee, just the two of you.

No. Most of the committees, I think, had seven members in the senate. I don't know if there were any nine-member committees. I'd have to think about that. But regardless, it doesn't matter whether it's seven or nine, the fact is we certainly did not have the majority. And sometimes *we* didn't necessarily see everything the same way—Jean and I.

Was it possible that it was the first time many of them had served with two women?

Oh, I'm sure you're right. Or two women such as Jean and myself. There were other women who had been in the senate, Margie Foote from Sparks, and there was a Helen Herr from Las Vegas. I have always liked Margie. We haven't agreed on everything, but I've always liked her. Helen Herr I hardly knew at all, but to be honest with you, she fit right in with the other guys in the senate, so she was a very acceptable type of person to have on a committee, because she wasn't going to pull any surprises, I guess would be fair to say. I suspect she's probably a nice person. I just never got to know her.

But had more of the same opinion, rather than a different viewpoint to bring.

Right. As I said, I don't know how else to say it, except that she fit in with the other senators. As I say, regardless of whether Jean and I voted alike, we did bring something different and had always, I'm sure, been perceived as bringing something different, whether we were in the assembly or in the senate.

OK. We want to continue on your first session in the senate, and I wanted to just ask you some general questions and maybe have you talk about each one of

these things. The first thing is that, by now, you knew the ropes of the legislature, because you had served several terms in the house. How was that different for you in terms of what you knew going into the senate, versus coming in as a brand new legislator in the assembly? What kind of knowledge do you think you took into the senate?

I think it would have been more difficult if I had started out in the senate initially, and I don't want to say there's a higher standard, because that's certainly not the case, but it's much more formal in the senate versus the assembly, and the committee structure and reliance on committee judgment is much more important in the senate than in the

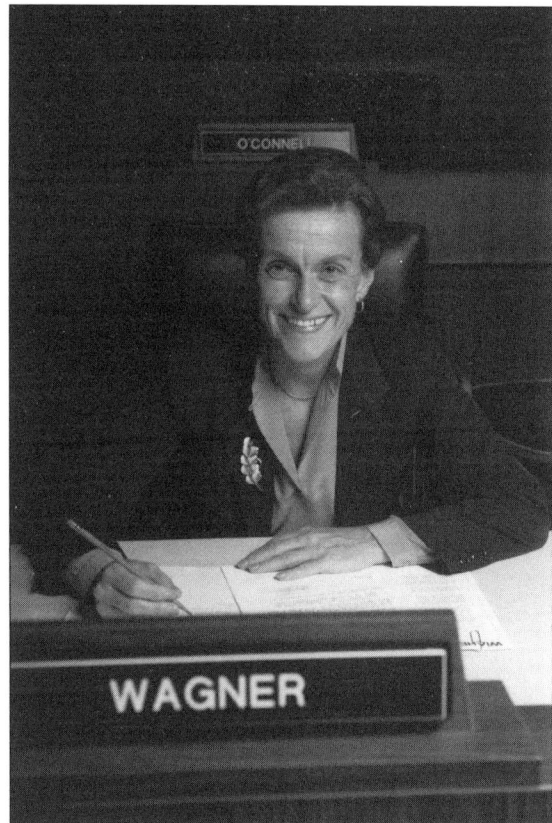

Senator Sue Wagner at her desk in the senate chambers.

Committee chair, Sue Wagner.

assembly. I think it would have been harder, unless you'd had a mentor who would have been very important to you, to start out right at the beginning and learn more about the process and the importance of the rules of each of the houses. If I had been a chair of a committee in the senate right off the bat, if I'd been in the majority party, I probably would have been at a big disadvantage. Whereas, I spent in the assembly—three sessions, six years—being in the minority and also was in the minority for quite a long period in the senate. But it did give you an opportunity to look at how other people ran their meetings, how people behave on committees as members. The senate, even though there was some humor, was pretty much all business.

I will talk about being the chair—that was the biggest difference. I'll finish that thought. Probably, the biggest difference being in the senate was that opportunity which I had not had in the assembly. I do remember many of my friends in the assembly asking me why I'd want to be in the senate, for all of the reasons that I've said. "Oh, they don't have any fun down

there. They don't even know the term 'joke'."

I thought, "I can't really believe that." But they were pretty much accurate, to be honest with you. [laughter] Although, certainly, that doesn't go across the board, but it was more formal, more business-like, more committee-structured. In the assembly, because there were always twice as many, people told jokes, and there'd be play on words, and even the speaker of the assembly, in many cases, was a little more fun than the president of the senate, although the president of the senate is the lieutenant governor.

I think that's probably the kind of general comments, and just by virtue of the fact that the chambers themselves are half as small in the senate as the chambers in the assembly, although there was extra room built in to add more desks, as belief that the senate and the assembly would have to increase in size at some point. One doesn't always think about things like that, but, actually, they designed into the new chambers an opportunity for seats to be added at both ends of the hall. Of course, we in our state of Nevada are limited by constitution to a maximum of seventy-five people total.

One of the big fights of our last session in 2001 was: should more members be added to both bodies? That would have been a plus for the northern part of the state, because you wouldn't have had to reduce seats so much when the population growth, of course, occurred so drastically in Clark County.

Because of the smallness of the chamber itself, you were just closer to people when you got up to speak. In the assembly, you actually had a dividing aisle, if you will, that goes down, and separates one half of the chamber from the other. It isn't that all Democrats are on one side and all Republicans are on the other. That's not exactly the way ours works. You get to choose your seat in the assembly. In the senate, you are seated by seniority—unless, you don't want to be. When they talk about the front row of the senate, those are the most senior people.

I had actually worked myself down to that front row when I didn't run anymore, when I ran for lieutenant governor. I probably am the only woman actually who has worked herself up to be one of—I don't know—eight? I don't know how many there are in the front row, but something like that. Just by the smallness, you got a sense of more proximity to the person you might have been arguing with, or agreeing with, as is the case.

You would think maybe, by virtue of the fact that we were closer together in the senate, we wouldn't have been as business-like, but that was not the case. It does give you a sense of actually not being able to reach out and touch somebody. The person was just closer because of the size. When I first got into the senate, of course, we were only twenty. Now that's increased one more—twenty-one. As we get back to the

discussion of the Equal Rights Amendment, to remember the discussion we had about the lieutenant governor, that was one of the important reasons. Certain people thought you must not have those kinds of procedural possibilities again. Parliamentary. We would need to add one more person, so it would not ever have to be a tie.

A tie broken by the lieutenant governor?

Right, breaking the tie, because of how he determined that not voting was to be recorded as a "no," if you remember.

Right, right. Also, one of the things you mentioned earlier was that when you first arrived in the assembly, you were sort of viewed as the same—Mary Gojack, Sue Wagner, Jean Ford—all were considered those "women legislators."

Yes, yes.

But, by now, I would guess that you were establishing your own separate identity. Would you address that a little bit and what that was?

Thank you. I know you asked me that question before, and I didn't answer it. Well, I think that my reputation had already been carved out. Clearly, when I got elected to the senate, I'm sure some people were, "Uh-oh," because at that time, Jean Ford was in the senate, I think, in 1981.

I think she was.

I know I did serve at some particular time with Helen Foley, who was at one time Jean Ford's intern, and I think Helen and Jean and I were all together in one session, and then it was just Jean and I one session. I really can't remember. I do believe that I did not have that same image again of being "just another Jean Ford," and, of course, Mary Gojack was not in the legislature at that time.

How would you say it was different—your reputation that you were carving out?

Well, that's a little bit difficult for me to explain, I guess, because maybe that's not true. Maybe, when I did come down to the senate, I certainly was known for being somebody who was very involved in women's issues. Clearly, Jean was, as well, when she was in the assembly. She had run once in the senate and lost and then changed her party from Republican to Democrat and then was elected.

Helen Foley was a Democrat from Clark County, as well. I think the difference would be that I was more of a known quantity, and, of course, coming into the assembly, judgments were made immediately, before I even got there, which was very unfair. Even if I turned out to be a carbon copy of one or the other, they didn't give me even a chance to find out if that was true.

As it turns out, it wasn't, because on some of the major issues that I've mentioned, particularly in terms of collective bargaining issues, they represented very different districts than I did, and we voted the way we thought our district would want us to vote on issues such as that.

However, when I got to the senate, this was different. The senate district, of course, was much larger. There were maybe five or six assembly districts, and I was elected in a multi-member district. That is a difference, because the multi-member district, as they used to be called, was when you elected more than one senator from a larger area. Before I ran with Bill Raggio it was Cliff Young and Bill Raggio. People got to vote for two out of, maybe, four, five, six, however many candidates—in the primary, anyway, depending upon how many were

running. Since Bill Raggio was already a known quantity, having run a number of times with Cliff Young, and then Cliff didn't run, and Bill Raggio and I were in the same political party, it kind of made sense to be perceived as maybe running together, although we really didn't run together. But it meant that the district was much larger, even than today, because they've all been carved up into single-member districts.

Basically, because Bill and I were elected in 1980, we represented all of Washoe County, with the exception of downtown Sparks. So, it was from the Carson City border to the Incline Village border all the way to the Oregon border, for that matter.

The district was much larger, and one's public voting record might change. If you remember, when I represented District 25, southwest Reno and talked about collective bargaining, clearly, my district had only single-family homes—no mobile homes, no apartments, no condos. I don't even know if they were building things called condos in those days, but there weren't any of those in my district, and so my district was rather homogeneous. However, when I was representing this larger area—Lemon Valley, Sun Valley, Gerlach, on and on—it allowed me, at least in my own mind, to be a little broader in my views. I felt that that was important, because I wasn't just representing such a homogeneous area, anymore. So that was a major change.

Another major change was the fact that you ran in a different manner. It was a very large district, so it was impossible for me to walk it like I did in the assembly. So other means had to be created in order to reach out and to let people know that it wasn't Bill Raggio and Cliff Young any longer; it was Bill Raggio and Sue Wagner—or Bill Raggio *or* Sue Wagner—you didn't have to vote for two.

A Libertarian and a Democrat, I believe, were our two opponents. As we know,

Libertarians have a very specific political philosophy of the less government the better—more so than even Republicans. However, I don't believe they've elected anybody to any office in our state. So, I guess one wasn't extremely nervous about that person as an opponent. The Democrat was a perennial candidate and someone who probably most people would think wouldn't have a chance, either. So I guess most people would have thought in that election that Bill and Sue were definitely going to win. Whether that really happens or not, you never really feel comfortable until election day, but it did mean that I probably advertised more, and I say "probably" because I, honest to gosh, cannot exactly remember.

One campaign from another?

Yes, I do remember the opponents, but more advertising—I don't believe I ever had any television until I ran for lieutenant governor. I know I didn't. I suspect maybe some radio spots. Clearly, it was a different campaign than one had run for an assembly seat.

Were your opponents using television?

No. Certainly neither the Democrat nor the Libertarian had any kind of resources—nothing more, I'm sure, than the resources that Bill and I would have had. Basically, we really are a two-party state. There are no write-ins, and the American Independent party is the more conservative party, the party of the Hansens, Janine Hansen and her brothers. That was really the party of George Wallace who had run in the South many years ago, but that was an established party, because they at some point did receive a certain percentage of the votes. The Libertarian party was an established party at that time. The person did not have to go out and do anything but get himself

on the ballot, but clearly they did not have the resources available to them to do that kind of thing.

When you were starting out in the senate, did you have some key issues in mind or some things that you were really hoping to accomplish?

Well, one of the things I'm sure we've talked about before was dealing with interim committees. There was an interim committee that I was involved in between my assembly career and my senate career, and that was one dealing with prisons. All the bills are drafted, and they're always given to the chair of that interim committee to introduce in whichever body they're in, so those are some of the first bills I introduced in the state senate.

Were you the chair of that interim committee?

Yes, I was. I think that this was my first "breakthrough," maybe, because I'm looking at the other names on the bills with me, and I believe that probably the other senators were even further down the "food chain," if you will, than myself. I don't think I'm going to say any more than that. I think that's probably why I got to chair it, actually. It was important to me, because it did establish the fact that that was the first committee I chaired. Even though it was an interim committee, it doesn't matter. It gives you the experience, because, in this case, I had some very competent staff persons. You were asking me what some of the bills were that I had, whether I had any issues that I carried over. This would have been a grouping of that, and I'm sure we'll find some others as we go along here.

Because you just got very interested in the whole prison system.

I did, and the reason I got interested in it was because it seemed to be more and more money was getting plowed into public safety. That is true, and I am sure it continues to be true to this day in 2002. When that happens, and you don't increase taxes or revenue source anymore, it means other money gets taken away from, i.e. education or a variety of other things that people think are very important. So I was always trying to look not only at how to reduce the impact, but also at other ways of just managing the prison population in a better way. I was talking about Bill Bible and Judy Matteucci. They both wound up working under Governor Bryan in a number of ways and still continued, actually, under Governor Miller, in some instances, and Governor Guinn.

I did introduce these bills by virtue of the fact that I did chair this interim committee between the legislative sessions, and that would have been probably in the year 1980. Those were some of the first bills I introduced, and I will talk a little bit about some of those to begin with.

The other thing was, it seems to me, that while you had all the advantages of having experience, you had the disadvantage of just having lost your husband, and it seems to me like this, in some ways, must have been a very difficult time to keep going.

It was, but the more people I know as I've gotten older, who lose someone important to them, particularly, their spouse, it seems as if one of the ways you're able to deal with it is to keep very busy. Or maybe with any traumatic experience in your life, if you have too much time on your hands, maybe, you dwell on those things more. I think in retrospect, maybe, who knows whether one does the right thing or not? But that's what I did at that time, and it *was* difficult.

I did have a friend, who was an older woman, and I met her through Business and Professional Women. This was the first session that I would have had away from my home without Pete there to take care of our children. Her name was Alice Hansen, and she just recently passed away. She retired from state government, from the Department of Agriculture, and she offered—this was her campaign contribution to me—to take care of my children during that session, up until a certain time. It was in May. First of all, Alice had never been married. Alice had, obviously, no children of her own, and all of a sudden she was going to come into a household with two

Sue with Alice Hansen (right). *"Alice Hansen . . . this was her campaign contribution to me—to take care of my children during that session."*

kids. One was in middle school, and you hear a lot of people say that is like the worst possible time.

Talk about middle school. Right. [laughter]

That was my son going into Swope Middle School, and my daughter would have then been in the fifth grade. I don't know how she did it, very honestly, but she did, and she never complained. Everything seemed to go very well, and I know it really didn't, but she never really bothered me with all of those facts. She just *lived* here; she just took over and stayed here, so I didn't even have to worry about getting back every single night.

What a wonderful gift.

It was incredible. She decided—during that particular year, 1981—that the kids would have to take over one night a week in fixing meals. In fact, I don't know why I thought about this not long ago—I think I was talking to my daughter or maybe my sister about it—that Kirk had this great idea. He got those ramen noodles in those cups that you pour the hot water in. That's what he had every single week. He just had a different kind. It was shrimp one week, pork the next week, I guess, beef the next week. [laughter] I don't know how many flavors they came in, but my daughter turned up her nose at that. That wasn't real cooking. She fixed pancakes or something like that. [laughter] I don't remember exactly, but I'll *never* forget the image of pouring the hot water into those cups, stirring them around, and plopping them down on the place mats. [laughter]

That was your dinner?

Yes, that was the one night a week. It just happened that I had emceed Alice

Hansen's retirement party, and I believe at that party, when we gave her all these gifts, she had an envelope for me saying, "Guess what you get?"

Great.

It surely was. In fact, when she left in May of that year, that was the same session that I had Spike Wilson's daughter, Ann, as my intern. So, of course, Spike was in the senate at that time, and I was having his daughter as my intern, and, of course, she'd sit there with me in the senate chambers, and then she could watch both me and her dad. When Alice had to leave in May, and the session went on and on—even in the 1980s, it went on a way long time—Ann and her sister, then, took over and babysat. They would share. First Ann would do it; then her sister would do it. And the kids *loved* them, because they brought the guitars, and they were college age, and they just thought that was great stuff. I don't even think they cared whether I came back or not. [laughter]

They were having fun.

Right. And I don't think they were quite as strict as Alice was—I suspect. [laughter] Ina Marie—that was Spike's other daughter's name.

We were talking about the difficulty of going into this after your husband's death, but how sometimes working real hard helps with the pain at a time like that.

Oh, there's no question about that. In retrospect, I think, "Did I do the right thing in running for office in 1980?" Even though we had decided that's what I was going to do when my husband was alive, I think probably for my own ability to carry on, it probably *was* the right thing.

I suspect, if you had asked my son and daughter at that time, they would have said, "No, it was the wrong thing."

I suspect that's a very difficult line that one has to decide what's right at the time. You never know whether it is right at that time or not, and looking back, you may question yourself, but you had to do what you thought was right at that time.

I suspect that I might not have felt that it was a good idea to do that. Certainly, I did not know that when I ran for office, but the fact that I had Alice offer to come and take care of my kids was incredible. Not only was it a generous thing to do under any circumstances, even if I lived in, let's say, Las Vegas, and I couldn't come back all the time, it would have been a wonderful thing. But, under the circumstances, it was essential. I probably hadn't thought that far ahead, to be honest with you, as to what was going to happen in the 1981 session. I expect that I would have figured that the kids just had to wait until I got home. The older they get, you hope that they're mature enough to know how to deal with, not problems, but when you leave them by themselves for longer periods of time, you really do start to worry. In fact, yesterday, the day before the day we're speaking here on tape, which is January thirty-first, the daughter of the governor of Florida was just picked up for forging a prescription, I guess.

Those are questions that you just don't know. As they get older, yes, they maybe are more responsible, but yet, they may have the opportunity to be more flexible, to do a variety of things, and, fortunately, I didn't have to worry about that.

That helped you go on?

Oh, yes.

OK. We've talked about how the prison was one of the issues. Did you want to go into that in more detail, or would you like to kind of summarize some of the issues?

Yes, I did speak to the fact of how those bills are assigned and to the fact that they were early numbers, low numbers, so that meant that I had chaired those committees, even if I don't remember them quite that well.

In some of the issues, I do remember, were the arguments that used to go on about where a prison should be sited, because if you got anywhere near where there's a population center, people absolutely would pack city hall, or the state legislative building or wherever it may be, saying, "We don't want a prison near us." And one can understand why they wouldn't.

There is the flip side of that, that the further away you build a prison, you, first of all, have to get employees to work in it, and the further away you get from a population center, where do the employees come from? Where do the inmates come from? There's a lot of material that suggests that when an inmate has visitors—families, spouses, children—they do far better than if they never see anybody. If you build a prison, let's say, a maximum security prison in Ely, which actually did happen, then, that's pretty much out there in hinterland, if you will, from the population basis of our state, particularly from Clark County, where most of the inmates come from, because that's the largest population base. In addition to that, that also has the difficulty of getting the kinds of people you'd want to run the prison, not only as correctional officers, but as staff persons themselves.

Some people may like living in a small town. I mean, Ely is a nice town. It's small, and a lot of people might like that environment, but it's certainly not going to have the kind of population base to staff it, so they have to be willing to give up wherever they are living and be able to move. Basically, it's the public outcry to elected officials. I don't think as many people were interested in penal philosophy versus where a good location would be, based upon some of those other criteria I just mentioned.

Well, I see that this bill had a very short life. It died in the senate committee on finance, and I have to ask myself, "I wonder why, if you just created the committee, you'd have to have money associated with it to be sent to senate finance." Maybe it was sent there to get it killed, or it's possible that, because it was a committee, maybe there was a small appropriation that went with it to pay the members of the committee or something of that sort. But, anyway, it didn't survive.

Which bill was that under?

That was SB28 of the 1981 session. Also, I believe that was one of the issues that we discussed with Warden Wolff, that the design was so inappropriate that there were going to be all these blind spots, and clearly even a layperson can understand why you don't have those, and so that's why that issue is important, too. I'm sure there are architects who do a lot of this kind of design, but that was a problem with Warden Wolff, and that was part of the questioning that I know I put him under one day. Currently, the ongoing concern is whether prisons should be publicly run or privately run—by private businesses. That was not the case back in the early 1980s. I don't believe there were any private companies that got involved in that business at that time.

I notice the next bill, SB29, extends the program of restitution, and using the word "extends" obviously means that restitution by certain offenders was already part of our law. It came out of this whole package of bills. Another one that came out of this same

interim committee did pass, and that revises eligibility for preliminary evaluation of convicted felons.

OK. Sue, talk about some of the bills you introduced in your first year in the senate.

Well, there are quite a few that didn't pass right at the beginning, and I guess that's why I don't have much memory of them. One of the ones that did pass was a bill that provided special license plates for prisoners of war. Currently, I don't know how many special license plates we have, but we have literally untold numbers. In the early 1980s that was not the case. There weren't that many, and each one was rather highly scrutinized by the committee on transportation. This was one that I was asked to introduce, I believe, by Congressman Santini's office, at that time. I think their staff person called me to do this. I remember a certain senator, Senator Lawrence Jacobsen, who was one of the cosponsors of this bill. When I got to the committee of which he was a member, he really grilled me extensively about why I thought POW's should have a special license plate, because, he argued, "Well, what if my daughter got into the car, or a POW's daughter drove the car? Everybody would think *she* was a prisoner of war."

The other committee members looked at me, "No, I don't think so. A teenage girl? I don't think so." [laughter] But anyway, he—I found out later—had a very proprietary control over license plates. He felt that if there should be a special license plate, he should have been the main sponsor, although he never said that to me, and he did become a cosponsor. Anyway, that did pass, and occasionally I see them around—and a myriad of others.

I introduced, I believe, one other—and we'll get to that when the time is right—in that particular session. There is one interesting one here that didn't pass, but I find it interesting based upon our previous discussion about multi-member districts and single-member senate districts. This created single-member districts in the senate. It requires each of them to consist of two assembly districts, which is *exactly* what happens today. Clearly, this was a bill that was before it's time, because that was exactly the race that I had been involved in in the election preceding this particular session, 1980. This is 1981, and, clearly, I found this multi-member district to be too large. People were representing from Sun Valley, which has a lot of mobile homes, to Incline Village, which has, probably, no mobile homes. The interests that they had were totally different, and I'm sure that's one of the reasons why I thought this would be a good approach. Again, it is now what we do, but it was not then.

There are some other bills. There's one here that passed, and I don't really remember it. It obviously didn't ring up on my register as being something that important. There is one here that's kind of interesting, and I remember two particulars, kind of anecdotal stories to tell about this, SB341. It designates the Lahontan cutthroat trout as the official state fish. We have, and most states have, official state trees. Well, we've gotten kind of carried away as we do with a lot of things, and, particularly, because school kids love to have contests and come up with a state animal or the state tree or the state fossil. In fact, we used to say when the bill came on the state fossil, "Well, that was really Senator Floyd Lamb," but he didn't think that was too funny. As I said, the senate didn't have a lot of humor, but we thought this was pretty funny. It really was the ichthyosaur, and Ichthyosaur State Park is out in Berlin, Nevada.

But anyway, this one provides for the Lahontan cutthroat trout, and I remember, at that time, Bob Rusk was in the assembly.

He represented an assembly district out in Washoe Valley, where he lives. He now runs a motel type of place down on the river. Anyway, Bob was concerned about this, because he wanted to make sure that it wasn't going to be any kind of endangered fish, or that it would hold up the progress of the water going anywhere, and I said, "Oh, no, no, no." Well, I do believe it *is* on the endangered fish list, I'm not quite sure, but it has become fairly important actually, and you do see it mentioned as a very important kind of trout and one that is very particular to our area of the country.

I remember Lawrence Jacobsen, the former senator who I was talking about, had invited me to go up to Marlette Lake, and they would milk fish, and many of them were Lahontan cutthroat trout, as a matter of fact. So, I did this before I introduced this bill. It's really cold, as you can imagine, where Marlette Lake is. We got in the water, and you pick up the fish and try to milk the eggs out of the female fish. So, when this bill came on the floor, he called me the "mother of the state fish." Of course, then he had to describe the story with graphic detail of how I was able to milk these fish. He probably helped me get that one passed, versus the other one that he didn't want to see passed. Anyway, it was kind of cute. This really did take on much more importance as time went on. I was asked to introduce this bill by the same fellows who asked me to introduce the State Duck Stamp. It was a wildlife group here in northern Nevada.

The next bill is one that I would guess a lot of people, depending upon what they were involved in, would think was one of the major bills that I'd introduced, and that was SB371. This bill set up the financial underpinning of all the domestic violence centers in our state. If you look at this bill, I had practically every senator on it, maybe all of them, and a lot of that work was done by my friend, who I first met during this session, Jan Evans, who then became an

Sue with Patty Sheehan (center) and Jan Evans (right).

assemblywoman and an important legislator in her own right. When I was asked to do this, following up on the bills I'd introduced on domestic violence in the assembly that changed the criminal code, this was the first one that addressed these centers.

It was beginning to be known at that time that this was a serious, serious problem. Where would these people go? Who would take care of them? If we wanted them to get out of the house, there had to be a place for them to feel safe, and if they didn't have family around then they sometimes said, "I don't know where to go, so I got to stay here." CAAW sent down a person who they thought would be helpful

to me, and that person was Jan Evans. She went around and educated most all of the senators on what this whole program was about, because the previous session, just a few bills were introduced. So this was still a fairly new concept, particularly, for many members of the senate, because I'm looking at all the names, and, with the exception of Jean Ford, all of the rest are men.

So that must have been the session that just Jan and I were there. I probably could not have done it without Jan. What we decided on as the vehicle, was marriage license fees, because we felt that, to a large extent, they were coupled together. We now know of many—and even at that time, but not as many—people who don't actually get married, but live together, and this same violence can occur.

We found that there would be some kind of a connection, and this is called "designated taxes". A lot of people don't like them. For example, if you wanted to increase the sale of liquor and designate that for substance abuse programs, some people don't like that kind of taxation. That was really what this was. This was the session where I'm really connected, as well, with Jim Joyce. Haven't I talked about Jim Joyce?

You just briefly mentioned his name but did not talk about your connection with him.

All right. Jim Joyce was the preeminent lobbyist, bar none. After his death, lobbyists scrambled to see who would be designated the "top dog," if you will, and I suppose that title would go to Harvey Whittemore today, although, their styles are so totally different. When we realized that Jim Joyce was lobbying for the wedding chapels, we realized that we needed to get his involvement, or, at least, for him to understand why we were doing this, because, clearly, wedding chapels were directly tied in with city clerks who issued marriage licenses. In many cases, wedding chapels are located as close as can be to the building where one gets a marriage license, so you could go right across the street and get married, particularly, in our state where there are so many marriages taking place, both in Reno and Las Vegas and in other places around our state.

I want you to remember that at some time I need to talk about how it used to be just done in the county seat. That will be people coming back to the legislature at a later date trying to expand that, because they're losing money, of course, if somebody from, let's say, Incline Village has to get married in Reno and get the marriage

license here, and they might like to have that money up there. So there is a direct connection between location and number of marriages.

This bill, to begin with, maybe it was five dollars extra, and it's gone up through other legislative sessions, of course, but I believe that's what it started out. Five dollars would be added to every marriage license issued, and that money would be designated to domestic violence shelters. That was considered to be unbelievable nationally. We were recognized for this tremendous advancement in terms of funding these shelters. Other states, of course, don't have the number of marriages that take place, particularly, if we'd look at our population base in the early 1980s. Now that both our communities, Reno and Las Vegas, have grown so rapidly, and our state, for that matter, they keep going up. But at that time, it was out of proportion to the number of our population base.

So this was logical funding, and as we go on in another session, we'll see how that really only subsidized the large counties, in the city of Reno and Sparks and also in Las Vegas. We had to do some tweaking of that funding formula so other counties would be able to take advantage of the funds, as well.

That was really a major step forward then, as you said, not only for this state, but it was being recognized all around the country.

It was. In fact, I do remember going to a National Conference of State Legislators, and I was there with Assemblywoman Myrna Williams. She and I went to the same workshop. She now is on the Clark County Commission, but she had been a powerful person in the assembly. They were talking about Nevada, and, of course, we wanted them to know we were there in the audience, and they were talking about how way out in front we were on this particular issue. Of course, mainly there were women in that audience, because this tended to be looked upon as an issue that women took on as their own, trying to take care of mainly women. I always hear that there are some men who have been involved in domestic violence, and I have seen a couple of those reports come across my desk, being on the Nevada Gaming Commission, but I have to say it's probably about ninety-eight to two percent, or maybe ninety to ten, to give it a little more liberal connotation. But, I have to give a great deal of credit to not only Jan, but also CAAW.

Most of these issues were driven by the northern part of the state, rather than coming from Las Vegas. Although, I just got a call yesterday from a domestic violence group in Clark County, where they want me to come to some event, because they're honoring people who've been involved with this issue for a long time, and I think they're celebrating their twenty-fifth anniversary. This was important, and, as I said, I think maybe because of our proximity to the capital, that some of these issues were driven by groups here in northern Nevada.

We're going to stop talking about the legislature for a little bit, and we're going to get caught up on the kids and a little bit about the job at DRI and some other family kinds of information that we haven't brought up to date.

Well, I think where we left off with the kids was at the time of their father's death. And the day we're taping this would be twenty-two years since March 2, 1980. The kids' lives changed incredibly on that day, and it still has affected how they've lived their lives ever since, actually. I think I'll try to not just glom them together as kids, because they were definite, distinct individuals. I think I'll take Kristina first.

I think Kristina was in the third grade when her father was killed, and clearly we can learn a lot from just watching programs, reading books, reading articles, and know how important a father is to a daughter's life. We can see patterns developing even from young girls: who they will date, what kind of boyfriends they will have. It is *directly* tied in almost every instance to their father, and when they don't have a father, that is even more troublesome and difficult, because they have no model at all, if they don't remember much. When you're that young, you don't really have a lot of memories. Although, I've tried to remind them of certain things, like that their dad was very involved in their lives. Peter was the Medicine Man for the Indian Guides; he was a Little League coach of Kirk's baseball team, and this is all, of course, before he died. But these are some of the things that my kids have forgotten, to some extent, and I need to remind them of that, because I think that's important, and they do readily admit that.

I may go back and forth from child to child and not take one separately, although they are separate individuals, but I'll make the point as to whom I'm talking about at the time.

Kirk, several years ago, was talking to me about his dad when I was over in Monterey. Often his memory of his dad was this: when he came home from work he went down in the basement and worked on wood; that he was a loner—and that is true, because Peter was not only an engineer, but also a scientist, and they do tend to be that loner type of a person. When I mentioned to Kirk that his dad had been the Little League coach and had been the Indian Guides' Medicine Man—and they had these vests with all their badges and stuff on them—he did remember that, but that was not the memory he had of his father at the *time* when he was talking to me. So I think it is important to make sure that they do have positive memories, because it is true what he said, but it's also true that the other occurred, as well. He probably doesn't remember also that his dad was an only child. His dad grew up in Alaska, and, in fact, there were many years that people couldn't even get in and out of his town, except by plane or by boat, because the road had not been built to any great extent from Anchorage down the Kenai Peninsula, where their dad was born, in Seward, Alaska. I suspect I've not talked about that either.

You just mentioned it when you talked about the honeymoon to Alaska.

Yes, but it did definitely in my mind determine who he was. Because he was an only child, because he *did* live in this kind of outpost where his dad was the dentist. The kids' Grandpa and Grandma Wagner used to talk about the fact, and they did, because upon their deaths I found containers full of gold fillings. He would trade Native Americans' fillings for food, for caribou, for whatever they brought in to barter with him. It was a different kind of upbringing than even other people would have had in the late 1930s and 1940s. I think of that as being important, though, because I was very concerned. I did speak to Peter a bit about the fact that he did spend a lot of time at his job, and doing things that he liked to do, that maybe one day he'd wake up and his kids would be graduating from high school, and he'd wonder where all the time went. As it turns out, that didn't even happen.

I think that Kristina had one little friend in the third grade to talk with about her dad, because the other little girl's father (whose name I'm not going to mention here) had committed suicide, and it was a very high-profile thing in this town at that time. So it must have been very difficult

for her, as well. Kristina has told me that she was the only person she could talk with, because everybody else in the third grade had their fathers, or, if they were divorced, they at least were here on this earth. Both of the kids, of course, being only eighteen months apart, were just a year apart in school, so they were following right along behind the other one.

Kirk was in a terrible accident in 1980, as well. It was Labor Day Weekend, and he was in a car accident. The car was being driven by the now new manager of Macy's here in town. Her name at that time was Kelly Condon. She's just returned to Reno as the manager of Macy's, and her name is now Kelly Bown. She was driving the car. Her brother was Kirk's best friend, Patrick Condon. He's an Allstate insurance agent now. He was Kirk's best man in his wedding, and Kirk was best man in Patrick's wedding. They were driving along Moana, going towards Lakeside, and Kelly was making a left hand turn to go into a 7-11, that is still there, and she turned, and she had to go across the traffic lane there, and somebody piled into her. She was fine. Patrick had a collarbone broken, but Kirk was in the back seat, and all of the glass of the front window came back. It was all embedded, mainly, in his neck.

I was someplace else and got called and went to Washoe Medical Center. I called my doctor, James Atcheson, and he tried to get who he thought was the best plastic surgeon in town at that time. George Greenburg was his name. He's since died, but he, at that time, I believe, was out of town. So they just got the plastic surgeon on call, who, interestingly enough, turns out to be the plastic surgeon of Bob Seale, who was piloting the plane when *I* had an air crash. His name was Grace. I can't remember his first name, but he was a young man at that time. He told me that Kirk had to stay over in the hospital, that the broken glass had almost cut his jugular vein. This glass was so deeply embedded in his neck and chin that he got out as much as he could, but he had to stitch him up, and he felt that some of it would come out in time.

It was not a very good year. It turns out that that was Labor Day weekend. It was *right* before both Patrick and Kirk were going off to their first year in middle school at Swope, because that was the first year they had moved the sixth grade out and moved it into middle school. Kirk also, of course, broke his glasses, which he was wearing, so he couldn't see a thing, and they were just *beside* themselves that here was their first day in middle school, and they were just beat up. Patrick had his little arm in a sling, but he had to kind of take Kirk around because Kirk couldn't see anything.

Anyway, I'll just finish this particular story. It turns out that Dr. Grace had done a very good job, because I was told about ten years later to take Kirk back to a plastic surgeon before I signed anything with the insurance company, which I did, and I did go to Dr. George Greenburg. He said it was a terrific job that had been done. The question was posed, "Did he need plastic surgery?" But because Kirk is so tall—he's six-foot five—most people could see up underneath his chin. But there wasn't very much showing, and Kirk has one of those strange beards that everybody has. I think maybe he's shaved it off now, because he's gone with a new law firm. But anyway, that was right after their dad died that all that happened, Labor Day weekend 1980. Well, no, this couldn't have been in 1980, because I remember specifically it was when Kirk was going off to middle school, and I thought Kristina was in the third grade. Well, anyway, I don't remember the exact dates, but I do know that this accident *did* occur right before Kirk was go to go middle school, so it would have happened after their dad died, anyway, regardless of whether or not it was the same year.

Kristina was then in the fifth grade, and it was interesting because I was just reading in the newspaper about cuts that the school district may have to make, and one of them has to do with the sex education course. And here's something else: my name is not on the bill that was the driving force behind sex and AIDS education in the public school system. I don't remember what year that was, but it was in the 1980s in the senate, and my name never appeared in the bill.

In looking at these cuts being made now, one of them discussed was the Academically Talented Program. I know Kirk, at least, was tested at this time. They did that maybe in the fifth grade. Somebody advised his counselor to test him. He did. He did pass whatever test it was, but he really did not want to go into this program at all. He was *absolutely* opposed to it because in his mind it would set him apart from his other guy friends, and he did not want to be set apart, but he finally saw the rationale of it. I guess we talked about his dad being a National Merit Scholar, that it was important, and that it probably would help him when he took his SATs, because he'd be having more difficult courses and so on. Then when Kristina came along, she also was in that program. I personally cannot say enough good things about our public education system in this county, particularly, in these classes, because they got what would be perceived, I guess, to be the best teachers in both middle school and high school, as long as you were on that track.

When they got to junior high, Kirk was on the basketball team, and there weren't very many activities for girls in sports at that time. I will say that Kristina was also on the Little League team that her brother was on. Her dad told her he was going to be going down there to coach, and she'd have to go with him, anyway, because I was at the legislature at that time. She finally said

OK, but then she got a list, and it was like a spreadsheet of all the names of the kids on the teams, and she realized she was the *only* girl, and she didn't want to be the only girl. Well, he still convinced her that she'd be wasting her time if she just went down there and sat in the bleachers, so she did play. And particularly, her grandpa came to watch them play. Kirk was much better than Kristina, but Grandpa was much more excited about Kristina, because she'd always wear like a pink shirt or something way out there in left field, so everybody would know she was a girl. [laughter] She had short little hair, which she still will wail on about me having her hair cut like Dorothy Hamill. But we'd just seen Dorothy Hamill, who was a comeback here at the last Olympics in Salt Lake City, although her hair is somewhat different now, but still short. But that was a big thing at that time—the Dorothy Hamill haircut. When she put a baseball cap on you couldn't really, necessarily, tell.

Anyway, I thought it was a fun time for the kids, and hopefully it was, because Kirk was more interested in sports at that time. When the kids got to high school that was a bigger change, because Kristina became very active, was a class officer, and ran for student body offices. To go to Reno High and to get to be what is called a song-leader was *the* thing.

What's a song-leader?

Well, a song-leader, I guess you'd say, is a pom-pom girl. *Better* than being a cheerleader. This was just it, and there were five girls, I think. Kristina had never tried out for cheerleader until her junior year, and everybody who got to be a song-leader had been a cheerleader before, because there were a lot of things that were similar. But she did go out for it, and she did get picked. So that was like, "Wow!" The

big thing. I remember coming in from Carson City and helping her put up signs when she ran for student body secretary, because she had been in office before then. She went to Girls State when she was a junior, as her mother had. In fact, she went to France with the American Field Service in her junior year, and *would* have gone, according to the people who ran Girls State, to Girls Nation, if she hadn't gone with AFS. So she was very much a person who was involved in high school.

Kirk was on two athletic squads, the basketball team and the golf team. They had both learned to ski earlier at Jessie Beck Elementary School and the Junior Ski Program. Kirk did basketball, and we used to go to as many basketball games as we could to see him, because usually they don't have huge crowds, unless they're really, really good—except for families and other kids.

They both really excelled at golf, and the reason, I suspect, is because after Peter died I had to get a job—I do know I've talked a little bit about going to DRI. There weren't any organized child care centers at that time, in the early 1980s, and so the kids did come home, to a large extent, after school and go next door. When it came around to summer, I had taken Kirk up, initially, to the golf course, because we lived so close to the Washoe County Golf Course that they could walk up there. They could cut through a field, which now has several homes on it, but I suppose they still could get through just to cut right up to Skyline. It might have taken them five or ten minutes to walk up to the golf course. I took Kirk up to meet the golf pro at that time. His name was Pete Marich, and he was very well known in town. There were very few golf courses at that time, unlike today. There were just the public courses, and I think the only private one was Hidden Valley. Kirk was left-handed, so at that time

Pete had told me that he never knew of any good left-handed golfers—the only one really today is Phil Mickelson—but he was right. So he taught Kirk how to play golf right-handed, and he actually found some old used clubs and cut them off to fit his size. They had kind of a junior program where the kids could go up and learn how to play. So Kristina went along, tagged along behind her brother. The golf pros and the other people who worked at the golf course always used to say that they were the Wagners' babysitters for many, many years, and that was probably the truth. It was outdoors; there were a lot of nice people who golfed; there's never been any kind of bad thing that's happened.

Ultimately, as they got to be older, they went to work there in different capacities, but at this time it was a real positive thing, because they then became very good golfers and were on the golf teams. The Reno girls team was just incredibly outstanding, usually won all the state tournaments. Now, that is not the case, because the teams in Las Vegas can play longer because of the weather, but that was true then. The girls had a very good coach, Mrs. Stevenson. Carol Stevenson was her name, and she was a terrific coach to the kids. I remember they always had to go to golf tournaments in buses, where the boys got to fly. So, needless to say, Carol made some kind of an issue out of that. I remember seeing them off at the airport their first time they got to fly down to Las Vegas, and it was kind of a nice thing to see them being treated the same.

Kristina and Kirk also played, I might say, in the WJBA, Washoe Junior Basketball Association. They may still have it. Both the kids were in that, as a matter of fact, and Peter was one of the coaches of that, too, because he had played a *lot* of basketball in high school. I probably mentioned he even went to Stanford to play basketball?

No. He got a scholarship to Stanford to play basketball?

Yes. Well, he also was a National Merit Scholar to Stanford. He went there also to play basketball. But when he got there he realized that he was just *not* as good as some of the guys. Actually, some of them went on to have long NBA careers, so he was right. Secondly, because he was in engineering, there just wasn't time to do both of those things.

Kristina's golf team, as I say, was very good. They used to let the parents follow the kids around on the golf course. It was not what you'd call a true spectator sport, because you had to walk the whole golf course to see the kids. But then I believe they *stopped* that later on, because there were people here in town whose kids were on golf teams, and they also happened to be golf pros, and evidently, somebody was mad at them. Or maybe they did it. I don't know. They alleged that someone was telling their girl what kind of club to use, et cetera, et cetera. So they didn't allow parents to go around, then, following their kids.

I remember Kristina was down in Las Vegas, and I was emceeing a dinner for the Nevada Women's Fund that night, and there were some people in the audience who were parents of another girl. So they would keep coming up to me and telling me what was going on, and I would announce it to all these hundreds of people who cared *little* about it, except that I had this opportunity to do that. As it turns out, Kristina was in a tie-breaker—I was so upset I missed all of this—and lost. I don't know how many holes they played, but she came in second.

I guess I'm getting ahead of myself, but we should talk about Kristina going to Stanford to play golf, if I don't finish that today. I was talking to Jennifer Satre about it the other night, as a matter of fact. Kristina was very involved in things in high school and had excellent grades. In fact, she had above a 4.0 GPA, because by being in the academically-talented class, she could actually get better than a perfect grade average.

Kirk also did very well. He was very smart. He did very well until he turned sixteen and got a car. Up until the time that both kids went to high school their school bus would take them to junior high, down to Swope. But when they got to Reno High, then they had to be a certain distance from school—I think it was at least two miles—or they had to get a ride. I couldn't take them because I was then working at DRI. Judge Chuck McGee's daughter took first Kirk and then Kristina *and* Kirk until Kirk got a car. When Kirk got a car, his grades went down almost a whole grade point average, from like a 4.0 to a 3.0. It was that time that guys had their cars, and they started to date, and they didn't care as much about other things. That was a real eye-opening experience for me, because I had to lay down the law. Here he is taking all these great courses, and neither one of my kids were *really* interested in going here to college if they could go someplace else, because they thought it was important, as did I, that they get away from home.

When you say you had to lay the law down, was that one of the first times you really had to be stern in that way with Kirk, that you can recall?

Well, I think that my kids were really, really, really good. I made it clear to them that I did not want to pick up the front page of the newspaper and read about my kids doing something that was wrong, whether that was drinking, whether that was drugs, whatever it was, because this just wasn't what should have been going on. I was gone a *lot* by the time they got to high school. I mean, they didn't have to go to anybody's

house or do anything like that because they were just too old. I'm sure my neighbors watched very carefully. In fact, I was talking not long ago with one of my neighbors across the street and talking about the kids, and I realized that I didn't know everything. I remember when my son told me one time that he was going with some girl whose parents had gone out of town, and so they had a big party there, and they totally trashed the house. Kirk said, "I'd *never* want to have it happen here." So at some level they definitely knew what was right and wrong. There's no question about that.

They also very honestly knew that talking about going to college wasn't even an issue in this household. Obviously, the expectation was, without even talking about it, that they were going to go to college. Having a dad who had a Ph.D. and mother who had a master's degree, clearly that was expected. As I say, neither one of them really had an inclination to want to go here, and I thought that was probably a good thing, although Kristina did win the John Ascuaga Scholarship, and then there was something else—I think it was a gaming thing that would have paid all her way to go here to school. I did have a letter from Dr. Crowley that I had saved, because at that point I didn't know what the future would hold for the kids. I don't know if the same is true now, but at that time, if you were on the faculty of the university system—and I suspect it's true maybe of other collegiate institutions as well—you could go free. I'm not sure that it's free now, but that was one of the benefits that people gave you.

By not now being on the faculty—and actually Pete *was* really on the faculty of DRI; he did teach a course or two in the engineering school—I wanted to make sure that that opportunity would still be there for my kids. And it *would* have been, because the kids did pretty well, and

Kirk, Kristina, and Sue at the South Shore Room, Harrah's Tahoe, June 1985.

Kristina pretty much paid her own way through college. But I guess I need to finish off, maybe, with high school.

Kirk got a golf scholarship, actually, in high school, and I was really very proud of both of them, because I went to an awards night prior to graduation, both years, where the students would be acknowledged for whatever they had won, or grades or those kinds of things. So I think they did very, very well being raised by a single mother most of their life. However, they were the winners. I told the kids that wherever they wanted to go and were admitted, I would make sure they could go look at the campuses. Kristina applied at a lot of

different places. Kirk just wanted to go to Boulder, Colorado, because he did like to ski. He just thought that he wanted to stay in the West, and it was a public institution rather than a private, which was cheaper. He did go there, and I'll talk a little bit about that in a minute.

Kristina had applied at Stanford, at Duke, at Notre Dame. I was at a convention in Boston, and I remember Kristina took her PSATs in her junior year, and then she flew back there and met me. When I was done with the conference, we traveled throughout New England to look at some schools. She was very interested in Dartmouth, and we looked at a lot of other

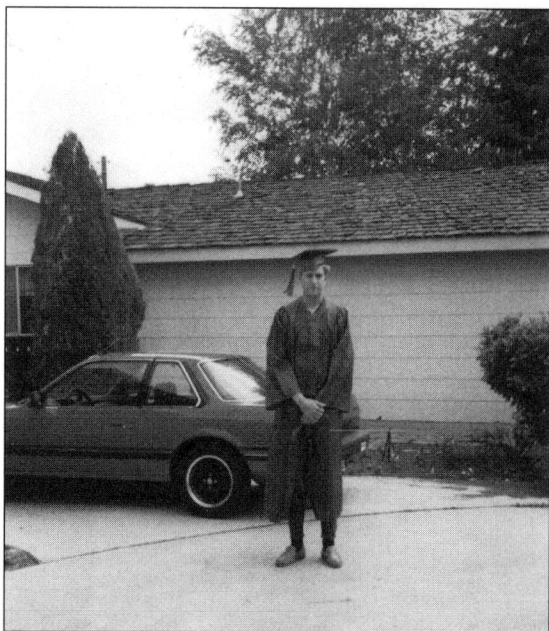

Kirk Wagner, high school graduation.

schools. I can't remember them all. I know we did look at Middlebury, Vermont, Smith, and some of the women's colleges. I suppose now they're probably co-ed; I suspect they are. So, she was kind of scattered throughout the country. She was admitted to quite a few. The last one she went to was Notre Dame.

She was the only student in the *state* that year to be admitted to Notre Dame, and she decided not to go after she had already gone to visit it. The people who supported her were really kind of irritated, because a lot of people wanted to go to Notre Dame. That is a big school, particularly, I think, for guys who want to be attorneys and their kids. They want their sons, particularly, to go there, to play football, whatever. But she just came home and said it was too homogeneous: everybody was just like she was—white, middle class, and a student-leader type.

I mentioned Jennifer Satre earlier. I'd just seen Jennifer awhile ago, and Phil, her husband, is the president of Harrah's. He was at that time, as well, president of Harrah's here in Reno. But now he's president of Harrah's everywhere—worldwide. He was a graduate of Stanford, as a *lot* of guys in town were, so they all wrote letters for Kristina. Of course, her dad had graduated from Stanford. At one time, that was a big thing, almost like being a legacy in a sorority house, and if you had a parent who went there, that was a big bump up to possibly getting admitted.

As I mentioned, Kristina had above a 4.0 grade average, and she had wanted to see if she could play golf at Stanford. So, somehow, arrangements were made. I drove her over, and I spent some time with a friend, and she spent the weekend with the golf coach. They have any girl that they're thinking about giving a scholarship to room with other girls in the dorm. So she did that. Had a great time. The girls loved Kristina. They all wanted for the coach to give her a scholarship. But he was very honest with me. He said he only had two scholarships, and Nevada just doesn't play that much golf compared to southern California or Texas, where the kids were so much more competitive. It was absolutely the truth. He said, "Besides, she can get in academically."

Well, she didn't, and she was really devastated. Interestingly enough, where a lot of kids from Reno High applied, none of them got in, except somebody who nobody knew. They *just* couldn't get over it. All these outstanding kids—none of them got in. But anyway, they didn't. She was disappointed for awhile, and I think that probably came before Notre Dame, I don't remember. The people she stayed with, I will mention their names, because they all have Nevada roots. The person she stayed with at Notre Dame was Nicole Lambol, and Paul, her dad, used to be chairman of the

Democratic Party in this state. Paul and his wife Stephanie have been friends of mine, and Nicole wound up being Governor Bob Miller's chief of staff here. She now works in San Francisco. Paul left Nevada to go to Washington, D.C., to become a member of the Interstate Commerce Commission, the ICC. Kristina then went down to UCLA and stayed with one of Janice Pine's daughters, and I don't remember which one it was now. Janice has been a Nevadan three or four times over, I suspect.

We're going to talk about Kristina going to college.

Yes. I've talked about some of the schools she applied to and got admitted to. She also got admitted to Dartmouth. And they had called the coach. The girls' golf coach had called her and talked to her. I kidded Kristina that that was at least better than Stanford as far as competitive golf, because Dartmouth would have a very short season based upon their climate, a lot of snow on the ground right away.

But Dartmouth in Hanover, New Hampshire, is just an absolutely fabulous location, remote but nice. I remember going back there with my husband when we took a trip, the trip that we took in the trailer before my husband died. The reason that I'm thinking of that right now is because we had gone to Hanover, New Hampshire, on that trip. So that was *my* first experience in seeing what Dartmouth looked like, and then we went back there again with Kristina.

We traveled all around through New England and looked at those colleges. The only reason I knew they were going to be beautiful was that I had seen some of them myself before. I had grown up in New England. We did a lot of the things—Kristina and I did—on that trip that I had done as a small child with my own family in the Adirondack Mountains, in Lake Champlain, which divides New York from Vermont. It's very bitter cold up in that area.

So Kristina had a *lot* of opportunities. I think it was right after she had visited Notre Dame, I don't remember, but anyway, she came back, and I remember we were sitting at the kitchen table, and she told me she had decided she wanted to go to the University of Arizona. I practically fell off the chair, to be honest with you.

She knew I was disappointed. A child *always* wants to see their parents be so excited, but I said, "How could I be excited?" *I* went there, and I *had* to go there because I had no other options. My parents couldn't afford for me to go anyplace else. It was like five blocks from my house. She had all these other opportunities! I had received a scholarship to Claremont, CMC, in Pomona. There are Scripps, Pomona, and CMC all in a cluster there together. But it was not for enough. I also was admitted to Bryn Mawr. Anyway, I did go to the University of Arizona because of those reasons. So, for Kristina to want to go there after she had been admitted to other schools—she hadn't even applied there! But if that's where they want to go, then that's where they want to go.

They start making their own decisions someday, don't they?

Yes, and you can't say, "You're not going there. I'm not going to pay for it." She didn't need it, as it turns out, but even if I'd said that, that wouldn't have been the right thing to have said. It's her life. Although, I very honestly thought it was a mistake. I now don't feel that way. At that time I did, because education was so important to both her dad and myself, that I thought if you can go to a place . . . and in my mind, UCLA would have been better than Arizona. I don't know if that's true or not.

Notre Dame was a totally different experience—smaller, a liberal arts school—but that wasn't what she wanted. So she did apply to Arizona. Needless to say, she got in and got a Regents Scholarship, which paid for all her tuition.

We can stop there and pick up talking about my taking her down there, and the sorority, and the dorm. Of course, I knew everything on the campus. I was on the National Alumni Board.

10

WORK AT THE DESERT RESEARCH INSTITUTE

We were just visiting a moment about the changes in your life, during this period right after your husband's death. We've talked about it only as it concerns your political career, but you mentioned, as you started talking about the children, that you had to take a full-time job, and it sounds to me like you had a lot to handle.

It was, but I guess the one thing I learned, both from my husband and from other people in this community after he had died, was that I guess people thought I was, quote, "A strong person. She can do anything." I guess it's nice to be thought of that way, and not so nice sometimes.

In what way?

Well, I can say that I remember when we were married we had very little money, even though, I suspect, for a Ph.D. it seemed like a lot, but it really wasn't. So the one thing we did not get was life insurance. And I remember my husband saying to me when he was only forty—and I have to keep emphasizing that that is very,

very young to have your life over—that if anything ever happened to him that I would be able to carry on. Needless to say, we never thought that would actually happen, particularly at that time. But anyway, we didn't have anything, so I did have to go to work. I think I did *talk* about that to some extent, in terms of Governor List offering me a job with the state and so on.

Only in mention, so we don't know anything about the job that was offered.

Well, I can't remember, to tell you the truth. I think it may not have been a specific job at that time. I do know that Governor Miller had offered me some specific jobs after I left being lieutenant governor, but with Bob List I really don't remember.

I do remember, Kathy, his then wife [Katherine Geary List], talked to me about this, as well, but I do know that Bob had made it very clear to me that there would be a job for me in state government. I'm not sure if he mentioned anything specific. I really didn't want to, at that time, make that kind of decision, because it clearly would have meant I would not have been in public office anymore. It was different than my not making the decision with Bob Miller, which would have meant a strenuous physical burden upon me. That was not the case. It was just that it's something I didn't want to do at that time. I also assumed, I guess, that the job would be in Carson City. That would mean my going back and forth again, and I felt that that would even be more than just being in the legislature.

So I suspect that because DRI felt responsible in some way—and I guess they should have—that the plane crash had taken my husband away, that they probably should offer me something. I have no idea what they thought, what they talked about. We just had a brand new president at that time, Cliff Murino, who wasn't even here yet when all of this happened, and here it was all newspapers, front-page stuff. So when he came on board—or maybe he hadn't even come on board then—he called and talked to me about being his assistant. I don't think he probably even had any idea what that assistant should do. I don't know any of this.

Although, as a matter of fact, there was a job by that same title, because at that time, the chancellor of the university was Mark Dawson, and Mark had had the same job that I was being offered at DRI. He went from being assistant to president to chancellor of the university system. So Mark and another guy named Joe Neumann were the people from the university or DRI to come over and deal with me in terms of all of the particulars about Peter's death in terms of insurance and that kind of thing. But clearly, as I just stated, we didn't have any, even life insurance, so there wasn't a whole lot there. So, for whatever reasons—and I can only surmise what they may have been—I did accept the job at DRI because, despite all that had happened, I really did

feel that the DRI job, the idea of it, was a really good one, and felt very strongly about it. There were other people who couldn't imagine my wanting to go to work for a place that had really been—and I really do feel that way—partially, if not big time, responsible for the plane.

Can you say in what way?

Yes, I think that the plane was . . . certainly the federal transportation system . . . . And it's interesting. My daughter is now going out with somebody who is looking at the entire report from the Federal Transportation Safety Board about her dad's air crash. And this is how many years later? What did I say?

Twenty-two, you said.

Twenty-two years later. But anyway, my memory serves me that they did not feel it was pilot error. I remember Peter talking about the pilot who lived around the corner from us. His wife, his widow, was Agnes Lapham. I think he was John Lapham. He had been an air force pilot, and I assume maybe had been stationed out at Stead, and this is the reason that they were living here now. He was no longer in the air force, but I remember Peter telling me that he thought he was a really good pilot—very capable. I remember a friend of both Peter's and mine, Peter Neumann—a different Neumann. I think it's spelled maybe the same way. But Peter Chase Neumann was a big personal injury attorney here in town. Still is. He went to college with me at Arizona, and he and Peter met by both being great and good skiers. So Peter did have his investigator—both for my airplane crash and for my husband's—follow the people around. I felt, regardless of what they found out, that it would be very difficult for me to sue the Board of Regents, because I was a publicly elected official, and I didn't think that would be an appropriate thing for me to do, whether evidence suggested that or not.

You said your husband said something about the plane, also. He said that the pilot was good?

Yes.

But had he also talked about the plane?

Well, I just think that the plane was fairly heavy in terms of all the equipment that was placed on it. Peter built the devices that then tested certain things in clouds or whatever it was that they were doing on any particular project. But anyway, I *do* know that the man, Dr. Jim Telford, from Australia, who had been with some Australian atmospheric science program there, was attracted to DRI. He had done similar experiments, and Peter worked for him. Actually, a plane had crashed in Australia, too. I did not know that the history of planes in my family, when we learned how bad things happened even before they happened to us, was pretty ironic.

I remember not very long ago, I was having lunch with Bill Raggio and Fred Davis. We were at the Prospectors' Club maybe a couple of years ago, and Fred sort of was doing what I did at DRI. He came over because he was good friends with Bill, too. At that luncheon I heard that a DRI plane had now crashed *again*, and that was just a couple of years ago. It wasn't doing the same thing, but it was another DRI plane.

I was pretty angry when I heard about the one happening in Australia, and then having the man who I had fairly decent feelings about . . . . I mean, it wasn't *his* fault that the plane had crashed, but I was angry when I heard a similar thing had crashed. He had gone to another country. And

maybe there was absolutely no connection at all, but you can't help sometimes how you feel.

I guess we're talking about DRI and my own feelings about having to go back to work and that kind of thing. At that time, as I mentioned, the kids were very little, and that's when they went over to the golf course, so we're kind of tying all these things together, because I didn't take a totally full-time job; I did three-quarters' time, because I just couldn't possibly have done that. I did want to come home earlier than five o'clock. I wanted to have a little flexibility. Very often, as a matter of fact, I would go up to the golf course and golf with the kids when they got to be a little bit older. I can't remember exactly when I started to go to work. It probably wasn't maybe until the fall. I can't really remember.

I'm thinking about where DRI and TMCC are located, on Dandini Boulevard. One little interesting item I'd like to mention is that I was the person who got that street named "Dandini Boulevard." Let's see, Dr. Murino, who was the DRI president I mentioned, called NCAR, the National Center for Atmospheric Research, which is in Boulder, Colorado, where my husband had gone to do a lot of his dissertation work. Cliff came from that institution here to DRI, and there were two things that he thought would be nice to do. I believe it was Cliff who wanted me to get the name of the street changed. I can't remember what it was called before, come to think of it now. Clearacre Lane? Could that be?

It could be. Clearacre attaches to it down the road.

Well, I learned the president wanted me to look into this. The other thing, and we should talk about it a little bit, was that Dr. Alessandro Dandini—Count Alessandro Dandini—had dedicated, oh, some of that

THROUGH THE GLASS CEILING

land between DRI and TMCC in the back. There was a parcel there that wasn't his, I think. I'm a little fuzzy on all this. I think we got Paul Laxalt to introduce a bill in Congress—was Paul Laxalt in the United States Senate at that time?

I'm not really clear on all the specifics of this, but I do know that Senator Laxalt was asked to introduce legislation that I think encompassed this whole area—made it whole, if you will—because the idea was to have a research park there. It seems to me that I left there in 1990, and that nothing has progressed on that. I don't know if that's true or not, but I suspect not.

But anyway, this gets into what I did on the job, so maybe I should go back and finish up.

Back to work full-time?

Sue and Paul Laxalt at a Republican Party function.

Right. Actually, I didn't really think much about it, because it was just something you had to do. You have to do it, so you do it. And I liked it. There weren't a lot of people around, so it wasn't quite as stimulating to me as, say, at the legislature, clearly, because you weren't seeing something begin and end, and all the things that goes on in a political process.

Of course, I had no intent of ever going back to work while I was still in the legislature until I had to. I always felt about DRI in a positive way, or I would never have gone to work for them. But I always felt, also, that people just never got it. DRI was always sort of like the fifth wheel of a car, and I still think it is today. I don't understand why they're not able to better promote themselves, because this was exactly the position that it was before I went to work there, when I went to work there, after I went to work there, and still today. I don't think people understand. Even when I could show to people that DRI hardly got *any* money from the state, hardly any at all, that everything mainly was on contracts that the researchers got for themselves, that it was such a good bang for their buck, and that many of the things they did had global implications. Very honestly, I see a TV ad on with some kids talking. And it's kind of cute, but I don't know. I guess they do need to promote DRI, unfortunately, in this state, because people even in Reno don't even know exactly what it is that they do.

What it is. They measure snow and they seed clouds, right? [laughter]

That's pretty much it. Well, I don't even think they measure the snow, but they seed the clouds, and that's what people know. That is probably not even a very scientifically astute program that they do. That's something a lot of people could do.

Anyways, to begin with, it may have been that the expectation was that I was

WORK AT THE DESERT RESEARCH INSTITUTE

going to go down and be a lobbyist for DRI at the legislature, but that was the last thing I was going to do, because I feel that those two things should be totally separate. Now I am talking a little bit about the job. I just think that, fortunately I was able to get a job, and I was able to pay for the things that one needed, but I really feel that the kids . . . all I can say is, they did a great job of doing as best they could under the circumstances. Clearly, it was not on *my* job description to come home and complain about the job, because they then would have felt bad about that, too. I certainly didn't want them to feel that way. So it was always done in a rather positive way. I have a tremendous amount of energy, so I don't think I ever felt that I couldn't do all of these different things.

The only thing that's kept me back now is my own plane crash, but I even, still to this day, have a lot of energy, relatively speaking. When people realize what I've been through, they're pretty surprised that I can even do what I can do, but I think the kids, even though they were young at that time, realized that Mother had to go off and do something else. Although, even to this day, I really think about whether I did the right thing in terms of going on with my political career. But I guess that, as I told my kids, if I hadn't been in the legislature, then I would have *never* been offered *any* job. There's no question in my mind. If I had just been Mrs. Peter Wagner, young widow, "Sorry about that." But young widow, "Well, have a nice life."

You don't have a place.

Maybe guys have a better understanding of it; I don't know. Maybe I haven't asked Kirk, specifically. Until I asked him about his dad, he didn't say anything to me either, unless I asked him a specific question. Or maybe it is more of a thing between a mother and a daughter, regardless of what the mother is doing, because they're the same gender. It might have been different if the other things were flipped, and *I* would have been taken, and it was just Kirk and his dad and Kristina. I don't know. But I think that even if I had had to have a job, there's no way that I could have lived on what the legislature pays—no way. If I hadn't been in the legislature, as I say, I don't think these things would have been offered. I mean, the governor is not going to call you on the phone and offer you a job just because he read about you in the morning paper. Didn't know you.

You'd already proven yourself as a hard worker and someone who understood what was going on in the political world.

Right. I was in the legislature, and I was in the same party as the governor at that time. I don't know if that had anything to do with it or not. Certainly, it didn't with Bob Miller and myself. But I think that at some level my daughter totally understands that. At another level she would like to have had me being home all the time. However, when I did do that for a few times, she *hated* it.

So, it was just one of those things where you can't be "all things to all people all of the time," I guess. I probably would feel comfortable in saying—although I don't have memories of this—that I probably wished I didn't have to do that, because I thought by just being in the legislature I was able to spend so much time doing what I thought was good stuff for my district, whether they thought that way or not, and time with the kids. Who knows? In fact, Bernice Martin-Mathews and I were just talking about that, and Nancy Cashell was talking about that with me not very long ago.

Certainly, if my husband had been alive, I would not have gotten out and gotten a job, let's put it that way, because his income was enough to allow me to go do that, because I wasn't bringing in any income anyway, I mean, just being a stay-at-home mother. When I went off to the legislature I made a *little* bit, but that's not why I did it. It certainly wasn't a strain on us financially, and that is what I would have preferred. I do know that we did talk about Dennis Myers and what he thought about Peter and that he was willing to go to Washington and do those things. I think it was a job that you had to create things to do, particularly, when they probably offered it thinking, "OK, maybe we'll have her do this and this and this."

I do have to feel that probably they did think that my being at the legislature would be a good thing. It certainly wasn't a *bad* thing, but it wasn't anything I was going to go out and do anything for. So maybe that wasn't a good thing. I don't know. But, needless to say, I was very aware of anything that dealt with DRI in a positive or a negative way. I could be right on top of it in that manner, understanding what was happening, because there were many times when UNR wanted to make DRI part of UNR. And, indeed, a former chancellor, Don Baepler, I believe, had thought that would be a good idea. Some of my fellow colleagues had introduced legislation to that effect. I don't think they really understood, again, what DRI was, and when they did, then the bill didn't go anyplace. There were a number of times when that happened in DRI's past history—not recently, though. Not in the last twenty, twenty-five years, I don't think.

So, during this 1980 to 1990 period, I worked at DRI, until I was elected lieutenant governor, actually. My first session in the senate was in 1981. Even though we meet every other year in Nevada, there are two committees, or commissions, that meet in the interim, and they're supposed to be only dealing with

issues that are fairly significant, but more likely in emergency, particularly, when you talk about the interim finance committee. That committee is made up of members of both ways and means and senate finance, because there are agencies or instances that come up that have to be funded in the biennium in the interim year, and they cannot wait until the legislature comes back into session. But they have to be careful. They have to be fairly careful, particularly, the finance committee, that they *do* only give stopgap measures, stopgap money on an emergency basis, because, basically, they're co-opting everybody else out [laughter] who were elected in the legislature, and they were making decisions for everybody else who may not agree. So they should be rather circumspect about that.

The other group that has been established—I don't know when it was created, but a long, long time ago, certainly way before I came on board—is the Legislative Commission. They basically deal with other issues, anything *but* money comes to that group. They, of course, cannot go ahead and make major policy decisions, because, again, they would be co-opting other people who did not serve on that. That commission is made up of members from both parties and from both bodies, and done, I believe, on a ratio of how many people are in each branch of the legislature. There may be only five Republicans in the assembly, for example, versus twenty-five Democrats. Well, that would then determine their membership on the commission.

Now, in 1979 I introduced a resolution. The commission is the group that decides which subject matter will be discussed in the interim out of many ideas that are presented to them. Then during that interim—and in this case 1980—bills will be drafted after important public hearings have been held. The bills will be presented then to the next legislature to determine their fate.

In 1979 I introduced a resolution that directed the Legislative Commission to study the Nevada prison system and alternatives to incarceration. It appears, from looking at some of the information in the beginning of this, that there was a major commitment appropriation to build a prison in Ely in the 1979 session. This then stimulated a lot of discussion about where should prisons be located and how much money is being spent in the arena of building a prison—it seems like every other year. I felt strongly that we needed to take a look and see who were we incarcerating, because so much money was funded to build these mortar buildings to place people in, and this money, of course, would be diverted from educational purposes or something else that people might think is important. In addition, there's always a saying that I remember a judge made one time, "Build a prison, and we will fill it." That is very true, because they feel more at ease sentencing people for higher crimes if they know there's a place to put them. There's a cause and effect there.

Anyway, each resolution is written so as to suggest the premise and why this idea is important and should be studied. It could be very important, and the Legislative Commission doesn't think so, and so it doesn't get supported. All of the ideas can't. This one obviously dealt with what I just described: the prison system and alternatives to incarceration. There were some ideas in here that did not go very far in the legislature, such as setting up a site selection committee. That was clearly something I was interested in, because when you build a prison in a place like Ely, think of the distances. Just to build it costs more, because you have to have people going out there and putting up this edifice,

and it was a maximum-security facility. In addition, you then run into problems, at least in my mind—and I think it has been proved since then—that you have to get correction officers and everybody to be willing to *live* out there.

I'm not saying anything derogatory about Ely, but it's a small community. There isn't a whole lot to do, and these people did not necessarily come from Ely or want to stay there their whole lives. There weren't that many people in Ely to man the prison, for instance. So I understand that people don't want it in their neighborhood. When it gets close to a district that they represent, then the outcry occurs, and the legislator normally responds to that and says, "I don't want it here." Ely seemed to be fairly interested in having it, because they felt it was economic development, and it really is not. That's not the kind of economic development, in my mind, that you should see.

The subcommittee did submit this concept to the legislature, and they said, "No, thanks. We want to be able to determine that place, ourselves." Of course, that's normally done by the finance committees. The bill that I introduced, that the subcommittee did, talked about the makeup of the committee. I read it over today, and it seems fairly reasonable, but obviously the legislature didn't feel that in 1981.

I'm spending a little bit of time here, because this really does point out the kind of issues that I think were important to discuss at that time, dealing with the whole issue of prisons. To me, the Department of Prisons really did not have an adequate means of determining population projection figures. That is extremely important, because if the warden just says, "We're going to have this many, x-number, fill in the blank," that is not the kind of thing that I think the legislators should make a decision on. There should be a reliable method of determining the inmate population projections.

Again, that was discussed quite a bit in the legislature, and I do not believe anything came out of that. But it did in a way. The bill didn't pass, but as I went along in the legislative process, particularly, when I chaired the senate judiciary committee, I had people come in from across the country, and they did work with the prison system, and they were able to teach them, basically, a much more sophisticated way of projecting population figures. To be honest with you, I have not had that much oversight of this whole area since I've been out of the legislature.

I'm going to talk about this right now. It was when Richard Bryan was governor, and I'm not sure if it was exactly this session or not. No, it wasn't; it was later on. There was

a time—it might have been 1987 or 1989—when I chaired the senate judiciary committee, and Bob Sader chaired the assembly judiciary committee. I talked to him about the whole subject of alternatives to incarceration, you know, using good judgment, and when to build the prison, what kind to build, and where to build it, and all of the other issues that come before us time and time again. We set up joint meetings, Bob and I, and we actually added some people, I believe, to the committees. Maybe it was not the judiciary committees; it was committees that Bob and I decided would be appropriate and would really look at the issue from all perspectives. In addition, we did speak to Governor Bryan at the time, because anything we got out of that committee then would have to go to the governor for his signature. Very often legislators are *very* afraid to vote for

Sue with Governor Richard Bryan.

anything except the real-tough-on-crime bills, because people can use it against them in their election. So we wanted to make sure if we did all this work that the governor would sign what came out of these committees. He agreed to sign certain things, which was very important and very beneficial. So Bob and I did get a number of things passed, and we'll talk about those, probably, in a little more depth as we go along, but, basically, it was this whole area that I've described.

When I was in the senate, the warden had said, "We need to have another prison." I know there was something that went on that I was able to get projected and make figures, which did not jive with the warden's. I'm a little fuzzy on this, but, basically, the bottom line is there were three people who voted against this prison. One was myself, Jean Ford, and I don't remember the third. People said, "This is it for you when you vote against the prison." But there was something—and I honest to gosh can't remember now—that I talked about on the floor that I felt justified my vote, and I was not all that concerned about it. As it turns out, nobody *ever* brought it up against me any time in any future election.

So that philosophy proved to be true.

Exactly. I think so. I think it does show that if you feel strongly, and you do have some facts and figures to back you up, then you can vote your conscience and still be safe.

This interim study committee that I'm talking about, in addition to doing the kinds of things, or suggesting the kind of things, that I've already talked about, tried to look at education and what was going on in the prison system with these inmates in Nevada, and it was clear there was not much. There didn't seem to be any cohesive educational component that you could even mandate

that prisoners go to, to get a G.E.D., for example, or offer other things. I'm convinced that some of the people in the prison system would take advantage of these things, because, otherwise, there's not a whole lot for them to do. There's this big hue and cry about inmates lifting weights and so on, that people think they get so buffed up that when they're paroled they go out and beat up somebody, or whatever. I don't think there's any correlation to that, either. And that was another component.

In addition, we tried to look at alternatives to incarceration. There were already established honor camps in our state, but there is a statutory provision that prohibits the Department of Prisons from assigning inmates who have committed an assault to forestry honor camps. We decided that should be repealed. The department has no statutory requirements in their other programs, i.e., "restitution centers and work-living programs, and is able to assign inmates based on their own classification findings." In other words, the honor camps are the only ones that have the statutory provision prohibiting certain inmates. The reason being is that someone had escaped from a forest honor camp and had done something, and there was an outburst from the public about that. So, evidently, somebody—and I know who it was, but I'm not going to mention it right now—introduced a bill to prohibit that kind of person, and I suspect that that did not pass.

There are all specific things in here that I think probably are just a little bit too involved to get into, but I think the general feeling that I had was that I did question, generally speaking, when I was in the legislature, what was coming out of the Department of Prisons and what was driving this unbelievable growth within the public safety budget. In fact, Nevada had the third highest incarceration rate *in the world*— our state.

There's nothing that shows that by virtue of incarcerating somebody you're doing anything positive, at all. The worst experience anybody can have is to go to prison, so what is the rationale for putting more and more people into the prison system? There is a high percentage—and I'm going to say 80 percent, maybe higher—of prison inmates that have had substance abuse problems—drugs or booze. There were *no* programs in the prison system to deal with their substance abuse problems.

When somebody gets on drugs, what do they do? They got to rip off people to get some money, or to get a TV or a VCR, to hock it so they can then buy their next joint or whatever. So it just seems it does not take a rocket scientist to figure out that in order to *reduce* the prison inmate population you need to have programs in there that are going to help these people. When they get out of prison they get like twenty bucks and a pair of shoes, or some ridiculous thing. That's a joke. But it is something that is certainly not going to prepare them for walking out of the doors in Carson City and coming back to Reno and making a life for themselves. To this day, hardly anything has changed, and this is twenty-some years later.

They do have some education now. Is that true? But in terms of long-term planning to bring them back into the population, nothing much has changed?

Well, there is a woman who is the new head of the Department of Prisons—this is the first time. My understanding is that this is her basic philosophy, and, hopefully, she'll be able to get things on. You know, there is a problem also with the things that were going on at the time, that what inmates could do didn't correlate with what goes on on the outside. Making license plates—hey, who else makes license plates? They're all made in the prison system. So

that does not provide you with the certain kinds of skills that you may need. And they did get into making furniture. In fact, I had in my office in the legislature furniture made by the inmates to show other people when they came into my office and so on, "Hey, look, they can do good stuff."

One of the problems was that the labor unions did not want—and this is a universal feeling—a lot of inmates getting very sophisticated and making products that could be sold *much* more cheaply than union type of jobs.

So you think, "Ah, that's a good idea. Let's try it." There's always some problem with a good idea, because if it's a good idea, normally it would have already taken place, it seems to me. But there is this whole area of the prison system and what to do about it, and an ever-increasing appetite to build more and more facilities to incarcerate more and more people. As I say, the recidivism rate is really, really high.

I think that this is something that's hard for people to get very interested in because, hey, the constituency out there that you're helping, they can't vote. If they're a felon, they'll never be able to vote again. Basically, the feeling is, "Who cares about those people that are incarcerated?" But 90 percent of them—I've gone up from 80 to 90 now, but I think it is 90—are going to be back out into the society at one time or another.

So it seems like we should somehow make them better. It's a whole argument, "Does prison rehabilitate anybody?" Not now, not in many instances they don't. It's not to say they can't, as long as there is leadership to provide those opportunities for inmates.

You mentioned that several things did get passed. Have we covered some of the major things that did get passed out of that study that came true?

I would have to go back and be very specific in looking at all of these things.

It may be better just to refer to the reports, since it's all documented there.

I think so. We were concerned about the low level of inmate participation and the low level of course completion, the lack of quality in the Department of Prisons academic programs, for example. I think there was one suggestion in here that the prisons then contract with the local school district and have *them* do the educational programs in the prison system, rather than "somebody," an officer who just will teach a class. We felt that the programs would be better. I'm sure nothing has been done with that thought.

Actually, I have a friend whose husband does teach. And I'm sorry that I haven't paid attention to what system he goes through to get there, but he goes into the prisons and teaches, and that's his area of expertise.

And he's not a correctional officer?

He's not a correctional officer. So there's some progress.

Right. I think there is, and I think some of these ideas are general in nature, because they were rather new. But the fact that those kinds of things are taking place is exactly what we were talking about in 1980.

But twenty years ago that wasn't happening, right?

No, that was not, at all, and that's why we thought these were good ideas to look at. Here's another recommendation, and it's coming right back to what we were talking about. They should try to develop to the greatest extent possible—this is talking about the course offerings—skills that are marketable in the outside job market. These were all things that were just very apparent to us when we had many, many public hearings.

Each one of these reports, that will be catalogued along with the oral history, talk about what was suggested, and if there were any BDRs, bill drafts, for example, right underneath the suggestion. It says in this example that this was setting up two multi-purpose centers, one in Washoe and one in Clark County, on a trial basis under the administrative supervision of the Department of Parole and Probation. These centers would be used to provide structured supervision to adult offenders who have not previously served time in any state prison institution. Two types of offenders would be housed in the centers. It would be convicted offenders as a condition of probation if the Department of Probation and Parole pre-sentencing investigative report recommended that kind of an assignment. The assignment could include, particularly in the case of, say, a property offender, restitution to the victim of the offender's criminal activities, and also convicted offenders who have violated the conditions of their probation. They could all be sentenced again for a period of structured supervision. That was a bill draft, as I say, and there were many things out of the sub-committee that *were* done: restitution centers, more expansive use of honor camps, halfway houses. In fact, it was interesting that one of the responsibilities of the Gaming Commission, which I am on now, has to do with work permits. Some individuals have had their work permit yanked, and you have to have a work permit in order to work in a casino. One man came and wanted his work permit back, and he had been in a halfway house. There was someone in the room with him, and he came before the Gaming

Commission. I remember one of the other gaming commissioners asked me, "Didn't you have something to do with that?"

I said, "Yes." And I've really never, ever seen anybody that has been in a restitution center or a halfway house, except for this guy. Actually, he did get his work permit back, because he told us what he was doing. He seemed like he was really trying to get his life back together again and had us believe that he would.

The concept of this is that it is much cheaper to house an inmate in one of these. Less supervision is necessary in a center, an honor camp, a forest camp, or whatever, but you can't assign people who have had violent acts against people. You couldn't trust them. So, normally, they are with low-level felons. I'm sure some people say, "There's no such thing as a low-level felon." But let's say, somebody had more than one ounce of marijuana. That's not a real serious crime. Burglary is the kind of crime that maybe somebody *could* be back in a restitution center. Anyway, the whole concept is that we're spending so much money in building these prisons that are going to be filled, that we better look at other places, other ways we can house inmates that are not as expensive. Also, a lot of people leave the halfway house, go to work, and then come back in the evening. A lot of those things have worked. In fact, I haven't heard of *any* horrible thing that's gone on in the last twenty years. Clearly, if something horrible had happened, it would have been in the paper. I'm sure of that, because it had been in the past.

So you have a feeling these things are working, right?

Yes! Yes, I do.

That's a good feeling.

Yes, it is. This really talks more about my philosophy, which other people agreed with, obviously, and that kind of followed me through at least the entire time I was in the legislature. I have to give Bob Sader kudos because he also was willing to go out on a limb, to some extent, and support some of the things that I did. That would have been in 1987 or 1989, somewhere further down the line. I guess my point here is that this was not just an issue that I had one session and didn't another.

Like the domestic violence issue, there were some things that were, in my mind, very important, that I thought it was worth my time to spend. I suspect if I went back to my constituents and said I'd spent all this time, they probably would not have thought that was a good idea. To me, it was not only a fiscally responsible thing to do, it made sense in the end, in the far end. It seems to me—and I've always been one who supported preventative measures—if you can assimilate somebody back into the workforce before they actually get back there full-time, that's a good thing. Or, if you are able to provide programs within the prison system to at least give them a heads-up, that they may make it on the outside, that's a good thing. And there are many other things I've thought that we dealt with at the end of the line, rather than at the beginning. Being in prison is certainly at the end of the line, unfortunately.

To wind up with this discussion on prisons, there were some bills submitted to the legislature out of that sub-committee, and one was to create that committee on sites and design for the prisons. I think I have told the story about the warden, Chuck Wolff, and the design of the prison. Well, it was during this interim when that incident happened.

In addition to that, there was a bill that established the programs of restitution, and that did pass. The previous bill did die in the senate committee on finance, which I think I've said before. This did die in senate finance again, and that was residential centers, the one I was just talking about. That did not survive. But the last bill did, and I won't get into that, because it's very technical. So some of the thoughts from that committee did survive, and some did not.

I talked about a bill that I was asked to introduce, actually, by Congressman Santini's office about special license plates for prisoners of war. I don't remember why. Fritsi Ericson and Lynn Atcheson, friends of mine, and Kay Zunino—they all worked in Congressman Santini's office, and I think they felt very comfortable in certain ways just to ask me if I could do something. I suspect somebody contacted his office and wanted a license plate. Of course, that's a state responsibility, not a federal one. So I did introduce that, and it did pass. Probably that was one of the first special license plates that we had in our state, because, actually, it didn't fly right through the legislature. Senator Lawrence Jacobsen, who was *on* the committee, and was on the transportation committee that this bill went through, and was also a co-sponsor of the bill, had a real problem with it by the time I was talking about it in the senate transportation committee. I remember him making one comment—and it's funny how you can remember specific things from a time long ago—but he kept saying, "Well, what if the prisoner of war's daughter drives the car. People will look at her and *know* she's not a prisoner of war."

And somebody in the committee said, "Well, Jake, what if your daughter drove your car that had senate license plates on it? And *she's* not a senator." [laughter]

It didn't quite click. It was not a substantial argument. So basically, the bill did pass. At that time, they just paid a certain amount more to get the special plate. To me, they seem like a very worthy group,

and if they want to identify themselves that way, I thought that was one thing we certainly could do for people who had been prisoners of war.

Another bill I introduced in that committee died, I see, in the senate committee on government affairs, but it did ultimately pass. I don't remember if I'm the one that introduced the bill that passed or not. This created single-member senate districts, and those senate districts would have been composed of two assembly districts. Now, when I ran for the senate for the very first time in 1980, I ran from at-large districts, which were *every* assembly district in Washoe County, with the exception of two in Sparks, and that was called multi-member, so the voters could select two people, in this case, Raggio and myself. We ran from these large districts, and people did say—although it was not that many—"Well, only people who raise a *lot* of money can run from these multi-member districts. If you made them smaller, it would give more of us a chance." That's the reason it died in senate government affairs. People who are already there don't want to make it easier for other people to potentially knock them off.

So that one died, right?

That did die, but as I said, that *is* the way it is now. Of course, Washoe County has lost a lot of seats in this last legislative session because of reapportionment. Did I talk about the bill about the use of guide dogs and canes by blind people?

No.

This was authorizing the use of guide dogs for the blind. They would be able to use both a guide dog and a cane, and those would be allowed to be taken into facilities, the store or something, because the person would need them in order for guidance around wherever it might be, to make it a little more accessible to them.

Some resolutions are more important than others, but there's one here that I sponsored, and it did pass, which urges Congress to use the Nevada Test Site for development of renewable sources of energy. It's kind of interesting that I see that, because I believe Harry Reid, our United States senator, is suggesting this very thing right now, because they've got a lot of wind there, and they have a lot of sun. As of the last session in 1991, there is a certain percentage of renewable energy resources—I think it's 15 percent—in the not too distant future that will be utilized to provide energy for people in our state. I don't know if Senator Reid had anything to do with asking Nevada legislators to make that part of their program or not.

In thinking back, this would have been in 1981, so that was some twenty years ago. It did remind me of another resolution that was *very* significant, that was introduced in 1975 or 1977 by an assemblyman from Clark County. His name was Zel Lowman. It was a resolution that basically urged— and I will use that word, because that's one that was used in the resolution—*urged* Congress to set up the nuclear dumpsite in our state. People have short memories, because nobody remembers that, but a reporter in the *Las Vegas Review-Journal* did, and maybe it's in some file that she can look up, but she called me not very long ago and asked me if I remembered this. I said, "Oh, yes, I *do*." As it turns out—and I've known this for a long time but didn't want to really remind other people of it— that Senator Richard Bryan had voted for that. Of course, as his career has blossomed, as to being governor of our state and then United States senator, he was a champion of not having the nuclear dumpsite here, and nobody went back and looked up the record.

I knew this, but, as I say, I have liked Richard. I think he's done a good job, and I'm certainly not the kind of person that's going to run out and tell his opponent, "This is something you could use against him." But actually, it would have been something. Although, you can always say, "Well, I changed my mind," or, "I've had more information." But it was interesting that *every single* legislator from Clark County, at that time, voted for it, with the exception of Jean Ford.

Of course, all the people from Washoe County voted against it. There wasn't a lot of information, if I remember correctly, that we said, "Oh, my gosh, look at this. They are going to build them in caskets or in barrels, and they're going to be able to drop them." Well, there was some of that, and it might have been at this time. I don't remember, but the chairman of what was then called the Atomic Energy Commission—Federal Energy Commission now—was a woman named Dixy Ray, who later on became governor of Washington. [Editor's note: Dixy Lee Ray was governor of the state of Washington 1977-1981.] They came out and had all these films for us to see and were showing these big barrels in a forklift, and they'd drop the barrel down from the forklift onto a cement floor to prove that it wasn't going to break open and spew all this nuclear waste into the air.

My husband, as I've mentioned, was a research scientist, and these kinds of things I talked about with him, of course, because I figured he knew more about it than I did. We talked about it, and it just seemed that, with the information I brought home to him, that they couldn't really prove that. I really did not believe that this was *not* going to be a danger at some point. Obviously, everybody from Washoe County felt the same way. But the reason this was introduced is because Las Vegas needed jobs. A *lot* of people were out of work then, and so this was a work program, a job resolution, if you will.

However, it has unbelievably poignant memories right now, when we are now *going* to get the nuclear dumpsite. So I guess all those people who wanted jobs or who are unemployed now will be happy about that, but I don't think very many people in our state really want us to have it. To me, I don't know if they can prove it any more than they could in 1980 that if there's a train crash . . . . And it's very interesting because since this has happened—and maybe it's just because you are on more notice—that there have been more trucks getting off the highway, there have been more train wrecks happening. As I say, maybe it's just because I'm more attuned to those than I used to be, but there's nothing to say that this could not happen.

Needless to say, it's true that we're getting it because we have the least members of a delegation in Congress. The other two states that were looked at were Texas and the state of Washington. Of course, Texas had a lot of congressmen, and not everybody just gets the two senators. But there was a senator—and now I'm off track here a little bit—named Bennett Johnson from the state of Louisiana, and they've got a lot of garbage in that state, and he was in charge of the committee that basically stuck it to us. It was called the "Screw Nevada Bill," basically, because, you know, anybody that has nuclear stuff in their state wants to get it out, and what do they care about some godforsaken place out there in Nevada.

In addition, people can say, "Well, you had nuclear tests *above the ground*, for God sakes." Yes, and a lot of people have died, too, with cancer—a lot of people. But anyway, that reminded me when I looked at that resolution.

Yes, that's a very hot topic right now.

I remembered that I hadn't talked about that at all. There are going to be things that will happen like that that I don't see on a piece of paper necessarily, because my name wasn't on it, of course. Yes, Zel Lowman was the main sponsor, and then I voted against it.

You voted against it?

Oh, yes! As I said, everybody from Washoe County did.

Vikki, maybe we could talk a little bit here about the issue of abortion, I guess, as a separate matter. I got this information from the Legislative Counsel Bureau in Carson City, from the research division. I definitely would like to thank Bob Erickson, who is the director, who put all of this stuff together. I mean, he assigned most of it, but Fred Weldon was unbelievably great, as he always has been. He was at the legislature when I was there, and he's still there. So he's helping a lot of other people along the way. There was a young woman at the bureau, Michelle Van Geel, and she did all of the information on the abortion issue for me.

This issue of abortion has been one that the legislature has dealt with a very long time. In fact, in my first session—and I believe that they obviously have gotten my vote wrong on this one—there was a resolution introduced by somebody who reminded Congress to consider the grievous ramifications of the *Roe v. Wade* decision by the United States Supreme Court on abortion, and to consider action to protect the right to life. In 1977 there wasn't anything. Excuse me, I'm going to digress here a moment. We did talk about Maureen Reagan and the Equal Rights Amendment—coming to Nevada and everything?

Yes.

OK. Because there were some other people who came to Nevada on this issue, so I was thinking about them. I can't remember when it was that they came.

Who was it that came? It doesn't matter about the time.

Eleanor Smeal. I believe she was the national president of NOW, the National Organization of Women, who led the fight for the Equal Rights Amendment. In 1977, evidently, there was nothing that was introduced, and, clearly, I'm somebody who's never going to introduce anything on this issue, because I'm comfortable the way it is now. The Supreme Court has decided that this is a right of privacy and has made that decision in *Roe v. Wade.* That was dealt with in 1973, before I ever got to the legislature.

Senator Margie Foote from Sparks introduced a bill that actually codified *Roe v. Wade* in our Nevada Revised Statutes, and that is important when I get to 1990 and what was done with that N.R.S. statute. I was not there at the time—and I've really not talked about this with Margie—but it seems to me as if people had told me that when she introduced this bill that it kept getting shuffled around from committee to committee, and it finally wound up in the agriculture committee, or something like that. But evidently it passed, because it was in the Nevada Revised Statutes. As I said, that will come to play as we go down the line here.

In 1979 there was something introduced that didn't pass, but I will mention it, because it's part of the history of this issue. Again, it was not enacted, but it exempted from prosecution persons who unlawfully serve minors under specified circumstances. This would have included situations where a minor, for example, used a false ID for an abortion. In other words, you should not prosecute the person who

assumed the ID was real, and might have performed an abortion on the person thinking it was somebody older, for example, I would assume. But that was not voted on. I have no idea if I put my name on that bill or not.

In addition to that, there was another resolution introduced requiring Congress to call a convention to propose an amendment to the national constitution to restrict abortion. I voted against that. Then there was an amendment exactly the same that came over from the senate requesting Congress to call a convention to propose an amendment that *was* passed, and I voted against that. The other one I talked about, coming from the assembly, the one I just mentioned, that was not enacted, clearly, it was something that the senate wanted to take credit for, and that's the reason the assembly resolution didn't pass.

It did pass in 1981, but as we know, Congress did *not* call a convention, and has not called a convention since the first convention, I believe, to propose an amendment. In 1981 this did pass. It says, "Requires the reporting of complications of abortion," and I voted against that. I really don't remember a whole lot about that. I will have to say, though, that this whole area of choice, or abortion . . . that the people who do not support abortion in any way, shape, or form have decided it's probably . . . and maybe we will see this happening if George W. Bush is able to appoint more people to the United States Supreme Court. However, because the United States Supreme Court appears that they would not vote against a *Roe v. Wade* issue, the anti-choice groups have chiseled away and have chipped away at *Roe v. Wade* from different perspectives to make it more and more difficult for someone to be able to have a legal abortion. This was an example of that. But many of the other issues that have come from other states, and that the Supreme Court has actually *looked* at, show that that's exactly the MO, and that is their plan of attack. You can see in Congress the numbers of bills that are introduced and what they're attempting to do.

In 1981, in addition to that reporting of complications—and I cannot remember why they thought that would be a good thing; I guess, maybe if they had a whole list of complications they could publicize it—this was enacted, as well, a bill from the assembly, which revises the requirements for consent and notice in cases of abortion. I really don't remember anything specific about that. I did vote against it.

Also in that same session the senate passed a bill and eliminated the requirement for corroboration of a victim's testimony in cases involving abortion or prostitution, if the witness is a peace officer. I voted for this. I guess the assumption here would be that if the witness is a peace officer, you'd accept the testimony from that person. I don't remember much about that, at all.

In 1983 there was a bill introduced. Well, it says here the senate did not vote on it. Basically, this young lady in the research department does not use the language that is normally used, because normally it would say this bill was placed on the "senate desk," or the "secretary's desk," and whether or not they voted on this. But the same thing—this bill in 1983 would have required a certificate of death and burial or cremation of an aborted embryo claiming that a fetus is a human. That, again, goes back to the whole idea that you make this uglier and uglier, if you will, to make people say that it is just getting to be *so* awful that you'd have to have a death certificate and then cremation of an aborted fetus, that that's something that's so distasteful to the average public, let's say, I'm in favor of that. But, again, that was not voted on.

The reason that that is done often—and it became more and more the tool used by the pro-choice people as the sessions went on—is that if you put it on the secretary's desk it dies, unless you have enough votes. That would be one more, then, to have to pull it off the desk, put it up on the board, and then vote on it. You wouldn't want to do that unless you knew you had eleven votes, let's say, in the senate, and eleven people would have to agree to take it off the desk. Maybe the same eleven would say put it up there on the board, and they'd vote for it. Sometimes those people might change. The numbers may change, but you got to have the eleven votes. Obviously, this just stayed there and died. I think I talked about a bill that I did have taken off the secretary's desk once, about naming schools after yourself.

No, I don't believe so.

Well, write that down, and we'll talk about that when I get done with this, because it's a perfect example of something like that.

OK. But what you're saying is that by introducing these horrific bills—the language—that's one of the ways that they kept chipping away, because they just keep hoping at every session that some things will get passed that chip away at Roe v. Wade.

Exactly. And, particularly, because we do have *Roe v. Wade* enshrined—I use that term loosely—in N.R.S., it's *there*. So, some of these things are not applicable to the trimester approach. This I can't imagine would. But it's just the fact that, clearly, somebody introduced it in the assembly. See, the way it's worded here, I think it was passed by the assembly, obviously, because I'm now looking at it as a senate bill. She said that the senate did not vote on this. So, it gets press attention. It gets people's names in the press. One doesn't know the real motive of what was going on here, but all of those things come into play.

Now, there's another bill in 1985, which it doesn't even tell you what it's about, because it just says, "Makes various changes." So the senate didn't vote on this, as well. That came from the assembly again. Then another bill from the assembly, and the senate didn't vote on this either, but it obviously passed. As I said, the assembly bill prohibits public funding of abortion, unless necessary to preserve the life or health of a pregnant woman. There are some people who would support abortion as a choice issue, but would not support the use of federal funds. Say, a poor woman who could not afford an abortion, that they don't feel that our taxpayers' money should be utilized for that purpose. That bill was, again, put on the secretary's desk and didn't survive the entire legislative process that session.

And there was another bill introduced. Oh, this was an active session—1985 was—for these issues. This one prohibits commercial use of the aborted embryo or fetus. I don't really know what that was addressed to, but I suppose you could think today that maybe a private lab could be able to use something like this for stem cell research, for example. I don't know. I doubt if that was the purpose *then*, because I don't even think we were that far along to understand in 1985 that stem cells did have a medical purpose, and certainly in this way, if a private company could use it in a commercial way. But, again, that did not pass. If you saw that in the newspaper you'd think, "Ah! Can't imagine anybody making money off of that."

Right, especially back then.

It has a negative kind of connotation.

I think you are right about the stem cell research. That's more recent, unless it was something that was going on and was not generally known back then.

I think not.

Fifteen, seventeen years ago.

Right. You could use that as an example *today*. What they might have been thinking of, I don't really know.

In 1985 a major bill was introduced, and all it says is, "Make various changes in provisions regulating abortion." This is a piece of legislation that was on parental notification, and that was very contentious.

What's the bill number?

The bill number was SB510 in the 1985 session. If you just looked at the title it wouldn't tell you a whole lot, but this bill was very contentious, and it was something that if you did not support it, you were really on the losing end of the stick, so to speak. Memory serves me correctly that there were three "no" votes: myself, Joe Neal, and Randolph Townsend, I think. I don't have the vote count right here. This bill passed and passed the assembly, and I'm going to talk a little bit about why I voted against it. I'm looking at the remarks I made in 1985, and the same remarks were made on my behalf on May 3, 1995 by a friend of mine, Edwina Prior, who was, when she was a bit younger, a very involved person in the Republican Party.

This bill mandated parental notification, and it also did allow for what is called the "judicial bypass," but it was later found unconstitutional by the Ninth Circuit in California, when I was lieutenant governor ten years later. The attorney general, Frankie Sue Del Papa, made it constitutional and sent it back to the senate again. So I then tried to get it killed again.

Kirk, Sue, and Kristina, opening day at the Nevada Legislature, Carson City, January 17, 1985.

I guess I felt very strongly that as a woman, a single head of household, and a mother of two teenagers—my fourteen-year old daughter and sixteen-year old son at the time—that this bill would *not* foster deeper, stronger, healthier family relationships. I argued on the floor that minors are going to tell their parents, that they're going to tell their mothers and fathers, if they are close, and if they're not afraid, and if they have a good relationship. I argued that this law is not necessary, because you could argue that this bill will have an *opposite* effect of the sponsor's intent; it could drive a wedge between members of the family. One could argue, as I did, that an increase in communication has not been the effect of the bills in the states where notification laws have been passed. You could argue that the youngsters might postpone good health care because of this bill.

I think I've made it clear in my history that I voted against resolutions calling for constitutional amendments and for a constitutional convention. Actually, I was opposed to that on any subject, but specifically on this one. As I mentioned, this bill that I'm talking about today was found unconstitutional, and didn't surprise me, at all, to be honest with you.

Thinking back on this whole issue, I am sorry, actually, that it had to become such a political issue. I personally felt, and have always felt, that my position as a Republican is a very conservative position, that I don't feel that government should be interfering in our private lives. I find it interesting that many Republicans can sort of somehow be consistent over here, but not over here, and change over here. Now, we're talking about possibly having the government interfere, in my mind, and make sure that people are prepared to be married. This is something that's coming under the Bush White House now. It's another invasion, in my mind, of government getting involved. Maybe people could make arguments that this is a good thing, that more people who have had counseling, their marriage tends to last longer, but I don't think that's government's role. I don't believe that this kind of legislation that was presented to our legislature will actually do anything good for families.

I'm trying to remember a case in the Ninth Circuit. I think the case was *Glick v. McKay*. Eugene Glick was a doctor here in town. I have no idea if he's passed away, or if he's moved out of the state, but I believe he sued the attorney general, Brian McKay, at that time, for this bill. Of course, that went to the Ninth Circuit. But we do see it coming back again. The attorney general took a look at the language. I believe that the Ninth Circuit found that the judicial bypass had no time element in it, and felt that because the *Roe v. Wade* decision is based upon a trimester approach, that the judge *must* make a decision by x-amount of time, or it could go on and on, and then it would be too late. The decision would have already been made for that child, and it wouldn't have been her choice.

Anyway, that was the most contentious vote that has taken place, I believe, in the senate. I'm going to just move along right now, and we're going to get back to something that took place in 1990. Another bill that the senate did *not* vote on was prohibiting use of public money for abortions. I've got, again, "Placed on the secretary's desk." Another bill was introduced in that same year, in 1987, and I don't remember what really was the fundamental part of this bill. The history tells me that it revises the provision requirements, certain care to be given to an infant born as a result of an attempted abortion. In 1989 there were no bills dealing with the subject matter. In 1991 it appears that there are two. Yes. The first was not enacted, and that required the humane disposal of an aborted embryo or fetus, and, as I say, it must have been put on the secretary's desk.

SB610 was introduced in 1991, as well. It prohibits certain persons from preventing *another* person from entering or exiting a physician's office or certain health facilities. That obviously pertains to people carrying picket signs or groups not allowing someone to go into Planned Parenthood offices, or wherever, and obstructing their access. I believe that was the term used, "acts of access" legislation. That *did* pass and is part of our Nevada Revised Statutes in 1993. In this case I, of course, was not in the senate; I was lieutenant governor at the time, president of the senate, where I could vote, as we know, only in cases of ties. And then, if I had that opportunity, it would be challenged.

Another bill was put on the secretary's desk in 1993, another bill that made certain changes regarding judicial review of a request from a minor seeking an abortion. That was put on the secretary's desk. That's been pretty much the practice of people, particularly the choice people, who don't want to have a bill out there, because then, again, they're probably going to lose it. It's clear if there aren't enough votes that are in the choice position that anything's going to pass. So their attempt has always been to try to put it on the secretary's desk and have nobody take it off. A lot of people, even if they're going to vote for it, don't want to have to, so they're not interested in really pulling it off the desk, either. There might be somebody—and I would use Maurice Washington as an example, the senator from Sparks—that these issues were very important to him, that he might be somebody who might take it off the desk. I think other senators have talked to him about the fact that this really isn't a good idea, and, I gather, if they have done that, that he listened.

You're saying they don't want to have to vote because it's a lose-lose, either way—no matter your position, you could lose constituents by going through the vote.

That's very true. They may have. And this happened, if you remember. We talked about the seven who lied. It's very possible that they had committed themselves to both positions hoping and praying—and maybe being part of the group who put it on the secretary's desk [laughter]—that they'd never have to vote. So both sides would know that somebody had told each that they would support their position. However, as you suggested, it is possible that the anti-choice group, that some of them are kind of squishy, and they *really* don't want to be thought of that way, but if it's brought out, they'll have to vote that way, because it is an issue that there is no middle ground on. There just isn't. It's either/or, basically.

Yes. Is this accurate, that it's also an issue where people aren't readily going to change their positions?

That's correct.

Some issues you can convince people.

Now we look at what's going on in the national legislative body, some of the most ardent pro-lifers are saying, "But I will support embryonic stem cell research." Senator Orrin Hatch from Utah *never* is going to change his mind on that fundamental question. But this is a secondary question, and that is: Can you use a part of the stem cell from an embryo for medical purposes? Clearly, even the president of the United States came up with

a compromise in his own mind of allowing this to be done on a certain number of stem cells that were viable at that time, either fifteen or eighteen. I guess you could say, "Well, that was somewhat of a compromise," but *nobody* was happy with that. The people who were pro-choice fought it more. I mean, it should be every stem cell that was available. The pro-lifers said there should be none. He obviously appealed more to the group that elected him.

It is a difficult issue, and I have never, never looked back. I have never thought I've been wrong. I suspect–I *know*—that other people feel the same way that I do, but I actually appreciate people who are consistent, if they believe there are to be no exceptions. They believe taking a life is taking a life. It's murder to them. I can understand it, rather than those who say, "Well, except in this case and this case and this case." Clearly, those people politically I would like better, because they're at least allowing some latitude for maybe the health of the mother, but I would be over in the opposite group. I cannot understand how someone can think that something the size of my fingernail is a living human being. Just cannot go there.

Now, we come to the end of the 1989 session, and the Supreme Court hands down an opinion in July of 1989, and it is called *Webster v. Reproductive Health Services.* We were almost wrapping up our legislative session when this came down the pike. I mean, we're like within the last week, working around the clock. I suggested to, I believe, Senator Raggio—and maybe we all decided this together—to leave this alone. We were too near the end of the session. If we opened it up again and some pro-life group or pro-life legislator wanted to have a decision dealing with Webster introduced in our legislature, that we'd be there for another month. So both sides agreed to leave it alone. However, because this came down the pike, the session was adjourned, groups started talking, and I remember a meeting on the second floor of the Planned Parenthood office about what was in store for us. In fact, I'm getting an award next month in Las Vegas, and I'm pretty sure it's for this action that I took. I tried to figure out how we could get around a lot of this problem happening to us session after session after session.

I worked with somebody—and I think for the oral history he probably should remain nameless, at least at this point. (Maybe I'll check and see if it's OK to mention the name.) So there were a variety of things to choose from, you might say, a menu. It appeared to me, with this other person—and it's not another legislator but another person—that maybe a referendum was the way to go. Now, a referendum is affirming an existing statute. If you remember, I talked about 1973, when Margie Foote put *Roe v. Wade* into the law. So we have an existing statute, and it basically enshrines the fundamental decision that I support. However, you can imagine that if it passes, then the only way that it can be changed is by another vote of the people.

This referendum then goes to a vote of the people, and the people decide, "Do I want that in the law?" I'm going to say, "Yes, I do," in the year 1990 when I go to the ballot box, or, "No, I don't. I want to get rid of it." That is taking a risk, and to me, it was just like my position on this issue. I didn't think there was even a question—we should do it. I believe, and I still believe—and this obviously proved it—that Nevadans are basically conservative by nature. They don't want to be told what to do. They want to have choices, and they don't think that government should be doing certain things.

Now, this is the way it read on the ballot. Basically, let me get back to the idea that everybody didn't feel exactly the way I did.

Even though we felt the same way about the issue, they felt this was too big of a risk to take, because if it is defeated, the existing statute will be void and of no effect, and the legislature will then have to decide what, if any, law will replace it. It's NRS 442.250. That's the existing Nevada statute regulating abortion. The question will be: will remain in effect and cannot be amended, repealed, or otherwise changed except by a direct vote of the people. That's what a referendum does.

Then it goes on. This is on the ballot, and it goes on to explain that the existing statute permits a woman to have an abortion performed by a physician within twenty-four weeks after the commencement of the pregnancy. A physician may perform an abortion after twenty-four weeks only to preserve the life or health of the pregnant woman. A "Yes" vote, again, is to vote to *approve* the existing statute, and a "No" vote would, of course, be disapproval. Then it went on to explain the arguments for passage and the argument against passage, and they even have a copy of the referendum position. Now, I don't know if I want to tell about the arguments for it and their arguments against it.

Basically, this is what people saw when they went to vote: "An abortion is a highly personal and private decision. It is our view that a woman should be free to make that decision without unreasonable governmental restriction or regulation. Some regulation is necessary to protect the health and safety of a pregnant woman. The existing statute provides that necessary protection. If legal abortion is not performed, then women may seek illegal and potentially unsafe abortions. The people of Nevada and of the legislature should decide how abortion is to be regulated." That was what appeared on the ballot *for* its passage.

Arguments against it: "Abortion should not be legalized. It is argued that life begins at conception, and the fetus is entitled to legal protection. The existing statute places the convenience of the pregnant woman *above* the protection of the fetus. There are other alternatives available to a pregnant woman who does not want to have a child." Adoption, I assume. "The legislature and not the people of Nevada should decide how abortion is to be regulated."

So that was what many, many, many women worked on for a year. It was decided that we would use this term "Campaign for Choice," and I thought it was incredibly good. I don't remember exactly who came up with it. I think it was me, but then I'm telling my history here, aren't I? [laughter] It might not have been me, but maybe I'll find out in June when I go back to get this award—what they think, anyway.

I also thought if something else comes up, and we need to whip out the slogan, "Campaign for Choice" could go for a lot of different campaigns, you know. I mean, we're just talking about one thing here. Fortunately, we haven't had to use it for anything else. But Jan Evans then got involved, because I was going to be running for lieutenant governor. Although I made it very clear that I was involved in this, I could not campaign for it, because I had to campaign for myself. As it turns out, I really didn't campaign for myself either, because of the plane crash.

I know Jan was pretty involved in this part. The initial part is getting it up and running and deciding what it's going to be called and what we're going to do. I was much more involved in that than later on. In the nitty-gritty work of trying to get it passed I was not as helpful. I know Jan and some of the people decided that they would hire a professional person outside the state to help us run this campaign.

So a man named Blair Butterworth was hired from Portland, Oregon, and he was terrific. I did not work with him that much, as I say, because I moved on to my own campaign. Maggie Tracey became head of the Campaign for Choice. I'm sure she remembers this way better than I in far more detail. [laughter] The disagreements among the women, the disagreements between northern Nevada versus southern Nevada, what we were going to do, how we're going to handle it, I guess, just drove people right up the wall.

When all was said and done, I think it was 64 or 65 percent of the people who voted "Yes" on this ballot question, and that vote then enshrined it into the law. It did not mean that other things could not be introduced; it meant that you couldn't change the twenty-four-hour period, any of the trimester approach. But it could mean, for example, as we've learned, that people introduce bills dealing with access to abortion clinics. I don't like that term, but that doesn't have anything to *do* with changing the language that was passed in 1973.

In most people's minds, that is the most important thing. And if the people opposed to abortion could have repealed that or done something different, that cannot be done. It's a heck of a lot of work, incredible amount of work, to do this and to get organized. It's like a political campaign. Of course, that's what it is. Instead of a *person* it's a *thing*.

It's an idea.

It's an issue. It's an idea, and it has to be handled in exactly the same way. So, to get them now, the other side, of course, they're organized all the time, the Eagle Forum and other groups that are more conservative. People are involved in work, they're paid.

That's why I'm convinced that they don't *want* to get rid of *Roe v. Wade*, because they might be out of employment if they're not there to have something to mess around with.

Fight against. [laughter]

Yes, exactly, to be opposed to. Anyway, I was very happy that it passed, and it's a great deal of satisfaction to me that I was even involved in it, at all. I really never felt concern once people bought into my idea that, "Oh, what if it doesn't pass?" I just had no doubt—no doubt. I thought maybe even more than 64 or 65 percent, but that's pretty darn good. In order then to change that substance there would have to be another referendum.

Did that really slow down all these different bills being introduced then? Did it accomplish what you wanted?

Well, it did. It did, but as I mentioned on my list of things . . . .

Access could still be an issue.

Right. And some of those other bills that were introduced, but they never went anywhere. They were always put on the secretary's desk, and we talked about the reasons for that.

I will say, I was having trouble comparing all the dates and the bill numbers, but in 1993 I was lieutenant governor, and the attorney general, Frankie Sue Del Papa, did send over a bill, SB59, which cleaned up the language that the Ninth Circuit found was unconstitutional. I've discussed that. It dealt with the time period the judges had in order to affect the judicial bypass section of the bill. I'm a Republican. There were no Democrats that testified against this. Everybody wanted *me* to be the spokesperson. I don't mean to be

sarcastic, but I'd already voted on this. There were very few people who had already voted on this. All those women who I work with and admire and like, they didn't want to have to talk about this, because they hadn't had anything on their record, ever, and they would be just as happy if they didn't.

I had been so outspoken about it that I can understand why they would think I should be the main sponsor, but I did have this feeling in the back of my mind that there were many other reasons why I was going to be the best spokesperson.

In addition, until just recently, when he decided he wasn't going to run, Senator Mark James from Clark County, who was first elected in 1990, very much wanted to get my endorsement. And I did not endorse people. I endorsed one person, a gubernatorial candidate, and it was Bob List in his first campaign. I was very, disappointed, and I decided I would not endorse anybody again. Mark was running for the senate against a woman, and it was very interesting because all my Democratic women friends once supported her, and she was anti-choice.

He asked you to endorse him?

Oh, yes. Mark asked me to endorse him. I hardly knew him. He was running against a former assemblywoman, Sandy Krenzer. They ran against each other in 1992. [Editor's note: Saundra Krenzer served in the assembly in 1991. Mark James first served in the senate in 1993. Per *Political History of Nevada, 1996*, Dean Heller, Secretary of State.] In fact, I just saw his opponent on the airplane coming back from Vegas a couple of months ago, and fortunately, I don't think she knew I endorsed Mark. [laughter] But anyway, I wanted to know how he felt on this issue, and I just did not want a response to, "Are you pro-choice?" because the real issues are, as we've learned, the secondary issues: notification, consent, access, et cetera, et cetera. Maybe even stem cell research.

He answered *every* one of them right. He won. They sent a brochure only to women in his district. With my endorsement he won by twenty-seven votes. Now, I've remembered that on many occasions when I wanted Mark maybe to do something for me. I'll remind him that I really personally take total responsibility for those twenty-seven votes.

Getting back to this hearing, Mark wanted to testify. I said he didn't need to because I was going to. He was a Republican, and no Democrats were to testify. He didn't need to do that, although I appreciated his saying he'd do it. He said no, he really *wanted* to do it. And he did, but he also did the same thing this last session.

I'll digress here a moment in talking about Mark. He came out against capital punishment, and he was *very* outspoken about it. The Republican caucus was *very* upset with him, mad at him. I talked to him about this one time, and he really didn't seem to care. I mean, he really felt very strongly. He had been thinking about running for attorney general, and pretty much knew he couldn't take that position and run for attorney general in this state. He's now decided he is not going to run, at all. He was not endorsed by the Republican caucus in Clark County, and I have a feeling it goes back to maybe not this issue, maybe the capital punishment issue, and maybe that issue and this one and maybe some others that didn't go along. Go along to get along.

Get along with the Republicans, yes.

So I was very impressed with that, personally, and obviously I remembered it, because I'm talking about it right now, because there aren't too many people that you can point to. I just did describe the fact that no Democrat testified, and no Democratic *women* testified. In fact, I was let in by the security police because the place was just jammed. They put me right up at the witness table, and other Democratic women were off to the side in another room, not even in the same room, urging me on, never to be seen, never to be heard from. In fact, Joanie Lambert, a former assemblywoman, and I always take pleasure in knowing we're the only two women, both Republicans, who have voted "no" on this issue. She feels the same way I do about it. But anyway, it's been an issue that will have life—that's maybe not a good description. That's not a pun.

Pardon the pun, right?

That will be an issue for years and years to come, unlike the Equal Rights Amendment, even though there are groups that try to get that on in Congress, which will not happen. It's not an issue anymore like it was in the early 1970s where women made this great change. In fact, you see women today such as Karen Hughes, who is George W. Bush's counsel, and, I believe, the female Ambassador to Pakistan—both women have recently resigned, or are going to, for family reasons. It may well be—I hope not—that there will be this great big swing back. I think we're in the right place right now, where women can do what they want. I mean, not all jobs are open to women, we all know. We look at the boards of directors of the *Fortune* 500, and most have no women. I'm sure at Enron, they're probably happy there are no women on that board of directors.

[laughter] There are cases.

There are not many that have broken through to the very top, but I still think it's possible today. I mean, running for office is just no big deal. Staying home with children is equally respected. Nobody thinks about gender anymore. Well, most don't.

I think that choice is going to be an issue because there is no middle ground on this. I have talked to Brian Sandoval, who, no question in my mind, is going to be the next attorney general. Of course, I asked him the same questions I ask anybody who wants my endorsement, and he did visit with me, because I represent to him exactly what I'm talking about today: a more moderate Republican woman who is pro-choice. In fact, almost anybody running for office comes and talks to me about this issue. [laughter]

A former GOP candidate, who ran for attorney general last year visited with me, and even though I didn't agree with him, he did feel that he wanted to come explain. [laughter] He did say, "Well, I'll support the law." Well, geez, duh! I would hope so, being the attorney general. [laughter] If you don't like it, that's too bad, it's the law.

I will tell another story, because this is a good one, and I think it deserves to be here. It deals with this issue. When I realized I wasn't going to be able to run for office any longer and made that announcement, it was just right after that I was asked to serve on the board of directors of First Interstate Bank, FIB, which was a big bank. I was very excited. That was the first overture to me for something like that. I was not going to be in elective office anymore, so hopefully that was good for them. I mean, that's why; I'm sure, they would *not* have asked me if I were going to run again. However, the president of the bank was a great guy and Mormon. There were no other women on the board, so a press release came out that I was going to be appointed to the board.

Pro-Life Andy Anderson, who ran against me when I ran for lieutenant governor in the Republican primary and changed his name legally to highlight our differences, called the president of the bank, called all the board of directors, and said don't put me on this board because I'm going to funnel all the bank money into abortion clinics. He went down to different branches in our town handing out fliers in front of the banks. He was still after me.

Well, I have to say there was a woman who was our legal counsel, Sarah Beth Brown, who is now legal counsel for IGT, vice-president of legal affairs. Anyway, she talked to the president of the bank about how ludicrous this was and about me, because he had just recently come to our state. Had a nice conversation with him, and I knew right away he was not going to accept any of this rabble-rousing. Even though he might disagree with me on the issue, it wasn't just something that should pertain to my seat on the board of a bank. I just couldn't even *believe* it, that somebody would be this vitriolic, I guess, to go out and do things like that when you would think he would applaud that I wasn't in the legislature anymore. [laughter] "Yea! She's gone."

Yea! She can't do anything. [laughter]

Yes, one more down. Anyway, I do want to mention, though, about Edwina Prior. I guess I did. She did speak for me in 1995, I think it was, and I was teaching my intern class and had a class that very day, at that very time, and she was very happy to do it. It was very interesting, because there was a female senator from Clark County and a Republican. In fact, she and her husband owned a couple of gaming casinos in Las Vegas. She's very attractive—used to be a TV news anchorperson, so everybody knew her. She beat up on Edwina Prior—and I say "beat up" in a verbal way. People couldn't even believe it. Edwina had been chair of the Republican Party of the state. She had no history of Edwina, but you don't treat anybody like that. She made a big mistake. But that's how some people treat others. And I have been told by people, except for Janine Hansen, but other people who were in the Eagle Forum and so on, that they've never had a problem with me, because they absolutely know where I stand on every issue. They don't waste my time; they don't waste their time. I've never personalized anything. If somebody doesn't agree with me, that's just the way it is.

In fact, I just saw Senator Ray Rawson at the airport last week. Have we gotten around to the sex and AIDS in the school yet? [laughter]

No. I think just a mention, but we haven't actually talked it over.

All right. Well, that's something we need to do. But Ray Rawson and I sat next to each other in the front row in the senate, and he and I went round and round and round on these issues, because he is a member of the LDS Church. But, hey, I was happy to see him the other day. We chitchatted. I mean, I've never, *ever* personalized anything dealing with any issue. I think that pretty much wraps up that issue.

Sue, let's go back and talk a little bit more about your time at DRI. You worked there after your husband's airplane crash, worked there for ten years, through three DRI presidencies. I think the thing we haven't talked about is what some of your day-to-day responsibilities were, and then I'd also like to have you talk about what you feel were some of your accomplishments. So there are about three main topics all in one question for

you. [laughter] We'll come back to each one of them. How's that?

OK. I've already alluded to this previously, that after the airplane that my husband was in crashed, needless to say, a job was mandatory. The new president, Clifford Murino, had just been selected and was coming from the National Center for Atmospheric Research in Boulder, Colorado. He had been head there. So this was a plum, I think, for DRI to get somebody from NCAR and, maybe, vice versa. Cliff really wasn't on board when this airplane crash occurred, and he had to come into that situation, which was, I'm sure, extremely difficult and stressful for him, as well, because this affected the entire DRI family and community. I vaguely remember that there was a memorial service at DRI.

This was, in a sense, a new position, even though one might go back and say that Mark Dawson and even Alessandro Dandini had positions of some sort, they weren't really this. I say that because Dr. Murino didn't really know what I should be doing. It was just, I'm sure, offered to me in an attempt at being fair, and maybe even trying to save face. I don't really know what term to put on it, but I think it was extending a benevolent hand, if you will, to a now young widow and two small children. Other people were also killed in that airplane crash, although none were of the rank that Peter was. But because of that, the job itself was not defined at all, so it was kind of feeling one's way.

I did only work three-quarter time, because I was at that time campaigning for the state senate and, of course, had children who were still eight and nine. So it was a lot of stepping around and trying to make one's way, not only in the job, but also in raising a family altogether by myself. It was, I think, an offer that would not have been made to me if Peter had not worked for DRI. I looked at it in that way, but wasn't going to say, "Oh, no. You really don't need to."

Although there have been times early on that I got a little angry when I'd think that this had occurred, and here I was working for the part of the university system that actually did take my husband's life. I mean, the plane was owned by the board of regents and thus DRI, but I've been a longtime supporter of DRI, which I'll talk about a little bit later, because I know my husband loved the job. I think he felt he was really contributing a great deal, particularly in instrumentation design to do experiments of one of a kind—that you cannot go out and buy something off the shelf. He had to design and build the instrumentation to place on the airplane to take measurements. In fact, there are two *volumes* of his patents and papers that were given to me by DRI, two big volumes. One, his parents received, and our family received another, because when you work for the university system—I assume it's the same at other branches of the university—you have to sign over to the university any design that you might come up with. It cannot be your personal patent; it has to go to the institution for whom you work.

Several things come to mind. Dr. Murino was the first president. He wasn't there that long because he left, and then came Dr. George Hidy.

When you say he wasn't there that long...?

Well, you know what? I cannot remember.

A year or two years?

Well, in a ten-year period we had three different presidents, some staying several years, probably two to three years.

Because this would have been during a time when time was pretty fuzzy for you, having just lost your husband.

Yes, it was. We'll say two to three years. I'm sorry that I don't remember more specifically, but I also don't remember what Dr. Murino did after he left DRI. I know that there is some kind of an unwritten rule, just a kind of a rule-of-thumb, that after four or five years you should apply for something else and move on. At least, that is what I've been told in the academic world. I don't remember. Cliff did marry his secretary at DRI at that time, and that becomes rather humorous as I go along. I like them both very much. In fact, I really became rather good friends with each of the presidents for whom I worked.

One of the major issues that Dr. Murino had me work on was getting a street named for Alessandro Dandini, which I did. I think I've discussed that, have I not?

You mentioned it. You didn't discuss the process. I don't know if there's a story in that.

Yes, there is a story. I might as well tell that, as we go along. That particular road is now Parr Boulevard on one side of the freeway, and on the other side of the freeway it is Dandini Boulevard. And then after it goes in front of Truckee Meadows Community College, it drops down to Sun Valley Boulevard. But on the other side of Sun Valley Boulevard, it is called El Rancho Drive, and then it becomes Kietzke Lane. Four names in all. And then there was a Clearacre someplace in there, too, I think.

Oh, Clearacre comes up and turns into Sun Valley Boulevard.

Well, I had to go to, I think, three different bodies of government in order to get this street changed. It was the Reno City Council, and I remember my friend Janice Pine, who now works for Saint Mary's Hospital as a lobbyist, and is married to a good friend of mine, Spike Wilson. She was on the city council, and I remember seeing her face, that she was just smiling, saying, "Yes, Sue, I'm going to go ahead and vote for this for you." [laughter] I just remember that. She didn't say that, but that's what her expression was saying to me.

Then I had to go to the *county*, because part of that was in the county. And oh, the third, I think, was in Sparks. There were three different entities, I believe, I had to go to. You know, you get one part done, and then if the other part didn't go, then you've only got a little stretch of the Dandini Boulevard. [laughter] But actually, the part that was most important was accomplished at the end of the day. That was very important to Dr. Murino, as was getting a piece of land that I believe I have alluded to, in Congress, through Senator Laxalt's good offices, to designate this as a business and research park called Dandini Research Park. Dr. Dandini, I'm going to be fuzzy on this, too, but I believe he had part of that.

Yes. There's something about the land you mentioned before. He owned some of it, but not all of it.

Yes. I think that's correct. When I was driving up there just the other day, going north on 395, I looked up at DRI, and it's grown quite a bit since then, but I looked at the research park, and there's really nothing on there. And this was a *very* long time ago. Almost what? Twenty-some years ago now. I don't know why that is. I do know that the board of trustees at one point had taken it on as one of their big tasks, and we do see a lot of business parks developing in the Truckee Meadows, but this is not one of them. It seemed to us that it was a great

relationship, where you might be able to have basic research and applied research working hand-in-hand. But it just did not happen.

Also, Dr. Murino—and things I remember about him dealt with the Dandinis, to be honest with you—wanted me to see if I could get the university to give Dr. Dandini a Distinguished Nevadan Award. I was not able to do that.

Did the Distinguished Nevadan Award exist at that time?

The one given by the university system? I don't know. It was something that came under the board of regents' aegis, and so I'm assuming that's what it was. Maybe it was the President's Medal. There was something that you needed to recommend people for, and I do believe it probably was what I've just said.

President's Medal maybe, or Distinguished Nevadan.

Why, do you know the Distinguished Nevadan's only been in place for so long? I've got one of those. But do you know when it started?

I don't know.

Anyway, it was some award, and it did not come to pass, and I'm sure he was disappointed, as was I. I do know that I did quite a few things with the Dandinis. We used their home, which is up by Washoe County Golf Course, or was. Angela may still live there. It is a very different home.

Mansion? No?

It is very unique. We felt by Sandro and Angela's hospitality that we'd be able to possibly raise money by having functions there, fund-raisers. They were very generous with their time and with their ability to do that and with their invitation lists—although I would put together a lot of those invitations, as well. They were very, very hospitable and would have dinner parties and receptions and a variety of kinds of things like that. So they were very agreeable to doing whatever they could to help DRI. That's kind of what I remember from the thrust of that administration.

I remember a small, little thing, but it was important to them, that I would take Sandro and Angela to see the Christmas lights out in Hidden Valley and other areas around town, and a variety of things like that. So I guess I'd say my memory thrusts me into the role of being a friend of the Dandinis in trying to do things for them, as they were doing for us, as well.

Under Dr. George Hidy . . . and I must have a little chuckle here—George also married his secretary. [laughter] With George and Doris, I probably have the best relationship, although I very much like Jim and Colleen Taranik. Now Jim is heading up the Mackay School of Mines as the interim dean. He was the dean before, left, and then there was a tussle between Dr. Lilley and the woman who was the dean there.

Jane Long, I think.

Yes. I don't know her. So Dr. Taranik is coming in again in an interim position.

Going back to Dr. Hidy. I'd say probably the most significant thing that happened under Dr. Hidy's administration was the fact that we started thinking about what we could do. First of all, I was always under the impression—and it wasn't just the impression; it was a fact—that DRI had hardly any visibility in our community. Nobody seemed to know what DRI did.

Most people thought DRI was part of the university—and it wasn't. It was a separate,

freestanding part of the university system—the research arm of the university system. There were bills introduced in the legislature off and on to remove that independence and freedom of DRI and place it under one of the branches of the university, because it would have brought a tremendous amount of research money into the university system. DRI received very little money from the state—a pittance, relatively speaking—because most all of the scientists and researchers would go out and get their own contracts. Their salaries and other things would come out of that money. So the state paid for very few positions. It was a very insignificant amount. It had seemed that that was something we constantly had to watch out for, but it was something that people would say, "DRI. Oh, yes." And there would be this vague description of what that might be, if you asked anybody on the street.

So I spent a lot of time giving speeches at groups, whether it was Downtown Rotary or whatever, with a slide presentation, or I had something else set up, if they wanted to hear from one scientist about a particular kind of research going on. There were some very interesting ones that were a little more, quote, "sexy" than some others, that people were more interested in, and were more easily understood by a layperson, such as myself. If I could understand it, probably most people could. So I did a lot of that.

The big thing that came under Dr. Hidy's administration was the science medal. Each of the other branches of the university system gives out awards at graduation—Distinguished Nevadans, President's Medal, Honorary Doctorate. Well, DRI was not granting a degree. So I worked with a member of the board of regents, Dorothy Gallagher, who was one of the more supportive regents with DRI. We came up with this idea of giving some kind of an award to a scientist, and we came up with the idea of a Nevada medal.

I have to tell you that I was really kind of laughed down by people, saying, "Who would want to get a science medal from a place in Nevada? I mean, get real! Nevada doesn't have anything going for it scientifically."

Well, as it happens, it wasn't ridiculous, but I was beginning to doubt whether it was really doable after I kept hearing how it wasn't possible, and it was kind of funny, et cetera. However, I was able to convince Nevada Bell to be involved with us, and they would give a monetary award. Well, from there I worked with Brian Herr, who just recently left Nevada Bell, a great guy.

I think this worked so well because of a person on our board of trustees—and I say "ours" being DRI. Art Anderson was a retired vice president of IBM, and he lived up at Incline Village. He knew many people in the National Science Foundation and other groups, so we would send out packets with a cover letter from him explaining what DRI was and that we were instituting this new award, et cetera, et cetera. He was just a terrific guy. If we had not had his knowledge and help, it would not have worked as well as it has.

The very first person we got was Dr. James Van Allen. It was the same year as UNLV won their national basketball championship, and I'll tell you why I remember that. We were going to have whoever won this award give a lecture for people interested in the subject matter at both UNLV and UNR. At that time we had a reception, not a dinner, but just a reception, and invited people. In this case it was in Las Vegas. We also duplicated it up here in Reno.

There's a Van Allen radiation belt that goes around the earth, and it is named for him. It's really what we now call the weather satellite, the spin-scan camera.

Because Dorothy Gallagher was not part of this—she was the board of regents contact—Brian and I took Dr. Van Allen and his wife—both just great people—around to meet all the weathermen on the news. Oh, and they were so excited to meet the guy who's responsible for getting their weather forecast.

I remember Sam Shad, who is still on TV. Sam was just so excited to meet Dr. Van Allen, but Mrs. Van Allen—cute, little, typical academic's wife—she was so excited about the UNLV basketball team winning, that she wanted me to see if I could go get autographs from all these basketball players. [laughter] No wonder I thought they were great. I watch Sports Center on ESPN almost every day. It was just so funny! And they were so delightful.

That was our first year. Everything about it was great, except for the unfortunate fact that few in the community came to any of these events. You'd have all these chairs set up for a speaker, and there might be twenty people. So that was a disappointment, but this was because it was new. You tried to get media coverage, and I have to say the *Reno Gazette-Journal* has been very, very supportive—always an editorial and stories about it. As the years have gone on, that award has become bigger and bigger, and Nobel Prize winners are getting it now.

They have two very large dinners in both ends of the state. Under Bob Miller, when I was lieutenant governor, Sandy Miller, the first lady, was very into science. She always used to tell me she was like a science groupie rather than a rock singer's groupie. So she was so supportive. They first started having the winner at the governor's mansion for a special dinner and things such as that. It's carried on, since Bob and Sandy left, with Governor Guinn and First Lady Dema. But the medal itself is now up to quite a bit more money than it was at one time, and there's a beautiful medal that has been crafted that is representative of the award itself.

So that was the big thing then, in Dr. Hidy's administration. Actually, it is one of the major things that DRI does, recognize and bring in someone of real scientific notoriety and renown. One would have probably never thought it would have turned out as well as it has. Dr. Hidy went to the Bay Area after he left DRI.

Dr. Jim Taranik was the next president. I would say that Dr. Taranik was probably the most politically interested. Well, I think they all felt that they were politically interested, but even today it is true that the chancellor pretty much represents the university. So the individual presidents of parts of the university system don't go down and lobby. In most cases the chancellor will say, "This is what I want to do," speaking from one voice, wherever they may go, whether it's to ways and means, the senate finance, or whatever.

Dr. Taranik, of course, came from more of a geological background, and each one came from a little bit different area. Both Dr. Murino and Dr. Hidy were in the atmospheric part of the DRI family. We have a variety of different centers, and they just would like to have somebody that had knowledge in one of the five centers or four centers.

Tell me where the five centers are. Or is that not fair? [laughter]

Well, they've changed names. I'd have to go look it up. I can give you some of them.

Don't worry about that. We should look that up. I'm just thinking in terms of not knowing.

Well, it'd be hydrology, atmospheric sciences. Another used to be called social

sciences, but now it's some paleontology type of a deal. That's one, two, three.

And you said geology was one.

No.

But Jim Taranik had a geological background?

Well, he came from that background.

Did your husband specialize in one particular area?

Yes. Atmospheric. He had a Ph.D. in atmospheric physics and electrical engineering. So, see, that's what he did. He designed.

So Jim Taranik, politically interested, geological background.

Yes. It was under Jim's administration that we reached out to southern Nevada. There was a plot of land that years before, another member of the board of regents, Bucky Buchanan remembered its stated purpose. It was just an absolutely incredible corner. It was on Flamingo; I don't remember the exact corner. It's where the DRI building is now. But as it turns out, because DRI was sort of the forgotten stepchild of the university system, some people saw this plot of land with different purposes in mind. In fact, at one time they wanted to turn it into a golf driving range. I mean, it is an incredible corner. You would never want to use it that way. [East Flamingo Road and Swenson Street.] Anyway, that's what was being discussed at that time. Fortunately, somehow the minutes were found, and it was very clear that that's what the intention was. So that's what ultimately happened.

DRI now has just received a gift—I can't remember the exact sum of money—from

Jim Rogers, who is a philanthropist for just so many different institutions. He graduated from the same law school my son did and has given the largest gift ever of any single individual to any law school in the nation in its history. I believe it was $150 million. So the University of Arizona law center is, guess what? Jim Rogers Law Center. It's the Boyd School of Law in UNLV, but Mr. Rogers has also given money to that. In addition, he gave the largest single gift to DRI just recently. [The name of the law school at the University of Arizona is: James E. Rogers College of Law. At UNLV it is the William S. Boyd School of Law.]

DRI then was expanding its horizons to both parts of the state, just like every other state agency or business or part of the university system has done, because, of course, that's where the population is. Jim, I think, had some vision for DRI and played an important role at that time in DRI history.

The one thing, though, I have to say that was a disappointment for me, personally, with Dr. Taranik, was the fact that when I was running for lieutenant governor, lieutenant governor was perceived as being a half-time job. It only paid, like $20,000 a year, and so I was going to work part-time at DRI. That was built into the budget. Well, after my airplane crash, et cetera, I was speaking with a friend of mine who also worked for the university, Assemblywoman Jan Evans, the day before the inauguration took place. We were talking about health insurance, because we took a leave of absence from our jobs. Well, she told me I needed to touch base with Dr. Taranik. This was on a Sunday. I called him at home, and we never got to the question I had, because somehow it came up that I could not work for DRI, because I could not accept two paychecks from the state, one from lieutenant governor and one from DRI, which was rather strange, because when I was in the

senate, that was not a problem. I was a senator, took a leave during session and paid my own insurance, and I then worked for DRI.

Well, as it turns out, the senate, the legislative branch of government, excluded themselves from every position, except they had forgotten—because the legislature doesn't make very much money—about this one executive branch position that doesn't pay very much. I learned this as sort of an afterthought, and I couldn't even believe it.

I then called our legal counsel, Mr. Lorne Malkiewich, at that time, got him at home in Carson City. He went down to LCB. He did not know the answer to this question. He looked it up, and this is the opinion. He came back and said, "You have three choices. Tomorrow you can get sworn in, resign from DRI. Two, don't get sworn in and work for DRI," and the other was, I guess, "Get sworn in and change the amount of money you make through the legislative process."

Well, as it turns out, I'd gone through a lot to get elected lieutenant governor, so I wasn't going to not get sworn in, despite that it was a bit difficult just getting down there physically. We issued a press release that day saying what had happened, and, of course, it was buried in all the inauguration day information. As it turns out, I would never ask for a bigger raise. I'd just have to live on the twenty thousand dollars a year.

It appears that the then budget director, Judy Matteucci, came up with this list of other things that the lieutenant governor could do to get a bigger salary. However, I declined that, because I felt that it would not be in the public's best interest, or mine, to get elected and then add responsibilities to my job and get a bigger paycheck. I also had a suspicion that some people who wanted to do this for me really wanted to do it to me, rather than for me, so I'm not pointing the finger at Judy.

So that's kind of what I was left with. If I really want to think about it too much, I think about the airplane crash with my husband and think about the fact of hearing about this only because I happened to call someone the Sunday before I was to get sworn in. I guess I probably wouldn't feel very good about DRI, but that's not true. You know, those things are in the past, and history's history.

I have actually set up two endowed fellowships at DRI in my husband's name. The first one was to a young researcher, because that's really how I looked at my own husband, that he was just really getting started in a research position. Forty years old was sort of on the youngish side at that time in working your way up the university ladder. And there've been some really, really neat people who have won. Now, this is an internal award given for somebody at DRI. It can be in any division, any one of the centers. There are no stipulations. There are committees set up to receive papers and ultimately make the decision. [The Peter Wagner Medal of Excellence was established in 1999. The medal and the scholarship are presented at the same time to the scientist who has outstanding accomplishments.]

When my mother-in-law died, I thought that probably one of the things she would have liked was to have set up another one in her son's name, her only child, for a woman in atmospheric sciences anywhere in the United States—it did not have to be anybody we knew. It's starting out sort of like the Nevada Medal did, that at first there were just a few. As we well know, there are very few women who even go into something like atmospheric sciences, because you have to be getting an advanced degree. So, you're getting down to just a handful.

As several years have gone by, the women have been just great. In fact, the one who won just this last year, in 2002,

was a woman who talked about the fact that she had no women role models when she was studying in this field, and that this was just a great thing because of that fact. She was getting her Ph.D. at the University of Washington. Besides, she just had a great personality. But all of them have been good.

So those are two things I have done for the institute, which, I think, is something I know my husband would have liked, and his family would have liked.

I'm going to go back and make a comment about DRI and the shock I received one day before I was to be sworn in as lieutenant governor, finding out that I could not have worked for DRI and be lieutenant governor at the same time. I'm looking at the legal opinion that was given to me by Lorne Malkiewich, who at that time was chief legal counsel, but is now a director of the legislative counsel bureau. This bill is dated January 6, 1991, my birthday, as a matter of fact, and the date that I was sworn in.

In fact, in an aside—and I'll get back to this—when the swearing-in took place in the year 2003, it was also on January 6. I told Governor Guinn that he really didn't need to do all this for my birthday party, to invite these hundreds of people. It was a lovely, festive occasion. He was sorry he didn't know that before, because he probably would have poked a little fun of me at my birthday. So that's why I didn't tell him before.

Getting back to this letter, when I talked to our chief legal counsel, there were three options. He was quite disturbed by having to give me this information, as a matter of fact. He cites all the different sections of NRS, Nevada Revised Statutes, which drove him to writing this particular opinion. He said that the salary of the lieutenant governor is set by law. That is true. He said that I'm prohibited from taking two paychecks from the state. It talks about three basic options that I had. The first was to propose an amendment to the law to allow the lieutenant governor to accept other employment with the state that does not conflict with the position of lieutenant governor, and he cites the sections of the law that that would probably be amended to make that possible

And that was the one that we missed previously.

Yes, it is. I was sort of on target, but not exactly. The other two options are exactly what I said: either resign my position with DRI or resign as lieutenant governor. He goes on to say that he's given me this legal advice because I've known him. But, as of that day forward, I would then be in the executive branch of government, so he urged me to contact the attorney general if I did not like this opinion, as I really didn't! [laughter] But I did not contact the attorney general, because I respected his advice. And that is a dilemma that confronted me.

There was this other option that I've discussed, that the budget director, Judy Matteucci, went in and tried to add more responsibilities to the lieutenant governor's job and then augment my salary. That was even a fourth option. But I took only the one of resigning from DRI. We did issue a press release, but clearly it was not big news, because that was the swearing in of the constitutional officers. And I think that that probably will wind up my discussion with my ten years at DRI.

You made a comment before that that was not your best time and for a specific reason.

Yes. I think it was because DRI felt a great deal of guilt in having many lives taken—four or five—because of a plane crash. They realized I was the one who was left behind with small children. Others were older; or some, I don't believe, were even married. So I think they created this job. Although the title was held by other people, previously, I think they had totally different responsibilities and some probably not much. I think that they sort of created this job for me, and as I mentioned, there was a new president of DRI, Dr. Clifford Murino, and I think he was just trying to find things for me to do. He was at a handicap, too, because he hadn't really even moved to Reno yet.

Did you find it challenging as a job, then?

Sometimes, and a lot of times no, because there was not a fixed responsibility, and so I tended to create things to keep myself busy. That didn't work as well many times, because there was not the support there to accomplish things, and there was no direction. Maybe I do better when I know exactly what the functions of a new position really are, rather than creating things out of the blue.

11

LIFE IN THE LEGISLATURE

We have a number of different directions we could go, and I think what we'd like to do first is to go back and do some pickup questions. There are some things we've mentioned, but then not followed up with the complete information. One is that you asked me to go back and check, and it's not there earlier, about Mary Gojack urging you to run for the legislature. Maybe you could start by just telling who Mary Gojack was, what roles she held for Nevada.

Mary Gojack was a very interesting person, and in thinking back on her life, I don't remember exactly when it was that I met her. She was elected to the assembly and, I believe, served one term, or maybe two there, and was then running for the state senate against a man named Corky Lingenfelter, a Republican who had held that position for some time. He lived in Washoe Valley, I believe, and people did not give her much of a chance, because she was a Democrat, and that tended to be more of a Republican district. However, I did meet her and got involved maybe for

the same reasons that I was interested in working for Pat Hardy Lewis at that time, because it was a woman running for office. She was *very* instrumental in getting me to run, maybe more so than AAUW, but, needless to say, she couldn't help me, at all, because she herself was running for office at that time for the state senate. Despite the fact that I was a Republican and she was a Democrat, she encouraged me and had me meet people who would maybe be helpful to me.

One thing I do remember specifically is that she invited my husband and me up to her place, and there were a number of women there who were interested in electing other women to office. Her husband really, I would say, almost pressured my husband and told him how terrific this would be and was very, very positive. I think that was important to Peter's decision, because here was another husband, who was obviously left behind in a certain way, encouraging yet another man to think in a positive way about this possibility.

I do remember during the discussion that one of the women who was active in

BPW jumped too quickly. My husband, I think, said something at this gathering such as, "Well, I'm anxious to let Sue run."

They jumped all over him because they said, "Well, you don't 'let' her anything. It's *her* choice." I was uncomfortable about the whole thing, because this was a big step for a young man, thirty-two or thirty-three, or in that age bracket, to feel this way. I thought they were being too harsh on him, but he had a great sense of humor and was also not dissuaded because of that comment. So I would have to say that both Mary Gojack and her then husband, John T. Gojack, were very instrumental in my initially running for the legislature. As it turns out—and I believe I might have mentioned this before—Mary Gojack *did* win and was elected a state senator, and actually I was placed in her seat on the assembly floor next to Jean Ford. And that may have been part of the problem that other people saw—that I was following in their footsteps, which we've discussed.

Very different in your beliefs and so on. OK.

To finish up, the Democrats encouraged Mary Gojack—and this was a very bad choice, and I did tell her that it was not a good thing to do—to run against United States Senator Paul Laxalt. He was extremely popular in our state and probably represented the state quite well in most areas. Mary lost very big, and then she turned around and ran for the new congressional seat that was created because of the increase in population in Nevada—against Paul Laxalt's former aid, Barbara Vucanovich, and lost that, as well. In my mind and in some of my friends' minds, we felt that the Democrats used her as a scapegoat, if you will, as a stalking-horse, and that they really could not believe that she could win, not because she wasn't a competent person, but because her philosophy was too liberal for Nevada at that

time. She was a good friend of mine and was very supportive of things that I did and vice versa.

She didn't run for any other offices after losing the congressional seat race?

No, she didn't. In fact, not long after that she got cancer and died at a relatively young age. In fact, she died when I was working at DRI, because I was going to see her in the hospital, and I was leaving from DRI, when I got a call saying that she had passed away. I think, Vikki, that several times I've mentioned that three of my good friends, women friends in the legislature, all died of cancer. I don't know if there's any correlation between stress and terrible disease, but all these women were under great stress and all died at about the time that they were involved in politics.

And perhaps under more pressure, more stress, than legislators today, women legislators

Oh, absolutely. No question.

Because of the time?

Yes. There's no question about that, because even the 1980s were to some extent carving out places for women, but specifically in the senate in the 1970s it was true, very true. Except for Jan Evans, Assemblywoman Jan Evans, all of them were active in the 1970s at the beginning of the women's movement.

OK. One of the other questions we wanted to talk about was DACOWITS.

Yes. I did talk a little bit previously about DACOWITS, the Defense Advisory Committee on Women in the Services. This was during the 1980s, and I got a call at DRI from a friend of mine, who I had only met maybe once in my life, so I guess I really wouldn't describe her as a friend at that time. Her name was Marybel Batjer. She called me from the Pentagon asking me if I'd serve on this committee, DACOWITS. I remember great surprise, because this was maybe ten years later, a number of years after I had first met her at a Republican convention. Have I discussed that?

I don't believe we've talked about that, at all.

I think it was in 1975. I was on the platform committee for the Republican Party, and she was, as well. I think she was representing high school students. I'm guessing she was about eighteen at the time, and I was about thirty-five. We both wound up in the women's restroom at the same time and started discussing how upset we were with the platform, that it was certainly not at all positive for women and women's issues. At least, *we* felt that way. And that was about it.

Ten years later I get this call from her, from the Pentagon, asking me to serve on the committee. I was surprised, and I told her I knew nothing about the military. She said that really was not essential, but she wanted to have Republicans—because this was a Republican administration under Ronald Reagan—who were moderate in their views, particularly about the advancement of women, and in this case, women in the armed services. So I accepted, and it was a three-year appointment. I remember there were only thirty women from throughout the country, and I wound up at the end being vice chair of this organization. In fact, Secretary of Defense Caspar Weinberger was the real appointing authority, but, of course, the names came from one of his assistants.

Marybel Batjer was at this time involved, I believe, as the head of all personnel decisions that dealt with civilians in the Pentagon. I know we think of the Pentagon as being a military complex, and it is, but there are *many* civilians who work in that building, not just the military people. She was able to appoint to that committee a number of women. In fact, later on, I met the former wife of Allen Neuharth, who created *USA Today* newspaper. She was a former state senator in Florida and Frank Carlucci's wife. Frank Carlucci then became secretary of defense in a later administration after Caspar Weinberger. So there were people on there that it was fun to get to know, and also it broadened my horizons on other institutions that I felt needed to be a little more open for women's advancement. I guess the startling thing about this organization was that we met four times a year, and each time we met at a different military base. We would alternate between, say, the navy and the marines, and then it would be the army; then it would be the coast guard, et cetera. So it was a very broadening experience for me.

I would go to these particular bases, and we were urged to travel in the interim, as well. For example, I went down to Nellis Air Force Base, where we did not meet as a group. There was a clear distinction between women who were *enlisted* and women who were *officers*. The women that were enlisted were interested in totally different things—hospitals, health care, childcare—those kinds of issues. Women officers were more interested in their advancement, their careers in the military, because that's what they wanted, was to move up within their own military branch. Talk about glass ceilings, there certainly was a major glass ceiling in the military, because most people in the military advance during wartime. You can take a general with four stars, let's say. Maybe he won two of those stars by having a tour of duty in Vietnam once and then came back and then went again. So he would get a star for each. That's a general description of how it works. But because women were not allowed to be in combat positions, they were hitting their head right against this very large glass ceiling. So this was something that those of us who were interested in *this* particular issue tried to help women advance, and we would, of course, pass this information on and meet with the secretary of defense at that time, Caspar Weinberger.

I met many people that way. In fact, I just saw recently the first woman astronaut, Sally Ride, at a Nevada Women's Fund luncheon. I had introduced her when I was on this committee at Vandenberg Air Force Base, and she spoke to our group. So it was a terrific experience for me, and one that I'll always remember. But clearly, it was only because of another friend, Marybel Batjer, that I was appointed to this position.

Then she asked me to select somebody else from Nevada, because she came from Nevada, and I will mention what she does now here in our state. I recommended Lynn Atcheson, a friend of mine, but she was a Democrat, and that did not work with the mix of the committee. So I then recommended Patsy Redmond, who was very active in the Republican Party and was a neighbor and *very* supportive when I first ran for office. She's the only one at this Republican state convention who kind of introduced me to people. She lived in my precinct, and she was a more moderate voice in the party. So she did serve.

Marybel Batjer's father was on the supreme court in our state. Cameron Batjer is a wonderful man, wonderful chief justice. He'd resigned from the supreme court because at that time there was a lot of dissension and arguments going on among the supreme court justices. Al Gunderson was one, and the other person was Noel Manoukian, and they had a real knockdown drag-out. Cameron Batjer was dissatisfied

with that. He was a good friend of Paul Laxalt, who was United States senator. He had a lot to do with Marybel Batjer getting the job in the Pentagon. He also appointed her dad as chairman of the pardons board, the federal pardons board, and he served in that position for quite some time. Marybel now has come back to Nevada and happens to be at this very day that we're speaking winding up the legislative session in Carson City, where she is Governor Guinn's chief of staff. So that kind of brings conclusion to the discussion of DACOWITS and how I got there and who was responsible for that.

Another question we wanted to go back to, and you did talk about this to some extent, was time limits on introducing and voting on bills, or the lack thereof, at the time that you were in the legislature, and how that compares to what's happening in today's legislature.

Yes. When I was first elected to the legislature, there were no time constraints. Everything just flowed whenever they wanted it to. Chairmen of committees could keep a bill forever, never have a hearing on it if they didn't want to, have a hearing at night, I guess. They really had total control. There was no ending date; there were no time limits. A bill had to be passed out of a committee on a certain date, let's say, fifteen days into the session, and then it had to be voted upon on the floor by the twentieth day, for example—that was not the case. I had introduced a resolution to do that very thing. I believe it might have been copied from the state of Michigan, but I don't remember that exactly. Well, it didn't even get a hearing, speaking about a bill not going very far. It actually was a resolution, because it would change the rules of our own bodies. It seemed to me to be a fairly good idea, but it did take away all power of the chairman, and that was a *major* thing. That's one of the reasons people *wanted* to chair committees and not just be a member, and to be in the majority party. So I have to smile to myself now, many, many years later, that that's exactly what we're doing in the legislative session. That was really stimulated by the passage of a constitutional amendment to limit legislative sessions to 120 days. When that occurred, there had to be the staff, I'm sure, working with the current legislators at that time—I was no longer in the legislature when that vote was taken—who came up with the processing of bills through the legislative process. A bill would be introduced in the assembly side; it had to have a hearing by X date, had to be voted upon by the people in that particular body by X date; going over to the other side, in this case, the senate, and going through the same process. That is what happens now, and, actually, it does work fairly well.

I, personally, was not supportive of limiting our sessions to 120 days, and some of the lobbyists were surprised when I mentioned this in my class this session, as they were on a panel, and they were a bit surprised. My reason for that was, we only meet every other year as it is. We are the fastest-growing state in the nation, and to limit ourselves to only 120 days made no sense to me. Clearly, since we've done this, we've had many special sessions—at least two, I believe, and maybe three. I'd have to think about that. I served for almost sixteen years in the legislature, and I only was party to two or three special sessions.

Now we have that in less than four or five years. I think it's because things are being done rather quickly. People don't have as much time to speak in front of a committee. I think it shortens the period of time where the average citizen could come and visit with legislators and also testify, but it appears that most everybody else is fairly

satisfied with it. It passed overwhelmingly, I must say, on the vote of the people. I think that people felt that if you had a certain day when it would conclude, that people's employers, for example, would know when that person was going to be able to come back to work. When it went on ad nauseam, in some people's minds, that was very difficult to pinpoint. I think that's why it passed. Thinking back on it, I suppose I could go back to certain people who served in the legislature with me—and there are quite a few still there—and say, "Nya, nya-nya, nya, nya!" [laughter] But I don't think I really want to do that!

We're going to be continuing with some questions that we just wanted to add information on them. One is some information on the domestic violence bills that went through. Sue, you can talk a little bit about how that changed over time.

Right. In the 1970s I actually had two victims of domestic violence come and testify. From the response that they got, I believe that if it hadn't been for them, this issue would have gotten short shrift. It would have been one of those issues that maybe the chairman would have kept in his desk for the whole session, but because of their import, it changed. It put faces on victims of domestic violence, very honestly. However, by the beginning of the 1980s, legislators had gotten a little more comfortable with people who fell into this bracket. Unfortunately, so many women do. Committee to Aid Abused Women, CAAW, sent down an intern to work with me. She was an older person at that time. Her name was Jan Evans, and she was getting a master's in sociology and had volunteered with Committee to Aid Abused Women. She'd recently been divorced, and so she came down to work with me. We became good friends, and she was *very*, very important in going around and visiting with many senators, particularly, on what this legislation was all about. It did set up the funding mechanism for domestic violence shelters throughout the state—well, actually not. It was based upon increasing marriage-license fees, because we did believe that there was at that time a correlation between getting married and being abused. Needless to say, there are many more people today who just live together, who don't get that marriage license, that abuse women. But at that time most people did tend to get married. It was less likely you'd have a partner that you were living with.

The funding mechanism—there was a problem with that in terms of the rural counties?

Yes. Actually, there was a major change in attitude from the late 1970s to the early 1980s. Jan Evans, who later became Assemblywoman Jan Evans, went and visited with all of the senators to get their support. So that was a major step forward. In fact, today there are so many bills introduced dealing with domestic violence that sometimes there are things that the domestic violence centers—Safe Nest in Las Vegas and CAAW, Committee to Aid Abused Women, in the northern part of the state—don't want them. They're actually harmful in some ways. That passed in 1981, a great success, and that was held up, as I've mentioned before, as kind of a national model. The problem was, because it was based upon a five-dollar increase in marriage license fees, most of the money was gained in Washoe County and in Clark County in Las Vegas, because that's where most of the marriages occurred. Well, clearly, it does not mean that the only victims of domestic violence *live* in urban areas. Actually, there is much need for shelters in the rural counties, or at least

programs. So their leadership—both Estelle Murphy, who runs the program then and now in Las Vegas and Joni Kaiser, who ran it then and now in Washoe County—realize they needed to spread some of this money around. They came back the next session, and we tweaked with the funding mechanism so that the rural counties, who had hardly any marriages occur there, did gain some of this money. That is the way it is even today, as we speak. There have been many changes in the laws, however. As I mentioned, everybody seems to have jumped on the bandwagon, and domestic violence seems to be, if you will, a comfortable social cause to be associated with, unlike in the very, very beginning.

Which is such a contrast to the time when you started introducing it, and people just didn't even believe it existed.

That's right. Or they didn't understand why people just didn't get up and walk away. Now, whole attitudes have changed, thankfully, but it is unfortunate that twenty-five years have passed. I have been to Las Vegas recently to commemorate them on their twenty-fifth anniversary, and also here in northern Nevada this year. It's a shame that they have been in business twenty-five years. The numbers have gone up astronomically. At each place, I said, "I hope that ten years from now, you will not have to invite me back." But, of course, I know that is not going to be the case.

So there are options for people who find themselves in that position, but it seems there's been no preventative found at this point. A lot of it's increasing.

That's absolutely true. In Las Vegas the difference in number between twenty-five years ago and today is *unbelievable*. People wouldn't even believe the numbers, and I would not want to give you numbers right now, because they'd probably be wrong, but in both counties it has just skyrocketed.

You've given a lot of information about the study of the prison system and a master plan for the prison system, but you wanted to mention the fiscal note that had to be added to the bills. Maybe you could explain that in more detail.

Yes. I believe that occurred in 1983. One of the dilemmas that we as legislators face is the skyrocketing budgets of public safety. Of course, when money is spent that way there's less of it to spend on education and a number of other interests that are as important or more, in my mind. So it seemed to me as if maybe one way to deal with that was to have a fiscal note attached to prison bills. Now, that's somewhat difficult to ascertain, because what you're trying to do is project how many more inmates there will be if you create a new crime—and believe me, there are all kinds of new crimes that are created each legislative session—or you increase the penalty of an *existing* crime. That then means that inmates are staying in there longer or staying in there at all, because, of course, only misdemeanants are sent to jails that are in the local communities. If it's a felony, then they must go to the state prison system. It seemed to me in my mind that we were increasing penalties, and we were creating new crimes so quickly that it was taking a larger and larger amount out of our general fund.

Needless to say, there are certain periods of time that legislators are tough on crime, and maybe several sessions go by, and you don't have to worry about that so much. In fact, one of the issues they're discussing right now is the meal allowance for the prison system—this particular session in 2003. Each of the money committees initially cut that money way

back. The director of the prisons has come and testified—and it is now a woman—saying that if you give them better food, they're not as likely to act up and to become hostile within the prison system. That's hard for legislators to understand, but both the governor and the director of the department of corrections have appealed to the money committees to increase that amount. And, see, that's even a soft-on-crime position, if you will, rather than, "Hey, look! They should have to drink water all day long and have bread in the evening, and that's about it." Well, that's not what legislators are hearing today, but we go through that process.

In order to have a fiscal note, at least the position of planner in the department of prisons will have to make a guess, but they can do that fairly accurately. In fact, because that has occurred, we have been a focus of some attention nationally. Actually, when I chaired the senate judiciary committee, I did invite national experts to come and tell us what these new crimes and enhanced penalties would do to our budget discussions. They've done a terrific job, and as the years have gone on, legislators are more interested in what they have to say, as are the staff people who work in the department of prisons. They have now, I think, received these people in a fairly amenable way.

The other thing I tended to do, when I was in that position of chair of the judiciary committee in the senate, was to hold all the bills that had a fiscal note dealing with the number of inmates, because sometimes you can introduce a bill that is actually so significant that you'd have to build a brand-new prison as a result of one particular piece of legislation, or two or three. And that is terribly expensive. Not only do you have to *build* it, but then you have to manage it by putting a lot of people in it and the rest of the operating costs.

So the point of holding those bills to the end of the session was to what? To see how the budget was going to end up?

Yes. The idea was to hold them to the end to see exactly what the accumulative result was. If all of them together was something like 130 new inmates, that would be a fairly significant hit on the state budget. So that was done, and I have to say my counterpart, Bob Sader, who chaired the assembly judiciary committee at this time—there were other assembly judiciary chairs who were not as, quote, "enlightened" as Bob Sader—also tried to do the same things I did, so we would be able to move ahead jointly, if you will.

So it wasn't just the budget. I want to try to be clear. It was the combination of how many of these laws were going to go into effect that would essentially increase either penalty or number of crimes, and the budget, the interplay between the two of those?

Yes, exactly. We would be able to then see what impact this was going to have on the budget, on the public safety aspect of our budget.

Sometimes people would say, "Doesn't matter."

The other legislators would say, "I don't care if it's 330 people. Good. We need to put all those people away."

Other times they may say, "Well, this is not really that necessary."

Needless to say, it was normally the first response, because on the whole, I did live during times of needing to be tough on crime. Interestingly enough, I suppose some people could say I wasn't, and yet I was not defeated. So who's to say?

There is one other thing here I might discuss, and that is another piece of legislation I introduced that tended to fit under this crime package, if you will, or the crime discussion we're having today. I'd introduced the legislation in 1985, I think it was, that in certain criminal cases property that was confiscated in the arrest of an alleged criminal would be forfeited, and that it would be utilized by either the local police departments or the state, and either used by their officers or sold at auctions. So that was a moneymaking proposition, or property that they would not necessarily have to buy themselves. I was asked to introduce that by local district attorneys, and I was happy to do that. So, needless to say, sometimes I was very supportive of prosecutors, and other times not as much so, but it all depended upon the issue. I think, generally speaking, that was a valid position for people to take.

You just touched on an issue that we talked a little bit about off of the tape, and that was that you said in this case you really weren't tough on crime in many ways, and yet you never suffered for that, as some people had advised you, "If you're not tough on crime, you'll never get reelected." You've mentioned a number of times, and I know you're going to continue to mention, bills you passed that weren't always popular with your peers—a bill to have time limits on legislation that took away power from the chairs of the committee, for instance. Yet you seemed to manage to do that without alienating your peers, and I'm just curious, how do you manage the power and the political realm, to be able to introduce things that would be unpopular with your peers, and survive? [laughter]

Well, you're assuming I survived. [laughter] Some people might say no.

That survived the legislature, perhaps, not the plane crash very well, right?

That's true. Yes. I think that maybe one of the ways is if you don't take yourself that seriously. If you know you're there to do a job and that people in your district respect you, and I think you know that by virtue of whether you have a lot of opposition, or whether, when you knock on doors, that people say, "Huh! Don't even bother!" and shut the door, smash it in your face, which I did have quite a few when I first ran. I always went back and walked and knocked in my assembly district door after door after door. In the senate it was a little harder, because I represented a much bigger area, but I did have open meetings throughout my district and took out ads and asked people to come and visit with me.

I think, probably, not taking myself that seriously and also having a sense of humor about things, although there were some things I felt passionately about and was devastated by the defeat, others not so much. Or others, I would think to myself, "Well, I'm sorry they didn't quite see it that way. Maybe later on they will." Very often you did introduce things time after time until finally—fortunately or unfortunately—they passed or they didn't. But after five or six times of looking at the same thing, hopefully people said, "Maybe it's about time we do pass this."

So part of it was your own personality of just not being obsessed with things that didn't pass the first time out, having a sense of humor about it.

Yes, I think so. Although, I do remember after my very first session, I'd introduced fifteen bills, and I think thirteen passed. That was always brought up in newspaper articles about me. I do believe part of another problem I had was that so much attention was given to me because I was a young woman with small children, and again, this was kind of groundbreaking, and I'm sure that people got a little tired of

reading about me—my colleagues, that is. I'm sure my constituents didn't as much, but my colleagues, because, hey, I'm sure they thought, "I'm down here. I'm doing things, too. How come it's all about her?"

I think that you can find that to be true even today, and I will allude to my friend who's just been elected attorney general, Brian Sandoval, as being the first Hispanic officeholder in our state, that it seemed like all the attention was on him and for that reason, and so there may be some feelings about people who are his peers, as well. I don't know that, and I'm sure at some point I will talk to Mr. Sandoval about that.

So there might have been some jealousy stirred up in terms of you getting all the media attention at that time.

I think that was probably true. I don't know if that answers your question or not.

I asked, "How did you manage to introduce bills that were unpopular and still manage to get along with the other legislators?"

And you said, "Very carefully." [laughter]

So perhaps there's a way you learned to go about the process that was successful for you in terms of talking to people, informing them.

Yes. I guess so. You know, one of the staff persons of the Legislative Counsel Bureau said to me just recently that he noticed a difference between the way I interacted with my male colleagues versus Jean Ford and Mary Gojack. He viewed me going down the hall one day and putting my arm around then speaker of the assembly, Keith Ashworth. He remembered that as something imprinted on his mind— and this was a male staff person—thinking to himself, he never would've seen either one of those other women do something like that, and he felt maybe that was one of the reasons that—I'm not going to say I was more one of the boys, because that certainly was not the case—I just had a more, I guess, cordial (I don't know if that's the correct word) relationship with some of my male colleagues, or was warmer toward them. That was his description of how he thought that I was able to have a more compelling career in the legislative body than maybe the other two did, or thought they did.

We have one more comment on that issue of your relationship with your colleagues, and it had to do with Carl Dodge and working on the ERA, and then another issue the day after that vote.

Yes. I guess this would be another example of my relationship with my colleagues. At that time I was in the assembly, and Carl Dodge was a very important member of the state senate. We both were Republicans. It was following the evening discussion that I referred to previously, where Lieutenant Governor Bob Rose broke a tie that was very emotional on ERA. In fact, it was even more so because it was at night. I don't know why that was, but that was the case. Of course, it was defeated, and some of the women who had come from around the state to be there for the vote were still there the following day. I obviously had a very emotional evening, too, but the next day is the next day. Even though for many of these women, this was their only issue—it was not for me. I was there for other things for my district and obviously for good government, hopefully.

I went down to the senate to ask Carl Dodge about a bill that I was going to hear in a committee that day on postcard voter registration. It was one of those bills that the Republicans always were against, just because they felt that droves of Democrats

would come in and vote on the last day and weren't interested enough in being registered earlier on. I don't really know what the exact reasons were, but because we were both Republicans, I was talking to Carl Dodge about it. He served on senate government affairs, and at that time I was on assembly government affairs, and those are the committees to which these kinds of bills were referred.

Carl and I were seen walking down the hall from the senate to the assembly arm-in-arm, discussing this. Carl had voted against the Equal Rights Amendment the previous evening. I then was chastised by women throughout the state for being friendly with an anti-ERA person. Well, I think, first of all, that shows that being a legislator is quite a bit different than being a lobbyist for a single issue. I tried to explain it to them, because I had many of them visit me on the floor of the assembly, asking me why I could do such a thing. I was like a traitor. It just surprised me, because here I was, one of their most committed votes, somebody who passionately believed in equal rights, and yet, they now the next day, were shaking their finger at me. I tried to explain to them that this was a different day and a different issue.

I think that is another reason possibly why, for example, I and Senator Dodge have been longtime friends. He certainly would be recognized as, well, a member of the good-old-boy system, but certainly one that thought for himself. He represented Fallon and still, I believe, lives in Fallon today. Wonderful wife, Betty. So I think maybe that's another part of it—that I did not look at Carl Dodge as an enemy, but as somebody who had a different opinion. Later on, I'd find out that he was pro-choice, and so he saw the issues as being the same but in a different way than I had. So I did not think of him as a hostile person or ignore him or turn my back on him, as some of the followers wanted me to, or expected me to.

Sort of non-personalizing a difference of opinion, taking that personally.

Exactly, because he certainly didn't feel that way about me, that I had supported it. I rose to his standard, I guess, if you will, rather than him coming down to mine.

I have said on a number of occasions, when people were not happy with what I had said, that I do not think you should vote for somebody only on a single issue. I said, probably, if somebody was pro-ERA and maybe pro-choice, you'd probably agree with them on most other issues, as well, but not necessarily.

Maybe because it was a constitutional amendment, it was perceived by some as only that, of the sacredness of amending our United States Constitution. Then, when people from pro-life, which I think is a great misnomer, came and wanted to add a constitutional amendment, prohibiting abortion, some felt the same way, that we should not keep amending the constitution. That's exactly the position that Senator Carl Dodge had. He was against ERA, because it was asking for a constitutional amendment, and he was against those people who wanted to add a constitutional amendment prohibiting abortion. So that was very consistent.

He appreciated people like that. I certainly did. I would not want anybody to have voted against Senator Carl Dodge based on that one vote, because, guess what? Some of those same people were pro-choice, and they would have found out that he was a good friend on that issue.

So it's important to look at the bigger pattern in your elected officials, of what they are consistent on. Like in this case, it was not changing the constitution more so than that particular issue.

That's exactly right. I do feel that voters should keep that in mind, but when I would say this, people would be upset with me, again, because they thought I should say, "If you're pro-ERA, then that's your candidate." And I really didn't feel that way.

Getting back to the question, I think that that may be one of the reasons I got along more easily, perhaps, than some of my female colleagues.

You were able to move past it when you didn't agree with someone else.

Yes, even though those two issues were very, very important to me, because they were philosophical positions that I couldn't understand why people could keep changing their mind. Carl Dodge didn't do that, and I use him as the example. Other legislators had, and we've talked about those who saw it as just like a bill that would change a penalty from a gross misdemeanor to a felony, or, let's say, banks would be able to sell insurance. Well, that's not quite the same thing in my mind as getting equal rights for women, but some people didn't see it quite that same way, either.

We had one other question that we wanted to touch on today, and that was your work with Spike Wilson on placing some BLM lands under the Forest Service. We're going to add to that some information about your relationship with Spike, and also, there's a related issue on conservation easements. So maybe we can start with the BLM land and then move from there.

Actually, both of these examples are environmental law. They occurred during the senate time of my life, during the 1980s. I worked on these with a former colleague of mine, someone who I greatly admire, Thomas R. C. Wilson III. We know him more affectionately as "Spike" Wilson. He did chair the senate judiciary committee prior to my taking over that seat. I had a difficult task, because Spike was so competent and capable and was such an articulate speaker. Of course, being an attorney, he knew a lot about almost everything that came through that committee.

Spike and I worked together closely on different things. One that was major, which probably very few people are aware of, dealt with working through a staff member, a public employee, on the National Forest Service, the Toiyabe National Forest, to move some BLM land. As most people know now, in Nevada 87.7 percent of the land is public land. Most of that is either BLM or Forest Service. In this case, it was a lot of BLM land that was prime potential to be under the auspices of the National Forest Service, because, generally speaking, most people identify the Forest Service as being

better stewards of the land, mainly because it's better land. It's forested; it normally is just more recreationally oriented, more beautiful. I'm sure some people would argue with me, but I think most people think of BLM land, in many cases, being used to raise cattle on, for grazing, but more of the deserty, hostile environment in many ways.

There were hundreds of thousands of potential acres that some of the Forest Service people came to Spike and I on and asked us if we would be co-chairs of an organization to try to move these certain acreages from BLM to Forest Service. I think the reason for this was because—this was under Ronald Reagan's administration— there was something happening under his secretary of interior and head of the Forest Service. I guess I've lost touch of what it really was, but something was precipitated at the federal level that was going to be even

Sue with Spike Wilson at the Tenth Anniversary Nevada Medal dinner.

more harmful, and we were called in to see if we could stop this from happening. Spike and I were asked to co-chair this committee to increase, augment the national forest lands, and we said we would.

It was explained to us the implications and the threat from the federal government, that we needed to do this rather quickly. The young man—and I will add his name later on—who presented this to us was quite a go-getter. He organized the hearings, and I'm not kidding you—there were hundreds and hundreds and *hundreds* of people who turned out for these hearings. Spike and I, very honestly, did relatively little to get the numbers of people there. We did go on television and talk about this and did some media, because this young man was quite a terrific organizer. And bah! We were just floored with the number of people who we would meet when we'd go to the hearings.

One was at the Reno Sparks Convention and Visitors Authority, and it was packed! Yes. I think maybe we thought a handful of people were interested. But evidently, whatever kind of an alert system they had was pretty impressive. So Spike and I did do this. We also had hearings around the state, and it was like a bandwagon and a locomotive train that you better get out of the way of. It was quite successful. It was a *fait accompli*. There was a lot of work done, and I have to say we did some, but I have to really give most of the credit to Forest Service people.

Spike and I did go back, or at least I remember *I* did. I think he did. I think we both went back to Washington, D.C., to meet with the head of the Forest Service, which comes under . . . .

Department of Interior?

Oh, no. The BLM comes under the Department of Interior. I believe the Forest Service is under USDA, United States Department of Agriculture.

We did go back and explain all this to him, because this was kind of a revolt underneath him. Of course, he has to get along with the person who makes sure he's there—that's Ronald Reagan in this case.

Senator Laxalt was a major part of that administration in terms of their friendship when both had been governors of California and Nevada. That was a real heady experience, if you will, and it's something that probably people have relatively little knowledge about, that we get the credit, but I have to say a lot of it has to go to the staff itself.

The head of the Toiyabe National Forest at that time was a man named Jim Nelson. I may have mentioned his name in terms of going up in the Monitor Range on the horseback trip with Jean Ford. Jim Nelson organized all these trips. It was a PR kind of an opportunity, because he'd take visiting people—I mean, if they were interested, or people who could make a difference—on these horseback trips, so they could see the lovely state that we have that most people think of as a vast wasteland. There are parts of Nevada that *are* that way, but not all of it, for sure. The young man who really orchestrated all the groundwork on this went off to Washington and moved up within the Forest Service, and I suspect that might have been part of his agenda. But that was really relevant to us. We thought it was something that needed to be done and was accomplished.

Spike was also a friend on much of my legislation when I was in the senate, particularly when other people were not. Spike was a good, old boy, but one that did his *own thing*, and he was very smart and was very respected. He was probably a more moderate Democrat than many of the others. I think most people may know, or may not, that regardless of whether you're a Republican or Democrat in this state, most everybody is somewhat conservative. That was true, at least, when

I was in the senate in the 1980s. I suspect this session, that some of those monikers will be quite different when many Republicans vote for tax increases and other things that they have decided are necessary because our state is growing so quickly.

Spike and I were involved in many other issues, and I'll probably talk about some of those—Ethics Commission and such—later on. But there was a bill that I was asked to introduce on behalf of the Nature Conservancy. I had the good fortune of meeting a young man, David Livermore, who was at that time head of the Nature Conservancy in Nevada. His father had been secretary of interior, or whatever they call it, in the state of California, under Governor Ronald Reagan. In fact, I believe the town of Livermore, California, is named after his family. He now has risen up in the Nature Conservancy; he's working out of Denver or Salt Lake and is in charge of the West—but a terrific young man. I'm sure he probably still is young at this time, relative to me. He asked me to introduce this bill, and I cannot remember exactly how I got interested in the Nature Conservancy. Maybe he came around and introduced himself in the legislature.

This was a piece of legislation that the Nature Conservancy wanted to pass in every state in the nation, which would allow individuals to dedicate their land. Let's say they had some certain kind of a water system going through it, a river, or a certain kind of wildflower. They would dedicate that land via a trust, a will, or something of that sort, to the Nature Conservancy, but it would be used at that time for *them* until their death, or until they designated in the future. Possibly, it was land that was ranchland, and they wanted to still have it ranchland, but there was something interesting about it or different about it. If you had a certain fish that was in a pond or lake or something there, then they would know ultimately it would be well taken care of by the Nature Conservancy.

This bill was introduced by very few people, and I know Spike was one of the other sponsors of that bill, but I think there were a couple of others, too. I've just looked at that recently. However, it was not perceived very well by ranchers, by the rural legislators. I think that they didn't quite understand what its purpose was, and I think they may have thought that land was going to be taken away from them, or something. I remember Norman Glaser, who was a great guy from Elko, had difficulty with it, and I think Floyd Lamb, who was then chairman of the senate finance committee, also had difficulty with this. Spike being a smart, articulate guy, went with me to discuss this bill when it was introduced in a variety of different steps that we had to go through. I think he was very important to me, because he was in the majority party at that time, and he got along reasonably well with some of these men I have just mentioned, in some cases, very well. So if I had difficulty with some of them, he did not.

That was an important piece of legislation for the Nature Conservancy, and, in fact, I was just looking the other day at a picture. In one of my bedrooms is a photograph, and it was given to me. When I looked on the back of it, wondering why I had this hanging there, it was from the Nature Conservancy for this particular piece of legislation. It ultimately did pass, and I think that they feel it has been successful. It has been successful in lots of other states in our nation. The Nature Conservancy, in my mind, is just an extremely terrific organization, and I've served on their board for many years. And that is a description of my legislative relationship with Spike.

He's been important to you all through your career?

Yes, he has, in the senate. Sometimes he served on different committees than I did, so I would visit with him about pieces of legislation that came out of other committees that I was not on, because you cannot be an expert on every single piece of legislation that comes to the senate floor. The senate relies to a greater degree on the committee system than does the assembly. The assembly is a little more free spirited and has more members, of course, so there are more different opinions and more discussion on the floors of each of the houses. I would visit with Spike about issues that I was not as familiar with, and he did at one time serve as chairman of the commerce and labor committee, so he was pretty knowledgeable about those issues. That was not his great love, so he left that and went over to chair the senate judiciary committee after the former senator either didn't run again or was defeated. His name was Mel Close.

Yes, I did respect Spike as much as anybody in the legislature. I felt he was there for the right reasons; he was, I would say, a statesman rather than a politician. Of course, many years later he did run for Congress, oh, maybe six years ago now, against our current congressman, Jim Gibbons, and lost. That was probably a shock to many people, but, because I had run once before for lieutenant governor and realized how fast this state was growing, I did talk to Spike about his lack of name ID. He had only run from Washoe County. I figured if I'd run for lieutenant governor again, I would've started all over, that I would assume I was starting from zero. I think that that was probably not his take on that, and that's one of the reasons he didn't win.

However, I think he would not have liked being in the House of Representatives, because there are so many people in it, so until you get a lot of seniority, you're kind of zero. I don't think that would have been a good fit for him. But anyway, it wasn't. When Spike left the senate, I found a vacuum there, and I think some of my other colleagues felt that way, not only about him, but about other people, who have left, and they had decided to fold up tent, because they felt there were not enough people in our current legislature who they could look up to, although, I know many that I could look up to, and I'm sure they could if they knew them as well as I do.

One of the other things that you just touched on and wanted to come back to was Jim Joyce. You had talked about him in relation to some issues along the way, and I believe one of those was domestic violence, and especially that he was the lobbyist for wedding chapels, among other things.

I have talked about that. I don't believe, however, I talked about Jim in my first session, or following sessions, until that one. Jim Joyce was the consummate lobbyist. His name was mentioned always as being *the* most influential and powerful lobbyist of all. Nobody even came close. He was so different from most other lobbyists, because he said very little; he'd sit in the back of a hearing room, if there was a bill he had an interest in, and work crossword puzzles. He was very bright, very articulate, very powerful and very smart. You always knew he was in the back of the room, not looking at anybody, just working the *New York Times* crossword puzzles, but it seemed like he was always able to get whatever bill he chose through the legislative process and signed by the governor. At least, that was the image.

Initially, I did not realize, being a freshman legislator and speaking out about things, that often I was speaking out against bills represented by Jim Joyce. Acupuncture passed the session before I came down, so that would have been 1973.

And the person whose place I took, whom I've discussed, Dr. Bob Broadbent, was so opposed, as you may well guess, being a medical doctor, to the acupuncture bill. My understanding is he spoke eloquently, at least by his description, against this, and nobody voted the same way he did. He was horrified that he was a medical person who was discussing acupuncture, and other people said, "Huh?" and just went ahead and voted for it. So we were the first state in the nation to legalize the use of acupuncture, and that bill was represented by Jim Joyce.

He had a number of other bills that were sort of different, and I will talk about one of them that dealt with laetrile and Gerovital. I may have discussed this, because I remember seeing Marvin Cravitts's name.

You did talk about that bill, but you said very little about Jim Joyce at that time.

He also represented that man. Jim Joyce—I don't remember him being very visible, although maybe he was sitting in the back row in my first sessions and working on the crossword puzzles. As I got to know him better, of course, I could pick him out of a crowd. I had voted against almost every single piece of legislation that he was lobbyist for in my first session, and I did not know that, but it was getting down to the end of the session, and there was a big discussion in Las Vegas of consolidation of the city of Las Vegas and Clark County. I didn't know what was the best thing. I wasn't on that committee, and I just would turn to look to my legislative friends from Clark County as to what they wanted, but it was a big split between them.

Jim Joyce was representing one side or the other, and he sent me down a note that said, "If you vote a certain way, you will have 100 percent voting record against me for the session. I just want you to know that." Signed, "Jim Joyce." [laughter] I

didn't know which way it was! He was going to hold me in suspense, so I could have this 100 percent voting record. It wasn't done in a threatening way. At least, how do you tell, by words written on a note, whether it was or wasn't? At one point I thought it was kind of funny. [laughter] I thought, "Wow! Maybe I won't be back here next time!" [laughter]

I can't remember how Jean Ford felt about that. I think probably in that case, I would have voted the way that she would have, because I sat next to her, of course, and it was an issue that affected her county, and I respected her. I believe I voted no, but the legislature let the county decide the issue, and that's really not important here. It was the fact that this was an unusual relationship between Jim Joyce and me from the first time I was there.

As sessions went on, it became clear that my voting record was going to be pretty much the same. He represented the gaming industry, the Nevada Resort Association, in addition to some kind of unusual bills, things that he probably believed in. He was very powerful. Really, I suspect our relationship changed, because I have discussed him, I believe, in relationship to laetrile and Gerovital. Maybe I've not attached him to that bill, but he was also lobbying for the people who wanted laetrile and Gerovital— Marvin Cravitts and other people. Of course, I was *adamantly* opposed to that, as I've described before, and I suspect that I was thinking that this was going to be the relationship I had with him, but he was not all that intrusive into elections in northern Nevada. He ran tons of campaigns in Clark County. Well, then he became a lobbyist. He'd gotten X number of people elected. Now, you don't think that they're not going to feel they owe him something? I suspect it did cross their minds once or twice—or maybe not. Maybe for some of them, it didn't. Maybe they didn't want to think about that, I don't know, but there was discussion that maybe we should separate those two. People didn't want to touch that, either, because guess who they were going to offend?

Well, in 1981, when I introduced the funding mechanism for domestic violence centers, as I think I've mentioned before, Jim Joyce did represent wedding chapels, or marriage license fees. Of course, that's what we were looking at for a funding mechanism. So Jan Evans and I, when we found out that this was the case, we thought, "Uh-oh." We decided we would go and talk to him about it, because he was known also for doing a number of things *pro bono* that he really believed in. In fact, he was very instrumental in getting money for the journalism school at UNR, because he was a journalism major, and that was something he just *did*. He did have that reputation, which most of the lobbyists today don't. They may do that, but they're not noted for that. Everybody knew that about Jim. So we decided we'd go talk to him about this, just so we would meet the lion, I guess, in his den. As it turns out, he was pretty impressed with what we were trying to do and said that he was not going to represent the wedding chapels anymore, because he felt that this was something really important. To be honest with you, maybe that's the reason we had eighteen cosponsors in the senate, in addition to Jan Evans doing a good job. I suspect that that did have something to do with it.

So that kind of changed our relationship—he and I—that I saw him in a different light. He did represent the Nevada Resort Association, though, and I have mentioned that in 1987 the last tax increase for gaming came when I chaired the judiciary committee. I remember him sitting in the back row, doing his crossword puzzle. Don Mello had actually leveraged this tax increase himself in the interim, and he had gotten the gaming people to agree to a quarter percent raise in one year of the biennium and another quarter percent raise in the second year. As it came closer to the session, the bill was introduced. I cosponsored it; Don Mello was the main sponsor, and several of the members of my committee did—judiciary committee. It was referred there, but it became clear that something happened that the gaming industry wasn't now committed to that second quarter percent in the second year. So the dilemma I had was not only getting the first year through, but the second year, and that was the sticking point. Most of the members of my committee came from Las Vegas. Charlie Joerg was from Carson City, and Erik Beyer was from Reno, and myself, and I think that was about it. So it was going to be difficult, but it did succeed. I don't know if I've told the story of that yet.

Yes, you did.

OK. But it did succeed, so I'm sure Jim was disappointed, and I suspect that probably they thought they could get it killed someplace else, but they didn't. So that I remember distinctly. Maybe I was fooled.

Then we move up to the time I'm running for lieutenant governor. Somebody I hired in northern Nevada, Jim Denton—I've discussed him before—had decided he wanted to reach out and become more of a player in Clark County, so he kind of tied in with Jim Joyce. Jim Joyce had told me at the very beginning, when I was thinking about running, that if I got these two men—Kenny Guinn, our current governor, and Peter Thomas, president of Valley Bank, which became Bank of America—to be honorary co-chairs in Clark County, it would scare off everybody else. I did that and, indeed, did scare off everybody except an opponent I had that Harry Reid had got involved named Jeanne Ireland.

Following my plane crash, Jim, again, played a major role in my life, because he then was pretty much committed to getting me elected against somebody from Clark County. Of course, I did get elected, and Jim and I actually became good friends. He died when I was lieutenant governor in the 1990s—smoked a lot and died of lung cancer. He *did* get me to go to the acupuncturist that he had lobbied for, Dr. Lok in Clark County, because he thought maybe that would help the pain that I have. I guess people had a hard time understanding that it was because of the fusion, which none of these things would help. But I did go as a courtesy. In fact, Jim was going to Dr. Lok when I would come down. He was thinking that Dr. Lok would be able to cure him of cancer. I was very sad, because, clearly, acupuncture isn't going to help. Sometimes people will go to traditional doctors until it's too late. And it probably was too late, anyway. So Jim died, and there's a table that's about chest high, in the main lobby of the legislative building, on the first floor. All avenues or isles come toward this place, and there's a little plaque in it saying, "Dedicated to Jim Joyce," because he used to hang around there, and he was pretty tall—he was about six-three—so it's about the height where he would rest and talk to people.

I did want to say some things about Jim, that he had a checkered career, but one that was positive at the end. When Jim Joyce decided he wasn't going to live much longer, I was one of a number of people he called to talk to. I guess that shows you how far our relationship had come.

Anyway, so there was a struggle to then become the next Jim Joyce. Of course, if you remember, this was in the 1990s, because he was very instrumental in my campaign for lieutenant governor in 1990. It was kind of a toss-up at that time between Harvey Whittemore and Sam McMullen.

They're both from northern Nevada, of course, though Harvey is now involved in projects in Clark County, as well, but at that time he was not. I would have to say there's no comparison between the clout that Sam McMullen has and Harvey. Of course, there are other very important lobbyists who may challenge somebody else, but most legislators know who these people are, who they represent, and what they may mean to them. You know, it's interesting to me to reflect on the taxation questions that are paramount today, and maybe tomorrow and maybe Sunday, in the Nevada legislature. The gaming industry wants a certain kind of tax to pass. Most legislators know that they are very, very influential in getting people elected or not elected, basically, because of the money.

Of course, labor unions have a huge impact on people in Clark County, too, because of the numbers of people who are members. They actually go out and work very *hard* going door-to-door and other kinds of things for legislative candidates. Some of the more powerful lobbyists are Harvey Whittemore and Greg Ferraro and one other person I will mention here, since we're talking about that, Billy Vassiliadis, who is from Clark County. He's the president of R&R Partners, which is the largest public relations firm in our state and actually has headquarters in Salt Lake and offices in a variety of locations throughout the West. In fact, at one time they had one in Moscow, I believe, which is very odd. Billy's wife is, I believe, the assistant in charge of McCarran Airport. I've not met her, but I understand she's very, very competent. Those people I've just mentioned are all extremely powerful; they all do represent many of the same interests, one of them being the Nevada Resort Association, which is comprised mainly of casinos in Clark County, *not* in the northern part of the state. They just can't seem to get together, and, of course, they're much, much smaller than the larger ones. Not all of them belong to the Nevada Resort Association; it's made up mainly of the big ones. They do a lot of work for the little ones, either getting something passed or getting something killed. The others kind of get hauled along with them.

I did want to say something about lobbyists, generally speaking, because clearly they have a major impact. Part of that is not all bad, of course, because we have a staff at LCB, Legislative Counsel Bureau, that is not partisan. They will work for a Republican legislator or a Democratic legislator. Most states have the Democratic people and the Republican people, but that's not true here. We have a small state, relatively speaking, and a small body. You only need eleven votes in the senate and maybe twenty-one, twenty-two in the assembly to be successful. In some states, and I think I've even mentioned a friend of mine in New Hampshire, there were hundreds of people in their body, because it's really based mainly on the town hall meeting concept that started in New England. We have one of the smaller bodies in the nation. So most people know who their lobbyists are and are friends with them. I'm sure some are not friends with certain ones, but they *can* be. Clearly, they make a huge difference in getting people elected or not.

Is it still possible for lobbyists to run a campaign and then lobby?

Yes.

So the situation that Jim Joyce had set up is still going on?

Yes, it is. Although—I'm thinking about it right now—I cannot tell you who that might affect.

Because, for example, Harvey Whittemore does not do campaigns, right?

That's correct.

He just strictly does lobbying. He's in Lionel Sawyer and Collins.

That's correct.

And that's his total thing is lobbying.

Yes. He is a land developer, did Wingfield Springs, or is partly responsible for that. He has another project in Clark County—I think it's called Coyote Springs—which will be forty-two thousand acres and is going to be a huge community, sort of like Summerlin in Las Vegas, land that was owned by Howard Hughes.

I know that R&R Partners runs campaigns, and then some of them I just mentioned, too. Greg Ferraro is the president, or was, here in the northern part of the state. He's a friend of mine. I mean, I am good friends with all these people I've mentioned, and Billy Vassiliadis. They're very sharp; they're very involved this session with taxes and the governor's package and so on. So I think that probably by the end of today or tomorrow we will know exactly who has been successful and who has not.

Because we're right at the end of this legislative session.

We are. This is May 30, and the session must be over by Monday, June 2. If it isn't, then the governor will have to call a special session, which I'm sure they do not want, because the only thing being discussed at that time will be taxes. So *everything* will be focused on that. I think the legislators would rather, if it's going to be focused upon that anyway, why not in the midst of a lot of other things, as well?

OK. Time to switch gears. Sue, you're going to talk to us about the study of foster care in 1985.

Yes, I am. Actually, the way these interim studies are developed is that very often a legislator will introduce a concurrent resolution outlining why they think something needs to be investigated between sessions. That does allow legislators to serve more year round, but it's certainly not in the legislative arena. This particular resolution I had introduced. It was cosponsored by most all the other legislators, and it directed the legislative commission—that's how they're designed—to study the foster care. This was a subject that I gained some information about as I was serving on the judiciary committee. Normally, if somebody introduces the resolution, then they expect to be the chair of that particular interim committee. Sometimes that happens; sometimes it doesn't. Very often there are a mix of senators and assembly people. In this case, I did chair this committee, and there were several senators on it with me, and two assembly people, one from Washoe County.

The dilemma of foster care really revolves around money. There isn't enough money for the foster care parents; there isn't enough money to hire competent staff; there just isn't enough money to really deal with a foster care program the way it should be done. It's really sad, and I found this to be the case as we got into studying the issue. Most of these studies tend to have public hearings. It depends upon where they're held; in fact, the ones I was involved in would meet both in Reno and in Las Vegas and then almost always once in a rural area, at least, because sometimes each of these issues takes on different concerns and

different problems in the rural areas as in the more metropolitan areas.

I was looking last evening to see who testified before the interim committee, and I was surprised I didn't see Linda Ryan's name. Linda Ryan was the head of the department of human resources at that time, and her husband was Cy Ryan, a well-known reporter for the *Las Vegas Sun* in Carson City. Anyway, I didn't see her name. We had foster parents and foster kids testify; we had professional people. It really did boil down to the fact that there just wasn't enough money to do anything that you would want to do to help out these youngsters. Very often they were shuffled from person to person. Sometimes the foster parents did it just for the money, and their hearts weren't really in it to help the children. As we know, the older the children become, the less likely they are to be adopted.

I'm looking at the summary of the recommendations that came from this committee. After the public hearings, then each committee is assigned LCB staff, and they write the report, and then the committee votes on what pieces of legislation they want to present to the next legislative session. In that case, since I chaired it, they would be introduced on the senate side, because that's the body I was in at the time, and then the other members of the committee in that body would be cosponsors, and anybody else that wanted to.

I'm looking at this, and almost every one starts with, "Providing funding. Providing funding. Providing funding," over and over again. I'm going to just mention some of the recommendations that we did have. One was to establish a statutory maximum caseload of thirty-five cases per social worker and to provide funding for additional staff positions in the welfare department, department of human resources. I believe Linda Ryan was head of the welfare department, not the department of human resources.

We realized that some of these social workers are so stretched out—as most everybody is in government, whether it's a probation officer or whatever—that they always have too large a caseload than they can effectively deal with. We realized that maybe a multidisciplinary team was something that would have been very valuable within the welfare department by utilizing even the existing staff to deal with these cases in somewhat of a different way. We encouraged exploring the possibility of coordinating the foster care operations in Clark County and in Washoe County and the rural areas to have one agency or jurisdiction.

Now, since this report, there have been changes occurring to combine Washoe and Clark County and to get some of this foster care into the county hands. That meant new employees would have to be hired, because you're getting rid of the ones at the state level, and that money would then flow to the counties. What was happening was that some of these children were being removed from their parental homes, and they would be in the county hands for a while; then they'd get shuffled to the state. And that was not a good thing at all, because different people were dealing with the same child.

I know this has been a major commitment of the legislature in the last couple of sessions, and I think this session, 2003, this will have been a *fait accompli*. We wanted to have formal training for social services staff again. We wanted to have background checks with the FBI, checking out people who were going to deal with children in the foster care system. We supported the efforts of the welfare division, for example, to have a comprehensive statewide computer system.

What we found was really archaic, not only in terms of their tools, but also the capital tools, in addition to the human tools. We asked for funding for emergency services to families to pay for food, medical care, shelter, transportation, those kinds of things. We wanted to have *respite* care for foster parents, so they could get a break occasionally from the obligation that they have assumed. We wanted to recognize some things that were more ceremonial in a way. We wanted monthly payments to be increased for foster parents, because we felt that they were not being paid enough for the work that they were undertaking and the commitment they have made in young people's lives. This was something that I was very involved in, because I realized there was not going to be enough money to do half of the things that we were suggesting.

I worked with the Junior League of Reno to have them take on a program, develop a program, to train and recruit foster parents. That was done, and it's been very successful, and often I see a Junior League member in town who remembers that. I happened to be a member of the Junior League in Tucson, and when I moved to Reno, there was no Junior League. There was later on, but I did not join it, because by then I was in the legislature and didn't have time.

You know, we need to have better emancipation services for young people ready to leave the home at the age of eighteen and all of a sudden be thrown into a totally different environment that they are not used to. We wanted more funding to subsidize adoptions. We definitely got into the area of termination of parental rights. In fact, a justice of the supreme court, Miriam Shearing, called me a number of years ago and asked me to reflect back on the discussion that was had dealing with termination of parental rights, because there was a supreme court case that she would be voting on, and she wanted to get a little more insight. As it turns out, I really couldn't help her. I felt somewhat intimidated, to be honest with you, to give a supreme court justice that kind of information, because sometimes the records were very well kept, and sometimes they were not, in terms of minutes of meetings. But that is a major area that judges get involved in: when and if they should terminate parental rights. That becomes a very emotional issue, as you might guess, and we did get involved in that to a large extent.

I would just wind up by saying that one of the last recommendations was to support a family court in northern Nevada, because there was something of that sort in Clark County. I would generally have to say that despite the fact of a few differences, most everything was asking for money, money, and more money. Obviously, I did recognize the fact that that wasn't going to happen, and that's why I went out to get the Junior League to at least give some kind of equal preparation for people who were going to be foster parents.

It was somewhat depressing, honestly, to be involved in something like this, because these kids were not there because they had done something wrong. As we know, it's very difficult for a child to be moved from one home to the next or even to be moved from their *own* to a foster home, because it does scar them later on for life, for practically all of their lives. I was very interested in trying to make some differences. As it turns out, I do remember that a lot of the money was not appropriated for this, and it just wasn't high enough on the pecking order of the finance committee or the ways and means committee in the assembly. You could only do so much and provide the background, the information, lobby, and testify yourself with your colleagues. Sometimes that works, and sometimes it doesn't.

At that time there wasn't money for many of these things. Have those things taken place since then? You said that the caseload is an issue that will probably be resolved this session.

Well, actually, no. The one agency is a big thing. And it hasn't really all culminated in that, because I know May Shelton is lobbying all the time down at the legislature to make sure that that does happen. She's now retired from the social services agency in Washoe County, and since she's retired, she does consulting in this area, which she knows very, very well. Some of these things have happened along the way, such as I've described, but some of it is just in a morass of other things that need more attention, but there's going to be more money appropriated this year, hopefully, for human services. I can't speak to whether foster care will be one of the recipients of that extra money, because all these things need more.

The family court, was it set up following this study, or did that come later?

Yes.

That did happen?

It did happen. I will talk about the long road that that had to becoming a reality in Nevada, but at that time it had not.

And it didn't happen following the study?

Immediately thereafter, I don't believe so. I have to think back on it, to when it did happen.

But it took a while.

Oh, yes. It did take a while. As a matter of fact, I know that it did not happen during this time period, because I was just thinking about what transpired and how long it took to get that on. If you want me to talk about that now, I can.

Yes. Let's go ahead.

I'm trying to remember how I was involved in this, but there was a grand jury examination of some of the issues that dealt with young people in Washoe County. I remember that there were some, I want to say, private meetings, but that's a little scary to think about. It was not a grand jury. I served on it, examining what was going on in the social services agencies in Washoe County. I don't believe much of this made the press, and I think that was done deliberately. In listening to all of this and hearing testimony, particularly from Charles "Chuck" McGee, who was a district judge in Washoe County, and his appeal for a family court, that struck a cord with me. After this examination was completed, I visited with Chuck McGee, and I decided this would be something really, really important. So I introduced a bill in the legislature, and it went to the senate judiciary committee, on which I served. There was one particular judge from Clark County named Charles Thompson, "Chuck" Thompson, who later ran for the supreme court against Miriam Shearing, and you remember to ask me a question about that.

Charles Thompson was well regarded in Clark County as a very competent, intelligent jurist. He had an unbelievably negative view of family courts. He would come to the legislature and always get it killed in the committee on which I served. It would be like a four-to-three vote. It was done one session; it came back again and was done another session. In fact, I was able to get a copy of the transcripts, when he made a statement. The substance of it was, and this is paraphrasing, "If I wasn't able to put a murderer away, I wouldn't want to be a judge," basically saying that these family matters are terribly unimportant, and it was even worse, but I cannot remember exactly. It was such a negative statement that I remembered it to this day—not exactly, but the gist of it.

Well, I was getting pretty frustrated, again, and obviously, Chuck McGee and other people would come and testify in favor of it. But Charles Thompson seemed to have all the power on the committee and in the senate and was able to come up, speak, and get it killed; come up again and speak and get it killed. So I discussed the possibility, just the idea of creating a family court. When I first discussed that with our chief legal counsel, Frank Daykin, at the time, there had only been one other court of jurisdiction, and I'm afraid I cannot remember exactly what that was. But there was only one special court of jurisdiction, meaning that a special court had been set up that dealt with only one thing. Today we know there are drug courts that people volunteer to preside over and mental health courts, but this is something that's coming later in the evolution of our state. The legal counsel felt that it could be done, and that was another difference of opinion that Judge Thompson and I had, that he felt that it could not constitutionally be done, creating this court of special jurisdiction. Our chief legal counsel did side with my proposal and gave me a legal opinion saying, yes, we could do that without amending the constitution.

However, it became clear that I was not going to be able to do this through the legislative process. So those of us who were interested in this—I still go back to Chuck McGee, and there were many other people as well—decided to amend the constitution publicly by having the people vote on it. I took it on the road, so to speak. I went and spoke to state PTA meetings that met in Tonopah. We'd drive all the way down there to talk about how important this was. I would actually read from the minutes what this judge had said, and everybody would go, "Oh!" They were so surprised and appalled that this would be said. Clearly, I did it for political reasons, because I wanted to get their attention. It was verbatim right out of the minutes, and I was saying nothing that had not been said. It was said in order to defeat this idea. Well, to make a long story short, it did become law, and so we now have family courts throughout the state. Now I don't think people even consider it as being different or unique, but it clearly was a part of the law that seemed to need change. Kids needed to be treated differently than someone who had murdered somebody. I mean, this is dealing with families; this is dealing with children; this is dealing with parents and their relationship to one another. I realize in many ways that it is a *very* difficult thing to deal with. Here you're dealing with mostly sad stories, because if your family was somewhat less dysfunctional than most, you probably would never see the court system. These need somewhat of a more compassionate, I guess, judge, someone who certainly doesn't look at everything as being about possibly sending someone away to the gas chamber.

I take pride in the fact that I was responsible to a large degree, at least legislatively, in making this happen. Actually, Judge Charles Thompson and Charles McGee were of equal import. They were at the same level; they were district court judges, but they had different attitudes and philosophies and temperament about the law.

Judge Thompson decided to run for the supreme court, as did Justice Miriam Shearing, both from Las Vegas. This was the first time a woman had run for the supreme court, and I was amazed. I was *absolutely* amazed. One time, when I was not watching my television, but was just listening to a commercial, it was touting Judge Thompson and talking about his commitment to guess what—family courts! Oh, I couldn't even believe it! You can imagine I about went right through the roof!

I can think you just about came out of your chair! [laughter]

I immediately called Justice Shearing, who I didn't know at all, but I knew a lot of my friends in Reno, women attorneys, were all supporting her and working very hard. So I was able to get in touch with her, and I told her this little story, and she found that to be very interesting. To be honest with you, I can't remember if she did anything with it. I don't think she did, but that became a very ugly, ugly race. For those of you who read this and think back on this or were living in Reno at the time, it was one of the ugliest campaigns I've seen.

I was surprised, to say the least, to hear that Judge Thompson took credit for that. The race was very bloody, very ugly. I mean, the commercials got downright mean. I was very happy to learn on election day that the person I voted for was elected, Miriam Shearing. She's done an excellent job; she's been reelected unopposed, I believe, at least twice and is retiring this year. There are people jockeying for her position already. She's such a *nice* person, as well as being very smart. I know when she was chief justice, and even another year, she spoke to my internship class, and they thoroughly enjoyed her.

Last session, Deborah Agosti was supposed to speak, because I wanted a woman to speak to my students, so they would understand that in the less visible branch of government there *are* women, and they can rise to that position as well as men. Something happened, and Deborah Agosti was not able to speak to the class last session, so Justice William Maupin, because he was chief justice at that time, spoke, as did Miriam Shearing. The class really enjoyed her because she's very down-to-earth. I've been involved in many different ways with judicial races, behind the scenes, but this was one that I felt very strongly about.

And just to clarify, your class is the one that you are currently doing. We should probably explain that, because we may refer to it a couple of times.

Right. The class to which I'm referring is a legislative internship class that I teach every other year at the Nevada State Legislature. It's mainly comprised of students from UNR. This year there were fifteen and six from UNLV, who come up and live in Carson City for the duration. And there were a couple from WNCC. I do have the major players in each branch of government come and speak, and other people. That's what I was referring to, and in this case, I actually was referring to the classes of 2001 and possibly 1998.

So that, Vikki, sort of tells about the history and evolution of the family court system. I would say, despite the fact that I took this on and spent a lot of time on it, most of the credit has to go to Chuck McGee, because it was his brainchild. He picked it up at some other meetings and readings that he's done, and it was something that he certainly convinced me was a good thing to do.

And he's very identified with the family court.

He is. Indeed. There are now—you can imagine—many family court judges in Clark County. Oh, I'm going to say eighteen to twenty. I may be wrong, but there are a lot. Whenever they come to create even more judgeships, there are all the statistics, the number of cases. They have to convince the legislature that that's the right thing to do. Because there's not home rule in our state, the legislature really has most of the power over local governments and even the judicial system in our state. They're the ones who have established the pay structure, even for judges, and the retirement system and all these things. That's something, of course, that local governments want desperately to have, and the legislature probably is not going to let go of it for a long time. [laughter]

But that's one of the power issues that we may talk about a little bit more.

Absolutely. Here is another interim study done for the same reasons that the other one was done that we've described. This was the study of alternative methods of resolving disputes, ADR. Because I served on the judiciary committee so often, every session, in fact, whether in the assembly or the senate, I really grew to love it. It dealt with issues, really, from birth to death, and not just things dealing with the legal system, but everything that has implications, whether it's a living will, et cetera. This was an issue that we really did not know much about; there weren't really any bills that stimulated this study. It rather was some people coming to me from Clark County who were interested in this whole approach of mediation, arbitration, taking things out of the court system and the judicial, contentious way. I think they came to me because I did chair the judiciary committee at that time. This was done in 1990 and was presented to the 1991 legislature, and it was something that I really thought had great merit to be discussed by the legislature.

Again, we had meetings throughout the state. Maybe the rural meeting was held in Fallon; another one was in Tonopah; but basically, it tried to cover the state. The committee heard a number of people speak about this—some attorneys themselves. Some attorneys did not think this was a good idea, and many did, people who were interested in issues that they felt would be better dealt with in a mediation or an arbitration way, rather than in a courtroom.

I introduced this resolution and did chair it. The assemblyman at the time,

Matthew Callister, who became a senator later on when I was lieutenant governor, was vice chair; he wound up also getting on city council in Las Vegas. Senator Charlie Joerg from Carson City served with me on the judiciary committee, as did Joe Neal, and both served on this interim committee. There was Assemblyman Gary Sheerin, who was an attorney and lived in Carson City, and Assemblyman Joe McGinness, and very honestly, I don't remember Joe, I'm sorry to say. I suspect he only served one session, because I think I would have known him if he had served in more.

This committee, after listening to all kinds of proposals—we had some national experts come in and talk to us, as well—decided to introduce legislation that revolved around these kinds of possibilities. We had a bill introduced that required mandatory nonbinding arbitration of all civil actions of twenty-five thousand dollars or less, incorporating disincentives to appeal, and authorized court-ordered, nonbinding arbitration in cases over twenty-five thousand. We did have a lot of discussion on the monetary fee and what exactly lent itself to nonbinding arbitration.

Really, it would not muster our judicial system to say that it had to be binding arbitration, I believe. You have to make it more attractive to do this, to take it out of the court system, and maybe to the disincentive programs that would accomplish that. We wanted to create a system of voluntary binding arbitration at any level of case. We required the state bar of Nevada to establish a pool of attorneys who will act as arbitrators without compensation, allowing the court to set fees and charge for arbitration in cases over twenty-five thousand dollars, allowing the court to appoint other qualified persons to act as arbitrators. Additionally, the bill would direct the state bar to offer training for the arbitrators, both attorneys and non-

attorneys, administer the program, and charge an administrative fee of not more than twenty-five dollars a year to all persons who apply to be arbitrators, and require that rules of law be used during the process.

One of the problems you have when you have legislation that has monetary figures in it is that very often inflation happens, and you have to go back and change the number. The classic case is in the constitution of Nevada, a requirement that we, being legislators, would get sixty dollars each session for postage. Well, you can imagine how far that lasts. You have to amend the constitution to remove that number. It has been tried several times, and it's been just words to this effect: "a reasonable sum." The public has not stood by and seen that passed. They think a reasonable sum might be thousands or hundreds of thousands of dollars. It just seems sixty dollars is a little archaic. That was 1864 or something.

You could do a lot then. [laughter]

Maybe they had leftover money. I don't know! [laughter]

They probably did!

They probably had Pony Express people delivering the mail. [laughter]

So that is a problem. Clearly, we needed to set a figure where civil actions would seem reasonable, after we heard the testimony, that this would be a nice cutting-off period. We wanted to create a pilot program in Washoe County, and if you remember, the makeup of the committee was pretty much geared to northern Nevada in this case. Usually, that's not a big deal, but I'm assuming, in thinking back, that that might be why we chose a pilot program in Washoe County for mandatory mediation of divorce cases involving children. The mediation will involve only issues of custody and visitation; the program will be supported by an increase in filing fees assessed against both parties. The supreme court will assist district courts in setting guidelines for the training of mediators. Mediators' reports to the court will be limited to whether the mediation was successful or not. No other facts may be disclosed. Allow smaller counties to increase their filing fees in order to institute a similar mediation program. We urge the supreme court of Nevada—and when we say "urge," it means that that's not a law; it's just a resolution expressing an opinion about something—to expand their rules, particularly Rule 171, to require attorneys to discuss ADR options thoroughly with each client, advising his or her client of the methods to resolve a dispute, which are available as an alternative to litigation, and explain the advantages, including the possible savings, of time, money, and other considerations that might bear on that particular case. We then wanted to urge the state bar of Nevada to inform the public to do a public campaign, if you will, so that the public of Nevada would know what this is all about and that they might even ask for it themselves or inquire about whether it would be a valid thing to use in their particular case.

On the other hand, in Clark County we established a pilot project for a neighborhood justice center. Actually, the people who interested me in this idea at all, this is what they were very much interested in, in establishing this neighborhood justice center in Las Vegas, again to be funded by filing fees assessed against both parties. The center would be based on ABA, the American Bar Association's program, establishing multi-door courthouses to provide a forum for local, small-scale disputes, such as landlord-tenant problems, neighborhood disagreements, and family disputes. It will also provide information and referral network linking the justices of the peace, municipal courts, lawyer referral systems, legal aid services, district attorneys, city attorneys, district courts, ADR programs, mental health services, and other governmental and private service agencies. This did happen, and my understanding is it has done quite well.

So it still exists?

Yes, it does. That I do know.

What happened to the pilot program in Washoe County?

I think that also got off the ground, and I think you can drive around town and even see outside of a law office, "ADR Provided Here," or whatever. I'm sure that many of us have seen it.

It might have not meant much at the time, until they realized what that's all about. We wanted to introduce a resolution to the supreme court on the judicial college, because we have wonderful opportunities in northern Nevada to work together to establish a specialized training program in ADR for Nevada judges.

At the judicial college?

Yes, as the judges are going through their training.

Let me understand. Was this saying that it could be attorneys or non-attorneys who were trained to do arbitrations and mediations?

Yes. The people who actually approached me about setting up this neighborhood justice center were non-attorneys. Clearly, they've got to have training, as do attorneys, because it is a different way you handle something. The hope was that this would be less contentious, it would be less expensive, and that it would take off.

And save court time?

Yes. Oh, absolutely. I think most people have sort of a fear of the judicial system, if they have to go, if they have to be confronted with it, anyway. It seems too formal; people wear robes. Then there are other people there deciding your fate, if indeed it is a trial by jury.

That feeling that your fate is being decided by somebody.

By people you don't know, who don't know you, who are just going to listen to some facts, and they may see the facts quite differently than you do. The fact may be presented in a fashion that you don't really like. You'd like to be able to tell it yourself, but you can't. So this is much more flexible and much more informal, and actually in many cases it has done quite well. It certainly has not revolutionized the judicial system, but nobody really expected that. Like anything else that's new and different, you have to have cheerleaders for it, just as we've discussed Chuck McGee being a cheerleader for the family court system.

This was, as I mentioned, presented to me by lay people who were very interested in it. In fact, they had a condominium or something in Hawaii, and Hawaii was utilizing it. For some reason, they thought it was great. I don't believe they had experience with it, but read about it and kind of brought the issue back in.

One of the things that LCB staff does for you is look throughout all the rest of the states, see what kind of programs, if any, other states have, how well they work, how the process was established, who could be arbiters, what the monetary cutoff line might be—those kinds of things.

So they really do help with the background research.

Oh. They are incredible. The staff of LCB—I cannot say enough about them—all of them—whether they're research, legal, audit, financial. I mean, they're just dedicated to government service. Of course, now it's so much easier on the Internet. At that time, it took a long time, but you felt very comfortable that what information you were getting was the best, reliable, true. This was something quite new, and not much was known about it. I can tell you that those kinds of things are still in operation. How successful it has been, generally, I really don't know, because clearly at that time I was running for a different office myself. In addition to that, I had an accident, so I sort of lost track of it.

One of the things that you wanted to talk about, especially when we were talking about foster care, family court, and working with families, was elementary school counselors.

Yes. It seemed to me, almost everything you deal with in government, if you can deal at the front end with prevention, then at the end of the day, you spend far less money; you don't have as many problems; you've taken care of the problems hopefully before they become major ones.

For example, in dealing with criminals, the total criminal justice system, if you're able to get some education in the prison system and have drug abuse programs in prison, wouldn't you think they would? Almost 75 to 80 percent of the people who are committed to prison are there because of substance abuse problems in one way or the other. The point being that if you deal with something at the beginning, you're better off at the end.

An example is elementary school counseling. It seems to me that in my day third grade was a big grade to have elementary school counselors. Unfortunately, we had very few in our state when I got interested in this issue. So I thought this would be something that if they could sort of pinpoint kids by third grade who might be having reading problems, maybe problems at home, a variety of things that somebody trained could pick up on, spend some time with, then that person would not end up in the sixth or seventh grade being a real problem—not being able to read very well, maybe not being able to write or do math or those things that really need to be done to live in our world today. So I decided to introduce something like this.

What I wanted to do, and this was hardly a big deal, I just wanted to have one elementary school counselor per three hundred pupils. That seems like a lot. It is. But at that time that was the national standard, and we weren't anywhere close. I don't remember the exact number, but this was a huge jump. If you think of one person being responsible for three hundred pupils, it may be that only four of them need help.

Yes. Or even 10 percent would be 30 students. Or 20 percent, 60 students.

Yes. Nobody challenged me on the logic of starting early and picking out students—that's not where I was challenged. I was challenged by the teachers association, much to my surprise, and I had been endorsed by the teachers association from the first time I'd run for office. I was so disappointed. They did not support this because of funding. They didn't want to disturb the distributed school fund. I was very disappointed in a group that had endorsed me, that I felt strongly about. Finally, as session after session went on—not because of anything I did; it was way after I was involved with this—there were some changes made. But the thing that disappointed me the most about this was the fact that the educational groups, such as WCTA, Washoe County Teachers Association, or Clark County Teachers Association, or NSEA, Nevada State Education Association, were not cheering and saying, "Wow! Here's a great idea! We totally agree with it, and we're going to support it." That did not happen at all. As I say, it seemed to me to be a moderate suggestion to have one per three hundred pupils, and that did not happen.

It didn't pass that session—or for several sessions?

It never did, because it wasn't a single piece of legislation. It would have been done in the finance committees when you're dealing with the distributed school fund. It needed a lot of expertise to do that, but that's not to say it could not be done. It was just that it was my first big moment of disillusionment and being disheartened with a group that I had supported and still did, and they still did me, as well, after that. Everybody who doesn't like the teachers association always says they're only interested in their paycheck and not the kids. Well, I don't want to believe that for a moment and don't, but it sort of did make me question it a little bit. It's one of those things, I guess, that you learn in the political process and try to work with it and move on.

I'm trying to understand, because I know that there are elementary school counselors.

Oh, there were at that time, yes.

So the issue that didn't get passed was having a manageable amount of three hundred students?

Exactly, the ratio.

The ratio. And that never got passed. It still hasn't to this day?

I can't say that. All I know is it didn't pass when I was making the attempt. I do believe, Vikki, that I've talked of one other jolt to me, when I had told the State of Nevada Employees Association that I'd support something, and when it came, I did not support it, because it had been amended so much. It was nothing like the original. That's another worrying experience that one has. I also believe I've talked about the fact that when you introduce any piece of legislation, and it affects anybody, you go and visit with them prior to having a hearing, whether it's a state agency or whatever it might be, and let them know what you're doing. You can work out any problems, if you can, and if you can't, OK. You take your best shot in a hearing. I think these are things you learn as you go along to make you, hopefully, more effective.

I understood that with the state employees association, where you said that you hadn't communicated as much as, you realized later, would have been helpful.

Yes. You're correct.

Was it similar with the state employees association?

No. No.

You had been communicating?

Yes, I had. Yes.

But they still didn't support it?

Yes, but that was different. With the State of Nevada Employees Association,

SNEA, I was clearly in the wrong, because I should have let them know. I just assumed they would have known. [laughter]

That they understood how much it had been amended.

Right! That it had just changed like 360 degrees. But they didn't. I had said one thing, did another, and hadn't told them. I think if I'd told them what I'm just saying to you, they would have had a different view. Hopefully, they would have, because that was the thing they said they were the most dismayed about.

As it turns out, though, as you work through this, they're not going to hold it against you forever, because they need your vote. I'm certainly not going to hold it against them, because in that case, I thought I was absolutely wrong. I was surprised that they were so upset, but then when they explained it to me, or maybe Jean Ford explained it me, then I did see.

[laughter] It was clear.

Yes. As long as you're there, you hope that you learn and don't do the same thing again, and I don't think I have, but in talking about one's life, regardless of what you're doing with your life, regardless of how old you are, or how much experience you have, there's always things you need to learn. It's life learning, I guess.

Life learning as you go along. The elementary school counselor issue obviously was related to funding and how funding was distributed. We had another topic to talk about, and that was the estate tax.

Yes, since we're talking about taxes. The estate tax, is really if you have an estate. If you have enough money, you set up a trust. Depending upon the amount in that, whatever the federal government law is at that time, you might have to pay half of it to the federal government, and half of it would remain with whomever you had expressly granted that to in a trust or a will. This was an idea that came to us from Bill Harrah, of Harrah's casinos. That was my first experience knowing anything about the estate tax. I was not on the committee of taxation to hear the arguments, but Bill Harrah had a very terrific lobbyist at the time, John Giannotti. Bill Harrah was very interested in having his particular estate tax wind up back in Nevada. Now, one of the things that a lot of people did not know, and I certainly didn't, was that this is really a rebate, that you pay it to the federal government, but each state had the right to ask for a certain percentage back. We were losing out on money by not buying into this. My first acquaintance with this was in the 1970s, that we were one of very few states that did not ask. I'll use lay language. I'm sure there are other ways of describing it—asking for this rebate back. The chairman of the assembly taxation at that time was named Paul May. He was a great friend of the banking industry. My mind is already working ahead, thinking I'm not going to be able to answer my own question. But Paul May would never let this bill out of the taxation committee, because the bankers were always opposed to it.

The question? Why? I can't answer that right now. But maybe they wanted to be trustees? That's another question that I need to explore before we're done with this project. Often Paul didn't even have a hearing or didn't even bring it up for a vote. You could imagine the lobbyist for a major player, as Bill Harrah was at that time, not being given the due he's expected he probably should, was very unsettling, to say the least. After a number of sessions of this occurring and just hearing about it, the way it was explained to me, I thought, "Well, for heaven sakes, why are we not doing this?" There was nothing negative about it. Again, you ask yourself, why would the bankers oppose this? I think it had something to do with their being often a trust officer, and maybe it meant that they would be losing some money, if you follow the money. You should on almost every piece of legislation. I suspect that had something to do with it.

After a couple of sessions of this, John Giannotti went around, and I don't know if he did it himself, but he went around with a roll call sheet, and these were little pieces of paper with everybody's names and "yes," or "no." He was going around and asking everybody, "Are you going to support AB32?" So you keep that as your little record. I remember he had this and asked everybody on the floor of the assembly—forget the committee—how they would vote on this. He had enough votes on the floor of the assembly—at that time there were forty people, so he obviously had twenty-one—to pass this. Now, the question is, how do you get it out of the committee when it's never brought up for a vote? We didn't have those timelines that we do now.

There's a process that we will get to when I talk about a bill dealing with high school freedom of speech, that this is almost the same kind of issue. There is a way of yanking a bill out of a committee, above, beyond, around—however you want to describe it—the committee chairman. So that's what he was going to do. And then, I don't know, a week later, whatever period of time passed, he came and let everybody know that he wasn't going to do that. The reason I heard—I was not on the committee, but it sounded like a good idea—was the fact that when one does this, it is a slap in the face to the committee chairman, and it would leave a lot of animosity, not only against the chairman, but against everybody who voted to pull it out from under the chairman. So it was discarded, and it was not done then. I don't remember exactly what year it was done, and that money, our estate tax rebate, was used for a variety of things—some at the university.

Of course, if the estate tax is eliminated or greatly reduced at the federal level, then that means all those funds that were being used for various programs won't be there anymore. I believe people are now looking at that possibility, I'm sure at other state legislatures as well as our own, thinking about, "Wow. What's going to happen if . . . or what's going to happen when . . . ?"

So that again is another little, interesting note about the process and how those things work or not work. Obviously, Bill Harrah and the people who work for him felt that that was not a positive thing to do at that time for whatever reason. Clearly, they understood, when they first started out, what exactly it was all about. So something must have occurred, which I'm not aware of, and would have no reason to be aware of, that made them stop and take a look at it again.

But it's a real serious issue today, with the federal government considering cuts in this.

It is. I suspect that the estate tax does change as time goes on, but it's never gotten to the point where it seriously has been considered and might indeed happen, that it's going to be pared way back or eliminated altogether. That will have a very negative impact on many programs. When you say to somebody, "It's possible that this is not a given amount of money every single session; it might not happen," people don't believe that.

It's always been there.

Yes. This is an aside, but when you think about reducing classroom size, the fact that that was done rather successfully, where are all those other students put? Where are they placed? That may mean more classrooms. And, of course, it has. Often you have trailers or mobile classrooms on the property. But those are things that at that time people think, "Oh, well. That's going to be in the future. We don't need to worry about that this session." There were a lot statistics that showed if you reduce the number of students in a classroom, particularly one through three, that the educational results are a lot better. I'm sure that's true. Makes sense. But on the other hand . . . .

But where do you hire the extra teachers?

Yes. Where do you put them?

Where are the classrooms for them to be?

Right. So all those things are hidden costs, if you will, and, obviously, in this case it was hidden well enough for a long time, the estate tax. But now it may be coming due, so to speak.

It seems like it's going to have a tremendous impact in terms of education, universities and community colleges and so on.

Well, I did mention universities. I don't know. I can't tell you today all the different programs that the money is going toward. I suspect it probably fluctuates a little bit, but once you start on that path, then I'm sure that the states expect it each and every time, for twenty years, I'd say. It may be greatly reduced, and then there's going to have to be some tough decisions made as to who does get that estate tax money and who doesn't. I'm sure the people who have the estates probably don't think of it in that way and probably would be happy if that happened.

Because it would mean more money for their heirs.

It had to do with the Midwestern part of our country, leaving farms, I believe, where this really took hold, and particularly when you're running for president of the United States, the heartland might be real important for you.

Now, we're going to start in on the study of grand juries. Why don't you give us some background.

Yes, I will. In fact, again, this is another and the last interim committee that I chaired. Of course, I served on many others, but we're not going to get into those.

But this was one you really wanted?

Yes, I did, because I've always been someone who wants to open up the process, whether it's been the legislative process, or the Reno city charter, changing that to allow people to be able to vote directly on a mayor. This again is slightly opening the door to grand juries, which are totally secret, and there was a reason for that. This was done in 1984, interim, and then presented to the 1985 session. The senate majority leader probably thought this is exactly why I wanted to do this and felt that this would not be a good thing for me to chair and had his person in mind.

Who was the senator majority leader then?

Jim Gibson. He was a very powerful man, in the same way that Bill Raggio is today. He wanted Jan Stewart [Janson F. Stewart], who was then the chairman of assembly judiciary and also a member of the same religious group that Jim Gibson

was a member of—the LDS Church. It was a shock to him, I believe, because an assembly person had told me that I probably wasn't going to get this, even though I'd introduced the resolution creating this. So this was the one time that I sort of got my ducks in a row prior to the legislative commission meeting when these decisions were made. So it was a surprise to the senate majority leader, I'm sure.

This was something of interest to me, not only from what I've just discussed, but because the American Bar Association had examined the role of grand juries in our country, and they came up with a set of rules and practices relating to the grand jury. What I thought would be appropriate is for us to examine those rules and suggestions and compare them with how we operated in the state of Nevada.

So they examined the rules that already existed? Is that what you're saying?

No. Actually, *they* came up with what they thought should be done.

Should be examined.

Yes. It was my idea to compare our laws, relatively speaking, to the suggestions made by the American Bar Association. So an interim committee was established, which I chaired, and Jan Stewart, who was a very nice guy that I just discussed, was vice chairman. Serving on it was Senator Bill Raggio, Senator Spike Wilson, Assemblyman Lonie Chaney, who was an African-American representing one of the Westside assembly districts in Las Vegas; Assemblywoman Jane Ham, who was a very close friend of Patty Cafferata's—they tended to vote alike; it was sometimes thirty-eight to two—and then Assemblyman Jim Stone, who was another attorney and, in fact, was a district court judge at one time in Washoe County.

So, we again had a number of meetings throughout the state: in Washoe County, in Las Vegas, and in the rural areas. There were some interesting suggestions made, and I'm going to discuss some of those now. Of course, the idea of the grand jury is that people don't know who's on it. It could be your neighbor. You're not supposed to say anything that's gone on there, unless at the end of the time, if some corrective action needs to be taken, then that becomes public, of course. I'm going to run through some of the recommendations that this subcommittee made, and it was based upon the ABA's recommendations.

Well, one of the biggest changes was the fact that this would allow a witness who is the subject of an investigation to be accompanied by counsel in his appearance before the grand jury.

And that had not been?

That's correct. That's one of the biggest situations that any person, such as myself or you, who do not know a lot about the law, would go in there all by themselves without any idea, and they might say something that was right but would be construed differently. Now, of course, the argument against this is, you don't want a grand jury to be like a mini trial, because that's not its purpose either. These things need to be examined more closely by the judicial system. So the compromise that was made was the fact that the witness and also the subject, of course, could have legal counsel there. But they were only to ask legal counsel questions, and then they would answer them. In other words, the attorney would not take over.

Would not speak for them?

No. Well, in a way they were speaking for them by helping them answer, but they weren't talking to the grand jury as an individual. I wanted to look here, and maybe I'll have to come back, so I can absolutely talk about that specific thing, because it was pretty important. If I may, I'm going to read this from the report, and these will become, of course, part of the record, as well. "Any person called to testify before a grand jury must now leave the grand jury room in order to consult with his attorney. This requires the witness to understand and recall in precise detail each question asked and to convey that information to the attorney who is waiting outside the grand jury room." So if he doesn't exactly phrase it the same way, or remember it exactly . . . .

Or he doesn't understand it.

Yes. Right. "To eliminate any prejudicial effect of a witness's exits." The fact that he gets up and leaves the room—some people are going to think, "Oh. I wonder why he needs help."

"To eliminate any prejudicial effect of a witness's exits from the room to confer with his counsel and to increase the efficiency of the proceeding, the subcommittee recommends that the legislature is allowed to be accompanied by counsel in his appearance before the grand jury. While the first ABA principle"—and this is obviously their most important suggestion—"urges that all witnesses be allowed to be accompanied by counsel"—that's the ABA principle—"the subcommittee determined that only a witness who is the *subject* of an investigation truly needs to be so accompanied."

Oh. So originally, it was recommended for any witness.

Let me finish up on this. But you're correct. "The subcommittee also determined that to allow the witness's counsel to elicit testimony or to address the grand jurors would turn the hearing into an adversarial proceeding. Therefore, the subcommittee will reflect and . . . ." Whenever we mention "subcommittee," it is the Nevada subcommittee. "The subcommittee believes that the role of the counsel allowed in the grand jury room should be limited solely to advising his client. The grand jury usually does not hear testimony from the subject of an investigation before an indictment is issued. Since there may be cases where an indictment might not be issued upon hearing the subject's side of the story, thus, avoiding the cost to the state and to the defendant of an unnecessary trial."

This is another suggestion. "The subcommittee recommends that the legislature allow the subject of an investigation to testify before the grand jury if he signs a waiver of immunity."

So those are two big things, but going back to the first, I think that sometimes this appears to be using the word *witness*, which has a different connotation to you and I than the subject, because—let me repeat it again—"While the first ABA principle urges that all witnesses be allowed, the subcommittee determined that only the witness truly need . . . ."

See, they're using the witness, that same term, who is the *subject* of an investigation. So clearly, they thought that was a fine idea but in a limited way. Basically, the grand jury is the prosecutorial tool, if you will. The DA is the one that normally takes issues to a grand jury. Defense attorneys aren't in there, except under these suggested changes, and I've discussed a bit number two, which I just read into the tape here.

Previously, they had not heard anything from the subject; the person was indicted without ever having a chance to say anything, prior to this study?

I can't answer that right now, not after the fact.

At least, that's how it sounds?

But the other one sounded different, too. So why don't you put a little question mark by that? "It requires district attorneys to make all reasonable attempts . . . ." Now, remember, I just said that this was a district attorney's heaven, if you will, being a prosecutor.

"It requires district attorneys to make all reasonable attempts to notify a person of his right to testify, unless notification may result in flight or endanger other persons or obstruct justice." I think that's fairly self-explanatory. When you ask the question, "Were these things different?" Well, obviously, they were different, or we wouldn't be recommending changes.

These are all the recommendations?

Yes. I think that I do have on one of those lists, which I've set over there, all the ones that were introduced into the legislature. They're phrased a little bit differently than these in the report are for some reason, because these have BDR numbers after each one of these suggestions. These first three things look like they all appeared in the same BDR down to number five. So there are a lot substantive things, it looks like, in one bill.

Then we can talk about which things actually passed from the recommendations or were introduced as bills.

Well, we could. What I have is the things that we introduced as bills, but the record that I have here does not tell me whether they passed or not. To be honest, I cannot remember. That was back in the mid 1980s; that's twenty-some years ago. I just can't remember that. We certainly could find that out.

OK. We don't have a list of those?

No. We have the list of them as we did with everything else; these were things I had introduced. Now, some things, obviously, I can remember in great detail, such as the abortion issues and Equal Rights Amendment. Maybe I should, but I just don't remember all of this. I remember what the thrust of it was, why we did it, and what we hoped to achieve.

Another suggestion, a summary of a recommendation, I guess: "Limit the period of confinement for a witness who refuses to testify before a grand jury and is found in contempt." I'm not going to be able to explain any more about that. Maybe I should just skip that one. "Prohibited district attorney from calling a person to testify before a grand jury regarding matters which have been determined to be within his constitutional privilege against self-incrimination."

So that would be a no-no for the district attorney. "Require the district attorney to inform orally any witness subpoenaed to testify before a grand jury of the general nature of the grand jurors in their area of inquiry." Because sometimes in the past witnesses would walk in, and they didn't know why they were there. They might think about, "What could this be?" "Could be this, and then I did that wrong." That seems to me as being *too* secret.

Obviously, that's what all of this is, opening up the process a bit more than it

has been. Most people, probably, if you ask them, "What is a grand jury?" they're not going to know. They're not going to be able to answer that. Grand juries sometimes go on for years, a very long period of time. But the average person wouldn't know that and shouldn't know that, actually.

"Allow a witness to review his previous testimony before a grand jury. Allow the subject of the investigation, if the grand jury does *not* indict him, to decide whether to make public the fact that no indictment was issued."

If you are brought before a grand jury and, when they're all done, they say, "You know, it's not enough to indict, to bring you into a real trial proceeding," then it would be up to you to make a decision. Do I want a press release on this, or do I want the DA to say anything? Because most people shouldn't even know that I *was* the subject of an investigation, because this is supposed to be all secret stuff. I'm sure you've heard the term "star chamber."

I have.

That is a description, very often, of the secrecy, not necessarily of this, but also when there have been periods where judges sometimes will decide among themselves, which, of course, they should not be doing that. But that's another whole issue, so we won't go there.

"Require a district attorney to disclose to the grand jury any evidence of which he is aware that would tend to substantially negate guilt." That seems like a logical thing but, obviously, up until this time, there was a question whether that was being done, because, if you remember, by listing all those people who were on the committee, most of them were attorneys. Attorneys add a lot of star power, if you will, on this subcommittee. Excluding myself and a couple of the other assembly people, all the rest were not only in leadership positions, but also considered to be pretty good attorneys. Of course, Bill Raggio used to be a district attorney, and this was a tool that he used, so he would be very interested in not opening this up too much. Spike Wilson is an attorney, who represents a variety of different positions, I should say, mainly civil, but both defense and plaintiffs.

So was he more in support of opening it? Spike Wilson?

Oh, I'm sure. But you have to understand that that's where Bill Raggio's head was coming from, because that was his first job before he got elected to the legislature—the DA of Washoe County.

And another recommendation was, "Prohibiting a district attorney from making any statement to a grand jury which would be impermissible at a trial," what we call a petit jury, small jury. "Require the district attorney to inform the grand jury as to the specific elements of the crimes to be considered by it before he seeks an indictment." That seems pretty self-explanatory. I can't imagine that was not done before.

It makes it sound like a person hardly stood a chance with the grand jury.

I suspect that's why all these changes were being made.

These are all the recommendations.

I think they repeated two pages in here. Yes. There were thirty recommendations, so I don't think we should go through all of them, or we're going to be here for some time. I think that one gets the sense of what

a grand jury was and what the subcommittee was about and what they tried to do. I was just gazing through here while I'm talking, and, for example, it talks about "requiring the recording of all matters before a grand jury by a certified shorthand, *except* any confidential communication between a witness and his legal counsel; and the legal counsel is allowed to accompany the witness before the grand jury and the deliberations and voting of the grand jury." Those are things that will *not* be in any kind of a record, and so, again, you can see that everything was not opened up.

I'm sure that somewhere in this report—here it is. All the recommendations of the ABA . . . well, commentary to the principles, "The American Bar Association has previously gone on record in 1975, supporting the right of a witness to have counsel present in the grand jury room. Principle number one represents a reaffirmation of that position," et cetera.

Was your study pretty much supportive of what the ABA was recommending then?

Yes. But I think you can tell right there that there was some massaging of the criteria to probably cut somewhere in between what it was at that time and what they wanted it to be and kind of split the hair down the middle. The Appendix A of this report lays out the ABA grand jury principles, so if anybody is specifically interested—actually, it is pretty interesting stuff—they can compare. Maybe I should read a couple of these principles, and we can compare them to what the subcommittee recommended.

The general idea of this report, without getting any more in depth, is the fact that a committee was established; we used the

ABA guidelines to check to see how our law stepped up to that; three, "to make suggestions to the next legislative session," that this subcommittee felt were where Nevada needed to change the law to be more similar to the ABA principles. I think in many cases they did take their recommendations; in some cases they did not; and in most cases they sort of moderated somewhat.

As you can imagine, we had many, many attorneys and people who'd been on grand juries, people who were targets of grand juries, and district attorneys testifying before the subcommittee. Each of these reports, by the way, does list everybody that testified before any of the interim committees throughout the state. So that's another value of these reports.

I was wondering if there were some pretty heated testimonies and discussions on the committee.

Oh, there were, particularly at first. Many of these reports—I don't know how they're done today—I suspect the same way. They take money to do this, because you pay the legislator, and, obviously, the staff's got to travel around, as do legislators, if you don't do it all in one locale. Now you can teleconference a lot of things, so that negates some of the travel money. The fact is that these are done at the very end of the session, or they used to be, so if you weren't really interested in things and didn't go to the legislative functions . . . . I don't know what it's called now, but it was basically a committee that oversaw what was going on within the legislature itself, then, say, a district attorney association, the state of Nevada might not have known when this was being approved.

Normally, the resolution itself is introduced somewhat earlier, and if they have a lobbyist, which they certainly do, then they will know that this is a possibility.

I know a lot of the arguments did come down to just what you would expect: district attorneys versus the defense attorneys, because if an indictment was handed down by a grand jury, then the target normally, if he or she could afford it, would hire a private defense attorney; if not, then a public defender would be appointed. But, as we used to say, this was the district attorney's "sandbox," a grand jury room, to play in. That was modified substantially by this report. So you're correct. There was a lot of heated debate, but very normally in interim reports, there were not big arguments back and forth between legislators and the persons testifying. I was very, very committed to this, and I was arguing with Mills Lane, let's say, when he would retort, "Well, I think this is a stupid idea," and then I'd get all heated. Normally, you didn't do that, because that took way too much time, for one thing, and secondly, you did want to hear what they had to say, because hopefully you're going to come up with a balanced product.

So if a DA said it was stupid, you wanted to know why, so you could get that information.

Exactly. Yes. These reports do not include minutes or anything of that sort. It's all summarized by staff. There's no record of what was successful or not. It was just the presentation to the legislature at the next session, which was 1985.

So we're going to talk about some that passed.

Yes, we are. It might be interesting to note that the descriptions of some of these bills are somewhat different than the ones that came out, and they really shouldn't be.

The recommendations.

Because each of these had a BDR number. Oh, as a matter of fact, they do. So let me just find them, and I can compare.

And the BDR number is what?

Bill draft request—that's what that stands for. However, if you remember, I mentioned that like the first five recommendations were encompassed in the same bill draft request. So when I look over here, I see a bill that I introduced, and I find that interesting because these bills were only introduced by me. You remember how many other senators I had on the committee? Maybe they were upset with the recommendations, I don't know. Well, Bill Raggio, of course, was back. Spike Wilson was there that session, because I took over for him in 1987. So I don't know. But this senate bill 103 changes standards for access: "Provides certain rights and privileges for persons likely to be indicted by a grand jury." Now, that has a certain bill number by it, but that's the bill number we had in the first five . . . . I don't have a copy of the bill here to tell you which of those five principles were encompassed. But that did pass, as did senate bill 104.

Another bill, number 105, did pass: "Enlarges the scope of confidentiality of proceedings of grand jury and increases penalty for disclosure." That bill draft request number seems to be attached to this: "Increases the penalty for breaching the secrecy for a grand jury proceeding and expands the group of persons to whom the penalty applies." Well, that even enhances the district attorney's power rather than the other way around, but that's not to say that the ABA didn't make that suggestion. I'd have to go back and look, because the ABA is not a defense attorney organization. It's something for all attorneys to belong to.

So by increasing the confidentiality and the penalty for disclosure, that's on the side of the district attorney to have it be a private matter until there is quite a bit of information.

That's correct. There were quite a few that actually did pass, but by looking at this list, it would be hard for me to tell, because the descriptions are somewhat different than we found in the report.

Here's one that we specifically know. It requires the grand jury to notify a witness of the general nature of the inquiry. And that was specifically a standard.

And that did pass?

That did pass. I can see there were probably about four or five bills that did pass, and that doesn't mean there were just four or five subjects, because oftentimes, if it's the same chapter, they will put them all together in one bill—more of an omnibus bill.

Did you feel successful about this committee at the end of it?

Yes, I did. I realized it was going to be a very tough row to hoe, particularly in a very conservative judicial state such as Nevada, which I think it is. This will be perceived as whittling away at the district attorney, who is more of a hero here in Nevada, maybe, than in some other states or jurisdictions. So, yes, I think just the fact that we had a discussion about all these issues itself is really important, because most people don't know what a grand jury is all about, or what they're supposed to be doing. What do they do, and how do we learn what they do? All of those issues, I think, are very important. So, if for no other reason than that, I think it was a positive.

The next topic we're going to address is regional planning and that always seems to be a hot topic any time it's being discussed these days. Give me a little idea of how things were when this all came up, the part that you worked on. Were there regional plans prior to this?

Well, I guess I can tell you that there was WCOG, Washoe Council of Governments. I've discussed home rule before, but the reason the legislature got involved, I was approached by many people, as were other members of our delegation, about the fact that people were frustrated that something would get zoned and right away would change, and the fact that there seemed to be *no* consistent policy of growth and planning in the Truckee Meadows. Not just this—they didn't want to isolate the city of Reno versus Sparks versus the county. A lot of people do feel they live in a meadows, in a countywide area, even though they may just live in the city of Sparks. We, the Washoe legislators were approached, and that's why we got involved, because people just said, "They fight among each other; they can't do anything; you can't trust them to do anything. If they do, it's probably going to be wrong." So they approached the Washoe delegation to say, "Can you help us in setting up some mechanism or way where we feel more comfortable? We realize that they're going to take a system-wide approach, if you will, or a county or a meadows approach." So we met, actually, as a full Washoe County delegation. Senator Don Mello chaired that group at that time. All of us who represented Washoe County were on that. That was our delegation. So that's what started the legislature's interest in this and why it wasn't left up to the local governments at that time, because it already *had* been, and clearly, our constituents didn't think they'd done a very good job with it.

What they wanted was something that would maybe tie their hands a little bit more and force locally elected officials to meet

with one another, to understand one another, and, hopefully, to make things that work better for others that live there. So this was a huge job. It occurred right in the middle of the session, At that time I was chairing the senate judiciary committee. The chairman, Senator Mello, appointed me as chair of this subcommittee, and he also appointed from Sparks Jan Evans, and, of course, Senator Mello came from Sparks. The other member was Assemblyman Bob Sader. He was then chairman of the assembly judiciary committee and from the county.

We did have LCB staffers who were very important, because not only were they dedicated, but they also had all been regional planners, or their background was in planning. The two I remember off the top were Bob Erickson, who at this time was director of the research arm of the Legislative Counsel Bureau, and Fred Weldon, who worked within that research division of LCB. So they were the staff, and particularly Fred Weldon, but they were appointed there because of their familiarity with the issue of planning.

So the subcommittee was set up, and we met over and over and over and over—not only just with ourselves, but including the local people. When you look at the record, you'll see that, in fact, at that time, the city of Sparks had a *great* manager, Pat Thompson. She went off to become the manager of Santa Rosa. It was a move up, anyway. Jim Spoo was the mayor of the city of Sparks at that time. I could go through and name other people, but they'll come to mind.

So we'd meet with them, and they acted a little bit better than they did in their local jurisdictions, because they were under the threat, to be honest with you, of a state law. In addition to those small meetings, we then had many hearings. We had hearings in Washoe County. In fact, one of them that I read about last night was the senate government affairs committee hearing before it was all introduced into the legislature. Just the process of having hearings and getting input and deciding what was going to be in a bill draft was incredible. We all were very busy. I just mentioned what Bob Sader's job was during that session. Jan Evans was on the money committee, vice chair, in addition to this major responsibility, and I was the chair of the senate judiciary committee. That's kind of who participated, and we did have all of these meetings. Then we took the show on the road after it was finalized.

As we went along, of course, everybody was not happy. Some people were still upset and, well, that's just the way it was going to be. Most legislation that passes, everybody's not happy about. But we did have all these hearings, and some of them were at night, so more people could participate. I know we had one meeting that was a senate government affairs committee, which I also was on, because this bill was referred to that committee. We had it at Wooster High School. So we made some real attempts to reach out, not only to the people who would have to implement this and work with it, *but* our constituents, because that's where this hue and cry came from. This was in response to that. This was really, really government in action, of having something be a problem for people we represented. We heard that; we did something about it.

There are many, many proposals in here, and I'm not going to get into all of them, needless to say, but one of the things we were *not*—we were not planners. We did not intend to be involved in planning. We were there to facilitate this, to try to come up with something that was different, to hopefully have the three locally elected bodies work better together. Yet, that was a major undertaking.

Since I was chair of that group, I then was the main sponsor of that bill. When you look at the bill, which was Senate Bill 367,

it was effective June 17 of 1989. Seven senators are on this. I'll mention the names: Wagner, Mello, Raggio, Townsend, Beyer, Joerg, and Rhoads. Now, those that are still *there* include Raggio, Townsend, and Rhoads—Rhoads being Dean Rhoads from Elko, because he had a part of Washoe County, actually, and he probably does today, I don't know. This is a fairly substantive bill, as you can imagine. I think the bottom line was, this was a lot of work. We did it in addition to everything else. We went through seven different versions before it was introduced, and each version would come back, and then it would be discussed by all the people I've mentioned. The list of people who came to these meetings is also included in all this mass of material. Of course, it passed easily, because it came from the Washoe delegation. So if you lived in Clark County, you were not going to mess around with that; that's not your business. That's the way that works in the legislature.

Clark County had something similar. For example, I mentioned just yesterday about the role of Jim Joyce and the fact that there was a bill that he was lobbying on. The consolidation of—guess what—Clark County. Sort of the same concept. Unfortunately, that delegation was split. If you have the whole delegation supportive of something, people who weren't part of that are obviously going to look to the delegation. So that was an easy thing. The difficult thing came before, that the three-person subcommittee itself met at least four times. We met, in addition to that, three more times with representatives of the local government, and we came up with the bill draft and then took that show on the road.

Is that essentially what we have in place now for the regional planning?

Yes, pretty much so. In fact, every five years you must go back and examine this.

I don't know if that's what's going on now. I guess we could think back, 1989, and add five years and five years.

I'm wondering if the review of the process is starting, because I know I received a card in the mail.

Well, that's what I'm saying.

You may have, too, that there's a review of the regional plan, and the meeting in our neighborhood was being held on a certain night.

Oh, no. I've not received a card like that.

Oh. I'll actually bring it with me when I come over tomorrow, just to show you and see if we think it's related.

Well, that could be easily figured, because if you took 1989 and then added five years from that date forward, you probably could at least see if that was the year.

Probably in the fourth year getting ready for the annual review. Or a five-year review.

We will have available to people who are interested in this subject a list of all the recommendations. Of course, some of the most contentious ones were, who's going to be on this or that? How many is each government going to have? How is an executive director going to be chosen? All of this was the jockeying around. It happened also with every other piece of legislation. I'm thinking the airport authority, all of these different things, so that the bill may be three hundred pages long, let's say, and the people who come and testify are only talking about paragraph A

on page one, because that's who's going to be on it. If you have three from one group and two from another, then that becomes very contentious.

But I think that this was a very good idea. I'm sure there were big difficulties with it, but the concept I absolutely am committed to. In fact, Assemblywoman Chris Giunchigliani, whom I may have mentioned along this oral history, from Clark County, has been very interested in doing something like this in Clark County. She has asked my opinion on a variety of things. She's actually used one of my interns to do a lot of background on this, as well, but she has not proceeded. I think one session she did introduce a bill, but I don't think she's done that this session. She may have, and it just wasn't in our newspaper, so I would not have known about it.

As fast as Clark County is growing, it's interesting to think that they haven't had a workable system or process in place.

No, they don't. The problem is that it's very difficult to do, because you're goring somebody in their sides or in their body when you do anything that seems to suggest you're taking the power away from somebody and sharing it—just as we're talking about the chairmen of legislative committees. It's quite different being a member versus being a chairman, because you're going to have more control. It's not equal, I guess we should say.

Lack of control, if you're just a member.

Yes. Well, in this case, if you had three members, and somebody else had only two, or if they didn't like the way the executive director was being chosen, all of these things were examined ad nauseam by the people sent from local jurisdictions. A lot of those people are planners. There's a John

Hester—I noticed he appeared. I think he was the planner for either Reno or Washoe County, and he switched roles. I think he is now a planner for the other entity than he was at this time in 1989. I could be wrong about that, but his name rang a bell with me. [Since 1998, Mr. Hester has served as Reno Community Development Director.]

I think that this is why it was created. This is generally what it attempted to do, and it's been on the books now since 1989. All you have to do is pick up the newspaper, from which I cut out a couple little articles along the way. This is in 2002, almost exactly a year ago, "Well Equipped to Seek Changes." It talks about the members of Washoe County legislative delegation, that they were thinking of jumping into the battle between—guess who—the county and the cities of Reno and Sparks over the recently approved regional plan update. So that answers that question. I might want to go back and read these editorials, which I did not do because I didn't see any point to it, but now I can see that maybe I should have.

Something that's going on right now, and what's happened since it went into effect in 1989—you've had a chance to look over some recent editorials. What is the gist of them?

It sounds exactly like arguments made in 1989, that all of the contingency issues are still squabbling between the three governments, and this was clear that they were updating the regional plan, which was mandated by the legislation of 1989. It talks about the tax system, that when that tax shift occurred, it was more beneficial to some entities than to others. Both of these editorials, by the way, are from the *Reno Gazette-Journal*. There had been a ton of articles about this subject in the last year, and that was the reason why there was so much going on. They were actually talking about having a super-agency, sort of like the TRPA, the Tahoe Regional Planning Agency, but there would be problems with that. They basically said, "There's such a difference between responsibilities of cities and counties. They blur their obligations and responsibilities, and this is a very difficult area. They suggest that you could always go back to the legislature again. [laughter] I can't really address the fact, but I suspect that has not occurred, that there've been many major changes made, because our newspaper is very involved in this, and we would have seen something. There hasn't been much this legislative session about anything like this.

No, I have seen that as a major issue.

Part of it has to do with the concern that local officials have in terms of the annexation policies of Reno, the sphere of influence, and that precipitated a great deal of discussion. Now in Carson City, the city and the county are together. There's just not Ormsby County; there's no Ormsby County. That was an experiment, and it seems to have worked fairly well. They also talked about the taxing issues, and even with a big box on the Wal-Mart that was going to be over the line that separated Douglas County from Carson City. These editorials just said, "Hey! A lot of problems. Don't jump in and change things just because of this or that, but look at it and see if it's really, really important and necessary." Clearly, it is a daunting task, but we're still living with it in one way or another since 1989, and they're following the law. Yes, maybe the law needs to be amended, but that's not my job anymore, although I have a great deal of interest in it.

The requirement that they continue to talk has remained in effect on that. That's happening; it's just that it didn't cut out any squabbling.

Oh, yes. That's very true. It's hard for me to believe, when you think about it right now, on this day in this year, that the squabbling is probably never going to go away, even if you have a super-agency, such as TRPA—squabbling goes on there all the time. I'm sorry that our newspaper does not cover it as well as it should, but you can think back on an issue this year between Lake Tahoe property owners and the secretary of state of Nevada, who is now the current chair of the TRPA, and his view that *visual* environment or problems should be addressed. Of course, the people up there think that's ridiculous. You have the League to Save Lake Tahoe versus the property owners and so on. So these things are very difficult.

Such a variety of interests.

Yes, a variety of interests and who has the power, how that power is utilized, whether beneficial or not. Maybe some land-use attorneys would be very interested in how they could tweak the regional plan. I'm not talking about TRPA anymore; I'm talking about Washoe County. Possibly, they happen to be very interested in the sphere of influence and so on. I thought that to myself through the last ten years or so. That's a possibility, but that's just conjecture on my part.

Getting back to the why this was done, how important it was, I still would never sit here and say, "I think it was a waste of my time." It was not. All I can hope is that judicious people will be elected to local governments with the best interest of where we live at heart. I really think, Vikki, talking about this, that people have no *clue.* I mean, they do have some clue in terms of particularly going I-80 West. Just take the Somersett project, the carving out of, oh,

all this land. The one good thing that happened out of all this is that the Ballardini Ranch is going to be saved. I think Canepa is the name of the people that had a lot of that beautiful agricultural land on I-80 West.

I'm really amazed that people, driving between Reno and Carson City, do see more developments, but they don't know the half of it. There are so many that have been already approved that haven't started to be built. People are going to be very dissatisfied, as they are now, in traffic patterns and traffic congestion. But you do what you can do. I'm not on a local governing body, would really not want to be, but this is one time that we heard from constituents when we tried to address it as best we could at that time. It's been many years later now that we're talking about this, so certainly things have changed, and in many cases it may depend upon who's on one of those bodies at any one time. Some may not be so aggressive in one way or the other. Anyway, I think it was time well spent on my part.

We're going to continue with senate issues that came up during your years in the senate.

Maybe I should finish up with TRPA.

OK. Since we were talking about planning, there's a topic of TRPA with Spike Wilson and Joe Dini, and a special session was involved. Maybe you can give us a little background on what was happening.

Yes. There was a kind of an ad hoc committee comprised of Spike Wilson and Joe Dini and myself. Joe was speaker of the assembly at that time, and I was a member, and Spike, of course, was in the senate. We were sent sort of representing Nevada, because anytime you change anything dealing with TRPA, you have to get both legislative bodies to agree in Nevada and in California.

And TRPA existed at that time?

Yes, it did. In fact, if I remember, I believe TRPA was created when Laxalt and Ronald Reagan were both governors. That's a *big* deal. I mean, to get one legislative body, which is *so* different from the other, to agree on anything is difficult.

I was reflecting on where we met. I just went on a little trip into California, and it was someplace in the Placerville area where we met in a café. The one person I remember being there from the California side was a man named John Garamendi. He was one handsome guy—he was big. He was born in Ely, Nevada, and at that time he was a state senator in California. Later on, he became the insurance commissioner of California and still is. You run for that office, actually. I suspect he had ideas of running for governor; he may have tried and lost. We were sort of talking to each other about changes in the TRPA. I believe this was the time we did this.

A major change occurred when we were talking about gaming casinos, actually, that they could not build anything more. They could only use the footprint of their existing building and maybe move things around internally. They could not add another floor or build out north, south, east, or west. So it was really attempting to create sort of a moratorium, if you will, on building. Now, some people would argue, probably rightly so, that the casinos on our side are a whole lot better than all these little strip motels and hamburger joints that were on the California side. There have been some big changes made at South Lake Tahoe with Embassy Suites and the Marriott Hotel having gone in there. I've not actually seen it, but read about it or heard about it. Those would be on the California side, I think. The

Marriott Hotel chain had actually looked at gaming at one point—not just there but throughout the country—but decided not to do it. I believe it's owned by members of the LDS church. I suspect that might've had something to do with their decision.

I was just pleased to be part of this, because this was a fairly important thing in my mind. It certainly still is—just the fact that it had to be done in a bi-state compact, so it had to be done with agreement between both legislative bodies. I do believe that we then came back, and a special session was called to approve changes in the bi-state compact. There may have been more changes than that, but I don't remember, because it affected Nevada. Interestingly enough, Harvey's Wagon Wheel—it was called at that time—burned. No. I think there was a bomb inside the casino that destroyed a lot of it. [A 1,000 lb. bomb was set off in Harvey's Lake Tahoe Resort Hotel-Casino in August 1980.] So they got to build a little bit differently. I believe that some newspapers had big question marks about that, suggesting that maybe they weren't quite convinced that this catastrophe happened accidentally. I don't have those thoughts, but there were some.

But the issue was raised.

Yes. There was some discussion about that. That really is all I wanted to say on that subject, because it does affect me, interestingly enough, in my now day job of being a gaming commissioner.

As long as we've kind of finished on regional planning, we wanted to say a few things about the gaming industry. You mentioned something about working on color-coding.

This was very interesting. This is probably one of the more interesting things that happened to me in my legislative career. I would put this up there with the laetrile, Gerovital experience. The Reno newspapers got hold of a "secret document" that was prepared by a lobbyist for a casino. This occurred in the mid-1980s, I believe. Richard Bryan was the governor. I can remember some of the people on the gaming control board at that time, because that does play into this, as well. What I'm going to discuss now is my involvement with this color-coded document. No legislator was supposed to know about this.

And this was the document that the Reno newspaper obtained?

Yes. This is the document that the Reno newspaper obtained somehow. It was prepared, as I say, for the president of a casino. However, this document was then sent around to other gaming CEOs. It hit the newspapers on the front page, and there were pictures of individual legislators, and we're talking now about northern Nevada, in the Washoe delegation. They had colors—there was green for very, very good legislators, and by that I mean those that the gaming industry could count on for anything and probably everything. Next, as you might guess, would be yellow, and I think there were maybe some other colors in between, but I'm only going to use green, yellow, and red. It had the pictures of the people who fell under that and actual comments about those individuals from this memo. Yellow was for legislators who, well, sometimes were and sometimes weren't with the gaming industry, and they had pictures of those people. And then there were red, and I was in the red column, and that means bad! Didn't support the gaming industry and kind of "thorns in our side." There were even things said about me and others. I obviously have blotted out what they said about me, but it was something

like what I just described, "Asked too many questions," or something like that. Well, this was *very* interesting to the readers, as you might guess.

And you didn't know anything about this before it hit the front page?

No. Oh, I may have known. Maybe someone called me to tell me that it was coming out the next day. I don't remember that.

But it isn't something that was general knowledge. It really was a secret.

Oh, it really was! It was only to be "eyes only" to the CEOs.

And if you knew about it, you only knew it shortly before it came out.

Yes. But I don't believe I did. In the text of the article, they did call the governor, who was Richard Bryan at the time, and asked him to respond to this. He basically focused on the other legislator and myself, saying that was the most ridiculous thing, that we were two of the best legislators—very complimentary comments from the governor. This was to be used, of course, in terms of reelection. You probably don't want those people who are reds to go back again.

Well, Senator Wagner decided to go and visit with each of the CEOs of these casinos and ask them what the deal is here. I remember my discussion with them. Of course, they were humiliated that this had gotten out and these negative things had been said. Now, some people, probably, were happy. I would not have wanted to have been green, very honestly. Maybe the yellow would have been good, but maybe just a compromise color. [laughter]

I remember my pitch. I thanked them very much, because I knew that was going to guarantee me reelection. People would not want to elect somebody who was in the *pockets* of anybody, particularly, at that time in the gaming industry. Well, that took the wind right out of those guys' sails, I'll tell you, because they knew I probably was right.

The fact is, I don't think I had any opposition that next time. The reason I don't know is because I was lucky enough not to have opposition a number of times. But I think that this did kind of guarantee no one was going to try to unseat me, because, needless to say, your constituents don't want that said about the person who represents them.

I can't imagine, unless you are married to a CEO of a casino or a gaming person high up in the administration or something. Anyway, I think that probably not very many people will have this in their oral histories ever, because I suspect it was not done again. Could have been, but they were just more clever about it. I do know how it got to be in the newspapers, but I'm not going to say that for my oral history, because that would be a very bad thing to do to this situation.

All right. You don't think anything similar to that goes on today, whether it's in writing or just understood?

I don't think so, but, to be honest with you, there are not too many people who ask really tough questions at the legislature. How would I know? Well, that probably is sort of a more conservative comment to make, but now being on the gaming commission, I have read a lot of the minutes dealing with bills that have passed, because the gaming commission must then adopt the regulations.

I don't know. I assume people know that passing a bill in the legislature is just the first step. To flesh that all out, you must have

regulations that are very specific. So I have particularly looked at the public gaming versus the private gaming, and that's something I will want to talk about at some other time. I've read all the minutes of that and did not think there were very many difficult questions asked. Hey, there may have been on other pieces of legislation, I don't know. Could go on today. I wouldn't know about it, even by being on the gaming commission. I *certainly* wouldn't know about it by being on the gaming commission.

And maybe the colors change, too. [laughter]

Maybe the colors went to fuchsia and lavender and black. That's kind of an interesting story to tell for my oral history— how the list was used in the exact opposite way from what they intended. I'm sure that the people who were "greens" made some quotes in the article. Part of this was used for contribution purposes, too, because people at that level in the gaming industry didn't go out and knock on doors for you. That was a way for them to know to whom they should commit financial resources for the next campaign.

How did you settle on the tactic of going in and thanking them for assuring your reelection?

I don't know. I just thought that was pretty clever. To tell you the truth, I was kind of nervous about it.

Were you? In going in and talking to them and starting off this way?

Yes! Starting off and taking the wind right out of their sails. I didn't know if they would be more furious at me or would feel like, "Ooh, she's got a good point." I really didn't know, but I do remember that each of the luncheons was fairly cordial. So I think they definitely got the point I was making. Now people knew this and that it had gone on before. We just didn't know about it before the color-coded list. Your question, "Does it go on today?" is a good one. I don't really know, since I'm not in elective office anymore, but I suspect, if it is, it's done in a totally different way.

Probably not in writing.

Probably not. However, just looking at some of the e-mails that some of the presidents write, e-mails that indict them right there, I'm amazed at what people do—put something down in writing in one way or the other, and think that no one's ever going to see it except those people who should.

Yes. And now with e-mail there's been an exaggerated situation, because it's easy to access.

Well, that's what I'm talking about, absolutely. So one doesn't know. But anyway, it happened once. Also, at that time you had to disclose—by the 1980s—the amount of money you got and from whom, so I'm sure that that was done very judiciously that particular election cycle. All people in the senate are not up for election at the same time, because we have staggered terms, and have always had staggered terms, as far as I know, even though the districts have become larger in size because we've lost legislators up here in northern Nevada.

Getting back to the color code, the only thing I remember is that it was done *here.* It was not done in Las Vegas, because Harrah's did not have other casinos in Las Vegas at that time. John Ascuaga's is locally owned, and the Atlantis and Peppermill weren't there. I think the Peppermill expanded in the mid-1980s.

The MGM would have been the only thing that was north and south.

Yes. Now, of course, that's the Hilton. Circus Circus—I don't remember when that was expanded up here to go into the Eldorado or Silver Legacy. I think that was probably *after* that. I do remember seeing other people's pictures. I can think of them in my mind right now, and they were all northern Nevada people.

There was another gaming issue. You talked about gaming industry invitations to meet abroad.

Yes, sort of in that same context in terms of the immense power that they have, and I will make some comments about gaming when I do the gaming section, because I don't want to appear that I'm negative on gaming, because I'm certainly not. I'm a regulator, and I feel *great* about the way we regulate the gaming industry in this state. I was not as aware of that as a legislator, not as familiar with the board and the commission. At that time—1987 and 1989—I was chair of the senate judiciary committee, and that is the committee where all the gaming bills flow through.

Bob Sader, as I've mentioned before, was the chair of the assembly judiciary committee. I got a call from a powerful gaming lobbyist and attorney. There is a group that's international known as the IAGA, International Association of Gaming Attorneys. It used to have very few members, because you'd only find them in Nevada, and some in New Jersey at that time. We do have some of the premier gaming attorneys in Nevada, even though it's spread throughout most of the other states. With the exception of Utah and Hawaii, each state in our country has some form of gaming.

They have an international meeting each year or every other year. I was invited, as was Bob Sader, to go to Australia free. Everything would be paid for, and I would be on a panel talking about gaming legislation, because I did chair the committee. At that time there weren't all these other gaming people, but it was growing even then. We're talking about worldwide now. Gaming goes on in other places besides the United States.

Right. Monte Carlo, and there are famous ones that you hear about.

Oh, yes. There's a big gaming industry in England, throughout Europe, many other places besides those that we always think of. Anyway, this was very tempting to go to Australia. I would have only had to be on a panel like one day, and the rest of the time, like a week, I could've done whatever. Well, maybe that stuff would have been arranged for me; I don't know. I declined, because I felt that the next session of the legislature, certainly there would be some gaming bills that came through the judiciary committee, that I would feel somewhat compromised if I had this great experience. I'm sure it would not have mattered to me, but I didn't want the appearance or the perception. Who would have known, for example, that the color code on legislators would have ever come out? That was my image, and it still is my image, and it is *real*. I've never done anything in all the years that I've been in government that I would ever regret. I was told that maybe my colleague on the assembly side was thinking about going, and I felt that was entirely his choice. He chose not to go, I believe. I never asked him, never talked about it. That was not my business. I was invited again by the same organization to Dublin, Ireland, and again declined to go.

It's sort of like the Barbra Streisand concert that I missed. I've talked about that, haven't I?

I don't believe so.

Oh. Well, that's another one of those stories.

I haven't heard about that one.

Well, yes, because that takes care of the gaming attorneys, and now I'm on the gaming commission. I thought about that when asking Governor Miller to appoint me.

There was another thing I really wanted to do. I just love Barbra Streisand, and she's had very few concerts. In fact, because I just happened to listen to her CD last night, I know it was twenty-seven years from one concert to the next. She was appearing at the MGM in Las Vegas, and, unfortunately, at that time there were informational pickets, an informational strike, against the MGM. I've maybe mentioned at some other time that the culinary union is so strong in Las Vegas that most of the large casinos just settle with them right off the bat, but this was not the case at the time. This was when I was lieutenant governor, so it was between 1990 and 1994 or 1995.

The CEO of the MGM at the time was a Republican, and he wanted the governor to be there. I don't know if the only reason he wanted him to be there was because all this turmoil was going on or not. He declined because he didn't want to cross a picket line, even if it was an informational picket, which I understand is slightly different. So then, the CEO calls the next person down the line, and that was me. Since he was a Republican, and I was a Republican, I'm sure he thought that I would definitely jump at the chance. I really wanted to, but I chose not to do that, as well, because I had been endorsed by the AFL-CIO when I ran for lieutenant governor, and I was the only Republican they had endorsed in a very, very long time. We now know, of course, that they endorsed Governor Guinn, but until that time, few and far between Republicans. So I felt that that was another commitment that I needed to keep. Oh, boy, did I want to go! It kept getting better and better, "Look, front row seats. We'll di-di di-di da." [laughter]

Because when he first asked me, I obviously said, "Oh, man! Do I want to do that? Yes!" [laughter] Then as he got on I kept thinking, "Oops!"

[laughter] Oops! Shouldn't have.

"Oops! I better not do that."

Shouldn't have let him know how much you want that, right? That's interesting.

Believe me. I am probably tempted far less than most legislators, but some of the temptations are pretty big—a whole trip to Australia or to Dublin, Ireland, or to do something else. In fact, with Barbra Streisand, I think that was the time when in the *first minute* that the Ticketron opened up—because this was before the Internet—everything was sold out.

Every ticket sold in the first minute?

Yes. In fact, the music I was just listening to last night was at Madison Square Garden, and it was three nights. Every single thing was gone in that minute.

It *is* amazing. I have to remember Barbra Streisand's appearance or the look on her face when she opened up the Oscar winner for the song for last year, and it was Eminem and the movie, *Eight Mile Road.* She looked like, "Aagh! Get *real!*" [laughter] She didn't say that, but that's exactly what was on her face! Because there's a big difference in her music versus somebody like Eminem. I suppose some people would think, oh, she's a fuddy-duddy

kind of singer—but not true. She cuts across *all* lines.

You said, "It was none of my business," whether Bob Sader accepted any of these invitations or not. Do you have a sense of how often people do accept or not?

No, I don't, but there have been other instances, and I think I've talked about the laetrile/Gerovital and how many people had bought into certain stuff with that. I've heard at other times when I was there that legislators really were very demanding. In fact, some of the people in the casinos resented it. Sometimes they were pressured into doing things that they really didn't want to do, very honestly. And that's the other side.

Asked for tickets or something like that, favors?

Absolutely that; or pushed, "I want to go up to this show at the lake, and I want to be on this floor, blah, blah." They're usually people you might not have a lot of respect for, anyway. You might question me, and I might think, "Oh, yes." If you mention that name, I'd say, "Yes. Doesn't surprise me," something like that. So, sometimes it works in reverse, particularly in this arena, because they have the entertainers, and you wouldn't probably put pressure on . . . well, I was going to say new-car dealers, but I take that back. [laughter] Maybe the pressure of them.

[laughter] Because they get pressured, too.

Well, let's say drugstores or something, I don't know, but, obviously, gaming is the one group you think legislators might go after. As of today, I have no idea. Actually, as a gaming regulator, I'm glad I have no idea, very honestly, because that is not my job anymore.

When you were speaking about the invitations from the gaming industry, you made a statement that you've never done anything that you were ashamed of, and that you didn't want to even present an appearance of doing something that would compromise your voting, which kind of leads us into a discussion of the ethics commission and when that was created.

Yes, but I hope if people said, "Who might be willing to introduce something like the ethics commission?" my name would be on a short list. Of course, this was one of those bills that people didn't take kindly to in the legislature, because it appeared to them that I was suggesting we *needed* something like this, because there must be a lot of unethical things that went on.

I do know that a lot of states have similar commissions or committees or oversight, because the Legislative Counsel Bureau staff, as they always do on most cases, look at what other states have done, what has worked, what hasn't worked. I believe the only other cosponsor on that bill was Senator Spike Wilson. I guess that sounds like a broken record, but it's the same kind of example as when we talked about the conservation easements in terms of the Nature Conservancy. It was the two of us, and I'm sure there were others on that. I decided that this would be a good thing to create and to even be able to give elected officials some way to go before a group and say, "I think I want to do this. Is this OK?"

People didn't see that side of it. They kind of saw, "She's pointing her finger at us."

There were a lot of different drafts of this, as you might guess. In the final analysis, it seemed to me to be a good idea. Now, people from Common Cause, of course,

were very much in favor of this. People of the ACLU were very much in favor of this. Unfortunately, those two groups don't have a whole lot of clout at the legislature.

What I decided might be fair was to pretty much structure who's going to be on here and *not* put Common Cause people or *not* put ACLU people on it. I felt this was a fair assessment, that they might have totally different concepts of what's ethical than we who serve, and that maybe it would be nice to have somebody who was a former city-council person on the commission. I suspect that maybe even Common Cause would think that this isn't strong enough, but at some point you've got to be fairly reasonable, and you've got to have people serving where they've not necessarily been there, done that, but they can better understand the dynamics of something that goes on.

So the composition of the commission right off the bat—this was fairly important— was structured so I believe you had a former legislator. Now, this may well have changed since that time, but the ethics commission is still in operation. You had the legislative commission, who were authorized to make an appointment of a former legislator that they thought would be someone who would represent the legislative body in a fine way, who had a good reputation themselves. There was also at that time an opportunity to appoint someone from a city council—same kind of criteria—a former city council person, someone of a great reputation in terms of ethics. That was chosen at that time by the legislative commission. Now, the governor was able to make some appointments, too, and he has up through the years. I say "he," because we haven't had a "she" yet as a governor.

I'll just give a general kind of description and the difficulty of getting this passed, as you may guess. Initially, it was deciding the number of people to serve on it, where these people should come from, what kind of backgrounds they should have. Was it going to have any staffing? Where would the staffing come from? What kind of jurisdiction would this group have? Of course, that was a very thorny issue.

I know Senator Wilson and Senator Wagner had to go to many different committees, and there were certain legislators, particularly in the senate—and we were both senators; it was a bipartisan approach—many were very, very offended that this legislation was introduced. Actually, it did pass. Now, it got watered down as it went along the way, as you can imagine. We start out with something that would be ideal. If you started out kind of further on down the food chain, then you probably wind up with something that wouldn't make any difference, at all. So it did pass, but it was amended substantially. I was very happy with that, and, needless to say, groups such as Common Cause did support it. It had a moderate amount of support, but the real tough audience was right there.

Right there in the legislature.

Actually the people voting upon it.

You were happy with the end result, even though it was watered down and amended quite a bit?

Yes, because this is the first, and I'm sure this would be true of any legislative body, that when you come up with something like this, people are going to be a little miffed, "Oh, why do we need that?"

Much like the checking on the police yourself, or is it that type of thing where you're actually evaluating your own behaviors, setting up a commission to look at you, and say, "Are we being ethical?" And some people don't want that.

Well, to some extent, but they don't just sit around and have a meeting and say, "OK. We're going to look at the senate this year, and we'll look at each other." In most circumstances, issues are brought to them.

People will file a complaint and say, "I think that the mayor of Reno has a conflict of interest because of abc." Take it to the ethics commission, and the ethics commission has an executive director. The recent and current executive directors have been attorneys. It used to be one of the functions of a deputy attorney general to be the legal staff for the ethics commission. Now, I suspect that's still true, but in addition to that, they have an executive director, and that happened under Governor Guinn's administration.

So, recently.

Yes. I think it might have been under Governor Miller's, to be honest with you, but it's been in the last few years that that has occurred, that they've had somebody separate. So in my mind, it was very, very important that first year to have somebody who was very credible to be the chair of this committee. Most people, if they know anything about it at all, will be reflective on who is running it, and I don't mean staff, but appointments. They probably couldn't name everybody on it. I couldn't do that even today, and I've kept an interest in this through the years. So the first person that was selected was Senator Carl Dodge, and he had a very good reputation, *very* intelligent guy, terrific person from Fallon, Nevada, and just a delight. He graduated from Stanford Law School, I believe, and I know he's got to be in his eighties by now, for sure. But he was very credible; he took his job very seriously, and the next session he came back with suggested changes. Obviously, *he* was looking at the changes as beneficial changes, not weakening it, but building it up, if you will.

I'm going to tell a story, and I think it might have been when Carl Dodge was the chairman. One of the members of the press came down to me one day. The press, as you might imagine, really thought this was a good idea. This will be something else I want to check on, because it's got big ramifications if I'm wrong. A member of the press was showing me, in the midst of the very end of a session when *everything* else was going on on the floor, that at the end of that bill there was a bracket, and at the beginning of the bill was a bracket, which suggested to this person that the whole thing was being amended *out*. In other words, if this passed, there would be no more ethics commission. That has significant importance, so I want to make sure I'm absolutely right, and I'm able to check this out as well.

I couldn't even *believe* it. At that time, there were like five amendments on other things pounding down upon us, because at the end of the session you suspend all the rules, so the same day you get all these amendments on your desk, and there's no time to go back and print them all into the bill. They do a great job in Nevada in the efficiency of our system, but when the rules are suspended, why, that's what's going on right now as we're talking.

Free-for-all.

Absolutely. And *major* things occur, and maybe three weeks later you look back at what you did and think, "Oh, my God!" But that's where all the very powerful legislators and lobbyists maneuver certain things, and you have to really be careful. So I think this is actually what was being proposed, but I want to check. I believe that the older male senators, several of them, were very interested in getting rid of this, but it didn't happen. So it survived for another day.

Following the chairmanship of Senator Dodge came Senator Spike Wilson, who obviously demonstrated an interest in this right from the beginning by being a cosponsor of the bill. He did a terrific job, as did Senator Dodge. I've been very thankful to have people who have impeccable reputations be head of this, because if they weren't, it wouldn't have any clout, at all. Most of the issues that come before the ethics commission are brought to that body; I want to emphasize that. We had examples here in Reno of constant citizen activists, I guess they'd like to call themselves, who have never won. They brought many issues against the mayor, particularly, former Mayor Griffin.

The ethics commission has not seen it that same way. I can tell you that right now I believe one of the senate representatives is a former senator who I knew quite well, Jim Kosinski. Jim—well, he became a senator—used to be in the assembly and represented an area that's somewhat similar, the north valleys, basically, above Reno, the Washoe County area. Jim had, in my mind, a very good reputation, as well. He's a member, not the chairman. In fact, the last chair was Peter Bernhard, and he resigned that position to become chair of the Nevada Gaming Commission, so I know Peter very well now. I heard very good things about him when he was appointed— a really smart, good guy. So that was a pleasant surprise, as well. And then Mary Boesch. From what I heard, she *also* did an excellent job. She followed Spike, and she was tough, knew the stuff. Clearly, the people who serve, that are attorneys, are more knowledgeable about many of the laws. I suspect some of the other members rely upon them to guide them, for example, but my understanding is there's a lot of reading that goes on. Well, [laughter] I don't know if there's any more than the gaming commission gets—that's no way. But there's a lot for lay people to assimilate and to understand.

In fact, during not this current administration, but the former one of Governor Guinn, Spike and I did go down. Scott Scherer, who was the governor's chief of staff and is now on the gaming control board, was on the ethics commission at one time. He might have been the chairman. He had been a former assemblyman, as well. There was a big question that we were concerned about, particularly Spike—I think he described it as a hole in the proposed amendments that you could drive a truck through. It became called by not only Spike, but also Jon Ralston, who is a columnist in Clark County and here for the *Reno Gazette-Journal*, as well. Jon Ralston was *very* high on the ethics commission; wrote a lot of columns about it, brought things to people's attention. I'm not going to get into the specifics, but particularly Jon and Spike felt—and I did, too, but they were more vocal about it—that there was a big hole where a lot of public elected officials could fall out, or *not* fall into, I guess, is a better description.

So I did go down with Spike to Carson City, and we had a meeting with Senator Raggio and other people—because this was going to go to the government affairs committee in the senate—visiting with them, pointing this out. It was not part of the bill that was sent to the assembly. The assembly, however, added it to close the gap. But then it has to go back, of course, to the other house to agree or not agree, and the senate did not agree, so that was dropped.

I do keep in touch with Spike about things such as this, and I know that there was a change made this year, but I think it was a fairly good one. It dealt with negative ads on television, and that really isn't what I envisioned the ethics commission to be involved in. First of all, there's a timing problem, that if you run a negative ad the weekend before, there's no way the ethics commission could call themselves together to read, to understand, to see it, et cetera, to make that kind of decision. So they tried it, and it didn't work. And with those kinds of things, you have to do things that are reasonable. But anyway, that's something that hopefully will be around a long time, because I think it does at least keep publicly elected officials on notice that there *is* something—there is a body that people can bring to its attention concerns they may have about elected officials. I suppose if there are elected officials that are *constantly* brought before them in an unfair way, I'm sure that they spend a lot of their time, their energy, maybe even money, to try to defend themselves. A lot of them bring their own attorneys with them, such as a little mini trial, I guess. I just hope in the future that other governors and administrations will be as supportive as the ones I'm familiar with.

Next we want to talk about a bill that involved naming schools.

Yes. The reason I would like just a little notation about this is because it was a learning experience for me and another fun kind of thing, or different kind of thing, I guess. During the 1980s—and this really affects northern Nevada—the school board members were naming schools after each other. Of course, they would abstain on the one with their name on it, but they'd get one of the other members to do it. If you and I were on it, Vikki, you'd nominate me, and I'd nominate you. Then we wouldn't vote on that, but everybody else would, because they knew that their time would come, and they'd get a school named after them, too.

Well, this became pretty apparent [laughter] to Washoe County voters, and they didn't like this too much. So an assemblyman named Steve Coulter, who actually taught in the journalism school at one time and was a TV anchorperson at one time, as well, introduced this bill that you couldn't do that anymore. It passed the assembly. I was then in the senate, and I totally agreed that that should not happen. So when it came over to the senate, Steve and I talked, and I told him that I would definitely make a big stand over this one. Well, unfortunately, not everybody agreed with me. I guess I could say a lot, couldn't I, through this whole thing? [laughter]

Some of the older senators didn't like that idea, because I'm sure they were hoping, from wherever they came, whether it was Las Vegas or elsewhere, that a school might be named after themselves. Even though this did not affect Clark County at that time, they thought it *might* at some other time, "If this passed, then guess what would come next?" Just like the regional planning idea.

I could mention some names of people who were on the school board at that time. I remember Virginia Palmer and Jerry Whitehead. Those are the two names that come to my mind. So it was in that era.

It got moved to the secretary's desk, and I really hadn't thought about the fact that if you move it to the secretary's desk, it's just lying there; it doesn't go in the wastebasket. It's there actually to the very last moment of a session. The motion is made to adjourn *sine die*, and the cheers go up, because everybody knows they're going to go home the next minute. But until that time, the secretary of the senate or the clerk of the assembly, who are the head of each of the desks, still have control over the business aspect of what goes on in each of their bodies. Actually, *we* all have control over them. They're just resting there.

So it happens that the secretary of the senate, Leola Armstrong, was the sister of Nancy Gomes. And I'm sure that name sounds familiar in Washoe County. I knew Nancy, particularly, because we both served in the assembly together. Nancy Gomes had passed away at this stage, but Leola wanted this bill to survive, because she didn't like what was going on. So she clued me in one day, "Hey! Now, this little thing is sitting here, and if you get eleven votes, you can take it off the desk." You have to have eleven votes to do that. Then you've got to have eleven votes to put it onto the general file, which is the place where you put bills to be voted upon. It could be a different eleven votes, but you've got to go through three stages: one, off the desk; one, to the third reading file, the general file, where bills have been amended and changed and go to be voted upon; then I'd have to have eleven "yes" votes.

So when she told me this, I thought, "Oh! This is kind of interesting." So I went around, and I remembered, of course, who had voted for it initially when it had failed. Of course, they were all with me. I was getting close. I think there were like eight that had voted for it initially. To make eleven votes, I needed to count upon two senators. They were great guys, but things sometimes passed them by, particularly when a lot of activity was going on. So I was a bit nervous about counting upon those two, but I had to. They sat to the right of me, and I put up a little sign that says "Yes on...," so they would know it was time to support me. And yes, they did! Then I held up another sign right after that *before* anybody else knew what was going on, particularly the guys in the front row. As you gain more seniority, you move up in the front row. There was Senator James Gibson, Senator Floyd Lamb—all of the real powerhouses, the longtime senior Democrats. They're the ones who didn't like this in the first place. So I had to do this very quickly, and I kept flashing the sign, which other senators, of course, saw down there. Most of them were laughing, because they'd never seen anything quite like this before! [laughter]

I'd never done anything like this before, but it worked! I got it from the secretary's desk to the floor of the senate, to the general file, and passed. The one glitch that happened was that Bob McQueen had just had a high school named after him. Assemblyman Coulter and others really did not want the high school named after Bob McQueen. But I felt I was being fair. It had already been decided, and if that was retroactively changing the name of the game, even though I might not have thought that this was the best person to have a high school named after him, I just didn't think it was fair. So he got his high school. Maybe if he ever reads this, he'll know how close he came to *not* getting a high school named after him.

Yes. Tell me the lesson. You said this was a real learning curve for you.

Oh! The lesson was that these bills laid there the whole time. When a bill dies, you think it *dies*. There weren't that many people who knew about this.

So was this the first time that you really understood you could, with the right number of votes, get that off and get that out?

Yes. Well, I've told you about other examples, like abortion bills, being placed on the desk, but this had *never* been done before in all the sessions that I had been in the legislature.

Wow. Was there any backlash?

Well, most of the time you can't get it back off the desk! That's the problem, because if it died, it died.

There's a reason why.

Yes! And most people aren't going to change their minds, but because I counted on these two, it may well have been that

they thought they were voting the right way in the first place. Who knows? But, yes, yes.

Did you get any backlash from doing this?

Oh, yes.

Yes? What was it?

Oh, yes. Well, I don't know. Probably something I wanted to pass. But some people thought it was really cool. [laughter] Even though they weren't in favor of the bill, yes, it was pretty darn cool! [laughter]

[laughter] The signs?

Well, they particularly liked the little flash cards.

Yes! [laughter] It's nice when you can win one.

I certainly would not pass any negative comments. It was just that it was pretty hectic at that time, and it was late. I'm sure it was. I don't remember what time of day it was, but sometimes we were up all night, for the next day. I don't exactly remember when this happened.

You're saying it could happen to anyone, that you would miss something in those final hours.

Yes. Well, that could happen, but the fact that a bill could be placed on the desk is not that unusual. Getting it *off*, you've got to go through three stages. The element of surprise is really important here. Absolutely. Unless it's agreed to that there were a whole lot of people that came later on and said, "Oh, you know what? I wish I'd supported that. Now I understand it better." Then that's different. But if you think it's going to be very tenuous . . . and we're going to talk about another thing that was very tenuous, too, here in sex and AIDs. But, yes, this was, I think, humorous, and actually, it's not done anymore.

Then the school board kind of got me. They made me the chair of the school-naming committee. Oh, the true story! [laughter] I came up with a good idea that we should go away from people and name it after geography, and the first one was Galena. We came up with sending three names to the school board, and then they had to select one of those three. But everybody who wanted a school named after them—of course, we were *deluged* by Rollan Melton supporters—I knew every single person well who wanted a school named after themselves, particularly high

schools, because you have sports teams. You have letter jackets. You've got all of these other things, so that it's real desirous to have a school named after yourself.

That's more visible often than the elementary or even the junior high.

Absolutely. When I realized that A, B, C, D, and E and F and G were all friends of mine, I thought, "Oh! This is a good idea," because I'd come from Arizona, and in Tucson we named schools after mountain ranges, after cacti—Saguaro High School, for example. However, I do know that Galena, well, Spanish Springs . . . .

Right. North Valleys.

Sue with friend, Rollan Melton. *"Of course we were deluged by Rollan Melton supporters."*

North Valleys. I guess Damonte was a ranching family that owned the land—or Caughlin—but that's a little more understandable.

It's a ranching family.

They own the land.

Turned into a geographical designation.

Right. [laughter] But I had to laugh that they would say, "You get to *do* this job now." [laughter]

That was one of the backlashes.

Right. It was.

One of the other issues that you wanted to discuss was alimony and child support?

Yes, and also increasing marriage license fees to help domestic violence shelters, even more. I wanted to point out two things: one, the ability of a committee chairperson to do things that they really want to do, as long as they can get it on with the rest of the committee; and two, issues that tend to be more important in the mind of a woman versus a man attorney, or a man chair, possibly. That's why these two issues—I wanted to couple them together.

As far as the law relating to alimony and child support, in most cases, though not all, you're talking about the female getting awarded child support and alimony from the male, although there are exceptions to that. This was a bill that came over from the assembly side, and most of the women legislators, assembly people, contacted me about this—not all, but a lot. They wanted something in the law, which I'm not very excited about doing. I mentioned putting

monetary amounts in law, and that they change over time, but this was a case for putting something, at least a percentage, into the law that would apply in these two areas. I think it is the first time this had been done with that much specificity, and it was done because I thought it was fair, and so did a lot of the other women legislators think it was fair.

It was interesting because I did have many male legislators and lobbyists, who had to line up to come through my office and tell me that this was not fair, that many of them—and I even know who they are right now; I can think of them—now had a second family, and they didn't think this was fair. But you know what? I didn't make them have a second family. That's none of my business. If they do, hey, you still had that first family, and you still had a former wife, in most cases, and children, so there were responsibilities.

This did pass, and I believe that today it's still there. I'm assuming that those percentages or monetary amounts have been changed with time. Every time you open up something, then there is the opportunity to get rid of it or to change it in a way that you'd not intend to do that. Same thing with the marriage license fees, because there was a bill that pertained to that section of the law.

Of course, I'm sure the male legislators and lobbyists who did not agree with me weren't happy about it. They attempted to change it on the floor, but were unable to do that. As I say, a lot of this now has passed me by, but I can talk about how things began, and hopefully they ended up somewhat similar to the way they began. Clearly, any legislator can create a bill and have that chapter, because we are unlike the federal government. You cannot amend a bill on any old subject. It has to be that same chapter, and that's a very, very important distinction, because now you hear that defense money is going to be put in, or family planning money has been stripped from a bill that was in the defense budget or whatever. That cannot happen in this state. I think that's a very good thing that it has to be *appropriate* to the significant bill. We deal with that with the chapter number.

If somebody wanted to do something different, of course, they could go in and get a bill drafted, but if it's sitting right there, if it's already been drafted, depending upon the time of the legislative session, then you open it up. Say, there was an example of marriages taking place, the way the language started out, that the marriage licenses were purchased in the county seat, Washoe County. Then Incline Village wanted to have an annex up there. See, that then dilutes, really, the opportunity to funnel that money into domestic violence shelters, although they're all in the same county. A large part of that stays in the place where it was purchased.

So those kinds of things have changed. But because of the fact that I happened to chair the senate judiciary committee, I was able to add two or three bucks on this time and maybe two or three bucks on that time. Those are the kinds of opportunities that are given to a committee chair and also, in a different way, if you serve on the money committees, but that's in a totally different fashion. It's usually with budgets and not with bills.

We're going to be talking about the issue of sex and AIDS education in K through twelve schools.

This was an issue that became paramount in the 1980s. There was a bill that came over from the assembly that had been amended substantially, I believe, in the assembly. It came over, and it was hardly related at all to this subject. I decided that I would use this vehicle, and I must have done it in conjunction with some

other legislators, and maybe one of them was Dina Titus, because I think she was on the human resources committee—Senator Dina Titus, now minority leader. I don't know who else, basically, at this time.

I thought I could probably get sex education into schools if I coupled it with AIDS, because AIDS was a big, scary thing. I don't remember exactly when it hit, but it was very scary in the 1980s. They both seemed to go together, but I didn't think that sex education would stand on its own. As I said, the bill was way different, but it was usable because it was in that chapter, as I've explained before. I wanted to have it be mandatory, because I was afraid if it was permissive, that hardly anybody would choose to do it in the school system. There'd be no point in it. I restructured the bill, and then I put the mandatory language in it, and it didn't pass.

Senator Ray Rawson, who sat next to me on the senate floor—we were both now in the front row—is a member of the LDS church, which is very much opposed to this kind of thing. He kept changing the language to "permissive." He thought that was going a stretch, and I suppose it probably was in his perspective. To me, it destroyed the entire intent in my mind of what I wanted to do.

This bill, I've been told, has been the most amended bill in our state's history. I believe that it was amended thirteen different times, so it went back and forth and back and forth. Some people didn't vote on it at all, so there was never a clear majority. I got up to like nine votes. I had the senator named Thomas Hickey, a good Irish Catholic, come over and shuffle up to me one day and say, "Hey, if you can get one more vote, I'll go with you." I was just shocked. He said, "I'm tired of religious groups imposing their views on the legislature." He basically said he had just had enough of it.

So I looked around, and I thought, "Oh! Who else am I going to get?" [laughter] That was ten. I looked at my friend, Senator Dean Rhoads from Elko, and I remembered that years ago, when we were both in the assembly, after a discussion about abortion, he had written me a note saying that he really agreed with me, but he could not vote that way because of his district. I thought, "Well! That's a start!"

So I went and asked him, and Dean is such a *decent* guy. He didn't go, "Whssh! Get real!" He just said, "Well, I'll think about it." He said, "Let me call my wife." His wife is just a delightful person, too, and she was on the school board in Elko. So that was a logical call for him to make. Not only was it his wife, but she was on the school board.

So the next day I remember exactly where I was. I was standing in the doorway of my office, which now has become part of Senator Dina Titus's office, but it's right at the top of the stairs on the second floor of the legislative building. I'm standing there talking to somebody, and Dean walks by and does a thumbs up, like that. I thought, "What's he doing?" Then I realized what he was doing it for, and I couldn't even believe it. Well, that gave me eleven votes.

I then had to go chair the senate judiciary committee, so I had to go into another room. I was very afraid what might happen between 8:00 a.m. and 11:00 a.m. Senator Foley, I think she was involved in this, too. I don't know, it might have been another bill. I believe she went down and took roll call for me, because I was chairing the judiciary committee. But anyway, I get down to the floor of the senate, and I see all of these senators surrounding Tom Hickey's desk, including the senate majority leader, the chairman of senate finance, Floyd Lamb, Jim Gibson, et cetera; and I couldn't even *see* him. I thought, "There goes that vote."

Then they turned around and came over to Dean Rhoads's desk, and, I'm sure, doing exactly the same thing. Well, I decided to vote on it at that time, and I couldn't believe it—not only did I get eleven votes, I got *twelve* votes, because Senator Lawrence Jacobsen had gone home and talked to his wife, Betty, and she thought it sounded like a good idea. So it passed!

That's why we have currently—and I say "currently"—sex and AIDS education in the school. As we know, tomorrow is the first day of June, 2003, and at this time tomorrow the school board in Washoe County is going to pretty much dismantle the entire thing, and I believe it'll never get back on again. My understanding is that there are only two school board members, Jonnie Pullman and Anne Loring, who will support it, and the rest won't. I think there's one that is a question mark.

There are seven members, I think, of the school board. I thought about going in and visiting with the superintendent myself, but I was told that that probably wouldn't do any good. I did serve with Mr. Hager on the United Way board, and I have met with people from Planned Parenthood about this, but this was during the legislative session. They've been very busy down there. We kind of devised a strategy, but I think it's too late. I think we should have been organized way sooner and had people show up at public hearings, because the people who seemed to show up were just, "We all know this."

If you show up, you're going to be listened to more than, "Oh, gosh! What are they doing to us? They're cutting my favorite project." Since there has been *no* input on this, at all, it's a little late in the game.

Was there no sex education in the school district before this? And you were doing this for all of Nevada or just for Washoe County?

No, it was all of Nevada.

So if Washoe County dismantles its sex education program, will it be the only one that has dismantled theirs since then?

I don't know that. I don't know. They're deciding what to cut; I'm sure it's different in every single school district.

It may be that there will be enough money, but once you even talk about it, the *only* individual who's going to be left is one person. Well, there are a lot of teachers who don't want to do this, aren't capable of doing it. In fact, after the bill was passed, then all of us in the Washoe delegation—and I've tried to impress this on Planned Parenthood people—*every* single one of us to a person supported this. We all not only voted for it, we all took turns going to school board meetings, sitting there, watching how they were going to put this committee together that was going to create the curriculum. It's called the SHARE program. I sat next to Pro-Life Andy Anderson—who actually ran against me later on—dressed as a ghoul, like with a Halloween costume on. We put up with all kinds of things to make sure this was done correctly. Interestingly enough, my own children's biology teacher, Judy Counter, was chosen to be the first overseer of this program, and I was very, very happy about that.

I have sort of given up. There's only so much one person can do. As I said, I have visited with Planned Parenthood personnel and tried to figure out a different strategy, but at least they did that. I've left messages over and over that we've got to do something about this, and I'm a big supporter of Planned Parenthood financially and every other way.

I don't know how they think they're going to get this back on again. They won't. It will not happen. Even at one other session, they wanted to come in and be part

of the teaching curriculum, and I said, "That's going to be very chancy, if you do that. Planned Parenthood sends off terrible signals." They have, of course, lists of people who contribute, and they could have at least called them and had them write letters. Call and not do the same old letter, so it looks like everybody's running it off, and they gave you what you're supposed to say. I have no idea if any of that's been done. I have volunteered to go and meet with the superintendent and other people, but they haven't gotten back to me on that either.

So I'm pretty disappointed about the whole thing, to be very honest with you, because it took a Herculean effort to get this mandated. Of course, each school district could do what they wanted. You cannot put into state law, "You've got to cover this and this and this and this." There's got to be some flexibility. We felt that Washoe County was considered to be the best in the state. There's no question, we put out a lot of energy, all of us, even after the session was over, showing up, rotating, taking different people, going on different nights. That was a pretty big deal.

The only other example I can think of is the regional planning, where the delegation got together wholeheartedly on an issue. I suppose now we think the regional planning is very controversial, but this was more controversial *at the time* than that was, certainly. Ray Rawson and I went back and forth and back and forth and back and forth. Actually, I like Ray very much, and he's a really good legislator in many, many things. He's been there with the governor with this session. He chairs a health committee, and he does an excellent job. It's just on these social issues that we tend to disagree.

I even spoke to him in the evening right after the state-of-the-state address. He told me he was very worried because he was up for election this time. I said, "Oh, Ray, I know you'll do the right thing." He has, and he's come right out for it early on. You could hardly call Bill Raggio moderate, and he's gone over the wall over this, too. The one way you could be beaten is in a Republican primary, and that's why I figured I probably would have a very difficult time. Ray is not perceived anywhere near as liberal as I am in the Republican Party, but he is more moderate than a lot of the other Republican legislators and really is a very thoughtful, smart guy. On that particular issue we weren't very good friends, because sometimes that gets in the way, particularly when you're tired and you're stressed out, and it's just the opposite of what you think is right. You're not going to call him names, but it isn't like smiling and sitting down and handing the microphone to him.

Twenty-some years later, when they interviewed a bunch of students in one of their articles, the students all said, "Oh, God, it was *really* important to me." There was not a negative comment said by any of the students that were interviewed for this article, and the fact is, our teenage pregnancy rates have gone way down, particularly in Washoe County. You have to assume that that had something to do with it. You just have to.

What else was being done?

Yes, exactly. What else is being done that would change this totally around?

It must be discouraging to have fought so hard for something that's fairly basic in terms of information.

You would think so.

And then to see it go, because the claim now is that it is a budget issue.

Yes. That is the thing.

That's why it would be cut.

I believe that. I'm not thinking they're cooking this up, because you've got athletics, and that's going to go *way* higher than this. You've got music programs; you've got academically talented programs. You've got a lot of really good things. Now, nothing has to suggest that some of those were put on there for *exactly* the reason that they know it would drive out a lot of parents, and the other was put on there because they know it wouldn't.

There are all kinds of things, having served so much of my life in the legislature, that what is perceived may not be real, at all. You would hope that really good criteria were used, but there's no question that the school district—Superintendent Hager—was up the creek. He believed he had to cut $6 million.

That's a huge amount.

That is a very large amount. When you look at some of them, even that's not very much, but it suddenly adds up, and it *is* something at the top of the food chain. I suspect that everybody thinks that their program is important. Their child is in music class, or your kid plays football, and you think that's the best thing for him, that he might drop out of school, whatever. Then those are very, very important.

I don't have children in the school system anymore, but that's totally irrelevant. The big thing I've noticed is that I could have gone down two weeks ago, three weeks ago, right after I met with Planned Parenthood. I'm not blaming it on Planned Parenthood. That's not *their* responsibility. My mind thought, "Who else can organize people?" Let's say, Fritsi Ericson is a Planned Parenthood member, but she could write and say this is very important to her. I don't know if she would say that, but she could say, "I was president of the Women's Fund, and I've seen these numbers go down." Lynn Atcheson could write from the perspective of Truckee Meadows Tomorrow and the quality of life indicators.

Clearly, if you compare this program and athletics, you know athletics is not going to die. Even if it died for, let's say, fall, which it isn't going to, then it's going to be right back. *This* will not be back. And if you think about kids having kids, it's a terrible way to raise a kid.

It really leaves the child at a disadvantage.

Huge disadvantage.

We were speaking about that over dinner with the situation in my family.

Yes, exactly, and that's what I was thinking when I said that. In most cases, young women, young girls, who happen to get pregnant probably come from homes where it has not been discussed, for whatever reason. If you're religious, you don't want to discuss it, or you're planning to do that next year, or whatever. I do believe that when you see teenage pregnancy go down, that is the only thing I can see that would suggest that it is the reason why. To me, that is a pretty big deal. Actually, that's more important in my mind than playing the violin in the ninth grade—versus having a baby in the ninth grade. No question.

No question. [laughter]

No question. [laughter] I don't think many of the parents would argue with me about that either.

Probably not. But they're probably not assuming that their child is going to be

the one who gets pregnant while, at the same time, they're playing the violin, that it's going to be an either/or.

Or they're playing the tuba. It's a little hard when you're playing the tuba.

Right!

Oh, you mean differently, at different times?

Right. [laughter]

Oh, I thought you meant playing it at the time. [laughter]

No. If they're choosing the program. [laughter]

I know what you're saying. Anyway, at this time that we are doing the taping, that is probably the biggest disappointment I have currently.

Out of all the things that you've watched over the years go up and down and change over time.

Yes. The things that I felt instrumental in—most of those things are still going, like family courts and domestic violence shelters. You can go back, and naming schools after members of the school board—that's still the policy. I don't think they'd dare . . . . You know what? I wonder if I could've traded that.

[laughter] For the sex education?

Told the school board, "Hey, you want a school named after you? I'll work it out, but you've got to make sure this stays in the school!" [laughter]

[laughter] There you go!

Oh, darn it! I just got that idea just this moment! Darn it! I should have thought about this sooner. "Lezlie Porter, do you want a school named after you?" She would not want me to have anything to do with it, though, I don't believe.

I don't believe.

Although, Lezlie Porter did nominate me for Mother of the Year. Did you know that? Did I mention that?

No.

Yes. In fact, looking at the honors in my list, I thought, "What's this American merit thing?" And then I remembered. Lezlie didn't know me very well, I suspect. I was very pleased about the fact, but when I got to the organization in Las Vegas, I realized that the woman who had the most children was most likely to win, and since I was the only one there who had just two, I took myself right out of it immediately. [laughter]

But she nominated you?

Yes, she did. I must have done a very good job of covering up my real *agenda*, huh? [laughter]

I don't know! That's an interesting combination. OK. We've finished on the sex education issue, at least until we hear what the end of this legislature and budget brings. We've talked throughout our interviews about the power—who has the power, where the power is on committees, and so on. There's a number of different topics.

Yes. When I first went down in 1975, of course, there was no office. There were no phones. I used the phone booth. The office was on the floor of the assembly. You only were rewarded with offices and maybe a secretary, with a phone on the desk, if you were in the majority party. Not only was I a freshman, but also, in the minority. It was said at that time, actually, that if you really wanted to go far in politics in Nevada, you had to be a Democrat. Well, I guess that's not true today. I don't know if it's taken all that many decades to come to this point or not, but being on committees that are of importance to your constituency, or of interest to you, is very important. I did, to a large extent, discuss my committee assignments. I made an outspoken comment that I was different than Mary Gojack, and I was different than Jean Ford.

In terms of explaining to me what the committees did, that was different. I chose government affairs, judiciary, and then this legislative functions, as it was called at that time, because you could see reform bills coming there, and the judiciary committee really dealt with birth to death and literally everything in between dealing with individuals. Government affairs dealt with relationships between the legislature and local governments and a variety of other kinds of things, and the legislative committee made all the decisions about how bills flow through the legislature, all of the kinds of things that happen internally.

So I did sit on those committees and did, really, until practically the end of my career. I do remember one time when Jean Ford was elected to the senate, and she served on those three committees, and I was on those same three committees in the assembly. And *literally*, people were *very* worried, because I was on that committee, and she was on that committee, and, well, I was in the assembly, so if that was forty and out of twenty, so out of sixty people, there was discussion that the two of us were probably going to wreak havoc over the legislative process! [laughter] That is kind of humorous, when you think about it today, because clearly, we did not have anywhere near that kind of influence. It was nice that people thought we did, but it didn't pay off in the long run, because we didn't do all the things we wanted done. [laughter]

We talked earlier about how that was probably the first time that many of those legislators, who were men, had served with women on a committee, and especially outspoken women.

But that was fine, and I learned a lot, looking at how other people chaired committees, et cetera. Then, finally, when you get to be in the majority party, you get the plum, so to speak.

So in the majority party come the plums.

Yes.

Describe that.

It's a big difference. I had to wait till 1987 to have that happen for me, starting out in 1975. I was selected—elected, I guess, too— as chair of the senate judiciary committee. I was handed off the same secretary that Spike Wilson had had the session before, who, of course, I knew very well because I already served on that committee. Then I received another secretary; then I received *another* secretary. Wow! I thought I'd died and gone to heaven! Marilyn Hoffman was the secretary of the committee, taking the committee minutes, and taking care of that kind thing, setting up the rooms, and keeping track of committee business. Marilyn lives in Tacoma, Washington, now, but she did come back a number of times to be Senator Bob Coffin's secretary until just last session. Judy Bishop became my personal secretary, and that was just terrific to have her. And then, I think it was Judy James, but I need to check on that. She did a lot of the committee work, too,

because I think I've mentioned that the judiciary committee has more bills referred to it than any other committee. That's the reason that it seemed to be manna from heaven, with the three secretaries. But it's a huge difference.

I actually got a nice office, the office that Senator Wilson had before me. Of course, now the digs down there are unbelievably plush. I'm sure if people travel around the country look at legislative buildings, they're going to say "Wow! This has got to be at the top!" I can't imagine a legislative building being any nicer than this, nor as advanced technologically. It is incredible. Actually, I learned a lot just this last session by going on a tour with my intern class and seeing behind the scenes, so to speak, because I really was never that interested in what happened behind the scenes, but it was pretty, pretty interesting. You do learn, hopefully, as you go along, particularly in the minority party, that maybe someday you will have things turn, so you watch people, how they handle themselves, how they run committees, and that kind of thing. So I thought that was really good training for me.

What did you observe that you really wanted to do or not do by watching others in the majority?

Well, I think that first of all, you should respect—even though you may disagree 100 percent—the person testifying, that they have the right to their opinion, that they are presenting the information to the legislature, and that people should not talk or write notes back and forth. That I saw a lot. Even when I met with my counterpart in the assembly judiciary committee in joint hearings, some of the people who he had on his committee, who will remain nameless, some of the judges now in other positions, were very rude. I could not believe it. If I had been standing out there watching this, I would have thought that they had no respect for anything I said. I did mention it to the chairman of that committee, but that was really up to him. I certainly couldn't rule them out of order or anything, because they were not senators at the time.

The other thing I always did, that I notice is not done at all as I'm serving on the gaming commission, is that I would let all my committee members ask all the questions they had first; and then if there were things that had not been asked, or I that I thought it important to get on the record, I would then clean up, be a cleanup hitter. I notice that Peter Bernhard, who I mentioned has gone from ethics commission chairmanship to gaming, asks all of his questions first. And that's just fine; it's just a different way of doing it.

Those are three things that come to mind right off the top. If people have to have limited time, only five minutes to speak or something—which usually did not happen too much when we didn't have these timelines to meet—then you did want to balance it out, if it was a pro and a con person. Usually, you'd always have the proponent go first. As a matter of fact, I always did—the person to present the reason for why do we have this bill before us, and then why should we not ever see it again? [laughter] So the con people get up there and discuss with us.

I think we've kind of touched on a number of bills I've introduced throughout my career that weren't really too exciting to a lot of my other legislative friends. Sometimes, that's just the way it is. As long as they don't think you're doing it for any reason other than you really care—like grandstanding or something like that—then I think that pretty much they understand that's just the way you are.

I did find that to be very much the case when I was selected to be chairman of the senate judiciary committee. I think that Senator Raggio, who was the majority leader, hardly did he agree with me on a lot of things, but hopefully, he knew I'd do a good job, and that things that were important to get out of the committee would go down to the senate floor for a vote. My goal at that time was to never lose a bill on the senate floor, and that's why I worked so hard to make sure that I could answer any questions that my fellow judiciary committee members could not, because I did not want this committee to look like they just let anything out, like they hadn't thought about it very well, and somebody could get up and shoot holes in it right off the bat.

You'd like to say that all of them are going to wind up on the governor's desk. Well, that's a great goal to have, but that doesn't always happen. At least, be able to defend it, because you're the one who's in your house. If it goes over to the assembly, I'm not *in* the assembly, so I can't jump right up and say something.

But at least be successful through your house, this process.

Yes, exactly. That was very important to me. I think that we've already touched on some bills, such as the school-naming bill, that clearly were not real popular. As I said, as long as you don't grandstand and go on and on, but it's just another deal in the day's work—move on from there. If the press tends to like you and so on, that is an added problem, really. Not that you're going to say, "Oh, I don't want another story about me." Well, clearly, you're not going to say something like that, because it was kind of an anomaly, and I was the first woman in the legislature, I believe, who had small children that age. That was a big deal.

And a single parent.

Well, at that time I was not a single parent, when I was first elected.

So first to have small children, period.

Oh, yes, ages three and four.

Jean's children were older, for example.

Oh, yes. Hers were in high school or college or way older. One of mine wasn't even in preschool yet. So that was a natural thing for reporters to want to report on, and how does that all work out, that sort of thing. I think, even though that comes your way, you don't need to act big about it. I guess that's a good way of putting it. One of the other neat things to get along better with your own colleagues, is to try to do as many informal things as possible. I suspect I've talked about my trip with then Senator Jean Ford down to Tonopah.

I think we've just mentioned that.

All right. This was a trip put together by the National Forest Service. Jim Nelson, whom I've mentioned before in the Forest Service exchange bill, put this together, but it was really stimulated by Senator Cliff Young, who was president of the National Wildlife Federation at the time. Cliff was just a great guy. He organized this horseback trip; I think it was five days. One of the rules was you cannot bring anybody else with you; it's just for the senator. But as it turns out, Jean was the only woman in the senate, and so they told her that she could invite one person, as long as it wasn't me. [laughter]

Well, that's not true. They didn't say that, but I think they probably figured that's who she would invite, and that's who she did, and it was a great, great opportunity. You'd be all filthy dirty, and somebody'd be cooking, and you'd just sit around the campfire and talk about stuff. I'm sure that

Jean was happy I was there, and I was happy to be there, because it was a way of getting to know the big major players. A lot of them went on this trip.

One of the funny stories that Senator Floyd Lamb used to say about me, and probably it was the only funny story that he would say about me, [laughter] was the fact that I fainted flat off my horse, just crashed down on the ground, and I was out. He says he revived me and that I looked up and said, "Oh! Floyd, thank you so much!" Now, I don't believe that for one moment! I had heard that he did help revive me, but maybe I did say, "Oh, thank you so much."

What caused that?

I don't know. I don't know. I think it was just going up to high altitude, because we were going straight up. The only time I'd ever been on a horse was when I was in the second grade, going around a little ring with another little person. All of a sudden, here it is all day for five straight days. One of the things I certainly noticed—I could *not move*. After about the third day, though, it was getting to be pretty good. By then it was almost time to be over. [laughter] It was painful.

Especially if you're not accustomed to horseback riding.

No. It was very painful. But in other opportunities that happened like that—well, the big softball game was our big deal, the assembly versus the senate. Evidently, I pitched well one year, so I was the pitcher for every succeeding session in the assembly and in the senate, as well. Later on we added a basketball game to our repertoire of athletic endeavors, and those again were fun, because people were outside, out of the building, kind of leaving their worries and the bills and the discussions back in that arena. Although,

I'm sure there was a little stuff that went on on the sidelines, because, of course, lobbyists all came to watch.

It was also good for them to see people in a different environment, I'm sure. Those kinds of things, I think, are very important for legislative bodies to have, or maybe even businesses to have, because it does break down some work barriers that you may have, and I think those are important opportunities.

We are going to finish some of the issues that came up during your terms in the senate. I'm going to let you start and introduce the first one.

Actually, this topic is general in nature, because I think we've touched on it, both in the assembly and maybe the senate, but it deals with campaign reform.

We have talked about it a number of times.

Right. I'm just going to briefly touch on the fact that throughout my entire career in both the assembly and the senate, I have always been involved in those kinds of issues. I guess I would generically say "good government" in terms of having the voters know more about who had contributed to your campaigns and what you had spent and who you spent it on. Being the legislator now, did you have a campaign manager? How much you spent on televisions commercials, that kind of thing?

I think that that is of interest to your voters, and it should be. Legislators should feel that that is an acceptable thing to disclose, because they're asking for the public trust to get elected. So, much of my career has dealt with putting a limit on the amount of money a legislator could accept.

I started out with fifty dollars, and I guess that was a hoot to the rest of the legislators. Mike O'Callaghan, the first governor under whom I served, had a much higher figure. Actually, I think it was five hundred—just added another zero, that's all. [laughter]

And you say it was a hoot. Tell us why.

Well, it was a hoot to other legislators.

Humorous. They thought it was funny.

Yes. "Fifty dollars? That's all? And you have to disclose everything above that?" That was shooting a little low, I guess.

They didn't want to have to do every little bit, right?

No, they didn't. It seems to me like constituents don't get all upset about it as long as they know. If you don't want to let them know, they think there's some reason that you don't want to, which sometimes is not the case, at all. I did have an ad in the paper one time, my first campaign. I don't believe I mentioned this, that I could only afford one ad right before the primary or the general, I don't remember which. But I made note of the fact that I had only accepted fifty dollars, except for the fact that my mother—and I had her name there—and my mother-in-law, had given me a hundred. Other than that, I really didn't have to worry about it, because I didn't get any offers of very much anyway! [laughter] I'm sure fifty dollars would have been high for me.

Campaign reform was one of the main issues that you ran on right from the beginning?

Yes, it was. In fact, it was *the* issue, and I had read a book by Common Cause called *Money and Politics*. As far as I was concerned, I took a lot of those ideas right out of that book. It made a lot of sense to me. I had been told by Republicans in the party—again, this is my first election—that those were very bad issues for me to take as a Republican, because I had a lot of people who lived in my district in southwest Reno who did contribute to campaigns, who were lobbyists, and they would not have liked this idea. Well, as it turns out, fortunately, somebody did, because I was elected. I think that's probably all I'm going to say on that subject, because I think we've touched on this already.

The one question that I have on campaign reform is, if you could give an assessment overall, did you feel like you made a lot of progress in your time in the legislature on campaign reform? Do you think that is continuing since that time?

I do. I think I made great strides, but I can't answer the second question, because I really don't know what the maximum allowable is. I would hope that there are other legislators who are watching over those things.

I think it started out with Watergate, though. That's the real reason I became interested in opening up government. It seemed to me that if you did *not* support these things at that time, you really became suspect. Of course, that is part of our American history, a long time ago now, in the 1970s. I'm sort of at a loss for words here. Because those kinds of issues are not paramount in either legislators' or constituents' minds these days, maybe there's always that slipping back sometimes. You should learn from history, but sometimes you don't. Hopefully those requirements are still in place. I do know that very often you'll read a political columnist—and normally it's Jon Ralston—talking about that X number of dollars were disclosed *after* they'd been elected. So there were periods of time where it was very

important to know *prior* to election, not just afterwards, because it didn't do the voters much good if they found out too late.

There are articles in the paper today around the election time—primaries and generals—mentioning how much somebody received. I don't know how many people read that and take that seriously. Clearly, you could not have an article on everybody in one newspaper column or press release. Jon Ralston—I'll mention him again—writes both for the *Las Vegas Sun* now and the *Reno Gazette-Journal*. It used to be the *Las Vegas Review-Journal*, the *R-J*, but he's become a part of the *Las Vegas Sun* family. He has whole Ralston Reports, which I subscribe to, and he will have three or four pages of lists of who we see. He sometimes makes editorial comments about that, because that's really what the purpose of the Ralston Report is. So clearly, it's still important to him, and hopefully it is to other reporters or media people, because that's how that will get disseminated.

I think I'm going to now kind of skip to smoking. I guess I should share my history on smoking, because I did smoke. I started smoking in college, which would have been in the 1960s. I quit once, practically overnight, for five years. Then I ran for office, and I started smoking again, and that was in the 1970s, of course. This is a story of so many people who have tried to quit. I did quit, as I said, literally overnight. Then I would bum one from somebody, and then it was a pack. Then I'd buy a carton, and pretty soon you're right back up there again. My husband hated it, and I didn't. You have to be the one that gives this stuff up.

After he died in 1980, I quit the next year, because my kids really gave me a hard time. And it wasn't just coming home and saying, "We saw this film at school. It showed your lungs, they were all pockmarked with holes," and all of this sort of stuff. No, it was far worse than that. They came home and told me that I guess I wanted them to be orphans. Well, that just about stabbed me in the heart. So I just quit.

Then I started running the next day, because normally when you quit, you sometimes gain weight. So I started running around Virginia Lake, and from that I got up to five miles a day. There's nothing worse than a reformer in some way, but because of that I was a reformer on smoking. I introduced a bill that would prohibit smoking in public buildings. I realized at that time—this was in the 1970s—that I couldn't expect people to vote for something that would infringe on the gaming casinos' dedication to having people be allowed to drink and smoke in their properties. I didn't even go there. In fact, here it is, 2003, and it's still *that* same issue.

I do want to mention, because I want to get back to this in a different part of my history, that I attempted to get smoking outlawed in grocery stores. Now, it is in most parts of the grocery stores, but around the slot machines it is not. Being a gaming commissioner, I tried to do that, but I lost there, as well as being in the legislature.

I did feel that a compromise was only public buildings. In the 1970s we didn't know as much as we do now about the addiction of smoking and the terrific correlation between that and lung cancer, although we did have a passing acquaintance with particularly *that* subject. Then in the 1980s we really understood the relationship. I did feel in the 1970s that I wasn't going to mandate that people who smoked all of a sudden had to give it up if they worked in a public building, so it said "Public buildings, except for designated smoking areas." That became

Sue jogging with her Brittany spaniel, Tahoya, at Virginia Lake, Reno.

a problem in itself, because some buildings did not have an appropriate place, so people had to go outside and smoke on the sidewalks. In the winter, if you're in northern Nevada, it gets kind of cold.

But, hey, that passed, although it was very difficult to get it passed. As you might guess, tobacco companies have a huge lobbying presence for their businesses. I do know there was an attempt made by a great legislator named Marvin Sedway—in fact, there's a building named after him in Carson City, part of the Legislative Counsel Bureau. Marvin was an incredibly brilliant guy. He chaired ways and means, the money committee, in the assembly. He was a big, big-time smoker. In fact, he'd already lost one lung from smoking. He tried to convince me that I should include in this piece of legislation that the state would have the presumptive right. That means nobody could pass anything more stringent than what the state did. We're discussing that, as well, this session. Polling has been done, and we had an advisory vote in Washoe County and one in Clark County just this last election in 2002, expressing the view that they would like to be able to have their local governments make more stringent laws than at the state level.

The legislature may be closing up today or tomorrow, and this is June 1, so that will not have been accomplished, because it was defeated early on, even though the cost of cigarettes goes skyrocketing, and I'm sure that taxes on them will be increased this session, as well, although it hadn't been as of yesterday or the day before. This is what passed, and it's still the law. I don't think much else has been passed since then to prohibit smoking in certain areas of buildings or restaurants or those kinds of places.

A lot of people now say, "Would you like to sit in a no-smoking area?" If you're lucky, you won't be right next to the smoking area, where it's all wafting over to your table! But

at least that's better than it used to be. You look at people who smoke now, and there are very few. Most of my friends do not smoke, and that was not true ten, fifteen years ago or more than that. People recognize how harmful it is, not only as an addiction, but also to your lungs. So I felt that that was something important to have mandated in the state.

When you said it was very difficult to get it passed, did you mean only because of Marvin Sedway, or is there more that you want to say about how you got that passed?

Heads of state agencies, even though they might have supported it, didn't know how this was all going to work. The big problem was: where are the designated smoking areas going to be? That was left up to each public building. I wasn't going to go around and choose each area in each building and who was going to be the supervisor of this. That was up to the agency to decide. That was a problem, as I mentioned.

Mr. Sedway, who I *really* liked, one day came to my office when I was in the senate. It was late at night, and he was smoking. I said, "Oh, Marvin, I don't want you smoking in my office." We started talking about how smart he was and why he would still do this—because he only had one lung. Of course, he then died of lung cancer several years later. I guess it was just impossible for him to quit; he didn't want to quit. But it was startling to me that someone who had had one lung removed already would continue to go ahead and abuse their bodies that way.

I don't know if it's in the public health part of Harvard University or not, but I read several articles recently that say researchers have identified an addictive chemical in the brain, and they find a high correlation, as we might guess, between gambling addiction, smoking, and liquor. That, of course, I'm sure the gaming casinos recognized early on. The people felt more comfortable, and that's the reason they didn't want to have to prohibit those other habits, I guess—I'm sure that they would think of it as entertainment. I know there has been a property in Reno, the Ponderosa Inn, that attempted to be smoke free at one time, and it didn't work out very well. Of course, the real impediment here was the lobbyists from the cigarette companies.

And the companies did send lobbyists into Nevada?

Oh, they sent them into every state. In fact, they'd hire somebody every session, who represented them, because of these constant attacks, particularly on the smoking. Problem gambling has just kind of come into its own now. We now know this session that even the Nevada legislature reduced the certain amount of liquor in one's body through a Breathalyzer test that would be utilized for a DUI, that you could not drink any more than that. It's now tied to money coming from the federal government in the area of transportation. So it's always been attempted and never has passed, but this year, even lobbyists who represented industries that didn't want it to happen, realized that it was going to happen this time.

One of the other areas I'm going to speak just very quickly about deals with another piece of legislation which I suspect people asked me to do, or I became interested in, because of my interest in metabolic genetic disorders. When you see the word "metabolic," you know that this can be corrected by dietary changes. When I talked about this testing for fetal defects— maternal serum alpha fetal protein screening—that was something that one

could learn through amniocentesis. I'm not going to go into that now, but I think that's inserting a needle and removing some fluid from the womb, and that is analyzed. I know that one of the illnesses, or diseases, that could be identified early on in this fashion, is Down's syndrome. Of course, a lot of people don't want to have anything to do with amniocentesis, because even if it gave a terrible result, and that information was given to the mother and the father, they don't believe in letting that couple make a decision to abort the fetus. But amniocentesis is used a great deal now, and in this case it was very important.

The *one* illness I remember was spina bifida. I'm not going to get into any clinical description of this, but it does potentially produce an offspring that is severely limited in physical movement. I'm not going to know the correct medical term, but in this case, one of the women who came to testify about this was from Fallon. She happened to be a Mormon young woman, and, of course, they are very opposed to the whole idea of amniocentesis.

So you're saying she had spina bifida?

Not her. Her child.

But even though she had a child with that, she was still opposed to the testing?

Oh, no. It was the opposite. Oh, she was there to support the testing. She said she wished she had known then. I suspect, knowing which committee this went before, senate human resources, that they asked her, "What would you have done then?"

Basically, it wasn't any attempt I had to have parents struggle with this decision, but it seemed to me people should know about this possibility. In fact, this young woman said they would have been far better prepared to have dealt with this situation when the baby was born. As a matter of fact, now that I think about it, she did keep the child. She didn't have the test done—it was not offered—but she said, yes, she would have kept it and been prepared for it mentally and physically. So that was, in other words, good information.

Right. Didn't necessarily lead to abortion, although there is the connection there.

Yes.

So the people who were against it were also generally opposed to abortion, that that was the connection in their minds?

Yes. Oh, absolutely. They were opposed to it under any circumstances. I was very pleased when the woman called me from Fallon and asked me if I'd like her to testify. When I heard her story, I said, "I'll come out and get you if you need a ride in," because it kind of took the wind out of opponents' sails in the fact that she was just a sweet, young woman. Anyway, in my mind it was something that, again, did not pass.

Was it to require testing?

No.

It was only to make it possible for testing?

Yes.

Now, has that passed in the meantime?

Oh, yes. You can have amniocentesis. Sure. And you could have amniocentesis then, as well. That's a very good question, and I can't really answer it. I don't know if the state would pick up the cost. There had to be something in that bill.

Something that involved the state.

Yes, otherwise it wouldn't have been necessary, because you don't have to have a law saying you can.

No. I wouldn't think so. Perhaps it did have to do with welfare picking up the cost.

It might have, because if you remember, when I talked about metabolic genetic screening, they did that. It just was the fact that they only tested for one thing at that time—PKU. Besides that, I wanted the state to pick up the cost of metabolic genetic screening. It was only like $1.75 per test, per child. In this case, it might have been the same. I might have traveled the same path. It might be something to look up, because I don't like to have these things hanging out there that I can't remember the conclusion. But I thought this is something I wanted to talk about, because again, it fits in with some general themes I have as a woman legislator and as a mother.

Did you introduce this when you were in the senate on the judiciary committee? When was that?

Oh, it didn't go through the judiciary committee. It went through human resources. I'm absolutely positive, because I can actually visualize what room I was in and what floor I was in. Unfortunately, I just can't remember what happened.

Right! [laughter] Can't remember the end result!

[laughter] No!

But that's easy enough. We can look that up.

We won't have to look that up, what room it's in, because we want to tie these things down.

OK, because you know that! [laughter]

I know that. I think that one of the other things I will just talk about at the conclusion is some awards and things that I've received. One of the things I will mention here, however, is that there were two national organizations for state legislators to be involved in. One is called the National Conference of State Legislators, NCSL. The other is the Council of State Governments, and that group is divided up into regions. For example, you'd be a member of the Western Conference of CSG, Council of State Governments. Their headquarters is in San Francisco. In fact, one of our research persons who helped do some

research for me, Mary Lou Cooper, I think, still is the director of the CSG for the Western part of United States, and she moved to San Francisco to do that. Somebody saw her at a conference. She was a staff person, and I thought that she would be excellent for that job.

I was able to rise fairly high in that organization, but never to be the president or the chairman or whatever, because, as you might guess, particularly in the Western part of the United States, it was pretty male dominated by a lot of—I don't mean this in a derogatory sense at all—cowboy-type legislators. Now, some people might use that about a president currently, and it would not be in a positive way, but I do

Sue with one of her idols, marathon runner, Joan Benoit Samuelson, who won the first women's Olympic marathon ever held in Los Angeles in the early 1980s at the Women Executives in State Government presentation of the "Breaking the Glass Ceiling" award to Sue. (Benoit Samuelson is the only American to this day to have won the women's Olympic marathon.)

mean that they were often from the rural areas. So that kind of philosophy was what permeated the CSG, unlike the NCSL. That was far more liberal, because it was national. You did become part of whichever region of the country you happened to live in.

They rotated chairmanships, and now I'm talking about CSG, the Western branch, but even nationally, they rotated the chairmanship of that through different regions. They did have a national meeting of CSG as well as the regional ones. I really liked that national meeting. One of the better experiences I had with that organization—I became chairperson of a couple of the committees and became very active in the committee on economic development and international trade,

which served me well when I became lieutenant governor. But one of the great experiences I had with this organization was with the president or the chairman of CSG as a whole. We were in Hawaii for a Western conference, and the president picked out a few people, I think like six or seven, to go with him to Taiwan, because we were already in Hawaii. I did make that trip, and I really enjoyed the people I traveled with, in addition to being in Taipei, Taiwan. That was pretty interesting.

And what was that connected with?

That was connected with the Council of State Governments. The chairman of the group just picked out people he thought he'd like to go on a trip with, to be honest

Nevada Medal Dinner. Sue received the award from the Desert Research Institute. Clockwise, starting at far left: Fritsi Ericson, Harry Ericson, Supreme Court Justice Deborah Agosti, Kirk Wagner, Sue, Marybel Batjer, Lynn Atcheson, Martha Romero, and Barbara Weinberg.

with you. [laughter] You could, I suppose, justify it by saying you were on the international trade or economic development committee. He was a representative in the state house in Massachusetts. He took another person from Massachusetts, Joan Menard. She's just great, so much fun.

Also, a woman named Sitech came who was in the New Hampshire legislature. At that time she wanted to be speaker of the house. She was telling me on this trip that her big commitment when she came back was to meet everybody. I said, "What do you mean, 'meet everybody'?"

"Meet everybody in the legislature."

I said, "You don't *know* everybody, and you're going to run for speaker?"

Well, there were like several hundred people in the house, because in some of the New England states, particularly New Hampshire, it was like a town hall meeting

Council of State Governments in Hawaii. Sue is to the right of the man in the center. Far left is Linda Sitech, who was running for speaker of the house in the New Hampshire legislature.

Lt. Governor Sue Wagner in the Taiwan legislative chamber with an official.

Joan Menard (left) and Sue with guard in Taiwan.

in a historical sense. For most people, it would be more equivalent to a precinct captain, in the normal parlance of politics.

It was fun to meet different people. We were the three women, and then the chairman was male, and then there were a couple of other guys. Oh, yes, one of them was in the state of New York, and I don't remember who the other one was, but it was pretty diverse. I think maybe I did represent the West, and we had a few from the East Coast, but since he was from Massachusetts, he probably felt more strongly about that, I don't know. But, yes, that was fun.

Working with the CSG and National Council of State Legislators, what was it that you felt helped you?

The advantage was really to meet other people, and I'm not going to say that it wasn't important; it was. First of all, you learned about what other people were doing in different parts of the nation, and that just because it comes from New York State doesn't mean that it's a bad idea, and that no one on the West Coast should think about it or possibly utilize it, and, hopefully, vice versa. If something was done in Nevada, somebody from South Carolina might hear about it and think that was a good way to do it. I won't use the example of California, because, clearly, a lot of ideas emanate from that state and then traverse across the country, I guess. Maybe it is a great idea from the state of Washington or Oregon. Oregon is another state, as a matter of fact, that is recognized for being on the cutting edge of a variety of trends.

Hopefully, people on the East Coast would consider those as something that they'd like to take a look at. I think there's a lot of discussion and debate in these groups, and so it's a clash of ideas, if you will, but sometimes good things come out of that.

The woman I was talking about in New Hampshire who I met on this trip to Taiwan, then ran for chairperson of NCSL, which is a *big*, *big* job. Her last name was Sitech, and I don't remember her first name. Her husband was like a professor in nuclear engineering or something. Of course, New Hampshire has a big nuclear plant, and they lived right across the border of Massachusetts; I guess a lot of people did, because the taxes were so low in New Hampshire, relatively speaking. She ran for this and lost, and I was not present then, but I knew she was doing this. It was interesting, because all the women who were delegates of NCSL and who were in favor of what I would describe as women's issues voted against her, because she was not pro-choice. They asked her flat-out during meetings where she was around trying to drum up votes. I knew, from being on this trip to Taiwan, that I still liked her, but I probably wouldn't have felt real close to her if I'd been a colleague of hers in a legislative body. But anyway, in that case, if she had won, I would have been one of very few people who would've known her in this kind of up close and personal way.

Nevada has held the NCSL National Conference twice, once in Reno—actually, they had it in Reno before—and then Las Vegas. We've never had, I don't believe, the national CSG meeting in Nevada, but I could be wrong on that. It might have happened after I was not part of the legislative body. I think that kind of ties up a number of issues I want to speak about today.

12

CAMPAIGN FOR LIEUTENANT GOVERNOR

I think at this point we want to talk about the plane crash, which everybody refers to as just "the plane crash," right?

Yes. I think so, distinguishing it, I guess, from the *other* plane crash. Plane crash one and plane crash two. You know, in 1988, when I ran for the state senate the last time, as it turns out, I didn't have any opposition. I had been picked out by a campaign-manager kind of guy named Jim Denton. He told me he met me at a function up at Mary Gojack's house, and I can't remember how he approached me about running my campaign. I had been elected to that position several times before without a professional person. It was clear when we had discussions that he was interested in having me run for statewide office, and it did seem to be a good time to think about it, because my kids had gone off to college, and so I was home alone, except for my Brittany spaniel.

So he actually approached you about running for statewide office?

Yes, I think so. It was a good time personally, but it also was a good time politically, because I'd just been elected to the senate. It's a four-year term. You do not have to resign that position, so you could run for something else, and even if you lost, you would still be in the state senate. I'd still be chair of the judiciary committee, I assumed. So the election for the state was an easy one, but it was a very *big* one. By that I mean there were very slick-looking brochures; I think we even used billboards at that time and a lot of signs, even though I had no opposition. The whole intent, of course, was to prepare me and to have my name identification known even more.

And did he help with the 1988 campaign?

Yes.

I see—as part of the move towards this.

Exactly. My friends, Barbara Weinberg and Patsy Redmond, had been the chairs of my previous senate campaigns. It was a friend/volunteer kind of an activity. But clearly, this one was being prepared for another race. It was at that time, I believe, that there were suggestions that Barbara Vucanovich might be chosen to be secretary of the interior. I had just run for the senate unopposed, and I had some people very interested in the moderate wing of the Republican party—at that time there were few people besides myself—who wanted to know if I would be interested in running for Congress if Barbara was chosen. It would be a special election, and that was kind of a nice thing to think about.

As it turns out, Barbara was not chosen, and so that was something that just came and went. Then there was a decision, what to run for. I thought, with the experience I'd had in the senate, I was not an attorney, so I wouldn't run for attorney general. Secretary of state was sort of interesting,

because it dealt with a lot of election reform. I really felt that lieutenant governor was a position, as far as chairing the economic development commission and the tourism commission, that covered about everything in the state. It's business, and in addition to business it's tourist business. With my background at the Desert Research Institute and the business park that we were contemplating developing there, it seemed like something I'd really be interested in and could really do a lot of different things. So that decision was made, and I announced in November of the year before the election, which would have been in 1989. Both Kirk and Kristi were there. We had the announcement in a room at the airport, a nice meeting room. It was packed.

I had at that time hired a young woman named Stephanie Tyler to run my day-to-day campaign. Stephanie and I had talked

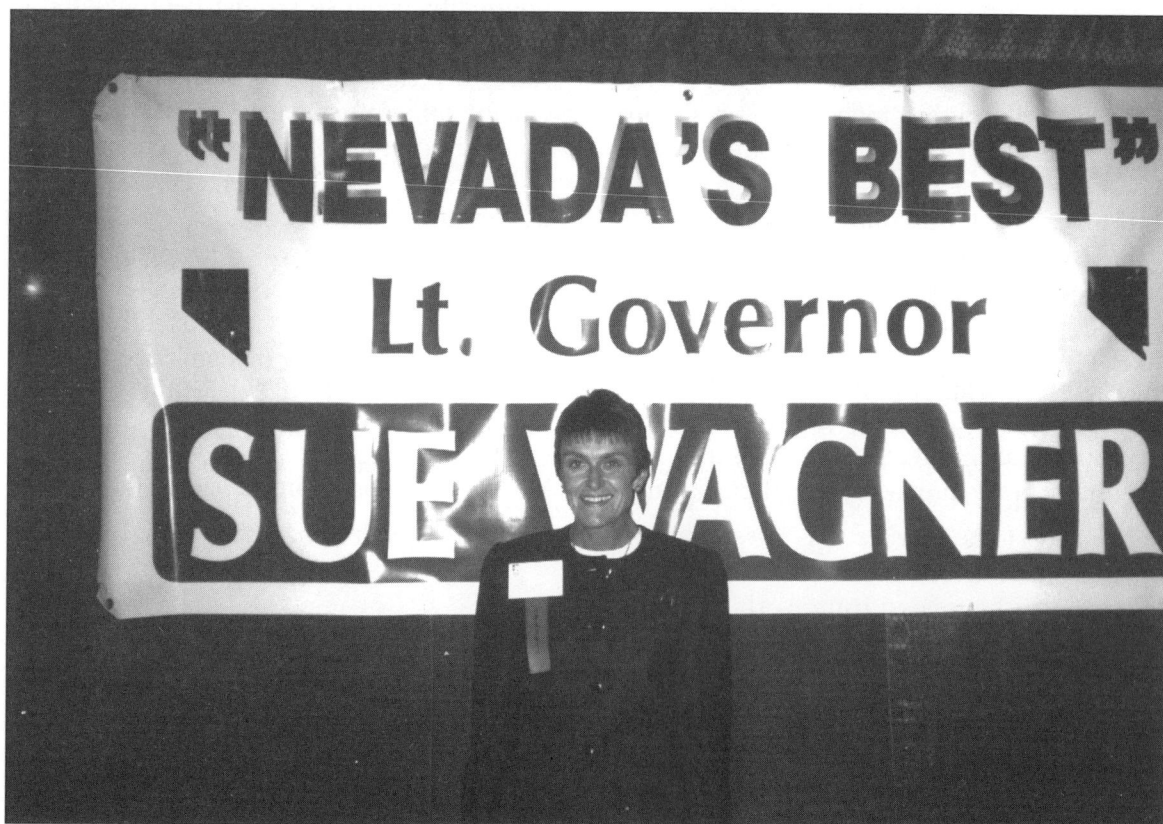

Sue with banner.

about running for statewide office a number of years before. At that time I was thinking about running for secretary of state. She was much, much younger than I, but very dynamic and personable, had a lot of energy, and she was very interested in politics. She had said that she would like to be deputy secretary of state. That's what she wanted out of running the campaign, which was something that was not unusual for her to ask.

Then I decided not to do that, and I visited with her again. I clearly saw that it would be a *huge* job to run a statewide campaign, because, though I'd been in the state senate, people didn't know who I was—maybe in northern Nevada they did, but not outside of the Washoe County area. You couldn't count on much in Las Vegas, because at that time in 1990, five thousand new people moved into Vegas every month. So, well, there were good things and bad things about that. You could start from scratch, and nobody else had the upper hand, unless they already were elected. There was nobody running at that time for lieutenant governor because the incumbent, Bob Miller, had been bumped up to acting governor. Richard Bryan had been governor, and Bob Miller had been his lieutenant governor, both of the same party. That gave Richard the luxury of running in midterm against United States Senator Chic Hecht. Richard did get elected, and so Bob became acting governor, and the lieutenant governor seat was then vacant, as was the secretary of state position. Yes. Well, wait a minute. I think Frankie Sue Del Papa had already served one term. I'm not quite sure.

I decided to run for lieutenant governor, and the announcement was made in November of 1989, and this room at the airport was just packed with people. I'm sure that had a lot to do with Stephanie getting people there, because I didn't. I knew what I was going to say. I had a focus in what I

was going to talk about in the campaign, and, of course, it tied in with economic development and tourism and my background for that and why I thought I would be the best person to run. We did not know of anybody else running at that time, but when you have a vacant constitutional office, you assume that people will be running. I was pretty sure there wouldn't be any other Republicans that I would be concerned about.

Anyway, that was a great sendoff, and then we went on the airplane down to Las Vegas and made an announcement there at a room at the airport, as well. I remember this very clearly, that Jon Ralston was there from the *Las Vegas Review-Journal*, and some other reporters. The first thing out of Jon Ralston's mouth was, "How do you think you could win this election as a Republican, because you're pro-choice, and your party is not?"

I answered that question. I remember saying that I thought really I represented the Republican Party, because to me it was a conservative issue of keeping government out of your lives, and here they were intruding. He didn't ask any more; that took care of that one.

Then the other question asked that I remember clearly was, "How do you think you can win, because you voted for the 300 percent pension increase?"

It was a big issue in that election for everybody who had been in the legislature in the 1989 session, and I had voted for it. We had gone back and repealed it at a special session. It really was generated by former Governor Mike O'Callaghan, who then was at the *Las Vegas Sun*. It was brutal on people who lived in Las Vegas, but then the rest of the press picked it up. They didn't explain how much the pension was—300 percent sounds like a big deal. Well, if they had been fair about it, they would have said it's twenty five dollars a month times number of years, but you have to serve ten years! So, you had to be elected five sessions, or four and a half for the senate.

I remember this was one of Jim Denton's bad ideas. Fortunately, I did not follow it, but most of the time you have to trust the people who are running your campaign when you don't have time to do every little thing yourself. He had suggested that I take out a full-page ad in the Las Vegas newspapers and apologize for it. I thought, "Wow. Talk about bringing attention to the issue—of people who might not have ever heard of it before." So I just explained that was one vote I'd made out of 3,632—make up a number—votes, or something. "If there's only one bad one, I don't think that's bad at all."

Nobody else asked me about it again, or that was the end of that discussion. So, you could go on, really, pretty much with what you wanted to do and how you felt you could serve in that position. Most things were focused on economic development and tourism, and that had just really come about under Lieutenant Governor Bob Cashell, who was right before Bob Miller. Bob Cashell was elected as a Democrat. He switched parties later on to Republican. Bob had actually created, when he was in that office, a couple of real responsibilities for the lieutenant governor. Before that, the only real responsibility was president of the senate. It's a responsibility that many lieutenant governors have across the nation.

Actually, the responsibilities for Nevada's lieutenant governor are much more substantial than many other states. There are a few states that don't have lieutenant governors, and the secretary of state is the next office in line of succession. There are less than ten, I think. In fact, Arizona, the state from which I came, does not have a lieutenant governor. So when I told my friends I was running for this,

[laughter] some of them didn't know what it was. They figured it was something like being vice president.

Fortunately, there was something substantial that you could get your hands around in terms of those issues. My kids went back to college again, and they did help me when summertime came and campaigned with me, particularly in Clark County. One of the things that we recognized immediately was that I had to spend almost all my time in Las Vegas, because I was as not as well known as in the northern part of the state and particularly Washoe County.

There were several good things that happened. At that time I was working at the Desert Research Institute, and they had not had a substantial office in Las Vegas like they do now, but they did have an office, and because my responsibility, to a large extent, was trying to promote DRI, that was something I could do there. I brought a slide show about DRI to breakfast and lunchtime meetings, and then in the evening I'd go to some reception with a member introducing me.

The problem you have is, who is going to introduce you? How are you going to make overtures? How do you make overtures to groups when you don't know anybody in the organization? You just can't walk in to somebody's cocktail party uninvited and start shaking hands.

One of the good things that happened to me at that time was that Jim Denton had wanted to expand his base of operations to Las Vegas, because he did have a pretty good record up here, actually, of getting people elected. I didn't know that at the time, but it made sense. So he was interested in tying up with Jim Joyce, who has been discussed before. So that was done, and all those things I just didn't bother with. I mean, all they wanted from me was money [laughter] out of the candidate. And that's exactly what it resulted in. Having Jim

Joyce involved was a very good thing, because he was very powerful, very well known. He told me, when we were discussing running for this office, "You know, I'm going to give you two names."

I had asked him, "How do I meet people?"

He said, "I'm going to give you two names. If you get these two guys to be associated with your campaign, you won't have any substantial opposition, because these two people are very well known, and it would send a signal that you are not to be messed around with."

He gave me the names, and I went to visit each of them. One was Peter Thomas, who at that time was president of Valley Bank, which was very, very big in Las Vegas and has since been sold to Bank of America. Peter Thomas was a young man and was very happy to be involved in the campaign. I don't know, but I suspect that Jim Joyce had spoken with him before. I did all the things that were necessary for the dinner or lunch or whatever.

The other one was Kenny Guinn, who, of course, now is Governor Guinn, and he was *very* helpful. I remember meeting with Governor Guinn and First Lady Dema and their children for lunch and learning a little bit more about him, as they certainly were learning about me. He was very helpful in getting me a campaign office as an in-kind contribution, meaning that instead of giving me money, they would provide other help, i.e., an office. The Las Vegas one was over near Fletcher Jones Ford dealership, so that was great.

I then needed to have somebody that was a Stephanie Tyler counterpart in Las Vegas. Actually, that's kind of a misnomer, because Stephanie was kind of the head of the whole thing, but, hey, that was a big, big problem. Stephanie and I had been talking about doing this for some time, and Stephanie went ahead and got some people to work with her, below her, and there were

a couple of young men who wanted to help, which was great.

One of them was Mike Dayton, and he went to Washington after this election with Jim Gibbons to be his chief of staff. He's back, I guess, in Reno. Stephanie preferred to ask a young man named C. J. Haddock, who she worked very well with, and they were just great together and got a lot of volunteers. Our office was in Independence Square on Moana. Herz Brothers Jewelers is in there. Anyway, it was a great office and had lots of room for people to stuff envelopes and mail things, et cetera, and that was something she set up.

Now that I had these two people, Thomas and Guinn, in Las Vegas on board with me to send out a political signal, then I had to get people to really work hard day to day to get me elected. So there was a woman I had met or that somebody had suggested to me. Her husband later on did run for lieutenant governor, and maybe his name will come to me, and hers will. I interviewed her, and she had all the skills that everybody told me she had, but when she heard about the magnitude of the job, she decided she just didn't want to do it.

So I thought, "Wow. Who do I get?" She recommended two other women she knew through the Junior League of Las Vegas. I interviewed one who was going to be the incoming president. Her name was Verona Pasquale, and it was absolutely one of the best decisions I ever made, period, as far as my election was concerned. She was absolutely terrific. She had not been very involved in politics, but she knew organization; she knew how to get along with people. She already had an image in the community by being incoming president of the Junior League, and she was an incredibly hard worker. I don't even know if she was a Republican. I suspect she was, because I did make Barbara Weinberg and other people register Republican if they were running my campaigns.

Sue with Nevada First Lady, Dema Guinn at annual Girls' Night Out reception at Sue's home.

Everything seemed to be great. I received another great in-kind contribution, and it was an apartment in the Whitney Ranch Estates, which was then *literally* on the outside of town. It was new. It had a whole lot of space, in fact, enough space for my children to come in the summer months or during vacations to help me campaign, which they did, and that was terrific. It meant that I could have everything there—clothes, all the kinds of things you need. I didn't have to keep shuffling them back and forth. I had a pool, and my kids certainly liked that. In fact, somebody gave me a membership to a gym as an in-kind contribution, because it was important to be able to keep up your stamina and energy, to be honest with you, during this period of time. It really is kind of a grueling exercise in American politics.

I had been up and down and around, gone to all these different small communities. For example, the big event that happens in Ely is the Pony Express Days. Being on the gaming commission now, we regulate those races, but I think that they don't do them anymore, because they just weren't financially feasible. It's a real shame. I had a good friend, JoAnne Wessel, who was working on the campaign. I think she got tied in with my campaign through Stephanie Tyler. JoAnne was from Ely, and her father still lived there, and she offered to take me and introduce me to people at the racetrack and other things. That's what you need; that's always terrific. We had a great time.

I selected a very sharp lady in Elko to be kind of my rural coordinator, and her name was Nancy Ernaut. It turns out that

Left to right: Judi Bishop, Verona Pasquale, Sue Wagner, Susan Haase.

her son was interested in politics, as well, and he later became Governor Guinn's chief of staff and now is a major lobbyist. Nancy looked like she came out of *Vanity Fair* magazine. She seemed so out of place in Elko, in a way. Now, she was very involved in the Republican Party, and that was very good to have in a rural community such as that, except she was more moderate than many of the people in Elko. I heard that they kept saying, "Are you sure you've picked the right person?"

I said, "Yes. I *know* I did." [laughter] I know I did, because, of course, she kind of supported the same things I did. Let me go back and say that I had met Nancy right before that. I had gone to Elko for a Lincoln Day dinner, and I don't know why, but I was on a plane with Brian McKay, who was our

attorney general, and Bill Raggio, who was the senate majority leader at that time. I think there was another person on the plane, but I don't remember. This precedes 1990, and it was the first time I met Nancy Ernaut, because she was in charge of the activity out there. On the plane, Brian McKay spoke with me about running for lieutenant governor with him, as he would be the gubernatorial candidate. That, of course, predates my previous discussion. That was the first time I'd really thought about it, because he was telling me, he and Bill Raggio and whoever else, why that would be a good match. Brian had lived in Las Vegas before. Of course, I was in northern Nevada. I was pro-choice, and I never did know what he was exactly. I think he was, but he was not as involved in it as

I. So I went on that premise, that this is what we were going to do, and then we tied in with Jim Denton, et cetera. But it had been in my mind before, because Jim Denton had been very involved in my 1988 campaign for the senate. I had already met Nancy, so she was a good choice for me later on.

But Brian McKay didn't run, as we know, and I was devastated. I now know *why* he didn't run, but he really didn't say then. I guess I understand why he didn't. In order to run for office, you have to be able to raise money, because running statewide, particularly, my gosh, you have to rely on billboards, and you've got to rely on television significantly, and that's why elections in America have become so outrageously expensive.

Did he think that you could not raise enough, much like Frankie Sue? That was what she said when she dropped out, too.

No. I'm not getting into that sort of stuff. I'm just talking now about my relationship with Brian McKay. And that was based upon a presidential, vice presidential . . . I mean, governor. Oh! Maybe that's a Freudian slip, huh? [laughter]

Maybe that was where you were headed, huh? [laughter]

Well, when Brian told me this—actually, he didn't; it was Karen, his wife, who called to tell me—maybe he knew I'd be really, really upset about it.

Brian McKay was the then attorney general and had a very good reputation. It was kind of like Robert Redford in *The Candidate*—good-looking guy, personable. When people talked about Brian McKay, they said the Robert Redford thing. So it would not be bad having him be at the top of the ticket with me. It does make a

difference who is heading the ticket up, because you then can rely on, for instance, logistical information. If there's going to be a pancake breakfast here or something that we need to know about, normally their being at the top of the ticket is very helpful. Well, as it turns out, there was no top of the ticket, and when he dropped out, then I was asked, "Well, why don't you now run for governor?"

I gave that about five minutes' thought and said, "No thank you." [laughter] I thought that would be a rather daunting task, because I would then be running against the then acting governor, Bob Miller. The person who did run, and I know this is going to sound like a man's name that we now have on the Washoe County Commission, Jim Gallaway—same name, same spelling. We have a county commissioner by that name, but he is not the same person. This person was independently wealthy to some extent; I believe he lived at Incline Village. Obviously, no one's heard of him since, and he didn't get many votes.

We had to do so much more work than under *normal* circumstances. One of the things that one does in a statewide race is set up two headquarters, if you will, in the northern and the southern part of the state, at a minimum. Then you need to know what's going on in the rural areas, particularly, because they tend to vote Republican far more than Democrat. The only county that is Democrat in the rural areas is White Pine, and that's where Ely is located. These places certainly don't have enough votes to determine . . . well, I suppose they could determine the result of an election, but it'd be highly unlikely. I did spend a lot of time in the rural areas. It wasn't that difficult, because I really liked the people. People were so friendly and so anxious to meet you and visit with you, and it was very laid back.

You always liked that.

Oh, yes.

It started when you were running for the assembly, going door to door.

That's right. I do. I very much like to campaign. Some people like to campaign, and they don't like to serve. Some people like to serve, but they don't want to mess around with the campaigns. I liked both of those.

You liked all of it.

I did. I really did. The rural areas—as I was explaining with Ely and White Pine and the Pony Express Days—a lot of these communities have something special. For example, in Hawthorne there's the Armed Forces Day, and so they have parades. Down in the Gardnerville-Minden area there is Nevada Days, I think it is called. They have a big parade. That's a hotbed of Republicanism in Douglas County.

Carson City has the big granddaddy parade, the Nevada Day Parade, which was October 31, and now it's been changed to make for a three-day weekend. Each year that I was in that parade, fortunately, the weather was pretty nice. Sometimes it was cold early in the morning, but the sun was out. Sometimes it has just been horrible. You could not be in that parade at that time unless you actually held an office. So if you were running against somebody who was a nonincumbent for anything, they couldn't be in the parade, and you could. I was able to be in the parade *prior* to my running for

Sue and JoAnne Wessell at Pony Express Days, Ely, Nevada, 1990.

lieutenant governor. This is the kind of thing that it helps if you've hired somebody to help you. I would never have thought of this, that I could run as a state senator from a next-door county, and it didn't look that politically motivated.

So you could go around to all of these little parades.

I could, but I really didn't. Only for that one, I think, I'm pretty sure. No, I didn't.

The other ones have these activities. Now, they do not all have parades, but there are several of them that do. Tonopah—it's the Jim Butler Day Parade, and that's fun, too. When I was elected lieutenant governor, the rural representative on the tourism commission was Bob Perchetti, and he's a really good guy. His family owned a motel—I think it was the Jim Butler Motel—

which I stayed in at that time. It's right on the main drag. That was fun, and they had a concert at night in the main street.

We're getting into the parts where I recognize some names now. [laughter]

Right. And I'm trying to think of other communities. Elko—I went there often.

Elko has a big Basque Festival every year. Did you know that?

Yes, but somehow that doesn't ring a big bell. The other things I did in these small communities was go and visit with the newspaper editors, so they could quiz me in what I would do in this position, if elected. That would lead either to your being endorsed or not being endorsed, but you hoped that you would be. Mel Steninger was

Nevada Day Parade, 1993.

at the *Elko Daily Free Press*, and he was *very* conservative. He didn't like me very much, but I was a Republican. That was kind of how he looked at it.

Jack McCloskey in Hawthorne was one of the greatest guys I've ever met, *ever*. Particularly in this campaign, he's way at the top of the list. He was the editor of the newspaper, *Mineral County Independent News*, and he had a great column called "Jasper." He and his wife were just great people. Talk about an oral history, I hope he's done his, because he's now dead. But he was an *incredible* guy and really made candidates pay attention to that little community. You were afraid for your life if you didn't! In fact, after I was elected, I went down to visit him occasionally.

Anyway, those kinds of things stick in your mind, because they are such exciting times, and you meet such unbelievably wonderful people. Now, I'm not going to pick out any other activities, but these were just things that I did [laughter] in my off hours, so to speak, because most of the time was then getting involved in the Las Vegas community. Interestingly enough, this happened to be at the high watermark of the UNLV basketball team, who won the national championship that year, so to go to the Thomas and Mack Center was the best way to campaign, and I knew an awful lot about basketball.

It was perfect for you.

Exactly. I had to be kind of quiet, because, in fact, one of the games was against my University of Arizona Wildcats. The oddest thing happened. What you wanted to do is go from box to box to box, around in a circle, because all the people in those boxes were big UNLV Rebel fans. They were large givers, and they were the people you would want to have know you for political purposes. I could obviously talk about basketball, too. You did not want to

butt into things. You had to have somebody take you around. There was a man who, after I was elected lieutenant governor, ran when I didn't run, and it was his wife I interviewed first about this job of being campaign manager. He was very helpful. His wife, of course, was very interested in my campaign, but just didn't want to work that hard, to be that tied up. So he took me around to all these different boxes and introduced me to people, and that was a very neat thing. That was kind of the first opening, but those people then were in all kinds of other different industries for their day job, so to speak, and that was a great avenue for me.

The Junior League was another avenue—many, many very active women. I had already captured the president's time, and she was very involved in many activities. So that was a real highlight. I met Diane Wilson, who I believe then became, or was at that moment in time, president of Junior League. Her husband was a medical doctor. She was just great to Stephanie and myself, and we stayed with her a couple of times. She knew a ton of people.

It was that kind of thing that you just had to network like crazy, because you just were starting from basically scratch. It was nice to be always introduced as "Senator Sue Wagner." Most of those people did not know whether I was their senator or not, because, as I said, the community had changed so quickly every month. If you'd said, "Who was your state senator?" *Really*, except *very* politically astute people, they wouldn't know.

Because so many were new. You've got ten thousand people a month.

Yes. But, of course, right now I'm talking about pretty established people. Say, you go to a luncheon, and somebody takes you as their guest, and you go around to table after table. A lot of those people may just be there, or they may not be interested. They may be a Realtor, and the only thing they're interested in is selling their next house. But you took advantage, or you made those things happen. The best thing was to give speeches there and be the one person they identified with. All attention was focused on you. The next best thing, of course, was going around and meeting people from table to table. The worst is just going in, sitting down, and getting up and leaving and maybe only meeting the people at your table or the people in sight of you. You really had to look at that as a waste of time, because you just didn't have that much contact.

You were still doing work for DRI, being a senator and campaigning.

Yes. Exactly.

So you didn't have much time.

Plus being a mother. Fortunately, at that point—and this is the reason I chose that time, particularly—I didn't have to be home all the time. I did have to get rid of my dog, Tahoya, though, because I was gone so much. My wonderful Brittany spaniel started howling and carrying on, so I found a real nice home for him.

It was just a crazy time but a really fun time. I would go down to Laughlin and speak to the Laughlin Chamber of Commerce. I remember telling them what I would perceive doing for that community, if elected. You try to reach out to as many groups as you possibly can, and you hope that they vote, and that they were registered to vote.

It was a really good mix of people working on my campaign. Of course, Verona Pasquale was down in Las Vegas, but she and Stephanie got along pretty well. Jim Denton was hired to devise a strategy.

He was not chosen because of his winning personality. I don't regret using him. I'm not sure I'd do it again, but I think that a lot of the things I might not have done, except he kept pushing me, pushing me. I think you do need somebody like that, when you realize how daunting this task is. You feel more comfortable being in a comfortable mode, which is not where you should be. You should be in an uncomfortable mode and doing just different things. But it was nice, because I had been in the legislature, so a lot of my colleagues in the senate were helpful. I think of Hal Smith in Henderson—he and his great wife took me different places.

The ball was rolling now, and it didn't seem like I was going to have much opposition. The only person who had filed in the Republican primary was a man named Pro-Life Andy Anderson. That was his real, legal name. He had it changed. So clearly, when people looked at the primary ballot—and that's all there was—they knew what that issue was for that man. You also knew what my position was on that issue, or else he wouldn't have been running against me.

Now, there were no Democrats. I remember Stephanie Tyler and I were at the airport on the very last day to file, and Stephanie went into a phone booth and called Rollie Melton at the *Reno Gazette-Journal*. Rollie told Stephanie that a woman named Jeanne Ireland had just filed as a Democrat, and Rollie knew her and told Stephanie all about her.

Stephanie was furious that somebody had actually filed against me. We were a bit worried, because Rollie knew her and told Stephanie that Jeanne and her husband knew people all over the state, because her husband had been the football and/or baseball coach of many, many, many high schools in the state. They were very well known in Las Vegas, because Bill

Ireland had been the UNLV athletic director and the Rebels' first football coach.

So it seemed to be, "Oh, my gosh! We've got to raise . . . ." And we wondered, why had she gotten involved? What were her issues? It appeared that issues were obviously not the reason. She was a woman, and, of course, she was a Democrat. It might have been worse if her *husband* had run, because he was a Republican, and I think he was the better known and the better liked, but she appeared to be very nice.

What do you mean when you say the issues were not the point?

Well, she didn't run because she was pro-life, for example. Andy Anderson ran on that issue.

She didn't have a strong central issue?

We didn't know. I don't remember her saying much about any issues. When she filed, I don't remember what the press release said, but it wasn't substantial. It appeared later on that actually United States Senator Harry Reid had got her involved in this race, which he had a capacity to do and has done ever since I've known him. I think Harry does a very good job in Washington, but, very honestly, everybody knows this about Harry Reid, that if he has any fear of anybody running against him, he tries to get rid of them before they can be an opponent. So if I could be defeated for lieutenant governor, then I probably would be disillusioned about running for the United States Senate.

This is an aside about Harry. [laughter] But after I got appointed to the gaming commission, he sent me a handwritten note, which I've saved somewhere, saying, "First in the assembly; then you're in the senate. Then you're lieutenant governor, and now you're in the gaming commission—

just like me." He was in each one of those; that's what he said.

"I certainly hope you're not going to be in my current office."

I'm sure at that time—in fact, I do know—that the one opponent who would give Harry the worst race was, you guessed it, a Republican woman, pro-choice, because he was a male Mormon and opposite of me on most of the social issues.

So it seemed as if that's why this person got in the race. Offers of money and help were forthcoming. But again, this is a pretty standard operation. In fact, he ran somebody against Randolph Townsend— Emma Sepulveda—because he thought Randolph was going to run against him.

He offered Brian Sandoval a federal judgeship in Las Vegas. Well, once you're a federal judge, you're not going to do anything else. That's for life. They would have had to move to Las Vegas, and, in fact, Brian and I talked about it. [laughter] He chose not to do that. Of course, he's now our attorney general.

So we are opponents, and we saw Jeanne and Bill Ireland along the way, but not all the time. They weren't always at the same occasions, but I did meet her at some point. She seemed nice. In fact, we met her, I remember specifically, at the Jim Butler Days in Tonopah. It just meant that we were going to have to work harder. So that activity took place from the time I announced in November to about the primary election.

And when did she announce?

She announced on the last day to file. That's when Stephanie called, because we had nobody at that time except Pro-Life Andy Anderson. We thought, "Whoa! Is this going to be fun!" [laughter]

We didn't know how many votes he'd get; we hoped and thought maybe not a lot, but in the Republican primary, you can't tell. You didn't know at that time.

Both my children, Kirk and Kristina, visited in Las Vegas during the summer, and they made absolutely incredible commercials for me. I'm sorry that they're now lost, because the cable television channel, A&E, did a documentary on small plane crashes—anyway, I'll get into that. They took all my campaign commercial tapes, and they promised they'd get them back to me. They were in Birmingham, England; that's where Granada Productions was located. They did these programs for A&E, but they were an offshoot of the *New York Times*. So they promised they'd tell me when it was going to be on, and I never heard. A couple of years went by, and all of a sudden, in Las Vegas, I ran into people who said, "We just saw you on TV! It was like a story of your life."

I kept thinking, "What could that be?" Suddenly, it dawned on me that that must have been it. I called Granada Productions in Birmingham, and it was on, because I have a copy of it now. This guy who came and did this wasn't there anymore. I was able to order it on-line from A&E.

Anyway, Jim Denton had a terrific guy, Ed Tuley. I still keep in touch with Ed. He left and went to Florida and got married and has darling, little kids and is a lobbyist in Tallahassee, in the state of Florida. He did the most wonderful commercials, and he did the production, and he worked with Jim Denton. The two of them did, I guess, an hour or so of just the kids, and he would throw questions at them, like we're doing here. "Tell me about your mother. Do you think she's a leader?" They were just kind of extemporaneously talking. It was just unbelievable. They looked like all-American kids. I just couldn't even imagine [laughter] that's how good looking my kids

are. In fact, in this A&E program, you see a little smidgen of it. He was very careful. I noticed it in other people's tapes, and they're not very careful about it, not like he was. If we did a tape that was made in Las Vegas, we wanted background or a park or something that was very well known, so that when people watched that commercial in Las Vegas, they'd know it had been made there. I noticed that, in fact, Jim Gibbons just had one not long ago, and it was right in front of the North Las Vegas fire station and was being shown in Reno. That would not have happened in my campaign, because they were very careful about that kind of thing.

Being sure the Las Vegas background was shown in Las Vegas?

Yes. For most people, it wouldn't matter. I remember the kids and I walking through this park—I don't remember the name of it now, but it was visible—so people would know that that was made there.

I remember Boulder City had a big parade, and Kristina and I were in that one. Kirk would drive the car, a convertible. While this is all going on, of course, billboards are appearing throughout the state.

Jim Denton has a tactic with billboards. I see it all the time now. I know exactly whose campaign he's running. I even know that anyway, but if I didn't, I could figure it out. He puts up great-looking billboards for a while, maybe a couple of weeks, and then they go down, because you can't afford to keep them up. But he puts them up right before the close of filing, so you think, "Oh, my gosh, look how organized that person is! I'm so far behind already." And that's true—you *are* that organized. In fact, when I announced in November of 1989, behind me is a *huge* banner. I mean, it's as long as this whole house. It's going to go up over my campaign headquarters, but it's behind the podium where I'm announcing. The right colors, the block printing, "FOR LIEUTENANT GOVERNOR." So that's all done. Those decisions have to be made early, but you *are* way ahead of anybody else—unless now somebody knows that, and they're equally as organized, and, I suspect, even *more* organized. That's how he gets ahead.

Stay one step ahead.

Yes. So that was going on. My mother, who is still alive at ninety-six in Tucson, came up on some kind of a little trip to Las Vegas. I was not there, but my chief of staff, Verona, took my mother around town to look at the billboards. [laughter] I think she took a picture of my mother in front of one of them. It was way up high in the air. It was expensive, but people would say, "Who is that? Oh, wow! That person's organized," or whatever.

Jim Joyce was obviously doing stuff down in Las Vegas, too, but the summer was a really good time with the kids. Kirk had at that time a girlfriend come over from Boulder, where he was going to college, and help out, and she was fun. I remember at the Boulder City party, they were in charge of blowing up the helium balloons, and you can imagine they had fun with the helium gas. Yes, blowing them up, because the balloons even said, "Sue Wagner." They were blue colored. Everything was coordinated. It was pretty well organized.

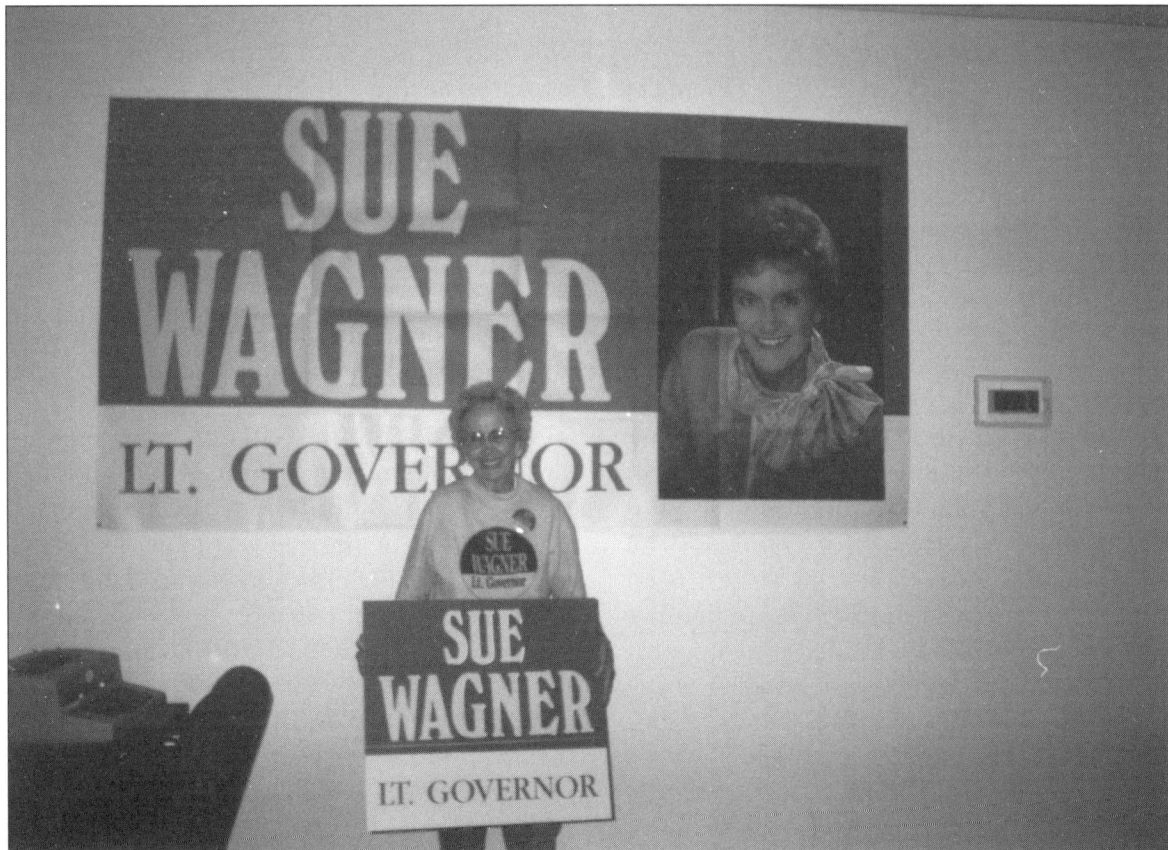

Sue's mother holds a sign for Sue's campaign for Lt. Governor.

Labor Day is the last hurrah before the primary election, which is right after Labor Day in September, so there are a lot of things like this that I've described going on throughout the summer.

Labor Day, I think we had something in Elko, and then there was another event in Winnemucca. I remember in Elko that the man who owned the Ford dealership let us have a truck. A truck with a roll bar was good, because you could stand up and hold onto the roll bar and then wave to people on each side, and you were up high. I don't remember the name of that. I'm pretty sure it was a Ford truck. Then I think we went to Winnemucca, because that was a busy weekend; there were pancake breakfasts at different places. We just went from one place to the next.

And this was 1990, Labor Day weekend?

Yes. This is going to be real difficult to talk about. This is Labor Day weekend, and as I said, there is a lot of activity going on, because the primary is right after that. In fact, I think that this year it might have been the first Tuesday *after* Labor Day, which would have been the way it fell. Monday is Labor Day, and then it's the next Tuesday. Labor Day fell on the first Monday of the month, I guess, is what I'm trying to say.

So the last place we get to is Fallon, where it's the cantaloupe festival. Fallon is noted for its Heart O' Gold cantaloupes. Everything is focused around the cantaloupes. I'm not sure this was the first time I had worn this or not, but I remember my mother-in-law made me an old-fashioned bathing suit, which was unbelievably great. She was a great seamstress. It was pink, and it had a pink and black plaid ruffle and then had a little ruffle plaid shower cap. It had the bloomer pants and a sash made out of the plaid, too. All the accessories were of the plaid, and the other was pink. She made it specifically

for all these picnics and things, because they'd always throw the ball at the person on the diving board, and if they hit it, you'd go in the tank of water.

In the dunk tank?

Yes. So it was a cute thing to wear and a good thing to wear for those. Of course, people thought it was funny, because guys would just wear shorts or something, if they even dared do it, because usually the water is really cold in those things. Anyway, I do remember that was something we did at that event.

It wasn't just a costume for fun. You were actually doing the dunk tank? Dunk the politician, right? [laughter]

Right. People wanted to do this, to get people in the water. This was a particularly fun thing for people to see, and they'd remember you, but it was a lot more comfortable to be in, too.

As I say, everything this particular day was built around the Heart O' Gold cantaloupes, because they are very, very well known. In fact, I remember getting a cantaloupe ice cream cone. Then we went to the airport, because we had flown there. I don't remember exactly where we'd come from. I'm assuming we had flown from Elko to Winnemucca and then to Fallon. Then we were getting ready to fly to Carson City at the end of the day, because they also had an event there. Actually, the only way you really could feasibly get around in our large state, particularly in the rural areas, is by plane.

I was flown into Tonopah by a man named Fran Breen, who is a well-known attorney in Reno. In fact, he had been chairman of the board of trustees of the Fleischmann Foundation and was a law partner of Cliff Young, who I told you had endorsed me to take his place in the state senate. Cliff was elected to the supreme court after being in the state senate. He was in Congress and all those wonderful things. Anyway, Fran Breen was one of his partners, and Fran had a single-engine plane, and it was very small. He flew Stephanie and I into Tonopah for the Jim Butler Days.

The plane that I was in at this time was owned by Bob Seale, who was a candidate for state treasurer. His wife was with us that day, Judy Seale, who was the surgical head nurse at Saint Mary's. What I've learned about Judy is that she was just very well liked, a wonderful person. Bob's campaign manager was a young man named Brian Krolicki. He and Stephanie Tyler were about the same age, late twenties, really young, and very, very interested in politics, as well.

All of us were together during this particular weekend. The plane was a Cessna 411, which I later learned was [sighs] a piece of junk. I didn't know that at the time, of course. It was a six-passenger plane. Of course, Bob was in the pilot seat, and Judy was in the copilot seat, and he referred to her as his copilot.

I have known one other couple who flew a lot, and it was Pete Neumann and Rénate Neumann. He's a well-known personal injury attorney in Reno. I went to college with him in Arizona, and Rénate knew how to fly very, very well. I jumped to the conclusion that this was the same kind of arrangement, that she was also a pilot, because he referred to her that way, but that was not true.

Anyway, I was seated facing backwards in the plane, and my back was to Judy's back. Stephanie had her back to Bob Seale's back, because she and I were facing the rear of the plane together. Brian Krolicki was seated across from me, and those planes are small when you get in them. His knees were kind of like up; our knees kind of met each other. So I was looking directly

at him. There wasn't anybody that Stephanie was looking at. That seat was empty.

When we had left Reno to go on this weekend, I remember Bob Seale talking to a mechanic on the ground about something, and I don't remember what that was, but he was obviously talking to a mechanic about something and probably shouldn't have been talking to a mechanic about anything as we were getting ready to fly on the plane. It didn't occur to me at the time that there was anything out of the ordinary about that.

Maybe it should have. Maybe I should have thought twice about getting in a plane at all, since Peter had been killed in one, but I can't blame it on anybody but myself. I mean, we're in the heat of a campaign, and Stephanie is telling them to go here and there on that day and this day and so on, and you just do it. Of course, her job *was* to get me to as many places as I could and most conveniently. Nobody at that time rode in a motor home or took a trailer or anything, which they could have done. It would be hard to do three or four events in one day, like was done on that particular day.

I remember taking off from Fallon, and I think it was Bryan Nelson, a Republican, who was running for attorney general against Frankie Sue Del Papa, and he was a deputy attorney general, which was interesting because he was running *against* the attorney general. I remember Bob Seale asked him if he'd like to fly with us, because we had an extra seat, and he said no. Lucky him. Anyway, we took off and didn't get very far. And I remember. [sighs] I remember [with emotion] Brian saying to me, "Don't worry. We've got a little problem."

Brian said that? He could see it from where he sat?

Evidently. Or he could feel it or whatever, because I was, of course, not looking toward the pilot. I don't know what he saw. And I don't remember anything for weeks.

Oh. That's the last thing you remember.

Yes. I've been told a lot of different things, and I'll relay some of those thoughts.

Do you remember being on the ground?

No.

No. Not anything.

Later I heard, of course, that Judy Seale was killed, and that the engine of the plane had crushed her. Bob Seale had some burns on his hand, and he had some plastic surgery done on that. Stephanie and I, because we were facing backwards, had all the damage done to our spine and neck. Stephanie's was pretty much in the lumbar area, and mine were in the cervical, the neck, and the thoracic part. I know that a doctor had subsequently told me—in fact, it was the doctor I had at University of California Davis hospital in Sacramento— that if Stephanie and I had been in the opposite seats, because of our age and our bones, that neither one of us probably would have lived. I don't know if that's true or not, but anyway, I'm sure it's maybe sometimes said to make you feel better.

But Brian was thrown out of the plane through the front window, which by this time, there wasn't anything there, so there was a wide open space. He landed on the ground with a little scratch on his forehead. That's all he got. And he then walked to get help, and help was brought to us by, I think, EMT guys out in Fallon. In fact, there is a young man who is serving his second term

in the legislature who I was reading about last night in the *Reno Gazette-Journal* newspaper. He is a captain in the fire department in North Las Vegas. Somebody introduced me to him last session. I had invited all of them down, though, to the senate when I got elected. But anyway, they obviously must have done a pretty good job, because they got everybody out, I guess.

Well, I was flown to Washoe Medical Center, and, of course, by now it's breaking news, I guess you'd say.

Yes, it was. The newscasters were there when you arrived?

Yes. Anyway, I think I was in a helicopter, because I've seen pictures of myself being wheeled in. Bob was taken to Saint Mary's, and Stephanie was taken to Northern Nevada in Sparks, and then I was taken to Washoe. I do know from people telling me, that they'd seen me there. Bill Raggio called my kids. [with emotion] The governor was there, I guess, and other elected people. I know my friend Marybel Batjer happened to be in town then and was there. Lynn Atcheson at that time, I think, had just started working for Washoe Medical Center. People tell me what I looked like and didn't think I was going to live and stuff, but I don't remember any of it.

They say I acted like I knew who they were and what was going on and talking to them. I guess I was on something that they'd strapped me to that was rotating me back and forth, and I don't know what that was for. But evidently, a decision was made that doctors didn't want to operate on my neck in Reno, so they flew me in a plane down to Sacramento, I don't how many days later. I think it was a couple days later. I still meet people today, particularly since I'm on the board of directors of Washoe Health System, who say, "Oh, yes. I was in the emergency room when you came in," or something of that sort. That was the day before the primary election.

Anyway, I was sent to University of California Davis in Sacramento, and they operated on my neck there. I was there for quite a while. I really don't remember how long it was, but it was several weeks at least, and all kinds of things happened. I had to have a body cast made to fit, but the worst thing, I guess, was the huge drugs that they had me on. I remember telling people—I think I told you—that nurses or orderlies or something would come in, and I actually believed they were SS troopers.

It's just a terrible feeling, when it's something like that, and you're so afraid, when it's really not normal thought processes that you're having. I was in intensive care for a very long time, and they wouldn't dismiss me from intensive care to just be on a floor, unless I could answer certain questions, and they were simple ones: What's your name, and what date is it, and who's president? Those kinds of things—where do you live? Finally, I guess, I answered those after a very long time.

I had a lot of people come down from Reno. I know I said that maybe I thought Lynn Atcheson was working at Washoe Med at that time. That is not true. She was with Harrah's, I believe, because Harrah's owned the Holiday Inns, and there was a Holiday Inn in Sacramento that was not too far from the hospital. So there was some kind of a deal worked out where people could come down to Sacramento and visit. Some of the people I know who came were Spike Wilson, Rollan and Marilyn Melton, Penny Mayer. I did not know this about Penny until, when I was thinking about buying a place in Graeagle, I called her, because she's a very good Realtor and very well known in Reno. In fact, she's president of the Nevada State Realtors Association this year.

I went to lunch with Penny and a woman Episcopal priest in Sparks about a year and a half ago, I guess, and hadn't seen her for a very long time. So she's telling the priest, Reverend Britt Olsen, about me, and she mentions that she had come to Sacramento to see me. I was just shocked! I said, "You did? I didn't know that, didn't remember that." The odd thing was that she was late, and she decided to stay overnight. She went to stay with her cousin—who was head of the orthopedic surgery department.

It's too bad he was not on that day, but he said, "What are you doing here?" She told him she was coming to see a patient. He said, "You mean that politician?"

And she said, "Yes."

He told her, "She had no business living."

So I think that's why they took me there rather than Washoe. Although, I thought it was because Washoe Medical Center was not a trauma center at that time. I'm wrong, because I was talking about this one day, and Lynn Atcheson corrected me and said, "Yes. We were a trauma center then." So I don't know why. I've heard other things, that doctors didn't want to operate on it. Probably, it looked so bad, or they didn't want to be responsible if something bad happened. I don't really know. But anyway, needless to say, an election was going on during this period of time.

Were your children there?

My children were flown in. Yes, they were there at Washoe. Then they came with me to Sacramento for a while. My brother lives near Danville, so he came up, and I think he made some decisions with the doctors, because the kids were nineteen or twenty, and they should not have been making those kinds of decisions.

Of course, it was really tough on them, because they'd lost their dad. [crying] And

I remember my friend Lynn telling me, oh, when she thinks about what terror looks like, she said, "I'll think of Kirk's face," that his face defined for her what that word meant when he came to see me. And that was at that time at Washoe Med.

Anyway, U. Cal. Davis's hospital for their med school—and they have a pretty good med school—was in Sacramento, and it was the county hospital there. I had the doctor who was on call that night, Dr. Pasquale. [laughter] Interestingly, he's got the same first name as the last name of my chief of staff in Las Vegas, Verona Pasquale. Dr. Pasquale Montesano—he very honestly loved having a patient who was possibly going to be lieutenant governor of the next state. That really was a big deal to him. He did some nice things in that arena, and he also did some things that were not good medical decisions.

But anyway, when I finally got out of whatever surgery and drugs and all that and moved to a floor, then I remember next to me was a policeman sitting in a chair in the aisle, the corridor, [laughter] because next to me was some guy who had murdered somebody, because it was a county hospital. But that was not top on my mind at the moment. I think it was Mike Dayton, the young man I had mentioned before, who bought a bracelet for me that's just beautiful. Brought it down and a little note.

In fact, I wore it several years ago—oh, I know what it was—at a DRI dinner where Kirk, my son, had flown over from where he lives now in California, because I was getting a little award. Mike was up at the bar, and I put my arm on the bar, so he could see I had this bracelet on. [laughter] He said, "I remember that!"

There were a lot of people who came down and all kinds of calls. The one unfortunate thing at that time, though, was that Jim Denton had made the decision that hardly anybody could get in to see me,

because he didn't think that would be good for my healing process or whatever. He also wouldn't let very many phone calls go through. When I was actually in a room recuperating, I remember Mother was very upset because she could not get through for the longest time.

That caused some problems within "the campaign." I kind of resented Jim for a while, but actually, I think he did the right thing. He took over, and he was telling the press that I was fine, and I'll be back soon, and all this positive spin on it, when, of course, he knew that was not true. But that was the thing to do, because he wouldn't have wanted to have said anything negative and then not have me elected. Actually, I was OK, I mean, mentally, but maybe not as much physically.

There's a friend of mine named Sandra Smolley. I had met Sandra at some political thing for moderate Republicans or something. Maybe it was a political caucus somewhere along the line. She was the chairperson of the board of supervisors for this very, very large county. I think it is Sacramento County. Anyway, it's the county that Sacramento is in. And, of course, she is in charge of the hospital. So she's downstairs showing Pete Wilson, who then became Governor Pete Wilson, around, because it was a campaign year for him, and somehow she heard I was upstairs, and she wanted to come up, and they said, "No, you can't. What's your name?"

She said, "You move out of my way, fella! I run this place! You just get out!" She charged up there, and it was just great. And she went out and got some things that I needed. Then the next day she sent all these balloons in the room—something to perk me up.

I *really* did not have any idea that I would not be just the way I was before. I was under this illusion, not because I was told that, just because I'd never been hurt, never been sick. Only time I'd been in a hospital was to have two children. Just got to get over this and get up and get going. And as time went on, of course, I realized this wasn't going to be quite what was going to happen, particularly when I started to get this body cast made, where they mold it to your body, and it came up over my head and supported my chin and, of course, the neck area. And if you moved one little way, it was just horrible, because it would give you sores.

I remember my brother used to say, when I had braces on, "You're going to be really glad you had braces on, particularly when you take them off. In about a month you're not going to remember how horrible they were. You're just going to look at what a great smile you have." I had to keep thinking about that, but the body cast was a little bit worse than the braces, actually, and I will talk about that.

Anyway, so I kept being told I could get released, and then something else would happen. Then it was another week and went on and on. So finally, they drove me in an ambulance from Sacramento to Reno, and I remember lying there all alone. The driver was up there, but you didn't talk to him or her, whoever it was. When I got to the top of Donner Summit and then feeling this going down, a bad, bad feeling—not only because you weren't sitting up and looking where you were going, but the other thing was just the feeling of going down . . . like, I guess, out of the sky. But I got home, and by that time my mother and sister were here.

So the ambulance brought you to your home, not to the other hospital?

Yes. To my home. And who was outside in my street but Pro-Life Andy Anderson!

Oh!

Oh, yes. And he had a Milky Way bar or something that he gave me, and my sister grabbed it and said, "This is going in the garbage can! You're not going to eat *this* thing. Probably poison!" I didn't hear any of that, but that's what she told me later. But anyway, they were pretty upset when they saw me.

Your mom and your sister?

Right.

That's the first they'd seen you?

Yes. I think at that time they had rented a hospital bed, and it was put in my room. Of course, I couldn't do anything, because literally you cannot do hardly anything in these body casts. At night, when you lie down, you can't move at all. You just have to be in one position because it just rubs on you. Fortunately, I guess, it was not in the hot heat of the summer, because that would have been even worse. My mother stayed for a while, and during that time she was very helpful, because I'd have to call people on the phone to get more money for the campaign. I had won the primary, and Pro-Life Andy Anderson didn't get a lot of votes. So that was a pretty good thing.

But you were really running against Jeanne Ireland at this point.

Yes. Of course, I wasn't going to be able to go anywhere. That's what I was told, and that was right. I don't know how many weeks had gone by now, quite a few, maybe a month. So I had to "dial for dollars," as I called it. And then my mother would write the name down of who it was I was calling and how much and so on. Most people were very good about it. Of course, they knew what had happened. I explained that I wasn't able to appear publicly, and that was going to be a problem in several ways, but that I needed to run more commercials. Fortunately, we'd made two. That's all I had, the one with the kids . . . and maybe there were three. But anyway, there weren't going to be any new ones, needless to say. So more time had to be bought and all of that sort of thing.

Were you still on lots of medication when you came home?

Yes.

Was it better?

Oh, yes! Oh, well, you couldn't get out of a hospital if you felt that way. No, as I said, you had to answer these certain basic questions just to get out of intensive care, and then there were other hurdles you had to get up over. You had to learn about the body cast. In fact, Sandra Smolley went out and bought all this stuff for me, because I had no clothes or anything.

You weren't going to put a body cast right next to your skin, and so that sort of thing had to be thought about. But, oh, yes, I pretty much knew what was going on. I felt, "Oh, once I get out of the body cast, everything is going to be the way it was before," because that's what you got the body cast on for.

As I say, I think there were a couple of mistakes made along the way about that, but I did have to have a press conference in my living room pretty soon after I'd come back from Sacramento, because there was a rumor going around that I had been brain damaged and that I could not possibly serve as lieutenant governor under those circumstances. So I'm sure that Jim Denton decided at that time that we had to diffuse this right away.

At that point, my two friends, Barbara Weinberg and Lynn Atcheson, took over my personal life—paying my bills, doing those kinds of things that needed to be done, and just left the campaign to Jim Denton. They had nothing to do with that, and they didn't want him involved in the other part of my life, which I'm sure he did not really want to be, anyway. So I later, of course, learned all this. By this time, my sister and mother had arrived, but my mother was going to be leaving soon. My sister stayed, I believe, until just before Thanksgiving. She had to get back to Flagstaff, because one of her grandchildren was being baptized, I believe. But anyway, she was there for quite some time. I mentioned that when my husband died, she was there for a long time, too, and also for my very first election. So we had this press conference in my living room and invited all the reporters who actually cover politics and local news and so on. Stephanie Tyler was there and my campaign manager and Dr. Pasquale Montesano.

Dr. Montesano came up from Sacramento, and he was there to answer any specific medical questions. That seemed like a logical person to have, who could explain far better than I could what had happened and what had broken and what the ramifications of all of this meant. And it went like it would have gone today. I mean, I looked funny, and Stephanie, I think, had her brace out, and she just had one around her waist. I don't mean *just*; she had had some big damage done to the lumbar area. She also had problems with that at another time in her life, as well, I think—bareback riding.

I remember my living room was just jammed, because I don't have a very large house, and, of course, all these lights and things had to be set up. But anyway, they decided at the end of the press conference that I was just as obnoxious as I used to be, so that must be an OK sign.

So that kind of took away that issue. I think, in retrospect, it probably was a good thing, because if there had been no public appearance, people would think, "Why? How come we don't see her?"

Well, she has a body cast on, but that doesn't mean she couldn't be propped up someplace or whatever. So I think that it probably was a good thing that the rumor came to our attention so early on, so it could be diffused.

So, I don't remember much. I mean, all it was, was pretty boring, because you couldn't move; you couldn't do anything.

But you were starting to remember things now.

Yes.

These are memories that you actually have of the press conference?

You mean, that I'm talking about now? Oh, yes.

The dialing for dollars?

Oh, yes.

So at some point in the hospital and before the trip home, because you remember the sensation of falling, coming down from Donner Pass, so you were starting to register again the things that were happening to you at this point.

Yes. But since that time, I don't remember anything more.

About the accident, itself?

No.

That is just gone, that period of time.

Yes, and they say that when you have a traumatic experience, that somehow your brain compensates and doesn't let you remember, because it's too horrifying to remember. And that's a very good thing.

A lot of this came back, however, or I learned a lot more during a trial that took place. But basically, I did a lot of reading, and I know this great guy, Ed Tuley, who I mentioned did the television commercials—he had a television put up high on my bedroom wall. I had to have a patch over one eye, because I had, and still do have, optical nerve damage that got moved around, so I had double vision and couldn't really see very well, but if I could only see out of one eye, that was a lot better. In fact, I think that's the way I looked when I got sworn in, in January of 1991.

The press conference went well?

Yes.

Everybody was convinced that mentally you were alert, but physically just not able to make appearances anywhere.

Right. I did go to one thing, though, and I remember it was at Reno City Council

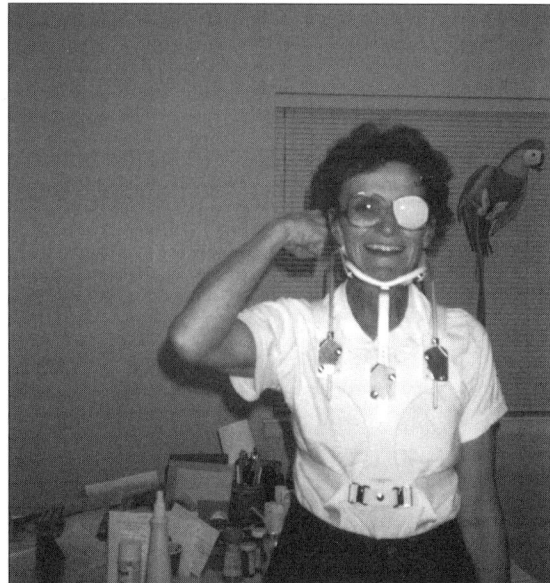

Sue with brace and eyepatch after airplane accident, 1990.

chambers. I guess it was something that Jim Denton wanted me to go to, because there were going to be television cameras there. Of course, that's pretty much what happened during that campaign. I don't have nearly as many interesting things to say about that, as I did from the time I announced to run, up to the time of the accident.

Where were you the day of the election?

Well, I was just going to get to that. I believe that the election headquarters for the Republican Party was maybe the Peppermill. I don't know if the Atlantis was up then. I think it was one of those places.

During that time, my friend Joanie Lambert, who was in the assembly—she's a great seamstress—made me a couple of skirts that had elastic waistbands and were kind of A-line, so I could put them on over my body cast. She made me a jacket and a big scarf, and so I was going to wear that on election night. Also, she made me a few more outfits to wear when I presided over the senate.

I remember this. I was escorted in by Senator Raggio and Senator Townsend, and, of course, people were real excited and very happy for me that I was there. And I won. It wasn't really close. You can imagine the amount of mail and notes and gifts and things that I received—it was pretty amazing. I had so many flowers. I made a decision early on: they would all go to nursing homes and senior citizen centers, because they would enjoy them, and I had way, way too many.

I actually have a cute, little doll that a friend of mine, Laura Myers, gave me. I haven't thought about her in years. She was the Associated Press person for the Reno newspaper, you know . . . wait a minute. She worked for the Reno newspaper and covered the legislature, and she then went on to become head of the Associated Press

in Washington. I think she's still like in her late thirties or something. She was way young when she did this.

I remember something I wore that Paula Dermody gave me. In fact, I saw Paula not long ago, and I said, "Do you remember?" And she said she remembered exactly what she'd given me. I remembered it, too, because I still use it. There were all kinds of things like that and a real outpouring of support and care. So, that's the first part of November.

When you say that you went to the Reno City Council, and you went to the election night, how difficult was it for you to get around? You were still in the body cast, is that correct?

Well, no.

No. You were out?

Well, I was at this event, whatever the event was. But by the time the election came, Dr. Montesano thought it would be just great if I could get out of the body cast. Now, I do want to talk a little bit more about the body cast. Anybody that's ever been in one knows what I'm talking about. It is just awful. I mean, even if you move half an inch . . . because it's molded right to your body as it was at a particular time and date. You cannot gain any weight; you cannot lose any weight. You cannot do anything, or it isn't going to fit right. Then you'd have to go in and have another one made. And, you know, fortunately, you don't remember . . . I do remember how horrible it was but, you know, not really, because it was so much worse than what I remember.

My sister was still with me, I remember, at the election night, so that was a really fun thing. As I said, I did win, and between the winning and up until about Thanksgiving, which would be a couple of weeks, or maybe two and a half, three weeks max, I don't have vivid memories of what happened during that period of time. I do know that after the plane crash I wasn't going to tell my daughter on the phone if she asked me what I was doing. I just said that we were doing this. I wasn't going to tell her what we were talking about.

They wanted to know if I thought they should stay at home and take care of me. It would have been a very loving thing to do, but my kids were not going to do it; I didn't want them to do it. I wanted them to go back and finish college. So I really was very emphatic about it, and it was very difficult for them, I think, particularly my daughter, or maybe because my daughter talks about things more than my son does. It was very difficult for them to go back and kind of deal with that, or deal with what was going on in Nevada in a very different way than they had, you know, the first part of September.

They had planned to come home, and they used to just come home at Christmas, because it got to be really expensive to have both of them come back from out-of-state schools, but they did come home at Thanksgiving, because the last time they'd seen me, was really, really bad. We went over to Dr. James Atcheson and Lynn Atcheson's house for Thanksgiving dinner. Dr. Atcheson is my primary-care physician and has been forever and ever. I wasn't feeling very well then. I felt like I had the flu.

We went home, and that weekend I wasn't feeling very well even more. The kids went off on the Sunday after Thanksgiving, I believe, to go back to school, and that Monday morning I realized there was something wrong, and it wasn't the flu. This is right after Thanksgiving.

And you're out of your body cast?

Yes, I am. Oh, let me get back to that.

He took you out for the election?

Yes, Dr. Montesano took me out of the cast, and it was *way* too soon, because subsequently, as we will get into, I've had other surgeries, and it's clear I should have been in this for six months, because things had not fused correctly. That may be the reason I have all this trouble, rather than that they did it wrong.

Well, they did it wrong, [laughter] because I shouldn't have been out of the body cast. And I know that, to Dr. Montesano's credit, he came up twice before that and helped my sister rotate me over, because, of course, I couldn't take a shower, or I couldn't get cleaned up or *anything*. She couldn't move me all by herself. So he did that twice and maybe because he didn't want to do that anymore—we didn't ask. We probably could've gotten somebody else around Reno to come and help her do this, as long as he showed somebody what to do.

And, you know, I'll make one other comment, one thing that stands out in my mind. The day of the press conference, obviously, we wanted me to look as good as possible. So I asked the person that cut my hair to come over, and, yes, he'd be there. Well, it was about half an hour before the press conference, twenty minutes before the press conference, fifteen minutes before the press conference. He wasn't there. So my sister finally had to wash my hair. And I remember she took like a big garbage bag, and had laid me out on the bed and had my head on top of this thing, so she could wash it, and the water would go in and stuff down there. So then Jim Denton got a really nice woman to come over and fix makeup and get my hair looking better. Actually, of course, I was now grousing about this guy that used to cut my hair, so she gave me the name of somebody else, and I've been to him ever since then. But I found out later that this guy, the one I was planning on coming, was so nervous about doing it, and all he had to do was call and tell us. We would have made other arrangements.

But anyway, people were either bent over backwards this way, or they were afraid, and they didn't know what to do, or they didn't know what to say.

So getting back to this Monday right after Thanksgiving, I felt tingly, like maybe your foot goes to sleep, you know?

Yes, like your fingers are asleep?

Yes, but it was more than that. It was like little pinpricks, and I particularly felt it in my toes and feet. My neighbors were really good, I mean, particularly, certain neighbors. I want to mention Hilda Hosley—she lives down the street from me—and my friend Martha Romero. Particularly, Hilda during this period of time was absolutely incredible. I think I got taken to my orthopedic surgeon, because there was something going on. He thought there was something going on with my spine, sent me back home again. Actually, what I found out was he thought I was depressed because my kids had left.

Well, *wrong!* I was getting paralyzed is what was happening. By that evening I couldn't feel anything from my toes almost up to my knees. So by that time, I did call my neighbor Hilda, who is, oh, way older than I, and she took me into the hospital— helped me get in the car and get to the hospital. Nobody seemed to know what was going on. They called neurosurgeons; they called neurologists. I know there was talk. I could hear them talking in the room or out in the hall. They didn't know what to do, but it appeared that other things were feeling strange. So they finally did a spinal tap, which in itself could be dangerous. They had an idea, and they did the spinal tap, and they finally figured out I had something called Guillain-Barré, which is named after two Frenchmen, and it's referred to as French polio. I guess they're

French. Of course, the name sounds like it. But it is exactly that—paralyzing your nerves. It's a neurological problem, and I could probably tell you more specifically about it, but I'm not going to right now. I can't remember right now, or I don't know.

Then were you hospitalized when they figured out what it was?

Oh, I was in there for another month. And the horrifying thing about this is that the polio ascends your body. It creeps up on you, starting at your toes, which is *exactly* what happened, and then it's up your leg, and then it's up the calves, and then it's up your knee, and then it's up your thighs. It's getting up to all your organs in your body. And I remember this.

I bet you Fritsi Ericson remembers this, too, because it was Monday night, and it was Monday night football. It was the Forty-Niners, I believe, against the New York Giants. Fritsi was going to that, or I *thought* she was going to that, because she had season tickets. I was thinking about her being there. The game was up on the television screen. Outside this room was a doctor for *every organ* in my body, whether it was the liver doctor, whether it was the lung doctor, whether it was the gallbladder doctor, whether it was the kidney doctor. One after another they came in and said, "You know, this is what we're going to have to do if this gets paralyzed," or, "This is what we got to do, blah, blah, blah." And [sighs] you just about . . . [sighs] this is just too much. It was really awful, because there were no drugs. It didn't hurt. Things just became heavy as stone. You couldn't move your legs or your arms or whatever. And because you were aware, you actually could see this progressing right up your body. And to me, that was worse—because I *knew* what was going on—than being in the plane crash.

Right before this, my sister had just gone home, and she, to this day, says, "I could not believe that I wasn't there." Well, she'd just *been* with me for six weeks.

So, this Hilda Hosley came to see me almost *every* day, and she's just a kick in the rear and so good. The newspaper—I don't remember who this was—it might have been Lenita Powers, who still writes for the *Reno Gazette-Journal*. Somebody did a whole story on my unbelievable recovery and had pictures of my sister and I, color pictures of walking around Virginia Lake with this body cast on. I was able to do five miles. That might have been not a good thing for me to do.

And the remarkable recovery was from the plane accident, not from the French polio, Guillain-Barré?

The story was about that. And all of the sudden I disappeared. All of the sudden, I'm not around anymore. So they called me or something and wanted some kind of quote for the story, and Jim Denton doesn't want to tell them I'm back in the hospital again.

I finally convince him that he needs to have a press conference and explain what's going on here. So there was a press conference downstairs in the Mack Auditorium with whatever doctor, neurologist, explaining what this is. They think I may have gotten it because I was worn out from not only the trauma of the plane crash, but trying to exercise, trying to build up my stamina again, and the fact that I had a flu shot.

The doctor said, "Oh, you got to have a flu shot. You *can't* get flu on top of all of this stuff." Back when Gerald Ford was president, there was a terrible Asian flu that was coming over from the Far East, and he made a great public appeal for people to go in and get flu shots, because this was killing people, et cetera. A lot of people got Guillain-Barré, and it's the *only* correlation

that they can think of. However, there was a person who died from this just about a year before I got it, and, for some reason, I had read a little article about him, and I remembered his name; I remembered what he was doing. I mean, this little article that had no relationship to me *at all* at the time, none. I didn't know diddly-squat, just read it, and it was one of those things I read in the newspaper and then blank out on.

Did you think you were going to die from this?

Well, the thought did cross my mind, because I heard the nurses whispering, and I said "What are you whispering about, ladies?"

"Oh, nothing."

And I said all of a sudden, "Gene Bobbagiletta." I mean, look at the name. How would I even remember the name? I said, "Are you talking about Gene Bobbagiletta? Is this what Gene Bobbagiletta had?"

"Yes."

I said, "Did he die?"

"Yes."

I said, "Well, I thought the doctor said that it might descend my body, as it ascended; then it might go out of my body."

"Yes. We're pretty sure that's what's going to happen."

Well, they didn't know. They keep changing how they deal with this. Prior to my having it, they used to just give you gamma globulin to build up more strength, to fight off the attacking of the nerves. When I got it, they decided you had to get rid of all of your blood plasma and throw it on the nuclear dump site or wherever they do that and then put someone else's plasma into your body, so it won't attack your nerves. That in itself is unbelievable. I don't know what being on a kidney dialysis machine is like, but they do something, and your temperature goes from burning up to freezing, and they keep putting blankets on top of you, because your blood pressure goes down or up or whatever. So they did that.

Jim Denton did have a press conference, and the doctor explained this, and I guess they did run that story at some point in the newspaper, but they didn't want to run it, because it appeared that maybe I *wasn't* coming back as well as I thought I had.

They did hook up a voice mail in the hospital, so people could call in and talk to me and leave messages and so on. It was the same all over again—cards and letters and things. It's getting closer to Christmastime now. Then I got sent downstairs—at that time the rehab was in the basement—because now I had to learn to walk again and do all that stuff. The one thing I remember specifically was that everything felt *so heavy*. They'd help me out of bed, and I'd put one foot on top of the other. I couldn't feel anything, of course. It was like cement. I suspect that is what it must be like for people who are paralyzed all the time. It does make you a lot more sympathetic and empathetic for all kinds of people.

When you were going into rehab, were you still paralyzed at that point, or had the paralysis receded?

It had to some extent. Do you know, since you worked for a newspaper, the Sanfords out in Yerington?

Yes.

His wife was in the rehab place the same time I was. She was paralyzed when they were out cutting wood—the brake on their truck didn't stick, and the truck rolled over. So we were down there together, and she just gave up. I still keep in touch with them to this day. They redid her whole house.

Hers was not one that you recover from. But they try to get you so you at least can stand up. There are certain things you got to do before you get out of there.

Next to me was Dr. George Greenberg, and he had had a massive stroke. He was a very well-known plastic surgeon in town, and one of his children went to school with Kirk and Kristi. The kids always came in and visited with me when they came to see their dad. It was nice, knowing a few people, because you're just there in bed.

Then I got released when the kids came home. They would not send me home unless somebody was there. They both came home for Christmas, and I remember Dennis Myers was over at the hospital the day that I got out. I was on crutches, and we went home, and I don't remember much about that.

I was going to be sworn in, and I've already talked about the problem I had of whether I was going to be sworn in or not under the DRI part.

The DRI and the income.

Yes.

After all of this, you find out you're not going to have an income.

Yes. That's right. Anyway, Governor Miller was very good and had all of the constitutional officers and their families over for breakfast in the mansion before the swearing in. I have a picture in my basement of everybody that came. I think he had to actually build on a little annex to have all my guests. I had my mother-in-law and my mother, my sister, her husband, and one of her daughters and a couple of her kids, my brother, his wife, a couple of his kids. Chief Justice John Mowbray swore us in, and that was pretty exciting. It was *snowing* that day; I remember that. And the crowd was . . . [crying] enthusiastic, I

Sue and her family on the day of her swearing-in as lieutenant governor, January 1991.

guess. So that's on January 6 or 7, and then somehow I had to get ready for presiding over the senate. We were able to get a high stool that had a back on it that I could sit on, rather than standing up all the time. It was a beautiful day in some ways, because it wasn't a horrible snow. It was just like little flakes coming down ever so nicely, but very, very cold. My kids helped me across the Capitol steps, where they have the swearing in. It wasn't the only swearing in I've been to. Actually, Governor Guinn has been very nice and invited not only past governors, which is a normal tradition, but he's also included past lieutenant governors. So I've been back a couple more times with

his administration. That was nice—and thoughtful.

So getting ready for the session is a big question mark. Joanie Lambert then made me a couple of more outfits, because standing up there in front of the senate I couldn't wear just the one thing. So she made a couple of things.

I rented a room over in the motel in the Carson Station. It's a Best Western owned by the Russell family, whose dad was governor, Charles Russell. They gave me a permanent room up on the top floor in the corner. We got a hospital bed in there, because it was just going to be too much for me to go back and forth every day.

This was the 1991 session. The day I was sworn in, the governor came up to me and said—and I don't believe I've recounted this, because it happened on this day—"You're going to have assigned to you a highway patrol trooper for your four years." I hadn't even thought about something like that. Like who was going to drive—I couldn't drive—how any of those things were going to work? I got to doff my hat to Bob, because he had thought about that and made the arrangements and introduced me to the guy at that time. You know, I don't know how he figured out who was going to do this.

Each governor, at least in our state, has the dignitary detail. I think probably some states have even more paraphernalia, but the governor *always* has a driver for the family—Governor Miller used to have the kids—for their use. So it was the same kind of thing for me. It turned out to be, in my mind, a great relationship. In fact, I just noticed in the paper the other day, "Scott Simon, president of the Highway Patrol Association."

The next big event was the inauguration, and my brother came to be my escort. [laughter] Bob told Sandy, "God, do we have to go behind her again? She gets all the applause, and I don't get any."

Inaugural balls are not my big thing, but everybody was very good and pleasant and so on. And then the session starts—maybe the inauguration came after the session—but most of the senators were really happy to see me back. Oh, I'm sure they all were. Some of them were probably glad I wasn't voting anymore. [laughter] Except *maybe* possibly in the case of a tie. I had been a creature of the senate, so to preside over it was not that difficult, because I pretty much knew . . . .

Knew all the rules and how things worked?

I did. I didn't know them as well as sometimes I thought I should, but I went to school with the secretaries of the senate and also the clerk of the assembly, Mouryne Landing, who is now married to Joe Dini, former speaker. But I wanted to make sure that I knew everything, and I wanted to make sure that I knew as much as Joe Neal, [laughter] Senator Joe Neal, because Joe was *really* good; and, you know, knowing the rules, you have a lot of power when you do that, particularly when other people don't know. You can actually make things up, and they *think* you know. They don't dare question you, because you may be right, and you may not be right.

It wasn't a difficult job. I mean, I did enjoy it a lot, because you could demonstrate your personality, your sense of humor, and you can see back there, whereas before, I was looking this direction, toward the front, toward the president of the senate. And now I can see people in the galley and who was signaling to whom to do what. Sometimes it was pretty disillusioning, to tell you the truth.

To sit up there in front now?

To see people appearing to be giving signals on how to vote on stuff. But it was fun. I think I particularly looked good after the next lieutenant governor, Lonnie Hammargren, became president of the senate. People thought my job was *absolutely* amazing. [laughter] But that's how I got by in the 1991 session. As far as what I did, there weren't a lot of things that I could do, because I was just coming back. If I'd had four years . . . but as we go on in terms of my service as lieutenant governor, I did do quite a bit and did things that had not been done before, and that was at the end of my term, because I was then a bit stronger. I kept thinking, if this hadn't happened, I had so many ideas and things that could have been done, should have been done, would have been done, but weren't. In retrospect, it was more than most people in that position had done.

And probably more than most people would try to do, given what you'd just been through.

Yes. And my daughter once asked me, "What I don't understand is why did you serve?"

I said, "Kristina, why wouldn't I have served?" I mean, to be elected to something and say, "Well, thanks a lot, but no thanks?" I mean, besides, I guess it's the same thing as after Peter was killed, that you keep busy, and you get through it. Each day became a week, a week became a month, and hopefully you got stronger.

I did go back, however, and had more surgery done, and when I say "go back," I do not mean to the University of California hospital in Sacramento. I did ask Dr. Montesano for some names of doctors, because there was a big part of my back that was broken that had not been recognized, or they hadn't fixed it.

I know he kept telling me, "You know what? It doesn't look too bad."

I think that at that point, he realized he had messed up, and he didn't want me to go back any place else. I did get names, and, as it turns out, I got names of *only* friends of his, and I should've known this. I went up and down the coast; I went to the University of Washington, to University of California, San Francisco, to UCLA, and they all basically said the same thing as what he had said, "You need to have these rods put in your back, and it will straighten that up." I did ask about a doctor that I'd heard of, Dr. White, who happened to be the San Francisco Forty-Niner quarterback, Joe Montana's orthopedic surgeon, and Dr. Montesano said, "Oh! He's not any good." As it turns out, he was *very* good, and that's probably who I should have gone to, and I

think it was kind of professional jealousy, if you will, because he did say, "The only reason he's any good is because he gets mentioned in the paper."

Well, as years have gone by, I know how many people have gone over to Daly City and have been operated on, including my friend Stephanie. It wasn't by this Dr. White, but it was the lumbar guy who was at the same center.

But, you know, it wasn't done, so I went back to Minnesota, to the Minnesota Spine Surgery Center, and that recommendation came from an orthopedic surgeon in Reno, Dr. Steve Cunningham.

I went to a lieutenant governors conference in Indianapolis, and since it was close to Minneapolis, I went over there. In fact, the lieutenant governor of Indianapolis, Frank O'Bannon, and his wife, Judy, are great people. He was elected governor after Evan Bayh, the son of Birch Bayh of Indiana, went to the U.S. Senate. He served two terms, and he can't serve any more. They were just terrific, *really* great people. And I do want to mention a couple of other lieutenant governors conferences, too.

The doctors in Minnesota said, "We can do this. No big deal." Dr. Lowenstein was the doctor, and he was at that time president of the American Scoliosis Society. He said, "You know what? Your back is going to be immobile, but you don't use your back for much of anything." He was the famous doctor. Well, of course, you use your back. You use your back a lot!

Later on, I thought, "Didn't they take *anatomy?*" Sometimes when you're so focused on surgery—that's all. You don't pay any attention to what happens after that.

I had a friend from high school, Catalina High School in Tucson, who I hadn't seen all these many years. Another thing I want to talk about is National Women's Political Caucus and other things that spun off from that. Anyway, I hadn't seen this gal . . . she

National Lieutenant Governors meeting, Indianapolis, around 1993. Sue is third from left, front row.

was a girl when I saw her. Barbara Calloway was her name.

I went back to Rutgers University, because there they have the Center for American Women in Politics, and it is an incredible place. The head of it at that time was Ruth Mandel. She's now head of the Eagleton Institute of Politics, which is also at Rutgers, but higher up the food chain. They brought women legislators back to Rutgers to prepare them, and they're only focused on women state legislators. They're not interested in learning more about Congress or the U.S. Senate; they are interested just in state legislators. I went back to give a little talk or something, and Ruth brought this woman in to see me, who was the provost of Rutgers, and she looked just like my high school friend, except she had white hair. Well, it *was* my high school friend!

She was provost at Rutgers, and she and her husband at that time were going to UCLA. She was writing a book. She has written three or four books that have been published. She was in Africa and wrote about some woman in Africa. She was writing a book either about the National Nurses Association or a very well-known nurse within that organization, but she was doing some research at UCLA.

So she and her husband, who was in the medical school in psychiatry, went to UCLA after I had seen them in Rutgers. In fact, after this event at Rutgers was over, I stayed with them in the town that they lived in, Princeton, New Jersey, for a couple of extra nights. It ties in, because then I go to UCLA, and I went to the Jules Stein Eye Center to see if they could do something with my eyes, and they really couldn't. I went to a neurologist there, and, you know, Barbara helped me get all these appointments to see what could be done and what should be done. The reason I mention this is because I decided not to go there, but to go to this Minnesota place. Because she felt in some way connected to that, she came with me to Minnesota and spent the day there. I do know that the surgery was twelve hours, because she told me that's how long she was sitting outside!

So, then I was in a hospital again for quite a while. There was a doctor in Reno, Rosenauer, and she was a friend . . . maybe it's her dad that's a doctor. Her friend is my friend, Marybel Batjer. So she came to see me. In fact, the governor, and the secretary of state of Minnesota came to see me. I knew the lieutenant governor of Minnesota through the lieutenant governors association, and so it really worked out well. I think that Nevada State Highway Trooper Scott Simon took me there, and we went over to the governor's mansion and had dinner the night before my surgery. That may have been the second time, because I had to go back there and have it done again.

These people came to visit, and I think it might have been the second time I went back there for surgery that they opened the Mall of America. It was the grand opening. And the highway trooper that came to pick me up from the Minnesota dignitary detail kept saying, "Do you want to go to this?"

I said, "No, not really," because I'm not a shopper. Besides, hundreds of thousands of people?

Well, he obviously wanted to, because he asked me about three or four times. He kept saying, well, his wife would be so jealous. So I said, "OK."

So we got a little golf cart and zipped all over the place. Actually, it was kind of fun, because we put a little back up there, but at that time I hadn't had all this surgery on my back. That's what they did there.

Finally, I was released from that and came back, and I think Scott came with me that time. That was when I learned that absolutely I should have had the body cast, because I had another body cast now. That's what I should have had the first time—at least six months in the cast. So when that six months comes up, now, we're getting into the 1991 session, and I'm kind of out of it. Then I go back to Minnesota and have this surgery.

My sister comes again, and guess what? When I get home, she's saying, "You know, there's this big swelling in your back."

So we go down to my orthopedic surgeon, Dr. Cunningham, and he has the X-rays that he took of me that day, in addition to the X-rays that came home with me. He said, "I hate to tell you this, but the hooks, or whatever, have come out of the spinal cord. You're going to have to go back again." So I go back again, and they have to do it again. [laughter]

Some of my legislative friends rented me the state airplane, so I could fly from Minneapolis to Las Vegas—put me on there, and then I could have flown right home without waiting around. So that's why I have such good friends at McCarran now.

They get me out to this airplane, the state plane. I can't get in it because I can't bend. There's just a little, bitty opening. I felt so sorry that they had invested all this money. Hopefully, they got it back. But I had to go in and, of course, lie down. Finally, I'm on the plane, and I see my friend Bill Bible. He says, "Hey, where you been?"

I said, "Oh, Minneapolis."

He said, "Oh, what are you going back there for again?"

I said, "Oh, I was just back there for a checkup," because I didn't want anybody to know that I'd had this done all over again. So the whole thing goes on.

I just want to know, how did you manage to keep facing surgeries? After the first round, I mean, going back in for a twelve-hour surgery and then hearing that you had to do it again, because the hooks weren't where they needed to be?

In fact, when I went back the second time, I was told that one of the surgical nurses knew—she wasn't there any longer, but I could have tracked her down—that the hooks were out before I was even sent home. I really don't know if that was true.

Sometimes I'll think about that and think I should have sued, but you know what? Having gone through one trial—and we need to talk about that trial, too—I didn't want to do it anymore. I'm not a very litigious person, and it just is very draining.

Yes. It leaves you with some pretty angry feelings, though, to think that people knew and didn't do the right thing at that point, and especially when your whole life is about doing the right thing.

Yes. I think if I have any anger, it's towards Bob Seale.

Because he knew there was something wrong with the plane?

Yes. I have a lot of friends who were very close to Bob—I wasn't a big buddy—and were very close to Judy and, oh, they can't say anything nice about him—selfish, blah, blah, blah, blah, blah. I guess my feeling is, you do the best you can, and, God, I don't want to be angry all the time. It gets back to that same thing. The only person it hurts is yourself. I really believe that.

I've seen people on the Oprah Winfrey show where a criminal has killed their husband or something, and they've forgiven him. Ha! That's pretty amazing. I'm sure that person feels a lot better about life than people who want to see that guy hung up by his thumbs.

And are just eaten up with the anger and vengefulness.

I can understand why they feel that way. I'm not sure I could say, "I forgive you," but what a better thing it is—not only better as a human being, but just better internally, I would think.

There are stages, too, that you go through. Maybe you can't always quite get to forgiveness, but you can say, "I'm moving past this. I'm not going to hang onto this and stay stuck on this."

Yes. My daughter said something that's very, very positive. I have told her and other people, "All I wanted from him was 'I'm sorry.'"

She said, "If he says that, then he's accepting responsibility for what he did. Maybe he can't do that." She's probably right. Do you remember Judy Simpson?

No.

What was that program, the neighborhood school thing? I was at an Easter brunch over with Margo Piscevich and Frankie Sue and a whole bunch of people, who obviously knew them a lot better than I. They were saying that he moved to Las Vegas, and then he became chairman of the Republican Party, and that he was still dating that Judy Simpson. I think her name was Judy Simpson.

I have a number of questions about things people might want to know from you. One is, you mentioned that a plane crash is the worst trauma of any accident, versus car accidents and so on. I was wondering if you would just describe some of the symptoms of the trauma that you still deal with today from that.

Well, I guess sleep is the biggest one that I can think of. I was never what you call a great sleeper, but it's become significantly worse. I don't go to bed sometimes until three o'clock in the morning, or even up to four o'clock. I've been to sleep clinics; I have sleeping medicine, which I have to take anyway. If I didn't do that, I probably wouldn't get any sleep.

They think maybe the reason that this has become so incredibly difficult and why my whole body clock is switched from most people's is that, psychologically, it's hard for me to close my eyes, because I'm afraid there's going to be another plane crash or that sensation that obviously I felt right before we met the ground. So, if I don't get up until eleven in the morning or something like that, then half a day is gone, and I need to get in touch with people or do things. I've given up any kind of activity, like committees that meet in the morning, because I just can't do it. The only one that I do is the gaming commission. That's somewhat different than a volunteer activity.

The other thing is my eyesight. One of the optic nerves got pushed around, and so I'm able to see better from the horizon up than the horizon down. I did go to UCLA, as I think I mentioned previously. I was at the Jules Stein Eye Institute to see if this could be corrected. All they could do at that time—and I think it's still true today—is flip it around, so I could see from the horizon down better than the horizon up. But to go through a surgery, they wouldn't be able to say, "Yes, we could fix it for you." Well, it didn't make sense. I'm not able to have

bifocals, trifocals, anything like that because of the optic damage.

And the surgery didn't seem to be worth it?

Right. I had asked, of course, about the lasers, whatever that's called. I guess it's *incredible* if you can have it done, but my ophthalmologist said no. When I see him every year or two, I ask if there's been any difference in opportunities to fix my eyes, and no, there hasn't been. So, it's just something I've got to deal with, but it takes me much longer to read. Fortunately, I'm able to do my gaming commission work at home and write my notes out. It takes me much longer than everybody else, but what difference does that make? In my mind it makes no difference at all. It just takes more time.

In addition to sleep problems and your eyes, do you have any difficulty with nightmares or hearing about airplane crashes or any of those types of things?

Well, I don't think I have nightmares, but I guess a lot of people don't remember if they did or not. But, in fact, when I do see something on television about an airplane crash . . . and there have been two since mine that involved someone running for office. One was Governor Mel Carnahan of Missouri; he was flying with his son in a small plane campaigning in a rural area of Missouri and crashed, and he and his son were killed. I knew Mel, because he was lieutenant governor prior to being governor, and, of course, at that time he was running for the United States Senate, and he did win, actually. He beat John Ashcroft. Then his wife was appointed to fill that part of his term.

The other one was Paul Wellstone, from Minnesota. I was in Minneapolis *almost* when that occurred to him. Everybody felt that he was a guy of principle. It was going to be a tight race for him, because he was very liberal, but, of course, Minnesota is much more so than some other states. Obviously, as we know, they do elect people who are kind of out of the box. Their governor, for example, is Jesse Ventura.

He was a former boxer?

No, he was a wrestler, which is, in my mind, even worse than boxing, if that's possible.

Paul was in a plane, and it wasn't a campaign trip, but he was flying up to the northern part of Minnesota to attend a funeral of a friend of his. That was catastrophic, because it was right near the election, but that's another story.

And was he also killed?

Yes, he was also killed. The plane, they found it in the woods, and everybody on board was dead, and there were aides of his and so on. What happens in those two instances is, it's in their computer or something, stored, because I always get called to comment on that in terms of, "How do you campaign in a state, any state, that has small communities that you must get to, so they know who you are, and they know what you support?" I don't know how else you do that.

Here in our own state, I had thought—and I will talk about it at the end of my lieutenant governor term—some people were very interested in having me run again and were talking about getting a camper and having somebody drive it, where I could lay down in the back. Of course, it would be difficult to go to two or three events; you couldn't do that. You'd have to be selective, but I guess people would have understood. I chose not to do that.

Even when I see on the television about a plane, not knowing who they are or anything, it does play around in my head. No question about that.

I can well imagine 9-11 was a very uncomfortable day for you.

Yes, it was. It was.

Does it bring back just the feelings, because you don't remember the actual details?

No, I don't, of course.

But the emotion is there, obviously, the fear of falling and that type of thing?

Yes, it is. [with emotion] I can't really explain why, particularly because I don't remember what happened, and, secondly, for the whole time I was sure that I'd be back exactly the way I had been before. But it does bring back the feelings.

Was there any particular time where it really hit you, or was it a gradual realization that you physically were not going to return to the way you had been?

Well, when I'd gone to visit the doctors in Minneapolis at the Minnesota Spine Surgery Center that I've discussed, they were very positive. Most doctors will cushion whatever they say in case it doesn't come out right, so you don't sue them for medical malpractice or whatever, but they were absolutely convinced that a lot of the pain that I felt and continue to feel would be gone. So that was a very positive feeling. I remember before I'd had that done, I was talking with two of my neighbors here, and I was telling them that I was going to go back and have some more surgery. One said, "Ah! Oh, that's horrible!"

And the other said, "Well, no. I think that's a great thing, because clearly it might take care of some of the pain." Of course, that was the point. I can't remember what number it was in the thoracic part of your spine, but anyway, I mentioned that that had not been fixed when I was at Sacramento, when I was having my neck operated on. So I guess that there was this other opportunity to get better.

So you think, "Oh, well. That didn't work just right in Sacramento, but maybe *this* will work." I did have that brace on for six months. That's why I knew that the other one had been taken off way too soon. Maybe that's the problem, I don't know. But, yes, I guess, obviously, years have passed, and I realize that the biggest problem in the aftermath of the accident is the fact that I'm in pain unless I lie down.

What they always say is, "It's a mechanical problem."

I keep asking what they *mean* by that. [laughter]

And they just say, "It's mechanical."

That's not an explanation for me, but anyway, that's what it is. So it's clear to me and to a lot of other people who have had the fortitude to bring it to my attention that the fusion was not done right over my spine. My head is forward, so I have all this pain in my neck, trying to get it to pull itself back into its proper place.

A chiropractor who goes to the same gym I do came up to me once and said something about this, and I was just shocked, very honestly. It was right before Christmas. My daughter had come home and was there at the gym with me. He told me there was a possibility that because this was not structurally correct, that it may cause paralysis in the legs. I could not believe, a) that he'd say that to me, and b) that he'd say it right before Christmas. [laughter] Because I saw him—he was down there all the time. I don't know why he happened to pick that particular day.

Actually, I've gotten over that and gone in and visited with him. He believes that he's on the cutting edge of chiropractic medicine. I read a lot of the articles that he had given to me, and I told my daughter at *that* time, when he first told me about it. She picked up the phone, and he was on it, and she got kind of mad at him. But he did fax us some articles, which I read. I then sent them on to my orthopedic surgeon here in town, and then I asked him later on, "Is there any truth to this paralysis-type thing?"

He didn't say no. He said, "Well, you don't worry about things unless it happens." Of course, it hasn't, but I asked him if the articles that the chiropractor had sent were from reputable magazines, and, yes, they certainly were. But I don't think about that, because, why would you?

The biggest fear I have, of course, is hepatitis C, which I did get through a blood transfusion in Sacramento. Of course, I did not know what it was, and I didn't know I had it until I was busy on a vacation in Palm Springs. I had to save a lot of pints of my own blood to use in the surgery in Minnesota, so it was there at this blood bank in Palm Springs.

I was lieutenant governor at the time, and I remember being in my office in the Capitol Building, and the phone rang, and there was a doctor from this blood bank telling me I had hepatitis C. I didn't know what that was. That was probably in 1991 or 1992 or something like that. About 1991 they did get the test perfected enough so they could test blood. So he told me about it, and said, "You should tell your primary care physician," which I did. In fact, Dr. Atcheson, who is my primary care physician, when I was in the hospital with Guillain-Barré, said this is what he was testing for, but it was right at the time that they didn't have it quite perfected. Six months later, it probably would not have happened.

The problem with hepatitis C is the fact that it's a blood-borne disease. About 80 or 85 percent of the people who have it first get cirrhosis of the liver, and then they get cancer of the liver. They have to have an organ donated, and, of course, that organ will then get hepatitis C, because it is a blood-borne disease and not a liver disease. I have done what I could.

I was just thinking today how it's been almost a couple of weeks since I've been down to the gym, and we're going to go Wednesday of this week, and then I'm going to be gone again. Those things, I believe, are helpful, and, of course, I don't drink. I don't have any liquor, because people who get cirrhosis of the liver, outside of having hepatitis C, it's because they drink too much, and the liver just cannot deal with that. So I've done that myself, and my enzymes in the tests that they do are pretty good.

The interesting thing about hepatitis C—and I learned this from the Gaming Control Board secretary—is that while it shows up, because you've got it in your blood, you are not sick, or the symptoms don't appear until about fifteen to twenty years *after* you've been in contact with it. Strange, but that is the truth. So you look back, and let's say 1990 I got it. So this is about twelve years. I should be feeling pretty good at this point.

They don't know how to cure it. They do the same thing, like chemotherapy. You give yourself interferon. There are two drugs that you do yourself, and you're very, very sick; it is chemotherapy, is what it is. So that obviously is the worst of all the aftermath of the airplane crash.

I could have gotten it either in Sacramento or by removing my plasma when I had Guillain-Barré. It appears more logical that it was at Sacramento. In fact, something humorous about this is that about, let's see, in the year 1999 or 2000, I got a form letter from the hospital in

Sacramento, University of California Davis. Basically, they're saying, "You may have contracted hepatitis C."

Blood banks were very against, absolutely opposed to, and continually killed bills in Congress that mandated that people should be notified, people who had surgery or had blood transfusions before a certain date. So it took all of this time to get this in operation. Well, of course, I learned about it years and years and years before. But I might not have. I might have been treating my body in a way that wasn't as positive as it could have been.

Could have been still drinking wine at dinner or something like that?

Yes, sure. I'm not going to mention the name of these doctors, but I did ask several doctors in town. In fact, one I was seated next to at a dinner when they were pouring wine, and I said, "Well, what about that?"

He said, "Phh! A couple of glasses of wine won't hurt you." I had that told to me by several different doctors. To be honest with you, I thought that didn't even make sense. So I did it myself, and now, four or five years later, that's exactly what they tell you. It just made sense, and, besides, why not try it?

Do everything you can.

Yes, it's something that you could have done. So those are pretty much some things that have followed me around, if you will, after the plane crash.

It seems like not very much positive came out of the trip to Sacramento. Is that how you feel, or were there some positives?

Oh, you mean after?

The surgery, yes. When they sent you down there for the surgery and so on, it

seems like you had a lot of problems; there were mistakes made.

Oh, right, but I think the way I look at it is the fact that, evidently, the doctors up here didn't want to deal with it. That must have been it. So they probably did the best they could. You've got to look at it that way, because otherwise you go around with anger at the doctor. I mean, I've been told he was not the best doctor they have, but that's who it was, and that's what happened.

You can't change it now.

No. Can't change it. In fact, I even told my son that when he was telling me about the doctor. I guess the doctor had several medical malpractice claims against him. But again, that's history. I wished I didn't even know that. Well, it doesn't matter. I guess my attitude's always been you move forward, because, as we've said, if you don't, then you've wasted a lot of your life eating away at stuff.

The only person that I think I've mentioned that I would have liked some comment from was the pilot, Bob Seale. Bob Seale and Brian Krolicki and Stephanie Tyler remained good friends. I believe that Stephanie had something to do with getting Brian elected. I think she worked on Krolicki's campaign.

She used to call every Labor Day and would talk. She hasn't done that for a while. She took my senate seat, actually, when I was elected lieutenant governor. They decided that this would be a district that they could get rid of in reapportionment, because, 1991 was the session of reapportionment. Since I was in the middle of my term, I wasn't going to run again, because I was then lieutenant governor.

Some people suggested that I run for the senate again, "Why don't you run for the senate? You're just down there for a short period of time." That wasn't something I wanted to do.

Stephanie and Brian and Bob Seale remained good friends. I mean, I think they talk to each other a lot, and I don't. That's just the way it is. I'm sure I could call them and get connected, but I have no interest in doing that.

So they're friends with each other?

I think so.

But you haven't remained friends with any of them.

That's correct. There is something that happened during the trial that I don't think I want to include.

OK. You mentioned that there was a trial, and what essentially was the trial?

The trial was suing Cessna, suing the maker of the engine. The right engine is where the problem was. Evidently, it had something to do with feathering the propeller. That's about all I can technically say about it.

Stephanie and I hired an attorney on the advice of Spike Wilson and Larry Hicks. They were both in the same law firm. Larry is now a federal judge and has moved to Las Vegas, but he's just a great guy. I've obviously mentioned Spike along the way. I actually had hired Larry. He'd been a former district attorney here in Washoe County. I had so many friends that were attorneys, and they were just dying to take this case.

I didn't want to get into that, so I picked somebody who I had a lot of respect for and who was a good attorney, Larry Hicks. That's not to say that Spike wasn't either, but I think through that whole trial Larry felt that I had hired Spike. In fact, I did find that out after, but it was the other way around.

This all happened, and Larry and Spike interviewed a lot of attorneys who didn't live here who had expertise in airplanes and that kind of thing. We hired a man from California—the San Francisco area—named Jerry Stearns. He had a great reputation. In fact, he had been involved in a case here in Washoe County before, and people had seen him. Friends of mine—maybe they worked at the courthouse, I don't remember—were saying, "Oh, wow. He won." He was a great guy. Kind of reminds you a little bit of, maybe, Abe Lincoln. Very tall. His wife was also in the firm, I believe.

He was here for about six weeks. That's as long as the trial had gone. The Cessna people wanted to deal with me, because I was the most injured, and probably they were concerned that I was most likely to influence a jury and maybe drag the rest of them along with me. They were willing to settle with me, but in a big company like that, they also have local counsel. I was told that the local attorney, whose name was Robert Hibbs, didn't want to do that, because he thought if he won this, it would be a real feather in his cap.

Among that kind of law, he was well thought of. Somehow we called him the "prince of darkness." [laughter] That's probably the perspective of my attorneys and myself.

The engine maker settled right away, and I'm going to give you a ratio. Let's say, there's a hundred dollars. They felt that Sue Wagner should get two-thirds or three-quarters of that, and Stephanie Tyler, one-quarter or a third of that. We did have the same attorneys. After I got mine, she decided to use Jerry Stearns, as well. Bob Seale had a different attorney; I know who it was. Brian Krolicki did file a suit, but that was kind of a har-har. I mean, a scratch on the forehead really was not the kind of thing

the jury would be impressed with. It lasted for six weeks, and, of course, everything was all revisited again. That was in 1993.

The attorneys did all the things you're supposed to do. They didn't want to do it in Fallon, because they felt people out there would be even more conservative. The only times I went down and actually sat in the courtroom . . . one day they were picking the jury. I went in; I looked around, and, of course, they invite a lot more people than they need. I must have seen about thirty people I knew who waved and said hi, and I thought, "Boy, I hope they get on the jury!" [laughter] But, of course, they weren't going to be, because that would eliminate them. That was one day I was there. Then I had to go the day I was to testify.

Most people don't have a trial involved with their life, and it's interesting that I've had, because, of course, when I was in the senate, I was very involved in all these issues—structured settlements, lump-sum payments, et cetera, et cetera. So I did have a passing acquaintance with it, *but* to be in the seat and be quizzed by a big attorney from Cessna, not the local guy . . . . He just threw me little softballs. He never asked me any question that was difficult, because he didn't want to irritate the jury. I know that they asked me if I thought I could run for office again; that was a big thing. I said, "I don't know, but I think probably not." At that time I really didn't know if I'd be better.

Probably, as it turns out, it would have been a lot better if I could've said, "No, I can't," because that's exactly the reason I didn't run, but at that time in 1993, I didn't know.

Yes. You were probably still hopeful.

Yes, I was, very much so. Then I came down, oh, when summation was going on, I think. So there were only three times. They would carry it on the local news or articles in the paper about it.

The jury really found that it was pilot error, even though the Cessna 411—I learned all of this later—was called a "death trap in the sky," and it had a *terrible* history with this exact same thing, this feathering of the right propeller. This particular plane—which, of course, I didn't find out until actually the trial was all over—was a piece of junk. It had been in another plane crash, and it had been patched back together. Of course, I'm exaggerating here a bit when I say "patched" or "band-aided," but it had sat in a warehouse or a hangar or something for a couple of years with no lubrication, nothing done to it. It shouldn't have been sold, and I'm sure it was bought for a very cheap price. I do hear that, because there's a whole group, as everybody might expect, of private investigators and all these people that kind of hang together. I'm friends with a lot of attorneys in town and so on, and even private investigators, so I've heard a lot of this stuff. I don't know how much it was sold for, but that's what most people think.

The reason I know any of this is that after the trial was over, Larry Hicks gave me, oh, a kind of a history of it, and it was used by Bob Hibbs in some mock trial juries. I guess they do that in big cases, where you would have a bunch of people sitting there, and then they'd try out different strategies to see what was impressive to them, what issue they might decide a case on, for example. There was all this stuff in it that I've just told you about. There was a lot more; I think I've got it in my file cabinet, but this is what I remember of it. Of course, I did *not* know that while it was going on.

As good as Jerry Stearns was, he probably felt that it was pilot error. I mean, in his own mind, he may have felt that. He was quite an expert in the area, even of Cessna, in addition to general airplanes. He felt that since Stephanie and I were seated facing backwards, that these seats were not supposed to be flown in that position.

I wondered about that when you told me. I had never seen that in any plane.

I guess they have little tables or something that you could sit at and have a little space between Brian Krolicki and myself, for example, but whatever they stick in to make the seat somewhat sturdy, there was nothing that would demonstrate that this seat should have been turned in the opposite direction. I guess the manual didn't say that, the Cessna manual.

Since we both had the most serious injuries, and they were spine injuries, that was his approach to the jury, and the jury was very, very conservative in that, I guess, until the very, very *end*. "Sorry, ladies. You were in a plane crash, but it was the pilot's fault, so too bad." There was one woman on the jury, and I don't know who it was, who insisted that I, particularly, get something. If it hadn't been for her, I guess, nothing would've happened.

Stephanie was not satisfied with the ratio that was used initially, and I think anybody who knows me knows I really don't care that much about money. It's not a big thing, never was. So I was kind of easy with her, and my attorneys were kind of mad, but I figured she was so much younger than me, and she had a long life ahead of her. I do know that she bought a black Porsche convertible or something, so I guess it was used in some way that was important to her.

She did take my seat in the senate, and I'm sure we're going to get a little confused here in chronology, but it was when I was in the hospital with Guillain-Barré, and, of course, I couldn't even write anything. Jim Denton, my campaign manager, cooked this deal up that Stephanie would get this seat, and the county commission had to vote on it. He figured that if I—being in *bed*, like in a movie, where you are barely able to write—would sign my name on the bottom of a statement that says, "I want Stephanie Tyler to take my seat," well, that's probably going to be pretty effective with the county commissioners, don't you think?

Yes.

I think so, too, and so did Jim Denton, because it was his idea. Of course, it was. So Stephanie fulfilled the other two years of my term, knowing the seat would go away after that.

Jim Denton—I don't know if I mentioned this or not, that they had a press conference and explained what Guillain-Barré is and so on? Most people I know today, they didn't get that part of it.

In terms of understanding the entire story of what was happening to you at that time?

Yes. So, anyway, most of the Guillain-Barré did descend out of my body, as we hoped it would.

Was that following that complete blood transfusion you described?

Yes. And that was not just once. We had to do that a number of different times. Now, they don't do that anymore. They go back to what they had done initially—gamma globulin. I don't know why, but, obviously, they didn't think it did the job as well as they expected it to.

Most people are left with a residual effect from Guillain-Barré. A lot of people have a dropped foot. I do know they put a big board at the bottom of my hospital bed where I could push it. Of course, you had no feeling, so I guess it was just laying up there, so my feet couldn't flop over.

Then after that, maybe when I was checking this pain I had, I kept thinking, what if it were Guillain-Barré that was causing that and not the fusion, and I went back and had all this other stuff done? It would be just terrible. I did see a neurologist

at UCLA when I was down there for other purposes, and she did whatever she did and felt that it was not neurological.

We have been talking about Guillain-Barré, but I still had some questions about the plane accident, and I didn't know about any conflict over the trial. I was especially wondering if Stephanie or Brian or Bob have similar symptoms to you in terms of trauma, and if you know.

I don't know. I don't know. I see Brian a bit at the legislature, and I talk to Stephanie occasionally. She had her rods removed, and I debated whether to have that done or not. You should do it at about a year, so nerves and muscles and things don't grow around it.

I don't think it's a very terrible thing to have them taken out—much easier than putting them in. Stephanie is back to the way she was, maybe even better. She is a lobbyist now with SBC, the big phone company. In fact, my friend Marybel Batjer, the governor's chief of staff, told me that Stephanie is now kind of centered in Sacramento. So she's obviously doing very well. She married an attorney from here who seemed like a very nice guy, J. J. He went down to Las Vegas to set up the legal firm's office there. They ultimately got married.

Bob Seale is in Las Vegas. He was chairman of the Republican Party, and I don't know exactly what he's doing.

Then, of course, Brian Krolicki did take Bob Seale's place as state treasurer and is in his second term. He has two little children—darling little kids—and wife. The last time I saw them was at the governor's inauguration.

Oftentimes if there's a death, similar to in wartime, there's a survivor's guilt type of thing, where that person died or you see other plane crashes where the people died.

Have you heard anybody talk about feeling guilty that Judy was killed and everyone else was not?

No.

That's not an issue?

No. It hasn't been, in my mind. I guess I would think maybe her husband might have some guilt, because he did know what the plane was like.

And the jury ruled that it was pilot error.

Actually, very honestly, politics is politics. If somebody had known what the jury had decided in that case—and it certainly was public information—one might question the judgment of running for statewide office, since the judgment in that case wasn't the best, at least from my perspective.

All of the others who were in the crash, other than you and Judy, have returned to their careers? They've been able to return to theirs?

Yes. Brian Krolicki was the assistant treasurer with Bob, so that was a natural progression for him. Actually, Brian had worked for some investment company like Goldman Sachs before he got connected with politics out here. Stephanie wasn't interested in running for office again but did like to "affect" legislation, which is a nice way of saying "lobbying."

One of the things we've talked off and on about is how you beat formidable odds in terms of health and a number of things. Some of the things you've said to me are that you stay busy. But if you could tell people, what is the formula that works for you? When faced with what seem to be impossible odds or just overwhelming

challenges, like the health issues that you've had, what is your approach to that? How do you manage that?

That's a really tough question.

I guess the other thing that you had said to me off tape is that some people always say, "You're so strong." We were discussing how, like with even very strong people, that isn't always how you feel.

Well, in thinking where I was born in the state of Maine, there is a perception—and it's not necessarily a perception but could be a reality—that the people who come from New England, particularly from that state, are a tough breed. I guess that that's part of it. I think obviously you're affected by the way you grew up and how you grew up. There was no pitying allowed for anything.

In your family?

Yes. I remember I was going with a guy at Northwestern. I went home to meet his parents, who lived in Kansas, and the parents said to Bruce something about the fact that I would be like a pillar of strength or something like that. They liked me and felt that that would be a good match. I guess I do leave that impression, evidently, with people.

I also feel you should, as much as you can, have a positive attitude. I'm alone now, except for my cat, and my daughter always kids me—she jokes about old ladies and their animals, particularly cats! [laughter] I'm not going to say it with a plural—just *a* cat.

That's difficult in itself, without being around people, but that's why, I'm sure, I keep busy. I do want to feel like I'm making a difference in some way or another and also to feel like I have contributed to my community or the state. But it's really hard for me to answer your question. I do think that you need to be positive, and sometimes you can't be that way all the time, obviously, but as much as you can.

Another example, which I don't think I've told yet: I was at the airport, and I saw Carole Vilardo, who's the lobbyist for the Nevada State Taxpayers Association. She got off the plane, came up, and said hello. My daughter was there, and Carole said, "Oh, Sue, how do you feel?"

I said, "Fine."

She left, and my daughter said, "Why did you say *that*? You feel *terrible*!"

I said, "Well, Kristina, if you say how you feel to somebody, they're not going to want to come up and speak to you again, because they don't know what to say in return. They'll say, 'Gee, I'm sorry.' And then that's it. The next time they may not want to visit with you about something else." I do think that's absolutely the truth.

It's like somebody that goes on a long trip. People say, "Did you have a good trip?"

"Yes." That's all they want to know. They don't want to see your entire itinerary and where you stayed, et cetera.

Don't give them the details! [laughter]

I guess that's about all I can think of in terms of answering the question. I think that when people hear about my life, it just seems like a soap opera to most people. It's just too much, they say, kind of too overwhelming, particularly just the significance of the airplane crashes. [sighs] Then all the rest of this stuff. I suppose it does.

My high school friend with Rutgers University, whom I've discussed, is in some organization, a women's group, and it's national. You're invited to be in it, and I'm going to say Jay Rockefeller's wife is in it. The woman who owns or manages the

Baltimore Orioles' baseball stadium, called Camden Yards, is in it. So there are all these interesting women, and she invited me to go speak about this very subject, about my life, in Monterey. I remember being really excited about it. I was in Las Vegas, and I wound up in the emergency room. We didn't know what it was, but it was kidney stones, and I couldn't go. So I taped it and sent it over, and I got a book back of messages from women who were there and just heard it. Since I taped it, they visually couldn't see it. It was people that I'll probably never meet, but they said things like, "I'm not going to complain any more."

My friend Lenita Powers used to be a columnist, but now she's back to writing stories. In one of her columns, without naming my name, she was writing something about whenever she feels down about something, or, "Gee, things aren't working out right," she thinks of me, and then she puts everything back into perspective again.

Yes. I remember that column, because she didn't name the person.

No, she didn't.

But it was so clear it was you. So you can tell that you are having a real influence on a lot of women, not only from the work that you did in the legislature and as lieutenant governor, but now simply because of your life and that you keep going.

Yes. I think that people will say, "Oh, my gosh, you're a role model," and I wish somebody else was their role model, to be honest with you, but that is in itself a positive thing. It's better to have somebody saying, "Gee, I wish you could have run for governor," or something, and it's nice that people say that rather than, "I wish she wouldn't have run again! I'm really sick of her!" The opposite. I think those are positive things.

13

THE OFFICE OF LIEUTENANT GOVERNOR

I don't know where you want to go right now, but I do want to talk about what I did in the office of lieutenant governor, because we've talked a lot about the senate, but we hadn't gotten to that, I don't believe.

It would be a good time to do that.

Yes. I did describe how I operated the first session, which was *just* managing the senate. There was an office there, which is now in the same quarters of the senate majority leader. I don't know who else is in that. It's called the leadership offices on the first floor near the senate chambers. I had an office there. The legislature bought me a day bed, so I could lie down. My secretary, Marilyn Hoffman, wouldn't let *anybody* in unless it was very important, and she knew them very well, because she didn't want anybody to see me lie down. She didn't want people assuming that maybe I wasn't up to full strength, which was true—I was not.

Anyway, I don't have really significant observations of the 1991 session, except the fact that it went very well, and I feel I

enjoyed it. I mean, it was hardly making policy, and sometimes you'd get so upset listening to these people. I used to send Dina Titus a lot of notes, because I figured Dina and I were on the same wavelength in many cases. Then I'd send her some information about something out of a bill that was going on. Or the young man I mentioned, Mark James—I would send him a note that would say, "Lighten up and smile, Mark," because he would get so serious, and he'd get so upset if somebody, particularly Senator Joe Neal, knew that he could pull his chains.

I was busy doing that sort of stuff while they were debating. So, of course, I was very interested in what was going on. There was one bill that I thought, "Wow, if it *is* a tie . . . . " And it looked like it might be. In fact, Stephanie came over to tell me about it. It had to do with when a settlement is made in a trial and nobody knows about that unless you want them to know about it. The trial lawyers, I think, would have been opposed to this. The press association or somebody wanted all of that to be public information. Well, that was about the only thing we could think of that would be a conflict for me in the position I was in at that time. So it looked like it was going to be very, very close.

Oh, a tie.

Yes, and in that case, I would have voted to break the tie just to see what would happen in the supreme court. So that's the first session, which was just being president of the senate. There were a lot of things I wanted to do, but obviously I just wasn't physically able to do them. I did have Scott Simon, my highway trooper, and that was an incredible relationship. If I gave a speech, he would make sure the microphone was working, and my notes were up there, and I really got very, very spoiled.

Then there was the 1993 session. Of course, in the meantime now, I've gone back to have the surgery done again, and then I had to recuperate from that.

Was this the second surgery in Minnesota, then?

Yes. My sister was with me that time. I had, as I mentioned, this great chief of staff in Las Vegas, Verona Pasquale. As a matter of fact, Verona, when she heard I had Guillain-Barré—and I don't think I've said this on the record here—she was just devastated, because she knew what it was and knew that sometimes it took a very, very long time to get over it. Of course, her role was so unbelievably more difficult, because I could not appear. I mean, I just physically couldn't get on the plane and go anywhere. So there was so much that needed to be done to promote my name there, and I've mentioned about getting more money to run the few commercials that I had.

The one great thing was that a lot of people particularly called her and said, "We want to help," after the plane crash. There were Democrats. I know Virgil Getto rode his horse in the Pahrump parade with my name on the saddle, I guess. And Dina Titus, a Democrat—there was just all this outpouring of not only support and sympathy, but I had offers of help. So that was somewhat helpful to Verona. We didn't really know each other all that well. We knew each other from the beginning of the primary, but I figured I'd win the Republican primary against Pro-Life Andy Anderson. Then I was going to focus all my attention in Las Vegas after the primary.

And then you couldn't be there at all.

And then I couldn't be anywhere, practically, so that was much more difficult for her, but she turned out to be an unbelievable person. I mean, I tend to be concerned about whether people are actually fulfilling their responsibility. If I said, "I'd like you to do this," I'd worry about whether it was done or was done the way I hoped it would be done. With her I didn't have to ever worry.

She became a very good speech writer. I had a small staff up here in Carson City. Now the lieutenant governor has a lot more. I think I had four people, a couple of secretaries and a couple assistants. Verona had been in broadcast. That's what she got her degree in at the University of Georgia, which actually gives the Peabody Awards, and that's where she got her experience—in broadcast journalism.

She knew a lot of people in interesting ways, and she knew somebody in Hollywood, because a part of the responsibilities of the lieutenant governor is the motion picture division. So she set up a trip for me to go to Hollywood. In fact, I took a reporter from the *Reno Gazette-Journal*, Susan Skorupa, who still is writing, and she went with us. I think that Wayne Melton, who was also at the newspaper at that time, was kind of disappointed he didn't get to go. I went in to talk about this with the editorial board. I can't remember which

Sue in Hollywood on a trip for the motion picture industry.

one came first, whether it was the motion picture trip or the trip to Mexico, but anyway, I took a reporter each time, and I'll talk about that in a moment.

The motion picture trip was really, really interesting, and we met with some mid-level people, I'm sure. It was amazing to me that the one thing I learned and came back to the Economic Development Commission with was that hardly anybody thought about us in any way other than gaming. There was something on television at that time that looked like it was in the Tetons or something, and, you know, it could be done here. In fact, Salt Lake now has a lot of television programs that are coming right out of Salt Lake City, Utah. In my mind we missed the boat again here, ten years, twelve years later, but I thought

it was pretty positive, and you have to keep doing those things.

Of course, the one thing that would have been terrific was a sound stage. That is an incredibly positive thing. You do tend to make a lot more movies if you have a sound stage. But it's very, very expensive, and to make it worthwhile, you've got to have it in use almost all the time, such as they do now in Vancouver, for example, in Canada, where they're making practically everything, including movies that are set in downtown New York City.

They've really stolen the business almost right out of Hollywood because of this exchange rate of the dollar, but that was not the problem at that time. Anyway, they did know we were on the map; they did know we had a motion picture division;

and they did know who to contact and those kinds of things. It was really fun.

I know Susan wrote some articles about it, who we met, and so on. I remember, when I returned from that trip, two things. Robin Hollabird is the assistant deputy motion picture person. She lives here. The Disney people wanted to come, but they needed a prison for one scene. Well, we have a new prison not very far from Reno. Somebody didn't get back to them in time, so they went off someplace else. That was a big disappointment.

There is a man that lives here in town, Tim Wilson, who does a lot of site selection. I guess that's probably not the appropriate description in motion picture jargon, but, in fact, he scoped out all the outside work done on *Dances With Wolves*.

I've kind of kept up a little bit with Robin. I mean, she sent me stuff. They put big books together now that they promote, and I really don't know how the new head of the motion picture division is doing. What I intended at one time was to take that division out of economic development and stick it with tourism, because I thought the man at the time who headed up tourism would do a far better job, but that didn't make it. The governor did sign off on it, but it didn't get through the legislature.

It wasn't a big thing, but I felt that it was something, that it's the best industry. It's clean, and it leaves a lot of money behind. Then, depending upon the motion picture, you get an image out to the rest of the country or world.

The legislature didn't pass the support, the idea of moving the motion picture division under the tourism department?

Right. I was not high on the head of the motion picture division, very honestly. It was kind of like if they called him, then he'll work something out, but it was not an aggressive campaign, at all.

The only good thing, I thought, about maybe having Lonnie Hammargren follow me—and it *is* the *only* thing I could think of that might have been positive—is that he was really into names and stuff. I thought, "Well, he's going to pick up on this motion picture thing." And he didn't, not at all. So that's too bad, because I cannot think of anything that happened while he was lieutenant governor that was ongoing.

The one big thing that I could think of was the fact that I got some regulations changed. For example, if you offer as an incentive a break on personal property or taxes, et cetera, in my mind they had to bring in businesses that paid at least the statewide hourly wage. That was a big thing to get through, because some people, of course, were opposed to it. They wanted to be able to promise a company, "You'll get this tax break," and they're paying like six or seven bucks an hour. At that time the statewide hourly wage was over twelve dollars an hour, and that was in the early 1990s.

And that was considered a living wage as opposed to minimum wage?

The statewide hourly wage is what it was known as, out of that division, out of the state agency. That was to me a very significant thing, and, of course, that's why the labor unions supported me for lieutenant governor, because I wanted to bring good-paying jobs here, not just jobs.

I did feel that the other part of the job as lieutenant governor is trade and promotion of our state. So I went to Mexico, and I made two stops. One was in Monterrey, where I opened a big trade show there, and I learned a few words in Spanish. They normally have governors and U.S. senators and so on, but they didn't at that time. I guess I was the highest-ranking person, so I got to open this. But while there we, of course, promoted Nevada. One of my fellow members on the Commission on Economic Development—which is a group that is appointed by the governor, as is the tourism commission—was Ray Vega. While there, Ray was able to nab the Mexican beer; I think it was Corona. He became the Corona distributor in Las Vegas, and that's not a shabby thing to get, I'll tell you. That was a real plum.

We took other business people. In fact, I think one member of the Mack family who is on the city council of Las Vegas went on this trip and wanted to open pawn shops down there. Of course, Mexico is very interested in gaming. They've not done that yet, but they have been very interested in that for a very long time. So the part of the trip in Monterrey was export, import, or business connections, as that is a business center in Mexico, and it is not very far into the interior. You go to Dallas, and then you fly south.

From there, we went to Mexico City, and I spoke at a luncheon, and it was related to tourism. We were very interested in direct airline flights to Las Vegas, for example, and that was a very important thing that we did achieve—the first charter nonstop to Las Vegas. In fact, when they flew their first flight, I went down to Vegas and cut the ribbon and that sort of thing. So when I think about all my buddies at the McCarran Airport in Las Vegas taking good care of me, part of that, of course, goes right back to the fact that I was interested in them at a time in my life.

Those were things that Verona organized, and we went to visit, for example, the ambassador to Mexico City while we were there. I took a reporter, John Stearns, who has been the business editor here for a long time at the *Reno Gazette-Journal* and just recently was plucked away by Sue Clark-Johnson, who is now the publisher of the *Arizona Republic*. It's the biggest newspaper in the Gannett chain. They have another newspaper in Detroit,

and I think those are the two biggest. But anyway, she liked John and thought he did a good job here and so wanted him to go down there. John wrote all these stories about the Mexico City trip, as Susan Skorupa did on the trip to Hollywood.

Well, all the people the governor appointed, I really liked. I did kind of try to convince Bob Miller to appoint some women to the commissions. The only woman on it, the Economic Development Commission, was Lynn Atcheson, and the one woman on the tourism commission is Claudine Williams, who was president of Harrah's. She's a very good friend of Thalia Dondero, who is on the Board of Regents, and they're lovely older women who I really enjoyed. In fact, I saw both of them not long ago. But I wanted to get, instead of like John Ascuaga on the tourism board, how about Michonne Ascuaga? Because she's the young woman, and she's moving herself up through Daddy's business.

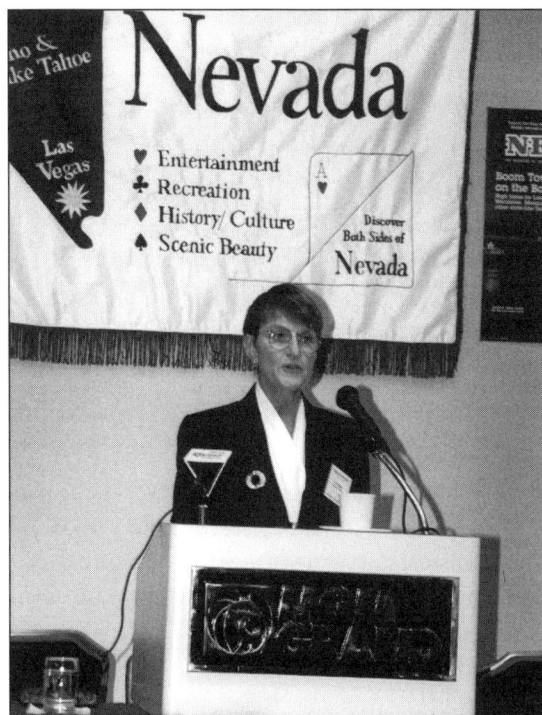

Sue, as chairman of the tourism commission, speaking at a tourism conference in Las Vegas.

I didn't succeed as much there as I would have liked, but I think that the commissions could be used in a different way. If I was up to it and was on the job all four years totally, we would have done some more. But as the newspaper said in an editorial when I decided not to run, as far as they were concerned, more had been done in those areas than ever before. To be fair about it, there haven't been that many lieutenant governors who had that opportunity, because that was just instituted under Bob Cashell when he was elected. And Bob Miller, of course, really was elected *only* to be a stalking horse, to wait around until Dick Bryan went off to the United States Senate.

It was still pretty new.

It's interesting. When that happened, I got a call—I was up at Lake Tahoe—from Sid Rogich, who is a very involved individual in Clark County and also in D.C. He called and asked me if I'd be interested in running for lieutenant governor, because they felt that then Dick Bryan could *not* leave and go off to Washington, because I, a Republican, would then become governor. Actually, I think they might have been wrong, because I think Dick would have left because we got along very well. [laughter] Who knows what would have happened. I got that call; then I started thinking about it, and then they never called me back, because I suspect they decided to choose Joe Brown, who is an attorney in Las Vegas. Nice guy but was much more, I'm sure, agreeable to all of the people that were making this decision. He lost, and, of course, Bob Miller did win, and Dick Bryan went off to Washington. So it worked out the way the Democrats wanted.

That was one of the questions that I wanted to go into just a little bit, because

there's been such a shift in power when certain things happen. For example, we talked about when Brian McKay didn't run, and that impacted you, and then everything shifted at that point. And then you decided not to run for lieutenant governor a second time.

Yes. I wanted to get into that a little bit.

Are you ready for that now, or is there more you want to say on things that you accomplished while you were in there first?

I should probably go and look at the editorial to remind myself. You know, it seems like that's probably it.

OK. So maybe you could talk about, well, two things—how you made the decision not to run, and then what you saw in terms of power shifting once that decision was made.

Well, I think that when you have a lieutenant governor of a different party than the governor, the governor never really believes that you might not run against him. There's always discussion about running as a team, in the same party, and it works in other states, not all of them, but I did not support that. Actually, this was important to Speaker Joe Dini, and I'd always heard that he was very interested in becoming lieutenant governor. That might've worked better for somebody from a smaller community to be on a two-person ticket, so to speak, but I think the voters should pick who they think is best for each job, myself. It would take a constitutional amendment. Joe said he was going to wait until I got out of office, because he didn't want it to affect me, at all. He didn't want people to think something I'd done was the reason he was doing this.

I think Governor Miller and I got along very well. In fact, we got along so well that when the next lieutenant governor, Lonnie Hammargren, came on board, I helped the governor out a lot, even though the next lieutenant governor was the same party I am. I think that even though they know you've been in this terrible accident, they know that you're not 100 percent; they *don't* know, however, with what you say . . . . They knew more from me than some others, because I usually did say what the truth was, but I had not said that I'm not going to run again, or that I can't run, or I can't run for something else. As I mentioned to you, even when I was presiding over the senate, I had a day bed, and my secretary just wouldn't let anybody in. So there was obviously an attempt to

Lt. Governor Sue Wagner with Governor Bob Miller

sort of not make me look better, but not make me look worse, I guess. I had been thinking about it for a while, and I realized how difficult it is to run statewide. I mean, that's what happened to me. I gave it a lot of thought.

The governor's chief of staff at that time was Patty Becker, who I knew well. She was a deputy attorney general of the gaming division, and she was also the only woman that's ever served on the Gaming Control Board in a full-time position, but at this point Patty was the governor's chief of staff, and the governor was good friends with Billy Vassiliadis, whom I've mentioned before. He is president of R&R Partners in Las Vegas. Patty lived rather close to me, and she wanted me to meet at her house with the governor and with Billy, because they were trying to convince me to run for lieutenant governor again before I made up my mind. They realized that they had somebody who wasn't going to muck around in their business or upstage the governor or try to. It's just not my style, at all. There were times when I thought I could, but I wouldn't do that. I guess there was something about wanting to be well liked or well respected or something.

I told them that it would be impossible for me to do the rural areas, and I'd have to cut back a lot. Of course, R&R Partners are very, very skillful in what they do, and Billy was trying to convince me that I could kind of run by tape. In other words, have more not just commercials, but more informationals or whatever. It just didn't sit well with me, because I like to campaign, and I would hate to be sitting home here in Reno while something was being run on television stations someplace else, because I'd miss out on all that.

So I have to say they gave it a good shot, and it was nice to know that they would have gone to bat for me. There would be no doubt that R&R would have done whatever they needed to do to get it done correctly.

Had you already made up your mind when they talked to you?

Probably. I don't remember that. Obviously, I had been thinking about it, because that's why they wanted to talk to me, you know. I know that R&R Advertising and other people have been real instrumental in saying that, "If you want to run for Congress, we'll support you." So there was that. If you don't have that kind of support, you might as well not run, because you're not going to win.

You had that support?

I had that support in my first race, not with those particular people that we're talking about right now. And then I did a good job as lieutenant governor. As I say, I knew I was lieutenant governor, and I didn't think I was "governor-in-waiting."

We would have a few jokes. We went over to the prison to get these new license plates. A bill I had introduced as lieutenant governor created a Running Rebel and a Wolf Pack license plate, something I learned in Arizona, and it raised a lot of money for scholarships, both academic and athletic. So we were over there, and they came off the press, and I grabbed number one and held it up! [laughter] Bob kind of knew I was joking around, but there still was, you know, some of that feeling.

One of the reasons that Bob and I got along very well is the fact that he was a big sports nut, and so was I. I don't think I've really talked about this *on* the record. I do believe this has something to do with getting back to our previous question about getting along with your colleagues. If you are interested in anything that someone else is interested in, of course, that person enjoys that. I enjoyed teaching my students

in Carson City, because they're interested in the same thing I am. That was a real icebreaker in a way. I could get involved in conversations with a bunch of guys and talk about graphite putters or whatever. That was another element of our relationship that was a very good one.

I do know that there are many women—I found this out when I taught my class on women in leadership—who have an athletic interest and/or background. I don't know if that's a connection with leadership, or if that's a way that gets women into positions with a bunch of males—whatever business it's in, whether it's university or politics, private sector— whether that's helpful and has helped them in any way. But I think it would make an interesting book to do.

Interesting study, to see what the correlation is.

Right, if there is any. And at the time I obviously had been thinking about maybe not getting involved, and I know my family really didn't want me to, but, you know, the thing is, if you don't do that, what are you going to do with the rest of your life, so to speak?

I always think about little people like that Tara Lapinsky, I think her name was, that won the gold medal in ice skating when she was thirteen, or Sarah Hughes who won it, again, at fifteen or something. What do you do for an encore? [laughter] I'm certainly not in that category.

I know that Verona didn't want to be chief of staff again, and that probably had some bearing on this, as well, because her husband was a CPA and had top-notch firms that hired him. One was Carl's Jr., a fast food chain. She was, if you wanted to say, not a stereotype, but if you met Verona, you could believe that she was in the Junior League. She and her husband were the most unlikely pair in the whole world. She

Sue hugs Governor Bob Miller at signing of legislation for the Wolf Pack license plates. Chris Ault (second from left), and Dina Titus (far right), with other university system representatives.

didn't like any sport at all except racing, car racing. They would go to all of these races, and she'd get down and change the tires, do all this stuff. Well, he got a job then at Toyota in charge of the racing branch of Toyota as a vice-president.

I guess it didn't turn out to be exactly what he thought. But anyway, he moved to Irvine, California, so she would go to see him on the weekends. They'd sold their house, or the house was up for sale in Las Vegas, so that was a problem, and, of course, I was very flexible. If she'd get something done, she'd leave on a Thursday or something like that, and it was a short flight. The campaign was the thing that was sort

of overwhelming—how to do it. And I've discussed that.

Because you wouldn't have your chief of staff, your family was against it, and you still had to deal with how you would reach people in rural areas.

How would I get around? Yes. Even if I was in Las Vegas—I mean, when I was there, I was busy from morning to night. You know, go to work, do a luncheon speech, go to work, come back, do something in the evening. I couldn't have done that.

As I mentioned, there's five thousand new people moving to Las Vegas every month. That was going on at that time, and it's still going on *today* in 2003. But you knew you had to start all over again. The governor doesn't have quite the same problem, because most people, if they know anybody in government, they're going to know who the governor is.

But the long days, the travel.

Oh, yes. All of those.

Because at that point, how long a day were you able to do? Because you would put in days, but you would take breaks and go lie down in your office.

Yes. I did take a break when I was presiding over the senate, though, if I absolutely had to. We do have a president *pro tem*, who fills in for the lieutenant governor, if I went someplace else like the lieutenant governors conference or something. I did go to quite a few, and I want to make sure I touch on that, as well. I don't know if you want me to touch on that now, or would you like me to just finish with deciding that I wasn't going to run?

Oh, why don't you go ahead and finish with deciding this, because we were talking about how much stamina you really had.

Well, actually, to be honest, I think I have quite a bit, considering.

But at that time was it different, because you'd been through three surgeries in four years?

Yes. Verona used to tell me that a surgery like that takes years to really get over, and there was one, and then there was another, and then there was another. For some of those reasons and probably many others, I decided not to run. I can't

remember who was helping me—probably Jim Denton or Verona. I wanted to have the head of the Republican Party, the highest-ranking Republican and then Bob Miller around while I'm sort of bailing out. Bob Miller did come down, and then in Vegas, I announced it first there. I asked Brian McKay. My line, I guess, was, "I'm going to take a break, but I'll be back." That kind of thing. I'm pretty sure that's what it was.

We had the press conference in a room at the airport, where the airport authority meets in Las Vegas. It was done really very quickly, like overnight, because these two guys were going to be in Vegas at the same time or something, and a woman that worked for R&R Advertising kind of put it together. Her last name was Scherer, and her husband is now on the gaming control board, Scott Scherer. He was in the assembly at the time, I think, or then he became Governor Guinn's chief of staff, too, for a period of time.

There were very few people there, as I say. Well, that was not the point. And who would appear? Lonnie Hammargren. He had no business being there. It was an emotional time for me. So when we got done with my decision, he ran up and grabbed the microphone and said he was going to run. The press ignored him totally, because they thought he deserved to be ignored. And to the gall of the guy, he later on asked me to endorse him, and he asked Verona to endorse him. Verona told him where he could go, big-time, and that's how I felt, too. He brought it up to people *all* the time. "She didn't endorse me. She didn't endorse." Well, if you knew him, you'd know hardly anybody would endorse him, to be honest with you. Just recently he ran for the assembly in Las Vegas, and he didn't win that, either.

Yes, I would think that that announcement would have been very difficult for you.

"I'm going to take a break, but I'll be back." Sue's announcement of retirement. Left to right: Manny Cortez (Executive Director, Las Vegas Convention and Visitors Authority), Joe Dini (Speaker of the Assembly), Bonnie Bryan, Governor Bob Miller, Dave Finley, Sue, and Kristina.

It was.

This is the work you love.

Yes. As a matter of fact, my sister . . . . [crying] Of course, she was happy, but she's a totally different person than I am, but Verona thought that would be a good idea.

To have her there with you for support?

Well, then we did the same thing here in the north. [with emotion] And by that time, I know Dennis Myers was there; Joanie Kaiser, and some other people, and they were very disappointed. It's funny that, right from there, I had to go to some function, and I think it was something with psychiatrists or psychologists. I didn't really remember much of it, except a year or so ago I was down where I work out at the gym, Sports West, and this woman was next to me. She introduced herself and said, "You probably don't remember me, but I was at this particular activity," she said, "right after you'd made this announcement." I didn't remember her, and to tell you honestly, I didn't remember the meeting, either, but I've been to so many things in my life that you couldn't possibly remember all of them, even when somebody tells you about it.

So that announcement was made, and then, of course some people were ready to run, to jump in, which is a very normal thing. In many instances I've thought to myself, when one of my colleagues died or something, that the vultures start flying over right away, picking up the pieces and

Left to right: Myrna Williams, Sue Wagner, Edith Sayre Auslander, Renee Diamond, and Dina Titus.

seeing how they fit in and where they fit in and if they do fit in. Lonnie wasn't the only person running. I'm pretty sure his name was Bruce Layne—the man that I had mentioned had taken me around the Thomas and Mack Center, because he was a big Rebel booster and other things. I had interviewed his wife to do the job Verona ultimately had—after what happened to me, I'm sure she was thankful. "Wow, am I glad I didn't take that job!"

It would have been way more work. [laughter]

Would have been way more. And that was something that you had to admire about Verona.

Yes. She stuck with you through all of that extra work.

Oh! Absolutely. Bill Briare, I think is his name, once was the mayor of Las Vegas, and he was a Democrat. And they were hoping, hoping, hoping. . . . Well, he did win the primary, and, of course, Lonnie Hammargren won the primary, and Lonnie beat Bill Briare.

Lonnie, in the primary, beat Bruce Layne, and Jim Denton did run this Bruce Layne campaign. He did things with that campaign that were so expensive and so underutilized, it was sickening. They made tapes—videotapes that you put in your VCR—and they talk about, "Here I am, and this is what I've done," and it was *unbelievably* expensive. But he had money, and he also didn't quite understand that you don't have to buy or do everything that the campaign manager may want you to do. I actually have not seen that particular approach in anybody else's campaign since. [laughter]

So what do you do after that? In thinking about what I wanted to do—something that I would enjoy, to look forward to—I talked to Joe Crowley, president of UNR, and told him that I'd be very interested in doing something with the intern program. I was familiar with that, because I've had the interns. Don Driggs had started this intern program at UNR some thirty-five years ago now, and he was a political science professor. I was familiar with that, and I thought, "Well, that would be something interesting to do."

I hadn't really seen it in operation when I was lieutenant governor. In fact, I did have Margaret Crowley, Dr. Crowley's daughter, as one of my interns. I was fortunate because Don Driggs kind of picked out one of the best students for me, and so I was spoiled. I had Spike Wilson's daughter, Ann, and, you know, they were way above, on the educational map, if you will.

They had some background.

Oh, yes. In fact, Ann was wheeling and dealing down there, like she was her own little lobbyist and stuff. [laughter] Fortunately, she and I agreed on everything, because it would have been terrible! I would have had to stomp on her, because she had so much enthusiasm.

I had also thought at that time that it would be neat to be able to help the university in terms of lobbying. I had been asked to be a lobbyist. It was something I really didn't think I wanted to do. Most of the things that I would want to lobby for didn't have much money, and I needed to get some kind of a job, because all of a sudden here I am, going from this high-paying $20,000 a year, whatever the lieutenant governor was being paid at that time, to nothing.

You had no income at that point, then?

No. I had been asked to be a lobbyist for the Nevada Trial Lawyers Association, which *definitely* would have paid me bucks. There were two things that I was concerned about with that, and they promised me that they would only use me on the big, big things, that I wouldn't have to go down there every day, but who knows?

I'd also been asked—and I do want to mention this—to be the interim director for the Nevada Press Association, because I had very good records in both those groups, I mean, in terms of my own philosophy. I believe Andy Engleman was, not the executive director, but the lobbyist of the press association. I don't know, maybe she was going to do something else, because it wasn't that they fired her or anything. Something else happened, because she kind of approached me on this, and Sherman Frederick, who's the head honcho down at the *Las Vegas Review-Journal*, really wanted me to do this, too.

I didn't do either one of those things, particularly the trial lawyers. I was going to be a member of the First Interstate Bank [FIB] board of directors, and I was a bit concerned if there would be any kind of a problem with that group versus the trial lawyers. I didn't know. I was thinking that maybe I could get on some other boards of directors. The trial lawyers have a very definite image and certainly one that I support, but a lot of other business people don't.

Was there some income with the FIB board of directors?

Yes, there was—every meeting, and then if you were on subcommittees, those kinds of boards, they're different. They're for-profit-type things, so you do get paid for being on the board. There were a lot of people I knew on the board, such as Bob List. That's kind of irrelevant now, but there were people that I see in later activities that I'm doing, such as the gaming commission, for example. There was a man named John O'Riley, who used to be former chair of the gaming commission, who was on the board. Anyway, it was really good for me, because I learned a whole lot and met a whole lot of nice, interesting people. I think I did mention this relationship to Pro-Life Andy Anderson, trying to picket against me for being on the board at a different time.

Right. Yes, you did. But you also thought then that, in relation to other jobs, this might be a conflict for you with the trial lawyers?

Yes, I did. Also, I was concerned that they said, "You only have to come down here for the big things." Sometimes it doesn't work out that way. I know that it would have been a good thing for them to have, particularly, a Republican to be able to talk to other Republicans.

It was interesting to me that I did do a few things for them just as a good person—calling on a couple of Republican legislators. It became such a partisan issue, trial lawyers. It was not quite that much when I was in there. It wasn't like the insurance companies are Republican, and the trial lawyers are Democrats. Well, that's basically what has happened, not only in our state but nationwide, because one of the things that President Bush has supported is a $250,000 cap on medical malpractice claims, for example.

That would be something I would have opposed in the legislature. Not only have I had personal experience—I didn't sue the doctors, but I could have, and I would hardly want to know that that was all you could get. You could hope you would get something more.

Anyway, so I have a couple of things. I really didn't want to wait until I had actually announced that I wasn't going to run and then start scurrying around. I wanted to know there was something there that would be of interest to me. So Joe Crowley did work with the chairman of the Political Science Department at that time, Eric Herzik, and worked it out. However, the opportunity to do lobbying was clearly not going to be something that they wanted me to do. But anyway, it didn't happen.

So at that time, of course, the internship class was absolutely nothing. There were no programs. In fact, the person that was in charge of it, I understand, is a *very* good teacher, John Marini, but he wasn't interested in this. Don Driggs had retired and left the state, and the Political Science Department felt they needed to keep it going, but that's all it was. They actually just had a student sign a piece of paper saying they wanted to be an intern. There was nothing else, no requirements, except you could write your own name, I guess. Dr. Marini never came down to the legislature during the session. Don Driggs used to appear occasionally. I have to say, Dr. Marini was so excited when he found out he didn't have to do this anymore. Actually, most of the Political Science Department was happy, because they were afraid they might have to help, which is very interesting to me, that they really don't want to participate in the real politics of the world. But anyway, that's true.

When that's what they're teaching.

Yes. Dr. Marini teaches theory and comparative, I assume, political systems and that sort of thing, and they say he's a good teacher, but this is not his bag. I remember even when Eric Herzik came down with me one day, we sat with, I think, Speaker Dini, and he was looking all over;

he had never been in the chambers before. So that was a good thing. I understand now he's interested in maybe running for my old assembly district. So anyway, that was of interest, but it was not a full-time job, and that would only happen—be getting revved up—right before the session.

I did teach another course in the Political Science Department, so I could be considered half-time and receive some benefits. One of the things that happened when I decided not to run for lieutenant governor was that I did not have enough years to vest in the PERS system. Now, I did have seventeen years in the *legislative* retirement system, which was totally separate from PERS. That was a bad decision that had been made years before, because if there was a small raise in coverage, you would have been with this other large group. You would not have separated yourselves out and have everybody focus on you voting on your own pension, which is politically impossible. So this also served that purpose, because I'd have to work, let's see, two years to make up that fifth year that I needed to vest. Obviously, I didn't want to have to run for lieutenant governor again, which I didn't feel I could do just to vest in the system.

So I don't know how many years I've done it now for the university, but it's not a big thing, because I make so little. I only now teach one class, but at that time I taught, and I had to create a brand-new class, in addition to taking over this internship program, which, as I said, there was *no* program.

So there was a lot of work in that?

There was a way lot of work.

To do a new class, yes.

There were no books; there was nothing. They wanted me to teach women in leadership. To tell you the truth, it got to be *so* overwhelming that I didn't have any time to myself, at all. I mean, I was grading papers, because most everything was, of course, essay. I did have a lot of women come in, though, and talk. Some of them did excellent jobs, because I gave them a section of the book that we were using to kind of encompass their job around the theories that were being given. I got a lot of good ideas from books from the Nevada Woman's Fund on leadership, women in leadership. You had to know what you were doing every week when you went in, because it was a three-hour seminar. I taught in the evening, mainly juniors, seniors, and I had a couple of grad students. In fact, one of them is now head of our health department in Washoe County.

Barbara Hunt?

Yes. Barbara was getting her master's in public administration. She was one of my better students. Actually, I taught it two or three different times.

Then there was the thought that I should teach another class, which we decided was going to be on campaigning. I did search out the nation on other colleges that had this course. I was in touch with a magazine, *Campaigns and Elections*. In fact, I saw it on CSPAN just the other night. I kind of got started doing that. I had accumulated all this material, and I got to thinking, "This is just too much. This is way too much." So I didn't do that.

After the two or three times that I taught the women in leadership class, I didn't do that again, either. It was a good thing, because in the meantime, in 1995, I was appointed to the Washoe Health System board of directors. And that was kind of a surprise. I couldn't actually go to some of the meetings, because they met on the last Monday of the month, and that's the night I taught this women in leadership class, but this was also a way in which I could get some income, because I realized I was not going to be teaching half-time anymore.

I had talked to Patty Becker, Governor Bob Miller's chief of staff, about being on the gaming commission, and it seemed to me like that would be a really good fit for me in many ways. It was of great interest and of great influence; I could do a lot of the work at home, and it was part-time.

I had other offers. My friend Judy Matteucci, who had been the budget director at one time, went over to be chair of the Public Utilities Commission, but at that time I think it was called the Public Service Commission. She called me and wanted me to get one of those jobs. There was an opening, and it would appear that I would get it. First of all, it was full-time. The salary was really good, and she kept saying, "Well, you could do a lot of the work at home," but if that was not what other people did, that's not what I would do.

Judy, wow, she's one *smart* person, one of the smartest people. She and Bill Bible are probably the man and woman I know who are one smart duo. I believe she thought I would have been part of her group of voting. It always appeared there were three-to-two votes, and I did not want that. I thought it would be a lot of stress, and besides that, the time spent. A lot of that had to do with the personalities. In fact, I recommended my boss, George Hidy, from DRI, because he would have fit it perfectly. He didn't get that appointment, because he was not political enough to get the job.

I had approached Patty Becker about the gaming commission, and, of course, I had to wait until there was even a seat available—someone's term *expiring* from northern Nevada, and a Republican. Scott Craigie followed Patty Becker as Governor Miller's chief of staff. Scott knew a woman in Reno, and she was a CPA, named Debbie Griffin, who I had never met and didn't know. She got an appointment to the gaming commission, and her four years were up, but she was reappointed, I think. There was one other person, Bob Lewis, who was a former officer in Sierra Pacific Power Company, who was on it. I think he was finishing up, or *would* in several years finish up with his third term, and so that was not available at that time.

I wasn't sure that the governor would appoint me anyway, because I am . . . I guess I use the word, the "c" word—it's hard to "control" me. I'm not saying that people on the gaming commission are controlled. What I'm saying is that I'm pretty outspoken. There was a national panel that was at that time appointed by Congress that was very, very important to Nevada, and we were able to get Bill Clinton to appoint Bill Bible, who was chairman of our gaming control board, to this panel. There were a lot of people on it who wanted to wrap up gaming everywhere, didn't want it going outside the borders of our state or New Jersey or anyplace else. They were very anti-gaming. Bill Bible, as I mentioned several times, is so smart, and it was a very good appointment, but there was a much brighter eye, or wide-open eye, on the whole issue of gaming at that time.

I don't know if this made any difference or not, but when I talked to Governor Miller about it, I told him, "Well, you know, you think about my reputation of honesty and ethics, and this would be a really good appointment at this time, when there's so much attention being brought to the whole issue of gaming." As I say, I don't know if that made any difference or not, but I was appointed, and I was just *really* pleased about it. I think my mother and other relatives were kind of scared, you know. The thought of gambling in some of the states is not always fair. I guess she thought maybe I'd wind up in the desert in some kind of a grave, buried there for not voting the right way or something. [laughter]

Sue and her mother, Kathryn Hooper Pooler.

With the cement shoes at the bottom of a lake.

Yes, yes. I was going to say a cement casket, but I knew that wasn't right. [laughter] That's exactly it.

The one class that I did keep was the internship class, and I do want to say a little bit about that, because I want to say what I've done to improve the class. I first thought that the students should be interviewed, that I should visit with them a bit; they should have a letter of recommendation, and they should fill out an application. Believe me, these things were not done—even an application. Well, I guess there was. I just saw a piece of paper with people's names on it. Maybe it actually was an application. That was the first thing. So that happened.

I interviewed them, and some of them didn't get to be interns. Not many, but some didn't. I had a certain grade average that I expected, and I also wanted juniors and seniors—upper-division students—because I think you need a certain maturation level to be thrust into that environment and to keep up and to enjoy it and get something out of it. It was kind of like, "Well, I got to be an intern." It wasn't like anybody could be. I mean, there was something there that looked like you need to jump through a few hoops.

You earned it.

Yes. I think that's important. My first was the 1995 session. I had to start this right after summer in 1994, because I had to let people know that this was available. They had to get the applications in by a certain date, because I was going to have interviews at a certain time. I wanted everything done by about Thanksgiving with the students, and then I had to go out and find the legislators and match them as best I could with a student. That's one of the reasons I interviewed them, because I'd ask certain questions that would give me some idea of their political philosophy. In my mind, it was always better if they agreed with the legislator they were working with, so that Assemblywoman Chris Giunchigliani could tell Jacques Pelham, her intern, "I want you to go over and research this about whether we should have the death penalty for people under eighteen," for example, which is something that did happen this year. You get a sense of the legislators and whether they do a good job with the interns.

Now, in the middle of all this, the constitution was amended to limit the legislative sessions to 120 days. I would like to say on the day Vikki and I are talking that today is the 120th day of the 2003 session. And it doesn't look like they're going to be done tonight.

Still going, as far as we know.

But this also, of course, impressed the time that legislators would even have to spend with their interns, because it doesn't work if they just follow you around. They've got to take the time, and it does take time. I know that from my own experience. No freshman legislator was going to get one of my interns, because they were learning the ropes themselves. I did have one. Her name was Ellen. She was in Special Collections at the university library. She's now retired, and her husband was in the electrical engineering department.

Anyway, so this was the process that I went through with the students. Then when they got down to Carson City, we had a big orientation, and then, I believe, the first year I might have asked the governor to come over and speak. I won't go through each session, but I'll just say that what I tried to do was to expose the students not only to the legislative branch of government, which is where they spent most of their time, but also to the executive branch and the judicial branch. The wonderful thing about Nevada is that it is small, that all of those government heads are right there in Carson City. It takes you about three minutes to walk from one building to the next, practically.

So I invited the chief justice of the supreme court, who at the first session was Miriam Shearing, who would share her views of our judicial system, explain it, and also anecdotally keep the kids interested. Then we added the executive branch—I think that might have been the first year as well—when I just had the governor come. I've added other constitutional officers as the years have gone by.

I now have a panel of lobbyists for them, so the students can know that there are different kinds of lobbyists: a contract lobbyist that actually signs a contract with a company; the executive director of an association who also is a lobbyist, such as NACO, the Nevada Associations of Counties; and then a nonprofit lobbyist, such as someone down there occasionally for the Committee to Aid Abused Women or the Girl Scouts or something like that. Then I've added the governor's lobbyist, who in this case was the deputy chief of staff, Mike Hillerby.

Joe Crowley, the president of the university, instituted something very nice, a reception at the end. He did it the first time I did this. Of course, I thought it was run out of the Political Science Department, and I found out it wasn't. Years later, I found out that it came out of Joe Crowley's budget, the *president's* budget, which was a surprise to me. Anyway, he threw this nice reception where all the legislators were invited along with their interns, and a great spread.

Well, all of these things were brand-new. So that first year was absolutely, incredibly busy. As the sessions have gone on, of course, it's become easier. The difficult part is selecting the students, and the *most* difficult is matching them up. This year, I got to say, everything worked absolutely terrifically, except for one little instance, and I was able to correct it. I do have a small office, I'd like to say, that the legislature has been very nice to share, and the director of LCB always laughs in saying how excited I am about having a closet! He said, "I wish the other people that are down here were as happy with something as she seems to be!"

I always worked well with the staff when I was there, and they are repaying me now, because they all come to speak to the students, the heads of each of the agencies. It's a terrific experience for young people, because you can't have this experience in many other places. To think that you got the chief justice this year, for example, Deborah Agosti, to come in, and she'd broken her foot or something and had her leg propped up and just was absolutely terrific. I've said it time and again to the students, "You could not have gotten this experience anywhere else." I think later on in life, they'll look back on it, because I do know that's the case. Also, they're smart enough to recognize that by being in that milieu, they're going to meet important people and that maybe their legislator will write them a letter of recommendation if they want to go to law school.

One of my students was picked up by R&R. They saw the student and thought he was just a sharp kid, and he went to work for them. So, there's a lot of networking that goes on, and they become part of it.

So you're really happy with the program the way you've worked on it over the years?

Yes, I am.

It seems like it's all come together.

Yes. I keep thinking, "No, I'm not going to add anything more," but I'm thinking about having the press come and explain how they choose their stories, all the kinds of things that I could think about. So, it's something that I have to get revved up for, as I say, in the fall of the year, prior to the legislature starting. Of course, it only goes as long as the university is in business. When the session's over, I cannot possibly make them come back. Many of them do. I'm sure there are a bunch of them right down there today.

Down there watching the final minutes?

Yes. So that is one experience that I've had that was getting too much for me to handle. And then the reason that I absolutely said I couldn't do the other teaching anymore is that finally a term expired, and Governor Miller did appoint me, as I mentioned, to the gaming commission.

So now today you have the gaming commission, Washoe Health System, and the intern class.

That's correct. Those are major things I spend my time with, but I'm involved in a lot of other nonprofit things, such as the Nature Conservancy or Pack PAWS, which is a group that supports women athletes at UNR, raising money for them. But those are my three main things.

Actually, in the year 2005, I will have to get off the Washoe Health System board, because remember Lynn Atcheson telling the chairman of the board, "You better hold your seat down," or something, "when Sue starts on your board," or something like, "Things are going to be kind of stirred up there." And I did. I thought that people had been on there way too long, and that we better have term limits. As a matter of fact, though, that came from the grand jury.

We've talked about grand juries before, that there was a grand jury investigation. I was on it, and this didn't have a whole lot to do with my life at the time. The hospital went from being a county-run hospital to not-for-profit, because the county commissioners then were very involved in the hospital. So some of these board members had been on there for a long time. I will be up in 2005, and my gaming commission term is up in 2005.

Of course, I've already decided I'm doing the university program again, so I'll have that in 2005, because, of course, we got a new president in the middle of all this that I did not know, did not meet, but Joe Crowley and Bob Dickens made sure that it was ongoing.

You had a few more things to say about Guillain-Barré and a few more things to say about your time as lieutenant governor.

Yes. I wanted to finish off with Guillain-Barré. It is kind of rare, and you can actually get it again, which is pretty horrifying when you learn that. They believe that you are so worn out that your resistance is low, and these things are floating in the air all the time, and so on. A set of circumstances—somebody gets it, and somebody doesn't.

After I left the hospital on crutches, I had to go to the physical therapist—who I still go to to this day—and learned how to walk again. Soon thereafter I was able to do that, and so that part of my life was back to what it had been before.

Then I had to be able to get around a little bit better, because I've got to preside over the senate as lieutenant governor. I did go to the first lieutenant governors conference that was in Charlotte, North Carolina. My highway trooper and I went, and it was a *beautiful* city—very Southern, very humid, very lovely. I decided to bid at that meeting on the lieutenant governors conference to be held in Las Vegas the following year or whatever year it was, several years out, I guess. Everybody seemed to want to come, but they were kind of afraid, per usual, of voting for it, and then everybody thinking they're going to go and gamble and not pay any attention to business, et cetera, but it *was* chosen. As a matter of fact, at that conference, I had to leave, because my mother-in-law, who lived in southern Arizona, was showing the first signs of Alzheimer's. Something had happened, and fortunately people knew how to reach me. So I left early and flew back.

Whatever year it was when we had it in Las Vegas, it was great. One of the opportunities that I had for them was to actually go to a part of Las Vegas where Ray Vega lived—one of the economic development commissioners that I spoke of going with me to Mexico. He had a beautiful home, and we had a cocktail party out by his pool. I don't know what this area is called in Las Vegas, but my chief of staff arranged for all this. We had a bus, and we drove in; there were all these beautiful trees overlapping the street, and it's like you could be in Des Moines, Iowa, or you could be *anyplace* in the country. I wanted them to realize that real people live in Las Vegas, and it's just not the Strip. That was very successful. We had a really good conference, and, of course, it was a lot of work for the staff, but it was interesting, because you're bringing all those people there to learn. Some had not been to Las Vegas before. The *Las Vegas Review-Journal* wrote a really negative editorial about my going to South Carolina, because I was wasting state taxpayers' money, even though I brought a convention back with me. That didn't seem to level out, so, you know, no matter what you do, you've got to get used to being knocked around a little bit, I guess.

Always the criticism, right?

Yes. Another lieutenant governors conference that I vividly remember was in Indianapolis, and there's a *lot* going on in that city that I think a lot of people don't know about. A beautiful place. They had a great lieutenant governor, and a second lady, I guess—I don't know what you call her—but Frank O'Bannon and Judy, and he then became governor. A lot of these people that I met as lieutenant governors have become governors. That may be one reason why they want to be lieutenant governor. Who knows? [laughter] I did have a good time, and I can feel I did a few things in that role. Hopefully those will be picked up by later lieutenant governors. Well, end of story.

OK. You have mentioned several times that since the airplane accident and the surgeries you had had a highway patrolman assigned to you as a driver, and you wanted to comment about this service.

I did. I think I mentioned how he was selected, that the governor had selected him and just announced it to me the day I was sworn in, without my having thought at all how I would be able to get around. Scott was a great guy. He was huge. He was like about 6'5" and 225 lbs. or something. So he ran interference for me, like he'd go onto airplanes and save me a seat, and nobody was going to tussle with him.

He really loved the job, because it got him off the road, very honestly, and into a whole different world. He got to meet so many new people. He knew everybody in the legislature. He would have to stop and pick up groceries. He was kind of like an advance person, I guess, that maybe the president or somebody has, that they go and make sure everything is done right. I might be talking to somebody, and he'd go up and check the microphone and put my notes up there and so on. Just so many things. I tried to take him to places that I've just mentioned, like a lieutenant governors conference. Of course, he's getting paid by the highway patrol, but it was a really good relationship that we had. He heard a lot of stuff in the car while I was on the phone and kept all that private.

Most governors have probably more dignitary detail than the governor in Nevada. In fact, I was just told the other day that a lot of the dignitary detail has gone because of budget cuts, and that they use the capitol police, but these people are very good drivers, obviously. I also had a driver in Las Vegas. I had a couple of guys, and I liked them all, but I finally said, "You know, maybe we should have a woman," because no woman had ever done this. So we did, and she was just great. In fact, she left the highway patrol and went to metro, because they paid more. That was an interesting experience that no other lieutenant governor has had, and it was one that worked very, very well.

The main thing we wanted to do next is to talk about the children. The last we've talked about Kirk and Kristina, they were headed off to college, and we heard a little bit about them coming home after your plane accident, but we aren't up to date with them.

Well, Kirk went off to the University of Colorado in Boulder and Kristi to the University of Arizona in Tucson. Kirk, of course, is a year older, and so this was a big change for him. Oh, it'd be a change for any of them, but at Arizona, actually, there were people involved in various ways that I knew. So it was different, but not as different.

We had never been to Colorado, but Kirk felt that would be a great place to go, and as it turned out, it was an incredibly good place for him to go. He majored in political science, and he is a real outdoorsman like his dad was. He pledged a fraternity his second year. I did encourage that, actually, because it is a large campus, although this campus isn't as big as Arizona is. I think there was one girl that went from Reno High to Boulder, as well, and, in fact, I know her parents. It's not like going to UNR. In fact, my kids did not want to go to UNR, either one, because they felt it would be a continuation of high school. I don't know if that would be fair—I had to go to my college that was in my hometown, and it was quite different—but I think pledging a fraternity was a really good thing, because he met a bunch of really, really nice guys, and they're still friends today.

I think I had mentioned in connection with running for office that one of his girlfriends was down with us in Las Vegas and campaigned, and we really liked her. I'm not sure if he became engaged in Boulder or not—not to the girlfriend that I just mentioned, but to a new young woman—and I have not met her. I think Kirk sent some pictures. I have to put this in context. This was right when I had had the accident—I mean, when all this was going on—and was trying to recover. So, you know, I can't really remember everything.

He graduated from Boulder, and he just loved Boulder. People who go there to school, they say they never want to leave, but there aren't enough jobs there, because it's a very small community, actually. Of course, at that time they had the number one football team in the country and won the national championship. It's an interesting campus. There were very few minorities there, because Boulder is a very expensive place to live, and the ones that are there are there on athletic scholarships, mainly. I say that only because I was talking about their football team.

So was Kirk on an athletic scholarship?

No. He got a golf scholarship, but that wasn't from the university. That was from a local golf place up here.

I went back a couple of times to Boulder. Of course, I went to graduation, but before that I think I went to an orientation for parents during his freshman year or before it. One thing they told us—and I'm glad they did, because I had planned on doing it—"Don't change your child's bedroom when they've just left." They said that's not a good thing to do, because it sort of, I guess, gives the child a sense that you're glad you're rid of them, and that their room isn't there

anymore the way they remembered it, even though you think, "Well, this guy is getting to be older, and, of course, he's not. . . ."

Well, they said, psychologically, don't do that, which was a nice little point, and I do remember that.

Boulder was a good school, and it was, evidently, just a great place to go to school. If you know where that is in Colorado, it is a beautiful spot. So he really had a good undergraduate experience at Boulder, still has a lot of friends, as I mentioned, met his wife there.

I'm sorry. I didn't catch her name.

Oh. Gabrielle. Sacett, I think. Her parents lived in Carmichael, California, at that time. When he graduated, the three of us—Kirk, Kristi, and I—went to Hawaii. I had mileage points, and at this time, I guess, you could do that, as we went on different airlines. Kirk went by himself on one airline, and Kristina and I went, right after graduation. I remember when we were there that a couple of his buddies were on the other island. We were in Kona, and they were on Oahu, and they flew over. What was it at that time? Twenty-five dollars to go from one island to the next. They came over, and they bummed around together. That was a very fun trip.

Kirk then applied to law school, and we were particularly looking at public schools, because it would be much cheaper. Bill Raggio wrote a letter of recommendation to Bolt Hall, and I know the governor wrote a letter to Santa Clara, the school that he went to. It was right in northern California, a private college. He went up to Oregon to look at that college, and he really didn't like it. I've never been there, but I had thought he would have liked it. In fact, I knew the dean of the law school, because he had been attorney general in Oregon and was a great guy. I was somewhat surprised when Kirk said he didn't like it—the University of Oregon in Eugene.

But anyway, of the schools that he had applied to, most of the private schools, he got admitted. He got admitted to Oregon, and I can't remember where else he applied. Arizona was really the target school, because it had the best reputation in how they rate them, like in *U.S. News and World Report*, which probably isn't a bible but gives you some idea. It was like in the ten best public universities that had law schools. Fortunately, he got admitted to that and went off.

While he was there, he got engaged, and that was kind of a little disagreement between mother and son. I was disappointed he got engaged while he was still in law school. I wasn't disappointed that he got engaged or to whom he got engaged, but I had been told by my friend Bob Sader . . . we're going to go back to Bob again. We were standing in line going somewhere, and we were talking about the kids and so on, and Bob is much younger than I am. He had small children, but we were talking about law schools and so on, because Bob was, of course, an attorney. He said, "You know, the divorce rate is higher going to law school than it is for medical school."

I was *really* surprised at that, and I had that in my mind then when Kirk told me this, so that's what I thought of, which was a very negative thing to think. I think he was pretty disappointed that I wasn't very, very wildly enthusiastic, but I'm surprised he would have thought any mother would have been wildly enthusiastic, going in the middle of law school. But, hey, maybe he knows different mothers than I do, I don't know! [laughter]

Law school is pretty rigorous.

It is very rigorous. But he did get married in his second year, and they bought

a condominium. The University of Arizona law school is in Tucson. In fact, I just introduced Harvey Whittemore a couple of weeks ago and gave him a hard time because he graduated from Arizona *State* University law school. I told him I was just informed that it had lost its accreditation, and, of course, all the kids thought that was very, very funny. [laughter] So did Harvey, actually. It was a very good law school.

Anyway, they bought a condominium, which I was a little surprised about, but they've been doing this wherever they've gone, and they've made a ton of money on everything that they've bought and sold. Of course, this was where I had grown up. Kirk then did graduate from law school. In fact, I was down there. Kristina and I were there when he was doing his moot court thing, and we were peeking through the window. I wanted to go in so much, but we were afraid we would just freak him out, you know, so we didn't, because we didn't want to ruin his grade or anything like that. [laughter]

Well, then Kirk, after he graduated from law school, came back to Reno, actually. I think I'd mentioned that after his first year, he came back and worked with the district court judge, at that time, Deborah Agosti, just to get a little experience and meet people. The second year he came back, he clerked—or I know the term is not "clerk." There's some term used where they work with a law firm.

I was thinking it was clerk, but I don't know if that's right.

Well, I think that goes with a judge, but anyway, the law firm at that time was Beckley, Singleton, Jameson, and List. He met this young guy who I had known through state government named Ken Creighton, I believe, and Ken was with that law firm that I just mentioned. Kirk just thought he was a great guy, so when he

Sue seated with Kirk, Kristina and Gabrielle, standing.

came back, he chose to work with that law firm. Soon thereafter, Ken left to go with former governor Bob List to Boomtown. Thereafter Bob List does something else—I don't remember what it is—and Ken Creighton then went to IGT as assistant legal counsel, and that's where he is today. That kind of left Kirk behind, because that was the guy that was mentoring him, I guess you would say. There were a couple of nice guys in the law firm, but they have now kind of split apart. They had a major law firm in Las Vegas and the one in Reno. Some of the other people left and went to other firms.

So, by that time, Kirk had gone. He left to go to California. Fortunately, after law school he took the Nevada bar and passed that, and then he also took the California bar the next summer. I'm sure he thought

he would be moving there, because his wife was anxious to get back, but it's a very good thing, even if you don't. If you only practice in Nevada, it's always nice to have that other association, because there's always the possibility of things that you would need to do in California, since we're so close.

Kirk now has three little girls. [laughter] Geez, it makes me smile just to think about it, going from law school to all of a sudden getting married and having three children. He has three little girls as we're speaking today, and he works with one of the best—if not *the* best, according to people that I know—law firm in the Monterey Peninsula area and seems to be on his way in his own life with his own family. That's kind of an exciting thing to see for a mother, you know.

Kristina—I believe I have talked about all the different colleges that she was

Kirk's three daughters, Olivia, Annabelle, and Grace.

admitted to and the options she had. Talk about being in shock, I guess. With both my kids I've had a big shock here about the same time of their life. When Kristina had come back from Notre Dame and told me that she was going to the University of Arizona, which she'd never applied to—not that she wouldn't get in—it was just like, "Wow!"

She was kind of mad that I reacted that way, but my goodness! Again, our kids have much higher expectations of their mothers than we're able to deliver. [laughter] I *had* to go to the University of Arizona, because it was very inexpensive, and it was like ten blocks from my house. Here, she had the opportunity to go any place, and it just seemed to me that, boy, if you had the opportunity, take it. But it turned out to be a good experience. I think what Kristina did not like about Notre Dame, particularly, was the fact that it was very homogeneous.

Everybody, she said, was like *her*. Most people were from middle-class or upper-middle-class families; most people were white; and most people had probably been student body presidents. They were very much the same. Like schools that we knew from Stanford to Duke, they look at the class as the class itself is homogeneous. Normally you think, "Oh, well. My daughter or son was student body president, and she or he was head cheerleader, and he or she was a star basketball player." That won't get you into a lot of colleges today. Now, in my day, that was what every college *wanted*, the star performer.

Kristina had very good grades. She had above a 4.0, because she took academically talented AP, Advanced Placement. So did my son, but she had like a 4.5 or some incredible grade average and graduated like twentieth in her class or something, and then was very, very active—the kind of student that I'm talking about, that we thought most schools wanted. Well, a lot of them did.

She did get into a lot of places, but as I say, she chose the University of Arizona, where I'd gone to school, and so I was a little surprised at first, but that's her choice. That's not my choice. We went down in the car and took all the stuff that she needed for the dorm. She got into the dorm that she had found out was the coolest—Coronado.

Then, of course, she was going to go through sorority rush in her freshman year, unlike my son, who waited a year to learn a little more about which fraternity he might like to be a member of. Kristina, I think, already had an idea of which sorority she wanted to be a member of. Since I was familiar with this whole process, since I'd done this myself at Arizona, I knew that it was very exciting for her, but I think she knew from the first day which one she wanted to belong to. That was not the case with me, where there were two or three.

I had a lot of my friends that I'd gone to college with that were rush advisors of different sororities, and they'd call me. They were very honest; they'd say, "Look, is she going to pledge Theta?" That's Kappa Alpha Theta, the sorority that I was a member of there. That would be your first thought, that a daughter is going to probably be a member of the same sorority her mother was. So they were trying to be honest. They said, "Well, you know, we're not going to carry her," meaning they weren't going to keep asking her back if she's not interested. I didn't know, and, of course, even if I did know, I wouldn't have said, because I wouldn't have wanted to disappointed her and have these sororities . . . .

It can be a little cutthroat. I'm sure that's the image a lot of people have. In some cases, that is true, particularly at a school like Arizona, where there are *so many*

people—hundreds and hundreds and hundreds and hundreds of girls, and you might be able to take thirty or forty. She did ultimately decide to be a member of Kappa Alpha Theta.

As it turns out, there were two other girls whose mothers I knew very well that pledged in the same class. So when they were being initiated—after they'd done their pledge class stuff and made their grades—they were then installed. And the three of us mothers—one lived in Phoenix, one lived in Tucson, and myself—were there. That was the only time I think I've ever left the legislature in the midst of things, but I flew down, and she didn't know I was coming, of course. When she saw me during part of the ceremony, it was like, somebody said, she levitated. It was almost like she just rose right off the floor! It was such a startling thing to her. Then we had dinner afterwards, and that was really fun. I *really* think she enjoyed the experience very, very much.

She made lifelong friends there, and she got very good grades. She was very active in college, in the sorority, on campus, and I think she really wanted to do that without thinking that she would have to study *every single minute*. I think that's why she chose Arizona—not that it wasn't hard.

She had time for some social life?

She did have time, yes. She had time for being involved in all the aspects of college. That's one of the better times in your life, you hope, because, as far as having fun and freedom, that's probably the last gasp for most people. You didn't have jobs; you didn't have families.

So when Kristina graduated, she wanted to go on. She had first gone down into MIS. I think that's what it is. Do you know what MIS is? It's signing on computer programs. That's what she started out in, but she decided that there were a lot of people in her class who looked like they were going to only be interested in computers, et cetera, so she decided to switch to just general business. Then, when she graduated, she decided she wanted to get an MBA.

She was very interested in international business, so she applied to the very well-known college that is in Arizona, the American Graduate School of International Management at the Thunderbird School. Students from all over the world go there and get a degree in international finance or international management. It's like a little, mini UN. In fact, my brother got a master's degree there many, many years ago. It was real nice; he came over when she graduated. She loved it and made a lot of good friends there.

When Kristina graduated with her MBA, she obviously had to get a job at some point. She's had *many* jobs, and I'm trying to think which one came first. She worked at the University of Nevada, Reno, in the Office of International Students and Scholars, and she worked for an investment bank in San Francisco, lived in San Francisco for a couple of years, and worked for First Interstate Bank in Las Vegas. All of her background fits in with all these things. I might be missing a job here, but then she went to Tucson and was employed by the Eller School of Business, which is the school that she graduated from, in working with MBA students. She had a title, and I would have to go look it up, find her card, but it doesn't really matter, probably. Then she decided to leave the university, basically because they haven't gotten a pay raise in I don't know how many years, and she was way underpaid, considering the education she had. So she's now with a private business, and she is doing what is called "cost structuring"—how you are able to depreciate commercial business in a certain way. She is learning all about this, and then she's going to go out and try to

sell to people in the community. She wrote a little article for a newspaper.

Kristina at this time has had probably twenty-five guys that she was really interested in, but not enough to get married to. She's always been very athletic. She was a top golfer in the state when she was in high school, and she's a great swimmer. At one point, she said all her life she just wanted to make enough money so she could do what she really liked, which was this, and she now is into triathlons and master swimming. She went to the nationals last year in master swimming.

She's bought a little townhouse near the university and likes to entertain. Of course, she has a lot of friends there, not only because she went to school there, but people that she's met through athletics and in her new job.

Well, I guess that's basically it in terms of Kirk and Kristina.

Sounds like both children are on their way.

Yes, they are. You know, they've been gone for a long time, although, Kirk came back and stayed with me when he worked with Justice Agosti. Kristina's been back occasionally. Well, no. She was back here when she worked at the university. But, you know, I realize that they're both gone now; they flew the coop. It's been a long time since they've done that, but now they *really* are settled. I don't believe Kristina would come back here. She likes Reno a lot but not enough, I think, to raise children here.

And her sports and everything are there.

Right. But I think that now there are so many new people here. I think at one time, when she came back, she knew everybody there was to date, and there wasn't anybody here she was particularly interested in getting serious about. But now that the town has grown so much . . . but I don't think that will happen.

So they're both gone. They're making their own ways, and that's the way that it's supposed to be. I'm happy for each of them and proud of each of them.

One of the things that you mentioned is that your daughter has said you have changed, and I think she was referring probably to now, compared to when you were in the legislature. Perhaps you want to address that specifically, but just a larger question of how you've changed from the time that you went into the legislature, changed by working in the government process, but then also going through this really life-threatening accident and these illnesses that you've had to deal with. Do you see yourself as changed?

Yes. I think what Kristi was referring to, however—and I will talk about that—is that I'm a lot more mellow. I think that I was so committed to doing a good job when I was first elected—well, hopefully all the time I was in the legislature—because that really was just opening the doors for women. I worked probably way too hard, took everything I was doing much too seriously. The times, I thought, demanded that in a way, because you hoped that because *you* had done a good job that other people would say, "Well, you know, women do a pretty darn good job," and they won't give the next woman a hard time about running. I'm just assuming that they're a good candidate, and it has nothing to do with their gender.

But I did. I spent probably more time trying to do the best job than probably, I'd say, 80 percent of the other legislators, maybe even 90. That was in a way a good thing and, in a way, not a good thing. The good thing was that people could not ever say that I didn't work hard, that I didn't care about my constituents, that I didn't take

these issues seriously. But maybe there were some things—I think I should have stayed home with my kids; I sometimes have that guilty feeling.

You know, part of this time, my husband was here, so he was here with the kids when I was gone, and the only reason I really chose to seek this office is because it was only every other year, but as we found out, it became more than every other year. You know, you were asked to do this or speak here or do that. Now, if I'd said, "No, no, no, no," it would have been a different commitment, and it probably wasn't one that I could personally do. I probably was not able to say, "No, no, no, no."

So it was kind of like a treadmill, I guess, that you're on, and you don't get off, or it's hard to get off it, but things were pretty good, because Peter was here. I know I've discussed the fact of how people thought we would get a divorce, or that this wasn't going to work or whatever, because they hadn't seen that kind of a model before, a family model, so to speak. Peter was just so supportive and didn't even hardly debate me on the issues, although he didn't always agree with me, I think. If we're talking about from there to now, I'd say that I'm just *way* more relaxed. That probably is a good thing in terms of my health, but it came *about* because of my health. I suspect that if I had not been in this plane crash, which forced me to take a look at what's going on in my life and what should be going on in my life, that I probably, without too much question, would have run for something else. I don't know if I would've won it or not, and if I had not won, I don't know if I would have thought about doing it again, because I had never lost an election. So I wouldn't know how I would have felt about that.

It was interesting, though, that when I made a decision that I was going to say good-bye, I really haven't pined away or thought, "Oh, I made a terrible mistake." Or, "Gosh, I wish I was down there doing that again." I really have never felt like that, which I think is really unusual, because almost everybody I know or talk to, it's very hard for them to say, "This is it," unless they're defeated.

I think with too many people that *that's* their identity—Senator so-and-so or Assemblyperson so-and-so. I might feel differently if I wasn't on the gaming commission, or if I didn't have a class, but you prepare for those times, I think, if you're smart about it, knowing that you're going to be on this fast track and all of a sudden the brakes are going to be put on. So you want to see what else you might be interested in that you think might be helpful, not only for you, but for whoever else is involved in it.

You have to think of that every time you run.

Yes! Exactly. Unless you're running unopposed, and then you don't give it a whole lot of thought, particularly, because it's very difficult to have a write-in candidate here in Nevada.

So you did relax, and you have slowed down, and yet in my own opinion, I still see you as a very hard worker and still a pretty high-energy person.

Well, I think that's probably true, but you didn't know me before. [laughter]

I can't imagine! [laughter] It would have been breathtaking!

It sort of was. [laughter] The secretaries used to say they used to hide under the desk when I came through the door! It was like a whirlwind! But, no, there was probably a little truth to that. I think that the interesting thing to me, though, is the fact that I was able to do this so easily. I got interested in flowers and gardening and

fixing up my house, things that weren't even on my radar screen before. My friends thought that was really a good thing, although most of my friends are very busy and active people, too.

I think that I've changed substantially in that way. I have not changed in terms of my interest in what's going on around me or being involved in issues. I feel very strongly about the state I live in and the community I live in. I worry about what's going to happen to Reno—that is, gambling and the threat of Indian gambling and all these kinds of things—because it's such a great place to live that you hope it's still going to be a great place to live.

Right now, I guess, it's a pretty good time in my life for me. I'm doing things that I really, really like. My family is doing well. My cat's doing OK. And, well, I like where I live and have a little time. I just took a road trip, which I haven't done, my goodness sakes, in I don't know how long, probably thirty years or longer.

Wow. And you weren't sure you could do that.

No, because of my spine, but actually, it did work out well, and so now I feel like, hey, I can up and do what I want, go wherever I want—a little more freedom.

Some more freedom. When we were talking earlier, you were talking about the gaming commission, Washoe Health System, those boards. Tentatively, your time on those might end in about 2005?

Yes.

So what do you see coming next?

Well, I really haven't given that a lot of thought, because I still have a couple more years to think about it. I probably—and we'll see—might hope that I would get another gaming commission appointment, but, you know, I'm really not clear in my mind that that would happen. The class will be ongoing. The Washoe Health System board is the one thing that I know won't be continuing. I don't see any need to duplicate that in some way.

So maybe you have more time for travel and some things that are positive.

This past year, when there's a session, then it is more busy for me, because I have Wednesday when I'm usually in Carson City in that office, just so they know I'm there, and legislators do. Interestingly, even when I'm there, there may be a hearing going on down the hall, but I don't feel this great need to run down there and sit there and listen.

And see what's going on?

No. I do keep my finger on a couple of things that I'm very, very interested in, to make sure that it passes, or it doesn't pass, something like that. When the weather is getting better—and I don't usually get out of the building till six or seven at night even then—I drive back home and think, "Boy, it's nice driving back, not worrying about this or that or the other thing." It's just there. I'm leaving it, and I'm not thinking about it.

I remember one time voting on the Sagebrush Rebellion, and I voted no, and there were only like three people that did, and I remember going through Washoe Valley thinking, "This is the reason I voted no," basically, because, in my mind, this was the nice part of Nevada. If you managed it in the state, rather than the federal, it would . . . . I don't know if that's even worth talking about.

But the idea that you were getting across is that it's different to drive home and not worry, to be done for the day, compared to when you were in the heat of the

legislative session and in voting and, you know, having to think through your vote and have answers for questions that were sure to come.

Yes. That's very true. So to kind of wind this up, I guess this is a good time.

INDEX